TAKING ON THEODORE ROOSEVELT

TAKING ON THEODORE ROOSEVELT

∾ How One Senator ∾
DEFIED THE PRESIDENT ON BROWNSVILLE
and Shook American Politics

HARRY LEMBECK

 Prometheus Books

59 John Glenn Drive
Amherst, New York 14228

Published 2015 by Prometheus Books

Cover images of Theodore Roosevelt and the Buffalo Soldiers from the Library of Congress; cover image of Joseph Foraker from the Society of the Army of the Cumberland, *Burial of General Rosecrans, Arlington National Cemetery, May 17, 1902* (Cincinnati: Robert Clark, 1903), p. 37.

Cover design by Nicole Sommer-Lecht

The Internet addresses listed in the text were accurate at the time of publication. The inclusion of a website does not indicate an endorsement by the author(s) or by Prometheus Books, and Prometheus Books does not guarantee the accuracy of the information presented at these sites.

Prometheus Books recognizes the following registered trademarks mentioned within the text: Springfield Armory®, Tabasco®, Mauser®, Winchester®.

Inquiries should be addressed to
Prometheus Books
59 John Glenn Drive
Amherst, New York 14228
VOICE: 716–691–0133
FAX: 716–691–0137
WWW.PROMETHEUSBOOKS.COM

19 18 17 16 15   5 4 3 2 1

Library of Congress Cataloging-in-Publication Data

Lembeck, Harry, 1944-
  Taking on Theodore Roosevelt : how one senator defied the president on Brownsville and shook American politics / by Harry Lembeck.
      pages cm
  Includes bibliographical references and index.
  ISBN 978-1-61614-954-3 (hardback) — ISBN 978-1-61614-955-0 (ebook)
  1. Foraker, Joseph Benson, 1846-1917. 2. Roosevelt, Theodore, 1858-1919—Adversaries. 3. United States—Politics and government—1901-1909. 4. African American soldiers—Texas—Brownsville—History—20th century. 5. Riots—Texas--Brownsville—History—20th century. 6. United States. Army. Infantry Regiment, 25th. 7. Legislators—United States—Biography. 8. United States—Race relations. I. Title.

E664.F69L46 2015
973.91'1092—dc23

                                                        2014027260

Printed in the United States of America

For Emily

"What a cleverly managed and malicious fraud the Brownsville business was."

Senator Henry Cabot Lodge to Roosevelt,
September 21, 1908,
Roosevelt-Lodge Correspondence 2

"Another method of investigating, with more patience and skill, might easily have brought all the facts to light, and resulted in even handed justice."

"An Unprejudiced Examination into the
Brownsville Affair," *New York Times*,
November 25, 1910

CONTENTS

"This is the true joy of life, the being used for a purpose recognized by yourself as a mighty one."

George Bernard Shaw, "Epistle Dedicatory,"
Man and Superman, 1903

PROLOGUE

ARRIVING EARLY FOR A meeting at the National Museum of American History at the Smithsonian and needing to kill a few minutes in its gift shop, at random I leafed through a book of photos of magnificent houses and buildings in Washington, DC, now torn down and forever lost. By chance I opened it to the home of Senator Joseph Foraker of Ohio. Sturdy and solid looking, the house was far more stately than his wife Julia's cheery description of "a big yellow house" and showed qualities her husband no doubt saw in himself—achievement, material success, respectability, and judgment.[1] I vaguely recalled Foraker from the so-called Brownsville Incident. President Theodore Roosevelt blamed black soldiers stationed at nearby Fort Brown for shooting up Brownsville, Texas. At the time of the shooting in 1906, the army was rigidly segregated; black soldiers served only with other black soldiers and were commanded by white officers. The Twenty-Fifth Infantry, the accused soldiers' regiment, was such a unit. After the army discharged the entire unit on Roosevelt's order, Senator Foraker came to their defense.

Considered the blackest mark against Theodore Roosevelt's legacy is his discharge "without honor" of what would come to be called the Black Battalion. More than one hundred years later, almost no one defends what he did. Some Roosevelt admirers soften their criticism by calling it merely an aberration or a blunder. On the other hand, Louis R. Harlan, Booker T. Washington's biographer, pulled no punches when he called it "the grossest single racial injustice of that so-called Progressive Era."[2] At the time, few dis-

9

agreed with what Roosevelt did. Most believed that some of the soldiers shot up the town and killed one man while wounding another, that other soldiers knew who the shooters were but refused to finger them, and that all of them deserved the punishment President Roosevelt gave them. Blunder, injustice, racist act, aberration, understandable mistake: whatever Brownsville was, that it only singes Theodore Roosevelt's legacy at its edges indicates his otherwise overall greatness.

Senator Foraker, formerly a successful trial lawyer and one-time Cincinnati judge, who saw the discrepancy between accusation and conviction, evidence and proof, said dismissing all for what may have been the acts of only a few was wrong. He took up their cause and worked tirelessly and publicly for them. Foraker understood that President Roosevelt, emulating his hero Abraham Lincoln, had strengthened his office with immense power and would use all of it against him brutally and personally.[3] He also had to know that Roosevelt had what Professor Lewis Gould has called the "unlovely aspect" of behaving unfairly with his opponents.[4] When Foraker took his stand for the soldiers, Roosevelt had been in the White House for five years and led an active government that, among other things, busted the big-business combines known as trusts and freely acknowledged that America was entitled to act as the world power it had become. Fighting in Cuba, digging the Panama Canal, warning European powers away from the Americas with his own corollary to the Monroe Doctrine, influencing affairs in the faraway Pacific Ocean region by mentoring a peace treaty that ended the Russo-Japanese War (and receiving the Nobel Peace Prize for it), and creating a special relationship with Great Britain that would help win a future World War II, Roosevelt stood second to no one in bringing about what *Time* magazine publisher Henry R. Luce would call the "American Century."[5]

With his intellectual restlessness yoked to a physical energy that was nothing less than astounding, Theodore Roosevelt seemingly was everywhere and knew what went on every day. To accomplish all he wanted for the future he foresaw for his country, and breaking with the more restrained presidencies of his predecessors since

Lincoln, he fortified the government with a greatly strengthened chief executive. In what would become an on-again, off-again process by most of his successors for the next hundred years, he expanded its scope, responsibilities, and powers. To justify his actions, he reinterpreted the Constitution his way and proposed bedrock changes to the federal system. Washington, DC, could not contain him. He often traveled away from the capital and thought nothing of going as far as California and the western states for extended periods. He even went to Panama in 1906 to see his canal under construction and to congratulate himself for bringing it about and showing the world what his America could do.

He changed the Executive Mansion itself. Almost immediately after his wife, Edith, unpacked their bags, he changed its name to the White House. Much better, he thought. It was natural, free from pretension, so purely American. Just as Roosevelt saw himself. It told the world that in a powerful America, even its leader lives in a simple, white house. But this was nonsense. As the presidential office grew, the office where he did business, and even the White House itself, seemed too small. Roosevelt expanded it by adding what is now called the West Wing, today the location of the Oval Office. The White House facade, reflecting the calm and restrained tastes of an earlier period, was an illusion screening a complexity that could not begin to describe the man Theodore Roosevelt was. Roosevelt found positively distasteful the way Senator Foraker saw America and how it should be governed. Where Roosevelt would increase government's sprawl, Foraker preferred it stay limited. Roosevelt was suspicious of big business; Foraker the lawyer represented it in court. When Roosevelt sought to apply the government's strength in court to restrain runaway companies, Foraker worked in Congress to protect them.

History has not yet been able to show Roosevelt was wrong in what he thought happened, even if it adjudges him wrong in what he did about it. Just who the shooters were is an enigma still unanswered more than a century later. Within the mystery is the tandem of Roosevelt and Foraker and their battle that continued beyond Foraker's days in the Senate and Roosevelt's time in the White House.

The Brownsville Incident was a snapshot of race in America in the early twentieth century and a pivot point in the struggle for equal treatment for black Americans. Voting rights were sharply curtailed. Jim Crow laws became a way of life in the South, segregating everything from streetcars to Pullman trains, toilets to restaurants, hotel accommodations to schools.[6] Black leaders were unsure of just how to deal with this. The greatest Negro leader of the day, Booker T. Washington, counseled accommodation and patience. So great was his influence, so respected was he for his accomplishments and position, for some time thereafter there was no effective counter-message from other black leaders. By 1906 and Brownsville, this would be changing, and others, notably W. E. B. Du Bois, were pushing hard for a more aggressive course of action. With his easy eloquence and forceful presence, Du Bois used Brownsville to chip away at Washington's leadership and redirect the movement for equality. The Brownsville Incident and Theodore Roosevelt's actions after it would be pulled into the collision between these two men. There were men, both black and white, who agreed with Foraker and stood with him in common cause. Others stayed with Roosevelt. Still others recognized there was justice in Senator Foraker's poking about but hung back from endorsing his quixotic pursuit. One was Booker T. Washington, who saw Roosevelt as a source of his own power and influence.

Roosevelt's personal magnetism beggars description, and those who attempt to do so sketch a phenomenon of nature. "He was his own limelight, and could not help it: a creature charged with such a voltage as his, became the central presence at once, whether he stepped on a platform or entered a room—and in a room the other presences were likely to feel crowded, and sometimes displaced."[7] Roosevelt's friend William Hard captured his extraordinary qualities when he said, "He was the prism through which the light of day took on more colors than could be seen in anybody else's company."[8]

A century later, Theodore Roosevelt is securely settled in as one of America's great presidents. In a 2010 poll ranking presidents, he was ranked overall number two, ahead even of Washington, Lincoln, and Jefferson.[9] On twenty-first-century problems ranging from immigration to war to conservation, his views are cited by one side or the other or both. Bigger than any man of his era, Theodore Roosevelt was considered as great as the country he led. When he left the White House in 1909 he was the most famous man in the world. Joseph Foraker is forgotten, and the Black Battalion is barely remembered.

"To him, principle and right were more important than political preferment. He should have our eternal gratitude. I wonder if again we will find another such friend and supporter."

William Sanders Scarborough,
former slave and president of Wilberforce University,
speaking about Joseph Foraker

CHAPTER ONE

THE IRON OF THE WOUND ENTERS THE SOUL ITSELF

"THE OLD MAN HAS fought for the reinstatement of our soldiers since 1906 and I do hope that his stand for justice will be appreciated by the black people of the country," wrote Ralph Tyler in 1909 to George Myers, an influential political leader in Cleveland's black community. Myers had been Tyler's mentor and at one time a close friend. "The old man" he referred to was Senator Joseph Benson Foraker, Republican of Ohio. "On the 6th of March," Tyler went on, "the colored citizens of Washington are going to present him with a loving cup at the Metropolitan Church and from the effort that is being made I am sure he will be given a great ovation."[1]

In his own mind, Myers must have questioned just how genuinely Tyler associated himself with Foraker and the effort to honor him. After the Brownsville shootings but before the incident became divisive, Tyler ingratiated himself to Foraker. On September 15, 1906, he complimented the senator on a "splendid speech" at the Ohio Republican Convention in Dayton. Tyler gushed, "You came, you saw, you conquered, as you deserved to do."[2]

Twelve days later Tyler ended another letter by fawning, "It is only my great admiration for you . . . and my desire to see you victorious in everything that prompted my writing. . . . You know, Senator, I am a REAL Foraker man, and am always with you and for you, whether in defeat or in victory."[3] Two months later, when Foraker took up Brownsville in the Senate, Tyler told him he was "our champion, and I thank you from the bottom of my heart."[4]

But shortly thereafter, when defending Roosevelt became the touchstone for loyalty to him and, even more important, a qualification for appointment to a federal job desired by Tyler, he jumped to Roosevelt's side and worked to persuade people to give Roosevelt a pass for what he had done. When Roosevelt made him fourth auditor of the navy, Myers, who by now had wiped his hands of Theodore Roosevelt over Brownsville, warned him not to undermine Foraker with Negro voters. "There is no doubt in my mind of Foraker's ultimate victory . . . [and] I am writing to you this fully, to demonstrate the futility of the President to corner or stop the stampede of the colored voters of Ohio by your appointment."[5]

By March 1909 and Roosevelt's last days in the White House, Tyler was back on Foraker's side and applauding the efforts of the man who had been the most active and visible man working to reverse President Roosevelt's order to discharge "without honor" 167 soldiers of the army's Twenty-Fifth Infantry, now being called the "Black Battalion," for their alleged involvement in a deadly shooting in Brownsville, Texas. He insisted the soldiers had been denied justice, publicly accused Roosevelt of punishing innocent men, compelled the Senate to investigate Roosevelt's action, and doggedly worked to reverse their discharges for as long as he remained in the Senate. In one of his final appearances in the Senate, barely two months before Ralph Tyler's letter to Myers, he pleaded to his colleagues and the nation, "They ask no favors because they are negroes, but only for justice, because they are men."[6] An enraged Roosevelt was forced to defend himself. Already fed up with Foraker for past differences of opinion, Roosevelt now made him an archenemy.

There was no doubt among Negroes that Foraker had worked his heart out. In the Senate committee hearings on Brownsville,

Foraker demonstrated why he was a very successful lawyer: attention to detail, thorough preparation, skillful argument, and forceful presence. He made hash of President Roosevelt's arguments defending the soldiers' dismissals. Even many whites believed Foraker was convincing and had shown Roosevelt to be wrong. Only a month into the committee hearings the *Washington Times* would write, "There is a strong feeling among many who have followed the testimony . . . that it already has been proved very doubtful if the soldiers did do it."[7] Black Americans, to whom Roosevelt had been thought a friend and an ally in their slow, painfully frustrating, and always disappointing push for the rights of American citizenship, now questioned whether Roosevelt could be trusted.

WHEN HE WAS OHIO governor in the 1880s, Joseph Foraker was known as "Fire Alarm Foraker" for his ringing, white-hot public speaking. On the stump he often used his blowtorch style and language to remind people of the rebellion of the Confederacy and the slavery the South sought to hold onto and was willing to split the nation to keep. Rhetoric like his was called "waving the bloody shirt," and Joseph Foraker employed it often to remind people what it had cost to preserve the Union. He believed it showed the voters he had "fire and courage."[8] He was not shy about using this for simple political advantage, coupling an "unwavering justification of the Republican stand during and after the Civil War" with a flair for partisan argument.[9]

In 1886, twenty-one years after Robert E. Lee surrendered his Confederate Army to Ulysses S. Grant at Appomattox to effectively end the Civil War, Foraker was still engaged in oratorical hostilities against the rebellion and its leader, Jefferson Davis. The Methodist Church withdrew its invitation for him to speak at a conference in Richmond, Davis's former capital city, after Foraker bitterly criticized Davis at a Grand Army of the Republic encampment in Cleveland. Foraker retreated not an inch and responded, "This man, Jeff Davis, represents only human slavery, the degradation of labor, the treason of secession and rebellion, the horrors and infamies of [the Confederate prisoner-of-war camps] Libby and Andersonville."[10]

A year later, as part of his reelection campaign for Ohio governor, Foraker tongue-lashed West Virginia governor Emanuel Wilson for criticizing the Union Army and for defending "those who organize Ku Klux Klans . . . and with the short gun and bull whip and all kinds of violence, with ballot box stuffing and all kinds of fraud . . . made the South solid." Having dispatched Governor Wilson, Foraker next welcomed the challenge from Georgia governor John B. Gordon, a former Confederate general, to defend his aggressive attacks on the South. "We want peace and union on the basis of the results of war and no other. We were right and they were wrong."[11] For Fire Alarm Foraker, that was all there was to it. When President Grover Cleveland thought it was time to return captured Confederate regimental flags held by Northern states, Governor Foraker's response was simple, direct, and what he knew Ohioans wanted to hear: "No rebel flags will be returned while I am governor." President Cleveland backed down, and Ohio kept the flags her sons had taken.[12] Foraker had not held back from confronting a president. It would not be the last time.

When he entered the Senate, Foraker tried to put the war behind him. Soothed possibly by the chamber's august serenity, he would speak not with the piercing clang of a fire bell but with the patient persuasion of the successful lawyer he had been and the statesman he hoped to become. Because of his impressive senatorial demeanor and bearing, he was selected by the Senate for the honor of reading George Washington's Farewell Address on Washington's birthday. He now addressed issues and took stands on matters broader in scope. As chairman of the Senate Committee on Pacific Islands and (what was then spelled) Porto Rico, he structured the territorial government for this island in the Caribbean that came under the protection of the Stars and Stripes in 1898. A critic nevertheless conceded it may have been "the most liberal territorial legislation in U.S. history."[13]

Becalmed as he now was, Foraker could still spit back. When President Roosevelt lumped him together with oil magnate John D. Rockefeller and railroad tycoon E. H. Harriman as part of the Wall Street "combination," Foraker deflected the charge by poking fun at it and, by extension, at Roosevelt. Piously he recalled the only time he had been with Rockefeller was "twenty years ago or more . . . at the laying of the corner-stone of the Young Men's Christian Association Building [in] Cleveland." As for Harriman, Foraker turned Roosevelt's accusation back onto him: it was true, Foraker admitted, he had been with Harriman, but only three times; two of them were at Roosevelt's White House, and the last time was when Harriman was an honored guest at the wedding of President Roosevelt's daughter.[14]

TODAY IT SEEMS AN odd way to say thank you. A century ago, a standard award to present to a man, especially a politician, was an oversize silver trophy resting on a heavy base, girded with two or three handles on its sides, festooned with Greco-Roman figures to suggest a classical pedigree, and etched with names, dates, and events being commemorated. It was meant as a measure of respect and admiration. They called it a loving cup.

On March 6, 1909, the black community in Washington presented one to Joseph Foraker, whose time in the Senate had ended three days earlier. The *Afro-American Ledger*, a Negro newspaper in nearby Baltimore, described his loving cup as "a beautiful work of the silversmith, standing nearly two feet high with three massive handles. . . . Around the base are the words, 'Twenty-fifth U.S. Infantry;' on the bowl the engraver has quoted from one of Foraker's speeches on Brownsville."

TWO DAYS BEFORE THE presentation to Senator Foraker, on the morning of the presidential inauguration, a storm seemingly from an ice age froze Washington to a stop. The National Weather Service deems the weather worse that day than any presidential inauguration in history.[15] "I knew there would be a blizzard when I went out," Roosevelt said.[16] Ten inches of snow fell overnight, and more than six thousand workers shoveled through the darkness to remove fifty-eight thousand tons of it along the route the inaugural parade would take. Winds made things worse, downing trees and telephone lines. Only the occasional spectator ventured out onto the snow-choked streets between the White House and the Capitol, where the outgoing President Roosevelt with satisfaction would witness the success of his efforts to make William H. Taft his successor.

President-elect Taft's swearing-in had to be moved inside to the warm Senate chamber, where, after taking the oath of office, President Taft delivered his inaugural address.[17] The fears of Republicans that Taft's role in the Brownsville Incident might drain Negro votes from him and the Republicans turned out to be overblown. During the campaign, Taft had made calming (though bland and limited) statements to reassure black voters he had no intention of abandoning their constitutional protections. In an otherwise broadly ranging campaign speech in Hot Springs, Virginia, on August 5, 1908, he made sure to praise the Negro for his remarkable progress since emancipation. Referring to the Republican platform plank that called for justice for all men without regard to race or color and the explicit declaration for enforcement "without reservation in letter or spirit" of the post–Civil War constitutional amendments that outlawed slavery and articulated equal treatment for blacks, he said, "I stand with my party squarely on that plank." In his first address to the nation as president, Taft's message for Negroes was discouraging. He expressed his "friendship for the south" and with an abandonment of syntax added, "It may well admit of doubt whether in the case of any race an appointment of any one of their number to a local office in a community in which the race feeling is so widespread and acute as to interfere with the ease and facility with which the local government business can be done by the appointee is of sufficient benefit by way of encouragement of the race to outweigh the recurrence and increase of race feelings which such an appointment is likely to engender." As muddied as this sentence was, its meaning was clear: fewer black federal appointees in the South.[18]

Negroes should not have been surprised. During the campaign, Taft told the South he believed that a "white man's government" was not inconsistent with the Constitution. The *New York Times* expressed sympathy for the idea. It editorialized, "The South has it in its power fully to protect itself from the domination of ignorant and unfit negro voters, and to secure that control of affairs by the more intelligent which for a long time at least, and probably for all time must be controlled by the whites."[19]

THE NEGRO COMMUNITY IN Washington, DC, at the turn of the twentieth century would have surprised the editor of the *New York Times*. In the nation's capital, the "center of the black aristocracy in the United States," black culture and intellectual life flourished without the control or even help of whites.[20] Washington contained a strong, smart, successful, educated, and vibrant community of what has been dubbed by a historian "Aristocrats of Color." Along with this black upper crust there was, because of the availability of government jobs on a more or less integrated basis, the strongest black middle class of any American city. Washington was where Joseph Foraker made his stand, and in Washington at the Metropolitan African Methodist Episcopal Church, the black community would show its appreciation to him.

The church was part of the African Methodist Episcopal (AME) movement founded in Philadelphia in the late eighteenth century by a former slave named Richard Allen, who bought his freedom and become a licensed Methodist minister. In 1816 it became the nation's first independent black denomination. A few years later in Washington, black parishioners in the mainly white Ebenezer Methodist Episcopal Church, chafing under its discriminatory treatment, divided into two AME churches that would recombine in 1870 into the renamed Metropolitan AME Church.

Its building, dedicated in 1886, was in the Victorian Gothic style. Though never as upper class as some other black churches in Washington, from its re-created medieval style, a passerby on the street might have thought it was a well-endowed white church. Frederick Douglass was a parishioner and spoke from its pulpit. His funeral and that of the United States senator from Mississippi Blanche K. Bruce were conducted at the church.[21] Many years later, Martin Luther King Jr. would speak to its congregation and to the world.

If the Metropolitan AME Church was the right venue, Archibald

Grimké, the principal speaker that evening, a man of talent and background, was the perfect choice to express the community's gratitude. He was a thoughtful speaker whose speeches were considered literary gems.[22] Born a slave, his father was Henry Grimké, a plantation owner in upstate South Carolina, and his mixed-ancestry mother, Nancy, was Henry's slave. Unlike the more common situation in which a master, to satisfy a sexual craving or simply on a whim, would ravish the slave of his choice, Henry, after his wife's death, developed as committed a relationship with Nancy as would be possible in the antebellum South. She even came to adopt the name Nancy Grimké when referring to herself. Henry allowed her and their sons—Archibald (as a boy, called Archie), Francis, and John—a house of their own with a small patch for a garden. He brought Nancy into his own house when she was ill and cared for her until she was well. At Nancy's insistence, he permitted the boys to get an education at a school in Charleston for free Negroes. Still, though he was affectionate with his black sons, more so Archie than the other two, Henry nevertheless never acknowledged them as his children.

Archie and his family may have benefitted from his father's favorable attention to them, but they would suffer the consequences of Henry's neglectfulness when he died. Trusting his white son Montague to continue the more sympathetic treatment his black family was accustomed to, Henry gave them to him in his will, believing that informal instructions would protect them. Henry was hardly in the ground when Montague ignored his father's intentions. Archie learned that blacks could pay for white people's carelessness as well as their cruelty.

But not all whites: not Henry's sisters Angelina and Sarah. Before the Civil War, revolted by slavery and their family's enthusiastic and profitable embrace of it, the sisters cut their bonds with them and the South and moved to Boston, the center of Northern abolitionism. After the war, when they found out they had black nephews, they reached out to the boys. The aunts thereafter stayed close to Archie and his brother Francis, established a loving and committed family relationship, and guided the boys into becoming strong and successful adults. Archie never forgot what they did for him and what he owed them. He would name his only daughter after his "Aunt Angelina."

With his Northern family's encouragement and financial aid, Grimké continued the education his mother made sure he began back in Charleston and eventually was admitted to Harvard Law School, where one of his classmates was Henry Cabot Lodge, who would be Roosevelt's best friend.

Grimké's first encounter with Foraker had left him disappointed. In 1906, when the Senate was considering President Roosevelt's Hepburn Act to regulate railroad rates, Grimké met with the senator and asked him to propose an amendment to the legislation to eliminate segregation on railroad cars. Foraker suggested the act require that railroads offer the same services and accommodations to all passengers paying the same fare. Grimké, though, knew the cars for blacks would never be equal to those for whites, and even if they were, segregating the cars was itself the evil he wanted eliminated. Foraker's suggested amendment implicitly blessed this indignity.[23]

Eventually, Republicans on the conference committee scissored Foraker's poorly considered language from the final bill but made no accommodation for what Grimké wanted. The Hepburn Act passed, Roosevelt had his rate regulation, and the hopes of Negro railroad travelers were left at the station.[24]

This was forgiven in the winter of 1906–1907, when Senator Foraker pressed the Senate to investigate Roosevelt's Brownsville actions. In his columns in the *New York Age*, Grimké praised Foraker and portrayed him as heroic for shouldering the challenge to Theodore Roosevelt.[25] Now, for himself and for all black Americans, Grimké was about to thank Foraker and make it clear just how much they appreciated his efforts.[26]

Coming to the pulpit, Grimké looked out at more than three thousand people. It was the largest event ever held in the city, according to the local Negro newspaper, the *Washington Bee*.[27] Police fretted over the danger from an even greater crush and ordered the doors from the street closed, denying entry to three hundred more. Conspicuously on the podium that night was First Sergeant Mingo Sanders, discharged from the Twenty-Fifth Infantry and from the army by President Roosevelt's order after twenty-seven years of service, which included fighting in Cuba alongside Roosevelt's Rough Riders.[28] Close by Sanders was a small bipartisan group of members of Congress who had supported Foraker against Roosevelt.

In a place of honor on the podium facing the audience sat Senator Foraker. Over six feet tall when standing, still trim at two hundred pounds, he was a handsome sixty-two-year-old man. With a full head of steel-gray hair and a carefully trimmed handlebar mustache to match, he looked every inch the United States senator he no longer was.

IN A VOICE GENTLED by the easy drawl of the Low Country of his youth, Grimké began to speak. His studies at Harvard and his many years in the North could not rinse the accent from him, and it was said it identified him as the gentleman he surely was.

He immediately took on Theodore Roosevelt, reminding people how unprepared they had been for Roosevelt's action. "[There] is no precedent." The act was "not warranted by law or justice," "cruel in the highest degree, and a wanton abuse of executive power." As if unable to get Roosevelt's betrayal out of his system, Grimké harshly criticized him again and again, calling what he did a "peculiar hardship," a "crushing injustice," a "cruel surprise." Even more grievous, "crueler than death itself," was that it was the "blow of an old friend" and therefore "the unkindest blow of all," something "one is never prepared for and when it falls, the wound which it inflicts cuts deeper than flesh and blood, for the iron of it enters the soul itself."[29]

For Grimké, Roosevelt's betrayal was personal. A Democrat for almost twenty years, in 1904, he went over to the Republicans to support Theodore Roosevelt and urged all Negroes to vote for him. "I am going to [vote for Roosevelt] because the South has taken from me any disposition to do otherwise, since it compels me to cast my vote for the man whom it hates as it hates no other man because he dared as President to have [Booker T. Washington] lunch with him at the White House. . . . What is the issue, the paramount issue, raised by the South between itself and the President is the right of the Negro to equal treatment with all other citizens."[30]

Four years later, after the lesson of Brownsville and what he saw as other Rooseveltian failures to appreciate and do something about Negro concerns, Grimké changed his mind again. "[Roosevelt] has nothing to say [about] the everlasting question of the rights . . . of the colored people of the United States. They are denied in every Southern state the right to vote, the equal protection of the laws, and discriminated against and oppressed in countless ways by bad laws and . . . are sent to death every day by mobs. All of which denials and oppressions and violences are in open and defiant violations of the Constitution of the nation, which guaranties [sic] to these people equal citizenship and equality of rights with all other races. The President's ears which catches [sic] all other sounds the world over fails to catch the bitter cry of 10,000,000 of his fellow citizens merely because they are black and their oppressors white."[31]

Having purged himself of his rage, Grimké calmed his speech as he turned his attention to Foraker. Adopting the language of war as a gesture to the soldiers Foraker defended and to make clear the stake each side had in winning, Grimké cried out, "The enemies of the Black Battalion . . . whether with their sappers and miners, or assaulting columns, there they found [Foraker] alert, dauntless, invincible, their sappers and miners hoisted with their own petard, their assaulting columns routed and driven to cover before the withering, the deadly fire from the flashing cannons of his facts, his logic, his law and his eloquence."[32] Every mention of the former senator's name by Grimké drew applause and wild enthusiasm from the audience. Using the oratorical flourishes more common to that era, he described "the grandeur of soul of a great man," who, "sleepless on the Senate floor defending a just cause" with the "genius of an orator, lawyer and defender of the first rank[,] . . . carried the case of the Black Battalion in his big and tireless brain, in his big and gentle heart as a mother carries under her bosom her unborn babe." Turning to face Foraker, Grimké asked, "Sir, did you know what love went out for you during those tremendous months of toil and struggle, and what prayers from the grateful hearts of ten millions of people?" Taking notice of the loss of Foraker's Senate seat and blaming it on Brownsville, Grimké told his listeners how this could have been avoided if the senator from Ohio had "chosen to play the part of the defender of President Roosevelt's wanton abuse and usurpation of executive power." "For he preferred to suffer afflic- tion with the Black Battalion and to suffer defeat for the Senator- ship rather than enjoy power and office as the price of desertion of the cause of these helpless men."[33]

Grimké, possibly remembering his own father's mixed feelings for his black sons, was sending mixed messages. Not once does he refer to Foraker as a friend. He used the word *friend* only twice, and both times in an unhappy context. Negroes are "without many friends." President Roosevelt, who proved faithless and discharged the Black Battalion, was an "old friend." This last use was a rebuke to Booker T. Washington, who regularly referred to Roosevelt as "our friend."[34] After Brownsville, when Washington refused to abandon his politically rewarding relationship with Roosevelt even while regretting Roosevelt's grievous blunder in Brownsville, he was fair game to a disgusted Grimké.

DID FORAKER SENSE GRIMKÉ'S suddenly detached language? Did he wonder if it had to do with his earlier checkered history when dealing with Negroes? He lost his first run for governor of Ohio in 1883, and the common wisdom of the day blamed it on what histo- rian Percy E. Murray called his "limited contact with blacks . . . and lukewarm support from black voters."[35] To say the least. Foraker had about the same contact with blacks as he had with the surface of the moon, and black support for him was no warmer than the blizzard at Taft's inaugural. Two years later, in a second run for the governor's mansion, he again found himself face-to-face with black hostility. Because he was a Republican and could expect very few Democratic votes, without the votes of blacks, almost to a man Republican, his election was again doubtful. Angry black oppo- sition presented itself in the person of Reverend J. W. Gazaway, who, wanting his daughter to attend a school closer to their home, went to court to confront the racially segregated Springfield, Ohio, schools. Foraker was the school system's lawyer and successfully defeated Gazaway's challenge. Ignoring how it looked, Foraker insisted he was acting only in his professional capacity and not because the segregation policy reflected his own personal feelings. Gazaway rejected Foraker's professional indifference and characterized Foraker's legal work for the schools as "an injustice against black people."[36] Talk against Foraker grew even more heated when Richard T. Greener, the first black man to graduate with honors from Harvard University, wrote in the *Boston Advocate* that Foraker was "an enemy to the manhood of the negro race" and asked Ohio's black voters to "whip" him in the upcoming election.[37]

Harry C. Smith, the editor of Cleveland's black newspaper, believed Foraker had a greater concern than blacks realized and urged Foraker to make a point of showing it. Meanwhile, to his readers he promoted Foraker as a friend of the black race. Working together they overcame black distrust for Foraker, and in November, Foraker won the governor's mansion with black support that he kept all the way to the Senate. And after Brownsville, no black person would question the extent and sincerity of his friendship with them on the march to equality. The Ohio Afro-American League was sure of this; its letterhead prominently displayed Foraker's photo, and above it was the legend "Our Great and Good Friend."

Foraker's attention returned to the pulpit as Grimké took his seat and lawyer Armond Scott formally presented the loving cup along with his own thoughts. To Scott, Foraker stood shoulder to shoulder with Abraham Lincoln, Charles Sumner, Wendell Phillips, Harriet Beecher Stowe, and Frederick Douglass. Those in attendance that night knew these heroes and understood what it meant to be included with them, and as Scott handed Foraker the loving cup, the ovation for him was deafening.

When it quieted down, it was the man of the hour's turn to speak.

"Close up your doors, boys, here come the niggers."

Joe Crixell's warning to men on the
sidewalk in front of the Ruby Saloon, August 13, 1906

CHAPTER TWO

"THEY ARE SHOOTING US UP"

IT HAS BEEN CALLED the shooting (to emphasize its violence), the affray (to minimize it), the raid (to make it bigger), the riot (to make it more brutal), and the incident (to expand its scope). Just as there are different names, there are different accounts of what happened. All agree there was gunfire around midnight on or close to Garrison Road, the street running parallel along and on the city side of the waist-high wall separating Fort Brown from Brownsville. From there it advanced into the city through Cowen Alley, which ran not quite perpendicular to Garrison Road, then turned corners and down streets until its strength ebbed three or so city blocks from where it started. It lasted no more than fifteen or twenty minutes. Along its path, homes and buildings were riddled with bullet holes, a policeman was so badly wounded his arm had to be amputated, and a bartender was shot dead.

Some townspeople, both Anglo and Mexican, who claimed to be witnesses were positive the men who rampaged through Brownsville wore army uniforms; some others saw they were Negro. Either way, this identified the raiders as soldiers from Fort Brown.

FREDERICK J. COMBE, A lifelong resident of Brownsville, was, like his father and brother, a physician. They lived together in a house at the corner of Tenth and Elizabeth Streets, a quarter of a mile from Fort Brown.[1] In 1902, after four years as an army surgeon starting

28

with the Spanish-American War and ending with the insurrection in the Philippines handed off to America by Spain after that war, he came home to practice medicine. With him on the troop transport ship across the Pacific Ocean was the Twenty-Fifth Infantry, also returning from the fighting in the Philippines, and Dr. Combe acted as its medical officer during the voyage.[2] Back in Brownsville, Dr. Combe stood in for the army's regular physician when he was away, and in that role he again cared for its soldiers.[3]

The Brownsville he returned to was a nondescript town deep in south Texas. Photographs taken right after the shooting show some sturdy buildings, telephone poles, and street lighting for unpaved streets.[4] Lamenting a bright but brief past of prosperity, the town's leaders were seeking ways to bring more people in and the good times back, not unlike so many Rust Belt cities and their chambers of commerce at the end of the century. Its population was about six thousand, and only about one-third of its citizens were white Anglos. Fewer than a dozen Negroes lived in Brownsville itself and only two hundred in surrounding Cameron County.[5] Except for the very bottom tip of Florida, Brownsville was the farthest south place in the United States. Yet the ways reflected more the American West. Some of this perhaps was the overall western character of Texas that sifted down from the rest of the state. A greater influence was the proximity of Mexico, just across the Rio Grande.[6] Unlike the rest of what had been the rebellious Confederacy, in which by far the largest nonwhite population was black, in Brownsville it was Mexican.[7] Mexicans, by ancestry and culture if not citizenship, were the majority of Brownsville's residents.[8]

After the 1890 population count, the US Census Office decreed the American frontier was closed. The raw society of the American West had been gentled by demands for civilization. But Brownsville retained something of the Wild West. As the newly returned Dr. Combe walked the streets of his hometown, he saw men passing along with one or two revolvers—sometimes as many as six or seven—strapped to their waists.[9] A man toting a rifle was not uncommon, even if he was simply taking the air as he strolled with his lady. This was not nostalgia nor a reluctance to let go of the robust pioneer era the

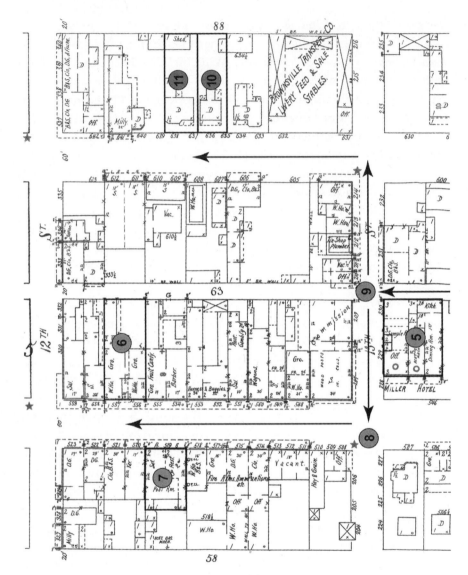

(1) Rendall residence/Western Union
(2) Cowen house
(3) Leahy Hotel
(4) Thorn house
(5) Miller Hotel
(6) Tillman's Ruby Saloon
(7) Crixell's Saloon
(8) location where Dominguez was shot

(9) intersection where raid split in two
(10) Starck house
(11) Tate house
(12) Company B barracks (barracks for
Companies A, C, and D not shown)

→ arrows indicate route taken by
shooters

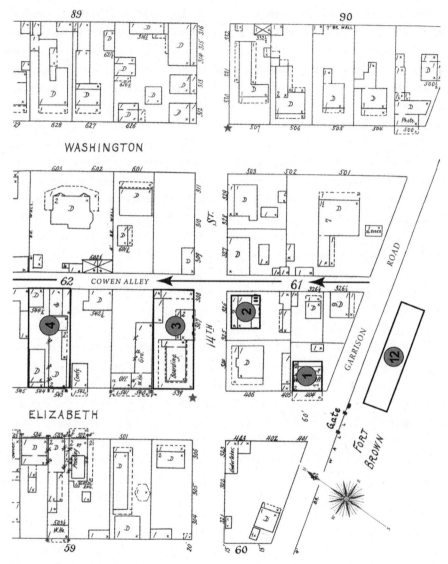

Brownsville map. From Senate Document 155, vol. 11, Parts 1 and 2, The Brownsville Affray, 59th Congress, 2d Session, 1906–1907. Washington: Government Printing Office, 1907.

historian Frederick Jackson Turner said helped define what it was to be American.[10] Men carried these weapons because they used them. Two or three nights a week, the streets crackled with gunfire. It was so commonplace that people stopped noticing it.[11] In Brownsville, a man felt he had to be armed to the teeth to protect himself because the city's woeful police department would not. Law enforcement was at best inadequate; at worst, it was a criminal enterprise. One problem was there were not enough police to accomplish anything. The city had only ten full-time cops, and only one spoke English. Police could supplement their pay by clopping civilians on the head with a pistol butt, throwing them in jail, and then demanding money to set them free.[12] Soldiers stationed at Fort Brown were especially vulnerable to this. One soldier in the Twenty-Sixth Infantry, the white regiment replaced by the black Twenty-Fifth, was shot in the leg. Another was badly beaten. The assaulting police in both these cases were not taken to court; instead, in pre-Combe Brownsville, it was the soldiers, the victims of violence, who were criminally tried (though both of these would be acquitted).

Dr. Combe set out to do something about Brownsville's lawlessness. In 1905 he ran for mayor and won. He wasted no time instituting "decided reforms."[13] The quality of men recruited for the police department increased measurably, though the force's size grew only modestly. With now a professional police force, for the first time wearing uniforms and badges, and with a new chief who instilled discipline and a professional attitude, civilian self-help would not be needed. Or tolerated. No longer would civilians be permitted to brazenly carry guns. Though Mayor Combe was a strict man, from his time in the army he retained a soft spot in his heart for soldiers, and he accepted some slack where they were concerned. He instructed his new chief of police that "a soldier is a soldier, and he should be allowed some latitude."[14] When the Twenty-Sixth Infantry made way for the soldiers of the Twenty-Fifth, the departing soldiers had come to think of him as a friend.[15]

THOUGH HE LATER SAID he never remembered a time the town was quieter and he had no reason to anticipate any trouble, on the evening of Monday, August 13, 1906, Mayor Combe was uneasy.[16] There was a disquieting incident the day before involving Mrs. Lon Evans, who lived with her husband in "the lower part of town" and claimed she had been assaulted in her yard by a soldier. The way the incident was treated in the headlines of the August 13 *Brownsville Herald* ("INFAMOUS OUTRAGE. Negro Soldier Invaded Private Premises Last Night and Attempted to Seize a White Lady") created, in Mayor Combe's words, "a good deal of excitement in the town," and in particular in the lady's husband. The outraged Mr. Evans and the mayor paid a call late that afternoon on Major Charles W. Penrose, the battalion's commanding officer, to demand the guilty soldier be found and punished. Brownsville was so stirred up the mayor cautioned Penrose that if soldiers went into town that night, they would be in danger. Penrose agreed to revoke all passes, keep the men on post, and send patrols into Brownsville searching out men violating his orders.[17] Calmed by this reassurance, Mayor Combe and the aggrieved Mr. Evans returned to town.

The mayor deliberately may have overstated his fears to Major Penrose to make certain the soldiers were kept on post. After the Evans matter and the incendiary treatment it had been given in the newspaper, it wasn't a bad idea to separate them from the townspeople for a while and buy a little peace and quiet. Or maybe he put on a show to calm the distraught Mr. Evans, who, according to Mayor Combe, had tears in his eyes as he told Major Penrose what had happened to his wife.[18] Nevertheless, it was clear to the Brownsville mayor that some precaution was in order. After meeting with Evans and Penrose, Mayor Combe made a beeline to Police Chief George Conner and instructed him to ensure his force was on high alert. "You will be especially on the qui vive—I remember using that expression."[19] As with the warning to Major Penrose, this stern directive may have masked the mayor's calmer assessment of the situation. Regardless of what he said to both men, he saw no signs of trouble and was confident that if any was brewing, he would have known it. Otherwise he might have coupled his warning to the police chief with a directive to increase the size of the force on duty that night and put them out on the streets to discourage hotheads from getting the wrong ideas. After reconnoitering the town and seeing nothing out of place, he headed home and, reclining on a cot on his back porch (called a *gallery* in that part of Texas), he quietly read until around 11:30 p.m. By then he was confident there would be no trouble. With the soldiers confined to Fort Brown, they and the citizens were safe from each other. Brownsville was quiet. Mayor Combe relaxed his guard and, without getting up from his cot, quickly dozed off.

Almost immediately he was awakened by gunfire.

THE RIO GRANDE SEPARATES the southern edge of Brownsville from Mexico. Because of a small oxbow in the river, a narrow part of Matamoros, the city's Mexican neighbor, stabs up into Brownsville, and were its streets to run true to the four compass points, this poke into its belly would interrupt their orderly arrangement. Brownsville's planners tilted its geometric grid so that streets ran northeast to southwest (generally those with numbers) and northwest to southeast (generally those with names). As a consequence, Brownsville's downtown was out of plumb with the compass, but its streets intersected each other at right angles and formed perfectly rectangular city blocks at regular intervals. This out-of-kilter city map conveyed the sense of order and orderliness Mayor Combe had been working to bring about in reality and not just on a surveyor's plat.

Fort Brown was on the western side of the oxbow's bulge. Brownsville's downtown and its inclined matrix of streets angled away from the post to the northwest, but Brownsville residents disregarded this and thought of the city as splaying out to the north.[20] The fort's main gate was at the southeastern (or as Brownsvillites would say, southern) dead end of Elizabeth Street (along with other named streets, it ran north and south; numbered streets ran east and west), where it met Garrison Road and the waist-high wall that divided fort from city. The first street east of Elizabeth Street was Washington Street. After it in sequence, matching the order of presidents, came Adams, Jefferson, Madison, and so on. In between them were alleys, usually named informally after a person or a family whose house backed onto it. Inside the fort, close to the wall and parallel to it, was a line of four two-floor barracks buildings. Since for strategic reasons the fort was built to face Mexico, the barracks had their backs to Brownsville.

The result of all of this was that outside the fort, Elizabeth Street, the presidents' streets, and the alleys started at the fort's wall and ran north (that's "Brownsville north") away from it. Immediately inside Fort Brown were the four enlisted barracks with their back porches (*galleries* in Brownsville) looking down Elizabeth Street, the presidents' streets, and the alleys; and on the other side of the barracks was the rest of the post, the Rio Grande, and, across the river, Mexico.

THERE IS AN ACCOUNT of the shooting most people, then and now, can agree on. It begins with the sound of gunfire just before midnight, close by the fort's main gate where Elizabeth Street deadended into Garrison Road. Most believe it took place at the mouth of Cowen Alley (named after the Cowen family that lived on it), half a block away from the gate.

While the exact number of shooters was never determined, it was not more than twenty, and probably fewer than that. They funneled through Cowen Alley toward the downtown. When they had gone one block to Fourteenth Street, the closest numbered street to the fort (the numbers getting lower the farther north one went from the fort) and running parallel to the waist-high wall, they came to the Cowen family home on their left and shot into it, then continued away from the fort.

At Thirteenth Street they divided themselves into two groups; one turned left toward Elizabeth Street and the other to the right toward Washington Street, where each group again turned to continue separately into the town and away from the fort. As they moved along, they kept shooting.

Before the one group could make the turn onto Elizabeth Street, a Brownsville policeman on horseback riding down Thirteenth Street spotted it as he crossed Cowen Alley. He continued down Thirteenth Street to warn guests at the Miller Hotel. To put distance between himself and the shooters, he sped up past the hotel to make a right turn onto Elizabeth Street. The shooters, still on Thirteenth Street but now behind him, shot at him, and just as he made the turn, one of their bullets struck him in the arm and another hit his horse. The animal fell dead, its body pinning the policeman's leg underneath. He managed to extricate himself from beneath the horse and continued on foot down Elizabeth Street in the direction of Twelfth Street.

Meanwhile, as these shooters followed him down Thirteenth Street, they repeatedly shot into the Miller Hotel. When they turned onto Elizabeth Street and got abreast of the Ruby Saloon on their right, they fired into it, killing the bartender inside.

The band of raiders that had turned onto Washington Street got a bit farther north, almost to Twelfth Street. It stopped at the house in which the Fred Starck family slept and shot into it.

By then, the riot's momentum slowed and the shooting ended, with the shooters on Elizabeth Street about two and a half blocks away from the fort and those on Washington Street almost three blocks away. The raid was over.

SO MANY PEOPLE CAN agree with the foregoing narrative because it leaves out so much. Who were the shooters? Why did they do it? What happened to the two clusters of shooters when the rampage ended? The Brownsville townspeople who claimed to see and hear the violence had their answer: the shooters were Negro soldiers from Fort Brown. The civilians were convinced of this because they wore army uniforms, looked black, and from the way they spoke sounded black. Some witnesses claimed they saw soldiers coming out of the fort and into the town by climbing over the garrison's waist-high wall. Most people said the soldiers were paying the town back for abuse received from whites since they took up duty at Fort Brown. As for what happened to the two groups of shooters when they stopped shooting, some were seen running in the direction of the fort to get back there quickly and avoid detection. This was further proof the shooters were soldiers.

Because it was very late at night, few of the eyewitnesses were in the street. Most were inside their homes when they first heard shots, and only a few of them ran outside to see what was going on. The others stayed safely inside and peeked through the curtains. There also were some people in saloons playing cards, eating, and drinking, and they stayed there. Yet almost all were very sure about what they had seen and heard. The shooters were well-armed soldiers. And they had to be from the Twenty-Fifth Infantry, the only unit at Fort Brown.

Inside the fort were the officers and soldiers, so new to Fort Brown they were still unpacking their gear; none of them witnessed what happened outside the fort. A few heard voices and shots and agreed with those townspeople who located the trouble as coming from inside the town. Unlike the townspeople, the voices heard by the soldiers inside Fort Brown were white, and they were cursing the soldiers. The soldiers believed the townspeople had it backward. It was civilians—not soldiers—shooting up Brownsville, and they might have been attacking the fort itself.

Other than that, the soldiers had nothing to say about the incident. Except for insisting that not one of them was a shooter.

IT WAS FOUR OR five shots that awoke Mayor Combe, and he thought they might have been from a pistol. These were followed immediately by several more shots, but these sounded like high-power rifles such as he remembered from the army. As he jumped out of his cot, there was a third volley of shots. All the firing seemed to be coming from the direction of Fort Brown. Pulling on his trousers, he yelled upstairs to his brother, Dr. Joe Combe, that he was going out to see what was happening.[21] He grabbed his revolver, and with his brother he raced off down Elizabeth Street in the direction of Fort Brown.[22]

GEORGE AND ELIZABETH RENDALL lived in a second-floor apartment above the Western Union office at Elizabeth Street and Garrison Road, about five and a half blocks from the Combe house, across the street from Fort Brown and only thirty-five feet from the garrison wall.[23] The seventy-two-year-old Mr. Rendall had been with Commodore Matthew C. Perry's voyage to Japan in 1853 that opened that country to the West.[24] Now burdened by age and "imperfect" hearing, Mr. Rendall nevertheless heard and was awakened by shots fired close to his house, shots he too thought came from a pistol. This may have been the same volley that jarred Mayor Combe from his sleep.

Getting out of bed, the Rendalls went to the window. Since firing a revolver was a common method to signal an alarm in Brownsville, Mr. Rendall's first reaction was that there was a fire somewhere in the town or, since the shots seemed to come from the direction of Fort Brown, on the post. By going from window to window, they got a good view of the fort and the entire city but saw no sign of flames. At the window facing the fort, they observed men in the fort moving this way and that. Mr. Rendall saw them firing weapons, one of which he could see was a pistol. He could see it elevated into the sky as it fired.[25] How well he could see this might be open to question; since 1866, he was blind in his right eye.[26] Meanwhile, a shot struck their apartment, showering Mrs. Rendall with splinters and dust.[27]

Mrs. Rendall could hear voices but could not tell "whether they were colored people or white people."[28] Mr. Rendall had no such reservations. The men he saw scurrying about were "colored men." He also saw them "vaulting the wall" and running into the street, but which way he could not say.[29] Half a minute later, he heard the shooting start again. It came "from the direction of the Cowen Alley."[30]

Inside the fort itself, Private Joseph Howard of Company D, a first-term enlistee in the army, was on sentry duty.[31] His post was the four barracks of the enlisted men, just inside the garrison wall, and he paced counterclockwise completely around them. When Howard was behind the barracks, to his right was the waist-high wall (about fifty feet away) and the town.[32] He heard two shots just as he reached the gap between Company B's and C's barracks. That put him almost directly across from Cowen Alley and not far from the Western Union office and the Rendall apartment above it. At first, Howard placed the shots "right outside the gate along the wall," which would have put them "close by" the Rendalls. He quickly changed this to say the gunfire was closer to the Company A barracks, which were then empty.[33] This would place the firing a block or so away from the Rendalls. While turning to look in the direction of the two shots, he immediately heard a fusillade of shots outside the fort and directly across from where he was standing. "The shooting seemed to be over in that little Valley" between Washington and Elizabeth Streets.[34]

Yelling to the sergeant of the guard, Howard ran through the gap between the two barracks and onto the parade ground. Elevating his rifle in the direction away from the town, he fired three times as an alarm to the post. He would have been standing in Mr. Rendall's line of sight about the time Mr. Rendall saw a soldier elevate what he thought was a pistol and fire. Howard said he saw no shooters and no soldiers on the fort's grounds.[35]

On sentry duty that night along with Private Howard was Private Charley Hairston of Company B, in the army only fourteen months. He was in the officers' quarters along a lagoon on the other side of the parade ground from the enlisted barracks. He also heard six shots at 11:50 p.m. coming from Garrison Road and Cowen Alley, the spot pinpointed by the Rendalls and Private Howard. When these six shots rang out, Hairston was standing next to Major Penrose's quarters. Seeing that the commanding officer had not yet gone to bed, Hairston rushed to Penrose's door, only to have it open just as he approached. The major and his wife had heard the same shots. "What is the matter?" Penrose asked, and later remembered Hairston answering, "They are shooting us up."[36] Penrose, wary from his meeting earlier in the evening with Mayor Combe, ordered Hairston to sound the "Call to Arms." In 1906 soldiers and Marines communicated with loud bugle calls that could be heard clearly over long distances and above the din of combat. The melody unique to each call and what it meant had to be memorized. "Call to Arms" told the troops to assemble with their weapons at a predesignated location without delay. Rushing across the parade deck, Hairston called out, "Trumpeter of the Guard, sound Call to Arms!"[37]

ASLEEP WAS COMPANY B'S First Sergeant Mingo Sanders, with more than twenty-five years' service, the most experienced and longest serving noncommissioned officer in the battalion. Because of his senior rank, he and his wife lived in quarters away from the enlisted barracks. Each of these quarters had three separate living units, which Sanders shared with the families of Sergeants Darby W. O. Brawner and Jacob Frazier of Companies C and D. It was Mrs. Brawner who first heard the shooting, and she slipped out of her bed to knock on the Sanders' front door. Like so many others, Mrs. Brawner thought the shots were nothing more serious than a fire alarm. She called through the door, "There is a fire out here or something." That got Sanders's attention, and he leaped from bed, getting to the door just in time to hear the bugler sounding the "Call to Arms." Sanders knew what this meant. "Why, that is not any fire," he said to his wife and Mrs. Brawner. Pulling on his uniform as he ran, Sanders raced to form up with his company at its barracks.[38]

Off post, Private Edward Johnson lived with his wife and baby at the intersection of Garrison Road and Jefferson Street, about three and a half blocks from the post's Elizabeth Street gate. Not a noncommissioned officer entitled to post housing for his family, he had permission to live in the town. Halfway through his fourth enlistment, with more than ten years in the army, all with Company C, Johnson was described as a neat man with character, a soldier who had exhibited good behavior. That is why he was picked to be the commanding officer's orderly and given privileges few other privates would have, such as permission to live off base.[39] Johnson's instinct was to get himself and his family out of bed immediately and down on the floor to wait for the shooting to end. It seemed to him it had come from "down toward the gate . . . right down in that part of town . . . where [Cowen] Alley is." He saw no shooters. Entering the fort the next day he saw no bullet holes or other marks in its walls or buildings.[40]

IN THAT ALLEY REFERRED to by the Rendalls, the two sentries, and Private Johnson, Mr. and Mrs. Louis Cowen and five of their children lived in a small frame house one block from the fort. The family had just returned from a visit to San Antonio and on the evening of the shooting threw a party for the older children and their friends. Around 10:30 p.m., as the party was breaking up, Mr. Cowen left for a restaurant to buy a sandwich for himself and a beer for his wife. The house was quiet. The only light came from the lamp above the dining room table where Mrs. Anna Cowen sat to await her husband's return.

Mrs. Cowen heard the gunfire and was sure it came "from the direction of the post." Then "the firing came right on us" and she knew "they were shooting at our house." Gathering her children, who were scattered throughout the house, she quickly herded them under the bed, just as Private Johnson did with his family, and they hugged the floor waiting for the shooting to end. She heard bullets whizzing through the house and smelled the gunfire. Bullets came into the dining room, the younger children's room, and her older son's room. When it was over, they counted twenty-three bullet holes altogether. No one in the house was hurt.[41]

HERBERT ELKINS WAS SEVENTEEN years old and had been in Brownsville only a couple of weeks longer than the men of the Twenty-Fifth Infantry. He came from Sutherland Spring, Texas, a speck on the map about two hundred sixty miles north, and he got a job in Brownsville working at a confectionary store. He boarded at the Leahy Hotel, across Fourteenth Street from the Cowen house. The same age as one of the Cowen daughters, he was at their party until it broke up around 10:30 p.m., when he walked some of the younger guests to their homes. By 11:30 p.m. he was back in his room on the second floor of Mrs. Leahy's hotel and in bed. The room's window looked straight down on the Cowen house across the street, and from it he could see the roof of one of the enlisted barracks at Fort Brown. The first shots seemed to come from "right there about the [garrison] wall and the barracks." Like others, Elkins thought there might be a fire, and he went to the window but saw no flames. Then he saw "two negro soldiers." They were coming onto Fourteenth Street just to the left of the Cowen house. Both men had rifles and were wearing parts of army uniforms. He "could see them plainly," and "they were colored soldiers." They "emptied their guns at the Cowen house." Once. Twice. Reloading their weapons, they walked back to the corner of Fourteenth Street and Cowen Alley, where another ten or fifteen soldiers joined them. After momentary confusion, a soldier hollered, "This way," and they turned "back up the alley toward the Miller Hotel."[42]

ABOUT HALFWAY ALONG ON Cowen Alley, between the Cowen house and the Miller Hotel, was the backyard of a house that fronted on Elizabeth Street and extended back almost to the alley. Dr. Charles H. Thorn lived and had his dental practice there. A fifty-year-old bachelor who lived with his mother, Thorn had gotten home late after a meeting at the Masonic Lodge. Reclining in bed but not asleep, he had a clear view through the open doorway into the adjacent kitchen. Because the evening was warm and the kitchen window was open, he could hear outside to the alley. Thorn was just about to fall asleep when he was jolted by the sound of gunfire—two or three shots. They came from the direction of the fort, possibly by the Leahy Hotel half a block away from the Thorn home. He remembered a policeman had been shot at that very spot a few years earlier. Fumbling for his slippers so he could get out of bed, he could hear the firing continue and get closer to him. It sounded like army weapons; he was sure it was not Winchesters or six-shooters. Just as he found his slippers, he heard men speaking outside in the alley: "There he goes" or "There they go," the voices were saying. He said the voices sounded like they were Negro. They continued, "Give them hell, God damn them."[43] Thorn never saw the shooters; he only heard them out on Cowen Alley as they came from the direction of the fort, passed his house, and continued in the direction that would take them to the Miller Hotel.

The raiders were now almost two blocks from the fort and working their way more deeply into the town.[44]

MANAGING THE MILLER HOTEL were S. C. and Helen Moore, a couple who had lived in Brownsville fewer than three years. Photos of the hotel show a three-story brick structure facing Elizabeth Street, with the rear of the building on Cowen Alley and its northern side running along Thirteenth Street. Mr. and Mrs. Moore lived in a second-floor room at the corner of the building, where one window faced toward Fort Brown and the other looked onto Cowen Alley.

From their room they could hear the shooters advance along the alley, pass their window, and turn onto Thirteenth Street.

Earlier that evening, Mr. Moore had been initiated as a first-degree Mason at the Masonic Lodge meeting attended by Dr. Thorn. Hearing the shots around 11:50 p.m., Mr. Moore's first thought, as that of so many others, was there must be a fire, which he believed from where the shots were coming had to be on the fort's grounds. Mrs. Moore disagreed. "No, it is trouble with the Negroes on account of Evans's wife."[45] She was familiar with the sound of gunfire from her own shooting experience, and the shots she heard suggested military weapons. Not sure she was correct, Mr. Moore sat at the window, watching for the flames that would prove him right, when he heard the shots that convinced him he was wrong. They seemed to be coming from the Leahy Hotel down on Fourteenth Street and close to Fort Brown. Keeping low, the Moores stayed in the hotel as the shooting outside came and went. They never saw the shooters themselves, but they could hear them. Mr. Moore remembered their voices as coarse and rough, and from his familiarity with the sound of black voices, he thought they were spoken by black men. His wife would not commit herself. But they both heard a shooter say, as the band came down the alley and approached Thirteenth Street, "There goes the son of a bitch on a horse; get him."[46] And then they heard more shooting as the shooters made their way up the alley and turned down "Thirteenth street toward Washington Street and toward Elizabeth street—both ways."[47]

Staying in the Miller Hotel in a large corner room on the second floor, one side facing Cowen Alley and the other Thirteenth Street, were Hale and Ethel Odin and their five children. Mr. Odin, an alumnus of the University of Michigan ("Graduated at Ann Arbor in the class of '72," he volunteered without being asked), had moved from Detroit to Dallas as a young boy.[48] Now living in San Antonio, his work in "land and immigration" took him on extended trips to many parts of the country, and on this visit to Brownsville he took his entire family with him. On the night of the shooting, they had been there six weeks.

Mr. Odin heard the first shots at 11:55 p.m. ("I noted the time," he said with some precision; "It was about 12 o'clock," Mrs. Odin more casually recalled).[49] She was in bed with their sick baby; her husband was sitting at a window on the alley side of the room. To him, the firing was down the alley in the direction of the fort. He called his wife over to the window. She left the baby and along with their young son came to the window. Looking out, Mr. Odin counted six soldiers ("3 abreast in two columns"), then a seventh (a "large negro soldier") running alongside, then an eighth who joined them. The large soldier gave the order to halt, then, "There he goes; shoot!" Because earlier Mr. Odin had noticed a stray black dog loping along the alley, he figured the dog was mad and still loose, and the soldiers were chasing it to kill it. Meanwhile four more soldiers came up the alley from the direction of the fort and joined the first group. The observant Mr. Odin counted seven soldiers wearing "their usual dark brown uniforms . . . four were without jackets and one was bareheaded." At least two volleys followed. Suddenly, a "large negro with freckled face fired point blank" at the three Odins. A bullet smashed through the lower sash of the open window, entered the room (its steel jacket later was found on the floor) and continued into the ceiling. The Odin boy fell back, and Mrs. Odin feared he was hit. Her coolheaded husband saw no blood and calmly remarked, "I reckon not."

Mr. Odin identified the shooters as black not only because he saw them looking directly up at the room's window; he also heard them. "They spoke in the manner and vernacular of the negroes."[50] Mrs. Odin heard soldiers hollering, "Shoot him; there he goes," as soon as she reached the window. She could see the soldiers were shooting at a man on a horse, whom she recognized as a policeman. Mr. Odin's chronology is slightly different. "There he goes; shoot!" was not yelled until the soldiers reached the corner of Thirteenth Street, then came the shot into the room, their son falling back, and after that, "We heard a heavy fall of a horse . . . and the groan of a dying horse . . . [and] the scream from a man." Both heard, "We got that son of bitch," after the shot that felled the horse.

The soldiers then ran south down Thirteenth Street in the direction of Elizabeth Street. There was a volley to the soldiers' right, into the King Building across Thirteenth Street from the hotel, then, crossing to that side of Thirteenth Street, the soldiers turned back and fired into the Miller Hotel. From there, according to both Mr. and Mrs. Odin, the soldiers went north (away from the fort) along the alley. This means they did not see the shooters divide into two groups and go in opposite directions on Thirteenth Street.

A few minutes later, the soldiers, now reversing their direction, were "running back toward the fort." That was the last the Odins saw of them. The next morning they took the train out of town.[51]

ALSO STAYING THAT NIGHT at the Miller Hotel were Charles Canada, a newspaperman, on the third floor facing Thirteenth Street and one room away from Cowen Alley, and Charles Chace, a locomotive engineer on a layover in Brownsville between shifts, also on the third floor facing Thirteenth Street. Canada saw five to ten men, a smaller group than the Odins saw on the alley, suggesting the shooters already might have split and Canada saw only those going to Elizabeth Street. He saw them when he heard the stricken horse fall to the ground, and he ran to the window to see what it meant. He heard the voices of "colored men," and he heard one of them say, "We have got him." He could see that they were wearing uniforms, "not citizens' clothes," but could not see their faces distinctly. He said nothing about the shooters splitting into two groups and moving in opposite directions on Thirteenth Street.

But Chace did. Sort of. He saw one man on Thirteenth Street coming from Elizabeth Street. He saw others, maybe fifteen, scatter, some coming closer to the hotel, presumably from the alley, but he did not say and was not asked to specifically state the direction these other men were coming from. It could have been from Elizabeth Street or from the alley on the way to Elizabeth Street. Chace saw the policeman riding the horse down Thirteenth Street as he passed his room window, and from Cowen Alley at the rear of the hotel he saw shooters fire at the horse and kill it.[52]

THE POLICEMAN WAS LIEUTENANT M. Yonacio ("Joe") Dominguez. Fifty-seven years old at the time of the shooting, Dominguez was a native of Brownsville and on the police force for twenty or so years, the last twelve as a lieutenant. He occasionally was called upon to arrest soldiers from Fort Brown but never had trouble with the men of the Twenty-Fifth Infantry.

Just before midnight, Dominguez was at the police station at the center of town between Eleventh and Twelfth Streets. He was waiting for the school bell, which rang at midnight every night, and his meticulous recollection of the moment he heard the first shots— 11:52 p.m. exactly—may have been because, with nothing else to do, he was staring at the clock waiting for the bell to ring. The firing came from "down near the garrison, on Washington Street."[53] (That would place it one block from Elizabeth Street and half a block from Cowen Alley.) Climbing onto his horse, Dominguez rode down Washington Street in the direction of the fort. Reaching Fourteenth Street, he came upon Genaro Padron, another policeman, who told him about the shooting at the Cowen house. Padron identified the shooters as colored soldiers and cautioned Dominguez to get out of the street. Dismounting in the intersection and moving close by the fence for cover, Dominguez tightened the strap holding the saddle to the horse and noticed four soldiers running up Cowen Alley, crossing Four-teenth Street in the direction of the Miller Hotel. Remounting, he raced back on Washington Street to Thirteenth Street and the Miller Hotel, where he turned left in the direction of Cowen Alley and Eliz-abeth Street. When he crossed the alley he heard (but did not see) the shooters walking in the alley toward Thirteenth Street. Once or twice he heard one of them say, "Give them hell!" Spurring his horse on, he rode past the hotel, yelling warnings to those inside. At Elizabeth Street, he turned his horse to the right, away from Fort Brown, and before completing the turn, he stood in his stirrups and turned his body to look back up Thirteenth Street in the direction of the alley. He saw between fifteen and twenty shooters coming out of the alley and turning down Thirteenth Street on both sides of the street.

It was then that he was wounded in the arm and the horse was killed. Pulling his leg from under the dead horse, he staggered down Elizabeth Street. Reaching its corner with Twelfth Street, he heard shots back on Cowen Alley, which put them near the back of two saloons.[54] Brownsville had more than its share of bars, and the Ruby was one of three saloons close to each other on Elizabeth Street, with John Tillman's Ruby and H. H. Weller's saloon cheek by jowl on one side and Joe Crixell's right across the street. When the Twenty-Fifth Infantry arrived in Brownsville, its men learned they could not mix with whites and drink in these saloons. Crixell fudged his refusal by telling the soldiers he preferred the "officer trade," and he figured enlisted men would prefer to do their drinking away from them.[55] Weller was more direct and just said they were not welcome. Tillman, either because he was more accommodating or just a better businessman, set up a separate, segregated bar in the back of the Ruby for the soldiers. There was no business back there this night; it closed early when the soldiers were confined to base.

In the back of his saloon, Joe Crixell and his card-playing buddies were playing "pitch," a game won by the player who came closest to his estimate at the beginning of the game of how many points he would win from the tricks he would take. Just before midnight they heard shooting. Crixell could tell it was gunfire but when one of the other players said it was nothing more than fireworks, the game continued. Immediately they heard another volley. Throwing their cards on the table, they jumped up to see what was happening. One player was worried enough about a bicycle he left outside to try to retrieve it. He changed his mind and scurried back in when a bullet hit the post the bike was leaning against. Crixell himself went to close the front door. Through the open door he saw people from Tillman's Ruby Saloon standing out on the sidewalk across the street. Though he had neither seen nor heard any of the shooters, he called out to them, "Close up your doors, boys, here come the niggers."

WHEN DOMINGUEZ LATER HEARD that the shooters killed Frank Natus, the bartender at the Ruby, he figured it was from the shooting he heard as he reached the intersection of Twelfth and Elizabeth Streets. He was right.

The Ruby extended back to the alley, but about halfway back there was an open-air courtyard for its patrons. John Tillman was sitting there with three friends. Frank Natus was at the bar. At the sound of the gunfire, the men got up and went out onto the side-walk on Elizabeth Street. They saw Joe Crixell across the street in his bar and heard his warning.[56] Natus closed and barred the front door. While he did this, one of Tillman's friends, a jeweler named Nicolas Sanchez Alanis, needed to use the toilet at the rear of the saloon, which was close to Cowen Alley. While in there, he heard voices in the alley. Connecting these voices with the shooting, he stayed put in the bathroom.

Meanwhile, Natus remembered that the gate that opened onto the alley in the back was open. He rushed through the saloon to close and lock it. Alanis yelled to him, "Don't go out there; they are firing from the alley." At that instant, Natus's hands flew up; he groaned "Oh, God," and fell to the ground dead.[57]

FRED STARCK RENTED A house for his family on Washington Street one block west of Cowen Alley and half a block north of Thirteenth Street. On one side was a livery stable with the noise and smells commonly associated with such a business. At midnight on the night of the shooting, the Starck family was asleep. Shots fired at the Miller Hotel only a block and a half away awakened them. No sooner were they up when they heard the terrifying sounds of bullets tearing through the rooms of their home. One ripped into the ceiling above their bed. Mrs. Starck became frantic for the safety of the children, who slept on the same floor as their parents. At least two bullets were fired into the children's room. Mr. Starck then heard men walking or running back toward Thirteenth Street, that is, in the direction of Fort Brown.

DRAWN INTO THE TOWN, the two Combe brothers were running along Elizabeth Street in the direction of the shots that awakened Mayor Combe, he in the street while his brother kept to the sidewalk. After going a block, Dr. Joe heard shooting down Elizabeth Street and called to his brother to hug the wall for protection. Another block farther on, Mayor Combe banged his pistol on an iron lamp post as a signal to summon police, but there was no response. Half a block later, he struck a brickbat against an iron post, and a few minutes later Genaro Padron, who had warned Dominguez of the shooting at the Cowen house, appeared out of the darkness. The three of them continued together until Twelfth Street, where a dark stain under a street light caught Mayor Combe's attention. He identified it as blood (but did not yet know it was Dominguez's). He asked Dr. Joe to follow its trail to find who was hurt, while he and Padron continued on Elizabeth Street.

By the time he got to Crixell's saloon, on his right just past Twelfth Street, the shooting was over.[58]

THIS ACCOUNT OF THE shooting is not complete. There is more testimony damning to the soldiers. James P. McDonnel saw shooting from inside Fort Brown.[59] So did Katie Leahy.[60] Jose Martinez saw men climb over the wall out of the fort at the beginning of the shooting.[61] The last time the Odin family saw what they claimed were soldiers, the men were moving quickly back to the fort. Katie Leahy, who lived across Fourteenth Street from the Cowens, saw the same thing.[62] So did her boarder, Herbert Elkins.[63] So did Ygnacio Garza, who lived with his wife across the alley from the Cowens, and whose home also was shot up by the shooters when the affray began.[64] On the other hand, there were witnesses who could not say they saw or heard soldiers. Some of statements were made under oath, others not. Not all were tested by cross-examination, and from those that were, wholly different inferences and conclusions could be drawn. There were so many investigations and statements and affidavits that over the course of the inquiries, many witnesses contradicted themselves, often in insignificant details, but occasionally largely modifying what they may have said earlier.

Nor is this narrative balanced. The imbalance is most pronounced when one considers there were many recollections of the details of the shooting by people in the town but very few by soldiers closed off inside the fort while the shooting took place.

From this narrative there emerges an understanding of the chronology and locations of the shooting itself and, even more significantly, why suspicion immediately, and some said logically, fell on the soldiers. And why it would be so difficult to convince people the soldiers had nothing to do with the shooting.

"To the men, not the least to be proud of is your record of good behavior in these Islands, proving your race is as law abiding as any in the world. I do not recall of the many places where the 25th Infantry has been stationed on these Islands that the inhabitants were not genuinely sorry when we had been ordered to leave their towns. For that matter, the same is true of your stations in the States."

Colonel A. S. Burt,
commanding officer of the Twenty-Fifth Infantry
during the Philippine Insurrection

CHAPTER THREE

A SPECIAL REQUEST

IN THE SPRING OF 1863, the *New York Times* reported that the nation was a step closer to forming army units made up of negroes (with the lowercase *n*) with the War Department's issue of General Orders No. 143: "Colored troops may be accepted by companies, to be afterward consolidated in battalions and regiments. . . . They will be designated 'U.S. Colored Troops.'"[1]

Blacks had already been fighting and dying for the country without waiting for permission from the War Department. Every American schoolchild learns about Crispus Attucks, the son of an African man and a Nantucket Indian woman. He was working on the Boston docks in 1770 when the brewer Samuel Adams encouraged demonstrations against British soldiers protecting the customs house. Jittery troops opened fire, and Attucks fell, the first American to die for the nation's independence. Many more free blacks would go on to serve in revolutionary militias and the newly formed Continental Army. Black slaves also served and, after the Revolutionary War, their owners tried to get them back.

In the War of 1812, blacks again took up arms on behalf of their country, especially with the navy, where there was a serious shortage of sailors. One captain complained about having to command blacks, but a fellow white officer vouched for the sailors' merits, and in battle, the captain found that "his black sailors performed so well that he wrote to the Secretary of the Navy, praising their courage."[2]

In the Civil War, the famous—and later bloodied—Fifty-Fourth Massachusetts Volunteer Infantry jumped the gun five months before General Orders No. 143.[3] Of the two million soldiers who fought for the Union, 180,000 were black, and forty thousand of these were killed. Their bravery became legendary to those who witnessed it. Turn-of-the-twentieth-century journalist Oswald Garrison Villard would write of the Negro cavalrymen riding gloriously into Richmond: "[They] went in waving their sabres and crying to the negroes on the sidewalks, 'We have come to set you free!' American history has no more stirring moment."[4]

AFTER THE CIVIL WAR, almost all army units—black and white—were disbanded and their soldiers mustered out of the army. In light of the lingering friction with Mexico, and because of the need for soldiers and army posts out in the American West and for federal troops to occupy the South during Reconstruction, on July 28, 1866, Congress enlarged the army and included four Negro infantry regiments. By 1906, there were two black cavalry regiments and two black infantry regiments, one the Twenty-Fifth.

Strictly speaking, the men of the Twenty-Fifth Infantry were not Buffalo Soldiers. Originally the term referred only to a cavalryman with the black Tenth Cavalry. According to the Buffalo Soldiers National Museum, "The most common explanation for the nickname goes back to the Indian Wars, when the Indians saw a similarity between the hair of the Negro soldier and the buffalo. Another account is that the nickname reflects the Indian's awe of the fierce fighting ability of the Tenth Cavalry."[5] It may have been both. According to some historians, in September 1867, Private John Randall of Troop G, Tenth Cavalry, was escorting civilians on a hunting trip in Kansas when, without warning, seventy Cheyenne attacked them. The Indians quickly killed the civilian hunters and shot Randall's horse out from under him. Shot in his shoulder and stabbed eleven times by Indian lances, Randall, using only his pistol, fought back with such ferocity that the Cheyenne warriors retreated. They told others of this black soldier, "who had fought like a cornered buffalo; who like a buffalo had suffered wound after wound, yet had not died; and who like a buffalo had a thick and shaggy mane of hair."[6] The soldiers of the Tenth Cavalry took to the name, seeing it as confirmation of their bravery and tenacity.

IT WAS THE CAVALRY, usually the white cavalry, that did most of the fighting in the American West. The infantry in the nineteenth century, white and black, served only marginally as soldiers, and its duties in the West were often unsoldierly. Most often the Twenty-Fifth Infantry guarded settlers, worked as laborers, and grew bored in garrison.[7] The garrisons in which its soldiers lived could be worse than the backbreaking labor. In 1875, the regiment's commanding officer wrote about conditions at Fort Davis, Texas, after every rainfall: "everything saturated with rain, the dirt floor full four inches deep of mud, and the men sitting at meals while their heads and backs were being defiled with ooze from the dripping dirt roof."[8] In Texas was a hard place to be. The climate, characterized by Brigadier General E. O. C. Ord, commanding general of the Department of Texas, was "rigorous [with] the extremes of heat in summer and cold in winter," and it was taking its toll. Referring "especially to the Tenth Cavalry and the colored troops," Ord recommended in his annual report for 1878 that the troops be rotated to "take their turn for duty in the vicinity of civilization." After much thought and discussion where this might be (including the question of whether Negro troops could adapt to a colder climate), in April 1880 the Twenty-Fifth Infantry was divided among three forts in Minnesota and the Dakota Territory. Only Fort Meade was any improvement over the previous posting in Texas, and that was because it also housed the Seventh Cavalry, back up to full strength after its annihilation at the Little Bighorn.[9]

After eight years in the Upper Great Plains, the regiment was ordered west to Montana, where again the regiment's units were divided among three forts, one appropriately enough named Fort Shaw to honor Colonel Robert Gould Shaw, the commanding officer of the Civil War's Negro Fifty-Fourth Massachusetts Volunteers. At Fort Missoula, Montana, the regimental band was a superb group of musicians, and not only the soldiers thought so. Its Thursday evening concerts quickly became a part of the city's social and cultural life. No civic or patriotic event in Missoula would be complete without it.

But even the band could not compete for the soldiers' affection with the regiment's beloved baseball team. Formed at Fort Missoula in 1894 by Master Sergeant Dalbert Green, the team was so popular that Colonel Andrew S. Burt, the regimental commander, made baseball teams a permanent part of the regiment to improve morale.[10] Because players on the regiment's first team had to provide their own uniforms, the nine men taking the field wore a variety of caps and jerseys. A photo shows one natty player wearing what appears to be a necktie. By 1899, the team had real uniforms, each with a large block number "25" sewn on the left front side of the jersey.

These soldiers knew how to play ball. In the 1920s, Green reminisced about the 1903 tournament for the Department of Missouri championship. Lieutenant John N. Stratt had marched his team from Fort Niobrara, Nebraska, 254 miles to the tournament at Fort Riley, Kansas. He arranged for games along the route of the march to enable the players on his newly formed squad to learn each other's skills, strengths, and weaknesses and to shape themselves into a winning team. Fort Niobrara won every one of these games.

At the tournament, it faced the other Twenty-Fifth Infantry team, Fort Reno, the cofavorite to win it all. Disregarding its fatigue from the march, Fort Niobrara, "to the surprise of the 'sure thing' betters," won and advanced to the final game against the other favorite, the Tenth Cavalry. The championship game was a close one and went into extra innings, but the infantry brought home the winning run and defeated the cavalry 3–2.[11]

ON A LATE-SPRING morning in 1897, Missoulians showed their affection for the Twenty-Fifth Infantry when they turned out to cheer on twenty soldiers as they began—of all things—a bicycle ride. Lieutenant James A. Moss had finished last in his class at West Point (an "honor" entitling Moss to be remembered as "the Goat"). Few of his higher-ranking classmates had wanted to serve out in the remote West; fewer still wanted to command black soldiers.[12] Moss the Goat wound up in Montana with the Twenty-Fifth Infantry and started thinking about military applications for the bicycle.

Moss figured bicycles were a good deal cheaper than horses to buy and maintain. They did not have to be fed, and this meant no feed costs and no land needed for grazing. They were smaller and less visible than horses. Bicycles never would attract attention by whinnying at inopportune times, so they were ideal for reconnaissance. Bikes could revolutionize how couriers got the message through. Moss was sure two-wheeled cycles could even transport most of the army's supplies, including food. He formally petitioned the army to permit him to form a bicycle corps to test his theories. Working its way through channels, his request came to General Nelson A. Miles, commanding general of the army.

Miles was a true army hero. He enlisted at the start of the Civil War, was commissioned a captain, and fought in practically every major battle other than Gettysburg, missing that only because he was recovering from a wound. A handsome man, whose opinion of his own skills and potential was monumental (Theodore Roosevelt would call him "the brave peacock"), his first postwar duty was commanding Fort Monroe with its prisoner Jefferson Davis. His second was to command the all-Negro Fortieth Infantry.[13] In the American West, Miles fought in the Indian Wars and went after Sitting Bull, Chief Joseph, and Crazy Horse. In 1886 he captured Geronimo; in 1890 he dealt with the Sioux. In 1891, General Miles watched a bicycle race in Madison Square Garden and came away wondering how to make use of bicycles in the army. When Moss's proposal came across his desk in 1894, Miles had not forgotten that race nor his time with the Buffalo Soldiers. He approved Moss's request. The new unit was called the Twenty-Fifth Infantry Bicycle Corps.

Imposing its designation may have been, but the "corps" consisted of exactly "one lieutenant, one sergeant, one corporal, one musician, and five privates, one of them a good mechanic."[14] And, of course, bicycles. A. G. Spalding & Bros., the sporting goods company, smelled an opportunity here to boost bicycle sales. This— and no doubt its spirit of patriotism—moved it to donate bikes to the army. They were strong and rugged, with frames and rims made of steel, which made them very heavy. Exactly what the army and Lieutenant Moss wanted.

In July 1896, testing of the bikes and the soldiers began. Moss had to come up with new commands for his new corps. "Jump fence" was for climbing over an obstacle. It alerted a rider to stand on his bike's seat, climb over whatever was in the way, then reach back and pull his "steel steed" across. Different physical conditioning was demanded. The men undertook long rides, up to 126 miles, in rain and heat, through mud and dust, testing themselves and their equipment. It all went very well.

The final test would be an almost-two-thousand-mile ride from Fort Missoula to St. Louis, Missouri, by twenty men, including Sergeant Mingo Sanders, who was responsible for the riders' morale.[15] They, the assistant post surgeon, and a reporter from the *Daily Missoulian* were off and cycling on June 14. As they departed Missoula at 5:30 a.m., an hour timed to meet the sun as it rose over the big sky of Montana, its citizens were in the streets, cheering for and encouraging them.

Moss set a goal of fifty miles a day, but this proved much too ambitious. Edward Boos, the accompanying reporter, wrote back to Missoula that the men were nearly "jolted to pieces." But on they soldiered. On July 24, as they prepared for the final leg into St. Louis, people from the city bicycled out to meet them, and together they crossed into the city, where they were welcomed by ten thousand people.

The biking Buffalo Soldiers of the Twenty-Fifth Infantry showed that Miles and Moss were right. The bike could be used by the army.[16] Alas, the idea had a short shelf life. Very quickly, the Twenty-Fifth Infantry, along with the other Buffalo Soldier units, white regular-army units, and volunteers, including Theodore Roosevelt, found themselves fighting in Cuba.

ON FEBRUARY 15, 1898, at 9:45 p.m., the US Navy's battleship *Maine* blew up while visiting Havana, Cuba. President McKinley's assistant secretary of the navy, Theodore Roosevelt, knew the *Maine*'s sinking meant war with Spain. Demanding thorough planning, preparation, and problem solving from others just as he did from himself, Roosevelt sent orders to ships at sea instructing them where to position themselves for the coming battles, alerted other ships gently rocking in port to be prepared to get underway, transferred big guns to New York to defend the city from attack by way of the sea, asked Congress for special wartime legislation, and ordered Admiral George Dewey to steam his fleet to Hong Kong to bottle up the Spanish fleet and begin offensive operations against it when war was declared.[17] He did all this on his own authority without consulting anyone.

A man did not have to have the foresight of a Theodore Roosevelt to see war coming. There was intense speculation at military posts, including those in faraway Montana, where Sergeant Frank Pullen of the Twenty-Fifth Infantry, a man who did not like the deep freeze in Montana called winter, was looking forward to fighting so long as it was in someplace warmer.[18] When the regiment received its orders to move out, almost a month before Congress declared war on Spain, the men "cheered as the order was read to them."[19] According to Lieutenant R. J. Burt, the Twenty-Fifth Infantry was the first army regiment ordered to war. When it reassembled in Tampa, Florida, on May 7, 1898, it would be the first time all its units had been together as a regiment in eighteen years. Training for combat began immediately. After all of those duties more appropriate for young laborers and old bank guards, the men of the Twenty-Fifth Infantry were going to war, where they would be soldiers, fighting soldiers. On June 6, the Twenty-Fifth Infantry received orders to embark for Cuba, and sixteen days later it landed on the beach.[20]

THE MEN OF THE Twenty-Fifth Infantry, and no doubt their fellow Buffalo Soldiers of the Twenty-Fourth Infantry and Tenth Cavalry, were no less delighted to be going to war than the man who may have done more than any other American to put them there—Theodore Roosevelt. Roosevelt now had his war, one he would be in the middle of as a soldier. When he resigned his position as assistant secretary of the navy to go to Cuba, his friends thought either he had lost his mind or that his wife Edith, in a sickbed recovering from surgery, must have died.[21] Edith Roosevelt would recover, thank you, without his help or even his presence. (He would say later he would have left her on her deathbed to go.) Roosevelt formed a regiment of volunteer cavalry and in time became its commanding officer. In that role he would display leadership, coolness under fire, and courage enough to earn him the Medal of Honor.[22] He came home from Cuba a hero. What seemed to other men a dangerous detour from his career would instead take him to the White House.[23]

THEODORE ROOSEVELT AND THE Twenty-Fifth Infantry brushed up against each other on July 1, 1898. The primary mission that day was to capture San Juan Heights, which overlooked General William Shafter's ultimate target, the city of Santiago and the Spanish army there. From San Juan Heights, Shafter would be able to lay down a siege to starve the city into surrender with minimal American casualties. First, though, he had to neutralize Spanish soldiers in an outpost known as El Caney. General Henry Ware Lawton's infantry, including the riflemen of the Twenty-Fifth, was ordered to secure El Caney on the morning of July 1. When he had it, he would turn his men west and link up with General Samuel S. Sumner's cavalry; together they would make the midday assault on San Juan Heights. Lawton was sure he could seize his objective in two hours. Shafter gave him three. Both were too optimistic; El Caney was not secured until 4:30 p.m.[24]

Waiting back at the bottom of San Juan Heights for Lawton's infantry to join them were the Buffalo Soldiers of the Tenth Cavalry and Roosevelt's Rough Riders.[25] The day wore on, and from his position along the bank of a creek, Roosevelt suddenly saw Americans beginning the advance he wanted for himself and his Rough Riders. This was all Roosevelt needed to order his men to move out. As the assault began, Spanish sharpshooters took a frightening toll on the Americans, but Roosevelt ignored this and remained high on his horse, encouraging his men behind him. To those hesitant to charge forward with him, he called back, "Are you afraid to stand up when I am on horseback?" To a regular army captain whose unit blocked Roosevelt's way, Roosevelt snarled, "*I* am the ranking officer here, and *I* give the order to charge." When the officer still did not budge, Roosevelt yelled, "Then let my men through, sir," and began what would be the famous charge up San Juan Heights, what Roosevelt would call his "crowded hour."[26] With Buffalo Soldiers of the Tenth Cavalry tearing away barbed-wire fence ahead of him and whooping and hollering Rough Riders behind him, Roosevelt, lashing his pony Little Texas, began his ride that would bring him a Medal of Honor, carry him to the White House, carve his face into Mount Rushmore, and solidify his place in history.

With San Juan Heights secure, Roosevelt, the Rough Riders, and the Buffalo Soldiers would pose at the summit with the Stars and Stripes snapping behind them in the wind. A photo of that triumph shows Roosevelt standing with hands on his hips, his head jutting forward in victory, with his men around him. Everyone who made the charge and survived is in the photo. Everyone earned his place in it. It appears in practically every Roosevelt biography published since 1898. What it shows may have been what Joe Rosenthal had in mind when he snapped his photo of Marines raising another Stars and Stripes on top of Mount Suribachi on Iwo Jima forty-seven years later. Only Roosevelt's had many more men in it. Many more faces. Many more heroes. All white.

It turns out the original photo included soldiers of the Tenth Cavalry, who risked just as much and whose bravery and heroism was just as great, standing on either side of the Rough Riders, but extending out from the American flag and Theodore Roosevelt, the man of the hour, just far enough to be conveniently cropped out of the picture and out of history. The Tenth Cavalry was there, but until the complete photo was rediscovered, no one knew it.[27]

As the men of the Twenty-Fifth Infantry arrived from El Caney and marched westward past San Juan Heights, they could see the Americans at its crest. One of its soldiers would say, "The next day about noon we heard that the Tenth Cavalry had met the enemy and that the Tenth Cavalry had rescued the Rough Riders. We congratulated ourselves that although not of the same branch of service, we were of the same color, and that to the eye of the enemy we, troopers [cavalry] and footmen [infantry] all looked alike."[28]

The Twenty-Fifth Infantry may have missed history that day by arriving at the bottom of San Juan Hill too late to take part in that famous charge, but it had seen its share of fighting at El Caney. One of its officers was killed and three were wounded; seven enlisted soldiers died, and twenty-eight suffered wounds.[29] Before it left Cuba, its commanding officer would tell his men, "the brightest hours of your lives were on the afternoon of June 1st. . . . You may well return to the United States proud of your accomplishments; and if any one [sic] asks what you have done, point him to El Caney."[30] A white southern soldier would say, "I've changed my opinion of the colored folks, for of all the men I saw fighting, there were none to beat the Tenth Cavalry and the colored infantry in Santiago, and I don't mind saying so."[31] Rough Rider Frank Knox, Franklin D. Roosevelt's secretary of the navy in World War II, said, "I fought with them shoulder to shoulder, and in justice to the colored race, I must say I never saw braver men anywhere. Some of those who rushed up the hill will live in my memory forever."[32]

Roosevelt called the black soldiers "Smoked Yankees" and said they were always welcome to share canteens with him.[33] When he used this odd expression, was he thinking of an incident Mingo Sanders of the Twenty-Fifth Infantry would recall a decade later? They had come together at a place called Siboney. The army had not resupplied the Rough Riders, and walking over to the Twenty-Fifth Infantry and by happenstance encountering Sergeant Sanders, Roosevelt made what Sanders would call a "special request." Would the Buffalo Soldiers share their hardtack with the Rough Riders? They would. In both his autobiography and *The Rough Riders*, his memoirs of the war in Cuba, Roosevelt never mentioned the incident. Mingo Sanders never forgot it.[34]

THE PEACE TREATY WAS signed by a rickety Spain and a rocketing United States, passing each other in different directions as one lost what remained of its empire and the other acquired what would be the beginning of its own. The war ended with Spain losing almost all of what had been a worldwide and fabulously wealthy domain. Its remnants—most important, Cuba in the Western Hemisphere and the Philippines in the Eastern—fell into America's lap.

For America, the question was what to do with them. For Cuba it would be independence. For the Philippines, so foreign and far away, this was out of the question. After agonizing over what to do, President McKinley decided the Philippines had to be occupied and Westernized. Filipinos wasted no time rejecting America's patronizing way. On February 9, 1899, only seven months since the Twenty-Fifth Infantry was at El Caney, they began an insurrection against the United States. The Philippine Insurrection continued into the administration of Theodore Roosevelt, who saw the Philippines as part of an American empire but not solely for economic purposes. Instead, anticipating the role America was to play from then on, Roosevelt wanted American outposts as listening posts in the rest of the world, especially in the Far East, where Roosevelt had his concerns about Japanese imperial designs.[35] As part of his plan, the navy's home port in Asia would be the Philippines. Having sent Admiral Dewey to seize them, Roosevelt intended to keep them.

With the Filipinos in revolt, retaining the islands would require detachments from every unit of the regular army. Less than a month after Congress authorized combat, the Twenty-Fifth Infantry, just settled into new posts in the Arizona and New Mexico Territories, got word that some of its units, including Company B of the First Battalion, later to be sent to Fort Brown, were going to the Philippines. By the beginning of August 1899, they were "in country."

They would stay there almost two years. As in any guerrilla war, combat was mostly a series of hit-and-run skirmishes, one side striking the other suddenly and viciously. The first fighting for the Twenty-Fifth Infantry took place in November. Men handpicked from Companies B, E, and K were ordered to capture a town called O'Donnell from insurgent forces. After a night march, the Americans reached their objective in the early morning and deployed to encircle it. More than one hundred insurgents were completely surprised, and the American force captured them, along with 273 rifles, several bolos (large knives similar to machetes), and thousands of rounds of ammunition. Mission accomplished without a casualty.[36]

Ahead lay the battle on Mount Arayat, where the insurgent General Servillano Aquino had his headquarters and where the Twenty-Fifth Infantry would be introduced to combat at its most gruesome. Aquino's main camp was at the end of a mountain trail. As they got closer to the top, an insurgent sniper opened fire. First Lieutenant William T. Schenck "yelled to one of the men on my right to kill the 'hombre,' and two of the scouts let drive and missed." The sniper continued his shooting. "Just then, someone in the rear opened up and then the whole outfit—about seventy men—turned loose. . . . Three bullets hit just below my feet, fired by my own men. . . . [I] yelled like a stuck pig to cease firing." When it ceased, Schenck and his black infantrymen rushed the hill "and carried it."[37]

Schenck described the "hill" he and his Buffalo Soldiers rushed and took as "a stairway made of logs held by forked sticks, and the drop here was fully 150 feet, and the slope was about 90 degrees. In fact, you could not get into the town without climbing a slope as steep as the roof of a house. The place is a regular Gibraltar and absolutely impregnable on all sides except from the mountain. American troops could never be ripped out of it, and when in future years the place is pointed out where the Twenty-Fifth charged the hill, the tourists will put it down as a lie."[38]

In his letter from Mount Arayat, Schenck wrote that the insurgents that day "were thousands in number. . . . They had evidently had all they wanted of the 'soldados negroes.'" With Schenck that day was First Sergeant Mingo Sanders of Company B. Having missed what Theodore Roosevelt referred to as the "charge" up San Juan Heights in 1898, Sanders took part in what Schenck called the "rush" up Mount Arayat. It was the proudest moment of his army career, and he would remember it just as he would recall sharing rations with Roosevelt in Cuba.[39]

For the Twenty-Fifth Infantry, there would be more fighting and skirmishing, but with Mount Arayat, the worst was over. By September 18, 1902, all units were back in America and at their new posts. For the First Battalion, this was Fort Niobrara, Nebraska, its last posting before Brownsville.

FORT NIOBRARA AND THE nearby town of Valentine welcomed the black soldiers. Not long after their arrival, the *Valentine Republican* complimented the soldiers on their behavior: "A more gentlemanly or better behaved lot of men never garrisoned Fort Niobrara than they have thus far proven themselves to be, and may it be said to their credit, they show a disposition to create less disturbance and noise than did many white soldiers who have been stationed here. . . . If they could know the compliments paid them on their conduct by Valentine citizens, they certainly would feel proud; and the *Republican* wants them to know this good feeling that exists toward them."[40]

Their stay in Nebraska would be short. By 1906, the government was reassessing the need for army protection from Indians. Confined to reservations, they no longer were thought to be a menace, especially in Nebraska, and it was not easy to justify the cost. What ultimately may have doomed Fort Niobrara as an army post, however, was not the end of the frontier but the near end of the buffalo and Theodore Roosevelt's determination to do something about it.

For Americans of the twenty-first century, Theodore Roosevelt's interest in conservation may have the greatest meaning. In *The Wilderness Warrior: Theodore Roosevelt and the Crusade for America*, the historian and writer Douglas Brinkley inventories the national forests, federal bird reservations, national game preserves, national parks, and national monuments that Roosevelt established. The total number is an astonishing 229. That is one for every ten days of his presidency. Not on the list is Fort Niobrara National Wildlife Refuge (it was created by Roosevelt's successor, President Taft, in 1912), but it owes its existence to Roosevelt and his determination to preserve the great American buffalo.[41] Fort Niobrara was in the middle of the Great Plains and an ideal home for the small group of buffalo raised and protected at the Bronx Zoo in New York. It was intended as the seed for the reinvigorated grand herds of the future. Before the buffalo could move in, the Buffalo Soldier had to move out.[42] On May 26, 1906, the War Department ordered the post closed and issued orders sending three companies of the Twenty-Fifth Infantry to Fort Brown, Texas.[43]

IN 1906, FORT BROWN was the oldest federal garrison on the Rio Grande. In his memoirs, Ulysses S. Grant told of how, during the Mexican War, Major Jacob Brown and his troops built what would be Fort Brown to protect themselves from Mexican guns on the other side of the river.[44] The 1848 Treaty of Guadalupe Hidalgo ended the war and confirmed that all land north of the Rio Grande, including Brownsville and Fort Brown, was American. During the Civil War, Confederates seized the fort, and when the war ended in 1865, Union General Philip Sheridan raised the American flag above what was left of it. Slaves in Texas never learned of President Lincoln's Emancipation Proclamation until Sheridan had Union General Gordon Granger tell them about it on June 19, 1865: "The people of Texas are informed that, in accordance with a proclamation from the Executive of the United States, all slaves are free."[45] "Juneteenth" is now celebrated every year throughout America.

BEFORE THE TRANSFER TO Texas was made, some of the Twenty-Fifth Infantry's officers worried about Texas. Colonel Ralph W. Hoyt, the regiment's commanding officer, requested that the orders be rescinded and that the regiment not be posted anywhere in Texas.[46] The War Department was unmoved. Three or four times before, the army had stationed Negro troops at Fort Brown, and now they were coming again.[47]

Some Texans also worried about the black soldiers. Brownsville businessman Samuel P. Wreford wrote to his US senator, Charles A. Culberson, objecting to the move. Added to whatever racial attitude he may have had, he was concerned that the presence of so many black soldiers would have a bad effect on the business community's efforts to recapture an earlier prosperity that had drifted away. It would be a very "unfortunate move."[48] Wreford was not the only one in Brownsville anticipating trouble or perhaps thinking of making it. Fort Brown's surgeon, Dr. Benjamin J. Edger, would later write to Senator Joseph Foraker that he "inter-mingled [sic] in social and professional ways with inhabitants of Brownsville," and "there was no one who said the colored troops would be welcome, and all were loud in denunciations of colored soldiers. My Mexican patients . . . were afraid of them."[49] Several prominent citizens, including Mayor Frederick J. Combe, had shared their concerns with Edger. The feelings of Brownsville's residents notwithstanding, Fort Brown would be the new home for the Negro soldiers of Companies B, C, and D, First Battalion, Twenty-Fifth Infantry, United States Army.

FROM FORT BROWN, ON Saturday, July 28, 1906, Major Charles W. Penrose, commanding officer of the First Battalion, Twenty-Fifth Infantry, wired the military secretary in Washington that his battalion "arrived at this post at 3.05 o'clock p. m. this date." Later he would recall that his men "were not welcomed the way other soldiers would have been. When we marched through the town going from the [train station] to the post people were standing along the streets, but there were no smiling faces or anything of that kind, as you might imagine when you are coming to a new post. . . . They did not seem to be happy over it."[50]

Trouble came quickly. Within days, Private James Newton of Company C was beaten with a pistol when he and another soldier did "not get off the sidewalk" for "a party of white ladies standing there." Three days later, Private Clifford I. Adair, also from Company C, was returning from Mexico with a writing pen he bought while there on a pass. An American customs official named Fred Tate, for no reason other than "You damned niggers are too smart around here," relieved him of it.[51] Only four days after that, there was yet another incident at the customs office. Private Oscar W. Reid, again of Company C, was pushed into the Rio Grande by another customs official for refusing to quiet down when returning from Matamoros. Reid, who had been drinking, admitted he may have gotten what he deserved.[52] Yet no one believed a white soldier from the departed Twenty-Sixth Infantry would have gotten the same treatment.

Worse for the soldiers, Reid's casual acceptance of his dunking to the contrary, the possible resentment by them over these incidents provided the motive for the shooting that became the Brownsville Incident.

"Does anybody know anything about this firing?"

Mayor Frederick Combe, early in the
morning of August 14, 1906, Brownsville

CHAPTER FOUR

ON THE GROUND

WHEN THE SHOOTING BEGAN, the battalion's commanding officer, Major Charles Penrose, was in bed but not asleep. Two shots—he was sure they were fired by pistols—got his attention. Then came a volley of six or seven more. Then another three "that stood out prominently, more so than the others," and which Penrose came to believe were those fired as an alarm by the sentry Private Joseph Howard.[1] Other than Howard's, all of these and another series of irregular shots that followed seemed to be coming from the town outside the post.[2] Pulling his uniform over his pajamas and shoving his bare feet into unlaced boots, he started for the door. Just as he got there, he heard Private Hairston's knock and his excited warning, "Major, they are shooting us up; they are shooting us up." Penrose ordered Hairston to sound "Call to Arms" and dashed across the parade ground to the enlisted men's barracks, where he found confusion among his soldiers and dead silence on the other side of the garrison wall.[3] The gunfire had ceased.

Captain Edgar Macklin, commanding officer of Company C, was Fort Brown's officer of the day. He was assumed to be somewhere attending to these duties, and his company was milling about outside their barracks without him. Some of them were not in uniform and were wandering around in their underwear. None had his weapon. Acting First Sergeant Samuel Harley, the man in charge of the weapons, claimed not to hear the bugle's call to arms, and without an order from an officer to release the rifles to the men, he kept them securely locked in their racks. An angry Major Penrose told the men to get their rifles, even if they had to smash open the racks to do it.[4]

Company B was a little better off: at least its men had their weapons. Its commanding officer, Lieutenant George Lawrason, also was absent. Its experienced First Sergeant Mingo Sanders, with more than twenty-five years in the army, took roll to see if any of his soldiers was missing. He was bringing order to his company, but it needed its commanding officer, and Penrose told a noncommissioned officer on the scene to find Lieutenant Lawrason.

Returning to Company C, Penrose saw it now had its rifles, but he was horrified to see the men loading them with ammunition. He ordered the soldiers to remove all bullets from their weapons and warned he would shoot any man who reloaded his rifle without a direct order from an officer. Because Macklin's company still had no officer to lead it, Penrose ordered Lieutenant Harry Grier, the battalion's quartermaster and acting adjutant, to assume command.[5]

Company D was not in the least confused or disorderly. Its commanding officer, Captain Samuel Lyon, had formed it quickly, and now he and his soldiers quietly awaited further orders. It was the best outfit in the battalion. In an army drill competition two or three years earlier, it won first place as the best drilled, most highly disciplined, and most efficient company-size unit in the army.[6]

From his own sense that the shots he heard were fired in the town and the soldiers' belief that the townspeople were shooting at the fort, Penrose concluded the post had to be defended.[7] He ordered his three companies of infantry to form a continuous line facing the town at the waist-high brick wall separating town and fort. With the shooting ended and his soldiers alert and in defensive positions, Penrose felt Fort Brown was secure from any further attack and turned his attention to his missing officer of the day and two soldiers from Company B who were also not accounted for. Worried about their safety, Penrose ordered Lyon and his company into Brownsville to search for them.

WHEN MAYOR COMBE REACHED Crixell's saloon, he heard a "chorus of remarks" from the men there. "The negroes are shooting on the town."[8] Police Chief Connor came up to him and said four policemen were missing. Combe worried they were victims of the shooting and possibly dead. He left Crixell's and started walking in the direction of Fort Brown, about two and a half blocks away. After half a block he saw in the dark street a large shape that turned out to be Dominguez's dead horse.[9] Disregarding shouted warnings to stay off the street, he crossed over to the Miller Hotel. He was going to find out what happened, and he was going to start there.

Standing inside the hotel's doorway, he called out to anyone who could hear him, "Does anybody know anything about this firing?" At that moment, a man in pajamas, whom Combe recognized as the cashier at the Merchants National Bank, came racing down the stairs and, without stopping to answer, if indeed he had even heard the question, ran past the startled mayor, out the door, and disappeared. "He was getting out of that hotbed as fast as he could."[10]

Combe stepped back onto Elizabeth Street and into bedlam. "People were running in, running in from all parts of town, armed with whatever they could find." They kept calling out, "The soldiers have shot up the town." Hotheads were collecting in the square, ginning up each other's anger and frustration, and Combe worried they would do something foolish, maybe even retaliate against the soldiers by assaulting Fort Brown. Pointing out that the soldiers in the fort were "efficient troops" and "splendidly armed," the mayor took the swagger out of the mob so that—reluctantly—it dispersed.[11] A potentially deadly confrontation between town and troops was, for the moment, avoided.

Learning nothing at Crixell's saloon or at the Miller Hotel, Combe continued on to the fort to see if anyone there knew anything. At just that moment, marching toward him on Elizabeth Street were Captain Lyon and Company D looking for the missing soldiers.[12] After exchanging their diametrically different versions of whether it was soldiers or townspeople who did the shooting, together they started off to the fort and Major Penrose, where Combe came right to the point. "Major, this is a terrible outrage. Your men have shot up the town, wounded the lieutenant of police, killed his horse, and generally shot up the town."[13] Penrose disagreed. He thought it was citizens who did the shooting and fired on Fort Brown. Where they agreed was that soldiers should be kept out of the town and civilians away from the fort. And they would meet again later that morning.

While they were talking, the missing Captain Macklin showed up. Excusing himself for being late, Macklin told Penrose he had been asleep the entire time in his quarters. The astonished Penrose ordered him to take command of his company at the brick wall separating town and fort.

The shooting was over. The town was tense but quiet. The fort was secure, but its soldiers were on edge. And as the smell of gunfire hung in the still, Texas air, the investigations began into what happened.

THE FIRST INVESTIGATOR WAS Mayor Combe himself. Walking back home from the fort, he got as far as the Miller Hotel when someone said he was needed at John Tillman's Ruby Saloon. There he saw the body of its bartender Frank Natus lying on the ground. Peeling away the dead man's clothes, Combe saw entry and exit wounds caused by what he believed was a "high-power bullet."[14] Moving on to the drugstore, where police lieutenant Dominguez was taken, he found a very badly wounded man. "His hand was pretty well torn up; the phalanges were hanging over . . . and it was badly shattered."[15] Combe and his brother, Dr. Joe Combe, realized that amputation was needed, but it could wait for later in the morning. The mayor asked Dominguez who did the shooting.

"The Negroes."

"Did you see that they were soldiers?"

"Yes, sir."[16]

Since Dominguez was shot as he was riding past the Miller Hotel, Combe decided to go back there before returning home. Walking past the front of the hotel, he turned east along Thirteenth Street to where Dominguez said the shooters had been when they shot him, "the mouth of the alley, when I stepped on something that gave a metallic sound." Combe bent down in the dark to feel with his hand what it was and discovered a cartridge. He felt around again and found more. Then a clip, which held cartridges before they were fired, then six or seven empty cartridge shells. He examined these under the light and immediately realized they all were from the army's new high-power Springfield rifle. "As far as I was personally concerned, this had been done by the soldiers."[17] Brownsville had its first hard evidence, and it was against the men of the Twenty-Fifth Infantry.[18]

AFTER A NIGHT OF no sleep, Mayor Combe returned early to Fort Brown, but not for his meeting with Major Penrose.[19] The post's attending surgeon was away from the fort and Combe was taking his place. He arrived for the 7:00 a.m. sick call, but there was not much there for him to do, and after a short time he drove back into town. Showing Penrose the shells and cartridges he had found in the darkness after the shooting could wait until they met later that morning. There was a "great deal of excitement" in the town, and Combe wanted to get a sense of what others were thinking.[20] The first man he met was John B. Armstrong, who preferred to be addressed as "Major," his rank from the army. Armstrong was, as Combe later made sure to point out to the Senate Military Affairs Committee and its majority-Republican membership, a "prominent Republican." Testing an idea, Combe asked Armstrong if it might be good to form a committee of "thinking people" to investigate what went on overnight. He knew of at least two men talking in a way that tended to provoke people, one of whom was the commission agent Sam Wreford, whose furiously indignant letter to Senator Charles Culberson back in May protesting the transfer of black soldiers to Brownsville made clear what he thought of such men. This committee might reassure the town something was being done.[21] Armstrong liked Combe's idea. Encouraged by this endorsement, Combe asked others, and all agreed it was a good way to learn what happened and, not incidentally, to calm people down. For men less amenable to this even-tempered approach, Combe "laid the law down" and threatened to arrest and jail to keep such talk off the streets.[22] Meanwhile, he called a meeting later that morning to form the committee he discussed. It was an essential element in the plan coalescing in his mind, and he needed to start pronto. Beforehand, however, he had his meeting with Major Penrose.

ARRIVING AT THE FORT at 9:00 a.m., Mayor Combe was waved through the gate by sentries alerted he was coming to see the commanding officer.

With Penrose was Commissioner Rentfro Creager. He had asked Creager to come to discuss how he might go about his investigation but quickly realized the man's mind was made up—the soldiers had done it—and he could not advise him in an unbiased way.[23]

Creager spent summer evenings at Point Isabel, a resort on the Texas Gulf Coast about twenty miles from Brownsville. He returned each morning on the train and hailed a hack to his law office, stopping on the way at the post office to collect his mail. He knew nothing of the shooting the night before until the Mexican hack driver broke the news to him. According to the driver, the black soldiers had "broken out of the post" and killed three people.[24] A crowd at the post office also told him the shooters were soldiers.[25] When Creager got to his law office, there was the call from Major Penrose requesting that he come to Fort Brown to meet with him.[26]

Combe could see that Penrose and Creager were discussing the shooting, and since that was why he was there, he joined right in.[27] He slapped the cartridge, clip, and shells he picked off the street down onto Penrose's desk and asked, "What do you think of that for evidence?" Before Penrose could answer, the mayor continued, "Your men did this."[28] After carefully examining the ammunition, Penrose reluctantly acknowledged this "was almost conclusive evidence, but who did it and how they did it we do not know." "Well, I am convinced," Combe snorted, and he went back to town to get ready for the citizens' meeting, leaving behind a battalion commanding officer now worried about his soldiers' guilt.

NOT QUITE SURE OF the other man's intentions or plans, neither Mayor Combe nor Major Penrose was completely candid at this meeting. Each hid from the other a second group of shells he knew of.

Penrose had gotten his from Macklin. When Macklin finally turned up and assumed command of Company C, Penrose decided that only it was needed to guard the fort's perimeter, and the other two companies were told to stand down. Macklin spent the rest of the night at the fort's main gate opposite Elizabeth Street, occasionally leaving to inspect his line of sentinels. When the "streak of dawn came," under Major Penrose's order he went outside the gate to look for spent ammunition.[29] He began by pacing inside the waist-high wall. He found nothing.[30] Then he walked along Garrison Road from the main gate to Cowen Alley, where he saw on the ground on the town side of Garrison Road, about thirty feet away from the wall, five cartridge clips and seven shells from fired ammunition. He saw they were for the army's Springfield rifle, issued to the Twenty-Fifth Infantry back at Fort Niobrara.[31] The seven empty shells were "all in a bunch," in a circle not more than twelve to fifteen inches in diameter. This puzzled him. Had the bullets been fired from a rifle, the shells would be scattered in a haphazard manner, and such a tight pattern would have been impossible.[32]

He glanced up and noticed civilians nearby bending down every now and then to pick something up. Quickly gathering up the shells and the clips at his feet, he carried them back into the fort to show Major Penrose. "I am afraid our men have done this shooting," Penrose said.[33] He told Macklin to hold onto what he had found. Macklin took them to his quarters and threw them in a drawer. In time, the desk and the shells disappeared.[34]

Combe also kept quiet about other shells and ammunition found that morning. On his way to Fort Brown for sick call, he swung by the Miller Hotel. It was about 5:30 a.m., not quite sunup, and he walked over to where he had found the shells in the street a few hours earlier. Other men were up and about, and they told him that at that same spot "quite a number of people" also had picked up shells. The mayor ordered Police Chief Connor to find these people and take possession of what they had.[35] Someone told him of the shooting at the Starck house on Washington Street, and he went over there. Sure enough, there were shells in the gutter in front of the house. Combe pocketed these as well.[36]

PENROSE'S SKEPTICISM WHEN THE mayor showed him the first group of shells may be why Combe said nothing about his newly discovered shells. Perhaps Combe realized they might not have convinced Penrose of his soldiers' guilt either. He was not aware Penrose was changing his mind after seeing the shells Macklin found on Garrison Road. Probably Combe no longer cared what Penrose thought. What was important to him was protecting Brownsville. In his mind there was no question some of the soldiers had rioted and at least one of them was a murderer, but it was not his job to determine who did the shooting and prosecute them. He was Brownsville's mayor, and his responsibility was to protect his city and the people who lived in it. The soldiers might go on a rampage again. No assurance from their officers that they could be kept safely within the confines of the post and out of the town was good enough for him. Only hours earlier, when he bumped into Captain Lyon and Company D looking for missing soldiers, he saw how difficult it was for Lyon to control his men. They nervously broke ranks, and when Lyon ordered them to get back in formation, they ignored him. It took a curse and a harshly shouted second command to bring them to order.[37] Their discipline might crumble entirely, and who knew what might happen to Brownsville if it did.

Combe also realized the town's own residents threatened it too. They could be just as uncontrollable as the soldiers. Brownsville's turn away from a frontier mind-set was too fresh to become a settled way of life. Last night's threat to attack the fort showed that. Harming the soldiers or even trying to harm them might trigger new shootings and lawlessness. Combe thwarted violence the night before by assuring townspeople that if they remained within the law, they would get justice.[38] How long would they sit tight? As mayor, Combe had to protect Brownsville from the soldiers, the soldiers from the town, and the town from its own people. The only way to do this was to get the soldiers out of Brownsville, and that would mean an appeal to the War Department, and maybe even to President Roosevelt, from a committee of the best citizens in Browns-ville, men above reproach. It would have to conduct a reasonably convincing investigation. Since it would not be a court of law, tes-timony and evidence need not be the kind admissible at a trial. If it came from enough people and reasonably showed it was more likely than not the shooters were soldiers, it would do the trick.

Combe left Fort Brown that morning with this plan and a deter-mination to carry it through.

HE HAD TO CLEAR his desk of all other distractions, including his medical practice. He told his brother and partner, Dr. Joe Combe, he would have to handle that himself. "I am going to occupy myself entirely with this matter."[39] His professional responsibilities no longer an intrusion, Mayor Combe walked through the town, talking to "influential and prominent citizens" until the hour he had set for the meeting. A large crowd of possibly five hundred, including trou-blemakers neither invited nor wanted and who had heard what was happening, showed up. They wanted to rush the fort and clean the soldiers out.[40] Combe asked people to continue to act as good citi-zens and not take the law into their own hands because it would lead to "the ruination of Brownsville." Meanwhile, he would take the matter up "to the highest authority in the land."

When things quieted down, it was time to select the members of what thereafter would be called the Citizens' Committee. Combe picked William Kelly as its chairman. Kelly was a native New Yorker who began his service to the Union in the Civil War with a New York volunteer regiment. Rising from the enlisted ranks, he was commissioned an officer in the Eighth United States Colored Troops. (More than forty years later, he liked to be addressed as Captain.) Coming to Brownsville with the army as the war was closing, he stayed there when he was discharged. A conservative and successful businessman, in 1891 Kelly formed the First National Bank of Brownsville and since then had served as its president. He knew everyone in Brownsville, the high and the low—and he knew which was which.[41] His son was making a career in the army and was then an instructor in modern languages at West Point. In an earlier tour of duty, the son served with Buffalo Soldiers in the Ninth Cavalry. Kelly knew Fort Brown and every unit ever posted there, from where else it was posted to who its commanding officers were. He knew the black units at Fort Brown before the Twenty-Fifth Infantry and had not a bad word to say about any of them. The Twenty-Fourth Infantry was "a magnificent organization," the Ninth Cavalry a "magnificent body of men . . . thoroughly disciplined and thoroughly drilled," and the Tenth Cavalry "as well-behaved a body of men as I ever saw anywhere."[42] Black soldiers were the equal of white soldiers and their units just as good, if, he cautioned, they were properly officered.

Combe must have thought that with Kelly he had hit a home run. Maybe it was just a triple. Kelly was not sure the Twenty-Fifth Infantry lived up to these standards. He was appalled to see its soldiers come into Brownsville out of uniform and sloppy, and he was astonished to see them pass by their officers without saluting. Discipline was lax, and he blamed this on their officers.[43] Kelly considered himself a man without prejudice,[44] but, a man of his time, he judged blacks not quite the equal of whites and hesitated to take their word against the word of a white man. He believed that "negroes . . . are the most secretive race of people on the face of the earth" and "that there exists in the four regiments of negro troops now in the Army of the United States an oath-bound society, by which they are bound to each other and together, to support each other in all cases, infractions of discipline, in crimes of any kind, and that the members of that society will not tell on each other or violate that oath under any circumstances."[45] Kelly had no doubts the shooters were the black soldiers. But then practically everyone in Brownsville thought the same thing, including Mayor Combe.

As committee chairman, Kelly selected the rest of its members. He selected "mostly northern men, who had no special animus against the negroes, as such."[46] Former Union soldiers, including some active in the local Grand Army post (equivalent to today's American Legion) were good. For another member, he picked the son of a Union officer who had died commanding Negro troops. The final Citizens' Committee membership included a county judge, the Brownsville city attorney, another lawyer or two, the superintendent of public instruction (a position Kelly himself once held), the chief of police, the Cameron County sheriff, a city alderman, another banker, the state quarantine officer, the editor of the local newspaper that flogged the story of the "assault" on Mrs. Evans, a doctor, and, of course, Mayor Combe.[47] They were ready to get down to business. "There is no time like the present," Captain Kelly exhorted his committee. "We will go at once to see Major Penrose."[48]

CAPTAIN KELLY REPEATED WHAT Major Penrose by now had heard twice from Mayor Combe. Penrose responded just as he had before and offered his counter-theory: it was an attack on the barracks by people from the town. But when confronted with the additional shells and other items found by other people in the town, he conceded he might have been wrong. "I do not understand. My men are good men. [But] I am afraid it is so. I would give my right arm if this had not occurred."[49] Satisfied Penrose now saw things their way, confident he would cooperate with them, Kelly and the committee members left the post and went back to town to take testimony.

MAJOR PENROSE COULD NO longer keep the shooting hidden from the army. Too much evidence damning his men was piling up. Before the day was over, he sent a telegram to his superiors at the Department of Texas, telling them of the "serious shooting," the casualties, and the shells and clips in the streets that supported the allegation that his soldiers had been the perpetrators. He promised full particulars would be mailed.[50]

FOR AN INVESTIGATION MAYOR Combe thought should be deliberate, the Citizens' Committee moved awfully fast. That very afternoon, with no preparation, it took the statements of thirteen witnesses. The next morning, another four told the committee what they knew. None of the testimony was under oath. None was cross-examined. None was from a soldier.

Other than when he testified himself, Combe was not present when the committee received the testimony. He was busy with unrelated responsibilities as the town's mayor. "I was in the committee room, backwards and forwards, but very seldom for any length of time."[51] In the end, the committee presented him with proof of a violent shooting committed by the dangerous men of the Twenty-Fifth Infantry, just what he wanted.

Only two of the twenty-four witnesses, Hale Odin and the teenager Herbert Elkins, testified they saw Negro shooters. Elkins may have gotten the hint when he was told before the first question to him, "We know that this outrage was committed by negro soldiers."[52] Combe had no interest in determining which soldiers in particular were involved in the shooting. That was the job of the law, not his committee. If what witnesses said was weak on some points, nevertheless they conveyed that what happened was more than a simple affray or brawl. This was a deadly assault on the town committed by more than just a few men. Its two casualties, including a death, were not the unfortunate result of a noisy quarrel gone too far but the foreseeable consequence of a well-planned attack with the violence one might expect of a military operation. That is what the testimony showed.

After only two days, Mayor Combe had his committee, its evidence, and its conclusion to send to the War Department and President Roosevelt. If the brutality of the raid did not speak for itself, in its appeal the Citizens' Committee would emphasize it. The soldiers were violent. They were dangerous. They might do it again. Officials at the highest authority in the land had to do something about it.

TO INFLUENCE THE WAR Department, who better to ask than Texas's two US senators? One of them, Charles Allen Culberson, could say to Secretary of War William Howard Taft that back in May, "I told you so." At that time, Senator Culberson wrote Taft, expressing his opposition to the move and including a copy of Wreford's letter to him. Three days later, Taft answered that objections already had been "very carefully considered." The War Department believed colored troops were as well disciplined as white troops, and there was no reason to anticipate the soldiers of the Twenty-Fifth Infantry would be any different. "It has sometimes happened that communities which objected to the coming of colored soldiers have, on account of their good conduct, entirely changed their view and commended their good behavior to the War Department."[53] The posting to Fort Brown could not be rescinded.

As far as Combe and almost everyone else in Brownsville were concerned, Taft and the army could not have been more wrong back in May. If Culberson was unable to keep them out of Brownsville in May, he damn well better help get rid of them now. He was only too happy to.

When the Twenty-Fifth Infantry was posted to Fort Brown, Culberson was just beginning his second term in the Senate. A native of Alabama, he moved with his family to Texas when he was only a year old. His father became active in Texas politics and was elected to Congress. After graduating from the University of Virginia law school, young Culberson returned to Texas to practice law in Jefferson, a flyspeck of a town in the northeastern corner of the state not far from the three corners of Texas, Louisiana, and Arkansas and strongly influenced by the Southern ways of the area. Eventually, Culberson moved to a bigger playing field in Dallas, was elected Texas attorney general, then governor. In January 1899 he was sent to the Senate, where he would stay until 1922.

Nothing like the stereotypical handshaking, yarn spinning, colorfully speaking Southern politician, Culberson was, if anything, aloof. Maybe this was because of his health. He suffered from Bright's disease, a disease of the kidneys, now called *nephritis*. A serious disease, then and now, in February 1884 it killed Theodore Roosevelt's young wife Alice only two days after she gave birth to their daughter, also to be named Alice. Just as serious to his health and his career, Culberson was an alcoholic. He was often missing from the Senate's business as he dried out at health resorts and spas. In his twenty-four years in the Senate, he missed more than half of its roll-call votes.[54]

Also no doubt trolling for votes in south Texas, the state's other senator, Joseph W. Bailey, was happy to join in the effort. Bailey was hardly a man to be outraged by the violence of other men. A native Mississippian, in 1883, he was accused of being the ringleader of a faction in a Democratic party there that used vicious tactics against another Democratic faction. When called to the US Senate to testify about this, Bailey stood mute on the ground he would be forced to perjure himself. He got away with it. By then, however, he was a spent force in Magnolia State politics and moved to Texas to start over. Texans overlooked his pugnacious past and in 1890 elected him to Congress. Eleven years later, the Texas legislature sent him to the Senate.[55] Old habits die hard. Not a year later, he physically assaulted Senator Albert Beveridge, a Republican from Indiana. The Senate did nothing about it because, according to an editorial in the *New York Times*, the assault did not occur while the Senate was in session.[56]

On August 15, Culberson and Bailey sent a short telegram to Secretary of War Taft. "We are advised that negro soldiers at Fort Brown have been guilty of the most outrageous conduct" and want them transferred "without delay."[57]

WITH THE WAR DEPARTMENT covered by the two senators, it was up to the Citizens' Committee to press the case with President Roosevelt. Not wasting any time, after hearing the last witness on the second day, it composed its appeal to him. On Wednesday, the same day Culberson and Bailey sent their telegram to the War Department, the committee's telegram was on its way to the Summer White House in Oyster Bay, New York. Since 1902 Roosevelt gathered his family and staff and left the unbearable heat of Washington's summer for his home on Long Island's North Shore. No matter the season, Roosevelt loved the home for its "birds and trees and books, and all things beautiful, and horses and rifles and children and hard work and the joy of life."[58]

Roosevelt's summer already had been interrupted several times. The government in Cuba, installed and maintained by the United States, was collapsing and a civil war looked likely. He would order Secretary of War Taft, the assistant secretary of state (and Harvard classmate) Robert Bacon, and a detachment of US Marines to go there and get things back on track. (This and other business kept the Secretary of War Taft out of the Brownsville loop for quite some time.) None of this slowed his plan to visit the under-construction Panama Canal. To Henry White, American ambassador to Italy, but for many years a fixture in one position or another at the embassy in London, Roosevelt sent a confidential letter with his thoughts about the discussions between Great Britain and Germany on how to slow down their "I'll see you and raise you one" competition to build the world's largest warships and the world's biggest navy. The next day, President Roosevelt congratulated Attorney General Charles Joseph Bonaparte, grandson of the youngest brother of Emperor Napoleon I of France, for his handling of a meat problem at the Navy Yard in Brooklyn. Roosevelt joked to Bonaparte that an editorial in the *Providence Journal* blamed him for a plan to decommission the Revolutionary War–era USS *Constitution* ("Old Ironsides") because he so hated the Constitution that formed the American government that he disliked anything with that name.[59] That same day, the telegram from Brownsville arrived at Sagamore Hill.[60]

The Citizens' Committee made sure its appeal was complete and respectfully forceful. It made clear it was appointed by Brownsville authorities and cloaked with civic authority. Eleven members of the committee, including Mayor Combe and seven other public officials, signed the telegram. Four of them were directly or indirectly involved in law enforcement, and two of these were a Cameron County judge and the Brownsville city attorney, who surely knew the committee behaved nothing like a court of law. The violence so frightening to Brownsville residents was emphasized unambiguously. This was an "attack." It involved "between 20 and 30" men, all well-armed with "rifles and an abundant supply of ammunition." About "200 shots" were fired "directly into dwellings, offices, stores, and at police and citizens." They killed one man and grievously wounded another. The committee identified the shooters as "Soldiers of Twenty-Fifth United States Infantry (colored). . . . Threats have been made . . . they will repeat this outrage," and there are not enough officers in the battalion to restrain them.[61] "Women and children are terrorized." Men are "under constant alarm and watchfulness." "No community can stand this strain." The telegram closed, just as Combe wanted, with the plea to President Roosevelt "to have the troops at once removed from Fort Brown and replaced by white soldiers."

The wire went out not quite forty-eight hours after the shooting.

NEITHER THE APPEAL FROM the Citizens' Committee nor the veiled demands from the senators worked. Two days after Roosevelt received his telegram, his personal secretary William Loeb instructed military secretary General Fred C. Ainsworth to tell Culberson, "No action can be taken on his request until a full investigation and report" have been made.[62]

It was Major Penrose's calm assurances that the situation in Brownsville was well in hand that foiled Combe's carefully orchestrated plan. Repeatedly Penrose told the chain of command above him that he and his officers had their soldiers under control while Combe was keeping the lid on Brownsville's residents.[63] "No trouble since shooting, and anticipate none."[64] Because of these calming wires, General Ainsworth and General J. Franklin Bell, the army's chief of staff, thought it was inadvisable to move the troops before the guilty parties were discovered and punished.[65] They convinced President Roosevelt, and for the moment the Twenty-Fifth Infantry was staying put. Mayor Combe had been checked. Additional effort would be required.

President Roosevelt, General Ainsworth, and General Bell's cool reaction to the Citizens' Committee had kept the matter orderly and within the army and its criminal-justice system. The army for the moment was doing the right thing. Politicians were held at bay. But two significant turns in the Brownsville Incident were taking place. Roosevelt was being squeezed by the Citizens' Committee, Culberson, and Bailey. The War Department, which itself was wavering in the face of pressure from Senators Culberson and Bailey, would be forced to turn to higher authority—President Roosevelt, its commander in chief—for guidance.

The Citizens' Committee asked Senator Culberson to turn up the heat. Culberson wired Taft, "Some time ago I called your attention to the danger of locating negro troops in Texas, especially at Brownsville." After this polite "I told you so," Culberson got down to business. "Can not these troops be removed at once?"[66] This letter landed on General Ainsworth's desk. A medical doctor who enlisted in the Army Medical Corps in 1874, Ainsworth's remarkable organizing and administrative skills and success in bringing order out of chaos led to duty in the Adjutant General's Office. Enjoying this kind of billet more than surgery, in 1891 he resigned his medical commission and accepted a line commission with the rank of major. In 1904 he was appointed military secretary in the War Department and given the rank of major general.[67] By the time of the shooting in Brownsville, Ainsworth had been in the army for thirty-two years and knew better than to ignore demands from US senators. And he knew how to pass the buck to "the highest authority" and, at the same time, use information and advice from others to influence this highest authority. He would be merely the conduit for passing information and requests up and decisions back down.

The same day he received the first appeal from Senators Culberson and Bailey, Ainsworth was pressured from another direction, the army itself. From the Department of Texas, General W. S. McCaskey described a gruesome picture of the situation in Brownsville. Mischaracterizing Penrose's somewhat hopeful and confident report, McCaskey instead reported that Penrose had said things were "grave," a word Penrose never used and a thought he never intended to express.[68] McCaskey recommended the soldiers be transferred away from the hostile situation in Brownsville. When Ainsworth asked Oyster Bay what to do about the second Culberson-Bailey request, he included McCaskey's warning and recommendation but repeated that he and the army's chief of staff thought this was not a good idea before "the culprits have been discovered and punished."[69]

Brownsville citizens sent a second and much-stronger telegram to President Roosevelt. This time, there were seven more signatories. No longer identifying themselves as the Citizens' Committee, they now were representative citizens of the city appealing to him "out of great necessity." Conditions were "deplorable"; families would not leave their homes, so great was their fear of another attack. Many were leaving town. "The accidental discharge of a firearm, any overt act of an excited citizen—and our citizens are fearfully excited—would precipitate upon the whole negro force at Brownsville." Combe's fear that citizens would attack the fort was clearly implied here. It was a tandem of threats designed to get attention. The town needed protection from the soldiers because five officers were unable to restrain them. Just as critical, the soldiers needed protection from the town. There would be a "fearful loss of life and probable destruction of city."[70]

When he saw this, General Ainsworth knew the troops had to leave. Accepting a suggestion in Culberson's telegram that he ask the man on the ground, the post's commanding officer, if he thought otherwise, he wired Penrose immediately and got right to the point: "Have you any doubt as to your ability to restrain troops from further violence? Have you any apprehension of collision with civilians or of other trouble?" Again Penrose was reassuring. "Have no doubt of my ability to restrain troops. Everything quiet in city. . . . Think Mayor has control of situation, and do not anticipate further trouble."[71]

Ainsworth backstopped Major Penrose by asking the same questions to Major Augustus Blocksom with the Department of Texas's inspector general, who had come to Brownsville the night before. Ainsworth wanted to know if Blocksom thought the colored troops should be removed from Fort Brown. Blocksom, in no uncertain language, wired back that he did. "I consider it necessary to remove colored troops, the sooner the better."[72]

MAYOR COMBE MAY NOT have realized it, but he was close to getting what he wanted. The initial reluctance of the army to relocate the soldiers and President Roosevelt's refusal to second-guess the army's advice were yesterday's news. By sending two scorched-earth wires to Oyster Bay, the Citizens' Committee changed the investigation from "Who did the shooting?" to "Should we get those guilty Negro soldiers out of there?" To frame the question this way guaranteed the answer would be yes. It was one thing to keep the Twenty-Fifth Infantry at Fort Brown if things were calming down, as the battalion's commanding officer said they were. But tension in Brownsville was swelling. There was a report that 150 armed men were positioning themselves between the town and the fort and promising to shoot any soldier who tried to leave it. The city appealed to the Texas governor for state troops to defend it, and he was considering sending a force of the fabled Texas Rangers to keep order. Business and commerce and almost all social interaction in the city came to a full stop.[73]

The appeals of the townspeople were too strident, too frightening, too threatening, and from too many of their officials and leading citizens to be ignored. The inspector general who was sent to Brownsville to find out what happened was worried after reading the mood of the town and surrounding countryside. Moreover, two general-grade officers (the military secretary and the army chief of staff) had changed their minds after the second appeal on August 18, and now they too endorsed moving the soldiers away.[74] The only one still advising that the black soldiers stay in Brownsville until things were sorted out was Major Penrose. While the opinion of the commanding officer as the man on the scene was important, this particular man on the scene said the mayor had things under control, but this same mayor was not so sure and twice signed appeals to save his town from "probable destruction" and separate the soldiers from it. The weight of opinion was too great to withstand. Roosevelt changed his mind. Combe's plan was working. In time, even Major Penrose realized the mayor was right. The following March, he would say, "In my opinion, he was solely responsible for the prevention of disaster."[75]

On August 20, President Roosevelt took the matter into his own hands and told his secretary William Loeb to wire General Ainsworth, "Send troops to Fort Ringgold."[76] Theodore Roosevelt now owned the Brownsville Incident.

WITH THE PRESIDENT'S BLESSING, the black soldiers would leave Fort Brown. But there would be delays that must have driven Mayor Combe to nervous exhaustion. Other units had to be found to take their place and brought to Brownsville. It turned out it would be the white soldiers from the Twenty-Sixth Infantry, who had been replaced such a short while ago by the Buffalo Soldiers of the Twenty-Fifth Infantry.[77]

An unforeseen problem was where to send the black soldiers. Displaying the zealousness of a convert, Major Penrose, once so sure Brownsville would remain calm and safe for his men, made an about face when he learned they were to go to another fort in Texas, only one hundred or so miles away. "I do not think," he wired General McCaskey, "the extremely bitter feeling existing throughout the southern part of the State of Texas over the shooting in Brownsville is thoroughly appreciated. . . . Situation at Ringgold would relieve the situation in Brownsville, but no wise alleviate the feelings of the people in this part of State, especially as similar troubles have occurred at Ringgold in the past. For the best interests of the service and the people of the State, the battalion should, in my opinion, be sent out of Texas." McCaskey agreed and forwarded Penrose's wire to Washington with the recommendation the new post be changed to Fort Reno, Oklahoma.[78] Roosevelt, now really in the weeds of decision making, agreed, and the next day the orders were changed.[79]

ENTER CAPTAIN WILLIAM "BILL" McDonald of the Texas Rangers, who arrived in Brownsville with the anger, bitterness, and aggressiveness that led south Texans to say he would charge hell with one bucket of water. And with no sense. Bill McDonald brought to Brownsville, its mayor, and the army a "good deal of trouble."[80] Of all the rabble-rousers in the Brownsville Incident, none was more dangerous than Ranger McDonald, who came to town to show the locals how Negroes should be dealt with and, possibly only incidentally, to prove the black soldiers were guilty.[81] Deciding on his own that Brownsville needed his skills if any progress was to be made in identifying the guilty soldiers, he sought from the Texas adjutant general the assistance of the Texas state militia, the forerunner of what would become the National Guard. He was turned down and told he had no authority to investigate the army.[82] He didn't care; he could take care of it by himself anyway. When his train to Brownsville stopped in Corpus Christi, District Judge Stanley Welch, who had been asked to come to Brownsville by District Attorney John Kleiber to assist him in his own investigation, came aboard.[83] Disputing the advice of the adjutant general, Judge Welch told McDonald that as a Texas Ranger he did have the authority to look for and apprehend the shooters. Fortified by this more agreeable clarification, McDonald got down to settling the business in Brownsville. But by the time he got there, President Roosevelt already had decided to redeploy the soldiers, and soon they would be away from McDonald and his authority, whatever it might be.

Unaware he might already be too late, McDonald started nosing around. First stop was a meeting with Mayor Combe and Captain Kelly to complain they had not moved the investigation along as quickly as he might have.[84] Kelly recalled he showed up with a battery of pistols ostentatiously strapped to him on a big belt. If these were insufficiently protective, McDonald also had a knife.[85] Accomplishing little else than antagonizing Combe and Kelly, the next stop was the Brownsville jail to speak to prisoner Mack Hamilton, a former Buffalo Soldier with the Tenth Cavalry. He had been posted at Fort Brown when it was stationed there, met and married a woman from the area, and returned after leaving the army. He supported his wife and family by running a lunch counter at Tillman's bar, where he had been working on the day of the shooting.[86] Right after the shooting, Sheriff Celedonio Garza of Cameron County got a tip that Hamilton might know something and arrested him. Garza had suggested McDonald talk to his prisoner.

"I got some good information from him against Corporal Miller," McDonald reported. Corporal Willie Miller of Company C was Hamilton's cousin and had been across the border in Matamoros on a pass that permitted him to be away from the post until the next morning. After returning to the American side of the Rio Grande, Miller made a visit to his cousin.[87] A few years later, Miller testified that Hamilton learned the afternoon before the shooting that white citizens were planning to attack the fort and seize the soldier who assaulted Mrs. Lon Evans. It is unlikely this is the "good information" McDonald was referring to, since it would hardly show the soldiers were the shooters, unless they learned of this and came into town to preempt the attack on them.[88] The next morning, McDonald went to Fort Brown, blustered his way past the sentries, and met with Corporal Miller, after which he snooped around the post, spoke to other soldiers, and decided he was on to something.

THE NEXT DAY, AUGUST 23, barely a day and a half after arriving in Brownsville, Ranger McDonald was ready to show the local rubes he had the goods. From Judge Welch, he asked for and received warrants to arrest twelve soldiers and one former soldier. The speed with which the soldiers were accused, with little or no evidence, shows how stacked against them the law and the system of justice were in Brownsville. Likewise, the speed with which Roosevelt accepted the soldiers' guilt—almost as quick as men like Ranger McDonald—tainted Roosevelt and showed his true feelings. General McCaskey was astounded by it all: "The manner by which their names were procured is a mystery. It seems to have been a dragnet proceeding."[89]

McDonald's haste was inexcusable. The evidence he had was thin, and he could expect little of it to be admissible in court or withstand a cross-examination by any halfway competent lawyer. All he had was conjecture. Yet it had a thread of logical thought to it:

- Of the twelve soldiers, six were members of Company C. It seemed to be in the thick of the shooting. Its gun racks were the ones that had to be smashed open with an ax. Its acting first sergeant refused to open them, and his excuse that he never heard the "Call to Arms" suggested he was trying to keep the rifles away from an inspection that would show they were fired. It was Company C's commanding officer, Captain Macklin, who was missing during the shooting and the formation of his and the other companies right after, and his excuse that he slept through it all sounded fishy. Two soldiers from Company C were away outside the fort on passes. They could have been in the town and participated in the shooting and not have been missed. Two others from Company C had altercations with citizens just before the shooting. This provided motives for the soldiers to shoot up the town and possibly target certain houses.[90] And an army cap of another man from Company C, identified by his initials, was found in the street where the shootings took place.

- Three men were from Company B. Its barracks were closest to the fort's main gate, permitting a quick way out of the fort to commit the offense and an easy way back in after hearing the "Call to Arms." One of its arrested men had charge of its rifles. His key would give access to them. Another was sergeant of the guard that night and therefore able to cover for the shooters. Another also was a sergeant, and some of the witnesses heard what sounded like a noncommissioned officer directing the shooting. One was the financial partner in the segregated saloon opened for the soldiers, a likely place for soldiers to gather and plan the shooting, and he often spent his off-duty time there protecting his investment and would have been there for such talk. It closed early on the night of the shooting, and perhaps McDonald thought this suspicious.
- A soldier from Company D was a sentry during the shooting, and he fired his rifle, supposedly as an alarm, something that would explain a "dirty" rifle if it had been inspected right afterward. A second man from Company D was in charge of its rifles and, like his counterpart in Company B, had a key and access to them.

None of this was anything more than speculation. Some was not even suspicious. Not a bit of this justified arrest. As a lawman, McDonald was acting irresponsibly. As an investigator, however, he may have discerned a pattern that fit a theory of what may have happened.

Penrose was just as baffled as General McCaskey and had no idea why McDonald thought these men had anything to do with what happened.[91] He also feared what would happen to these soldiers once Ranger McDonald got his hands on them. When McDonald tried on August 23 to serve the warrants and take possession of the twelve soldiers, to keep them away from him, Penrose made a suggestion to Judge Welch. He would confine the men in Fort Brown's guardhouse and not take them from the post without the judge's permission. Welch accepted this arrangement and in return did not enforce the arrest warrants issued to McDonald. When the order came to leave Fort Brown, Penrose had to tell the army why they might not be able to. If the judge now insisted these men stay behind, Penrose was in a box. Both orders—the army's and the judge's—could not be obeyed.

Penrose wired the Department of Texas in Austin that the men could not get a fair trial and he feared for their safety if they stayed behind. Major Blocksom sent a solution: turn the confined men over to the detachment from the Twenty-Sixth Infantry on its way to secure the base. "Authorities pledge themselves able to keep prisoners from violence." General McCaskey forwarded Blocksom's wire to Washington with his own opinion that the men's lives would not be safe, urging they be confined elsewhere. To make the point, he separately forwarded a wire from Company D's Captain Lyon: his men were "absolutely innocent" and would not get a fair trial in Brownsville.[92] The messages from Penrose, Blocksom, Lyon, and McCaskey hit their target. The next day, General Ainsworth sent two wires directly to Penrose. The first ordered him to delay his departure from Fort Brown.[93] The second, marked "Confidential," ordered Penrose to keep the confined men under proper guard. If civilian authorities demanded their custody, Penrose was to send Ainsworth the demand along with authorities' assurances the men would be safe and would receive a fair trial. Without these assurances, which Penrose and the others already had said were unlikely, the War Department would keep the men in its custody, and Judge Welch's order be damned. Then Penrose was asked if he was sure he could protect his men while they were at Fort Brown, and, if not, could he escort them safely elsewhere?[94] If he said no to the first and yes to the second, the twelve men would not even be kept at Fort Brown.

Now it was Judge Welch's turn to find out what was happening.

Violating the confidentiality of the second telegram, Penrose showed his orders to the judge. With Welch was Ranger McDonald, who somehow knew what was happening, probably from a leak to him by the Western Union agent handling the telegrams. McDonald demanded the prisoners be turned over to him. Penrose refused; he had orders otherwise. The judge postponed his decision until later that night, when he asked Mayor Combe, District Attorney Kleiber, Congressman John Nance Garner of Brownsville, and James Wells, the most prominent lawyer in town, to join him. McDonald showed up too. This time he blundered and in so doing took himself out of the case, giving Combe and by now everyone else what they wanted. His first mistake was carrying a shotgun into a judge's office. Judges frown on that sort of intimidation. His second was, in the presence of a judge, getting a little "excited." Judges dislike that even more. Lawyer Wells tried to calm him down: "If you attempt to interfere with those soldiers down there, this matter will break out anew and we will lose a great many lives here." As the now-triumphant Combe would recall, Judge Welch felt that "it was dangerous for [McDonald] to hold this bench warrant, and Judge Welch said, 'I am going to withdraw that bench warrant from [him].'"[95] Judge Welch had heard enough and had had enough of Ranger McDonald. The formerly arrested men were free to leave with the rest of their battalion, and all soon would be gone from Brownsville.

Had Judge Welch wanted to keep the men in Brownsville and had Ranger McDonald persuaded him to affirm the arrest warrants, it would not have mattered. Even before the judge's ruling, President Roosevelt, in a telegram over his name and not William Loeb's, decreed the battalion would be transferred and the confined men taken with it.[96] The last two words in his telegram were "Act immediately."

The Citizens' Committee had accomplished Mayor Combe's purpose. But in showing the soldiers were dangerous, Combe and his committee established their collective guilt. This presumption of guilt colored every investigation thereafter. Their battalion commander, the commanding general of the Department of Texas, his inspector general, the army's chief of staff, the acting secretary of war, and in the end President Roosevelt thought the anguish expressed by the residents of Brownsville might be justified.

MAYOR COMBE FORMED A committee ostensibly to investigate a crime and find evidence showing who did it. The committee was to make a prima facie case against the soldiers that would be enough to get them out of Brownsville. How could President Roosevelt ignore advice that he had to protect the town and its citizens? The protection of Brownsville became more important than the protection of the soldiers' rights.

Crucial to the history of the Brownsville Incident is understanding that Combe and his committee changed the focus of almost every subsequent investigation. Any crime investigation has to have two parts: finding out who did it and developing the evidence to prove it. After the Citizens' Committee, subsequent investigations skipped over the first and went right to the second. Quickly it became apparent that the only way to prove it was soldiers was to get other soldiers to say so. The army was never able to do that, and the government soon determined it did not have to.

And so Combe and his committee manipulated Theodore Roosevelt into taking charge of the Brownville Incident.

"Now tell who did the shooting
And how it all begun";
But not one word escaped their lips—
That noble band stood mum.

Well, if you will shield the guilty
Your fame as soldiers is erased;
You are discharged, every man of you,
Dishonored and disgraced.

Ah, but who can say dishonor,
In this land of toil and strife,
When men stand by their comrades
For the protection of their life.

Poem appearing in the
Colored American Magazine, January 1907, pp. 62–63,
quoted in Lewis N. Wynne,
"Brownsville: The Reaction of the Negro Press,"
Phylon, 1972

CHAPTER FIVE

A MORE AGGRESSIVE ATTITUDE

WATCHING FROM THE PORCH of the Miller Hotel, Mayor Combe was relieved to see the battalion form up at Fort Brown's main gate and prepare to leave Brownsville. His jaw dropped when he saw the soldiers about-face and march back into the fort. Major Penrose had just received the telegram from General Ainsworth ordering a delay until the army resolved the problem of Ranger McDonald and the soldiers in the guardhouse. "Your message this date received as battalion was forming to march to train," Penrose wired back.[1] When the snarl was straightened out, the new plan was to leave around midnight. Now it was Mayor Combe who wanted a delay. Violence from townspeople was more likely in the dark, and Penrose agreed to wait for daybreak. Mayor Combe used this time to bulk up the police presence with hand-picked deputies stationed at regular intervals along Elizabeth Street between the fort and the train depot. No disruption would be tolerated. The police would arrest any man demonstrating against the soldiers and shoot anyone firing a weapon.[2]

A story later that day in the *Brownsville Daily Herald*, cited by Brownsville historian John Weaver, described the scene: "Not a word was spoken by the men as they left and only the briefest commands given by the officers as they marched through town."[3] As soon as the soldiers boarded the waiting train and left, Brownsville stopped holding its breath, and very soon the streets came alive with women and children no longer afraid to leave their homes.[4]

There would be no replacement for the Twenty-Fifth Infantry; Fort Brown would be deactivated and shuttered. Interest in the Citizens' Committee and its investigation soon dwindled and the committee itself would fade away. Texas Ranger McDonald left town to bring his kind of peace and justice to other parts of Texas, and Brownsville was as happy to see the end of him as it was of the soldiers. Judge Welch returned to his regular judicial duties, but only briefly. A few weeks later he was murdered, and, just as with the investigations into the Brownsville shooting, his killers would never be identified.[5]

EVEN BEFORE THE BATTALION left Brownsville, the army started its own inquiries. At sunrise after the shooting, Major Penrose ordered the men's rifles inspected and sent Captain Macklin to walk the brick wall separating the fort and the town to look for spent ammunition. Later that day, when for the first time he notified his superiors of the raid, he told them, "Am doing everything in my power to find guilty parties *if* they be in this command" (author's emphasis).[6] For the next five months, the army investigated and reinvestigated, and over the following four years, there would be at least twenty investigations, seven by the army.[7] Each sought to redress the inadequacies of those preceding it, each made its own mistakes, and all failed to learn who the shooters were.

MAJOR PENROSE HAD TROUBLE getting started. He had no idea how to go about it. His thought to seek help from Commissioner Rentfro Creager got him nowhere when he realized the man was too prejudiced against the Negro soldiers to be of any use. Meanwhile, the demands from higher-ups to know what happened pressured him to respond too quickly. His hopelessly hurried one-day inquiry relied on Citizens' Committee testimony.[8] Because it was neither under oath nor cross-examined, it had little probative value. It allowed Penrose to describe the raid in greater detail, but it was one-sided. Its conclusion was untested.

Penrose's telegram of August 14 alerting the army to the shooting and his report of August 15 made two statements with important consequences. The raid "was carefully planned beforehand [and the shooting] was done by . . . men of this command, abetted by others in post."[9] That made it premeditated. For the moment, the army and the War Department's only interest was finding out *which* soldiers were conspirators. Penrose could not tell them. His report ended with an optimistic prediction: "through [the soldiers themselves], rather than my own efforts, the perpetrators of this wanton crime will be apprehended."[10]

Curiously, he said nothing about Macklin finding shells, just as he also hid this from Mayor Combe. In time, the Macklin shells vanished along with the desk Captain Macklin so casually tossed them into.[11] The mystery of who shot them and why Penrose never mentioned them remains.

MAJOR PENROSE'S INVESTIGATION, COMPLETED in double time, was unsatisfactory and his report's findings poorly thought out. He was not the right man for the job. He was not a detective and he was not a lawyer. He was not part of the army's office of the inspector general. On his own, he had no authority to investigate the civilians (the opposite problem for Texas Ranger McDonald, who was told he had no right to investigate soldiers), and without this, the army should not have expected his investigation to be complete. There should have been formal coordination of his and civil authorities' investigations, not the informality of his offer to cooperate with the Citizens' Committee, itself something of a rump band, most of whose members were selected for reasons other than backgrounds in investigative training.

Another investigation was needed.

MAJOR AUGUSTUS BLOCKSOM, ASSISTANT inspector general for the army's Southwest Division, was in his office at the division's head-quarters in Oklahoma City, when he received his orders to "go down there and investigate this trouble."[12] A graduate of the US Military Academy at West Point, Blocksom had seen a lot of fighting during his almost-thirty years in the army. He was a cavalry officer in the Indian Wars in the American West, helped put down the Boxer Rebellion in China, and received the Purple Heart for wounds charging up San Juan Heights in Cuba.[13] Now fifty-two years old, Major Blocksom's inspector-general duties brought him in from the field to inspect troops, find out the condition of their discipline, and investigate infractions of military duty. These were matters he was "quite familiar" with.[14] If he had experience in off-post criminal behavior and working with civilian police agencies and prosecutors, he never mentioned it.

Blocksom claimed he knew very little about the shooting before he got off the train in Brownsville. He never saw any of the swarm of telegrams that buzzed along the Western Union wires since the raid or even knew there were any.[15] He had an open mind, no bias or prejudice, and no preconceived notion of the soldiers' guilt.[16] But it did not take him long to make up his mind. To help decide if the soldiers should stay in Texas or go to Oklahoma, General Ainsworth asked Blocksom for his "conclusions as to cause of Browns-ville disturbance."[17] In his response that same day, Blocksom told Ainsworth, the "causes of disturbance are racial." White residents did not want black soldiers at Fort Brown and instigated "several encounters," and the soldiers knew this and resented it. Angry, the soldiers made what Blocksom called a "preconcerted" raid.[18]

Once the soldiers were on their way to Oklahoma, Blocksom got down to business. He started his investigation by speaking to citizens and witnesses, learning the thoughts of the members of the Citizens' Committee, and interviewing the Twenty-Fifth Infantry's commissioned and noncommissioned officers and army hospital corpsmen. As he absorbed what people told him, his conclusions did not change at all. The shooters were soldiers. He supported Penrose's conclusion that the raid was premeditated; therefore any questionable act by a soldier could be interpreted as part of the plan. Thus when the first shots were fired from inside the fort as an alarm, this was further evidence of the plan.[19] Did the sergeant of the guard sound the "Call to Arms" on his own? This was a signal to the shooters and part of the plan.

Blocksom said he was determined to conduct an investigation as thoroughly as he could. But he took no notice of facts that simply got in the way of his conclusion. For example, Major Penrose thought the first two shots were fired from pistols, and others heard pistol fire too.[20] This was significant because pistols were common among Brownsville civilians,[21] but the soldiers' pistols were in their shipping cases and under lock and key.[22] Blocksom's report, like Penrose's, ignored possible pistol fire and the logical inference that it probably would not be from the soldiers.

He secured no new written testimony (or any written statements for that matter), either sworn or unsworn. If someone made a comment exonerating the soldiers, he considered it false and tossed it aside, as with Private Joseph Howard, who denied seeing who was shooting. Blocksom thought he was lying.[23] His entire perception of the soldiers and what they said began with skepticism and ended with doubt. He scoffed at First Sergeant Mingo Sanders's assertion that his record in the army was perfect, without bothering to look at it.[24] Had he done so, he would have found more than twenty-five years of military service with no record of any court-martial or reprimand.[25]

He failed to critically question the officers. Astonishingly, his quizzing of Penrose and Macklin was so incomplete, he never found out about the shells Macklin picked off the ground.[26] He never asked about them; Penrose and Macklin never told him about them. (This would be the third time Penrose failed to mention it.) He gave no weight to the opinion of the only officer who thought the soldiers innocent, Captain Samuel Lyon of Company D. Instead, he accepted at face value what the residents told him. The "evidence of many witnesses . . . *is conclusive*" (author's emphasis).[27] He never tested, for example, whether witnesses could tell a shooter's race in the dark. The soldiers' defenders looked into this and learned they probably could not.[28] When Blocksom heard this, he later conceded this would bear on the witnesses' credibility.[29]

He did not consider that revenge worked both ways. He thought the soldiers wanted to get even with the town for the harassment it gave them; was it not just as likely angry townspeople wanted to get even with them for the alleged assault on Mrs. Evans? Blocksom acknowledged people were "excited" after the Evans "assault." Excited? They were so enraged the next day that Mayor Combe told Penrose that if soldiers came into the town he could not be responsible for their safety.

He insufficiently grasped what the harassment and humiliation meant to the soldiers, some of them proud combat veterans, and what they were forced to live with in Brownsville, especially after postings in the Jim Crow–free Northwest. (General McCaskey, the man who ordered Blocksom to Brownsville, was aware of it.) He explained away some of the nasty treatment of the soldiers by whites as "in the manner of the South."[30] Tate may have been "too drastic" when he battered Private James Newton on the head with a revolver, but Newton was "rude and probably insulting" when he refused to walk around the ladies. Customs Inspector A. Y. Baker probably did use too much force when he pushed Private Oscar Reid (misspelled as "Reed" by Blocksom) into the water; then again, Reid may have been "drunk and disorderly."

The result of a one-sided investigation was an inevitable conclusion. His report could have begun and ended with its first line, "Sir,

I have the honor to report investigation of *trouble caused by soldiers of the Twenty-Fifth Infantry*" (author's emphasis). Race was the reason there was a shooting. And, he made clear, race was the reason for his failure to find out who did it.

IN HIS TESTIMONY BEFORE the Senate Military Affairs Committee, Major Blocksom tried to explain how race kept him from accomplishing what he was sent to Brownsville to do. Awkwardly expressing himself, Blocksom blamed the soldiers and said their actions were "external to the ordinary affairs of discipline."[31] Regardless of race, "I know when a man commits a crime in a company that the men all know it. They are bound to find it out." He was "morally certain" of it.[32] Add the racial component to the Brownsville raid, and "the soldiers stuck together and so intended to do so through thick and thin, so far as they could."[33] "Many of the old soldiers who had nothing to do with the raid must know something tangible as to the identity of the criminals."[34] If pressure was applied to these men, some of them would identify the raiders to save their own careers. If they did not, "they should be made to suffer with others more guilty, as far as the law will permit." If they did not know who the raiders and conspirators were, they should find out or be thrown out of the army along with them.[35]

Blocksom ended his report with a revealing statement, nowhere justified by what he learned in Brownsville. New ideas of the times prodded Negro soldiers into reacting in new and unsettling ways to provocations formerly quietly endured. "It must be confessed the colored soldier is much more aggressive in his attitude on the social equality question than he used to be."[36]

WITH THE ARMY'S INVESTIGATIONS down a blind alley, it still had to make a decision regarding what to do with soldiers who might be singled out as shooters and conspirators. At one point, it seemed to consider trials by Texas authorities. The idea made sense. The raid was off the base and in the town itself, the victims were civilians, and Texas had a criminal court system. But would a south Texas court protect black soldiers? In a letter to Secretary of War Taft dated the day after the Black Battalion arrived at Fort Reno,

General Ainsworth wrote, "We propose to continue the investigation with a view to discovering the guilty parties if possible, *so that they as well as any others that may be demanded may be turned over to the civil authorities when the President is satisfied that this can be done with reasonable assurance that the men turned over will receive protection and a fair trial*" (author's emphasis).[37] Four days later, both Blocksom and Assistant Attorney General A. C. Hamilton, sent to Brownsville by the Justice Department specifically to find out if a fair trial there was possible, in separate reports to their respective superiors said it was not.[38]

The question became moot. Texas might not have a reason to try the men. Technically, the moment Judge Welch withdrew the arrest warrants, the confined soldiers were, as General Ainsworth advised William Loeb, the president's secretary, on September 3, "free from any charges so far as the civil authorities are concerned." However, the Cameron County grand jury had not met to consider the affray; it soon would, and it was possible it might indict the soldiers. Both Blocksom and Hamilton thought this was doubtful, and using identical language both men said so in their letters of September 2. They were right. Three weeks later, the grand jury adjourned without returning verdicts against any of the soldiers. That same day, Judge Welch advised the army the men were "entitled to release."[39] Trial by Texas was out.

TRIAL BY ARMY COURT-MARTIAL was the obvious alternative. Three days before Ainsworth's letter to Loeb, Loeb wrote Ainsworth about a request from a Negro lawyer in Jacksonville, Florida, J. Douglas Wetmore, for an interview with President Roosevelt concerning Brownsville. Loeb had put Wetmore off by telling him, "So far as the President is advised the men will be tried before a military court." Now Loeb was having second thoughts. "I was correct in this statement, was I not?" he asked Ainsworth.[40] He was. General Ainsworth already had the army, with Roosevelt's knowledge and consent, charge the confined soldiers under the military's Articles of War.[41] If Texas decided to bring the men to trial and Roosevelt had no objections, he could determine the Texas courts could protect the men and their rights and allow civilian trials. If, as Ainsworth suspected, Roosevelt wanted to keep control in his own hands, he could, with the two warning letters from Hamilton (which Ainsworth thoughtfully included in his response to Loeb), find Texas justice lacking and order courts-martial for these military charges. The decision was Roosevelt's to make.

SOON AFTER BLOCKSOM'S REPORT, General McCaskey at the Department of Texas told Ainsworth nothing had been learned since the men arrived at Fort Reno.[42] Eight days later, Ainsworth, still empty-handed, advised Loeb he would let him know when there were any results.[43] That same day, President Roosevelt, working on his annual message to Congress, was irritated he had nothing conclusive to include about Brownsville and was growing increasingly frustrated. Even the Secret Service, whose use in the Brownsville investigation he had authorized, had come up empty.[44] His mind went back to Major Blocksom's report and its prediction the crime would not be solved because no soldier would tell on another. He looked again at its recommendation that the threat of discharge be used to force the soldiers to tell what they knew. A month after the shooting, all else having failed, this seemed to him the only way to get the names of the shooters and those who cooperated with them. The next day, September 13, 1906, a month to the day after the shooting, his secretary Loeb wired Ainsworth, "the President . . . is much concerned over [Blocksom's report]. . . . If the guilty parties cannot be discovered the President approves of the recommendation that the whole three companies implicated in this atrocious outrage should be dismissed and the men forever debarred from reenlisting in the Army or Navy of the United States." Roosevelt's concern had turned to anger.

EVEN WITHOUT HEARING FROM President Roosevelt, the pressure to crack this nut was building. If the soldiers shot up Brownsville because of Brownsville's treatment of them, it might be a good idea to learn just how bad this treatment was. General Ainsworth directed the Department of Texas to look into this, and the Department of

Texas instructed the Twenty-Sixth Infantry to send someone back to Brownsville to find out. According to two of its officers, it was pretty bad. So scorching were two affidavits that, toward the end of September, Lieutenant Colonel Leonard A. Lovering was sent to Fort Reno to "make an investigation and report on the matter."[45]

In his report two weeks later, Lovering confessed it was "difficult to obtain testimony about troubles between soldiers and civilians in Brownsville."[46] Since this would have meant a thin report, one not pleasing to Generals McCaskey and Ainsworth, Lovering showed some initiative and inflated the meaning of "the matter" he was told to investigate to include more than the attitude of people in Brownsville toward the Black Battalion. As long as he was speaking to the soldiers to get an idea of what they really thought about the harassment, he might as well ask them about the shooting itself.

Lovington's report is by far the most thorough of the army investigations that took place in the two months after the shooting. He took the sworn testimony of Major Penrose, Captains Macklin and Lyon, Lieutenant Grier, and practically every noncommissioned officer and enlisted man in the battalion. He asked for and received evidence showing which soldiers were at the post or nearby on that fateful night. He made lists of those soldiers with alibis, those absent from the post on duty elsewhere, and those seen by officers while the shooting was in progress. Lovington asked soldiers where they were when the shooting began and had they been harassed by civilians, and a surprising number neither had trouble nor heard of any soldier who had.

He also questioned Major Blocksom about items in his report, including why men who heard the first shots were so sure they were fired from the town into Fort Brown. Carefully inspecting buildings and other structures in the post, Blocksom "could find no bullets striking anywhere in the post." His theory was that the early shots supposedly fired into the post were intentionally aimed *high and over* the post to justify an impression the fort was under attack.[47] (This might explain why the next morning Captain Macklin found army shells *on the town side* of the waist-high wall.)

After all this, Lovering's conclusions were disappointing. His report joined those from Penrose and Macklin in failing to identify any shooter. It did not advance the ball at all.[48]

WHILE LOVERING WAS WASTING time at Fort Reno and President Roosevelt was working himself into a fury in Oyster Bay, the Black Battalion was languishing at Fort Reno, its military effectiveness withering away from inactivity and the late-summer Oklahoma sun. Major Penrose despaired for his battalion and its men. On September 20, the same day the battalion's Company A arrived from Wyoming to bring it to full strength, he knew he had to make it clear to the army that things could not go on this way. He reminded the Department of Texas that adding the time they were confined to Fort Brown after the shooting and their days at Fort Reno, his men "had no liberty of any kind or character for over a month." They endured extra guard duty, extra drills, roll calls when bugled back to their barracks, one or two surprise inspections each night, and unending policing (cleaning up) of their area. Penrose had thought this might persuade soldiers who knew something about the shooting to come clean. None had. More frustrating to him, this make-work had the opposite effect. All his officers and many of the black noncommissioned officers agreed with him that only a few men knew anything, and they were continuing to resist.

The next day, General McCaskey wired Washington that the men of the battalion were practically prisoners, and he recommended the restrictions be ended.[49] Three days later he forwarded a letter from Penrose suggesting that restrictions be ended (as a carrot) and discharges be implemented (the stick), but in stages to encourage men to talk before they were out of the army and it was too late; McCaskey commented that Penrose's proposal of discharges was "excessive."[50]

PRESIDENT ROOSEVELT DISAGREED. His displeasure with Penrose's variation of Blocksom's recommendation was that it was at best a half measure and, if not immediately successful, it would take too long to reach a result that would put him and the army right back where they had been all along, no suspects to deal with and no justice to dispense. On October 4, 1906, the acting secretary of war ordered the US Army's inspector general, Brigadier General Ernest A. Garlington, to Oklahoma to get the matter over with quickly.[51] Gone was the need to learn what happened. "The President directs that you . . . secure information that will lead to the *apprehension and punishment of the men of the Twenty-fifth Infantry* believed in the riotous disturbance" (author's emphasis). Garlington was told to tell the soldiers, "The orders given by the President [are] 'If the guilty parties cannot be discovered . . . the whole three companies . . . should be dismissed and the men forever debarred from reenlisting in the Army or Navy of the United State as well as from employment in any civil capacity under the Government.'"[52]

Evidently, no thought was given to the legal basis of such a presidential order or the precedents for such an action. With his mind free of any such concerns, on the same day Garlington was sent to Oklahoma, Roosevelt was off to dedicate the new Pennsylvania State Capitol in Harrisburg ("the handsomest building I ever saw") and talk with the state's Republican bosses about the off-year elections coming up the next month.[53]

ON HIS WAY TO Fort Reno, Garlington stopped in Oklahoma City to speak to Major Blocksom, where, other than finding out for the first time about Lovering's investigation, he learned "nothing new."[54] Then on to Fort Sam Houston in San Antonio to examine the twelve soldiers (he referred to them as prisoners) still in the guardhouse there. He believed these were the men more likely to be shooters or conspirators. Each of them denied any role in the raid or knowing anything about it. If this small group had been involved in the raid, Garlington's chances of getting one to admit it were slim. The smaller the conspiracy, the less likely one member will break away. An active player was unlikely to admit his own guilt and buy himself a court-martial. Better to play dumb and be returned to civilian life. What made no sense to Garlington was that, although all of them knew the whites in Brownsville did not want them at Fort Brown and knew of Newton's, Reid's, and Adair's abusive treatment, none felt any animosity or resentment. Garlington's better chance was at Fort Reno, where he was more likely to find a soldier guilty only of hearing what others had done and now willing to tell what he had heard to stay in the army.[55]

At Fort Reno, Garlington met with the battalion's officers; they had learned nothing new to tell him. He turned to noncommissioned officers with longtime service in the army and careers and pensions to protect; some were aware of the ill-treatment in Brownsville, but all were mystifyingly indifferent to it. None knew anything about the raid. He assembled the entire battalion and read President Roosevelt's order with its threat of dismissal. He appealed to their pride as members of the Twenty-Fifth Infantry and in themselves as soldiers. It was futile. In a last effort, General Garlington said he would make himself accessible to any soldier who wanted to disclose privately what he knew. One soldier came to him, and that man, unnamed by Garlington but later identified as First Sergeant Mingo Sanders of Company B, showed up, "not to give information, but to urge his own case for exemption" from the discharges.[56]

Recognizing he failed to "secure information that will lead to the apprehension and punishment of" the raiders, Garlington returned to Washington to make his report. There was "a possible general understanding among the enlisted men of this battalion . . . that they would admit nothing." He repeated every previous investigation's conclusion: the raid "was done by enlisted men . . . at Fort Brown." Acknowledging the innocent soldier would be punished along with the guilty, he nevertheless recommended every enlisted man who was at Fort Brown that night be "discharged without honor."[57]

THE THREAD OF LOGIC for a conspiracy of silence was a straight line starting with the May announcement of the battalion's transfer to Brownsville to the salvo of shots on August 13: the townspeople did not want them; attempts were made to keep them away; the black soldiers came anyway and were greeted by an unwelcoming town and sullen townspeople; unhappiness with the soldiers' presence quickly led to racial discrimination, harassment, and violence; the soldiers' resentment quickly became anger and a plan to get even, which all soldiers thought a good idea; and to protect their comrades who did the shooting, a conspiracy of silence was agreed to.

Garlington scoffed at the notion that no one could say anything because no one knew anything. There had to be "a possible general understanding . . . as to the position they would take." "The secretive nature of the race, where crimes charged to members of their color are made, is well known."[58]

Speaking for himself and a great many other people at the time, journalist and author Arthur Wallace Dunn believed that "Brownsville showed a characteristic of the Negro little understood. Negroes will not tell on each other. . . . A chief characteristic of the Negro is secretiveness regarding himself and his people."[59] Alvred B. Nettleton, Civil War veteran and self-described "anti-slavery advocate when that phrase had a meaning," was so sure this was happening in Brownsville, he sent a letter to Secretary of War Taft telling him "a very large proportion of the command" knew what happened but was not saying so.[60] The soldiers' defenders were just as sure the soldiers never talked because they were not the shooters.

The argument goes on today.

The army was at the end of its rope. The fox could not be caught. Let it go, but at least get it out of the hen house. Garlington recommended the dismissal of every enlisted man "serving at Fort Brown, Tex., on the night of August 13, 1906, and forever debarring them from reenlisting in the Army or Navy of the United States, [and] from employment in any civil capacity under the Government."[61]

IF THERE WAS SUCH an agreement among the soldiers to keep quiet to avoid criminal prosecution and army court-martial, it worked. The Cameron County grand jury, probably just itching to prosecute the men arrested by Texas Ranger McDonald, could do nothing. It had no hint of whom to indict. The army had the same problem.[62] Those who doubted the conspiracy-of-silence theory were helpless to undermine it. One of the regiment's staunchest defenders, Brigadier General Andrew S. Burt, who was, except for the time in Cuba, their commanding officer from 1892 until 1902, refused to believe it. Pressed by the Senate Military Affairs Committee, "So that you would not expect the members of the battalion who had nothing to do with the shooting try to conceal the facts in regard to it, and prevent the detection of those who were guilty?" "No, Sir," the general emphatically replied.[63] Even General Garlington admitted he "could find no evidence of such understanding."[64] But without evidence, a reverse logic took hold, and the idea of a conspiracy of silence became self-supporting; the longer soldiers claimed unawareness of anything, the more they were lying, and this itself was proof of their agreement to say nothing about what they knew.

Some saw this as a good thing, a sign of progress. Colonel Thomas W. Higginson, a white officer who led the First South Carolina Volunteers in the Civil War, was convinced it was "a long step forward" for the black race. "When I commanded them in the South, I feared they would never learn to stick together and be loyal to each other." Higginson was elated the Brownsville soldiers "can neither be forced nor bribed to reveal who did it."[65]

If the conspiracy was planned and implemented right after the shooting, how was it possible to maintain it? Their champion General Burt didn't think it could be. The fact that it did not leak out was proof to him there was no battalion-wide conspiracy. His reasoning was oddly racial. He stood with the soldiers because "the colored man is essentially a vain man, and if a number of those men had been in a conspiracy, some one man in that crowd, if he would have been in it, he would have wanted to tell, so as to aggrandize some credit to himself. They are naturally a vain race." Among only fifteen to twenty men, maybe the secret could be kept, but among all the enlisted men at Fort Brown, it would be "simply an impossibility."[66]

PRESIDENT ROOSEVELT ACCEPTED THAT there was a conspiracy of silence in Brownsville and brooded about it. Such a thing could "not be tolerated in any soldiers, black or white." Worse, it foreshadowed "the gravest danger to both races."[67] What worried him was that it suggested the black race was particularly likely to shield black criminals and would therefore, as a race, be thought untrustworthy.[68] This was "the greatest danger." Four months after the dismissals, he wrote he was "really deprest over this." He said before Brownsville, he dismissed "the claim of Southern whites that the decent

Negroes would actively or passively shield their own wrongdoers."
Now he wasn't so sure, and it gave him "the most serious concern,"
because it showed that "colored people . . . [have lost] sight of every
real movement for the betterment of their race, of every real wrong
done their race by peonage or lynching, and to fix their eyes only
upon this movement to prevent the punishment of atrociously guilty
men of their race."[69] "The respectable colored people must learn not
to harbor their criminals, but to assist the officers in bringing them to
justice. This is the larger crime. . . . The two races can never get on
until there is an understanding on the part of both to make common
cause with the law-abiding against criminals of any color."[70]

The idea that the black community has a code of silence for
black crime has proven durable, even among African Americans of
the twenty-first century. In 2010, more than a century after Brownsville, Bill Maxwell, an African American syndicated columnist for
the *St. Petersburg Times*, wrote of three black women in Tampa who,
after hearing gunshots, rushed into the street to find two police officers on the ground dying. Maxwell writes that for calling 911 and
remaining with the dying officers until help arrived, the women
were "ostracized by many other black people. . . . Their sin, considered by many to be perhaps the worst in American black culture,
was helping 'the enemy'—the police."[71]

ON MONDAY, NOVEMBER 5, President Roosevelt, just as he had threatened, ordered "that the recommendations of General Garlington
be complied with."[72] Every enlisted soldier who had been at Fort
Brown on the night of the raid was to be dismissed without honor.
Not one was to be spared.[73]

One question—at the time and ever since—is why it took Roosevelt two weeks to do what Major Blocksom recommended back
in September, which Roosevelt himself supported when Blocksom
proposed it.[74] Was it that the 1906 off-year elections were the next
day and Roosevelt did not want to antagonize and scare away those
who were probably the most loyal Republican voters—Negroes?
The *New York Times* reported two weeks after the election from a
"leak" (never identified by the *New York Times*) that "political con-

siderations were not wholly overlooked" and the order was kept hidden until "it was too late for the colored vote . . . to be affected."[75] Three days later, the *New York Times* seemed to confirm the connection between the delay and election day when it wrote that Republican leaders in Washington were congratulating themselves "on the President's foresight in holding up the publication of the order," otherwise "some well-known men in Congress . . . would have lost."[76]

Roosevelt had a lot on his plate at the time. Bids for work on the Panama Canal had to be sorted out. The attorney general needed guidance on the ongoing prosecutions of trusts, especially the Standard Oil case. There was the frightening possibility that Japan, fortified by the way it humbled Russia in the Russo-Japanese War, might turn hostile to the United States over treatment of Japanese workers in western states, most importantly California. A vacancy on the Supreme Court had to be filled.[77] Possibly the biggest domestic mess was the Department of the Interior, where charges of fraudulent land acquisitions in the American West by wealthy ranchers (almost all Republican and some elected officials) to take advantage of favorable terms and cheap prices under the Desert Land Act of 1877 would not go away.

ALL THIS WAS NOTHING compared to the Niagara of Roosevelt correspondence. In the same ten-day period, he wrote letters dealing with investigations by the Interstate Commerce Commission into railroad rates; the as-yet unratified treaty with Great Britain to resolve the use of nets by American fisherman in the waters of Newfoundland; the consequences to the American navy if disarmament meetings in The Hague actually accomplished anything; and the ongoing disarray in Cuba. He was telling anyone (and it seemed everyone) how he disliked William Randolph Hearst (he aligned Hearst's "thoroly" disreputable life with that of Winston Churchill, then a low-ranking member of the British government) and how, as his spelling of "thoroly" indicates, conscientiously he was working to simplify spelling. He was also thinking about whom he might want for the 1908 Republican presidential nomination.[78] Catching his breath, Roosevelt sent a "private and personal" letter to a different

Winston Churchill, the American writer from New Hampshire, complimenting him on his recent book about Granite State politics.[79]

IT CANNOT BE DENIED that the off-year election was important to Roosevelt and something he worked on with care, perseverance, and worry. Roosevelt always put his heart and soul into winning his own and other Republicans' elections. Presidents are not only the heads of state and heads of government; they are also the head of their political party. Working on party affairs is part of the job and in election years especially so. The 1906 election would be the last one of his administration, and for him too much of his legislative program and legacy were still at stake. Historian Barbara Tuchman understood that Roosevelt always had "a haunting fear of being defeated in elections."[80] As Election Day got closer, Roosevelt spent more time immersed in it. The men of the Twenty-Fifth Infantry, in limbo at Fort Reno, were part of the election's equation, and they had to wait for it to be over.

From October 22, the date of the Garlington Report, until the end of the month, Roosevelt had almost-daily conferences and meetings with Republican politicians and officeholders about the campaign. In a letter to his daughter Alice, newlywed wife of Republican of Cincinnati Congressman Nicholas Longworth, he added a handwritten note, "I hear that Nick is all right and will win hands down."[81] Nick did win, but by fewer votes than in 1904.[82] In another letter to Alice, Roosevelt congratulated husband and wife "upon the successful way in which both of you have run your campaign."[83] Enough other Republicans joined Longworth in the House of Representatives to keep the Republican majority, but it was down from 251 seats to 223. In the Senate, happy Republicans would have 61, up from 59.

There had never been anything to worry about.

MEANWHILE, THERE WERE PERSONAL distractions, one of which would become an embarrassment when critics of his Brownsville actions saw hypocrisy in Roosevelt. In Cambridge, his son Ted Jr. got into a scrape with the police when he and two Harvard friends were "in town together at the theater" and one of the friends "got a little drunk." In an undated letter to his father, young Ted described how the two friends had a "disagreement" that quickly became a scuffle. Two plainclothes policemen thought they had witnessed an assault. One tried to collar the drunk friend, who, again according to young Ted, now thought *he* was the victim of an assault, and he knocked down the plainclothes policeman and ran. At the station house, the police wanted Ted Jr. to identify the friend who ran away. He would not. According to the *New York Times*, a policeman suggested his father would have advised him to give the name, "But [Ted Jr.] said, 'I don't think he would.'"[84]

The incident became grist to be ground for a news cycle, and the blessing Ted Jr. thought his father would give to his "conspiracy of silence," so at odds with what his father later would punish the black soldiers for doing, was noted and commented upon.[85]

ANOTHER INTERRUPTION WAS LESS aggravating to Roosevelt. He received notice he was awarded the Nobel Peace Prize for ending the Russo-Japanese War, and he had to decide what to do with the $40,000 prize money that went with it (worth more than $1 million today). He used it to establish a committee for industrial peace in Washington.[86]

DID ROOSEVELT'S DELAY AFFECT the elections? Any answer is speculative. As we shall see, a year later, the 1907 off-year elections were inconclusive. In the presidential election of 1908, Negro emigration from the Republicans was not a factor at all. Still, in 1906, when Roosevelt's discharge order was made public, black reaction was white-hot. That might have affected an election here and there, but as the resounding Republican triumph that year showed, overall it would have had little impact. (Though Nicholas Longworth won his race for reelection to Congress in Cincinnati, the voting patterns in his district worried him. It was possible he would have lost enough otherwise-expected Negro votes to keep him home in Cincinnati.

Had he been unlucky enough to lose the election, he would have needed better luck to keep his wife, Alice, there with him. She was bored to tears by her in-laws and loathed Cincinnati.[87]) Senator Joseph Foraker thought Roosevelt's delay had little importance and made no difference. He devoted ninety-six pages in his memoirs to Brownsville and another twenty-seven to his differences with Roosevelt. He never mentioned the delay. [88]

Would Roosevelt, whom Speaker of the House Joseph Cannon called "first, last, and all the time, a politician, one of the greatest of them all," who unduly focused on elections and always felt stress and pessimism before polling day, have taken the risk of an earlier announcement?[89] Of course not. That's why he waited.[90]

"These [racial] prejudices are something that it does not pay to disturb. It is best 'to let sleeping dogs lie.'"

Booker T. Washington,
The Story of My Life and Work

CHAPTER SIX

THE EDUCATIONS OF THE ROUGH RIDER AND THE WIZARD

THEODORE ROOSEVELT WAS FROM New York, came from a family of wealth and position, as a young boy traveled with his family to Europe and Africa in style, and knew and loved his father and credited him with much of his success.[1] Booker T. Washington lived his whole life in the rural South, he and his family were slaves, he never knew his father's name or who he was, and when his siblings left where they had been born, they walked several hundred miles to their new home.[2] Roosevelt knew tragedy when his first wife, Alice, died in childbirth. Overcome with grief, he never spoke in public or wrote of her again. He was so emotionally lost, he gave their baby, also named Alice, to his sister to raise until he married Edith Carow and had a wife who could be her mother. Washington also was a widower, twice actually, and just as Edith raised Theodore's baby Alice, Fanny Washington raised Booker's baby Portia. Washington already knew how tragic life could be, and he bore his losses stoically.

Both men achieved much while they were young. Neither lived to see old age (Washington died at fifty-nine; Roosevelt barely two months after he turned sixty). Both men knew how to get what they wanted and, for a time, defend what they had. Both died with their influence a thing of the past.

BOOKER T. WASHINGTON WAS for a while the most famous black man in the world, the greatest black leader in America before Martin Luther King Jr. He abjured any role as a politician, but he hobnobbed with those who were and used their methods to keep running smoothly what was called the "Tuskegee Machine," a tight web of Washington lieutenants supporting and supported by him. Through it he dispensed favors, secured federal appointments and other jobs for Negroes, backed their businesses and other ventures (especially influential black newspapers) with loans and capital, marginalized those who opposed him, and—always important—ensured no one could challenge him as *the* black leader. During his lifetime, his critics, mostly confrontational blacks in the North looking to snatch some of his influence for themselves and chip away at his leadership and ideas, derisively called him "the Wizard."[3] Much of the Negro philanthropy of men like John D. Rockefeller, Andrew Carnegie, Jacob Schiff, and Sears, Roebuck president Julius Rosenwald passed through Tuskegee.[4] The Wizard knew how to handle these titans. When a new dormitory at Tuskegee built with Rockefeller money cost $249 less than expected, Washington returned it to the man worth more than a billion dollars. Rockefeller, surprised at this gesture and impressed that Washington's sharp eye on the bottom line brought the project in under budget, sent it back with his congratulations.[5] If Rockefeller was not the richest man in the world, then Andrew Carnegie was, and he donated even more to Tuskegee. His first donation was a modest (for Carnegie) $20,000 for a library. He thereafter annually donated $10,000 to the school, and in 1903 he gave its endowment fund $600,000 (an astonishing $15 million in today's dollars). Only Booker T. Washington, Carnegie believed, could solve the race problem in the South.[6]

It was not only the superrich Washington could handle. He possessed remarkable people skills. When he went North seeking donations for Tuskegee, aware of the suspicions of potential white donors, he brought with him letters of introduction from trustworthy whites.

He also secured a written promise from the Alabama state school superintendent that the state would allow any money he raised to stay with Tuskegee, and to make sure that is what would happen, he asked the Alabama governor to endorse the letter. As donors gave him money, he would ask *them* for letters of introduction that he would use with others.[7]

IN 1903 BOOKER T. Washington's leadership was beginning to be questioned publicly. W. E. B. Du Bois published *The Souls of Black Folk*, a collection of fourteen essays on being Negro in America. The open and determined assault on what had been Washington's impregnable position began with an essay in this book. Du Bois started softly. "Easily the most striking thing in the history of the American Negro since 1876 is the ascendancy of Mr. Booker T. Washington. One hesitates, therefore, to criticize such a life which, beginning with so little, has done so much. . . . The time is come when one may speak in all sincerity and utter courtesy of the mistakes and shortcomings of Mr. Washington's career, as well as his triumphs, without being thought captious or envious, and without forgetting that it is easier to do ill then well in the world."[8] The shiv has to be teased out of these exquisitely equivocal sentences: *However did we allow such a thing to happen?*

Du Bois was right. Washington started life with "so little." Born a slave in Franklin County, Virginia, he never knew for sure when he was born, but when the Civil War ended and he was free, he was about seven years old. In his influential autobiography, Washington tells of the degradations of slavery as experienced by a young boy. He remembered those days and understood as well as any man how awful they were, but for him there were better times ahead. In his autobiography's title, *Up from Slavery*, the emphasis he intends is on his passage "up."

His mother's husband, who was not young Booker's father, had escaped the plantation before emancipation and sent word to his mother that she and the children were to join him in West Virginia. Booker's stepfather, as the man now became, took Booker and his brother to work with him as salt packers. The observant young boy noticed the supervisor scrawled something on the barrels they packed that he could not read (it was the number "18" and identified the barrels they would be paid for), but he copied it over and over to practice writing until he could do it legibly. He was teaching himself to write. He asked his mother to see if she could secure a book for him, and she got a spelling book.[9] From it, Booker taught himself how to read. Another step "up."

Booker's stepfather did not permit him to leave his work for school. He needed the boy's diligence, youthful strength, and energy for the hard labor of packing salt, and he needed the money Booker earned. When Booker said he would go to school only at night, the man said go ahead. Eventually, he was able to spend less time at the salt furnace so he could attend the day school. On the first day, he faced an unexpected problem. The school required a last name, which he did not have. He had only a few minutes to think of one. With the bold confidence that would be his as an adult, when he was asked, he calmly said, "'Booker Washington,' as if I had been called by that name all my life."[10] Not surprisingly, Booker wanted a way out of the salt mines. The mine owner's wife, Mrs. Viola Ruffner, needed someone to help in her home, and he applied for the job and got it. (The five dollars a month he earned went to his stepfather.) To please Mrs. Ruffner, he had to go about his responsibilities "promptly and systematically. . . . Nothing must be sloven or slipshod; every door, every fence, must be kept in repair."[11] That is precisely how he went about his work for her. Above all else, she wanted "absolute honesty and frankness." He gave her that, too, and she soon trusted him implicitly. Booker did more than please Mrs. Ruffner; he became just like her. As an adult, scattered papers around the house or even in the street triggered an impulse to clean them up. A dirty yard had to be cleaned; an unpainted fence had to be whitewashed. A missing button or a spot of grease required attention.[12] These lessons were for him as valuable as any education he got anywhere else. In the more casual and forgiving twenty-first century, such habits might be called obsessive-compulsive; for an ex-slave in the nineteenth century determined to make something of himself, they were essential, and the grown man would always impress this point on others seeking their own way "up."

ACQUIRING THIS STRONG WORK ethic was an important step in the development of Booker T. Washington, but he knew he also had to be educated. He made up his mind to go to a school in Virginia and, unaware of just how far it was from his home in West Virginia—he later recalled it was about five hundred miles—Booker started walking.[13] When he realized his mistake, he continued on anyway, begging rides and working odd jobs to earn food and pocket money. He would not be denied this chance. He reached Hampton Normal and Agricultural Institute with "exactly fifty cents with which to begin my education."[14] The teacher in charge of admissions kept putting him off. After a few days she told him the next room needed to be swept clean and he should take the broom and get to it. With the thoroughness of a boy trained by Mrs. Ruffner, Booker did more than he was asked. He moved tables and chairs and anything else on the floor to get to hard-to-reach places. He dusted the furniture and woodwork and cleaned the closets. When he finished, the head teacher inspected the room and found no dirt or dust. Booker knew he had passed his entrance exam. This reaffirmed to him that skills and personal habits unrelated to book learning were also an important part of a person's education.

General Samuel C. Armstrong, who founded and operated Hampton Institute, was a Civil War veteran. In 1863, after fighting for the Union at Gettysburg, he was assigned to command the Ninth Regiment, US Colored Troops. While still in the army, he formed a school to educate his black soldiers and, after the army, founded Hampton Institute to educate Negroes.

Before emancipation, Southern states made it illegal to educate slaves, and, when freed, there were millions of liberated blacks still chained to ignorance and illiteracy. How were they supposed to become productive, learn what it was to be citizens and active in the nation's democracy, and, not incidentally, compete with educated and skilled whites? Unskilled and uneducated as many were, the reality was that manual labor was the only kind of work they could do. Anything above it required technical skills, working with numbers, reading, an ability to start and continue a task, a persistence in working at it, a patience to stay with it until completion, a desire to do it right, and a sense of pride in a finished job well done. Rarely was this part of a slave's work; a slave was just supposed to follow someone else's orders. From Hampton, Washington learned and then taught at Tuskegee that to move up, a free man needed to know the three *R*s, but just as crucial, he had to understand the moral value of physical labor and the skills needed to do it. Once learned, these values had to be taught to others, who, in turn, would replicate the Hampton style at schools elsewhere, and their students then could go out and teach others.

Booker T. Washington came to believe in Hampton's education and its emphasis on industrial training as the way to advance the black race. Industrial education was a program of self-improvement that would allow poor youths to work their way through school and learn a trade. The Hampton idea was not so much polytechnic training as the inculcation of virtues such as hard work and thrift, the so-called Puritan work ethic. At Hampton this was "a quasi-religious principle, for the salvation of the Negro race."[15] Washington believed in this with every fiber of his soul. Not only would industrial education give Negroes skills for themselves as individuals and as a race, just as important, it would make them useful to their communities and thereby improve relations between the races. For himself, and by extension for the Negro race, such an education was superior to that of an Ivy League school.[16] When he left Hampton, he transplanted the Hampton idea to Alabama at the Tuskegee Institute, where he became the principal.[17]

TUSKEGEE BECAME THE TOUCHSTONE of what his biographer Louis R. Harlan called his "phenomenal energy," his ability to roll up his sleeves and work hard to get an impossible job done and done right, his sure understanding of people and what motivated them, and his genius for visualizing and then implementing solutions acceptable to people with antagonistic goals.[18] Arriving in the spring of 1881, the new principal was astonished to see there was nothing there.

There were no buildings, no land to build them on, and no students. He, his school, and his students would have to create what they would need to take themselves up from slavery. That is just what they did.[19] Independence Day 1881 was the day the school would open. A chicken coop and a church would be its first buildings, and Booker T. Washington its first and only teacher. Prospective students applied and were accepted. Slowly, more teachers were added. (The first, Olivia A. Davidson, later became Mrs. Booker T. Washington.) Washington knew he would not get all the money he needed from Alabama public officials, so he and Miss Davidson raised it from donors.[20] Using Mrs. Ruffner's principles of "promptly and systematically," Tuskegee's students first learned how to make their own bricks, which they then used to build their own classrooms. This combination of donor money and student labor became the pattern for the school's expansion.[21] By July 1884 Tuskegee was an up-and-running school, and Washington was an up-and-coming man.

WITH PEACE AT APPOMATTOX, the federal government governed the South as if it were a foreign conquest, which in a sense it was. It was called Reconstruction, and it included enacting and implementing the Thirteenth, Fourteenth, and Fifteenth Amendments to the Constitution.[22] Reconstruction protected newly freed slaves, made an effort to educate and otherwise help them through the Freedman's Bureau, and was enforced by federal soldiers. Southern whites didn't like any of it. From their point of view it was as if the North saw itself as Rome and the Civil War as the Punic Wars. "To the South lay Carthage."[23] Short of resuming the war, there was nothing Southerners could do about it.

In the presidential election of 1876, neither party won a clear majority of electoral votes, which meant the House of Representatives would decide the new president. This reshaped an electoral contest into a political tussle, and the House considered it the same way it dealt with legislation—by horse trading. Southern Democrats saw their opportunity to rid themselves of Northern occupation, Northern soldiers, and Northern ideas, and they agreed to support the Republican Rutherford B. Hayes in return for an end to Recon-

struction. The deal was made, and the era of Jim Crow began.
Named after a Negro character in a minstrel show, Jim Crow laws
imposed a society rigidly segregated by race and denied Negroes the
rights acquired during Reconstruction, everything from the right to
vote to the ability to get an education to the freedom to mingle with
whites in public places.[24] (Although not codified by statute as much
outside the South, the discrimination these laws enforced was not
"limited by latitude" and existed throughout the country.[25]) No part
of everyday life was untouched.

By 1894 Jim Crow was tightly woven into the nation's Southern
quilt. Booker T. Washington realized that unless a way of surviving
it could be devised, the plight of Negroes would be hopeless, especially in the South, where almost 90 percent of the Negroes lived
and where the status quo was more than burdensome—it was
deadly.[26] He took it upon himself to come up with a plan by which
Negroes could become economically self-sufficient and not dependent on whites, and whites would realize they needed blacks, not
as slaves in all but name and not as field hands and pack animals,
but as people who could help bring the South into the future. To
achieve this, black people had to overcome what must have been for
him as an educator the bitterest legacies of slavery—ignorance and
illiteracy—and considering the era, they had to learn in a way that
would not threaten whites. Do this and they would be taking a big
step "up." He used an invitation to speak to the National Education
Association in Madison, Wisconsin, to test his thoughts.

Ever the realistic man, Washington acknowledged in his speech
that the separation of the races was a fact of life that would not go
away anytime soon. To live and advance in such a world, the Negro
had to make himself "through his skill, intelligence, and character, of
such undeniable value to the community in which he lived that the
community could not dispense with his presence." When Southern
whites saw they too would benefit from educated and productive
Negroes, they would accept the formula to bring this about. This
white cooperation was essential; without it, the proposal would fail.
For this reason, and because it would ensure black "prosperity,"
industrial education—for a time, nothing higher other than in excep-

tional cases—should be pursued by Southern blacks.[27] He saw the results of an industrial education justifying his faith in it as a bridge between the races that both whites and blacks could cross to learn to work with each other. "As the people of the neighborhood came to us to buy bricks, we got acquainted with them; they traded with us and we with them. Our business interests became intermingled. We had something that they wanted, they had something which we wanted. This, in a large measure, helped to lay the foundation for the pleasant relations that have continued to exist between us and the white people in [the area]."[28]

Nothing was said directly about Negro political rights (to vote and otherwise participate in government) and social rights (an integrated society). Washington hinted that in exchange for an education and working-class economic rights, these could be shelved until the future. He made this point elliptically when he said, "*in relation to his vote*, the Negro should more and more consider the interests of the community in which he lived, rather than seek alone to please some one who lived a thousand miles away from him and from his interests" (author's emphasis). It was a message of black accommodation to the reality of white power and white authority. His program of industrial education would *prepare* blacks to live with whites *socially and politically*. In other words, not now full equality; only after adequate preparation. Washington's speech was so short and his manner so reassuring it is likely most listeners missed this last point.[29] Washington would be more clear a year later in Atlanta.

IN 1895 WASHINGTON ADDRESSED the Cotton States and International Exposition in Atlanta. He was introduced by Rufus Brown Bullock, a New Yorker who was raised by abolitionists yet fought for the Confederacy, then served as Georgia's Reconstruction governor. Georgians took to Bullock no more warmly than to boll weevils, and his time in the governor's mansion was marked by financial mismanagement and allegations of bribery. In *Gone with the Wind*, Margaret Mitchell captures his rascality by making him a friend of Rhett Butler, something of a scamp himself.[30]

Washington emphasized to both races the point made in

Madison: the blacks were in the South to stay. It was blacks he began speaking to. There was nothing in the North to tempt them, and the Hampton/Tuskegee education he offered was the key to bettering their lives where they were.

> Cast down your bucket where you are—cast it down in making friends in every manly way of the people of all races by whom we are surrounded. Cast it down in agriculture, mechanics, in commerce, in domestic service, and in the professions. . . . Our greatest danger is that in the great leap from slavery to freedom we may overlook the fact that the masses of us are to live by the productions of our hands. . . . No race can prosper till it learns that there is as much dignity in tilling a field as in writing a poem. "It is at the bottom of life we must begin, and not at the top."[31]

Then he turned to whites, and his disgraceful pandering to their racism grates on twenty-first century ears. He told them their support for Negro self-improvement would not endanger their own ways of life:

> You can be sure in the future, as in the past, that you and your families will be surrounded by the most patient, faithful, law-abiding, and unresentful people that the world has seen. As we have proved our loyalty to you in the past, in nursing your children, watching by the sick-bed of your mothers and fathers, and often following them with tear-dimmed eyes to their graves, so in the future, in our humble way, we shall stand by you with a devotion that no foreigner can approach, ready to lay down our lives, if need be, in defense of yours, interlacing our industrial, commercial, civil, and religious life with yours in a way that shall make the interests of both races one. In all things that are purely social we can be as separate as the fingers, yet one as the hand in all things essential to mutual progress.[32]

Then he dropped the other shoe on both races:

> The wisest among my race understand that the agitation of questions of social equality is the extremest folly. . . . *It is important and*

right that all privileges of the law be ours, but it is vastly more impor-
tant that we be prepared for the exercise of these privileges. (author's
emphasis)

Because of its often-repeated catchphrase, "Cast down your
bucket," the address originally was referred to by that name. As
time passed and doubt about Washington's ideas set in, calling it the
"Atlanta Compromise" seemed more appropriately to reflect what
he was saying.

AFTER THE ATLANTA SPEECH, Washington was viewed by both blacks
and whites as a man standing apart from all other Negroes. There
was no Negro leader that could be considered anywhere near Washington in the impact he had on articulating the relations between the
races. His thoughts and conclusions were thought to represent the
views of all Negroes. From then on, if Booker T. Washington said it,
that's what Negroes thought. And what whites liked to hear. Clark
Howell, the managing editor of the *Atlanta Constitution*, wrote the
next day to the *New York World*, "The whole speech is a platform
on which the whites and blacks can stand with full justice to each
race." Full justice certainly did not mean social equality to Howell,
because, as Harlan wrote, Howell was "particularly gratified" that
it was eliminated as a factor.[33]

Not until Martin Luther King Jr.'s "I Have a Dream" speech
would the words of a black man so alter the course of the nation.
"Cast down Your Buckets" was only five minutes long, but it had
an impact disproportionate to its brevity. The spontaneous applause,
cheers, and shouts of approval by those who heard it in Atlanta told
those there, including Washington himself, that here was a man with
the answer to an insoluble problem both blacks and whites would
accept. But Washington would be a flawed messenger. He was, as
Harlan noted, the perfect Negro for whites because he "shifted from
whites the responsibility for racial problems they were thoroughly
tired of." By making the problem of race an economic one, Washington took it out of politics, and this too was what fatigued whites
wanted so many years after emancipation.

It has been impossible to read the Atlanta Compromise today

with anything less than astonishment. How could Washington counsel his fellow Southern blacks to accept and accommodate themselves to their decidedly second-class status? How, we ask ourselves, did anyone accept such an idea? What were they thinking? What was Washington thinking?

For one thing, he was thinking about getting the country behind his program of industrial education. For another, he was thinking about Jim Crow. In the South in 1895, Negroes were forced to think about it, live with it, and often suffer and die because of it. W. E. B. Du Bois was Washington's analytical opposite in dealing with Jim Crow and Negro inequality, and the perfection that was his way of writing shows how dehumanizing its petty humiliations were when lived with day after day.

> Did you ever see a "jim-crow" waiting room? There are some exceptions but usually no heat in winter and no air in summer; undisturbed loafers and white train hands and broken disreputable settees; to buy a ticket is torture: you stand and stand and wait and wait until every white person at the "Other Window" is waited on. Then the tired agent yells across (because all the tickets and change are over there): What d'y want? WHAT? WHERE? He browbeats and contradicts you, hurries and confuses the ignorant; gives many the wrong change; for lack of time compels a number to purchase tickets on the train at a higher price and sends them all out on the platform burning with indignation and hatred.

> The "jim-crow" car is up next to the baggage car and engine. The train stops out beyond the covering in the rain or sun or dust. Usually there is no step to help one climb on, and often the car is a smoker cut in two and you must pass through the white smokers and then they pass through your part with swagger and noise and stares. Your apartment is half or quarter or an eighth of the oldest car in service. Unless it happens to be a through express, the old plush is caked with dirt, the floor is gummy and the windows dirty.

> . . . It is difficult to get lunch or drinking water. Lunch rooms either "don't serve niggers" or serve them at some dirty and ill-attended hole in the wall. Toilet rooms are often filthy. If you have to change

cars be wary of junctions which are usually without accommodation and filled with quarrelsome whites who hate a "darky dressed up." You are apt to have the company of a sheriff and a couple of meek or sullen black prisoners on part of your way and the dirty colored section hands will pour in toward night and drive you to the smallest corner. "No," said the little lady in the corner (she looked like an ivory cameo and her dress flowed on her like a caress), "We don't travel much."[34]

All this was sanctioned in 1896 by the US Supreme Court in *Plessy v. Ferguson*, when it permitted Louisiana, and by extension everywhere else, to segregate railroad cars, and by extension everything else. As the painful reality of Jim Crow chafed on both Washington and Du Bois, their differences would clash head-on over Brownsville.

THEODORE ROOSEVELT'S FIRST PUBLIC office was from the voters. In 1882, he had just turned twenty-four when he was elected to the New York state legislature as a Republican. His immaturity and brash manners made for rough navigating at first, but when he got his balance, in his own words, "I rose like a rocket."[35]

His agony after his wife's death took him out of public life, and he became a cattle rancher in the Dakota Territory. Historian and Roosevelt biographer Peter Collier wrote, "Something in the grim and desolate environment" of the Dakota Badlands connected with Roosevelt's now-anguished mental state.[36] He loved the raw and unfinished country, the hard work, the cowboys, even the harsh climate. He met, worked with, and genuinely liked people he never would have encountered back east. He saw an America and Americans that expanded his view of his country—its youth, strength, promise, and future. It was in Dakota where, for the first time, he saw himself as a part of that promise and future. His time there changed him.

But a bitter winter a couple of years into the venture killed his cattle and brought the ranch to ruin. Roosevelt told Arthur Parker, editor of the *Bad Lands Cowboy*, that he was leaving Dakota to do public and political work back east. "Then you will become President of the United States," Parker said. He would "remember distinctly that [Roosevelt] was not in the least surprised."[37]

Meanwhile, because of the crushing financial losses from his Dakota hiatus, he had to earn a living for his daughter and new wife, Edith. The family moved from New York City to Oyster Bay on Long Island and to the home he had built and named for his wife Alice, now renamed Sagamore Hill. As an undergraduate at Harvard, his interest in the navy had led him to write *The Naval War of 1812*, which became a book in 1882 and was very well received. He decided to become a writer of biography and historical narrative. This interlude in his life would pass, but he used it well to make himself a better writer and someone who, back in public life, could effectively use his pen to persuade men to his ideas.

President Cleveland was defeated for reelection in 1888, and the Republican whom Roosevelt campaigned for, Benjamin Harrison, showed his appreciation by appointing Roosevelt to the Civil Service Commission. Roosevelt handled the job well—too well. He antagonized fellow Republicans thirsty for federal appointments from Postmaster General John Wanamaker, the administration's spoilsmeister, when he set out to tidy up Wanamaker's Post Office. In the end, Roosevelt learned that clean politics can be the best politics, and in 1892, when Harrison lost his own reelection race to the Democrat he had beaten four years earlier, Grover Cleveland kept Roosevelt in the job. By the spring of 1894, Roosevelt was ready for a change.

The Republican reform mayor of New York, William L. Strong, thought the man who cleaned up the civil service could do the same for New York's streets. Literally. He offered to make Roosevelt the street-cleaning commissioner.[38] For a man with his eyes on the White House, whether he admitted this to others or even himself, cleaning streets was not anything he wanted for his résumé. But there were four seats yet unfilled on the city's police commission, and by April 1895, one was Roosevelt's. The Roosevelt family, now with four more children, headed back to New York.

AS POLICE COMMISSIONER, ROOSEVELT perfected the art of favorable public relations. He learned how remarkably easy it was for him.

Later, when he was president, still a young man, physically vigorous, and with an attractive family of young children, it would be a snap. It was all in how you cultivated and handled the press. It helped if you liked the reporters and they liked you.

Jacob Riis, a reporter for the *New York Sun*, was one of Theodore Roosevelt's firmest admirers. In 1890, he had written a book about the ghettoes of poverty in New York. Riis's reporting often took him into the city's Lower East Side, where immigrants from eastern and southern Europe were crammed as they began their transformation into Americans. Through his dealings with crooks (both criminals and police), Riis developed a cynicism but retained an immigrant's faith of what America could be. With scorching prose and electrifying photos he taught himself to take, he depicted the slums and indicted America for tolerating such a thing. His book was titled *How the Other Half Lives*, and it is in print to this day. One evening, not long after its publication, Riis came back to his desk at the *Sun* and found a gentleman's calling card. On it was written, "I have read your book and have come to help." The signature beneath was Theodore Roosevelt's. A friendship was sealed.

Roosevelt took to patrolling the city's streets late at night—he called them midnight rambles—to catch the police loafing. Riis often went with him and nudged him to detour into slum apartments to see how the other half lived. He would take what he saw to the White House, and it prompted many of his Progressive Era programs. "For two years we were brothers on Mulberry Street," Riis wrote in 1904, when Roosevelt was running for the White House, in a book called *Theodore Roosevelt: The Citizen*.[39] Readers were told Roosevelt was always cordial, gracious, gentle, and approachable. The book showcased Roosevelt's leadership. Riis's laudatory biography was Roosevelt's public relations at its best. No president before Roosevelt did it so well.

IN 1896 ROOSEVELT DECIDED to seek an appointment from President-elect William McKinley. After the Civil Service Commission, Roosevelt knew important jobs in Washington depended on the kindness of others, and he would need help from those who had McKinley's ear, such as Mr. and Mrs. Bellamy Storer of Cincinnati. Mr. Storer was a lawyer and would be appointed to a succession of ambassadorial posts in Europe by President McKinley and to his last one in Vienna by President Roosevelt. Mrs. Maria Storer was the better politician in the family. It was she who never forgot—and never forgot to remind McKinley of—a Storer gift of $10,000 when he was on the ropes. When her nephew Nicholas Longworth, also from Cincinnati, became a member of Congress and later Speaker of the House of Representatives and married Alice Roosevelt in a White House wedding, Mr. and Mrs. Storer became distantly related to Theodore Roosevelt. A decade later this didn't keep President Roosevelt from firing Mr. Storer from his post in Vienna.

Roosevelt had invited the Storers to Sagamore Hill for the weekend during the summer, while the McKinley-Bryan campaign still was raging. He was a charming, witty, and thoroughly entertaining host. Taking Mrs. Storer on a rowboat ride, he told her as he pulled on the oars that he would like to be assistant secretary of the navy. He was working hard for McKinley's election and thought he might be entitled to consideration. Would she help him? She would.

Another boost was from Senator Henry Cabot Lodge of Massachusetts, Roosevelt's closest friend. Early in December, Lodge met with Major McKinley (his Civil War army rank, still appropriate because he was not yet sworn into office) and urged him to appoint Roosevelt. McKinley knew of Roosevelt's tendency to act on his own and not as part of a team. Lodge assured him Roosevelt would do as told. Roosevelt thanked Lodge and added, "Of course I have no preconceived policy of any kind." But Roosevelt's unpleasant tendency to do what he wanted no matter what others thought came up again just three days later. Lodge spoke with Senator Thomas Platt of New York, whose role as the Republican boss in the Empire State was more important to him than his seat in the Senate, and who was worried that as assistant secretary of the navy Roosevelt might make war on him—or as he put it, on the "organization," by finagling with the Brooklyn Navy Yard. Roosevelt told Lodge he would not do anything deliberately to interfere with Platt. Lodge next lobbied Secretary of the Navy John D. Long, a former governor of

Lodge's home state of Massachusetts. Again he faced the problem of Roosevelt's use of any position to promote his own agenda. Lodge calmed Long down.

It worked. On March 23, Roosevelt wrote Lodge, "The machine people here [Senator Platt's organization] have it in their heads that I am to be made Assistant Secretary of the Navy, and evidently approve of it as a means of getting me out of New York." For Platt, distancing the hard-to-control Roosevelt from his fiefdom trumped any fear he might have over the Brooklyn Navy Yard. Roosevelt had overcome his ornery personality and self-centered nature to get what he wanted. He needed more than the assistance of others; he needed to overcome his own reputation.[40]

While earning his right to ask for the appointment by campaigning for McKinley, Roosevelt, as Edmund Morris described it, "went about his familiar business of emasculating the opposition."[41] Morris cites how Roosevelt wowed the crowds by likening Democratic candidate William Jennings Bryan and others favoring free silver to "the leaders of the Terror in France in mental and moral attitude." He went after Governor John Peter Altgeld of Illinois for pardoning rioters from the Haymarket bombing in 1886, calling them "these foulest criminals, the men whose crimes take the form of assassination." This manner of speaking—harsh language, abrasive condemnation, and take-no-prisoners attitude—would become standard Rooseveltian vilification of people who did not support him and his ideas or when he felt he had to defend his actions.

"Because the world is judged by its majority, and an individual too is judged by the majority of deeds, good or bad, if he performs one good deed, happy is he for turning the scale both for himself and for the whole world on the side of merit; if one commits one transgression, woe to him for weighing himself and the whole world in the scale of guilt, for it is said, 'But one sinner.' On account of this single sin which this man commits he and the whole world lose much good."

Rabbi Eleazar, son of Rabbi Simeon

CHAPTER SEVEN

ROOSEVELT DOES JUSTICE

THE TRAIN CARRYING THE soldiers of the Twenty-Fifth Infantry ran straight as the crow flies almost due north from Brownsville. Around 9:00 p.m. it stopped at San Antonio, where the commanding officer of Fort Sam Houston and armed guards took custody of the prisoners from the Fort Brown stockade, then continued on to Fort Reno, a post with room to absorb four companies of infantry (including the straggling Company A on September 20).[1] Penrose wired a greatly relieved General Ainsworth of their arrival at Fort Reno early Monday morning and added, "No trouble whatever during the journey."[2]

Fort Reno dated back to 1875, in what was then called the Indian Territory (which combined with the Oklahoma Territory to form the state of Oklahoma). A 1901 drawing shows flat Oklahoma land on which barracks and administrative buildings formed a square for the parade ground. Outside and parallel to one side of the square and extending away from it in both directions was a wide street with its own buildings and access to the town that took its name from the fort's, El Reno. For the Twenty-Fifth Infantry, it was a detention center away from the regular army, where they could be questioned about their roles in the shooting, probed for information they might have about others more deeply involved, and threatened with punishment for not cooperating.

While the army's investigation proceeded unsuccessfully, the soldiers tried to crack the case on their own. More than anything, they wanted to avoid dismissal from the army for something they did not do. The oldest soldier in the battalion, First Sergeant Mingo Sanders, was candid enough to say his concern was his own self-interest. "I'm for Sanders. . . . I wanted to do all I could to relieve myself of this responsibility."[3] First Sergeant Jacob Frazier of Company D, who thought soldiers might have done it, tried to find out which ones. "Yes, sir; I did. I tried in a secret way. . . . I just spoke about it as though I didn't care much if they had killed the whole town. I wanted to see if I could get any information from anybody. . . . My time that I put in the service, it has been honest and faithful. . . . I did not want to lose my time [and] that is why I did that. I didn't want them to go and throw me out of the service, to cast me out, not even to allow me a job in the civil employment of the government. I wanted to be a man."[4] (His commanding officer, Captain Samuel Lyon, did not want him thrown out either. After the discharge, he gave Frazier a letter addressed "To any recruiting officer, United States Army" and recommended his reenlistment and return to Company C.[5]) Quartermaster Sergeant George McMurray of Company C testified everyone wanted to know who had done the shooting, and, "I would ask among the men, have you found out yet who did the shooting?"[6] Sergeant Samuel C. Harley, also from Company C, a wounded veteran of the assault on the blockhouse at El Caney in Cuba: "We did possibly all we could in the time we had . . . but [I] could not get a single hint."[7] Even the lower-ranking enlisted men with not enough years in the army to worry about losing pensions and benefits worked at it. While still at Fort Brown, Private Len Reeves of Company D "called [my section] all together . . . and explained the matter to them and told them that if any of them knew who did it, or had heard, or anything about it, they would let me know [and] after we got to Fort Reno also, but I was never able to find out anything. Everybody seemed to be trying to find out, just like I was."[8]

ON MONDAY, NOVEMBER 5, because no soldier confessed to a part in the raid, because no soldier identified anyone who had any role in it, and because no soldier was able to persuade the army or President Roosevelt to protect him from discharge, no soldier was rescued from Roosevelt's decision. In a short, fifty-word letter on White House stationery, President Roosevelt directed the secretary of war to comply with General Garlington's recommendations. Four days later, with Secretary Taft away from Washington and unavailable, Arthur Murray, a lost-to-history acting chief of staff, issued Special Orders No. 266, which listed the names of the 167 soldiers to be discharged "and forever debarred from reenlisting in the Army or Navy of the United States, as well as from employment in any civil capacity under the Government." (There was no legal authority to keep the men from future federal civil employment; Roosevelt corrected that in his special message to the Senate on January 14, 1907.) General Garlington's report carefully noted the names of soldiers who had been at Fort Brown on the night of the raid but whose enlistments ended before Special Orders No. 266 and had been honorably discharged. Roosevelt's order would remember these men and change their discharges to "without honor."

Secretary of War Taft was enjoying his vacation in Quebec and not really in the Brownsville loop, but perhaps he should have been. Scrupulously and judicially mindful of the obligation to act only with full knowledge of the facts and the law, he might have tried to dissuade Roosevelt. Such advice would have been worth listening to. Since Ainsworth had the matter under control at the War Department and Roosevelt was incrementally becoming more directly involved, Taft was not asked for his opinions and could tend to other business.

SUCH AS CUBA. BY the summer of 1906, President Tomás Estrada Palma had lost control of his country and asked for a supportive show of force from his American patrons.[9] President Roosevelt responded with Assistant Secretary of State Robert Bacon, thousands of US Marines and the navy, and, following in their wake, the man who never failed at any task Roosevelt gave him, William Taft. When Bacon disembarked the Marines, an angry Roosevelt wired: "You had no reason to direct the landing of those troops without specific authority from here. They are not to be employed in keeping general order without our authority."[10]

Taft, meanwhile, feared he too knew far too little about Cuba. "I am so lacking in knowledge that it is quite embarrassing to me to go," he said to Secretary of State Elihu Root.[11] Nevertheless, on September 19, as the men of the Twenty-Fifth Infantry were drilling in Oklahoma, Taft arrived in Havana, where he promptly named himself Cuba's provisional governor.[12] Quickly stabilizing the situation, on October 3 he returned to Washington. Taft came back not to the Brownsville matter or anything else dealing with the War Department. There was the election campaign going on, and President Roosevelt drafted his military leader into its ranks. Brownsville may have shared presidential attention with Cuba and the election, but by November, very little of the secretary of war's time was available for the plight of the Twenty-Fifth Infantry.[13]

THE ACTUAL ADMINISTRATION OF the War Department was for Taft an insignificant part of his job.[14] The government money he controlled and could dispense on behalf of Roosevelt made Taft a "star salesman" for the administration's policies and programs.[15] So off he went, campaigning in early October through the middle and far west. In Cheyenne on the day Roosevelt ordered the discharge of the Black Battalion and in the presence of Wyoming's Senator Francis E. Warren, Taft inspected Fort Russell and the new barracks and other buildings built with $750,000 of federal generosity. This expenditure and the deference paid to Senator Warren reflected his control of Wyoming and the power he held back in Washington as chairman of the Senate Military Affairs Committee. Taft went on to Fort Sam Houston, where the arrested men from Brownsville were confined, but there is no indication that he questioned them or otherwise sought to solve the Brownsville dilemma. He may not have been aware they were there.

A DISCHARGE WITHOUT HONOR is not a dishonorable discharge. Under the Articles of War, a dishonorable discharge could be awarded only after trial by court-martial. Discharge without honor had its roots in the Civil War, when soldiers were summarily discharged after doing something to "disgrace the service" but not necessarily a crime, and therefore could not be dishonorably discharged.[16] Even serious offenses—desertion, for example—could be handled this way.[17] A soldier discharged without honor was entitled to travel expenses back to his place of enlistment, and those with at least twenty years' service, such as First Sergeant Mingo Sanders, could still be admitted to the Old Soldiers' Home in Washington, DC.

And it was not considered punishment.[18] President Roosevelt would use this to parry accusations he was "punishing" men not found guilty of any crime.

IN THE AFTERNOON OF November 8, President Roosevelt sent a cable to King Edward VII of Great Britain, the world's foremost sea power. The next day was Edward's birthday, and Roosevelt wanted his congratulations and best wishes to arrive punctually.[19] That evening, with the highly satisfying voters' decision behind him and the order to discharge the soldiers issued, President and Mrs. Roosevelt boarded the USS *Louisiana* for Panama. "It seems a strange thing to think of my now being President, going to visit the work of the Panama Canal *which I have made possible*" (author's emphasis).[20]

THE SHOOTING ITSELF HAD attracted little attention in the newspapers.[21] The *New York Times*, in three short paragraphs, incorrectly reported its cause was Negro troops angry over efforts to arrest one of their own for the Evans assault. It got the number and type of casualties right but misidentified the wounded policeman as Joe Dominge.

Politicians and office holders, except for Brownsville's congressman and Texas's two senators, reacted to the news with a yawn. Whites normally disposed to work on behalf of Negro rights were just as indifferent. On October 10, 1906, John Milholland, the organizer, driving force, and hefty financial supporter of the Constitution League, an active biracial organization supporting Negro efforts to gain equality, spoke "to the Afro-American Constitutional League mass meeting in Cooper Union, which I hired for them, and in my speech boldly attacked Roosevelt's infamous policy towards the Southern Blacks and Whites, declaring that he [is] likely to go down in history bracketed with James Buchanan." Milholland said nothing about Brownsville.[22]

It was the horrible race riot in Atlanta a month later that overwhelmed any attention that otherwise might have been given Brownsville, even among blacks.[23] George Myers and his friend and hanger-on Ralph Tyler exchanged many letters right after August 13, but not one mentioned Brownsville. Tyler made a point to compliment Senator Foraker's comments on the race riot in Atlanta, but he ignored Brownsville.[24] The usually very sure-footed Booker T. Washington, generally the first to recognize the significance of events ignored by others, paid it little attention. A week after the raid he spoke to the National Negro Business League in Atlanta and had nothing to say about it.[25] David Levering Lewis's Pulitzer Prize–winning biography of Washington's bête noire W. E. B. Du Bois makes no reference to any comment by him. The energy of the Brownsville story soon depleted itself, as the shooting "receded to newspaper back pages and then disappeared."[26]

A CYCLONE OF ASTONISHMENT followed President Roosevelt's discharge order. Brownsville was back in the news. The *New York Times* declared Roosevelt's action "Unprecedented . . . dismissing in disgrace from the army an entire battalion of colored troops because of their failure to disclose the identity of some of their number who had been guilty of violence and murder."[27] The *Washington Post*, unaware that discharge without honor was not considered punishment, said, "While the President's power to discharge a soldier cannot be questioned, it is not conferred for purpose of punishment. Punishment is supposed to follow a trial." The *New York Sun* saw the problem for what it was. "By the old law the individual is entitled to trial and must be proved guilty. . . . By the new law . . . the individual must prove his innocence."[28] The *New York Evening Post* was afraid Roosevelt has created "a most pernicious precedent." The most bitter damnation, no doubt felt by many others as well, was from the *New York Evening World*: "executive lynch law."[29]

The South, as usual in those days, marched to an off-key and different drummer. The *Atlanta Journal* applauded Roosevelt for this "most commendable" act.[30]

The Negro reservoir of good will toward Theodore Roosevelt quickly drained away. Beginning with his invitation to Booker T. Washington to dine at the White House in 1901, all hopes for real change had converged in him. With him had come the hope for the beginning, at long last, of equal participation in all America had to offer: economic advancement, political equality, social acceptance, liberation from the isolation and humiliation of Jim Crow, a chance at education that would lift Negroes out of sharecropper poverty and indenture, and, most important, the end of the physical violence, even horrible death, so many lived with day after day.

Overnight Theodore Roosevelt went from being "our friend," as Booker T. Washington referred to him, to, as Negro columnist Richard W. Thompson wrote to Washington's secretary Emmett J. Scott, an "anathema with the Negroes from now on."[31] In his autobiography, Washington wrote that, "as a consequence of this order, the song of praise of ten millions of people were turned into a chorus of criticism and censure."[32] For W. E. B. Du Bois, "The door once declared open, Mr. Roosevelt by his word and deed since has slammed most emphatically in the black man's face."[33]

Here and there, the expectation remained that Roosevelt could be counted on to do the right thing. Charles V. Richey, a former soldier in the Twenty-Fifth Infantry who had fought at El Caney, held on to this belief. He wrote to the *Washington Post*, "Let us give the President a little time, by which I think he will save the innocent boys in blue, without discredit to himself. . . . Teddy can still be

Teddy indeed, and that we may love him more for not retreating to rehear an issue which he can meet in an honorable manner during his march forward."[34]

The revulsion's vanguard was the Negro press. Ignored in the pages of what today would be called "mainstream" broadsheets and tabloids, cohesive black communities developed separate newspapers that kept Negroes current with local and national news, political and cultural events, arts and literature, black leaders, personalities, and opinion. One of the most influential was the *New York Age*, edited by the talented but emotionally troubled writer, poet, and journalist T. Thomas Fortune. A week after the discharges, the *Age* published a sample of comments and criticisms from its sister black publications. In Richmond, the *Planet* called Roosevelt's decision "out of harmony with the principles of this Republic" and tore into him for "the most monumental blunder of his administration." The *Washington Bee* called the discharges "shameful." Acknowledging "a large number [of the soldiers] knew who the real perpetrators of the crime were," the *Bee* nevertheless characterized what Roosevelt did to the other soldiers as "shameful in the extreme." Also seeing politics in the announcement's delay, the paper wondered whether it might not have affected the New York governor's race, in which the Republican Charles Evans Hughes defeated Democratic newspaper publisher William Randolph Hearst.[35] The *Baltimore Afro-American Ledger* saw Roosevelt as "tinctured with colorphobia."

The *Age* characterized Roosevelt's action as "an outrage upon the rights of citizens who are entitled in civil life to trial by jury and in military life to trial by court-martial."[36] In Boston, two months after Special Orders No. 266, *Alexander's Magazine* pounded away at Roosevelt in every editorial into January except one.[37] In Washington, DC, Calvin Chase chose to lash out at a Roosevelt defense: "If this is military discipline, then we say to h—l with military discipline."[38] Ralph Tyler alliteratively wrote Booker T. Washington that "Negroes are depleting the dictionary of adjectives in their denunciation of the President."[39]

Meanwhile, the War Department was deluged with letters from "nearly every section of the country" angry over the discharges.

Ignoring its army officers' recommendations relied upon by their commander in chief, it absolved itself from any responsibility and said it was Roosevelt's doing.[40]

At the Metropolitan AME Church in Washington, where two and half years later Senator Foraker would be honored, a mass meeting of protest was held on November 20. "Those present refused to sing 'America' on the Chairman's call." The *Washington Bee*'s editor Calvin Chase (a Roosevelt delegate to the Republican convention six years earlier) spoke bitterly but illogically when he offered a fifty-three-year-old receipt kept by Roosevelt's maternal grandmother from her sale of a "young woman slave" to raise money for Roosevelt's mother's trousseau as proof that "the President is against the black man." A former commanding officer of the Twenty-Fifth Infantry, General Andrew Burt was supposed to speak that evening but, claiming he was physically "broken down" from his exertions to save the Black Battalion, he could not come.[41] Burt loved the regiment and retained a respect and affection for its soldiers for the rest of his life. When asked if they were good fighters, he would reply with relish, "Fight, did you say? Why they would charge into hell, fight their way out, and drag the devil out by the tail."[42] In New York, Gilchrist Stewart, a black lawyer who seemed to be everywhere working on behalf of the Black Battalion, referred to Roosevelt's efforts on behalf of Japanese laborers in the American West and demanded he show similar concern for the "black citizens of America."[43]

The most fiery words were by Negro preachers in their churches. Reverend J. E. C. Fernanders of the Metropolitan Union AME Church in New York said Roosevelt was sacrificing Negroes "upon the altar of Southern prejudice." Reverend Adam Clayton Powell of the Emanuel Baptist Church in New Haven repeated this thought but focused the blame on Brownsville. "Say what you please, these soldiers were dismissed because the white people of Brownsville wanted them dismissed, and for no other reason under the sun." He continued, "[Roosevelt] has greatly disappointed us."[44] A few Negro churches and their members saw the discharges differently. In Cincinnati, home of Secretary of War Taft and Senator

Foraker, the largest black church in the city passed a resolution supporting Roosevelt and criticizing the soldiers who did the shooting and hid behind their shielding comrades.[45]

In his speech, Reverend Powell also had harsh words for one of his own race, Booker T. Washington. Reverend Powell said Roosevelt's order was consistent with advice he got from Washington, "a man who believes it best to submit meekly to wrongs and has sold himself for a little political sop," and he minced few words when adding "Dr. Booker T. Washington is . . . responsible for the change in the President's attitude towards the Negro-American."[46]

Whatever Washington may have been responsible for, he was not to blame for Special Orders No. 266. On October 30, Roosevelt secretly summoned him to the White House and alerted him to what was coming. Washington tried to talk him out of it but could not. On Brownsville, Roosevelt wanted no advice from the one black man whose past guidance he had solicited and paid attention to. This matter had nothing to do with federal appointments or rebuilding the Republican Party in the South, matters generally in Washington's portfolio. It certainly affected Negroes, and therefore had something to do with the man from Tuskegee, and it is hard to believe Roosevelt did not see this. More likely he did, but his mind was made up, and he ignored any advice to the contrary from Washington. Pledging Washington to absolute secrecy, he sent him on his way. Eleven days later, Washington wrote he "did [his] full duty in trying to persuade [Roosevelt] from the course . . . but got nowhere."[47] Washington saw that, having made a decision, Roosevelt was intellectually and emotionally incapable of changing his mind. But Washington kept trying.[48] He had to. Negro unhappiness with Roosevelt carried great risks for him, his prestige, and his influence. Knowing he had no safe harbor save with Roosevelt, he wrote, "I cannot [be] disloyal to our friend, who I mean to stand by." Besides, Roosevelt "always comes out on top."[49]

WASHINGTON WAS NOT THE only Negro to stand with President Roosevelt. For all his militancy on the question of Negro rights and hostility to Roosevelt's order to discharge the soldiers, the middle ground was W. E. B. Du Bois's position. He accepted there was a conspiracy of silence and agreed the shooters should be severely punished, and those who knew who their identities should be too, only not as much.[50] In Baltimore, preachers at its AME churches by resolution advised Roosevelt that they accepted that the Twenty-Fifth Infantry's soldiers were shooters; they stood resolutely against this behavior and just as firmly against any of the soldiers' shielding the shooters from discovery; they believed it was reasonable for the army to maintain discipline; and they did not question the president's right to throw the guilty parties out of the army. But once the army had "exhausted its efforts without success to discover the guilty . . . the duty of the authorities has been fully discharged," and granting all of the above, the president was wrong in what he did to punish the innocent along with the guilty. Taking his support for Roosevelt further even than Booker T. Washington's, the principal of the Hearne Colored Schools in Texas wrote to Roosevelt on November 8, thanking him "for this great and priceless lesson and its future bearing to my unfortunate people."

John Milholland of the Constitution League noted in his diary on November 18, "The week has been spent trying to save the Negro soldiers in Texas whom President Roosevelt has ordered to be dishonorably discharged because they refused to 'peach' upon their comrades who shot up Brownsville to answer the *assaults* [Milholland's emphasis] and infamies upon them by the local Bourbons. . . . The effort is great. . . . I sent a long cable, costing about $25, to Roosevelt in Panama telling him of the . . . attitude of [the] Press." A man whose history with Theodore Roosevelt went back two decades, he decided it would be more effective if Gilchrist Stewart, who worked for the Constitution League, signed the telegram.[51] But together they were planning their next steps.

THIS WAS NOT THE first hint there might be organized pushback against Special Orders No. 266. Washington had warned Roosevelt of this when they met in October. Governor Curtis Guild Jr. of Massachusetts, a fellow Republican, asked in a telegram marked "Personal and Confidential" for reconsideration on behalf of "the most prominent colored soldiers of Massachusetts . . . strongly moved by the proposed punishment." How strongly? Guild's wire was sent *on the morning after the election*, when most people in America still were unaware of the discharges. Somehow these soldiers managed to organize themselves that quickly and face Governor Guild in his office and demand that the telegram be sent. Pulling out all the stops, Guild went on to say that some of the men "served under [Colonel Robert Gould] Shaw" and "carried the colors [of the black Fifty-Fourth Massachusetts Volunteers] at Fort Wagner," where the unit's manpower was gutted by Confederate forces. With a request there was a threat. "These men are all your friends and do not desire any political capital by public attacks on you."

Livid at this impertinence, President Roosevelt wired back that same day, "The order in question will under no circumstances be rescinded or modified." He felt only "profound indifference" to public attacks.[52] A few hours later, a nervous Governor Guild, his office by then presumably empty of the Negro veterans, surrendered with presumably his last comment on the matter. "Cannot see why you should take offense friendly message . . . will simply tell them affair is closed."[53] Like Booker T. Washington, he would not pick a fight with a man who always seemed to win.

THE CRITICISM SWELLED WHILE Roosevelt was on his Panama trip. On November 15, while he was enjoying a leisurely train ride from Colón to Panama City, the New York County (Manhattan) Republican Committee unanimously voted to ask him to cancel the discharges. "Roosevelt's Own Personal Machine against Him," reported the *New York Age*.[54] It was big news. In the sixty-six years since Abraham Lincoln's election, the nation had sent only one Democrat to the White House. Repudiation of a president by his own party in his home city was a seismic tremble potentially foreshadowing a tectonic shift by black voters. (The *New York Times'* coverage of the committee's vote was tranquilized: Gilchrist Stewart introduced the resolution; there was unanimous approval; end of story.[55]) Stewart wired Roosevelt the next day about the Republican Committee's resolution along with a plea to reverse his action. Angrily Roosevelt fired back in his own telegram, "Unless *facts* as known to me are shown to be false," nothing would be changed. If

Stewart or anyone else had such facts, "have them before me at once on my return."[56] The Brownsville Incident was awake, opposition was strengthening, and Roosevelt would return to an increasingly difficult problem.

ON NOVEMBER 9, THE day Roosevelt left for Panama, Military Secretary Ainsworth sent a telegram to General McCaskey at the Department of Texas. "Orders will be sent today directing discharge without honor of all enlisted men of Twenty-Fifth Infantry present at Fort Brown at time of disturbance there." It was marked "Confidential" because he feared violence when the soldiers learned what would be done with them. Ainsworth ordered a battalion from the Twenty-Sixth Infantry commanded by a "discreet officer" to Fort Reno to keep an eye on the black soldiers until they left the "country" and there was no danger of trouble from them. The black soldiers were to be disarmed when these white troops got there. Discharges and final payment of what was owed the soldiers were to be staged "so that no large body shall go on same train or at same time." The whole process was to be expedited and over with quickly.[57]

On November 11, the Twenty-Sixth Infantry arrived. General Garlington's threat was about to be made good. Testimony a few years later from Private Boyd Conyers of Company B, a young soldier from rural Georgia, captures the soldiers' despair, hopelessness, and shuddering fear of the darkness about to descend on them and their families. "When we was to be disarmed the soldiers fell about on their bunks, and it was one of the saddest things I have ever seen in my life. The soldiers were crying, even Mingo Sanders was crying and his wife was screaming, when we was disarmed. I never experienced such sadness in my life." Private Conyers's certainty that no man in the Black Battalion had anything to do with the shooting in Brownsville became unshakeable. "I believe if any man had been implicated in that shooting he would have told something about it. I know I would."[58]

WITH ONLY DISCHARGE AHEAD of them, the soldiers kept drilling. Their behavior was, according to Major C. J. T. Clarke, the "discreet officer" from the Twenty-Sixth Infantry, nothing less than excellent.[59] "As they were paid off and dismissed they remained orderly and well-behaved. None displayed any ugly feeling. Their officers were mute."[60] Major Penrose was with his soldiers to the end, and many came up to him to say good-bye. In El Reno, while awaiting the trains to take them to their hometowns or wherever they were going to restart and rebuild their lives, the now former United States soldiers comported themselves properly. The El Reno police chief had no call to report any misbehavior, no soldier needed to be arrested, and there was no instance of drunkenness or any misconduct. "He would hardly have known the men were being discharged during this period."[61]

By November 27 it was over. Every man was gone.[62] "Here goes the last of the best disciplined, best behaved, best regulated battalion in the United States Army," Major Penrose told a reporter for the *Washington Herald*. When asked if this was for publication, the bitter officer said it was and added, "I will add there was but little evidence to convict these brave men."[63] "The discharged soldiers feel that when Mr. Roosevelt hears their side of the story he will grant them a hearing."[64] In Washington, Senator Foraker believed so too. "I was all the while hoping that with the truth established . . . the President would in a manly fashion undo the wrong he had done."[65]

That night, President Roosevelt returned to the White House and Brownsville.

"[My enemies] will, as usual, try to blame me for all of this. They can talk; I cannot, without being disloyal to our friend, who I mean to stand by throughout his administration."

Booker T. Washington in a letter to
Charles W. Anderson, November 7, 1906

CHAPTER EIGHT

FRIENDS OF THE ADMINISTRATION

ROOSEVELT HAD IGNORED BOOKER T. Washington's warning of danger on October 30, 1906, but Washington, sure Roosevelt was committing a blunder, kept at it.[1] A few days after their meeting, he sent a newspaper clipping "from a recent address delivered in Montgomery in which I spoke out against Negro crimes, *even more strongly than you have done*" (author's emphasis). With his bona fides thus reconfirmed, he segued into what he knew Roosevelt considered *the* Negro crime of the moment—Brownsville. "If you possibly can avoid doing so, I very much hope you will not take definite action regarding the Negro soldiers in the Brownsville Affair, until your return from Panama."[2] A thoroughly irritated Roosevelt replied dismissively, "I could not possibly refrain from acting as regards those colored soldiers. You can not have any information to give me privately to which I could pay heed, my dear Mr. Washington."[3] The matter was closed. The Wizard's influence with Roosevelt was cresting quickly, and Roosevelt was in danger of becoming a pariah to black Americans.[4]

IF WASHINGTON SUPPORTED ROOSEVELT, his good standing with him might survive. But his position as the nation's recognized black

142

leader, already increasingly rocked by Du Bois's attacks on him for not making life better for Negroes, might not. He would be a victim of Brownsville just as surely as the soldiers were. Still, as much as he disagreed, he knew he could not cross Roosevelt, so for himself as much as anything else, he would not give up trying to change Roosevelt's mind. He would have to work through someone else, Secretary of War William Howard Taft.[5]

Taft was returning from a tour of the West November 17; Roosevelt was due back at his desk on November 27. Washington would not have much time. But Washington correctly suspected Taft did not agree with Roosevelt's shortcut justice and thought he might be offended by the injustice of the discharges. Because he was out of Washington, DC, and not involved in Brownsville, Taft knew little of its details and was therefore a tabula rasa on which Washington could persuasively press his own ideas and suggestions.

On November 20, Roosevelt was cruising home. "Our visit to Panama was most successful as well as most interesting," he wrote that day to his son Kermit.[6] That same day, Washington sent a "Personal and Confidential" letter to Taft. As was his style, he began obliquely. He politely asked if the War Department intended to "enlist additionally colored soldiers to take the place of the three companies which were dismissed?" "I very much hope, by the time the President returns, some plan will have been thought out by which to do something that may change the feeling of the colored people now as a whole have regarding the dismissal of the three colored companies. I have never in all my experience with the race, experienced a time when the entire people have the feeling that they have now in regard to the administration."[7] This gentle threat would remind Taft that he was part of the administration, it was in his name Special Orders No. 266 was issued, and whatever angers, disappointments, and frustrations the Negroes had would touch him as well.

Washington was playing a clever game here. Changing Taft's and Roosevelt's minds would be a complete victory; exerting any influence on Taft would build political capital for the future; getting the Black Battalion rebuilt would look good for now. (On the last point, Washington had better hopes of success. By law the Twenty-

Fifth Infantry was Negro; the army could hardly do anything else than rebuild it as Washington was suggesting.) In all this Washington was careful to wall himself off from Roosevelt's wrath. If Roosevelt lashed out, it would be at Taft. Washington was merely pointing out the political implications to Taft, something Roosevelt, politician par excellence, might understand and forgive.

Three days earlier, as Washington knew, Taft had in fact decided to suspend Special Orders No. 266. Brownsville historian John D. Weaver credited Mary Church Terrell and John Milholland of the Constitution League with nudging Taft toward that decision, and he was close to the truth. On Saturday, November 17, the day after the discharges began at Fort Reno, Milholland made a long-distance telephone call to Mrs. Terrell in Washington and asked her to go to Taft on behalf of the Constitution League. She would be glad she went.[8]

Mrs. Terrell met Milholland when both were in Europe in 1904. She had spoken in Berlin to the International Congress of Women about the place of who she called "colored" women in America, and because she was fluent in German she was the only speaker able to deliver her address in the language of the host country. According to the *Washington Post*, she was the "the hit of the congress."[9] Returning home via London, she met William Thomas Stead, English journalist and editor of the *Pall Mall Gazette*, who arranged for Mrs. Terrell to dine with John Milholland.[10]

Her father was Robert Church, a former slave who became wealthy investing in Memphis real estate. When she was six, he sent Mary to Antioch College Model School in Ohio and then to Oberlin College, also in Ohio, where she majored in classics. Her freshman year she was named the class poet and later was editor of the *Oberlin Review*. She stayed at Oberlin for a bachelor's and a master's degree and then taught at Wilberforce, America's oldest private black college.

Ohio could not hold her, and in 1887 she left for Washington, DC, to teach Latin at M Street Colored High School. A year later, she went to Europe, where the absence of racial discrimination almost persuaded her to stay. As she later wrote in her autobiography, "I knew I would be much happier trying to promote the welfare of my race in my native land, working under certain hard conditions, than I would be living in a foreign land where I could enjoy freedom from prejudice but where I would make no effort to do the work which I then believed it was my duty to do."[11] She returned to America and M Street High School and reunited with teacher and former suitor Robert H. Terrell. His father, "Faithful Harrison" Terrell, had been President Grant's manservant, and in the summer of 1883 Grant helped young Robert get a job at the Boston Customs House to earn money for his senior year at Harvard University. "I should feel an interest in any young man, white or colored, who had the courage and ability to graduate himself at Harvard without pecuniary aid other than what he could earn," Grant wrote.[12] When Robert and Mary married in 1891 he decided to change careers and become a lawyer. In 1910, President Taft would appoint Robert Terrell to the District of Columbia Municipal Court, making him the first black judge in the nation's capital.

Secretary Taft's "personal sense of justice had been aroused," and this motivated him as much as anything else to help Mary Church Terrell.[13] So might have been his political sense of justice. Roosevelt's order inflamed people, yet it was Taft's run for the White House that would be burned by it. "I do not think [Roosevelt] realizes quite the great feeling that has been aroused on the subject," Taft wrote to his wife.[14] On his just-completed trip out west, Taft got an earful from fearful Republican politicians worried about Brownsville's shadow. He was "deluged with protests" that what Roosevelt did was anything but a "square deal." Kansans told Taft the state might be lost in 1908, Oklahomans were almost as pessimistic, and even Texans in San Antonio were scared (though about what is unclear; the state had not voted Republican since the Civil War and would remain safely Democratic for another seventy-six years). Particularly crushing was the drift in his home state of Ohio. "He was assured that the negro vote in Ohio carries the balance of power, and every bit of it would be alienated from the Republicans."[15] Roosevelt's sleight of hand with the timing of the discharges may have avoided any problem in 1906, but 1908 was looming.

Roosevelt was setting foot that Saturday morning on Pana-

manian soil. Ignoring a downpour that soaked the bunting, dec-
orations, and cheering people awaiting him, he was enjoying
the moment and what he had brought about in the jungles of
Central America.[16] Back home, Taft knew he was facing a storm
of his own and not one he created. Arriving at his office at the
War Department, Taft perused the newspapers that told of more
trouble.

AFTER WAITING THREE HOURS at the War Department, Mrs. Terrell
sat across a desk from the secretary of war. Getting to the point,
she asked Taft to suspend Roosevelt's order. "Is that ALL you want
me to do? ALL you want me to do is to suspend an order issued
by the President of the United States during his absence from
the country?" Sensing sympathy from Taft's smile and what she
recognized as "good natured sarcasm," Mrs. Terrell pressed her
case, emphasizing the pride "colored people . . . take in our soldiers" and how bravely they had fought in previous wars. The dismissals were "more than we can bear" until a thorough investigation has been made. She recalled, "The smile left Mr. Taft's face.
He became serious and remained silent for several seconds. Then
he said with an intensity and a sympathy I can never forget: I do
not wonder that you are proud of the record of your soldiers. They
have served their country well."[17]

Milholland's plan worked.[18] Within the hour, Secretary of War
Taft decided on his own to suspend the discharges without President
Roosevelt's consent or knowledge. He told his secretary to send a
cable to Roosevelt in Panama advising him what he was doing.

But Taft's insubordination was short-lived. On November 20 he
got back to Washington after a visit to Yale University and found
Assistant Secretary Oliver and Military Secretary Ainsworth
waiting for him. Roosevelt's private secretary William Loeb soon
joined them, and by 6:00 p.m., they persuaded Taft to back down.
Or maybe they made it clear that when Roosevelt found out what
Taft did, the explosion might be heard in Washington without wireless transmission. However they did it, they convinced Taft he had
made a mistake, and that night, just under the wire, he ordered the

discharges to start again.[19] By cable that night to Porto Rico, he told President Roosevelt.

Taft never heard from Roosevelt because of the unreliable communications of the early twentieth century. Roosevelt got Taft's first wire on Saturday evening, just as he was leaving Colón for home. Enraged at what he read, Roosevelt sent his answer that night from the *Louisiana* via wireless, but because of atmospheric conditions, it never arrived in Washington.[20] When he landed in Porto Rico on Wednesday and there was no confirmation that Taft's actions had been reversed, he got angry all over again. Taking no chances Taft would not get the message this time, Roosevelt sent his order in three separate cables: "Discharge is not to be suspended unless there are new facts of such importance as to warrant your cabling me. I care nothing whatever for the yelling of either the politicians or the sentimentalists. The offense was most heinous and the punishment I inflicted was imposed after due deliberation. . . . Nothing has been brought before me to warrant the suspension, and I direct that it be executed."[21] However, by then the pressure from Loeb and the others had accomplished what the atmospheric pressure over the Caribbean kept Taft from finding out.

In a public statement the next day, Taft said he had been unaware how fully and exhaustively President Roosevelt considered the arguments against the discharges.[22] He wrote his wife the same day and, not mentioning his meeting with Oliver, Ainsworth, and Loeb, said he changed his mind because too much time had passed since he notified Roosevelt of the suspension, and not hearing anything, he was uncomfortable continuing it.[23] He also told her his action had been misinterpreted by some as "an act of disobedience," but he did not think Roosevelt would think it was.[24] A few days later he wrote to Richard Harding Davis, the reporter and war correspondent who made Roosevelt a national figure with the stories he filed from Cuba in the Spanish-American War, disingenuously pleading his own ignorance. He was away from Washington when Roosevelt ordered the army's investigations and again when he ordered the discharges and had no knowledge of why these decisions had been made. He also was not told that President Roosevelt already turned down the "same gentleman" (meaning Washington) who asked him to suspend the discharges to afford time for a rehearing.[25]

TAFT'S DICEY DISREGARD FOR what President Roosevelt wanted did not help the soldiers. Milholland unkindly referred to this as Taft's "flip flop."[26] Mary Church Terrell saw it differently. She always believed what Taft did for her and the soldiers was commendable and courageous and later wrote, "I shall never cease to thank him for trying to save those three companies of colored soldiers from dishonor and disgrace."[27] Meanwhile, Booker T. Washington's attempt to piggyback on the Constitution League's approach to Taft—and then take the credit—had failed. Taft's eventual response ignored completely everything Washington had said and implied, except to confirm the plan to rebuild the Twenty-Fifth Infantry with blacks.[28]

On November 26, five days after Roosevelt's three angry wires to Taft, Major Charles Penrose reported by telegram from Fort Reno, "Discharge of all men . . . completed at 9:30 AM this morning.[29] That evening Roosevelt disembarked from the presidential yacht *May-flower* at the Washington Navy Yard. His victory cruise to Panama and his indifference to the bubbling indignation over Brownsville were over.

THE TRIP BACK FROM Panama gave Roosevelt time to think about Brownsville. A man could spend just so much time reading books and writing letters to people like the secretary of the navy about how to improve coal delivery on the *Louisiana* or his son Kermit about the beauty of Porto Rico.[30] Sitting on the ship's deck in the warm sun, he would put aside the small library of books he brought along to read and allow Brownsville to advance to the front of his mind. He had received two pieces of news he did not like. There was the demand from Gilchrist Stewart and the New York County Republican Club to reverse the discharges. He knew Stewart was acting on behalf of John Milholland's Constitution League. His relationship with Milholland went back to New York City and Roosevelt's time as police commissioner in 1894, and Roosevelt knew Milholland had no political skill or muscle. He could be annoying and arouse others like him to make a lot of noise, but he could not do a thing.

Then there was this Taft suspension business. Taft might not be as hardheaded as he should be, but he knew right from wrong and he knew the law.

What is it he would want me to do? Trials? Even Texas knew this wouldn't work.[31] *I kept Taft's skirts clean by keeping him out of Washington and away from this mess. I sent him out to meet people who could help him in 1908. Maybe I should have asked him what he thought I should do. Maybe I should have told him what I wanted to do and asked him how to do it. Some opposition from Negroes was to be expected. The same with white wobblies like Milholland. And of course the Progressive press, like the* New York Sun. *But where was the rest coming from? Why was nothing said between the shooting in August and my discharge order in November? That three-month delay shows I did not act impulsively. I waited for the results of at least five investigations, and while the one by the citizens' committee may have been sloppy, the others by the army were trustworthy. No one doubted the soldiers did it. In fact, the discharge idea was not originally mine; it came from the army itself. This conspiracy of silence made sense; not one alternative theory did. Every adviser I spoke to, except Booker T. Washington, counseled me to discharge the soldiers, and Washington didn't like it because of its political consequences, for him especially. I know how he thinks. And for God's sake, what is the complaint? No soldier was hanged, no soldier went to jail, no soldier was punished—they all went home to their families and a new life. Not just those who kept their mouths shut, even the shooters and murderers.*[32]

How could I be expected to keep murderers and those who shielded them in the army? What community would accept them at a nearby post? What community wouldn't be afraid they would do it again? I could not try them in court; they'd be acquitted and right back in the army, and I'd be right back where I started. Then there's this rubbish I did it because these soldiers were Negro. They say it's a part of my new Southern strategy? It's not. What's so bad anyway about my plan to build the Republican Party of the Great Emancipator Lincoln in the South? What could be better for the South, the country, and the Negro? What have the Democrats done for the Negro in the South or anywhere else? Who would ever expect any progress from a political party with

*creatures in it like "Pitchfork" Ben Tillman of South Carolina—why,
I don't allow this foul man, even if he is a US senator, to set foot in the
White House.*[33]

That people would think he behaved unjustly, that he did not do justice with the Brownsville soldiers, was particularly unsettling to Roosevelt. "To love justice, to be merciful. . . . That is my religion, my faith," said the teenaged Roosevelt.[34] And he believed as a grown man that he did justice. Years later, in a trial unrelated to Brownsville, he was asked, "How did you know that substantial justice was done?"

> *Roosevelt:* Because I did it, because I was doing my best.
> *Question:* You mean to say that when you do a thing thereby substantial justice is done?
> *Roosevelt:* I do. When I do a thing I do it so as to do substantial justice. I mean just that.[35]

Unfortunately, in the Brownsville Incident, Roosevelt forgot he must not only do justice, but he must also be able to show that he was doing justice. The opposition had very little to do with the soldiers' guilt. It was the perception that, for most of the men, the discharges were unjust because there had been no proper finding of guilt. The investigations simply were not sufficient. Without open hearings, the right to counsel, the right to cross-examine witnesses against the soldiers, and the opportunity to present witnesses and other evidence of their own, there was no justice.

Then there was the soldiers' race and the feeling that, were they not Negro, they might have been treated differently. But Roosevelt would never admit their race had anything to do with his decision because he didn't think it did. When he made federal appointments, "I certainly cannot treat mere color as a permanent bar to holding office any more than I could treat it as conferring a right to hold office," he told the owner and editor of the *Atlanta Constitution*.[36] Around the same time, he acknowledged to the editor of *Century Magazine*, Richard Watson Gilder, that his way of making appointments policy "decreased the quantity [of black appointments]," but defended it because it "raised the quality." Five years later, he was still saying this as a way of defending the shrinking pool of blacks when he wrote Gilder that he raised the bar higher so that only "those few from the very best colored men . . . to be found" could hurdle it.[37] By itself, this fine-tuning does not indict Roosevelt. For a practical politician also seeking to help the black race advance (as he would put it), working with anything less than the very best was self-defeating. But working with the best did not always ensure success.

Minnie Cox was the best of the best, and she was run out of town. She and her husband, Wayne, were prosperous and respected Negroes in Sunflower County, Mississippi, and Republican to the core. President Benjamin Harrison appointed her as postmistress in its county seat, Indianola, and when President McKinley reclaimed the White House for the Republicans in 1896, she reclaimed the post and held it when Roosevelt took office in September 1901. Both Mississippi senators voted to confirm her in 1897, and three prominent whites in Indianola served as her bondsmen.[38] She took her job seriously and handled it well. Desiring cordial relations with the town's whites, Mrs. Cox went out of her way to avoid friction. With her own money, she installed a telephone in the post office for her patrons' use and covered past-due post-office-box rentals from her own pocket. The white (and Democratic) postal inspector for the area vouched for her. Everything was fine until she ran into Roosevelt's plan of action to rebuild the Republican Party in the South. When Roosevelt, with Booker T. Washington's advice and cover, appointed a white Democrat as US marshal for Mississippi's Southern District, the few white Republicans there feared a purge of white Republicans. They wanted Mrs. Cox's job and its $1,000 salary for themselves.

The fight to get rid of her soon became an all-out assault on blacks. A Negro porter in a general store owned by a Jew had to be fired. A Negro physician in Indianola was given three months to pack up and leave. Fearing the worst, on December 4, 1902, Mrs. Cox tendered her resignation. Roosevelt, with the assent of the white postal inspector, refused to accept it. Detouring around the legal requirement that there be a post office there, Roosevelt suspended postal service in Indianola. It still had a post office and Mrs. Cox still was the postmistress (and drew her salary), but mail had to be picked up in Greenville, inconveniently thirty miles down the road. When Mrs. Cox's term ended in 1904, she chose not to ask for another. This time Roosevelt accepted it but refused to appoint as her replacement any Republican involved in the clique against her. He picked a local Democrat who had been one of her bondsmen and "her staunch friend" during the trouble. More important to history and to an understanding of Roosevelt, he was, as historian Willard Gatewood said, "never plagued by misgivings about his support of Mrs. Cox."[39] In the context of Roosevelt's efforts to build the GOP in the South, standing by Mrs. Cox was not smart. Maybe he thought amends to her were required for the clumsy implementation of his plans that helped bring on the confrontation. Maybe it was principle.

Roosevelt's support for Minnie Cox did not mean he was not sensitive to the political consequences of black appointments. Planning strategy for the 1904 Republican presidential nomination he still worried about, he wrote the chairman of the National Republican Executive Committee, "The most damaging thing the *Times* can do is to give the impression that in what I have done for the Negro I have been actuated by political motives." It is just that he did not see race in Brownsville. Wrapping the mantle of the Great Emancipator around him, hoping it would inoculate him from such criticism in the North, he added, "I have acted . . . on the Negro question . . . [as] the heir of Abraham Lincoln."[40]

IN HIS FOREWORD TO Joshua Hawley's *Theodore Roosevelt: Preacher of Righteousness*, Pulitzer Prize–winning historian David M. Kennedy suggests Roosevelt's racial views were tainted in his youth and reinforced as a young man. "[Roosevelt] had read and mastered [Darwin's *On the Origin of Species*] by the age of fourteen. . . . Darwinian notions of evolutionary progress through struggle continued to color his thinking about issues ranging from politics to warfare to racial categorization."[41] On the other hand, Progressive Era historian Sidney Milkis credits Roosevelt with freeing "himself from the most noxious views of an Aryan race," and at least by 1910, he "no longer subscribed to a perverse understanding of evolution, common in the United States at that time, that championed white supremacy."[42]

Roosevelt's mind and what he thought specifically of the black race are glimpsed in a letter, written on his first day back from Panama, to the man he appointed chairman of the Isthmian Canal Commission. Pleased overall with what he saw in Panama, he was unhappy with conditions tolerated among "West India Negroes" working there. Roosevelt wanted to "teach them some of the principles of personal hygiene, notably having one suit to work in and another to sleep in."[43] There is Roosevelt's racial theory: some races are more advanced than others; acting in loco parentis, those more advanced have the responsibility to teach the lower races to improve themselves; in the meantime, those being taught have equal civil rights, but not necessarily equal privileges.

Historian and forceful Roosevelt admirer John Gable has written, "Roosevelt generally subscribed to the views of Booker T. Washington. That is, he believed that many years of educational, vocational, and self-help training for blacks would be needed before the problem facing the Negro could be solved. . . . Thus, he found American blacks as a group 'inferior' to American whites as a group, because he did not think that the long oppressed blacks had yet reached as high a degree of education, economic success, and social and cultural achievement as the majority of whites had."[44] As with the "West India Negroes," Roosevelt's impulse to "teach them" illustrates his belief that blacks as a race had to be treated as a father treats a child, with care and an awareness they possess some rights now and, with growth and maturity, full privileges in the future. (He felt the same way about the American Indian.[45])

Not that Roosevelt applied this consistently. His "relations with Negroes" were whimsical and impulsive, "unhampered by the tedium of logical coherences or consistency of procedure."[46] Sometimes he did the right thing. While Civil Service Commissioner, when the Bureau of Engraving and Printing was charged with "discrimination . . . upon the basis of color," Roosevelt said the law did not authorize him to do anything about it[47] and asked President Harrison to correct this by promulgating a rule. A year later, Roosevelt added, "The spirit of the law undoubtedly meant there should be this equal treatment. . . . When the blacks were discriminated against we intended to make public the fact, so that we might at least excite the indignation of honest men about them."[48]

Other times, however, the logical conclusions from his assumption of a race's shortcomings led him to behave foolishly. In Cuba, black soldiers made a mixed impression on him. Some enlisted men could fight as well as their white counterparts but were "particularly dependent on their white officers." Black noncommissioned officers "occasionally" had initiative as much as "the best class of whites . . . [although] this cannot be expected normally, nor is it fair to expect it."

The mixture of his racial views and his well-known impulsiveness could be volatile. Spotting Buffalo Soldiers in Cuba he assumed were running away from battle, "I . . . drew my revolver, halted the retreating soldiers . . . [and said] that I would shoot the first man who, on any pretense whatever, went to the rear." When later told the men were not cowards or shirkers but only following an officer's orders to remove wounded men, Roosevelt went back to these men and apologized.

Five days after the Brownsville raid (but unconnected to it), he was considering an odd choice for the Supreme Court, Democrat and former Confederate soldier Horace Lurton, because he "takes just the attitude we take as regards . . . the propriety of the National Government doing just what it can to secure certain *elementary rights* to the Negro" (author's emphasis).[49]

Roosevelt's use of "the Negro" was criticized as an indication he failed to see individual differences among black people, preferring to see in each one traits common to all because of their race.[50] Nevertheless, he recognized individual exceptions when he believed he met with them; Booker T. Washington was an example. A consideration of Theodore Roosevelt and race is incomplete without including his relationship with the educator from Tuskegee.

For Booker T. Washington, it began when the hero of San Juan Heights was running for New York governor in 1898. Washington saw Roosevelt as someone on the way up and asked his intelligence agents in New York what they thought of him. "Two men we have in N.Y. whom we admire & are proud of but who are like a pair of Race horses on traces beyond the control of all but their own mood and cannot be led are Roosevelt and [T. Thomas] Fortune. We never know what they will do next," was the judgment of newspaper reporter J. M. Holland.[51] Fortune, the other uncontrollable man, was less cynical in his impression of Roosevelt. "He seems to be a very open and honest man and I rather like him," he told Washington. He added that Roosevelt's admiration for Washington was "unstinted," something Fortune knew would please the educator.[52] Washington would not have been Washington if he did not grasp Roosevelt was a man just like himself. A man not to trifle with, just like himself.

For Roosevelt, it began while he was vice president and planning for the 1904 presidential nomination. His intention to build a new Republican Party in the South arose to counter Senator Mark Hanna's control of Southern Negro delegates to the Republican nominating convention. He asked Booker T. Washington to help him. (This scheme shows how global Roosevelt's solutions to problems could be and how much work he was willing to put into them. To win the 1904 nomination, he needed delegates from the South; to get them, he had to bypass Mark Hanna; to bypass Hanna, he would build a new Republican Party down there; and to do this, he needed Booker T. Washington.) Washington agreed, and a trip to Tuskegee by Roosevelt was planned for November. By then, he was President Roosevelt and suggested they meet in the White House over dinner. In a handwritten note, Washington confirmed he would "accept your invitation for dinner."[53]

No black man ever had dined in the White House with a president before. Even though this meeting had nothing to do with black rights or social equality and was exclusively to talk politics, the blowback was intense. Roosevelt admitted to Albion W. Tourgée (the lawyer for Homer Plessy of *Plessy v. Ferguson*) he had a "moment's qualm [that] made me ashamed of myself."[54] Henry Cabot Lodge assured him, "Everyone here, literally everyone, is with you heart and soul on the Booker Washington matter. Needless for me to say how utterly right you are,"[55] and Roosevelt became adamant he did the right thing. "If these creatures had any sense they would understand that they can't bluff me."[56] Outwardly, Roosevelt stuck to his guns and said he would invite anyone he pleased to the White House. But he may not have been so sure he was right. A week after Washington's visit, Roosevelt bumped into Mark Twain at an awards ceremony at Yale, and Roosevelt asked Twain if he had done the right thing. Recalled Twain, "I judged by his tone that he was worried and troubled and sorry about that showy adventure, and wanted a little word of comfort and approval."[57]

The Theodore Roosevelt–Booker T. Washington collaboration shows the Jekyll and Hyde of Roosevelt and race. The good Dr. Jekyll saw Booker T. Washington every bit as entitled to meet and eat with him as anyone else. The dishonorable Mr. Hyde never had a black man to dinner again. The Roosevelt-Washington relationship also paralleled the overall relationship between whites and blacks at the beginning of the twentieth century. Roosevelt would be dominant, occasionally dismissive; Washington was content to be secondary and obsequious, just as he counseled Southern Negroes to be. Publicly, Washington would understate his influence, though few believed him: "Whatever conferences I have had with the President or with any public official have grown out of my position, not as a politician, but as an educator." After that dinner, their partnership prospered for almost five years, until it was stunted by Brownsville.

IN A BOSTON SPEECH in May 1907, John Milholland condemned Roosevelt's race policy as having "done more to strengthen the Bourbon Democracy in the South than any administration since the days of Buchanan."[58] Oscar Straus, a Jew and therefore a legatee of group hatred and one who understood what it was, attended a dinner at the White House after the 1906 election, where President Roosevelt and others discussed his upcoming message to Congress. "First there was the negro question. . . . His position plainly was that he would do anything in his power for the white man South without, however, doing a wrong or an injustice to the colored man."[59]

These three descriptions of Roosevelt and race, two at opposite extremes, one in the middle, suggest three different Theodore Roosevelts on the question of race. Not one of them comes near describing a man who would cashier three companies of infantry soldiers from the army simply because they were black.

Roosevelt was a product of his youth and a man of his era. On race, his beliefs and behaviors were more advanced than most but nowhere near those of the twenty-first century. He has to be judged by the times he lived in. But we may test him by more than his actions. We are entitled to judge him on his words as well, and as we shall see, they were angry and cruel, and they shaded what he did. As the debate over the Brownsville discharges boiled over, Roosevelt would overheat his words and rhetoric and aim them at the black soldiers and their defenders.

*"Ohio had such a plethora of aspiring statesmen that they
jostled one another and were in one another's way."*

James Beauchamp ("Champ") Clark,
Speaker of the US House of Representatives,
My Quarter Century of American Politics, vol. 1

CHAPTER NINE

THESE ARE MY JEWELS

O N THE GROUNDS OF the Ohio Statehouse in Columbus is a
statue of Cornelia of ancient Rome. When a friend boasted
about her fine jewelry, Cornelia pointed to her sons and said, "These
are my jewels." Cornelia represents Ohio, and on her pedestal surrounding her are life-size statutes of seven Ohioans who served the
nation during and after the Civil War, including Presidents Ulysses
S. Grant, Rutherford B. Hayes, and James A. Garfield. By 1906,
three other Ohioans had been president, and it looked like two more
were competing against each other for the prize in 1908.[1] Both were
from Cincinnati.

IN SIX NARROW COLUMNS on page one, crammed with small typeset
but no pictures or drawings, the *Cincinnati Daily Enquirer* on August
16, 1869, reported that Parisians were celebrating the one hundredth
anniversary of the birth of Napoleon I.[2] In England, the Harvard
crew was racing on the Thames. Closer to home, Columbus had
an attempted robbery of a jewelry store, but an alert policeman
caught the burglars in action. In Cincinnati, four businessmen had
formed a partnership to distill alcohol and whiskies. From Indiana
came news of "Another Steamboat Disaster." And another on the
Mississippi River seven miles below St. Louis, in which eighteen to

twenty lives were feared lost. In a river city like Cincinnati, this was important news. But as a transportation hub, Cincinnati already was losing out to other Midwestern cities with steel railroad tracks going almost everywhere. The railroads were cutting into Cincinnati's steamboat business. The newspaper had ads from a score of them; one, the Old Reliable Little Miami Railroad, claimed to be the shortest and fastest route to the "Eastern cities, towns, villages and stations." The local news was on page eight under the heading "City Matters." A building owned by Mr. George Martin was destroyed by fire. The Mayor's Office reported weekly receipts of $183, including $77 from peddlers and $1 from dog licenses. The Eckford Base-Ball Club from Brooklyn, "champions of the United States," were staying at the Gibson House and preparing to play the Red Stockings at Union Grounds. (The next day's edition happily reported a "victory for our boys," who beat the champs by what sportscasters today would call a "football score," 45–18.) From the single "Law Card" by H. S. Brewster, attorney at law and master commissioner of the Court of Common Pleas, who would have guessed there were already three hundred lawyers in Cincinnati?[3] Not Joseph Foraker, who came that day to practice law.[4]

WILLIAM HOWARD TAFT'S WEIGHT always had been a problem, though as a young man he carried it well. He loved sports, especially baseball.[5] Playing the infield in high school, he was a quick-footed second baseman able to make the out and then pivot to throw accurately to first base to get the back end of the double play. He took jokes about his weight in good fun and loved repeating Secretary of State Elihu Root's response to his telegram from the Philippines when he was governor there. Taft wired he had ridden a horse that day and was "feeling good." Root wired back, "How's the horse?" As he aged, Taft added more pounds (at one point he reached three hundred), and they became the visible image of his other frustrations.

His father, Alphonso Taft, was a lawyer and later a judge in Cincinnati and achieved respect enough for President Ulysses S.

Grant, trying in his last year in the White House to scrub away the stain of scandal, to bring him and his good name and character into the cabinet as secretary of war and then as attorney general. Taft's mother was Alphonso's second wife. In time they would have five children, four of whom would be boys, the first "the large and smiling Willie."[6] He was "good nature personified."[7]

SITTING ACROSS THE OHIO River from the slave state of Kentucky, Cincinnati was while Willie Taft was growing up there a Southern city in a Northern state. Ohio was a free state, and before the Civil War both free and slave blacks crossed the river to get to it. Because of this next-door accessibility to the South, it was a station on the Underground Railroad, the lacework of secret routes used by slaves to escape slavery. Harriet Beecher Stowe, who wrote *Uncle Tom's Cabin*, the book Abraham Lincoln is said to have joked "started this whole war," lived in Cincinnati, and she and her husband hid fugitive slaves in their home. (Her father, the abolitionist minister Lyman Beecher, lived on Gilbert Avenue just a few steps from its intersection with what is today Foraker Avenue.) Not all white Cincinnatians supported the abolitionists; in 1862, Wendell Phillips was booed and pelted with eggs and rocks and caused a riot when he spoke there against slavery.[8] By the time Foraker decided to stake his future there, of the 216,000 or so people in Cincinnati (it was the nation's sixth-largest city), 5,900 were Negro.[9]

The Ohio River was not the River Jordan, and Ohio was not the Promised Land. Its black residents may have been free, but legally they were not equal to whites. Ohio had "Black Laws." Negroes could not testify against whites, serve in the militia or on juries, or enroll in public schools.[10] In 1829, relying on an 1804 law prohibiting blacks from entering Ohio, and aware many slaves came anyway and simply remained there, Cincinnati expelled them. Irish immigrants hastened blacks on their way, leading to riots between the two. Before things quieted down, more than one thousand Negroes (half of the pre-riot black population) had abandoned Cincinnati.[11] Those who stayed lived with the violence that could be brought to bear on them.[12]

Still, just before the Civil War, the city had a small, educated, and affluent black upper class. Robert Harlan "exemplified [its] life style, tastes and self-perception."[13] He was able to see to it that his son, Robert Jr., attended Woodward High School, where a class-mate was Will Taft.[14] The senior Harlan's white half brother, with whom, according to historian Willard Gatewood, he shared a rela-tionship of "intimacy and mutual respect," was US Supreme Court Justice John Marshall Harlan, who wrote in his dissent in *Plessy v. Ferguson*, "Our Constitution is color-blind. . . . In respect of civil rights, all citizens are equal before the law. . . . The law regards man as man and takes no account of his surroundings or of his color when his civil rights as guaranteed by the supreme law of the land are involved."[15]

BORN INTO A LARGE family with nine children (two more died in infancy), Joseph Foraker used his childhood to acquire the disci-plines—hard work and thorough preparation—necessary for a family farm "where there was always more work to do."[16] In school, his favorite subject was history, especially military history. He had "an aptitude for declamation" and later remembered how well he recited "Henry V at Harfleur":

> Once more unto the breach, dear friends, once more;
> . . .
> In peace there's nothing so becomes a man
> As modest stillness and humility:
> But when the blast of war blows in our ears,
> Then imitate the action of the tiger.[17]

Young Joe, at fourteen years still only a tiger cub and unable to enlist in the Union Army when the "blast of war" began with cannon fire at Fort Sumpter, stayed behind when his older brother Burch joined the Twenty-Fourth Ohio Volunteer Infantry. Two years later, just after his sixteenth birthday, he lied about his age and enlisted in the newly formed Company A, Eighty-Ninth Ohio Volunteer Infantry, as its first volunteer.[18] It can be said of Foraker's wartime service that he did his duty and he did it well. But he saw practically no fighting himself, and when the Eighty-Ninth was bloodied at Chickamauga, he was by "a great piece of good fortune" back in Ohio on recruiting duty.[19]

His most significant recollection from the war was learning of Lincoln's Emancipation Proclamation in September 1862.[20] From then on, the war "was to involve . . . the abolition of slavery [and] had been placed on a higher and better plane, both morally and patriotically; that Union victory in consequence meant something worth fighting for, and if need be, dying for."[21]

RUBBING SHOULDERS WITH THE officers, Foraker learned that he was uneducated. When he left the army (he bookended his regiment's existence as the first man enlisted and the last mustered out), he prepared himself to get an education. After a year he was ready for Ohio Wesleyan University in Delaware, Ohio.[22] "It was there I met, courted and became engaged to Miss Julia Bundy."[23] There must have been something in Delaware, Ohio, that encouraged future leaders of the nation from Ohio to woo and win the young ladies at Wesleyan's sister college, Ohio Wesleyan Women's University. As Julia coyly put it, "It was quite against the design of the founders of old Delaware that 'the sexes,' students-under-the-elms, should meet. (Ah, but didn't they . . . !)"[24] Future president Rutherford B. Hayes and future vice president (in Theodore Roosevelt's second term) Charles W. Fairbanks also did the trick.

Julia was as lively and vivacious as her husband could be dour. She would add balance to him and, from her father, Hezekiah Bundy, a congressman from Jackson County, Ohio, she supplemented his political perspective. Of course there were activities at college not quite as absorbing as Julia that also brought perspective to Foraker. The Lyceum Circuit would come through Delaware, and Foraker would often attend the lectures, hearing, among others, the former slave Frederick Douglass and Wendell Phillips.[25] These hardened Foraker's views on the antebellum South and the mistreatment of Negroes.

He decided to become a lawyer and left Ohio Wesleyan to join the senior class at Cornell University where in July 1869 he was part of its first class to graduate with a law degree. When he and Julia then married in the Bundy home in Wellston, Ohio, their nuptials had to be at 9:00 a.m. so Mr. and the new Mrs. Joseph Benson Foraker could make the only train of the day to Cincinnati and their new home.[26] Where they would thrive.

IT WAS NOT LONG before Foraker felt the tug of politics. He started with local elections but was spectacularly unsuccessful, losing a run for Common Pleas Court judge in 1876 and, in an election tainted by outrageous fraud unconnected to him, for county solicitor in 1878.[27] He tried again the next year, and this time he rang the bell and was elected to the Superior Court of Cincinnati. He served for three years, when, "on account of a temporary illness that gave my friends as well as myself serious concern," he resigned.[28] "The year following my resignation . . . I was nominated by the Republicans of Ohio for the office of Governor."[29] He lost to George Hoadly, also of Cincinnati and once a Republican, but who left the party when it split over the sale of liquor.[30] In losing the election, Foraker nevertheless mastered the art of the stump speech.[31] He was learning to be a compelling speaker, a "fire alarm."

"AS FAR BACK AS he could remember, there had always been a Yale for William Howard Taft."[32] His father, Alphonso, and his brother Charley were Yale alumni, and it would be Old Eli for the young man now calling himself Bill. It was at Yale where he developed a love for scholarship and critical thinking, and he graduated second in his class of 132 students. When still a young man, he set his heart on appointment to the US Supreme Court, and this dream reflected the pleasure and reward he enjoyed by exercising his wits where knowledge, thoughtful reflection, and clever reasoning were the stock in trade.

He learned the law at Cincinnati Law School but gained no

practical education or training. Classes and studies left more than enough time for other work, and he became a cub reporter with the *Cincinnati Commercial*, assigned to the court beat. He used this experience to fill in the gaps by watching how the law worked in the real world of trials and hearings. When he left the world of ink, he had little interest in lawyering, and when President Chester A. Arthur offered him the position of collector of internal revenue for Cincinnati, a position that had nothing to do with the law and would advance his career not at all, Taft jumped at it.[33]

FORAKER MEANWHILE STEPPED AWAY from politics to build a "prosperous" law practice. Keeping a toe in the water, he was a delegate to the 1884 Republican National Convention in Chicago. There he met Theodore Roosevelt, whom he found to be without discretion. Mrs. Foraker had a vivid memory of Roosevelt standing on his chair, shaking his fist, and conspicuously demonstrating what she called, "a very beagle's flair for political tactics."[34]

Roosevelt supported Vermont senator George F. Edmunds for the nomination, while Foraker managed Ohio senator John Sherman's campaign. For either to prevail, Senator James G. Blaine of Maine had to be turned aside. With their interests coinciding, they worked well together on an early test of Blaine's strength, the election of Negro John R. Lynch of Mississippi as the convention's temporary chairman. Julia would say it was a black man who first brought Roosevelt and Foraker together.[35]

In 1885 Foraker ran again for governor, and this time he won. A year later, a seat opened up on his old bench, the Superior Court in Cincinnati, one of the trenches in which lawsuits are battled out. Its judges were elected by the voters, but when a vacancy occurred the governor appointed someone to fill the rest of that term. These appointments were valuable to governors, who could use them to repay existing political debts or create new chits to be redeemed in the future. The man on whom fortune and a governor smiled could expect to keep the job as long as he wanted it. No one knows why

Foraker picked Taft. Taft's biographer Henry Pringle suggests the governor may have decided it would look good in the upcoming gubernatorial campaign to make a nonpolitical appointment. Maybe it was affection for the younger man. According to Mrs. Foraker, theirs was a friendship that went back to when court reporter Taft covered Superior Court Judge Foraker. "There was an instant sympathy between the twenty-one year old collegian and the thirty-two year old magistrate. Foraker liked Taft's smile, liked his agreeable manner, liked his type of mind."[36]

So the appointment was made. Taft put on his judicial robes. He, his father, and his brother sent notes to Foraker warmly thanking him.[37] Foraker responded cordially with a note of his own. He now had a Taft family IOU in his pocket.

EVEN BEFORE UNION VICTORY in the Civil War, Ohio courts and judges were uneasy with the Black Laws. In a case in which two whites were accused of murdering a black man, the question was whether the victim's obviously black wife could testify against them. The court noted the legal definition of a white person (one with more than 50 percent "white blood") and held even persons with clearly dark skin could qualify and be allowed to give testimony.[38] Further help came from state officials, especially those in Columbus. Democratic governor George B. Hoadly shut down a skating rink closed to blacks. Members of the House of Representatives protested on behalf of a black colleague not allowed to eat in a Columbus restaurant.

Foraker opposed the Black Laws and, after he was elected governor in 1886, got the Republican-controlled state legislature to repeal the last of them. Foraker later said their end "accord[s] to the colored people of Ohio . . . that full measure of manhood to which they are entitled."[39] In his 1887 campaign for reelection, he emphasized his support for repeal and solidified his black support.[40] It would not fade away.

By 1888 Foraker had been governor for two terms and was a force on the national stage. The year before he spoke in New York City, and in what was called a stem-winder, he brought people to their feet cheering him. Without declaring himself a candidate, Foraker passed James G. Blaine, the unsuccessful 1884 Republican presidential nominee and another undeclared candidate in 1888, and became lead dog for the 1888 nomination. The *New York Sun* was giddy over him. Better watch Foraker, it warned his rivals; he might snatch the nomination for himself.[41] Before the delegates met, Blaine declared himself out of the race. He went so far as to be out of the country during the convention, traveling through Scotland with Andrew Carnegie. Mrs. Blaine found the dreary Scottish summer cold and wet ("It rains . . . every day and at all hours. . . . And it is so cold. When we go out driving we bundle up, as we do in Augusta only in winter.").[42] Back in Chicago, things were just as chilly for the supporters of the disinterested Senator Blaine. Ohio's John Sherman, in his third try, seemed to have captured the lightning in a bottle. With Blaine out of the way and a united Ohio delegation headed by Foraker, the way seemed clear to him. But it turned upside down again.

Ohio may have been united for Sherman, but not strongly so. Some delegates yearned for Blaine. Others looked to William McKinley. And Foraker was miffed. As leader of the Ohio delegation, he expected to make the nominating speech. Sherman would not hear of it. When the time came for nominations, Foraker would instead make the seconding speech, and as he strode to the platform to perform his assigned task, a floral wreath with "No rebel flags will be returned while I am governor" stitched with red flowers against a white background was placed at the speaker's stand for all to see. These were the words flung at President Cleveland by Governor Foraker when Cleveland, as a gesture to help end sectionalism, thought it was time to return captured Confederate regimental flags held by Northern states.[43] This defiance had become part of the Foraker lore. Appearing visibly embarrassed, Foraker had the display removed before he began to speak, but the lethal effect of these delicate blooms lingered along with their fragrance. His speech was a great one, but when balloting came, Sherman's support dropped like petals on dying flowers. After three ballots, he was in the lead but still 172 votes short of what was needed.

His goose was in the oven but not yet completely cooked. On Saturday morning, a fourth ballot was held; Benjamin Harrison gained momentum, while Sherman lost strength.[44]

And then came the unexpected. Julia told the story in her memoirs. "At 2 AM, on Monday Foraker and I, very sound asleep, were awakened by a knock on the door. It was Kurtz, my husband's secretary. [The Blaine men] were outside waiting in the hall. They wanted to hold an immediate conference with my husband. Well, the only place to receive them was in that bedroom, the only thing for me to do was to leave, and the only place for me to go was the bathroom. So there I hid."[45] From there she heard what went on. Blaine men "crowded into the bedroom." They told Foraker they wanted "to throw the entire Blaine strength to [him] on Monday morning if [he] would accept the nomination for President." He turned them down.

On Monday, the vote went to Benjamin Harrison, as it would in November. It was a Republican year, and it could have been Foraker's. Julia ends the story, "Husbands know best, that is understood; at the same time . . . I tremble to think of the unfolded future had Foraker been in a position to say 'yes' to that two-in-the-morning offer of the presidential candidacy."[46] Eighteen years later, in 1906, people wondered if his time had finally come.

BEING A TRIAL JUDGE WAS fine, but Taft still dreamed of being a justice on the US Supreme Court. In July 1889 Justice Stanley Matthews, another Cincinnatian, died, and President Harrison offered the seat to yet another lawyer from Cincinnati, Thomas McDougal, but he declined. Taft—only thirty-two years old, never elected to any public office, his only judicial experience in superior court, and about his only qualifications that he taught constitutional law and was a Republican—saw a chance and jumped at it. His most important advocate was Governor Joseph Foraker, who wrote President Harrison and even spoke to him on Taft's behalf.[47] But the summons from the White House never came; Harrison selected David Brewer, a fellow Yale alumnus. But Harrison remembered the young man from his birth state, and when he needed a solicitor general, then the counselor to the attorney general and the one usually representing the government before the Supreme Court, Taft got the job as a consolation. Much of the credit went to Governor Foraker, who now considered himself to be Taft's guide and mentor and again had gone to bat for him with Harrison.[48] When Taft was appointed, Foraker sent his congratulations and added, what "lies beyond that office is the other position to which I can clearly see that it leads . . . the bench of the Supreme Court."[49]

In Washington, Taft met and became friends with civil-service commissioner Theodore Roosevelt. Seven years later, Taft petitioned his fellow Ohioan, President William McKinley, to appoint Roosevelt assistant secretary of the navy.[50]

In the meantime, McKinley appointed Taft to the Sixth United States Circuit Court of Appeals in Cincinnati. Taft's wife, Helen ("Nellie"), wanted him to stay in Washington and in touch with Washington "bigwigs," but risking her displeasure Taft accepted the appointment and returned home. He liked being a judge again and saw it as a Supreme Court résumé builder. Nellie didn't like it and let him know how she felt. She had a sharp tongue that pierced her husband across the room, but he never felt any pain, and she always apologized. "I know that I am very cross to you, but I love you just the same."[51] In 1900, when Taft received a telegram from President McKinley, Nellie was overjoyed. She sensed something was in the works and she and Taft would be getting out of the judicial rut. She would be frustrated.

JUDGE TAFT SUPPORTED THE war in Cuba in 1898 because he felt it was unavoidable after the sinking of the USS *Maine*. After the war and President McKinley's agonized decision to Westernize and Christianize the Philippines, someone had to go there to do it. The telegram that so excited Nellie Taft dashed her hopes. McKinley wanted Taft to take the job. A constitution had to be written, laws drafted, an administration and civil-service bureaucracy set up, and an uprising suppressed. The army under General Arthur MacArthur for too long had been running the show, and to some extent it had to be suppressed too. Taft hesitated. This required skills he was not sure he had. And it would take him across the globe and off the judicial track to the Supreme Court he thought he was on. McKinley parried this objection by promising to return him to his career path when he returned home.[52] Taft accepted the job and replaced Cornell University president Jacob Gould Schurman, who, back in Ithaca, stayed in touch with Joseph Foraker, class of '69.[53]

Expecting the job to last no more than six to nine months, Taft and Nellie would stay in the Philippines more than four years, during which time McKinley was assassinated and Roosevelt took his place in the White House. Taft tamed the rebels and the American army. "He established a civil-service system, a judicial system, English-language public schools, a transportation network, and health care facilities. He also negotiated with the Vatican . . . to purchase 390,000 acres of church property in the Philippines for $7.5 million," which he resold "by way of low-cost mortgages to . . . Filipino peasants."[54] This solved the problem of inequitable land ownership and persuaded Spaniards in the church hierarchy in the Philippines to go home and make room for Filipinos.

Taft came to love the islands and their people, and they loved him. His job there became his mission. An offer of a vacant seat on the Supreme Court, his life's dream, could not tempt him to leave. He refused it, citing the need to stay in Manila to finish the job he agreed to do. "Looking forward to time when I can accept such an offer but even if it is certain that it can never be repeated I must now decline."[55] The offer was repeated three months later; again he said no.

WHEN TAFT ACCEPTED THE Philippines post, Foraker had been in the Senate for two years. His appearance, bearing, and demeanor were nothing if not senatorial. It was said he was the most handsome politician in Ohio, "a very handsome man, over six feet in stature, weighing slightly over two hundred pound, with as fine a shock of iron-gray hair as was ever on a man's head; possessed of brilliant talents and great personal charm . . . a smart constitutional lawyer, and an audacious fighter, [who] displayed . . . patience in exposition, alacrity in compromise, poise under attack," and even withering wit.[56] (When someone spoke reverently of William Jennings Bryan, who had been called the "Boy Orator of the Platte," Foraker reminded people "the River Platte was only six inches deep but with a mouth six miles wide."[57]) He joined comfortably with the Senate's Old Guard, the Republicans who narrowly interpreted the Constitution as creating a limited federal government and judged legislation cramping the growth of business enterprises with government regulation by this standard. His law practice had at its core the representation of corporations and other large business entities, and in the Senate he would resist Roosevelt's efforts to pull the teeth from corporate interests. Most especially did he oppose building the presidency and its executive agencies into a stronger and, as he would see it, a more meddlesome branch of government.

After working together at the 1884 Republican convention, Roosevelt and Foraker continued to get along rather well. Each man had a combativeness the other admired, so long as it was asserted against other men. If they can be believed, a shared attitude of defiance is what motivated Foraker to seek the Senate and Roosevelt to take the nomination for vice president.[58] Foraker said, "If they had not made up a combination to prevent me from going to the senate, then I would not want the position. Now I have made up my mind to go after it."[59] According to Foraker, Roosevelt told him he accepted second spot on the ticket in 1900 because "he had learned the administration did not want him." Foraker can take partial credit for encouraging Roosevelt to agree to it by persuading him he would strengthen the ticket.[60] When President McKinley asked Foraker not to support Roosevelt, Foraker said he had to because of the commitment he made. This suggests that as late as the 1900 election, the Roosevelt-Foraker relationship was calm, cordial, even friendly. Foraker wrote that before the 1904 election, they had no serious differences over public affairs.[61] But right after, they found themselves at opposite corners in the ring, discerning the nation's problems and the ways to solve them.

DURING OHIO'S ODD-YEAR campaign of 1905, Foraker spoke in Bellefontaine to oppose President Roosevelt's proposal to stop the rebates and other tricks railroads used to discount shipping costs to big shippers by giving the Interstate Commerce Commission power to set rates. Foraker thought rate setting was "too complicated, delicate" for a government agency to take on and just might be unconstitutional.[62] Roosevelt's scheme was introduced in Congress as the Hepburn Bill, and its final version passed the Senate in May 1906 with only three votes against it, one of which was Foraker's (the only Republican). It's easy to see why Roosevelt was happy with the Hepburn Act and Foraker was not. A railroad, a private enterprise, no longer could decide what it could charge for its services. That decision was now made by the government. What is not easy to see is why Foraker didn't swallow hard and accept it, like every other Republican senator. In an address to the Senate on May 18, two days before it passed the Hepburn Bill, he did not back down: "I have acted as I have spoken and voted as I have spoken, in accordance with my own judgment and my own convictions."[63] Foraker would pay for his convictions and his vote. No one could say he had not been warned. Two weeks after his Bellefontaine address, even before the Hepburn Bill was introduced in Congress, the *New York Times* reported, "Friends of the Administration have . . . let it be known they will oppose Senator Foraker's activities in Pennsylvania, as well as Ohio [and he] will find himself in the attitude of a foe of President Roosevelt." Looking to 1908 and the competition for the Republican presidential nomination, the *New York Times* predicted, "From now until the convention of 1908 . . . Mr. Taft [will act] as the spokesman of the President and Mr. Foraker as the representative of the opposite element in the party."

Roosevelt was angry at Foraker because he could not see the Ohio senator as a man with another point of view, only as one standing in his way, and as Justice Oliver Wendell Holmes Jr. learned when he dissented in the *Northern Securities* case and voted against applying antitrust laws as Roosevelt wanted, Roosevelt "couldn't forgive anyone who stood in his way."[64] Roosevelt called those who opposed him for "asserting and exercising a genuine control . . . over those great corporations" his "*enemies . . . the railroad senators*" (author's emphasis).[65] That would include Foraker, no longer just an opponent, now an enemy. Woe betide a Roosevelt enemy.

ROOSEVELT ORDERED TAFT BACK to Washington to be secretary of war in February 1903. It is strange that a man who did not share Roosevelt's appetite for war and never appreciated the martial values that Roosevelt found so necessary for strong men and strong nations would become, of all things, head of the War Department. One reason Taft accepted was because the Philippines were under its jurisdiction and he could stay involved.

Taft would spend much of his time on assignments that had little to do with the War Department: he became Roosevelt's chief agent, confidant, and troubleshooter in foreign affairs and made several voyages around the world (traveling more than any other cabinet member); supervised both the construction of the Panama Canal and affairs in the Philippines; for a while was the provisional governor of Cuba; and, after the death of Secretary of State John Hay, he acted as secretary of state during the Morocco crisis in March 1905 and took part in the negotiations among France, England, and Germany to resolve it.[66] And there was the politics he would be thrown into. "It seems strange that with an effort to keep out of politics and with my real dislike for it, I should thus be pitched into the middle of it."[67] Nellie was happy; he would be back in Washington with the "bigwigs."

TAFT WOULD SAY IT was the Philippines that put him in the White House.[68] He was wrong. What did it was Theodore Roosevelt's decision to put him there. Roosevelt believed there was no space between how he governed the country for almost eight years and how Taft would in the future. "He and I view public questions exactly alike."[69] Besides, for Roosevelt, Taft was the last Republican standing. Elihu Root, Roosevelt's first choice, was unelectable. Others on the left were too much to the left. None on the right satisfied him. Foraker made his skin crawl. Taft made sense. As the Black Battalion drilled at Fort Reno in the autumn of 1906, Will Taft still wanted to be on the Supreme Court. But he knew Theodore Roosevelt and Nellie Taft dearly wanted him in the White House. He was coming around to them.

After a cabinet meeting one day, Roosevelt asked Taft, Secretary of State Elihu Root, and Postmaster General George B. Cortelyou to stay behind and chat about a vacancy on the Supreme Court and the 1908 election. They ganged up on Taft and told him he "stood the best chance among the Republicans." Roosevelt, realizing he had an ally in Nellie Taft, told Taft he would speak to her. Five days later she was in his office telling him why her husband should not be on the Supreme Court. That morning, Roosevelt had a letter from Taft arguing why he should not be president. The Tafts were a house divided, and Roosevelt knew how to exploit this and get what he and Nellie wanted.

Answering Taft the next day, Roosevelt said he read Taft's letter as not expressing a preference for the Supreme Court over the White House, which, Roosevelt confessed, he had always thought was what Taft wanted. He now realized that "your decided personal preference [is] to continue your *present* work" (author's emphasis), and the dilemma for Taft was whether to stay with it (and finish the work in the Philippines) or go on the Court. That decision, said Roosevelt, "no other man can [decide] for you." A decision about the presidency was another matter, something to think about in the future, but since he had happened to discuss it the previous day with Nellie, "you are the man who is most likely to receive the . . . nomination and . . . have the most chance to succeed." Until then, Roosevelt had an empty seat to fill. If Taft wanted to wait for another chance by not seeking the 1908 nomination, he should keep in mind, "the shadow of the Presidency falls on no man twice."[70]

Roosevelt's cleverness and ability to persuade men to do what he wanted has never been better displayed. He framed the problem for Taft a whole new way by showing it as three choices, not two, and by taking the third, Taft could easily lose both of the other two, one of which was his life's dream. In the letter's last words, Roosevelt piously disclaimed any desire to counsel or influence Taft. "No one can with wisdom advise you."[71]

Not long after this, the Tafts attended dinner at the White House. Roosevelt teased them about the decision as yet unmade. "I am the seventh son of a seventh daughter. I have clairvoyant powers. I see a man weighing 350 pounds. There is something hanging over his head. I cannot make out what it is; it is hanging by a slender thread. At one time it looks like the Presidency—then again it looks like the Chief Justiceship."

"Make it the Presidency," said Mrs. Taft.

"Make it the Chief Justiceship," said her husband.[72]

Despite this wish, Taft was now letting the winds carry him to where Roosevelt and Nellie wanted. But he wasn't quite ready to tell people. In a letter to Colonel William R. Nelson, founder of the *Kansas City Star*, after telling the similarly weight-challenged Nelson of recent dietary success, he wrote, "So far as the Presidential election is concerned, . . . there are a good many reasons which I could explain to you which would militate against [it]."[73] But only a couple of weeks later, he had apparently overcome those reasons, assuring Nelson his presidential hopes had the support of another important Kansan, Senator Chester I. Long.[74]

Having hooked his big fish, Roosevelt could allow some slack in the line connecting them. The following month, the day before the Brownsville shooting, in a "personal" letter to another Kansan, William Allen White, the influential editor of the *Emporia Gazette*, he wrote, "Of course I am not going to try to nominate any man. Personally you know how highly I think of Secretary Taft, but I am not going to take a hand in his nomination, for it is none of my business. I am sure Kansas will like him." Then he added in ink, "He would be an ideal President."[75]

Knowing Nellie Taft suffered a case of the vapors whenever someone else's name was mentioned for 1908, during the 1906 fall campaign he spoke to her glowingly of Charles Evans Hughes's campaign for New York governor, sure she would misunderstand this as a possible endorsement of the New Yorker and get to work on her husband. Sure enough, she told Taft. Never one to push, Taft wrote Roosevelt, "Mrs. Taft said that you might . . . have to support Hughes for the presidency. . . . You know what my feeling has been in respect to the presidency, and can understand that it will not leave the slightest trace of disappointment should your views change and think it wise to make a start in another direction."[76] Roosevelt must have sighed heavily. It was a good thing Will Taft was working on his diet; he would need a lot of pushing.

IN A CHAPTER CALLED "Surrender" in his Taft biography, Henry Pringle wrote that is exactly what Taft did as early as the summer of 1905.[77] It is hard to imagine, nervous as they may have been when occasionally Taft looked to be falling off the wagon, that two people as perceptive as Theodore Roosevelt and Nellie Taft did not see it and start measuring Cornelia's pedestal in Columbus to see if there was room on it for one more jewel.

"This is the true joy in life, the being used for a purpose recognized by yourself as a mighty one; the being thoroughly worn out before you are thrown on the scrap heap."

George Bernard Shaw, preface to
Man and Superman: A Comedy and Philosophy

CHAPTER TEN

TWO SETS OF AFFIDAVITS

THE DIFFERENCES BETWEEN ROOSEVELT and Foraker burst like overripe Ohio buckeye nuts in the spring and summer of 1906. It was bad enough when Foraker was the only Republican senator to vote against Roosevelt's railroad rate-setting Hepburn Act, but it got worse in September when he sent a telegram to Roosevelt cautioning against acting in Cuba on his own. "I do not like Foraker's action at all," Roosevelt wrote Henry Cabot Lodge. "He is a very powerful and very vindictive man. It is possible . . . that he intends to fight me hereafter on every point, good or bad."[1] Their disagreement was more than petulance or personal pique. Foraker's disapproval of Roosevelt acting in Cuba without consulting Congress reflects how uncomfortable he was with Roosevelt's expanded view of the powers of the presidency and is seen in the arguments he made against the discharges of the Brownsville soldiers.[2]

Roosevelt's displeasure with Foraker had been sensed quickly back in Ohio by those who counted most, other politicians. Blood was in Roosevelt's eye and dripping into Ohio's power struggles. The opportunistic Congressman Theodore Burton from Cleveland believed that by antagonizing Roosevelt, especially when he opposed the Hepburn Act, Foraker had committed political suicide, and now "only a 'little shove' was necessary to shove him over the

176

precipice."[3] In an August speech in Cleveland, he spoke of the way Foraker had split himself from Roosevelt's legislative programs and suggested such disloyalty merited only a barely lukewarm endorsement for the 1908 Senate race at the party's state convention in Dayton in September.[4] Foraker was unconcerned and was going to skip Dayton and stay with his family at a rented summer cottage in Sea Bright, New Jersey. But early in September he was alarmed by a warning from an acquaintance in Columbus. "Many of your former friends here have deserted you—some—a few—because of your attitude towards the rate bill, some because of your co-operation with [Senator Charles] Dick [Ohio's other senator], some because they think you are down, some for other reasons. I have also talked with some from other parts of the State, and they describe the situation where they are, in about the same way."[5] Foraker changed his mind and got to Dayton just as the convention was gaveled to order.

Though he was not scheduled to speak, after a very long opening speech by former Ohio governor Myron Herrick (one of the insurgent leaders), cries from the delegates and galleries for a Foraker speech lifted him from his seat and carried him to the podium. Speaking with heat that night, he incinerated Burton's scheme. Delegates saw him as the old Foraker, eloquent and aggressive, and his name was "on everybody's tongue."[6] There were demands that the convention "adopt a resolution then and there endorsing [him] for the Presidency in 1908," but using a technicality that made such a resolution inappropriate, Foraker discouraged it. He enjoyed the success of the moment and heard from, among others, Vice President Charles Fairbanks, his longtime friend from their days at Ohio Wesleyan University. Fairbanks was thinking there might be a way he and his family could move into the White House when the Roosevelts moved out and therefore was careful to exclude himself when he wrote, "I found Mrs. Fairbanks and [son] Freddie had saved your speech which they read with delight. They most heartily rejoice in your triumph."[7] Foraker's success was not the end of it. He may have foiled Burton and the insurgents at the convention, but they and President Roosevelt would not stop working against him, and Foraker knew it. He also knew Roosevelt had twisted Burton's arm to run for Cleveland mayor the following year to pump up his résumé for his shot at Foraker's Senate seat. Further presidential plotting against him could be expected on behalf of Burton and Taft. Foraker could consider the capriciousness of timing. A person's life moves on parallel yet unsynchronized tracks. An opportunity can be there when one is unprepared for it but gone when he is ready. Proffered help and assistance could not be tucked away in a political piggy bank and saved. As a younger man, he had many friends. Now they were not there for him. He had been a man with a future. A few quick years later, he had only a past and maybe not even a present. Could his seasoning and skills bring him to that high office he turned down when it was offered eighteen years earlier? Could they keep him in the Senate? The politician in him controlled his thoughts. There were two years until both elections; he had time to get control of the situation. But for which office? Taft was, for the moment, his only competition for the White House, and unless Taft held to his Supreme Court dream he would be hard to derail. Should he settle instead on returning to the Senate, he had an ever more crowded field to contend with, and they were still sharpening their knives after Dayton. What—or who—could hold them at bay? There was only one man. Theodore Roosevelt. The same man who wanted Taft to succeed himself in the White House and Burton to succeed Foraker in the Senate. But why would Roosevelt help Foraker? The answer was because it would help Taft too. Roosevelt would cast off Burton if necessary to help Taft. If Foraker put up a good fight for the presidential nomination, Roosevelt might accept his decision to stay in the Senate if he stepped aside for Taft. It would ensure Taft's nomination by clearing Foraker off of the road before the nominating convention. It was something to think about.

SEPTEMBER MAY HAVE ENDED with a hopeful sign for Joseph Foraker, but for John Milholland it was a time of continuing anguish over race in America. On the day Foraker spoke so well at the Ohio Republican convention, Milholland told his diary that on "the Negro question . . . The Republican Party is morally dead—almost."[8]

The tinkering and inventive Milholland had developed a system for moving mail through large cities by a system of underground pneumatic tubes. In 1897 he signed a contract with the Post Office to operate a system in New York that eventually would run throughout the city.[9] His business expanded to Philadelphia and elsewhere. With this success, he was able to turn to what became his life's work. "My time has come at last to lead this Crusade for the Negroes' Political and Civil Rights . . . the Issue, the Supreme Moral Issue of the Hour in this Republic. Oh let me be free, Good Lord, that I may free others!"[10] As his vehicle for this struggle, he founded the Constitution League in 1903 to "attack disfranchisement, peonage, and mob violence by means of court action, legislation and propaganda" and to reject Booker T. Washington and his program.[11]

He had always been a Republican, but by the early 1890s Milholland was fed up with its "machine politics" and set about restructuring the party in New York. It was inevitable he would fail and just as inevitable he would cross paths with Theodore Roosevelt. In 1892, as supervising immigrant inspector at Ellis Island, Milholland tangled with Cornelius Bliss, the machine's leader in the Eleventh Assembly District, and learned a thing or two about how things were done in New York. Bliss took their dispute to Washington, DC, and got Milholland fired from his plum patronage post. Unaware still just how the system operated, Milholland compounded his blunder with Bliss and appealed his dismissal to the Civil Service Commission headed by Theodore Roosevelt. "It will give [Roosevelt] an opportunity to make one of his thorough investigations to see if there has been a violation of the spirit and letter of the civil-service law in the Eleventh District," the *New York Times* predicted.[12] Roosevelt disappointed Milholland and the *New York Times* by expertly dodging the problem. The chastened John Milholland went back to editing the *New York Tribune* and wondering about Theodore Roosevelt.

In 1894, still knee-deep in efforts to correct inadequacies in the Republican party, Milholland was elected president of the New York County Republican Committee. Elected with him as the committee's recording secretary was a black man, T. Thomas Fortune, the editor of the *New York Age*. Fortune was as militant then as W. E. B. Du Bois would become. As early as 1882 he argued before the Colored Press Association that the Republican Party was ignoring the principles of Lincoln and abandoning Southern blacks to their fate in the post-Reconstruction South. Milholland's association with Fortune exposed him to this sort of thinking and shook his faith in the Republicans' ability or desire to help blacks in any meaningful way.[13]

Originally respectful to Booker T. Washington, Milholland became disillusioned with him for selling out his own race by accepting a quasi-permanent denial of Negro equality and voting rights. "You will pardon me from saying it, the most enlightened sentiment is not reflected in the course you have marked out," he wrote Washington.[14] In 1906, before the shooting in Brownsville, his Constitution League held a meeting at Cooper Union in New York to "protest against disfranchisement of the negro in the South." Milholland reached beyond his own organization for the conference's speakers, and among others he asked Kelly Thomas of Howard University and W. E. B. Du Bois, then of Atlanta University. There was no one from Booker T. Washington's Tuskegee Machine.[15] With Brownsville, their break became final.[16]

Milholland's break with Theodore Roosevelt came much earlier, in 1896. It was an election year, and Milholland was threatening to bolt the party, thereby jeopardizing the Empire State's big basket of electoral votes. Theodore Roosevelt, now New York City police commissioner, tried to stay out of it but could not shield himself from Milholland's hostility. Milholland's irritation with the party had to do with fraudulent voter enrollment, but Roosevelt took it personally and saw it as something between Milholland and him. He wrote Lodge that he had broken with Milholland over this intraparty squabble, which he characterized as "a very ugly fight. Of course it began when I refused to give [the *Tribune* the police department] advertising, and let it out by open bidding."[17] In time Theodore Roosevelt came to personify for Milholland the denial of human and constitutional rights, the debasement, and the humiliation black Americans had to deal with. On October 10, 1906, his diary condemned Roosevelt for interrupting a meeting at the White House to shake hands with Sheriff Joseph F. Shipp of Chattanooga, who had been charged with contempt of the US Supreme Court for his complicity in the lynching of a black man whose appeal had been before the Court. When in Washington for the Court's oral argument, he and the others were invited to the White House to meet President Roosevelt, and in his diary Milholland wrote, "Roosevelt shocked me into profanity by shaking hands with the 27 Chattanooga Lynchers yesterday."[18]

The Brownsville Incident was one more Roosevelt outrage. Milholland resolved to do something about it.

UNLIKE JOHN MILHOLLAND, FOR Joseph Foraker the Brownsville shooting initially held little interest. Reading about it in the newspapers he was sure, like almost everyone else in the country, that the soldiers had done it and claimed to not give it further thought. About three weeks before President Roosevelt ordered the discharges, Foraker decried the lack of black progress since the Civil War. "In every war through which the country has passed, so far as we have permitted them to do so, [the black man has] borne an honorable part." Referring to the possibility of troops going to Cuba to protect the tottering government there, Foraker said, "It is even more important to protect [black] Americans in America." Despite his allusion to black soldiers, he neither mentioned Brownsville nor made any connection to it.[19]

Then came Special Orders No. 266, and the protests put Brownsville back on the front page. Negroes, sensitized to injustice after thirty years of Jim Crow discrimination, were united in anger. Almost exclusively Republican, they directed it at President Roosevelt. Since the convention in Dayton two months earlier and Roosevelt's unseen presence there, Foraker had been seeking something that might sap Roosevelt's influence on his 1908 prospects. He gave Brownsville a second look. The discharges seemed harsh; it was improbable every man in the regiment could have been involved, and none had been convicted or even charged with anything. This could be what he was looking for.

In his memoirs, Foraker declared that his change from uninterested observer to crusader for the soldiers was sparked by a righteous anger over their treatment. At the time, the press and politicians, including President Roosevelt, saw a more pragmatic impulse: "[Foraker's] own presidential aspirations."[20] Brownsville historians accept both reasons.[21] A narrative of the Brownsville incident is incomplete and meaningless without looking into Foraker's motives. Was he a sincere advocate for the soldiers or a determined politician out for himself? Or both?

What we know about his turnaround comes almost exclusively from his and his wife's respective memoirs. Julia's *I Would Live It Again*, written a quarter of a century later by an eighty-four-year-old widow, is consumed by another Brownsville injustice, what it did to her husband's career and life. This pain was so fresh in her mind and so important to what she wanted to say that she began her memoirs with Brownsville and President Roosevelt's intention to use Brownsville to destroy Joseph Foraker, as if everything else in her life was the backstory.[22] She agreed it was the soldiers' "harsh punishment" that got his attention.[23] Foraker called it "summary punishment" and "drastic punishment," and because of it he "read with some care the testimony on which the President acted."[24] It was "flimsy, unreliable and insufficient and untruthful." He spent hours and hours studying "a thickening jungle of newspapers, clippings, letters, and calf-bound books," as he "gave himself to Brownsville that November." He reacted to what he so carefully read by speaking softly to himself as unexpected revelations overcame him, and Julia remembered what she overheard. "No, no, that isn't true. . . . That doesn't follow at all. . . . No, no, there is nothing in that."[25]

According to Foraker, he may have reconsidered the situation when he examined the testimony, but that was not why he got involved with the soldiers. It was affidavits from the soldiers that he claimed "*caused me to doubt their guilt and to conclude it was my duty . . . to cause an investigation*" so the guilty could be discovered and punished and the innocent absolved (author's emphasis).[26] He further claimed he had learned of these affidavits when they were "*announced by the newspapers* and that in them every man in the battalion positively and unqualifiedly denied guilt, or any knowledge of guilt." The only newspaper reports about affidavits that Foraker could have been referring to were on November 25, 1906.[27] He would ask for the investigation on December 3, only eight days later (which included the long Thanksgiving holiday weekend). Not much time for him to prepare. *Unless he knew before then the affidavits would be forthcoming.*

THE NEW YORK TIMES' report of the affidavits said the black lawyer Gilchrist Stewart obtained them from the soldiers at Fort Reno. Stewart was a real estate dealer, lawyer, and reform Republican. Theodore Roosevelt thought him a "cheap and noisome agitator."[28] Booker T. Washington saw him as untrustworthy, a danger to the Tuskegee Machine, and a man to be watched closely. Washington's man in New York warned him that Stewart was trying to lure the local Colored Republican Clubs to the Constitution League (and away from Roosevelt and Washington) and added that Stewart was "informing both groups on each other's moves during the [Brownsville] investigation."[29] In other words, Stewart worked with Milholland but was a double agent.

Stewart went to Oklahoma to get the soldiers' affidavits because of Roosevelt's response to the New York County Republican Committee's rebuke. Stewart had cabled the president in Panama about it and in his wire concluded, "Developments and new facts warrant. Ask immediate suspension order." Unlike the Taft wire after the meeting with Mary Church Terrell, Stewart's got to Panama before Roosevelt left for home, and Roosevelt was able to reply. "Unless facts are shown to be false, the order will, under no circumstances, be revoked, and I shall not for one moment consider suspending it on a simple allegation that there are new facts until these new facts are laid before me. Inform any persons having new facts to have them in shape to *lay before me at once on my return*, and I will then consider whether or not any further action by me is called for" (author's emphasis).[30] Like men hearing only what they want to hear, Milholland and Stewart read this as good news. Roosevelt was willing to listen. Two days later, on November 18—one week before the affidavits were mentioned in the newspapers—Stewart left for Fort Reno to get them and to give Roosevelt his "new facts."

Roosevelt said he wanted them "at once" upon his return to Washington, but Stewart first missed and then disregarded this deadline. Stewart took two more days to have anything at all for Roosevelt, and that was nothing more than a promise to deliver *synopses* of "the affidavits [of the soldiers] and statements of officers by Saturday, December 1."[31]

That would be two days before Congress reconvened, December 3, 1906, a date circled on Senator Foraker's calendar. It seems more likely Foraker, a man addicted to thorough preparation, made his decision before the November 25 newspaper articles about the affidavits and without seeing them, because Stewart did not have them as late as December 1, the date he promised Roosevelt synopses, not the affidavits themselves. Foraker jumped into the Brownsville Incident when he knew soldiers' sworn denials of guilt would be forthcoming. He knew this because either Stewart or someone else with the Constitution League must have alerted him.

There is evidence this is what happened. Foraker and the Constitution League had worked together before, most recently on the Hepburn Act. And there is evidence they already were working together on Brownsville.[32] He and its secretary Andrew Humphrey had been exchanging letters and information. On November 25, Humphrey asked Foraker to send him a copy of the War Department pamphlet, "The Affray at Brownsville." Four days later he told Humphrey he had been "looking it over with some care [and in it] there are some damaging circumstances, but I think all can be accounted for consistently with the entire innocence of the men, *but without positive proof to overthrow these circumstances I hardly know what course should be taken*" (author's emphasis).[33] Positive proof was what Roosevelt had demanded from Gilchrist Stewart, and Foraker was telling Stewart's colleague at the Constitution League he would need it too.[34] Foraker's eye also was on the calendar, and with the Senate convening on December 3, he needed the proof fast.

NOVEMBER 29 WAS THANKSGIVING. The White House visitor log for the day shows no meetings or callers, as President and Mrs. Roosevelt and their family enjoyed the holiday. Two days earlier the president had attended to thank-you notes to Horace Voss of Westerly, Rhode Island, for his gift of the Thanksgiving turkey ("The White House Thanksgiving would be not quite regular without your turkey.") and Senator John Kean for the roast pig he presented to the First Family.[35]

Before sitting down at the table to enjoy them, he looked over the telegram from Gilchrist Stewart that arrived earlier that day. Four pages long, it set out what Stewart said he had learned in his investigation and promised affidavits to support his conclusions, which he would present in two days at the White House. This was hardly the "new facts" Roosevelt had demanded. Worse, it was inexcusably sloppy. It incorrectly referred to the soldiers as members of the Third Battalion (it was the *First* Battalion), said a customs inspector knocked Private James Reed into the Rio Grande (there was no Private James Reed; there was a Private James *Reid* in Company B, but the dunked soldier was Private Oscar Reid of Company C), more than once misspelled as "Howd" the last name of Company D's Private Joseph Howard, and thought Private Frank Lipscomb was Private Liscomb. Stewart proffered as new evidence soldier and officer testimony already known along with the inferences he drew from it. It was woefully, almost embarrassingly, inadequate, and nothing at all what Roosevelt told him he wanted.[36] If this was all the Constitution League and Stewart had, Roosevelt knew he had nothing to worry about. Stewart's investigation could be swatted away. But Roosevelt still had to face down the Senate.

His eye lingered over the synopses of the affidavits. An affidavit is a written statement made under oath. Because any false statement in it may give rise to a criminal charge of perjury, it has greater weight in a court of law and a greater impact in general on anyone reading it. To effectively counter what it says, one needs at the least a statement also made under oath, that is, another affidavit. Roosevelt understood this and reached for a sheet of paper and wrote a memorandum to Taft. It was short and emphatically insistent. "We must not fail to have a full set of affidavits in the Brownsville matter *when Congress meets* [author's emphasis]. *Very important* [Roosevelt's emphasis]."[37] Roosevelt was not lulled into inaction by Stewart's ineffective efforts. He was aware of the situation, his opponents' advantages, and what he had to do to confront them, and he was planning his own course of action. He was only starting.

The Senate would convene four days later.

"[Booker T. Washington's] doctrine has tended to make the whites, North and South, shift the burden of the Negro Problem to the Negro's Shoulders . . . when in fact the burden belongs to the nation."

W. E. B. Du Bois, "Of Mr. Washington and Others," in *The Souls of Black Folk*

CHAPTER ELEVEN

BETWEEN TWO STOOLS

ON DECEMBER 6, THE day the Senate voted to accept both the Penrose and Foraker resolutions, Mary Church Terrell wrote to First Sergeant Mingo Sanders on Washington, DC, Board of Education stationery, asking him to come to her home (she helpfully penned the address beside her printed name on the letterhead).[1] Realizing Sanders might not know who she was, Terrell told him of her role in Secretary of War Taft's suspension of the discharges. When they met, it seemed to her that his countenance was as "unruffled and as free from any trace of melancholy as is one of Raphael's angels" and his attitude as "serene and mild as a May morning." He told her it was because "I know that I am innocent and I am sure the other fellow is just as innocent as I am."

As a young boy watching a military parade in Charleston, South Carolina—the prettiest sight he had ever seen—"I made up my mind right then and there that I would be a soldier some day."[2] It was a good choice of career for a black man not well educated and with few job skills. Sanders's entire career was with the Twenty-Fifth Infantry, from his first duty assignment at Fort Snelling, Minnesota, to Cuba, the Philippines, and finally Fort Brown. He saw combat overseas, tangled with Indians in the West, endured boredom at garrison duty, and along the way trained other soldiers in the ways of the army. Mrs. Terrell wrote, "He has been a veritable father to the young men of his race, who have enlisted in the army."[3] But he was not able to protect his family of soldiers—or himself—from Special Orders No. 266.

WHEN W. E. B. DU BOIS predicted that the "problem of the twentieth century is the problem of the color line," he added it was "the question as to how far differences of race are going to be made . . . the basis of denying . . . the opportunities and privileges of modern civilization."[4] When he said this in 1900 he had not yet fully embraced agitation and confrontation as the way to deal with this problem. Nor was he persuaded that Booker T. Washington's answer was wrong. But he was getting there, and when he did, the two men would lead the opposing sides within the Negro community. The fracture was called *factionalism*. As already explained, Booker T. Washington believed his accommodation might not solve the problem, but for the time being it kept things from getting worse and over time would make them better. W. E. B. Du Bois scoffed at this. Things *were* getting worse, much worse, and what Washington offered was "hypocritical compromise."[5] Their split became bitter and personal and played itself out over Brownsville.

Washington and Du Bois split on three basic issues. Both knew education was the path to full racial equality, but they differed on what kind. From his own experience Washington was sure one that trained the race for entry-level jobs and developed personal habits, everything from personal hygiene to a strong work ethic, was the answer. Du Bois agreed, but Negroes with greater talent and intelligence, who made up what he called "The Talented Tenth," were entitled to more. They should be able to go to college and beyond and become professionals, scholars, and people of letters and science. They would use advanced education for the benefit of the entire race.[6]

Washington and Du Bois also disagreed on the necessity for equal political rights and social integration for blacks. In his Atlanta Compromise of 1895 Washington hinted that the right to vote and participate in American democracy be shelved until his industrial education developed black men and women into more useful citizens. In return for these concessions, whites would permit the advance of black Americans and allow them the security of a peaceful life. When whites in both the North and the South cheered these ideas and accepted Washington as the race's leader, he thought they were agreeing to the bargain. But in practice they accepted only what the Negro gave up. When Washington realized this, it was too late for him to change. He was by then a "player" and wanted to stay in the game. Du Bois, always the outsider, saw from the beginning whites would not give in.

The third issue was how to deal with whites. Washington was not one to push ahead with sharp elbows. It would only antagonize whites and without white support, the race would go nowhere. Du Bois saw the necessity of support of whites as an illusion. Equal rights should be demanded now and white sensitivity be damned.

One man was willing to accommodate himself to reality and be patient. The other would confront the reality and demand the vision right now.[7]

DU BOIS WAS A sociologist, a teacher, and a writer, formally educated at Fisk University, Harvard University (both schools awarded him bachelor of arts degrees), the University of Berlin, and again at Harvard for his doctorate. Informally he acquired an education in racial denials from experiencing them. Fortified by both educations, he decided to topple Washington.

He was born into what was for that era the integrated society of Great Barrington, Massachusetts.[8] His grandfather Alexander Du Bois was the son of the white James Du Bois, whose family in New York had remained loyal to the British crown and was rewarded with property in the Bahamas. James ran the family's plantation there and acquired a black mistress, with whom he had Alexander. He took Alexander and a brother back to New York for schooling, and after his death the white Du Bois family disowned them. Alexander's son Alfred, who like his father could have passed for white, was a rootless, wandering man, who tried and failed at many low-rung occupations. He happened to be in the Berkshires, where he met and married Mary Burghardt, whom their son William Edward Burghardt Du Bois described as "dark shining bronze."[9]

Du Bois's first awareness of racial differences came when he was ten years old. He and his white playmates decided to exchange visiting cards, as they saw adults doing, and one girl "refused my card—refused it peremptorily. . . . Then it dawned upon me with a certain suddenness that I was different from the others . . . shut out from their world by a vast veil."[10] He progressed from this realization of being different to seeing the harm it caused Negroes, to believing there was little to be done, to understanding something needed to be done, to thinking as did Booker T. Washington that gentle persuasion might work, and to putting his faith in the Tuskegean. For a while. When he got to know Washington better, he did not like him. When he understood what he saw as the failure of Washington's accommodation idea, he liked him even less, and he broke away to clear the road ahead by agitation.

IN 1899, WHILE DU Bois taught sociology at Atlanta University, he and Washington worked together to defeat a bill in the Georgia legislature that would make it impossible for Negroes to vote. On paper, its qualifications for voting applied to blacks and whites, but the exceptions, most notoriously the "grandfather clause" that waived these barriers for Georgians whose grandfathers had been qualified voters, applied unfairly to blacks whose grandfathers had been slaves and therefore were unable to vote. In a petition to the Georgia legislature Du Bois pointed to this and other tricks hidden in the manipulations of other provisions and lobbied for its defeat.[11] Washington, working in tandem with him, gave an interview to the *Atlanta Constitution* and made the same arguments. The legislation was defeated (with help from upper-class whites fearful of a deluge of newly enfranchised white "redneck" voters), and the effort reinforced in Du Bois the need for continuous efforts just to keep white racism at bay and the futility of making any progress at all by an accommodation with it.

Washington meanwhile thought they had worked well together on this project and decided to offer Du Bois a position at Tuskegee. But it ran aground on clashing egos and misunderstandings, and the opportunity to talk about their different ideas and shake off their mutual suspicions and dislikes was lost.[12]

Two years later, however, when Du Bois was upset that the Rhodes Scholarship Foundation would not include Atlanta University in its scholarship conference for Georgia colleges, he turned to Tuskegee for help. Washington went to bat and wrote Du Bois that black college men would be considered in the future.[13] But though they were cordial with each other and again worked well together, Du Bois remained uneasy over Washington's insistence on farming and industrial education for Negroes and his indifference to higher education for the race. He also resented the Tuskegee Machine's political machinations that Washington kept to and for himself. Du Bois wasn't the only one.

CENTERED IN BOSTON WAS an informal group of "talented tenth" blacks already combative with Booker T. Washington. It was known as the Boston Radicals, and its leader was William Monroe Trotter, a graduate of Harvard and the first black elected to the honor society Phi Beta Kappa there. Trotter sneered at Washington's pretensions as an educator. He agreed with Du Bois that they were only a cover for his acquisition of political power, which he used for his own ends primarily and the good of others only as an afterthought and when necessary to preserve his position. Washington and his Tuskegee Machine were no better than the political bosses and their rings in Northern cities, and the machine's national presence through President Roosevelt made things worse. In 1901 Trotter established the *Boston Guardian*. From its beginning it was bitterly anti-Washington, and Trotter made no apologies for what his newspaper said and how it said it.[14] Its "articles, editorials and cartoons flayed Washington with his pose of morality."[15] Washington was called a coward and a self-seeker, even a liar. One cartoon showed him as "Mammy" at an ironing board, taking on too many tasks and doing none of them well.[16]

At the 1903 meeting of the National Afro-American Council in

Louisville, Trotter led the chorus of complaints against Washington. The Council had been formed as an umbrella for civil rights organizations, and its politics embraced them all. One of the council's founders was T. Thomas Fortune, and he helped shade its positions to accommodate Washington. At its first meeting in Rochester, New York, in 1898 the speakers had included Ida B. Wells Barnett, journalist and early civil rights leader; Frederick Douglass, former slave, abolitionist, writer, and black leader; Professor Kelly Miller of Howard University; Mary Church Terrell; and Booker T. Washington (to discuss industrial education).[17] As these names and Du Bois's presence suggest, there was a range of black leadership, but it tilted to the Bookerites.[18] They controlled the meeting that year in Louisville and outfoxed Trotter's plan to have it criticize Theodore Roosevelt and separate itself from him when he maneuvered the council into passing a resolution endorsing Roosevelt. Trotter's anger swelled.

Later that month, Washington came to Boston to speak at its African Methodist Episcopal Church. Trotter had taunted him in the past as a coward who was afraid to show up in Boston because of its nest of radicals. Washington could not ignore this dare. Preliminary speakers T. Thomas Fortune and William H. Lewis, both members in good standing of the Tuskegee Machine, were heckled and booed whenever they mentioned Washington's name.[19] By the time his turn came to speak, the mood in the church was ugly. He got as far as his beginning words when pandemonium erupted. "We don't want to hear you, Booker T. Washington. We don't like you," the Boston Radicals shouted at him. Police were called in to calm things down, but their success was only temporary. Trotter, to embarrass Washington and to show him to be inconsequential, stood on a chair and in a high, shrill voice shouted damning questions he never intended Washington to answer. He called Washington's leadership a calamity. Things got completely out of hand. Men were yelling and hissing at Washington, stink bombs were set off, and one man was slashed with a razor and had to be taken to the hospital. Trotter used his umbrella as a weapon, and his sister Maude did same with a hat pin. Back in came the police, this time with a vengeance. Trotter and his sister were arrested, and he would stay in jail for a month.[20] (What the Tuskegee Machine could do was made even clearer to Trotter after the Boston Riot. It made sure he stayed in jail for the full sentence.)

It was Trotter's public confrontation with Washington in Boston that first exposed whites and many blacks to black factionalism. Du Bois himself in his autobiography credits Trotter's jailing after the Boston Riot as the reason he sent out "a call to a few selected persons" to organize the first Niagara Movement conference in July 1905.[21] Du Bois knew the Tuskegee Machine's strength was real and to oppose it he had to create a counterbalancing and more confrontational organization. The Niagara Movement was to be it. With a program of confrontation, Du Bois and his supporters thought they had the means to tear away the veil of trust between Negroes and Booker T. Washington, and by extension, to the Republican Party and President Theodore Roosevelt.[22]

A year later, Brownsville would help them.[23]

ON FRIDAY, AUGUST 15, 1906, the second day after the Brownsville shooting that Du Bois no doubt was aware of by then, he addressed the second annual meeting of the Niagara Movement at Harpers Ferry, West Virginia, and said, "We will not be satisfied to take one jot or tittle less than our full manhood rights. We claim for ourselves every single right that belongs to a freeborn American, political, civil, and social; and until we get these rights we will never cease to protest and assail the ears of America."[24] He was by then an agitator.[25] The following March in the *Voice of the Negro* magazine, referring to himself he wrote, "Here then comes the agitator. He is the herald—he is the prophet—he is the man who says to the world: There are evils which you do not know but which I know and you must listen to them."[26]

Only three years earlier he had penned "Of Mr. Booker T. Washington and Others" and signaled if not the end of Washington's near monarchy, then its tarnished crown. The two men knew and took the measure of each other. Washington recognized the genius in Du Bois but never confused merit with reality.[27] The reality for Du Bois was that Washington was too much the icon of black leadership to chuck aside. But his angry rhetoric and growing impatience with the glacial pace of change could, with his allies, make life difficult for Washington and chip at his leadership pedestal.[28] Brownsville and Washington's defense of Roosevelt would help Du Bois tip it over and ultimately change the direction of the civil rights movement.

TO A POINT, BOTH Washington and Du Bois saw Brownsville the same way. Both believed the shooters were soldiers, and they agreed those men and those others who helped them, either directly or by keeping quiet, deserved severe punishment. But because of the factionalism in the Negro movement, they had opposite motivations: Washington to prove Roosevelt was right; Du Bois to prove Roosevelt wrong. Washington and Du Bois assembled their alliances and sharpened their knives, and each prepared his plans to thwart the other. For each of them and the nation, the consequences were ordained.

BEFORE LEAVING DU BOIS'S turn to confrontation with Washington and seeing it only as either the result of his disappointment with the bare (if any) gains realized from accommodation or his tendency to think radically when Washington sized things up realistically, it is well to consider a personal story.

His son, Burghardt, died in Atlanta when he was eighteen months old. The limitless love a father has for a son, sharing with him the excitement and glee of seeing the world for the first time through his son's eyes (and rediscovering it for himself), and feeling pride as he sees the boy grow, was now gone from Du Bois's life forever. The boy died of diphtheria when his father, frantic with fear and dread, was unable to find a nearby white doctor who would treat him and ran out of time when he sought one of the black doctors who lived too far away in the neighborhood Atlantans today call "Sweet Auburn." He would write of its devastation as a chapter in *The Souls of Black Folk*, and in his grief the father would try make his son's "life and death monumentally symbolic" for himself and the race.[29] He begins the chapter titled "Of the Passing of the First Born" with a stanza from the poem "Itylus" by Algernon Charles Swinburne:

O sister, sister, thy first-begotten
The hands that cling and the feet that follow,
The voice of the child's blood crying yet,
Who hath remembered me? who hath forgotten?
Thou hast forgotten, O summer swallow,
But the world shall end when I forget.[30]

For Du Bois, there were many things he could not forget. His son, Burghardt. And injustice.

WHEN MINGO SANDERS MET Mary Church Terrell in Washington, he had come to the nation's capital on a mission. He wanted to get back into the army. He wanted justice.

"This has been an extraordinary week. [I] think we have done some good work not for the soldiers alone, not for the Republic, for Justice."

John Milholland,
diary entry for December 6, 1906

CHAPTER TWELVE

GRIM-VISAGED WAR

THE WEEK BEGAN PRECISELY at noon on Monday, December 3, when the US Senate was called into session by its presiding officer, Vice President Charles W. Fairbanks. It was customary on the first day of a new session to recess quickly after some brief and perfunctory business. Normally it would receive President Roosevelt's nominees for federal positions, one of whom today was, as he promised Jewish New Yorkers, Oscar Straus as secretary of commerce and labor and the first Jewish member of the cabinet. The secretary of the navy (then a cabinet department) Charles J. Bonaparte was posted to the Justice Department to replace as attorney-general (as it was then hyphenated) William Moody; Moody would succeed Justice Henry Brown on the Supreme Court (Secretary of War Taft was offered the seat first but turned it down because he was running for president). James R. Garfield (whose father James A. Garfield was handed the 1888 Republican presidential nomination when Joseph Foraker said no to it in his hotel room in Chicago) was nominated to replace Ethan Allen Hitchcock as secretary of the interior. Hitchcock's stern and often-unyielding leadership there antagonized too many important Republicans, especially Senator Francis E. Warren of Wyoming, chairman of the Senate Military Affairs Committee. Getting Hitchcock out of his hair was not the only good news Senator Warren received that day; Roosevelt asked the Senate to approve the promotion of his son-in-law, army Captain John J. Pershing, to brigadier general, skipping three ranks. For his old position as civil-service commissioner, Roosevelt selected John A. McIlhenny, a hunting buddy and, most important for Roosevelt, a former Rough Rider. (More important possibly for later generations, McIlhenny's family made Tabasco brand Original Red Sauce a part of the American diet.) Ernest A. Garlington, who had recommended discharging the soldiers for what he saw as their conspiracy of silence, was to be formally approved as the army's inspector-general and promoted to brigadier general.[1]

These presidential appointments, however, had to wait when, senators barely back in their seats after Reverend Edward Everett Hale's invocation, Pennsylvania senator Boies E. Penrose came to his feet. Addressing Vice President Fairbanks in his role as president of the Senate, he called out, "Mr. President. I submit a resolution asking for certain information, and if that is not out of order I would ask for its present consideration."[2]

AS PART OF ITS constitutional responsibility to pass legislation, Congress has the right to investigate why new laws may be needed, existing laws changed or repealed, and just about anything and anyone else it has an interest in. This goes double for the Senate, which often serves as a check on executive authority. A treaty agreed to by the administration has no effect unless the Senate ratifies it. A selection for the US Supreme Court must be blessed by it. As the nine-page-long list of appointments presented to the Senate on December 3 showed, other appointments for positions as high as federal judges and not quite as high (though probably harder working) as surgeons in the Public Health Service had to be approved by this most august body, the US Senate. The Senate considers itself the "upper house" of Congress, which for the Senate means the only important house. The biographer and historian Robert Caro has written that to make the Senate stand for all time, our Founding Fathers made it very strong.[3] They also made even the president occasionally dependent on it and fearful of what it could do.

The Senate is where Roosevelt expected any potentially wor-risome attack on Brownsville to come from. He knew all about Senator Foraker's preparation.[4] With his thoroughness and elo-quence, Foraker could capture the Senate's attention and persuade it to take the one step Roosevelt most feared—a formal Senate investigation of Brownsville. There was no telling where it might lead, what dragon's teeth it might sow, what consequences Roos-evelt's enemies might reap.

His first defense would be to argue his order discharging the soldiers was issued as commander in chief, and this made it practi-cally untouchable, so why waste time questioning it? If this failed, and he expected it might, he could try to limit the scope of the Sen-ate's inquiry with a mandate so limited and a reach so short, the investigation would, as Theodore Roosevelt the boxer might say, be unable to lay a glove on him. He therefore had to preempt Foraker by asking for a resolution in a way better suited to defending himself. He would have his own resolution, one more to his liking, intro-duced by a cooperating senator, and try to get it approved in place of Foraker's.

THE PREVIOUS WEDNESDAY, THE day before Thanksgiving, Roosevelt met at the White House with Pennsylvania's "Boss" Penrose, one of the most colorful "scoundrels of American politics," or less gen-erously, "among the most unscrupulous senators."[5] He was from Philadelphia, where, so said Tammany Hall's George Washington Plunkett from New York, politicians plundered the public with great daring. "The Philadelphians ain't satisfied with robbing the bank of all its gold and paper money. They stay and pick up the nickels and pennies. Why, I remember . . . a Republican superintendent of the Philadelphia almshouse stole the zinc roof off the buildin' and sold it for junk. That was carrying things to excess."[6]

Excess was how Penrose defined himself. Even physically. Weighing 350 pounds and standing six feet, four inches, he had extra-size furniture made for home and office. When Pennsylva-nia's other senator, the pint-sized Philander Chase Knox, came to Penrose's office he had to dangle his legs over the edge of the chair, to Penrose's great enjoyment.[7] Penrose gained his gargantuan girth by indulging his enormous appetite. A foolish bettor whose appetite was then legendary wagered Penrose that he could not eat more oysters and drink more bourbon. Penrose started off with three dozen oysters and a bottle of Old Crow bourbon and did not stop eating and drinking until the other man had to be hospitalized.[8] For breakfast he could eat a dozen eggs and a seven-pound steak as he drank a quart of coffee. He got so overweight he could not fit into seats in movie houses, so he bought his own $3,000 projector for his Washington apartment. The first time he turned it on, it blew out the building's electrical system. He had the power company dig up the street, lay a special cable, and extend it up the building's side and into his apartment. He paid the cost himself.[9]

His father, Dr. Richard Alexander Fullerton Penrose, was a prominent physician and a professor of medicine at the University of Pennsylvania. His brother Charles also was a physician, and his brother Spencer a businessman, entrepreneur, and philanthropist in Colorado Springs (he financed development of the Broadmoor Hotel). A very bright man, Boies graduated from Harvard second in his class in 1881. (Theodore Roosevelt, overlapping three years with him, graduated a year earlier and was twenty-first in his class.[10]) He remained in Cambridge to get his law degree. "Privately, he surrounded himself with books on history, biography, economics, philosophy, and psychology. He was fond of reading the classics in the original Latin. Like Roosevelt, he enjoyed the outdoors; unlike Roosevelt, they were only for looking at while being motored in his car, where he might talk about the birds and trees he saw. He prided himself on knowing all the bird species of Pennsylvania."[11] Theodore Roosevelt admitted, "Penrose was better informed about the flora and fauna of this part of the United States than any other man in public life," and then added, "except me."[12] Penrose would get out of the car to hunt, an activity he loved, but none of that "small" game, such as moose, deer, or caribou (such a hunter, he said, "would shoot a cow and call it sport"); for him the only worthwhile quarry was a grizzly bear. On one hunt in the Wyoming Tetons with his brother Charles, they stumbled onto a grizzly and her two cubs.

When Charles killed one cub, the enraged mother charged him; he managed to get a shot into her, but in her death throes, she smashed one of his arms, broke some of his ribs, and almost severed a leg. Boies, ignoring the guide's insistence he could not carry Charles out of the woods to safety, did just that through forests until then penetrated only by Indians, and in three days he delivered his bandaged brother to the Mayo Clinic.

PENROSE CLAIMED HE HELPED make Roosevelt vice president in 1900.[13] He told despairing New York boss Senator Tom Platt, at the end of his rope trying to get Roosevelt out of New York and out of his hair, "I went to college with Theodore. I know Theodore very well. If you can get enough people for him hollering to take the job—common people, mind you, not nice people—he'll insist on being Vice-President. Just tell Theodore that the people need him in Washington and then start people out West writing to him begging him to take it. I've known Theodore a long time."[14] Platt took this advice, and that helped persuade Roosevelt to accept the nomination.

As Penrose said, he and Theodore knew each other a long time. Neither man could stand the other, but political to their cores, they could deal with each other when they had to. On November 5, the day before voters went to the polls, they had met at the White House to discuss the campaign. To the *Washington Herald*, Penrose said the meeting was about "several departmental matters,"[15] but to the *New York Tribune*, he was more forthcoming. "The President is in hearty sympathy with us [in Pennsylvania], and I see no reason to fear the result."[16] But he must have been biting his polished fingernails down to the first knuckle over the election. A fusion of Democrats and independent Republicans running against his slate of machine candidates throughout the state threatened to end his rule there. Roosevelt was worried, but not about the same thing. He needed a solid Republican delegation in the new Congress to help push his legislative program. Penrose had little interest in either Roosevelt's legacy or the Republicans in Washington. Like any political boss, he had to protect his turf—and patronage—back home. That was where *his* power was. Any loosening of his grip in Pennsylvania could foreshadow catastrophe for him. Happy election results in the Keystone State therefore were in both men's interests.

Roosevelt had sent administration officials to Pennsylvania to campaign. Senator Philander Knox, perhaps with Penrose's massive furniture in mind, wasn't sure he wanted to go, but Roosevelt showed him the true light. On September 20, he had Senator and Mrs. Knox as overnight guests at Sagamore Hill, where he brought up the subject.[17] In a handwritten report to Penrose he wrote, "I had a most interesting talk with Knox. Make him speak in the campaign."[18] On September 22, he followed up in a letter to Knox, "It is of the utmost consequence that you should speak in the present campaign. . . . We have the right to expect [your] leadership."[19] Knox did his duty in his hometown of Pittsburgh and throughout the state, and it looks like he did it well. After the meeting with Penrose on November 5, Roosevelt wrote Knox, "Accept a belated word of congratulation on your speech. I was mightily pleased with it."[20]

Roosevelt had led from the front and in Harrisburg had spoken to more than one hundred thousand people on a cold, drizzly day at the opening of the new Pennsylvania State Capitol.[21] Supposedly a nonpartisan speech, it was clear the politician in chief was pumping for Republicans in the campaign. It all worked. The Penrose Machine triumphed. The fusion candidate for governor lost to Penrose's man by more than one hundred thousand votes. Three of the winners in the races to replace the four vacancies in the congressional delegation were Republican.[22] Both Roosevelt and Penrose were happy. Roosevelt more so; he now had Penrose's IOU in his pocket. On November 28, Roosevelt had him come back to the White House to talk about Brownsville, Senator Foraker, and repaying his debt. There is no record of what the two politicians said to each other, but Roosevelt, as more than a conversation icebreaker, no doubt recalled the recent election.

ROOSEVELT'S DETERMINATION NOT TO give in to Foraker had the strength of reinforced steel, but his instincts as a politician to make a deal if necessary had not corroded. The surest way to deal with

Foraker, though not the easiest, was to persuade him to drop his plans to seek an investigation. The Ohio senator may have been too invested in Brownsville to agree to this; still, it was worth a chance. A story in Julia Foraker's memoirs suggested the outlines of such a deal and, at the same time, what else Roosevelt and Penrose may have spoken about. Mrs. Foraker wrote of an unexpected visit to their home by, of all people, Senator Boies Penrose with a message from Roosevelt. He would like to offer an ambassadorship, perhaps in Paris, if only Foraker agreed to drop the Brownsville matter. Julia recalled that her husband's answer was to throw Penrose out of the house. Julia remembered the visit took place later in the Brownsville business, but this may have been the failing memory of an elderly widow. The visit could have happened earlier, say, around November 28. Something else in Julia's recollection does not sound right. It is hard to imagine Foraker bullying Penrose out the front door. Foraker was too polite a man, and, though physically a big man himself, Penrose had the edge by almost two inches and one hundred pounds. What is easy to accept is that Penrose, having taken on the assignment to introduce his resolution on December 3, would, while he was at it, agree to act as Roosevelt's emissary to make this offer.[23]

The arrangement to turn Foraker as described by Mrs. Foraker having soured, Roosevelt had one more trick to play. As Roosevelt saw things, Foraker had his own pressures. His position was weak, and Roosevelt felt sure he was unlikely to achieve the reinstatement of the soldiers, if that was what he wanted. Unlike the Senate itself, with its institutional advantages in opposing a president, he would be a lone senator working against not just any president, but Theodore Roosevelt, as determined as any man and as unyielding as a Roman legion.[24] Foraker also had to know he had not seen the last of Theodore Burton and the Ohio insurgents, and they very shortly would be coming after his Senate seat. President Roosevelt could put a stop to them if Foraker gave him a reason to. The Roosevelt-Foraker relationship had gone from warm to frosty to deep freeze, but it could be thawed. It might be a good idea to talk to Foraker himself. On Saturday, Roosevelt asked Foraker to come by the White House for a chat that very evening.[25]

Neither man left a record of their discussion. If third parties were present, they kept mum too. One man probably there, although there is no record of it, was Boies Penrose, because it seems likely the purpose of Foraker's visit that day was to arrange a charade for the Penrose and Foraker resolutions on Monday. Another would have been Vice President Fairbanks, who would learn his lines and be expected to use his powers as the Senate's presiding officer to see that no careless actions or comments by senators would foil things. And just in case, Roosevelt allies, Henry Cabot Lodge, for instance. And perhaps someone else with skin in the game, Senator Francis Warren of Wyoming, for example, happily expecting to be rid of his archenemy Interior Secretary Hitchcock; any slipup might keep his daughter's husband from becoming a brigadier general, so he could be trusted to protect the agreement from Foraker's irresponsible behavior. (Nine days later, when Warren showed Roosevelt he would do his bidding in return for pushing Hitchcock out and promoting Pershing, he would gleefully announce agreement with Roosevelt to his people back in Wyoming.[26]) It is highly likely Roosevelt's secretary William Loeb was present. Roosevelt would expect him to coordinate things.

Roosevelt may have asked Foraker what he knew of Gilchrist Stewart's investigation at Fort Reno, and Foraker probably said he knew all about it. In fact, he even had copies of the same affidavits and other statements the White House had finally received from Stewart that day. Taft, a caller at the White House that day, may have told Foraker that they were preparing to deal with whatever Stewart collected, and he had already ordered Major Blocksom to send him "any affidavit or other papers . . . bearing upon the case."[27] He also alerted the military secretary to find precedents for Roosevelt's summary discharge of three entire companies and discharges without honor.[28] (On Sunday Taft also would have his secretary send "four galleys of proof concerning the Brownsville incident" for printing with instructions to return "clean galleys" to him before noon on Monday.[29]) At some point, this preliminary pawing at the ground led to a discussion of what Foraker planned to do. Nothing, he probably responded, until after he had a chance to discuss his plans with other senators, many not yet back in Washington. But then he planned to move ahead with his demand for an investigation. Roosevelt told him he was going to fight back hammer and tong. Now they were ready to talk.

Most likely Roosevelt first mentioned a settlement. Foraker was unlikely to bring it up and show he realized his position was weak. Better to tough it out. He would have waited for Roosevelt, who was aware Foraker could cause trouble, disrupt the Senate's business, delay consideration of his legislative program, and perhaps imperil some of it. Roosevelt would ask for a resolution that would gain the Senate nothing; Foraker would go for the home run and, possibly to deflect attention away from the president, address his resolution to Secretary of War Taft. Foraker would go to bat first, followed by Roosevelt's man. Let's see who wins.

Except Roosevelt reneged on the deal enough to let Foraker know how deadly serious he was. He instructed Penrose to jump the gun. A resolution that called for just enough disclosure to satisfy the Senate's sense of self-regard and dignity might be enough, and with the help of his vice president's parliamentary rulings, the efforts of his friend Henry Cabot Lodge and some of the other Republican senators joined by Democrats who, with scant care for what happened to the black soldiers, could be counted on to support him, it might work. And that is why the normally slow-moving Senator Penrose was so quick to get the vice president's attention as the curtain rose on John Milholland's "extraordinary week."

CONDUCTING THIS BUSINESS BEFORE receiving the White House's message *was* out of order, and according to the *New York Times*, "an absolutely unprecedented interruption of the regular proceedings." Fairbanks after momentary hesitation told Penrose his transgression was not the "usual practice," then quickly added, "there was no rule to that effect."[30] Taking this as a cue to press on, Penrose asked consent from his fellow senators to offer his resolution. Fairbanks could have ruled Penrose was out of order, preventing his resolution from even being heard, but he kept it alive and available for adoption that day by asking the clerk to read it, "for the information of the Senate." It was polite, short, simple, and it asked President Roosevelt, only "if not incompatible with the public interests," to present to the Senate "full information bearing upon the recent order dismissing from the military service of the United States" the soldiers of the Twenty-Fifth Infantry.[31] Hearing no objections, as presiding officer Fairbanks could rule Penrose's resolution was before the Senate.

But before Fairbanks could make that ruling, Senator Joseph Foraker, taken by surprise, called loudly, "I offer as a substitute the resolution which I send to the desk, and I will ask that both may go over for consideration on a subsequent day." This was quick thinking. He was asking that his resolution replace Penrose's ("as a substitute"), and if the Senate approved his, Penrose's would be eliminated from consideration. By asking that both resolutions "go over," he was postponing consideration that day of either one, giving him time to catch his breath and figure out his next move. Immediately Senator John C. Spooner of Wisconsin, an experienced lawyer and sure-handed with the Senate's tangled rules of procedure, tried to bring the Penrose amendment back to its "first in line" place before the Senate. He asked that it be reread. Senator Warren, noting that Foraker's request that both resolutions be postponed had not been acted on and wanting to make sure Foraker's resolution stayed alive, asked that consideration of it be postponed. Warren was playing his own game, and while this may have been helpful to Foraker, he had his own unrevealed personal interests in mind. Senator Lodge immediately piped up and asked that Foraker's resolution be read, only as a "courtesy to the Senator from Ohio." The *Washington Post* would report anyone who knew Foraker knew how thorough and far-reaching a resolution drawn by him would be.[32] Lodge certainly knew Foraker and did not want his colleagues to leave the Senate without hearing just how long and complicated his resolution was compared to Penrose's. They got an earful. Its 276 words (more than the Gettysburg Address) were confusing and hard to follow and seemed straight from a textbook on how to write government jargon. It demanded all information and just about everything else the War Department had about Brownsville. Unlike Penrose's, it was addressed to the secretary of war, not the president, and it demanded, not requested, information.[33]

Foraker, no doubt sensing his proposal had little chance of approval (much less of being understood) that day, wanted nevertheless to make sure Penrose's did not somehow sneak in, and he echoed Senator Warren and asked that both resolutions be put off. Fairbanks "so ordered." And the Senate adjourned.

In his diary that evening, John Milholland wrote and underlined, "Wait on the Lord; be of good courage and He shall strengthen thy heart; wait I say on the Lord."[34]

PENROSE'S HASTE AND VICE President Fairbanks's indifference to tradition and precedent, usually as holy to the Senate as scripture itself, were more than an indiscretion by a brash senator and an accommodation of him by the presiding officer. They were part of a plan by President Roosevelt to stop Senator Foraker in his tracks and end the threat of a potentially uncontrollable Senate investigation of the Brownsville Incident. A headline in the next day's *New York Sun* revealed Roosevelt's hand: "President Roosevelt Said to Be behind the Penrose Resolution."[35] Indeed he was, because for him the ominous-sounding Penrose resolution was an empty threat. It asked for information "not incompatible with the public interests," and Roosevelt would judge what those might be. He could respond by sending nothing at all to the Senate, if he so wished. It was a resolution he could live with, because it was one he could disregard.

Brownsville historian John Weaver believed Vice President Fairbanks was so surprised by Penrose's action he "hardly had any time to recover," Foraker was just as surprised and had to go "fumbling through his pockets" searching for his own resolution, and other senators were nothing less than "astonished."[36] The truth of all of this is something else. It was no secret in Washington that Senator Foraker had been preparing a resolution. But Penrose's surprised everyone. Almost everyone. Senator Foraker and Vice President Fairbanks knew about it. That's why when faced with Penrose's disregard of custom, Fairbanks was quick to put on the record "there was no rule" to stop Penrose. And that's why Foraker "just happened" to have his own resolution in his pocket. What the senator from Ohio had no warning of was Penrose's timing. As the *New York Times* put it, "The Pennsylvanian took no chances on letting anybody get ahead of him."[37] "Anybody" could mean only Senator Foraker. A script worked out two days before had Foraker putting forward his resolution first. "Senator Foraker's resolution, which came into the open . . . as soon as Mr. Penrose submitted his own, *was designed to make its debut later on in the form of an initiatory resolution rather than a 'trailer'*" (author's emphasis).[38] Fairbanks hesitated because Penrose changed the order of things. The *New York Evening World* agreed, "The action of the Senator [Penrose] caused some embarrassment [to Fairbanks], as it was understood that Senator Foraker was to make the opening move."[39] Foraker fumbled in his pockets for his resolution because allowing Penrose to get his on the floor ahead of him might cost him the game.

Weaver's characterization of all of this may have been grandly sensational, and the reaction of the *New York Times* mildly melodramatic when it reported on December 4, "Grim-visaged War was present and in his seat in the Senate . . . and with unprecedented promptness he exhibited a wrinkled front," but the *New York Times* hit the mark when it added, "The Brownsville resolutions plainly portend trouble."[40] Both of them, however, missed Theodore Roosevelt's preparation for the Senate session, his strong hand shaping it, and his determination to come out the winner at the end of the day. The dominating Speaker of the House, Joseph "Uncle Joe" Cannon, wrote in his memoirs, "Nobody who ever came in contact with [Theodore Roosevelt] when he was President will ever forget that he was first, last, and all the time, a politician, one of the greatest of them all."[41] His preparation for the Senate's session that day shows why.

He realized the hostility over his decision to discharge the soldiers went deeper than anger that he waited until after Election Day to spring it. There was resentment that regardless of its timing, his discharge order rubbed against the grain of America's system of justice and was fundamentally unfair. Men suspected of crimes should not be treated as guilty with no opportunity to dispute the charge in court. Regardless, Roosevelt was positive he did justice and wanted no one to overturn what he did. Only one force on earth could try to do that, and that was Congress, most likely the Senate.

ON MONDAY EVENING, AFTER the Senate session, there was quite a bit of Brownsville business at the White House, and Roosevelt had to cancel dinner plans at Lodges' home. He told Mrs. Lodge he would be "engaged this evening."[42] He had not won his Penrose gamble in the Senate that day, and he now might face Foraker's more demanding resolution.

Many newspaper stories were after-the-fact explanations of Roosevelt's hand behind Penrose. The *New York Tribune* wrote that Penrose had "submitted [his resolution] to the Executive before introducing it to the Senate," and Roosevelt "cordially approved it."[43] The *New York Sun* reported, "It was really President Roosevelt who was behind [the Penrose resolution].[44] The *Dayton Evening News* agreed Roosevelt was the inspiration because he knew Foraker had his resolution ready to go, and he acted "to forestall him by having Penrose introduce [his] resolution first."[45]

Other newspaper articles questioned Foraker's motives. The *New York Sun* wrote, "Everybody takes the Foraker resolution as an undisguised attack on the President." The *Brooklyn Daily Times* interpreted it the same way and questioned Foraker's sincerity because it thought he was working in league with the unscrupulous Boss Penrose. "Neither . . . is inspired by any zeal for the negro troops. They and the interests they especially represent . . . have a grudge against the President for reasons which they dare not avow."[46] But the next day, Joseph Pulitzer's *New York World* was satisfied that with his resolution Foraker would bring out the facts in the case.[47] After all, that is just what Foraker said he wanted to do.[48]

Other business was put off on Tuesday as Congress heard President Roosevelt's annual message. In 1906, it was not yet delivered in person before a joint session of the House and Senate. The clerk in each house read it aloud. Roosevelt's that year, one of the longest in American history at almost twenty-four thousand words, tested the patience of members of Congress and the stamina of the clerks reading it. Those who dozed off while it was read to them may not have been aware of something curious about it. There was not one word about Brownsville.[49]

BOTH THE SENATE AND the War Department got down to the business of dealing with Brownsville on Wednesday. Releasing an extract from his annual report, Secretary of War Taft discussed under the heading of "Discipline" what he called "The Brownsville Affray."[50] Taft acted forcefully as defense counsel for President Roosevelt (after the way Roosevelt brought him up short for suspending the discharges the previous month, he was "once bitten, twice careful") and was "very severe in his condemnation of the enlisted men."[51] Among other things, he took the "facts" as Major Blocksom found them and ignored Lieutenant Colonel Lovering's investigation completely (permitting him to overlook the soldiers' claimed indifference to the mistreatment of their comrades by Brownsville residents; instead Taft could misstate these were "the cause of much discussion in the barracks of the three companies"). Without any foundation, he also said the shooting began when "shots were fired in the fort toward the town."[52]

Taft carefully distinguished the soldiers' "discharge without honor" from a "dishonorable discharge" given only by sentence of a court-martial. *That* would have been a punishment, and he went to great pains to make it very clear Special Orders No. 266 was not "in itself a punishment either of the innocent or the guilty." (Which Taft must have realized got neatly to the nub of Senator Foraker's initial concerns: there had been no trials.) He acknowledged the word *penalty* had been used "in the proceedings" but this was a mere misnomer and unfortunate. The headline writer for the *New York Times*, heedless of Taft's splitting hairs, saw the discharges the same way as the public: "Taft Defends *Penalty* on Negro Battalion" (author's emphasis).[53] This "chop logic" clarification would be an essential part of Roosevelt's defense thereafter.

Taft denied the soldiers were treated more harshly because of their race. Such an argument "hardly merits notice." And he held out hope that if future evidence turned up showing the innocence of certain men, this would "render such persons eligible for reenlistment."

Taft certainly was entitled to an A for his efforts and, for releasing this part of his annual report while the Senate was still considering the two Brownsville resolutions, an A+ for his timing. It is doubtful, though, if even he believed it would turn Foraker aside. A consensus already was gelling that some sort of investigation might be acceptable to the Senate. Roosevelt's ploy may have been responsible for this. Had he left well enough alone, Foraker's resolution standing by itself may have been too much for the Senate to approve. Penrose's offered a lifeline to senators who wanted to do something for the soldiers while not antagonizing Roosevelt. Because Roosevelt saw and approved Penrose's, it suggested he welcomed an inquiry, albeit one he thought would be worthless.

BOTH HOUSES OF CONGRESS spend what seems to outsiders an excessive amount of time on matters with no discernible importance to the American people. On Wednesday, for example, before it could take up the Brownsville resolutions, the Senate first had to receive an estimated accounting for eighteen dollars of expenses in making the proper returns for the Salmon Lake voting precinct in Kougarok District, Alaska; accept a publication from the Austro-Hungarian ambassador describing the new Hungarian Parliament building in Budapest (and, appropriately, refer it to the Committee on Public Buildings and Grounds); consider a report "in detail" on receipts and expenditures of the Government Hospital for the Insane; and accept eight petitions asking for investigations into conditions in the Kongo Free State (one from the Patrons of Husbandry in Walpole, Massachusetts). Waiting patiently for the Senate to work itself through business such as this, at long last Senator Foraker was able to bring up his resolution and ask that it be voted upon.

The vice president had the clerk read both Senator Penrose's and Senator Foraker's resolutions, thereby bringing both before the Senate. Rising to this challenge, Foraker noticed that Penrose was absent from the chamber, and rather than taking up the Penrose resolution while its author was not there, he would like his considered independently.[54] Not so fast, Warren of Wyoming said in not so many words. He wanted to offer his own substitute resolution combining the two from Monday and incorporating Foraker's "exactly as it now reads, excepting that it calls on the President for all the information." Foraker, not caring to depend on Roosevelt's good humor or unilateral interpretation of what he had to do, demurred. "I do not care to call upon the President about the matter. I do not feel disposed to bother him any further. All I want is certain specific information, which is on file in the War Department, in the custody of the Secretary of War, and I specify what it is we want." He had no objection to the Senate adopting Penrose's at another time, but he would like his own adopted now.

Roosevelt's chief protector Lodge came to his feet. He professed to want both the Penrose and Foraker resolutions, but advised the Senate be "a little more considerate" of the absent Penrose and not ignore his while approving Foraker's. The other Pennsylvania senator (and Roosevelt's former attorney general) stood up to play his role in frustrating Foraker. Knox pointed out Penrose was not only absent, but also his resolution's "parliamentary status" had been changed by Foraker asking that his "substitute by amendment" be characterized as an "independent substitute." Warren, to muddle Foraker's concentration by bringing up the question of which committee the proposal or proposals ultimately would be sent to, proposed the one he chaired, the Military Affairs Committee.

Vice President Fairbanks, no longer confused as he was on Monday, kept his eye on the ball: keep Foraker's resolution away from a vote. He agreed with Senator Knox; Foraker's resolution must be put off. Foraker tried one last attempt to get a vote. He reminded the vice president that if unanimous consent was given by the senators present, the vote could be taken. No doubt gazing across the Senate podium in the direction of Senator Knox, Vice President Fairbanks asked if there was an objection. Knox dutifully replied, "Mr. President, I rise for the purpose of making an objection." Game, set, but not quite match. Roosevelt's men were not yet finished with the crestfallen Foraker.

It had become a game of hiding the pea under the walnut shell. Foraker was unsure who next would say something to throw him off track. Senator Culberson of Texas, who never wanted the Twenty-Fifth Infantry at Fort Brown to begin with, wanted his own amendment to Foraker's resolution; Senator Warren interrupted to ask whatever happened to the amendment he offered a little earlier. Fairbanks wasn't sure but in the meantime wanted to hear what Culberson had to say. The Texan, still angry that the twelve men in confinement at Fort Brown were kept from Texas Ranger McDonald, wanted to see the order to this effect to Major Penrose. Foraker, knowing he was beaten, if for only that day, responded with fatigue, "Mr. President, if I have the power to do so, I accept the amendment." He saw no reason to light another fire that might burn away his chance of getting the investigation. Spooner got in his own last lick and said he had never heard of a resolution taken up when its author is absent from the Senate. Foraker, who did not want it taken up that day and suggested it be considered only so there would be no argument it was not, agreed to postpone both until the wayward Senator Penrose presented himself. Finally, Warren, still mindful his amendment somehow had been ignored, asked that it be dealt with. Vice President Fairbanks, knowing Warren had no real interest in seeing it passed now that Foraker had been stopped for the day, ordered it to "lie on the table," that is, to live in a sort of halfway house in which it could die or be resuscitated if needed.

PROCEDURALLY, THE DAY ENDED pretty much as it began. Neither resolution had been passed; neither had been killed. It is clear from the comments by the other senators and the amendments they offered to it that they would vote for Foraker's resolution and it would pass. Penrose's would too, but that was acceptable to Foraker so long as his retained its punch. But if he did not know it before, he certainly realized now what he was up against. He was opposed by the cleverest and most experienced senators, those who knew the Senate's rules and procedures as well as they knew the names of their wives (and might exhibit greater fidelity to the rules), each supporting the other, and all supporting President Roosevelt. And President Roosevelt supported them.

Foraker was alone.

THURSDAY WOULD BE THE day of decision. It began, however, not with Brownsville but with a lengthy debate on the canal across

Central America, forced on it by Alabama senator John T. Morgan, the Confederate cavalry officer who led the charge at Chickamauga that Foraker missed by his stroke of good fortune. By 1906 Morgan was eighty-two years old and had been in the Senate for the last thirty years. Canal historian David McCullough quotes Senator Shelby Collum of Illinois on crossing Morgan: "He was so intense on any subject in which he took an interest, particularly the inter-oceanic canal, that he became vicious toward anyone who opposed him."[55] He had strongly favored Nicaragua as the site for the canal, but by now that battle had been lost for some time. Morgan was expressing his unyielding frustration in a resolution seeking to "bring the alleged corporation of the Panama railroad within the direct control of the United States Government."[56]

When at last Morgan concluded his speech, Foraker asked to bring up the Penrose resolution, which, since his was considered to be an amendment to Penrose's, brought his resolution up for discussion as well. Penrose, in the Capitol but not the Senate chamber, rushed in to find his resolution before his colleagues.[57] He agreed his and Foraker's resolution could be considered separately and asked for unanimous consent to permit this. Things seemed to be going Foraker's way, as if Penrose's presence calmed the Senate in the way an itching palm would be greased to tranquility by a fifty-dollar bill slipped into it. Then an inflammation from Senator Spooner caused a new itch. Did not the Penrose resolution imply that but for its passage the Senate would not be entitled to the documents it requested? Foraker responded that is why he did not want the two resolutions combined. He feared the *request* from Penrose to President Roosevelt would weaken his *demand* to the secretary of war. Colorado's Henry M. Teller, who switched parties twice while in the Senate, from Republican to Silver Republican (his fortune was in silver mining) to Democrat (which he was by now), wondered aloud what difference it made. A president could tell the secretary to ignore a demand made upon him, and that would be the end of it. Thomas H. Carter of Montana began to say something potentially supportive of Foraker, when Foraker, who missed something Carter said, interrupted to ask what it was, thereby offending

Carter. Culberson of Texas disputed the weight Foraker gave to some evidence. Ben Tillman wanted to know why Foraker had the War Department pamphlet, but he did not and had to learn it existed in the morning's newspapers.[58] Penrose got up to say Spooner's comments made no sense to him. The Pennsylvanian added, with no segue from what anyone else was saying, but merely to show he was close to the black community and independent from Roosevelt, "I introduced the resolution without guile, out of a natural relationship to a large colored constituency in the State of Pennsylvania, whose race prejudice has been aroused and who felt that perhaps an affront had been put upon them.[59] I did not know that I was going to create such a disturbance in the minds of some of my colleagues as was developed when I heard the anguished tones of the Senator from Ohio informing this body that he had a similar resolution which he would like promptly to get before us."[60] Foraker asked him to repeat the adjective that described his tones; he did not hear it clearly and thought Penrose said "angry." Now it was Penrose's turn to be defensive. Foraker tried to calm him down, but Penrose burned even hotter, at one point refusing to yield the floor to him.

Interruptions interrupted interruptions. Sore feelings had to be soothed. Potentially misunderstood arguments had to be restated. A session that had begun calmly was in bedlam.

Then Senator Foraker brought it back to order and gave it purpose. He pointed out the consequences of doing nothing. It would act as precedent to restrict Congress's ability to act as a check on the executive office. He did not introduce his resolution on Monday because it involved race. Deliberately addressing the Senate's institutional touchiness, he said the bigger question was the president's authority. "If the President may disband one company he may disband three, as he has done here, and if he may discharge a whole battalion, he can do away with a regiment if he so likes, and if he can do away with a regiment, a brigade, and, as I say, the whole Army." Beyond that, "The broader question is one of constitutional right. . . . No such discharge can be granted by any order . . . when as a result of such discharge punishment is inflicted as though it had been in pursuance of the sentence of a court-martial."[61]

Penrose, to conclude the matter, asked that both resolutions be approved. Foraker, still irritated by Penrose's refusal to yield to him earlier, did not yield. "I will be through in a little bit, and the Senator can then take the floor and deal in questions of anguish and anger as he may see fit."[62] Senator Teller helped out by telling his colleagues they simply did not have the information needed to discuss the Brownsville Incident intelligently and the only question was how they would get it. Even Roosevelt's defenders were past worrying whether there was any merit in discussing the difference between a president being asked and a secretary of war being directed. Along with Culberson's amendment asking to see the order denying Ranger McDonald custody of the men he sought from the army, both resolutions were passed.

STRICT COMPLIANCE WITH THE Foraker resolution soon would inundate the Senate with paperwork. According to the *Dayton Daily News*, Taft would be forced by Foraker's resolution "to send to the Senate everything in the war department bearing upon the case—all of the correspondence, all of the reports of officers, all of the investigations made, the record of every man dismissed, the military history of each, the files of all the companies, and every blot of ink that in any way touches the merits of the controversy.[63] This cut two ways. Senators would be overwhelmed by this flood and unable to use it effectively against Roosevelt. But Senator Foraker could be counted on to study this rockslide carefully, ferret out those crystals helpful to him, interpret them favorably to the soldiers and in a way showing Roosevelt at his worst, and prevail upon the Senate to ask for more. He was a member of the Senate Military Affairs Committee, ground zero for the paperwork, and if he got the Senate to take another step no doubt it would delegate to that committee the responsibility to undertake further investigation and take appropriate action. Its chairman, Francis Warren of Wyoming, had shown no sympathy for Foraker's position. In fact, he would be identified in the *Washington Herald* the next day as a leader of those who spoke against him.[64] Still there was no telling where things would lead. Later that day President Roosevelt asked Senator Warren to stop by the White House.

And so John Milholland's extraordinary week ended victoriously for him, Senator Foraker, and the soldiers.

*"We are not better than our fellows, Lord, we are but weak
and human men. When our devils do deviltry, curse Thou the
doer and the deed: curse them as we curse them, do to them all
and more than ever they have done to innocence and weak-
ness, to womanhood and home.*

Have mercy upon us, miserable sinners!"

W. E. B. Du Bois, "A Litany of Atlanta"

CHAPTER THIRTEEN

STRANGE FRUIT[1]

PRESIDENT ROOSEVELT MADE NO direct mention of Brownsville in his annual message to Congress on December 4.
He planned to deal with it later that month in a special message.
In the meantime, lynching was very much on his mind. His
address devoted some time to it and seemed, without saying so,
to connect it to Brownsville through the idea of conspiracies of
silence.

He told Congress, and through it the American people, there
were two problems with crime in the black community: black criminals and other blacks who hid them. When he said the crime that
most often led to lynching was black men raping white women and
came within a breath of blaming the accused black men for their
own lynching (most of whom, like the Brownsville soldiers, had
never been tried in a court of law), the reaction by Negro leaders
and others was seismic. For him to say the crime of rape was primarily a black-on-white problem was delusional, and to ignore
the racial undertone to the crime of lynching was blindness. So
soon after the Brownsville discharges, this message to Congress
prompted black Americans to rethink Roosevelt, his party, the

man now seen as his minion, Booker T. Washington, and W. E. B. Du Bois.[2]

THERE IS NO CRIME in American history as chilling as lynching. Human degeneracy continues, but few group acts can compare with it. Behaviors such as parents encouraging their children to engage in suicide bombings against innocent people and Nazis murdering six million men, women, and children because they were Jewish (or performing gruesome experiments on them in the name of medical science) are comparable, but these are no longer ignored or excused by civilized people or tolerated in civilized nations. Lynching was. Before he talked about it, President Roosevelt might have done well thinking more about what it was. Kelly Miller, a president of Howard University, said this:

> The cruelty and barbarity of lynchings are indescribable for horror and atrocity. . . . Victims have been drowned, hanged, shot, burned alive, beaten to death, dismembered while thousands gloated over their groanings with ghoulish glee. Women with child have been disemboweled in the public gaze. The United States enjoys the evil distinction of being the only civilized nation of the earth whose people take delight in the burning and torturing of human beings. No where else in the civilized world do men, women and children dance with glee and fight for ghastly souvenirs of quivering human flesh, and mock with laughter the dying groans of the helpless victim which sicken the air while the flickering flames of the funeral pyre light up the midnight sky with dismal glare.[3]

Miller was right, but even this fails to describe the horror. But he was wrong when he said only Americans "take delight in the burning and torturing of human beings." He should have known that the Imperial Russia of his day was just as bad. Describing a 1906 massacre of Jews there, only one of the recurring pogroms egged on by the czar's government, a clipping from the *New York Times* pasted by Mark Twain into a draft of his autobiography reads in part:

> Merely saying that the bodies were mutilated . . . fails to describe the awful facts. The faces of the dead have lost all human resem-

blance. The body of Teacher Apstein lay on the grass with the hands tied. In the face and eyes had been hammered three-inch nails. Rioters entered his home, killing him thus, and then murdered the rest of his family of seven. When the body arrived at the hospital it was also marked with bayonet thrusts.

Beside the body of Apstein lay that of a child of 10 years, whose leg had been chopped off with an axe. Here also were the dead from the Schlacter home, where, according to witnesses, soldiers came and plundered the house and killed the wife, son, and a neighbor's daughter and seriously wounded Schlacter and his two daughters.

I am told the soldiers entered the apartments of the Lapidus brothers, which were crowded with people who had fled from the streets for safety, and ordered the Christians to separate themselves from the Jews. A Christian student named Dikar protested and was killed on the spot. Then all the Jews were shot.

In this one pogrom in Bialystok, encouraged by the police and civil authorities, as many as two hundred Jews were killed.[4]

W. E. B. Du Bois said the problem of the twentieth century would be the color line. He died in 1963, two-thirds of the way into the century, and by then he would know of the Armenian Genocide by the Ottoman Turks during World War I; the starving of the Ukraine by Stalin in the early 1930s; the Rape of Nanking a few years later, where Japanese soldiers used Chinese babies for bayonet practice; and the Holocaust by Nazi Germany.[5] Had he lived a little longer he would been witness to the death of millions by Pol Pot in Cambodia, the Rwandan genocide in East Africa, and Saddam Hussein killing human beings in shredders designed to tear apart metal. By the twenty-first century, Du Bois might have changed his mind and said the problem of the century just passed, as it has been since history was recorded, was the way humans treated other humans.

But of course America should have been different. It should have been better. Even the Russians pointed out the hypocrisy to the Americans. In a letter to Jacob Schiff two weeks before the Brownsville shooting, Roosevelt mentioned a letter from the American ambassador to Russia: "The [Russian] Minister of Foreign Affairs refuses definitely to discuss, even informally, the Beilostok [*sic*] massacre, and claims that we have no more right to meddle in the matter than they would have to take up the lynching of negroes with us."[6]

IT IS NOT KNOWN for sure where this act of murder got its name. Usually cited is one man or another with the surname Lynch. Perhaps it was William Lynch, a Virginian who wrote a compact among the slave owners of Pittsylvania County to deal with errant slaves. Or a different William Lynch, whose father was the founder of Lynchburg, Virginia. Charles Lynch, yet another Virginian, tried accused criminals in his front yard and, after finding them guilty, tied them to a tree and whipped them. Some suggest its etymology was Irish, in the person of James Fitzstephens Lynch, a fifteenth-century mayor of Galway, who hanged his own son for robbing and murdering a Spaniard.[7] Wherever it began, it found a home in the post-Reconstruction American South. From there it metastasized elsewhere in the country. Kelly Miller claimed that between 1889 and 1920 there were lynchings in every state and territory except Connecticut, Massachusetts, New Hampshire, Vermont, and Utah. Even faraway Alaska had four. In those thirty-one years he counted 3,372 lynchings, and overwhelmingly the victims were black (2,656 versus 716 white). The eleven states of the Confederacy witnessed 2,426 lynchings (more than 91 percent of the total); Georgia had the most in the nation with 416. Sixty women and girls were lynched, of which forty-nine were black. The offenses charged to the victims were murder (1,219; 900 black, 319 white), rape (523; 477 black, 46 white), an attack upon a woman (250; 237 black, 13 white), crimes against property (331; 210 black, 121 white), and miscellaneous crimes (438; 303 black, 135 white). The rest of the victims had not been charged with any crime.[8]

Lynching's continuing presence in the American republic was like a disease for which there was no cure in a patient who had no other choice. Resistance was futile.

Roosevelt began his discussion of lynching in his annual address by saying, "The greatest existing cause of lynching is the perpetration, especially by black men, of the hideous crime of rape—the most

abominable in all the category of crimes, even worse than murder."
This was not a good beginning for him. Of the 3,372 lynchings
counted by Miller, only 477 were of black men accused of rape. This
hardly justifies Roosevelt's claim that rape was "the greatest existing
cause of lynching." It's not clear he believed it himself. In 1906, after
the shooting in Brownsville, in a letter to John M. Parker of New
Orleans ("You are a mighty good friend," he began the letter) he said,
"You are of course aware, however, that three-fourths of the lynchings are not for rape but for other offenses."[9] At different times he
found different reasons to explain lynching. Just after he was elected
vice president, it was delays in the criminal justice system.[10] Three
years after that, in a letter marked "Personal" to his attorney general
Philander Knox, he suggested it might be because of a general era
of lawlessness the country was passing through.[11] (He repeated this
thought in the 1906 annual message, calling the nation's attention to
"the prevalence of crime among us.") In that same letter he thought
too many "clever criminal lawyers" secure too many acquittals for
too many guilty men, and this was disturbing enough to drive other
men to lynching. He repeated this idea less than two weeks later
to Indiana governor Winfield Taylor Durbin after a three-day race
riot in Evansville, Indiana.[12] People seemed to share Roosevelt's
discomfort with how criminal trials were conducted and, like Roosevelt, saw a connection between this and lynching. After a mob
in Wilmington, Delaware, lynched a black man accused of killing
a white man, the grand jury wanted to condemn the judge for not
bringing him to trial faster. This tardiness, it was said, encouraged
people to take matters in their own hands.[13]

In his annual message, Roosevelt, of course, did not say these
or any other circumstances excused lynching. It was "inexcusable
anywhere." But at the same time, seeing it as a natural consequence
of "the perpetration, especially by black men, of the hideous crime
of rape—the most abominable in all the category of crimes" took all
life out of his censure of lynching and made its victims the problem.

Then Roosevelt carried his argument too far. Into the braided
lynching and rape he now wove the notion of a conspiracy of silence.
"The white people of the South indict the whole colored race on the

ground that even the better elements lend no assistance whatever in ferreting out criminals of their own color. The respectable colored people must learn not to harbor their criminals, but to assist the officers in bringing them to justice. Every colored man should realize that the worst enemy of his race is the negro criminal, and above all the negro criminal who commits the dreadful crime of rape; and it should be felt as in the highest degree an offense against the whole country, and against the colored race in particular, for a colored man to fail to help the officers of the law in hunting down with all possible earnestness and zeal every such infamous offender."[14]

Then he tied rape to a lack of education. "The lowest and most brutal criminals, those for instance who commit the crime of rape, are in the great majority men who have had either no education or very little." (He added a plug for Booker T. Washington, "Of course the best type of education for the colored man, taken as a whole, is such education as is conferred in schools like Hampton and Tuskegee; where the boys and girls, the young men and young women, are trained industrially.")

What the message seemed to be saying was that lynching was unfortunate, but if black men stopped raping white women, and if black citizens would help the police find these men, and if black men and women all learned a trade, the whole awful mess would go away.[15] Roosevelt, without mentioning Brownsville, had opened a window into how he thought about what he did to the soldiers. If black civilians could hide black criminals, black soldiers could just as easily remain silent about black wrongdoers in the army.

A WEEK EARLIER IN a letter marked "Personal" to Silas McBee, editor of the quasi-official magazine of the Protestant Episcopal Church, Roosevelt said it was Negro indifference to Negro crime that "had an undoubted effect in helping to precipitate the hideous Atlanta riots."[16]

The riots in Atlanta joined Brownsville in making up what biographer David Levering Lewis called the watershed summer and fall of 1906, and like two fire alarms they sounded the turn against Roosevelt's man in the Negro community, Booker T. Washington and his

Atlanta Compromise. The break can be seen in the different reactions to two of his speeches, one made in August as Brownsville was unfolding and Atlanta was heating to a boil, and the other in October, when the riots had scalded the city and burned Washington himself. In August, as the Twenty-Fifth Infantry soldiers were on the train from Fort Brown to Fort Reno, Booker T. Washington was telling people what he thought of black criminals. In the keynote address before the Atlanta convention of the National Negro Business League he said, "The negro is committing too much crime," and the race's leaders had the duty to see that "the negro criminal is gotten rid of" or the race will "suffer permanently." Black crime was as great an enemy as lynching. "Our southland today has no greater enemy to business progress than lynchers *and those who provoke lynching*" (author's emphasis).[17] He was applauded. Two months later, speaking to the Afro-American Council in New York, he said again that blacks had to get rid of their criminals. This time he was ignored.[18]

Less than two months after that, in his annual address, President Roosevelt, now completely out of step with Negro thinking on the matter, said Negro crime and Negro refusal to help do anything about it was "the larger crime, and it provokes such atrocious offenses as the one at Atlanta." Roosevelt had embraced the idea as his own.

"MY DAY OPENED WITH hearing the massacre of Negroes in Atlanta. A horrible, horrible affair," John Milholland wrote in his diary.[19] The rioting would be worse than any the country had seen since the New York draft riots during the Civil War.

Race riots, inevitable as summer humidity in the South, regularly occurred mainly there but also throughout the United States in the late nineteenth century and continued well into the twentieth.[20] Over the summer and fall of 1906, there had been a series of assaults reported in Atlanta. T. Thomas Fortune, in Atlanta in August for the National Negro Business League meeting, later would say, "The better class of black men knew that . . . trouble was coming."[21] On September 22, stories of new assaults that day by blacks on whites were spoken of on the street. Neither of these involved rape; one was a "negro rough" supposedly pushing a white woman off the street when she refused to make way for him, and another was a black *woman* assaulting a white *man*, who in turn pushed her.[22] That was all it took. A man got up on a box on Marietta Street downtown and cried out to the crowd, "Are we Southern white men going to stand for this?" Cries of "No!" were followed by "Kill the negroes," and the mob was off and running. Its first victims were two innocent black men riding a nearby trolley. The first was killed with a knife; the other pulled into the street and trampled to death. The rampage went on for four days, and only after the governor brought in the state militia was order restored. The official death toll was fourteen, twelve of these blacks, but unofficial reports place it at twenty-two, twenty blacks and two whites.[23]

The rumored assaults the first day of the riots were said to have been the spark, and white anger at earlier alleged assaults by blacks was considered the tinder. Atlanta's Mayor James G. Woodward blamed it on "black brutes who assault our white women."[24] A contributing reason was thought to be Atlanta's skyrocketing population after General William Sherman depopulated the city in the Civil War, with blacks increasing at a far greater rate and racial tensions growing apace.[25] One factor might have been the three-way contest for governor that year among Tom Watson, an out-and-out racist; Hoke Smith, almost as bad; and Clark Howell, who gave Watson and Smith as good as he got. In Washington, DC, Archibald Grimké's brother Francis said the riots were "the result of envy, born of hatred. It hurts this class of whites to see the Negro prospering. They don't want him to succeed; they don't want him to get along."[26]

When the riots began President Roosevelt was enjoying the last few days of summer at his home in Oyster Bay, New York. He had been there since July 1, badly in need of the rest and recharging he found at Sagamore Hill.[27] The stresses of the legislative program he worked hard to get through Congress over the winter and spring had been calmed briefly and only slightly by the summer pleasures of that rambling and beloved house and his family before Brownsville broke and gave way to Atlanta. Booker T. Washington was not far away, attending a meeting in New York City to discuss indus-

trial conditions for blacks there.[28] Receiving reports of the horror in
Atlanta as the brutality torqued itself up, Washington asked President Roosevelt to send in federal troops. Roosevelt refused, saying
he lacked the authority to interfere in a local matter.[29] Just as the brutality was easing off, Washington sent identical letters to the editors
of the *New York World* and the *New York Times* to remind them and
their readers he was "against the crime of assaulting women and of
resorting to lynching and mob law as a remedy for any evil." The
immediate solution was for the "best" of both races to get together
and change things.[30] Though he encouraged people to think he had
rushed from New York to Atlanta to work to calm things down, he
did not arrive there until September 28, two days after the city was
declared secure.[31] Two days later he was back in Tuskegee.

Du Bois was living in Atlanta while teaching sociology at the
Negro Atlanta University. When the riots began, he was in Alabama
doing research for the Census Bureau but rushed home to protect
his family in a nonaccommodating and very confrontational way—
sitting on the steps with a shotgun in his hands. He was prepared to
use it against any threatening white rioter. He never got his chance;
they never got that far.[32] It was on the train back to Alabama, in the
Jim Crow railroad car, where he composed "A Litany to Atlanta."
In it he asked God to pay whites back for what they had done to his
race. President Roosevelt made no public comment about the riot's
causes until his annual message in December. By then, as we have
seen, he settled on Negroes for not turning in their own criminals
to the police. Six months after the riots, he adopted the opinion of
journalist Ray Stannard Baker:[33]

> For months the relation of the races had been growing more
> strained. . . . In Atlanta the lower class—the "worthless Negro"—
> had been increasing in members: it showed itself too evidently
> among the swarming saloons, dives, and "clubs" which a complai-
> sant city administration allowed to exist in the very heart of the
> city. Crime had increased to an alarming extent; an insufficient and
> ineffective police force seemed unable to cope with it. With a popu-
> lation of 115,000 Atlanta had over 17,000 arrests in 1905; in 1906
> the number increased to 21,602. Atlanta had more arrests than

New Orleans with nearly three times the population and twice as many Negroes. . . . Race feeling had sharpened through a long and bitter political campaign.[34]

Booker T. Washington would say nothing about the riots while he was in New York, using as an excuse he spoke of race matters only in the South.[35] No one was taken in by this preposterous answer, and when he had time to think of what to say, ever the accommodator, Washington condemned both alleged black rapists and white rioters evenhandedly.[36] Du Bois, however, signaling how he intended to use the riots and Brownsville to topple Washington, pointed his finger at the man he called the "Arch-Tempter," who, in the city now devastated by the riots, sold that bill of goods known as the Atlanta Compromise. That compromise was now a dead letter; none of the parties had any use for it. The South had changed since 1895. Its leaders no longer were willing to live up to the bargain made by their predecessors, who themselves had failed to live up to it anyway. They would not allow blacks to advance patiently and painfully; they would not permit them to advance at all. They would not control the violence. Black Americans were beginning to understand they had denied themselves the rights they were entitled to as American citizens and had not gotten anything for it.[37] Du Bois biographer Lewis called Washington's accommodation a "fatal trap."[38] Washington biographer Harlan recognized it had become a "Faustian bargain."[39]

The devil had come for his due, and to the Wizard his face was that of W. E. B. Du Bois. Du Bois's message was starting to get through. In 1906, after the Brownsville Incident, Du Bois was overtaking Washington. He was gaining a growing number of black leaders, and Washington was seeing them fall away. Archibald Grimké once had a foot in both camps. He tended to see Washington's point of view but was tugged in a different way by men like Monroe Trotter, whom he knew from Boston. August Meier, historian and prolific writer on the era, believed Brownsville was the "turning point" in how Grimké saw things. Now he was firmly in Washington's opposition.[40]

The Atlanta Compromise of 1895, tottering from the awareness it was not working, was now shaking dangerously from the Atlanta riots and the Brownsville discharges of 1906. The riots came *after* the Brownsville shooting but *before* Roosevelt ordered the soldiers' discharges, so it was Atlanta that broke the dishes and Brownsville that cleared them away. After Roosevelt's Brownsville order was made public in November, the table would not be set for Washington again.

By the time of Roosevelt's annual message, this was clear to Washington. When he wrote Fortune that he had tried unsuccessfully to get Roosevelt to modify the annual address, Fortune wrote back, "I am sorry that the President did not let you blue pencil his address. . . . His advice that Afro-Americans who know nothing of their criminals shall help to hunt them down and his adoption of the lynch law method of slaying the innocent with the guilty are vile propositions calculated to do us great injury."[41] Fortune was through with Roosevelt; soon he too would break with Washington.

CHAPTER FOURTEEN

A DIFFERENT
BURDEN OF PROOF

ROOSEVELT WAS WELL AWARE of the racial element in the opposition to the discharges, and though he denied race had anything to do with what he did, it was a problem that had to be faced. His favorable relations with Negroes were based on just a few things: having Booker T. Washington to the White House for dinner (but this was now five years ago), the protection Washington gave him through the Tuskegee Machine standing with him on issues affecting black Americans, the federal jobs he dispensed to qualified blacks (in hindsight not very many), and the fact he was not a "Pitchfork Ben" Tillman and the others like him in Congress who protected the South's Jim Crow culture and laws. This was no longer sufficient. Facing a Senate investigation and the attention the nation's newspapers would pay to it, he had to do better. Help came from the man in Tuskegee.

Someone sent Booker T. Washington a clipping from the *New York Age* that cited a *Chicago Daily Tribune* story about a white army officer's recent inflammatory comment about black soldiers.[1] Colonel William L. Pitcher of the Twenty-Seventh Infantry was said to have wondered aloud why the army had sent Buffalo Soldiers of the Tenth Cavalry to Fort Sheridan, Illinois. It never would have happened, he said, "without a protest if I was to remain in command here. . . . For the life of me I cannot see why the United States should try to make soldiers out of them."[2] As a young second lieutenant, Pitcher had been assigned to the Tenth Cavalry and may have formed his opinions then.[3] Or they may have had their genesis earlier, when his father, General Thomas G. Pitcher, was superintendent at West Point. The general ordered a court-martial for a black cadet who was alleged to have falsely accused white cadets of racial harassment. The black cadet was convicted and sentenced to dismissal from West Point. But President Grant, stating "that the ends of public justice will be better subserved and the policy of the government, of which the presence of this cadet in the Military Academy is a signal illustration, be better maintained by a commutation of the sentence," allowed him to stay.[4] The younger Pitcher might have seen this as an uncalled-for rebuke of his father.

Aside from race, Colonel Pitcher's army career was an uneven one, and as recently as 1904, he was censured by Secretary Taft for "unceremoniously breaking" an engagement to a young woman in Washington. Pitcher made things worse for himself with the "language he used in communications to the [war] department" about the matter.[5] The Wizard saw Pitcher as an easy mark, and so did Roosevelt. He ordered the War Department to get an explanation from Pitcher about his antiblack remarks, and if it was not satisfactory, to court-martial the white officer for what he said.[6] He would show he was an evenhanded man when it came to race. Perhaps it was coincidence that Roosevelt's Pitcher order was made public the same day as his Brownsville order and both appeared in the same article in many newspapers.[7] Three months later, when Pitcher denied even having given an interview in which such comments could have been made, Roosevelt accepted this and the matter was closed.[8]

WHILE PRESIDENT ROOSEVELT WAS in Panama, talk began circulating quietly in officers' clubs at army posts that insufficient attention had been paid to the officers' actions at Fort Brown at the time of the shooting. Some said the delay in beginning an investigation, in particular not inspecting the soldiers' rifles in time to reveal whether they had been fired, was a neglect of duty.[9] The grumbling soon became public. One week after the election, the *New York Times* reported that the battalion's commanding officer, Major Charles Penrose, was almost certainly to be taken to court, and every other officer at the post was a potential defendant. Two days later it said the army was under "tremendous pressure" to do something.[10] There things stood until December 5, the day before the Senate would approve the Foraker and Penrose resolutions, when Roosevelt told Taft he had made "a careful study" of Major Blocksom's report and of a letter from a former army officer named A. B. Nettleton. He was now uncertain the Black Battalion's officers "are or are not blamable." He asked for a thorough investigation and report.[11]

Major Blocksom's report by itself should not have raised any concern about the officers. His report defended their inattention before the shooting ("Who could imagine that American soldiers in a body would try to murder unoffending women and innocent children?") and said Major Penrose did the right thing after the Evans assault by keeping the soldiers out of town and away from civilians. It may have been something Penrose did much later at Fort Reno that upset Roosevelt. As the battalion was discharged at Fort Reno, Penrose was reported to have told Gilchrist Stewart, "There goes the last of the best disciplined, best behaved and regulated battalion in the entire United States Army." Stewart asked if this was for publication. "Yes, indeed, I would say that anywhere." Stewart told it to the *Washington Post*, which published it on November 27, the day Roosevelt returned from Panama. The *New York Times* ran with the story that same day. On Thanksgiving Roosevelt would have read in the *Post* that morning that Penrose's statement had caused indignation at the War Department. "It was flagrantly insubordinate, and his court-martial would surely follow." President Roosevelt may have seen this as a message to him.[12]

The Nettleton letter more likely pricked Roosevelt's curiosity. Nettleton zeroed in on behaviors and practices uniquely military for which officers have the responsibility and in which the martinet Roosevelt would have an interest. Nettleton was "surprised by several facts relating to discipline," amazed "that neither the commanding officer, the officer of the day, nor the officer of the guard should have known anything about the bloody event," and "that the officer of the day . . . had undressed, gone to bed, and was sound asleep throughout the entire occurrence."[13]

Taft ordered wanted the general staff "at once" to confer with General Garlington, Major Blocksom and the "Judge-Advocate-General."[14] By including the army's senior lawyer and making the matter a priority, it was clear where this was going. Garlington, experienced in how the army operated, hedged. In the army problems roll from higher to lower ranks, and although he told the general staff he did not think that any criminal charge "would hold before any court," he pointed to the man sent to Brownsville to investigate the original trouble. That would have been Major Augustus Blocksom. Blocksom stood his ground. Major Penrose may have made an "error in judgement" but not one of "intention or neglect," and certainly none of the other officers "didn't do his full duty." Less than a week later the general staff recommended courts-martial for Penrose and Captain Edgar Macklin, and in quick order, the judge advocate general agreed, Secretary Taft concurred, and Roosevelt noted, "Approved: Make the necessary order." Total time between Roosevelt telling Loeb he had some concerns to Roosevelt's approval of court-martial: nine days.[15] Roosevelt could show he was just as willing to go after white officers as black soldiers.

ON SUNDAY, DECEMBER 1, Roosevelt had Loeb ask the War Department for precedents for the discharge of an entire battalion of soldiers. Knowing what Foraker was planning, he also ordered Blocksom to review Stewart's synopses of the testimony and evidence and come to Washington to meet him, and the next night Blocksom was on his way.[16] Before leaving Texas Blocksom asked Mayor Frederick Combe and Captain William Kelly in Brownsville to forward him the papers and proofs he anticipated Roosevelt would want to see. Blocksom was learning how to play the game.[17]

It seemed like a large part of the War Department was devoting itself to defending the discharges and had been since Taft tried to delay them.[18] The effort continued into the next weekend. On

Friday, Roosevelt made it to the Lodges' for the dinner he had canceled on Monday. Brownsville was on the menu. Saturday he wondered why he still had not received the final Constitution League/Stewart Report.[19] He had Loeb send a wire asking for it, and later that evening Gilchrist Stewart replied, "Telegram from Loeb received. Regret delay exceedingly." He promised the report would be in Washington on Monday evening.[20]

Stewart's reply came from Milholland's office in New York, where the two of them and other leaders of the Constitution League were meeting to get the report finished and sent to an impatient president (and to Foraker, who also was expecting it).[21] The pressure on them to finish must have been intense. One reason no doubt was the effort that had to be made—ultimately without success—to clean it up. Forty years later, historian James Tinsley, who was sympathetic to the soldiers, would describe it as "hastily prepared[, reflecting] in part a bias and prejudice in favor of the Negro as strong as the bias of which it complained."[22] Calling it "hastily prepared" was an act of charity. It was an awful mess. There was a terrible inattention to detail. Jacob Frazier's name was spelled two ways in Affidavit L, "Fraser" and "Frazer," and neither was correct.[23] It was signed and notarized on November 24, 1906, but the notary's commission expired the previous June. In John M. Hill's affidavit (Affidavit M) the commission for the same notary was shown as unexpired. Both could not be right. Furthermore, on some affidavits the notary was shown as E. T. Barbour, and on others as E. J. Barbon.[24] Wilbert Voshelle (Affidavit B) was not a soldier and not sent to Fort Reno, but according to his affidavit, that was where he signed it. Affidavit G was by twenty-five soldiers and not notarized for any of them. Affidavit H was from thirty-four soldiers but evidently signed by only one. Affidavit T was called a "general affidavit" and signed by thirty-five soldiers, but not one signature was notarized.[25]

Before sending the wire to Roosevelt, Stewart and Milholland talked and probably decided it was not a good idea to go into these details.[26] Who could blame them? In Stewart's defense, while he was working with the soldiers, they were either still in the army or discharged and away from Fort Reno. No one knows what sort of secretarial and stenographic help he might have had. Joe Smith, a friend of Milholland's and a Constitution League man, had been sent ahead to do the spade work, but he was the wrong man for the job.[27] Most crucial, Stewart had three days, four at the most, to travel to Fort Reno, interview those of the 150 or more soldiers Smith and Barbour did not get to, put what they said into written statements, and have them signed and notarized. The rush was necessary to satisfy the demand for Stewart's new facts by Roosevelt returning from Panama and by Foraker returning to the Senate.

AS CASUALLY AS THE affidavits were prepared, one might have expected an inferior presentation of the soldiers' defense, but all in all it was good. As Professor Tinsley noted, Stewart laced it with the bias of an advocate, but that is what he was expected to do. That aside, it was well organized and well written and presented as a lawyer might argue in court for clients. He disputed the "prosecution's" facts and argued the soldiers had not had an opportunity to interpret them in a way that supported their innocence or to present their side of the story. (He was right. They had made statements to investigating army officers, but those did not reach Washington, DC, until the day General Garlington was told to go to Oklahoma; by then the army's and Roosevelt's minds were made up. They had concluded soldiers had been the shooters before any of their statements denying it were looked at.[28]) Stewart pointed out the Brownsville residents' bias cast doubt on their incriminating testimony; those who thought they saw soldiers only because the shooters wore khaki could have been mistaken since khaki was "the usual garb of numerous civilians"; some of the witnesses were unable to identify the shooters cither as soldiers or as Negro, and this was just as meaningful as those who saw black soldiers; bullets and shells found on the streets and identified as army ammunition could have fit into "the rifle in common use in that part of Texas"; and, of course, the case had been prejudged by the investigators.[29] But for Roosevelt, he needed to do more; he had to show facts disproving the soldiers were the shooters.

Significantly the report omitted any discussion of the law or Roosevelt's authority to discharge the soldiers. That would be something Foraker would face shortly in the Senate, and by leaving it out Stewart may have been responding to a suggestion from Senator Foraker.

ON DECEMBER 7 JOHN Milholland made a note in his diary that a meeting of the Constitution League in Philadelphia was "not a howling success."[30] There is no mention of the resolution approved at that meeting "respectfully" urging the Senate to investigate the Brownsville Incident. In New York on December 10, Andrew B. Humphrey, the Constitution League's secretary, signed Stewart's report (addressed to "The President" and prefaced with the resolution), and he and Stewart took it to Washington. Milholland would note with relief that the two were on their way.[31] The next day at 5:00 p.m. Stewart handed it to William Loeb at the White House.[32]

Roosevelt would have recognized the name of Andrew Humphrey; they went way back. To Roosevelt, Humphrey was another "goo-goo," with his eyes on the stars and his feet in the air.[33] Running for New York governor in 1900, Roosevelt promised the voters he would clean things up in Albany. After he was elected he directed his aim at the state's insurance department and its superintendent, Lou Payn. Payn, who later would admit he knew nothing about the insurance business when he was appointed (by Governor Roosevelt's predecessor), somehow obtained loans from insurance companies that inexplicably were not reported. He ran the department in a fairly relaxed manner and was said to have allowed one company to write its own annual report for the state's records rather than imposing on the department, which normally took care of it, and he received $200,000 for this gesture. Roosevelt the governor found it more difficult than Roosevelt the candidate thought it would be to ease Payn out of office, but with the assistance of Andrew Humphrey he did it. Some residual anxiety over how he accomplished it must have stayed with Roosevelt, and in June 1904, in the middle of that year's presidential election, he invited Payn to visit him at the White House, where the two of them and George Cortelyou, the chairman of the Republican National Committee, had a cordial discussion about old times. Payn evidently scratched whatever itch

Roosevelt had, and when he left the meeting he told reporters, "I took occasion to assure the President that I was for him and should exert my influence to the limit for his election."[34]

In later years Humphrey would become active in the peace movement so generously supported by Andrew Carnegie, but like the "Cold War Warriors" of the Democratic Party in midcentury, most notably John F. Kennedy, he recognized that for the country's security from foreign threat, he had to plant his feet firmly on the ground. Shortly after World War I began, he joined with others to demand the United States start preparing for a war.[35] On this issue, as with Lou Payn, he and Roosevelt stood together. On the matter of civil rights and black equality, Humphrey had none of Roosevelt's equivocations.

SOMETHING IN THE STEWART Report bothered Roosevelt. Stewart's forceful arguments that *none* of the soldiers had done anything wrong were to Roosevelt naive and foolish, but he had known all along *some* of the men had to be innocent of any involvement, and now he wondered what to do about them. The Senate would wonder about this too, and giving these soldiers a way back into the army, no matter how difficult it might be, would make it easier to uphold the discharges of the others. It would be the right thing to do for more than one reason. It would be justice, of course. And some of the exonerated men might be more willing to identify the guilty ones. He decided it was a good idea to make a show of permitting reenlistment. He had Taft come up with a plan that allowed it but only after a soldier proved he was innocent. The burden of proof—some said an impossible burden—was settled on the soldiers.[36]

THERE WERE TWO SEPARATE Stewart reports—one for the White House and the other for Congress. They were virtually identical and both included the Constitution League resolution. The one addressed to "The President" asked him for nothing. He was not asked to unwind Special Orders No. 266 or otherwise rescind the discharges. The "petition" to Congress asked for an investigation. It was as if Milholland and Stewart knew Stewart had failed to turn up new facts showing the soldiers' innocence and were handing this task over to Congress. Reinstatement of the soldiers seemed to have been set aside by them for the time being. If asking Roosevelt for no relief was their indirect way of asking him to stand aside and allow the Senate to move ahead, they showed zero understanding of the man they were up against.

WILLIAM LOEB IMMEDIATELY SENT Stewart's report to Secretary of War Taft with no instructions or other comment. He knew the efficient Taft would do his duty. Copies were sent to General Garlington and Major Blocksom, each of whom answered within a few days that they interpreted the evidence differently.[37] This back and forth over what the evidence did or did not prove illustrates the red herring distracting anyone trying to figure out who was right in the Brownsville Incident. *It should not have been the soldiers' responsibility to prove anything. That was the government's burden, not to do so "conclusively," as Roosevelt would later say in his message of December 19, 1906, but "beyond a reasonable doubt."* Gilchrist Stewart understood this. In his telegram of November 29, he tried to shift the burden back onto the army and President Roosevelt. He tried to make the point that President Roosevelt, acting as the prosecutor (and, though he didn't say it, judge, jury, and executioner), failed to meet this burden. In his report of December 10, he also tried to persuade Roosevelt that if the soldiers had any burden it was whether "there is *fair reason* to believe that the commotion on the night in question was created by parties not soldiers" (author's emphasis). Stewart said there was. Historians considering Brownsville have tended to think Roosevelt did not meet his proper burden of proof, and while Stewart did meet the one he set for himself, he should not have had to. President Roosevelt, however, did not see himself as a court of law, and he did not see these rules as applicable to the discharges.

TWO DAYS LATER MAJOR Blocksom, pursuant to prior orders, was on the train to Washington to meet with President Roosevelt. With time on his hands and no distractions, he supplemented his response of December 4. He made note of Stewart's misspelling of the names of

Privates Howard and Lipscomb and wondered how soldiers could have been shooters and still gotten back for the roll calls. "I never believed the first roll calls were accurate," because officers and many noncommissioned officers thought principally of defending the post from attack and not taking roll.[38] He also recounted the number of soldiers not at the roll call and came up with a slightly higher number (but not enough to match the number of shooters).

Most important, whether he realized it or not, he lessened the burden for defending his recommendation of discharge. Discharge was justified for reasons of "public safety [rather] than punishment."[39] With such a lower and meaningless burden, he changed the game.

"All I care for is an investigation of the whole affair, in order that the real facts may be laid before the Senate."

Senator Joseph Foraker, editorial in the
New York Sun, January 22, 1907

CHAPTER FIFTEEN

CORDIAL COOPERATION

I T WAS CLEAR TO Senator Foraker that the December 6 resolutions weren't enough. Penrose's was weak, and Roosevelt could dodge its intent easily. His own was a fishing expedition for all information "in the possession of the [war] department," but after plowing through it all, then what? The word *investigation* was not in either of them. Roosevelt agreeing so quickly to abide by both showed he feared neither one.

THE DAY AFTER FORAKER presented the Constitution League/Stewart Report to the Senate, President Roosevelt met with John C. Spooner of Wisconsin, who had told senators he liked Foraker's resolution over Penrose's. Spooner disliked Penrose's use of the word *request* because it was appropriate only when disclosure of information was potentially harmful to the public interest, something not present here.[1] This did not mean he favored an investigation. He accepted the discharges because he felt Roosevelt had the authority to order them.

Earlier in his career Spooner had championed the Negro right to vote. In 1890 he spoke strongly in favor of then-representative Henry Cabot Lodge's legislation to reduce Southern representation in Congress for denying voting rights to Negroes (a denial not so implicitly blessed by Booker T. Washington's Atlanta Compromise).[2] "The guaranties of the Constitution and the majesty of the

238

law are not for any race or class."[3] Historian James R. Parker characterized him as one who adopted and used the Republican "talk" of equality, but did very little to achieve it. Mostly his "talk" was used to score political points against the Democrats and not as a sincere and sustained effort to resolve the problem. When the party's interests were involved, as in Brownsville, the party came first.[4] Spooner denied he was anything but genuine but admitted he was discouraged. "I took great interest . . . for years, until it seemed hopeless."[5]

Roosevelt and Spooner met five times in December and January "to discuss the case," beginning, according to Spooner's biographer, Dorothy Ganfield Fowler, on December 3, the day Penrose and Spooner introduced their resolutions.[6] "Shortly thereafter the Wisconsin Senator began to receive from Secretary of War Taft batches and batches of material on the Brownsville case."[7] All this mutual affection, courting, and some accommodation by Spooner did the trick. Spooner became a secure member of Team Roosevelt.

On December 19, along with a special message he claimed would put to rest all objections to the discharges, end Foraker's insurrection against him, and discourage any further opposition, Roosevelt sent the requested documentation. It must have landed on the senators' desks with a thud. The government later would publish it in book form as part of volume 11 of Senate Document No. 155 for that session of Congress, and it would be 545 pages long.[8] Its chronologic order meanders and makes frequent U-turns; there is no list of the documents, table of contents, or index; and there is barely any coherence in how it was assembled. It is confusing and hard to follow. That it had been prepared and delivered to the Senate so quickly may be an endorsement of the hard work and diligent attention devoted to it. Or a deliberate carelessness intended to make it unusable to Senator Foraker.

The first attachment to Roosevelt's message was a memorandum from Taft.[9] (The many exhibits and attachments to Roosevelt's message are really the exhibits and attachments to Taft's memo. Taft referred to them as the "full information bearing upon the order of discharge."[10]) Taft defended the discharges on the facts and the law. He disputed the conclusions in the Stewart Report and presented those he considered more likely and consistent with the facts. He analyzed the law, including how it was applied in past examples of discharges without honor, and incorporated the opinion of the army's "Judge-Advocate-General that confirmed the complete power of the President to discharge every member of any [military] organization."

Roosevelt's message itself was one of the most disturbing documents ever prepared by a president.[11] Its argumentative tone, abusive language, inflammatory imagery, and irresponsibly divisive rhetoric resembled a tirade by the generalissimo in a banana republic junta. Although Roosevelt began reasonably (in the first sentence he called what the soldiers did "misconduct"), immediately he stopped mincing words. What a sentence or two earlier had been characterized as "misconduct" was now "an attack, as cold blooded as it was cowardly," nothing "blacker [in] the annals of the army," "a dastardly crime," "mutiny and murder, treason," "atrocious conduct . . . under cover of night."[12] The attackers "leaped over the walls," "hurried through the town," "shot at whomever they saw moving," and "into houses where they saw lights." Their victims were "women and children," some "sleeping" in their beds, and innocent guests sitting by a window in a hotel. This was only the beginning of their criminal behavior. Evoking his recent annual message, Roosevelt told the Senate a second crime was banding "together in a conspiracy to protect the assassins." This was a "conspiracy of silence" disregarding that they had "sworn to uphold the laws of the United States, and [were] under every obligation of oath and honor not merely to refrain from criminality, but with the sturdiest rigor to hunt down criminality; and the crime they committed or connived at was murder. They perverted the power put into their hands to sustain the law into the most deadly violation of the law."[13]

He was speaking of men not convicted of a crime.

Though the army's report was "most careful," the guilty shooters could not be identified because "the streets of the town are poorly lighted."[14] He had no choice but to discharge them from the army without trial or hearing. And he had the right to do it because "these men were all in the service of the United States under contracts of enlistment, which by their terms and by statute were terminable by my direction as Commander in Chief of the Army. . . . It was my clear duty to terminate those contracts when the *public interest* demanded it; and it would have been a betrayal of the public interest on my part not to terminate the contracts which were keeping in the service of the United States a body of mutineers and murderers" (author's emphasis).[15] President Roosevelt here was invoking the rationale inspired by Major Blocksom while on the train to Washington earlier that month when he wrote, "All enlisted men of the three companies present on the night of August 13 [should] be discharged [from] the service" for reasons of "*public safety*" (author's emphasis).[16] President Roosevelt was making his case not as commander in chief but as "protector of the public." He was arguing that decisions made in this role overrode concerns with trials and due process of law. It would have been an impossible case to make in the twenty-first century, but Roosevelt was seeing if he could make it stick in 1906.

Turning from public protector to public executioner, he reminded senators what he did was not punishment because "discharge from the service" was "utterly inadequate." He regretted being unable to punish them with "death."[17] If he had not already crossed the line separating discourse from demagoguery, he went on to obliterate it. In his annual message two weeks earlier he "gave utterance to the abhorrence which all decent citizens should feel for the deeds of [in almost all cases white men] who take part in lynchings," and astonishingly he accused Brownsville soldiers of committing a crime just like lynching. "In the case of these companies we had to deal with men who in the first place were *guilty of what is practically the worst possible form of lynching*—for a lynching is in its essence lawless and murderous vengeance taken by an armed mob for real or fancied wrongs—and who in the second place *covered up the crime of lynching* by standing with a vicious solidarity to protect the criminals" (author's emphasis).[18] Negroes reading or hearing these words must have shivered.[19]

The next day the *Washington Post* reported, "The virility of language and forcefulness of expression . . . excited much wonder among the Senators." In an accompanying editorial it said, "The

President comes back with terrific force." But it could not, nor would not, disguise that *Roosevelt was declaring war on "a group of his Republican colleagues"* (author's emphasis).[20] President Roosevelt already had, seemingly with little concern, antagonized black voters, virtually all of whom were Republicans. Now he was threatening to create a second front in the intraparty conflict and widen the split. His enemies now were fellow Republicans.

IN HIS MEMOIRS WRITTEN a decade later, Joseph Foraker said Roosevelt's message was "of the most vitriolic character. His language bore evidence on its face of intent to make it nearly offensive to all who disagreed from him."[21] But that day he responded "as soon as the reading [of the message] was concluded." Before Penrose or anyone else could gain a step on him, he was on his feet: "Mr. President I ask that the message, with the accompanying exhibits and all paper connected therewith, may be printed as a document and referred to the Committee on Military Affairs, with instructions to take such testimony as may be necessary to establish all the facts, the expense so incurred to be paid out of the contingent fund of the Senate."[22] This was clever. A request to print the message and its exhibits required practically no permission from senators and normally would be accepted by the vice president saying quickly and indistinctly, "Hearing-no-objection-it-is-so-ordered," as if it were one long word. Foraker's feint was to couple the printing request with an order sending it to the Military Affairs Committee and hope no one would notice or object. If he could get way with that, then the other language ("with instructions to take such testimony as may be necessary to establish all the facts, the expense so incurred to be paid out of the contingent fund of the Senate") was enough for the committee to start and maintain an investigation. Foraker was trying to avoid a formal investigation resolution that would have to be introduced, accepted for discussion, debated, amended, hashed out and in the end approved. Or not.

Who would have expected him to disguise the investigation by folding it into a routine request that a document be printed? Henry Cabot Lodge would. Coming out of his chair, the senator from Massachusetts spoke quietly, "The last part ought to be a separate reso-lution. The usual motion is, of course, that the message be referred and printed, to which there is no objection, but I think before we decide to enter on a Congressional investigation the matter ought to be presented at least separately."[23] The battle had begun.

It was clear to both sides that an investigation eventually would be approved. The fight was to frame its scope in terms favorable to one side or the other. Foraker wanted an unhampered inquiry, in which he as a member of the Military Affairs Committee could probe Brownsville as a frontier surgeon probed a wound until he found the bullet and could begin to work on its damage. Lodge, acting on President Roosevelt's behalf, wanted the investigation cor-ralled for the same reasons Foraker did not. The less it could do, the less it could accomplish.

Foraker tested Lodge's determination. Presenting the inves-tigation separate from the printing was fine, he said, but was there an objection to "testimony being taken in regard to the facts of the matter?" Lodge ignored the question and shot back, if an investiga-tion is what you want and what the Senate wants, let us do it right. Foraker tried again. We don't know "whether all the evidence is there [in the documents included with the special message]." Isn't it better that it goes to the committee for it to sift through and see if it is com-plete and, if not, what to do about it? Again ignoring Foraker, Lodge repeated to the vice president, "I ask that the motion be divided."[24]

Boies Penrose came to Lodge's assistance with "a suggestion to the Senator from Ohio." Why not simply print Roosevelt's special message, send it to the Military Affairs Committee, and see what it wants to do. If it wants a resolution, it can ask for it.[25]

Senator Joseph C. S. Blackburn of Kentucky, a Democrat and his party's leader in the Senate, spoke up. Neither he nor the Demo-crats cared a bit what happened to the soldiers, and an investigation, the tougher the better, was fine with him. Let the Republicans tear each other and President Roosevelt to pieces publicly for the next few months. His interest was to make mischief. Blackburn said he saw no reason why the request for printing would be a problem, but in his haste to take the floor and sneak his non-resolution resolution past the Senate, Foraker had not bothered to write out what he wanted. Write it down, said Blackburn, so we may see whether your purpose is "to instruct and direct the Military Affairs Committee . . . to make an investigation, or whether . . . to leave it to the committee to determine whether an investigation is to be made."[26] Foraker could see he had gotten all the mileage he ever would out of his verbal resolution and sat down at his desk to write out what he wanted the Senate to do. While he did this, Vice President Fairbanks pronounced that the part asking for the printing was agreed to.

While Foraker was scribbling at his desk, deciding what to ask for and how to ask for it, Lodge used the dead space to point out that Roosevelt sent over "a considerable amount of printed testimony" and added, "which I for one should like to examine." Before he agreed to an investigation, "I should like to see the papers first."[27] Foraker continued to gather his thoughts and put them in writing while the Senate temporarily turned to other business. When he was finished, he presented it to the Senate. It said that if after reviewing the documents given to the Senate the committee wanted an investigation, it was authorized to conduct it.

Lodge said this was fine with him, because, as he understood this proposed resolution, it did not order an investigation. That was left to the Military Affairs Committee, which "by bill or otherwise" could ask for one. Or not, if it chose. Foraker and Lodge were talking past each other and getting nowhere. Senator Francis Warren was unsure where they were going but knew whenever they got there the problem would land in his lap as the chairman of the Military Affairs Committee. He reminded the Senate that payment of the committee's expenses first had to be approved by a different committee.[28] Another hurdle for Foraker, something he did not anticipate or, if he did, he thought he could finesse; it was potentially more delay. Spooner of Wisconsin wanted to hear the resolution again. After it was read, Foraker, still hoping to get the matter into the Military Affairs Committee that day, modified what he wrote down to omit this funding problem. Before it could be discussed, Alexander Clay of Georgia, a Democrat, wanted more time to read the testimony. Like schoolyard bullies they were starting to pile on Foraker.

Clay objected to any consideration of a resolution, whatever it was. Shelby Collum, an Illinois Republican, wanted the Senate to move on to other business. Foraker tried to speak; Collum would not let him, insisting upon his motion.[29]

Here the "debate" ended. Its deliberate tumult and confusion, disguised as sincere questions and honest expressions of opinion, were a warning to Foraker. This is what he was in for. They were only starting.

THE WASHINGTON POST WOULD write the next day that Roosevelt's message was "as much a defiance as an explanation."[30] John Milholland wrote in his diary, "Began the day by sending Foraker a ringing telegram. He is leading the fight in Congress on behalf of the Negro Battalion Roosevelt dismissed. The President fired another message yesterday in defense of his undefensible action, seeking by violent language to force the public to accept his 'hot air for evidence and conclusions.'" His friend Joe Smith called it "sewer gas."[31]

Roosevelt wanted Foraker to know he was not afraid of an inquiry. Foraker already knew that, and he knew he was in for a fight. Roosevelt's point man in the Senate that day, Henry Cabot Lodge, did well on his behalf but once or twice needed some help from colleagues. Foraker never got his resolution accepted; in fact, he never got to formally introduce it. He tried to deal with objections by accommodating them rather than meeting them head on. But he was still in the game. He showed he was prepared, clever, and able to adjust to the debate. He would be more careful about giving in to objections from here on. His opponents had not killed his resolution. He would bring it up again tomorrow.

The day was a draw.

Except no one stood with Foraker. No senator was there to come into the debate and spell him for a minute or two so he could collect his thoughts. Not one member of his party spoke for his position. None was his ally.

He was still alone.

AS VICE PRESIDENT FAIRBANKS brought the Senate to order the next day, the visitors' galleries and those for the press, diplomats, and

VIPs were full. Senator Foraker was to reply to President Roosevelt's special message and nobody wanted to miss it. Sitting on the floor of the Senate were two former secretaries of war, now Republican senators. Redfield Proctor of Vermont led the War Department under President Harrison, and Michigan's Russell A. Alger under McKinley. Both may have whispered a quiet thanks to the heavens they never had to face anything like Brownsville or an angry president like Theodore Roosevelt. In the reserved-seating areas were Congressman Nicholas Longworth from Cincinnati (President Roosevelt's son-in-law) and Joseph Cannon, the Speaker of the House of Representatives.[32] Both had come over from the other side of the Capitol to hear what Foraker had to say. Both knew they were in for a great performance by Longworth's fellow Cincinnatian. The vice president asked the clerk to read Foraker's resolution coming over from yesterday, and when the clerk finished, Fairbanks turned to his college friend from Ohio Wesleyan and gestured that the Senate floor was his.

HE BEGAN NOT LIKE a fire alarm but as an experienced lawyer, quietly and earnestly pleading his client's case with simple words and without the need for histrionics. Roosevelt the day before was a loose cannon, firing off one misstatement after another.[33] Foraker, with the confidence of a debater, would have the facts at hand to support what he said and could cite them quickly and correctly. He was quiet, almost conversational, as he started off with what appeared to be a yarn. When he got home last night, he told the Senate, he had a chance to read for the third time what President Roosevelt said in his message. "I may be mistaken but in my opinion," President Roosevelt has no authority to discharge the soldiers, and even if he does the evidence does not support it. In this rural manner, the big-city lawyer expressed the situation in a way anyone could understand. For the record, he repeated it more formally: "He has misconceived . . . his constitutional powers" and "misconceived the testimony upon which his action is based."[34]

He remained formal and studied as he analyzed the constitutional text. According to Article II, Section 1 of the Constitution (which he read from his notes), "The President shall be Commander in Chief of the Army." He stopped. "I have read far enough. That's all [it] says." But "*Congress* shall have the power, 'To make Rules for the government and regulation of the land and naval forces'" (author's emphasis).[35] So, for example, a president can say "where they should be stationed in time of peace." But Congress determines "how . . . men shall be enlisted and men shall be discharged [and] the rights that shall accrue to them on account of their service."[36] Foraker was beginning a logical, step-by-step argument. First an undeniable statement, followed by another just as undeniable, then another, and so on, until at the end a listener has agreed with each link in the chain and must accept the strength of the conclusion. Foraker forged the next link. The military forces were governed by the Articles of War enacted by Congress.[37] He took the time to read nineteen separate articles, showing the Senate that Congress had identified offenses that seem to have been what the Brownsville soldiers were accused of, and in every one of these it was *a court-martial that must decide guilt and a court-martial that must impose punishment. Not the president*, whether as commander in chief or in any other capacity. He next cited a treatise on military law by General George B. Davis that said "refusing to testify . . . and give evidence" (which Foraker did not have to say is exactly what a conspiracy of silence is) came within Article 62. Therefore such a charge too must be tried by court-martial and guilt must be punished by court-martial, not by President Roosevelt. This General George B. Davis happened to be army's "Judge-Advocate-General" advising President Roosevelt and Secretary Taft on their actions in Brownsville.[38]

Senator Lodge had heard enough to be worried, and he attempted to distract Foraker by asking why then were 352 enlisted men discharged without honor in the past two years without first being court-martialed under Article 62? Foraker asked for his patience: "I am going to take that up separately." But to avoid the impression this response was simply a dodge to avoid answering, he told Lodge these were men primarily who had to be discharged because they enlisted when they were underage or were otherwise barred from military service, but not because they were accused or found guilty of a crime. The men of the Black Battalion are not seeking a discharge, *they want to stay in the army*. Lodge sat down, sorry he asked the question.

Foraker was not finished. He disputed Roosevelt's assertion this was no punishment. Even Garlington said that was what it was. In front of the Senate, Foraker consulted a dictionary, and it agreed with him. When he finished, Lodge said to him and the Senate, "I will not interrupt the Senator again." This was not an act of courtesy; he had learned his lesson.[39]

Having disposed of Roosevelt's misunderstanding of his constitutional authority, Foraker began to show that Roosevelt misinterpreted the evidence and misdescribed it to the Senate the day before. Roosevelt said there were "scores of witnesses." Last night at home, Foraker confided to the Senate, he carefully counted them using the reports and investigations Roosevelt said *he* relied on. There were not scores, only twenty-one, and slowly and distinctly so as not to be misunderstood, he read off every name, in effect daring anyone to disagree with his count, from George W. Rendall, "the first," on down to G. W. H. Rucker, "the twenty-first." He paused so this could be absorbed.

Not all twenty-one were *eyewitnesses*. He read the testimony of each witness that on its face disqualified that person. After the first was eliminated, for the benefit of those not keeping score he said, "The number is down to twenty." He continued counting backward until, after reading G. W. H. Rucker's statement, he told the Senate, "So he saw nothing. That cuts the number down to eight." From Roosevelt's "scores" the number was down to only "eight."[40]

AND THEN HE COMMITTED what may have been his only mistake that day. He felt he had to respond to something President Roosevelt said the day before. "He has seen to point out . . . that Major Blocksom . . . is from Ohio." Was he saying that Blocksom's report "should be strengthened thereby?"

Foraker had received an unsolicited letter from "a most reputable, a most honored man in the State of Ohio, a man of the highest character who has known Major Blocksom all his life." Because of what this unidentified correspondent wrote, Foraker believed Major Blocksom was "unfitted" for investigating Brownsville. "He [Major Blocksom] is not aware of it. . . . Unconsciously he is the victim of early influences" from his father. Foraker read from the man's letter that Blocksom Sr., "an active and radical Democrat politician [was] of the Vallandigham type." Clement Vallandigham, Ohio governor during the first two years of the Civil War, was what President Lincoln called a "wily agitator." He disliked Negroes, supported slavery, opposed the war, spoke harshly and disparagingly of Lincoln personally and the Union cause generally, and did so every chance he got. He was eventually convicted of violating a military order against publicly declaring sympathies for the enemy. Vallandigham was to the Civil War what Quisling was to World War II, though his tongue-twister name never entered the English language as a synonym for traitor. Putting the letter down on the desk, Foraker continued with his own thoughts after receiving this letter. "[Major Blocksom] was the son of that kind of a father and in his youth that kind of political affiliation and that kind of political atmosphere. It is natural that he should inherit that prejudice and carry it with him and be insensibly influenced by it in the discharge of this very delicate duty. I think anybody could see, by simply reading his report, that there was some kind of a screw loose with him."[41]

Blocksom's report shows nothing of the kind. Nothing in it or his telegrams, letters, and conversations during the Brownsville Incident suggests he was anything like that. Whatever feelings common to that time Blocksom may have carried with him on the train to Brownsville the previous August, to stain him with his father's political passions, with which there was no evidence he agreed, eroded Foraker's otherwise-admirable speech.

HAVING REFUTED PRESIDENT ROOSEVELT's claim of authority and weakened his explanation of the evidence from the shooting, there remained only the conspiracy of silence to deal with. General Garlington said the denials themselves were proof of the conspiracy. Foraker showed this was absurd: "In Heaven's name, if a man is absolutely innocent, as these men claim to be, what else could he say?"[42]

Then, because he probably saved it for the end to make a stronger impression, he recalled Roosevelt said "there were plenty of precedents" for discharging an entire battalion without honor. But he showed none to the Senate. Because there was none. His military secretary had reported a "protracted examination of the official records [failed] to discover a precedent." Foraker agreed, "Senators will study in vain to find any precedent with the United States Army."[43] Certainly not the case of the Sixtieth Ohio cited by Roosevelt, because it was "disorganized, mutinous and worthless."[44] Foraker knew the Sixtieth Ohio well; he and it both came from Highland County. Its colonel, "I knew as intimately as a boy could know a man of full age and full of the affairs of the world."[45]

At this point the vice president, perhaps afraid Foraker was about to retrieve his handkerchief to wipe his tears and suggest his colleagues do the same with their own, stepped in to halt, even if only temporarily, the Foraker onslaught. He asked the Senate if it could turn its attention to the unfinished business of railroad employees' working hours. Senator Robert La Follette objected, saying they should keep to the topic at hand.[46]

Foraker returned to the slandered Sixtieth. Its parallel with Brownsville was an illusion. Those Ohioans were guilty of nothing and had not been discharged for anything questionable; "almost every man of them immediately enlisted in other regiments and went to the front, and every one of them made a good record as a soldier." Senator Nathan B. Scott, Republican from West Virginia, who had yet to speak a word, could not restrain himself and leaped up to echo Foraker. Some soldiers from the Sixtieth Ohio became members of his company in the war, and they would not have been allowed in had they been given a tainted discharge.[47] At last, a senator standing with Foraker before the Senate.

Foraker ended by mentioning how valiantly and heroically black soldiers had fought for their country. They deserved nothing less than what President Roosevelt said he wanted for all Americans: "a square deal."[48]

Senator Lodge realized how well-argued and powerful Foraker's appeal was, and he could not let senators go home for the holidays with it as the last words ringing in their ears. He wanted to change the soldiers' choirboy image Foraker had drawn. Lodge began, "If this regiment or these companies were entirely innocent of this shooting with which they are charged, as the Senator from Ohio alleges—" The senator from Ohio stopped him cold: "I do not allege that. Only that their guilt has not been conclusively challenged. I think there is testimony to show that they are free from guilt, but I do not know what the facts are, and I want to find out."[49] Lodge could not have been a bigger shill for Foraker if he had auditioned for the part. If Lodge thought he would get in the last licks, Senator Scott surprised him. Having found his courage defending the Sixtieth Ohio, he now stood up for the men of the Twenty-Fifth Infantry. He was aware one of its former commanding officers would vouch for their reliability, and he hoped the Military Affairs Committee would take his and others' testimony. Then he took a swipe at President Roosevelt. Were it not for the bravery of the Tenth Cavalry (a colored regiment, he made sure to point out), "we might not now have the privilege of having in the White House that brave soldier and . . . patriotic President of ours."[50] *That* was the last thing the senators heard about Brownsville before the Senate adjourned for the year.

WHO WON THIS DAY? Foraker. Except for the Vallandigham-Blocksom mistake, he spoke without resort to subterfuge, misstatement, or bombast. As the *Washington Post* put it the next day, he did it with "his own picturesque style of oratory."[51] And he was scoring points outside the Senate. The *New York Evening Post* called for a full Senate inquiry.[52] Other newspapers already had, and still others would join them. Roosevelt was in for a battle.

FORAKER'S EFFECTIVE COUNTERATTACK WOUNDED any satisfaction President Roosevelt may have felt after his special message. Roosevelt energized his fight. He tried to intimidate the Senate by promising a hard and unending fight. He said he would veto any legislation to give any relief at all to the soldiers; if Congress overrode his veto, he would ignore it; if this brought about his impeachment, he would welcome it.[53] And he took out his frustration on discharged Brownsville soldiers who claimed they were innocent and wanted to reenlist under the arrangement he had Taft set up. He added a new condition that they help discover the shooters.[54] To get back in, soldiers had to be innocent *and be detectives for the army.*

But more was needed to rehabilitate the evidence Foraker had fractured so effectively. Roosevelt met with the two lawyers he had the most faith in, his secretaries of state and war, Elihu Root and William Taft. According to John Weaver, these two men suggested he refute Foraker with sworn testimony.[55] Roosevelt saw the merit in the idea, and on December 22 he ordered Assistant Attorney General Milton D. Purdy to leave for Brownsville, and to meet Major Blocksom, and "to conduct a thorough, careful, and impartial examination of the witnesses as to the issue who were the perpetrators of the crime."[56] To General Garlington, Taft wrote, "The President wishes me to say that Major Blocksom does not go as a prosecuting officer in the trial of an indictment, but only as an examiner, to elicit the truth and to put the evidence in respect to the matter in convenient and permanent form. The President has reached a conclusion as to what the facts are, but this should not influence Major Blocksom in his examination, for if the President's conclusion in the matter is wrong he earnestly desires that it be put right."[57] If indeed this is what Roosevelt told Taft to pass on, this was a "posterity letter," a communication designed to purify what he was doing for history. The *Washington Post* saw through it; Purdy and Blocksom were headed for Brownsville to "secure legal evidence tending to prove that the shooting was done by members of the battalion."[58] The *New York Times* agreed. Roosevelt wanted them to "bring back the absolute proof that the rioting at Brownsville was the work of the men of the Twenty-Fifth Infantry and not of residents of the town."[59] In a letter to Democratic senator W. A. Clark of Montana a few days later, Foraker said the new investigation was because of his response to the president's special message.[60] Roosevelt biographer Henry Pringle said the same thing but in a different way: "Roosevelt must have agreed the evidence was insufficient."[61]

IT WAS CLEAR TO Booker T. Washington as early as November 5, when President Roosevelt coldly refused a plea to reconsider the discharges, that his mind was set and could not be changed.[62] Washington's fight now was as much for himself as for the Twenty-Fifth Infantry. He continued to tell others of his disappointment but, sure this would sour Roosevelt's attitude toward blacks and further damage his own now-wobbling relationship with the White House, did not publicly condemn Roosevelt. When a mass meeting was held in Washington on November 18 "to discuss the matter," he refused to attend, "as I do not believe in abusing the President; but I think all of the colored people should go slow on him hereafter."[63] In a letter to Ralph Tyler, he advised others to control themselves. "If our people make the mistake of going too far, there will be a reaction in the North among the people and newspapers who have stood by us."[64]

Meanwhile, Washington was working to shore up his position of influence for the future. After urging Secretary Taft to refill the Twenty-Fifth Infantry with black soldiers, he had Emmett Scott suggest black musicians be appointed as chief musicians in "colored army bands." Taft accepted the idea and issued the necessary order. This was a good start; black newspapers such as the *Indianapolis Freeman* praised the idea.[65] Those Washington most wanted to impress, of course, were other blacks. He was increasingly dealing with whispers he had lost his touch. Du Bois was the main concern. Brownsville, assisted by the Atlanta rioting, "gave [him] additional justification for attacking Washington."[66] The new year would see Washington increasingly under siege and increasingly fighting back.

FORAKER WAS ON A surge and used the Senate's holiday recess to build on it. It now seemed only a matter of time before a resolution all could agree to would be approved. He and Milholland met in New York on Christmas Eve to come to an understanding to work together on the Brownsville matter. Milholland noted in his diary,

"Saw Foraker. . . . Cordial cooperation agreed upon all around."[67] An alliance was formed.

ON HIS WAY UP from Washington, Foraker may have stopped in Philadelphia to see his brother James, hospitalized there with what would shortly be diagnosed as terminal cancer. At one time the brothers were law partners in Cincinnati, but it does not appear they were especially close. Foraker's niece Ethel Marie was with her father, and news of his illness came regularly in letters to her "Uncle Ben" (short for Benson, his middle name).

A month earlier Foraker had written their brother in Albuquerque, "Dear Creighton: I saw brother James at the University Hospital in Philadelphia yesterday. I had seen him also Tuesday and Wednesday, last. I was surprised to find him yesterday apparently much worse. I would have remained with him, but some matters here require me to return to Washington. The doctors think it will be necessary to operate on him again, and they have concluded to do so at 1:30 today. I fear the result, or rather I fear the operation will do no good. His present affliction is of a cancerous character, and it gives him constant and intense suffering and pain. I write this to prepare you for the unwelcome announcement which I fear I will have to send you soon. Hoping you are well, I am, Affectionately &c."[68] The operation was postponed, but the news from Philadelphia remained grim. Ethel wrote Foraker, "I know how you suffer when others are suffering."

On November 25 she gave him reason for further agony. "Papa has been suffering so intensely that the Doctor says he must be operated on immediately." After the surgery the doctor wrote Foraker, "I regret to say that we found much more extensive disease [and] some brain symptoms developed which appear to be secondary to a [newly discovered] growth in the base of the brain. . . . This has been a disappointment."

On Saturday, December 1, while planning for the Senate's opening session and meeting with President Roosevelt at the White House, Foraker wrote to cheer up his brother, "My dear brother: I would have written sooner, but I was hoping I might return to

Philadelphia and have a chance to talk with you, but each day has brought me some new demand, and in consequence I have been kept here. . . . I am so glad you underwent the last operation, and that you are recovering from it so nicely. We gave more thanks here on [Thanksgiving] on that account than any other."

On December 5 Ethel wrote, "[Papa] is very interested in your interest in the dismissing of the Negro troops. I have read to him about it." But Jim's condition worsened. On December 7, the day after the Senate approved the Penrose and Foraker resolutions, Foraker wrote his niece, "I feel a little disturbed by your last letter saying your father now has some kind of bad feeling in his head. Kindly keep me fully advised." On December 10 Creighton arrived in Philadelphia from New Mexico and wrote his brother Ben, "I arrived here this morn and I went to see Jim. . . . He seemed delighted to think that I had come to see him. This has been a bad day for him, he has been suffering with pain in the head and side of face. . . . He likes to joke a little yet. He told the nurse that I would be here to see him to day and that I was very tall & slim and was a Conservative so when I presented myself she did not know whether to let me in or not. . . . If you could come over during this time I believe it would do him good to see you as well as myself."

Brownsville kept Foraker from joining Creighton in Philadelphia. He was torn between the obligation he had taken on for the Twenty-Fifth Infantry and the one he owed Jim. Creighton came through Washington on his way back to New Mexico and "was in the Senate when I was speaking on the discharge of the Negro troops, but I did not get to see him afterward. He had to leave, as I was informed, on account of his train." The three brothers would never be together again.

MILHOLLAND ALSO NOTED IN his diary after their meeting in New York, "Foraker had said Roosevelt had sent 5 or 6 Secret Service men to Texas on advice of Dept. of Justice."[69] Right after the holiday, the story broke in the newspapers. The Secret Service was in Brownsville probing for evidence Roosevelt could use against Foraker and to "forestall an investigation."[70]

The idea originally was not Roosevelt's. Right after the shooting, General Fred Ainsworth wired William Loeb that it would be a good idea for the president to "suggest" to the secretary of the treasury that the Secret Service get involved. Loeb passed this on to Roosevelt, who agreed.[71] Ainsworth met with John E. Wilkie, the Secret Service's chief, to discuss the shooting and later sent him a copy of Blocksom's report and said he stood ready to discuss it so they could "discover the guilty parties."[72] Roosevelt was merely continuing the practices of previous presidents. "Like other presidents, TR relied on the Secret Service for investigations," including those by Attorney General Bonaparte into land, postal, and timber fraud, and ominously, congressional misbehaviors.[73] One member of Congress he looked into was South Carolina's Ben Tillman. Roosevelt went too far with this one. Members of Congress shuddered at what the Secret Service might know about them and prohibited its agents from any tasks other than "physically protecting the President and hunting down counterfeiters."

Roosevelt fretted over this restriction for the rest of his administration. In his 1908 annual message he snorted this benefitted "only the criminal classes," and "the chief argument in favor of [it] was that the congressmen did not themselves wish to be investigated."[74] He was right. When he proposed members of Congress permit themselves to be investigated but grant themselves immunity from prosecution, they declined the suggestion.

In 1906 Roosevelt sicced the Secret Service on Joseph Foraker.

GILCHRIST STEWART AND A man named Richard Le Roy Stokes accompanied Foraker on the train back to Washington. Milholland noted in his diary on Christmas Eve, "Decided to send Stokes to Brownsville armed with letters to US Marshall Houston of Texas." Milholland didn't know it but Stokes was a spy for Booker T. Washington. At one time Washington's stenographer at Tuskegee, he was sent to New York to work at the *New York Age* with T. Thomas Fortune in 1905.[75] He remained Washington's mole at the *Age* until the beginning of December 1906, when Fortune had to let him go during one of the newspaper's recurring financial crises prompted by

Washington's capriciously opening and closing the money spigot as a way of controlling Fortune.[76] While Stokes was at the *Age*, Washington had trusted him enough to think of him replacing Fortune at the National Negro Business League meeting in Atlanta just before the riots there.[77] After leaving the *Age*, he hooked up with Gilchrist Stewart, the other double agent. According to Constitution League secretary Charles Anderson, "Stewart . . . informed me that Stokes had played false with both him and the Constitution League. . . . He had advised Milholland to send Stokes to Brownsville. . . . Stewart now claims that Stokes has gone over to the other side.[78] In fact, he double crossed Milholland, who had given him a letter from Joseph Pulitzer's *New York World* stating he was one of its reporters. Milholland told him to send anything he learned back to the *World*. What Stokes sent, and what appeared in the paper on January 14, proved "that the soldiers actually did the shooting—which of course, nobody doubted."[79] Milholland was stunned.

Booker T. Washington had liberally salted the Constitution League with spies. He himself would take a shot directly at Milholland, who made a fortune supplying pneumatic tubes for moving mail between post offices, when he wrote to Postmaster General George Cortelyou: "[Milholland] who is more responsible than any of the others put together for stirring up trouble against the administration on the Brownsville affair draws the money he is using in this fight from your department. [If it were not for him] the whole Brownsville Affair would have been almost forgotten before this time."[80]

The Stewart-Stokes saga and the letter to Cortelyou are typical of the fanatical attention Washington was by now paying to his enemies within the black movement. He was running a spy network against them. Du Bois, Monroe Trotter, and others for whom the scales had fallen from their eyes when looking at the Wizard would use Washington's inattention to the real problem to snatch the agenda away from him.

BACK IN WASHINGTON, FORAKER, while waiting for the Senate to reconvene in January and get back to considering the investigation, worked to get whatever mileage he could from the December 6 resolutions, just in case an investigation was not approved. He asked Taft to provide various documents of questionable value to him.[81]

A FEW DAYS LATER, John Milholland wrote his New Year's resolutions in his diary: "To get my temper, my passionate nature in hand. To that end, I've appealed to God for divine aid. . . . To go forward in the Crusade for Justice to the Negro."[82]

"In appointing you, I have only one qualification to make. Colonel [George] Goethals here is to be chairman. He is to have complete authority. If at any time you do not agree with his policies, do not bother to tell me about it—your disagreement with him will constitute your resignation."

Theodore Roosevelt's charge to new
members of the Panama Canal Commission, from
David McCullough, *The Path between the Seas*

CHAPTER SIXTEEN

MOST IMPLICIT FAITH

O N JANUARY 3 THE Senate reconvened after the holidays and picked up where it had left off in December. Before Foraker could present his case, senators sat through Charles Culberson of Texas raging for two hours against the very idea of blacks in the army. When he finished, Henry Cabot Lodge offered an amendment to Foraker's resolution, which presumed "the President [acted within] his constitutional and legal authority as Commander in Chief." This would be voted on *before* a vote on Foraker's resolution, and to vote against it would be to deny Roosevelt's authority. Roosevelt and Lodge knew even Foraker was not willing to go that far, and the amendment would pass and become part of Foraker's resolution. If Foraker's resolution then passed, no matter what an investigation turned up, the discharges could not be overridden because Roosevelt's authority to order them would be undisturbed. This, said the *New York Times*, "was a very shrewd move, which [put] Mr. Foraker badly in the hole."[1]

Actually it was a blunder, and the *New York Times* corrected itself the next day. In an editorial it called Lodge's amendment "irrelevant, impertinent, and incompetent." The Senate could keep presidential authority out of the discussion simply by saying it was not pertinent to the Foraker resolution.[2] Besides, Foraker's resolution did not question Roosevelt's authority; it limited the investigation only to "facts." He knew all along it would be easier to get his resolution adopted if it did not question "presidential authority." On Sunday there were rumors some senators were asking Lodge to withdraw his amendment to avoid any constitutional discussion.[3] They feared it might establish a precedent diminishing Congress's power. Not wanting a fight with Republican senators, one he (and Roosevelt) might lose, Lodge withdrew his amendment. Roosevelt, who had a deaf ear to the crescendo against him by party regulars from his double-cross the previous spring over the Hepburn Bill, was perhaps more sensitive to it now.[4] Lodge and Roosevelt caving in was seen for the defeat it was.[5]

While Lodge was speaking to the Senate, Wisconsin's Robert La Follette was tending to correspondence with an ear to the debate. In a letter to his wife written on US Senate stationery, he told her what he was seeing and hearing.

> Monday afternoon,
>
> Dear Ones at Home,
>   The Senate is in session and Lodge is speaking in support of the Pres. in dismissing the Colored Troops. The galleries have been crowded all day. It is strange what interest the people have manifest in this subject. No legislation last session drew larger crowds.
>   . . .
>   Lodge has just finished and has made a very good speech. Foraker is getting up to reply to him. He sees this as I. Gives him the chance to slap the Pres & Taft—who supports the Pres. He also sees a chance to get the colored people with him. He is really a candidate—everyone thinks—or ready to be one. He is showing great feeling in his talk. . . . As a speaker [Foraker] has shown off to a better advantage than at any time I have heard him.[6]

NO ONE EVER EXPECTED to see what happened a few days later. Senator "Pitchfork Ben" Tillman, who yielded to no man in racist views, was going to speak and, of all things, defend the black soldiers of the Twenty-Fifth Infantry. Negroes wanted so badly to hear it, they lined up early in the day to be allowed into the Senate's public galleries, and so many of them made it in, the "galleries looked dark brown from the other side of the Chamber." Northern Republican senators gave passes to black friends, who thus were admitted to the reserved galleries, where they sat "cheek by jowl" with white matrons there courtesy of Southern Democrats.[7] The *Washington Post* would report Tillman was, when he spoke off the cuff without his notes, "lurid, vehement, and picturesque and always entertaining."[8] His siding with Negroes may have been what brought the people in, but for Tillman the soldiers' plight was merely a sideshow. His real interest that day was, as it always was, pummeling President Roosevelt and expressing his own primitive, even for those days, views on race.

Tillman's face was deformed by a missing left eye. When he was seventeen, the left eye had to be removed from its socket when infection set in from a swim in a millpond in rural South Carolina.[9] He wore no patch over the hole, and photos of him generally show his right profile. It was as if, with only one eye, he saw only half the world, and there was no room in it for any but white people. A lifetime of abusive racism warped his mind just as the missing eye deformed his face.[10] Only two colors—black and white—were permitted by his remaining eye to pass into the darkness of his mind, and everyone he encountered was tested by this stark duality. That which was white was biologically superior and developed, civilized, talented, decent, and diligent. That which was black was barbarous, savage, low, and degraded.[11] For Tillman, Brownsville showed Negroes and Roosevelt at their worst, but Tillman could use each to go after the other.[12] If he had to form an alliance with blacks and Joseph Foraker to bludgeon Roosevelt, so be it.[13]

It was the brutal, unimaginably bloody, stomach-turning, savagely cruel violence that set him apart from any well-formed human being, and he was only too ready and too happy to visit it on blacks. On the Fourth of July in 1876, Captain D. L. "Dock" Adams, a black Union Army veteran, led a black state militia company in the Independence Day parade in Hamburg, South Carolina. The small town across the Savannah River from Augusta, Georgia, was a showpiece for black advancement during Reconstruction. What happened forecast the end of both. Depending on which version you believe, either a carriage with two young men from well-to-do white families deliberately drove through the militia's columns, or the militia deliberately refused to allow it to pass.[14] Ben Tillman, who was then twenty-nine, lived not far away in the town of Edgefield and was the commander of its paramilitary unit dedicated to terrorizing Republican officeholders and restoring white rule in South Carolina. He chose to believe the white men. He led his troublemakers to Hamburg and joined other whites in the coldblooded murder of the black militiamen. They then burned the town to the ground.[15] John Hope, who in 1906 was the president of Atlanta Baptist (now Morehouse) College, was then eight years old and living in Augusta. He recalled hearing men shout from across the river, "This is the beginning of the redemption of South Carolina."[16] Tillman, no doubt exaggerating his part in the massacre, would later say the leading white men of Edgefield had decided to seize the first opportunity that the Negroes might offer them to provoke a riot and teach the Negroes a lesson by killing as many of them as was justifiable.[17] In post-Reconstruction South Carolina, this was a boast and a career boost, and it was certainly that for Ben Tillman. The Hamburg Massacre and how he described his part in it made him a leader of the white supremacy movement in the state.[18] He was admired and supported by white farmers and workers he said he would protect from aristocratic whites (the so-called Bourbons: bankers, merchants, and landowners mostly from the Low Country and around Charleston) and, most important, from blacks. In 1896 the farmers and workers elected him to the US Senate.[19] Five years later, Roosevelt's dinner with Booker T. Washington would drive him to say, "The action of President Roosevelt in entertaining that nigger will necessitate our killing a thousand niggers in the South before they will learn their place again."[20] Five years after that, he would defend the rights of 167 black soldiers against an evil just as great: Theodore Roosevelt. Tillman had no interest in clearing up what happened in Brownsville and bringing justice to it, but like an actor on a stage, he used the soldiers as handy props to help him better play his role bedeviling Roosevelt.[21]

HE ADMITTED THE "RIDICULOUSNESS of the situation," he told the Senate: the Negro soldiers being defended by him, "who is supposed to have a broiled negro for breakfast [here the *Congressional Record* indicates 'laughter'], who is known to justify lynching for rape, and whose attitude is one of not hatred toward the negroes, but of a feeling akin to it, in the belief that white men are made of better clay than negroes and that white men alone are entitled to participate in government—I say this alliance is an odd one." He immediately attacked President Roosevelt. "The President of the United States has . . . dealt with certain men of the Twenty-fifth Infantry very unjustly. . . . Even he has no right nor any authority to punish an innocent man because some men have been guilty." "I see nothing in this oath of enlistment which makes it obligatory upon a man . . . to tell something that he does not know or to tell something that might incriminate himself. The Constitution, I believe, protects a man from being compelled to answer questions like that."[22]

He agreed it was soldiers who shot up Brownsville and committed murder. "I have no more doubt that the negro soldiers did these infamous things than that I am alive and standing here." He also agreed there was a conspiracy of silence. "Every man familiar with the negro character knows that they will bear torture with stoicism in defense of one another rather than act as traitors. . . . It is inherent in their nature and can not be eradicated by discipline or anything else. Then why upbraid the poor negro and punish him because he is true to his nature and his race and color?"[23] The real responsibility lay with President Roosevelt, who encouraged them "to be satisfied with nothing less than absolute equality everywhere [and] they naturally were upset when the bitter, vindictive, nigger-hating Texans" refused to treat them this way.[24] [Roosevelt] should have been "happy and proud to see how well they had learned the lesson."[25] "The whole issue involved is one of race, and the President is more responsible than any other man for the position the

negroes in the South have taken on the question of negro rights. He
gave recognition to Booker Washington in a social way."[26] Tillman
went on to predict a race conflict in the near future. "With a negro
majority of 225,000 in South Carolina, a race conflict is inevitable,
and when it comes, those in Colorado [a reference to Colorado
Democratic senator Thomas M. Patterson, who earlier that day had
tangled bitterly with Tillman] who stand off and theorize will not be
there to participate on the throat-cutting or get their throats cut."[27]
"America for the Americans, and this is a white man's country and
white men must govern it."[28]

Every one of the Black Battalion's supporters agreed with Tillman's accusation that Roosevelt railroaded the soldiers. Nasty language aside, Foraker himself could not have said it better. But it
came from a man who, later that day, when the debate turned to
lynching and the South, would say, "As long as the negroes continue
to ravish white women we will continue to lynch them."[29] This was
why President Roosevelt called Tillman "one of the foulest and rot-
tenest demagogs in the whole country."[30] This was Foraker's and
the soldiers' ally. Senator Foraker must have shaken his head. Was
Tillman's vote for his resolution worth it?

AS EVERYONE WAITED FOR Roosevelt's next message with its report
from the Purdy-Blocksom investigation, Foraker's resolution was
held aside as Republicans tried to maintain the presumption of presidential authority, and Democrats came up with tactics to harass
them. On January 11 Assistant Attorney General Milton D. Purdy
met with President Roosevelt at the White House to go over his
and Major Blocksom's investigation. It supported Roosevelt's conclusions. Roosevelt would use it in his special message to the Senate
when it convened four days later on January 12.[31]

President Roosevelt's second message in twenty-six days about
Brownsville was a world apart from his first.[32] There was no
bombast and he presented his evidence coolly and in an organized,
step-by-step manner. Particularly effective was his—really Taft's—
astonishment that anyone could seriously consider the townspeople
shot up their own town. "The only motive suggested as possibly

influencing anyone else was a desire to get rid of the colored troops, so strong that it impelled the citizens of Brownsville to shoot up their own houses, to kill one of their own number, to assault their own police, wounding the lieutenant, who had been an officer for twenty years—all with the purpose of discrediting the negro troops. The suggestion is on its face so ludicrously impossible that is difficult to treat it as honestly made." The soldiers' defenders never would be able effectively to counter this argument.[33]

The message made a point of discussing the shells found on the ground that implicated the soldiers since they were from the army's Springfield rifle. Yes, they could also fit in a civilian Winchester rifle, "but . . . rarely if ever go off." Bullets "picked out of the buildings" had four lands; had they been fired from the Winchester, there would have been six. A bullet from a Krag rifle would have four lands, but the Springfield's cartridge would not fit into a Krag. By elimination, therefore, the only rifle that matched the shells and the bullets was the Springfield.[34]

Roosevelt's witness list shrank from twenty-two in December to only twenty in January, and in a nod to Foraker's dramatic countdown to eight witnesses even fewer were eyewitnesses, but still twice as many as Foraker's (Roosevelt had sixteen, fourteen of whom saw Negro shooters and two who saw only that the shooters were soldiers). However, in a highly inventive category he called "earwitnesses," Roosevelt placed four other civilians. So he was up to twenty, close enough to his original twenty-two to not be called a liar. He also had twenty-five more he called "corroborative."[35]

In a departure from the standard of proof required in a court of law, Roosevelt's message abandoned "beyond a reasonable doubt" and adopted "beyond possibility of honest question." He claimed the evidence as a whole met this standard and so did the testimony of the witnesses, even with "a conflict on some of the minor points."[36]

Just before ending, he said of that part of Special Orders No. 266 debarring the soldiers from future civilian employment with the government, "I am now satisfied [it] was lacking in validity . . . and I have directed that such portion be revoked." He ended with reference to his authority: "The order was within my discretion, under the Constitution and the laws, and can not be reviewed or reversed save by another Executive order. The facts do not merely warrant the action I took—they render such action imperative unless I was to prove false to my sworn duty."[37] With a gesture to any soldier who can clear himself of guilt in the shooting or the cover-up, "I will take what action is warranted," without saying what it might be, and emptying this of any value he added, "Any such man [has] the burden of this clearing himself."[38]

Roosevelt's hope was that what he said about the facts of the shooting would soften up the Senate for Senator John Spooner (whose job the next day was to show that with these facts the law permitted the discharges), and together they would convince the Senate there was no reason to investigate Brownsville. Spooner's role was critical; if what Roosevelt did passed constitutional muster, his position was impregnable, and no one could touch him. The legal impossibility of Congress overruling his action made an investigation a waste of time.

ON JANUARY 15 THE Senate entered what would be its final week of considering Brownsville. It had grown tired of this endless debate. The momentum favoring an investigation had generated a sense of inevitability that one would take place. Spooner knew this and was not comfortable. He agreed Roosevelt had the authority to discharge the soldiers but believed he was wrong to do it. He gave in to White House coaxing and said he would defend President Roosevelt, but only if he could confine himself to the question of his authority. He had hoped to fulfill his obligation by drafting the poorly received Lodge amendment. When it was withdrawn, Spooner was in for the duration and wound up making this final appeal. He had negoti- ated a further concession: rescinding the prohibition against future federal civilian employment.[39]

Spooner neatly turned the question of authority on its head. Instead of questioning presidential authority, he questioned the Sen- ate's authority to investigate President Roosevelt. Congress may "make rules for the government and regulation of the land and naval forces . . . [but] can not in the guise of [making these rules] impair the authority of the President as the Commander in Chief."

If the Brownsville discharges were an abuse of Roosevelt's power as commander in chief, the proper action would be to impeach him in the House of Representatives. Then the Senate could investigate what he did in order to see if it should remove him from office.[40] Otherwise it would be jumping the gun.

Spooner felt more comfortable when he echoed the "public safety" argument invoked by Major Blocksom and adapted by President Roosevelt in his December 19 message as "public interest." Roosevelt was right, he said, in concluding soldiers had been the shooters but it had been impossible to identify any of them as guilty. "What should the Commander in Chief do? Nothing but transfer . . . the murderers of that battalion to some other community, emboldened by successful concealment of identity to do the same and worse the next time somewhere else . . . ?"[41] This was his strongest argument, and he should have stopped there. Instead he confused civilians' fears of murderers posted in their communities with the soldiers' fears of retaliations from civilians who viewed them as escapees from justice. "Even Mingo Sanders . . . is served with notice by the Senator from South Carolina [Tillman] that he must not go to the State of his birth lest he should be shot down. . . . What about the . . . other communities and other States?" To which Tillman retorted, "Would you like to have him sent to Wisconsin?" Spooner shot back, "I would not have the slightest objection," taking all the wind out of the public-safety argument he had just made.[42]

Sensing he was not doing well, he turned to criticizing Senator Tillman, a man he hated, perhaps thinking he could persuade senators to oppose anything Tillman advocated and support Roosevelt solely to oppose a man like Tillman. He denounced the South Carolinian for threatening a race war when he spoke a few days earlier. "I do not know of a more certain way to precipitate a struggle between the two races in such an environment than to be constantly and violently declaring it to be imminent and inevitable." The *Congressional Record* reflects at this point there was "applause in the galleries."[43] With it ringing in his ears, Spooner sat down. That night the Roosevelts and Spooners both attended a dinner party at the Taft home. In her diary, Mrs. Spooner gushed, "John spoke 4 hrs.—A great speech—all say—John was the hero of the hour." She said nothing about praise from President Roosevelt.[44]

THE NEXT DAY, SENATOR Joseph C. S. Blackburn brought back the question of President Roosevelt's authority. Modifications to Foraker's resolution and his own denials that it authorized consideration of that authority should have put this matter to rest. Foraker shuddered at yet another detour.

Blackburn was a Democrat, and recalling the discomfort Lodge's amendment caused Republican senators he saw an opportunity to make further mischief. He noted that as it stood the resolution said the investigation would not "question" President Roosevelt's authority. He wanted an "express disclaimer" that it would not "deny" it either.[45] This put the Republicans in the same corner as Lodge's amendment had earlier in the month. It implied the authority might be deniable, only that in Brownsville it would not be questioned. It was a masterstroke. Roosevelt would favor Blackburn's amendment to slam the door on any possibility that his authority would be questioned.[46] Foraker said he would vote against Blackburn. Which of course made it more likely Roosevelt would want it approved. Republican senators would have to line up behind one man or the other, exposing the split in the party's ranks. Democratic senators were delighted. Their Republican counterparts were in knots, and Roosevelt would accept nothing less than their full and enthusiastic support for the Democrat Blackburn.

Republicans tried to get Blackburn to withdraw his amendment. He refused. "He had them in a hole and he knew they knew it." Republican Nelson Aldrich threatened to conduct "an investigation of the race question" in the Senate Judiciary Committee to see whether any state had violated the Fourteenth and Fifteenth Amendments. This was really a threat to reduce congressional representation from Southern states, and "how would Blackburn and the other Southern Democrats like that?" Blackburn called his bluff.[47] "Fine. The South had been trying for a long time to get the attention of the country focused on the difficulties it was having with its race problem, and if the Senate would give it a general investigation it would be delighted. Nothing could suit it better." The Republicans had to go back and think about all this. Blackburn had put Foraker's resolution off until the next week.[48]

TO HIS SON KERMIT Roosevelt wrote, "[The senators] are nearly at the crisis. . . . I do not know how it will come out [but], it will not make the slightest difference in my attitude." In fact he was anything but blasé.[49] On January 20 he left the White House for Senator Lodge's home, where he met with Republican senators dragged there by Lodge and made it clear that a vote against Blackburn or even a vote to table his amendment was a vote against Roosevelt. He was there for two to three hours, no doubt knowing it would be hard to say no to his face, and he got what he wanted. The *New York Times* reported that "the less courageous of his party supporters in the Senate [got] a new stiffening of the backbone." They would support Blackburn "as the President desired."[50]

Meanwhile Foraker said he would agree to changing his resolution to accept language that neither the "legality nor the justice" of the president's act was to be questioned. Blackburn said there was "not a shadow of difference" between this language and his proposed amendment.[51] With everyone's concerns at long last addressed, Foraker's resolution was laid before the Senate for consideration the next day.

IT SHOULD HAVE TAKEN no time at all. It took quite a bit. As the session opened, Senator Julius Burrows of Michigan wanted to be recognized and jump ahead of Foraker's resolution and everything else to talk about Reed Smoot of Utah, who had been elected to the Senate in 1903 but whose Mormon religion still provoked efforts to unseat him. The previous summer the Committee on Privileges and Elections had reported to the Senate by resolution that Smoot was not entitled to be what he had in fact been for more than three years, a member of the Senate. Senator Burrows wanted something done about it. He held the floor for more than fifteen pages of the *Congressional Record*, including questions asked and comments made by other senators. When he concluded, the Senate did what it had been doing since 1903. It put the Smoot matter aside.[52]

Then it turned to Brownsville. But not to approve the resolution everyone had agreed upon. Stephen Mallory of Florida was not sure—really sure—everyone understood that consideration of Roosevelt's authority was off limits. He had an amendment to correct this. It had to be debated but in the end was rejected. Porter J. McCumber of North Dakota, a Republican, had an amendment to spell out in detail what the investigative committee could do. It too was turned away. Charles Culberson of Texas still was not ready to risk any investigation; he feared it might end with the black soldiers back in the army. After forty-four days of debate, he now wanted the resolution to simply say the President did the right thing and discussion of the Brownsville Incident "will be closed."[53] Culberson had to accept his amendment's defeat.

And then, "with a great sigh of relief that the month-long flood of talk was over at last," it was done.[54]

> *The Vice-President:* The question is on agreeing to the resolution of the Senator from Ohio [Mr. FORAKER].
> *Mr. Foraker:* I move that the resolution, under the rule, be referred to the Committee to Audit and Control the Contingent Expenses of the Senate.
> *[The motion was agreed to.]*
> *Mr. Kean:* I ask for unanimous consent for its presentation.
> The resolution was agreed to by unanimous consent and agreed to.[55]

IN HIS MEMOIRS WRITTEN a decade later, Senator Foraker described with brevity the events over the forty-four days it took the Senate to decide what to do with his resolution. "[There was] a running debate that continued until January 22, when my resolution authorizing an investigation was adopted." He added, "I was all the while hoping that, with the truth established, as I believed an investigation would establish it, that the President would in a manly fashion undo the wrong he had done."[56] It is hard to believe after all Roosevelt had said about him and the soldiers that he could expect this to happen.

President Roosevelt did not see it the same way. He thought Foraker had taken a drubbing. As he said in a letter marked "Personal" to George Spinney, an old friend from his New York days, Foraker accepted the amendment with no inquiry into either the legality or the justice of his action. "There has never been a more complete case of backdown and humiliation than this of Foraker's."[57] Lodge agreed. In a letter to W. Sturgis Bigelow of Boston, both his and Roosevelt's friend, he wrote, "We came out completely on top in the Brownsville fight, which was very satisfactory, especially as they had us down at first."[58]

Unsaid by Foraker was what he failed to gain. There is in our Constitution an unending tension among the three branches of government to gain power at the expense of one or both of the other two. In his time in the Senate, Foraker boldly stood up to presidential action that he and others believed intruded in the business of Congress. Roosevelt pushed back, drawing into the executive branch authority that, once there, would be hard to evict, thereby strengthening him and his successors and correspondingly weakening Congress. By yielding to Roosevelt's demand that the investigation have nothing to do with his right to discharge the soldiers, Foraker weakened what the Senate would be able to do in Brownsville and thereafter what Congress could do as a legislative body, nourishing a stronger Roosevelt and a more dominating presidential office. The tension exists today.

THE BATTLE OVER BROWNSVILLE continued in the House of Representatives. Back in December, Republican Ernest W. Roberts from Massachusetts introduced a bill to permit the soldiers "to be eligible to reenlistment . . . with the same standing, rights, and privileges to which they were entitled at the time of their discharge."[59] Democrats took the opposite view. The day after the Foraker resolution was approved, Thetus W. Sims of Tennessee introduced Resolution No. 785, which said Roosevelt's action "was within the scope of his authority and power and is approved and commended as a proper exercise of same."[60] It was referred to the House Military Affairs Committee, where it died in its sleep when the Fifty-Ninth Congress ended. John Nance Garner, Brownsville's congressman, introduced a bill that "called for the elimination of all Blacks currently in the military and barring Black enlistment." When it did not pass, he introduced similar bills in each of the next three sessions.[61] The War Department, citing gallant service of Negro troops, always opposed it.

BROWNSVILLE BECAME AN EXCUSE to ask for presidential involvement in other soldier disturbances. On the day the Foraker resolution was approved, the *Columbus Citizen* reported, "President Roosevelt may be called upon to investigate into the conduct of the United States soldiers at the Columbus barracks, who ran amuck . . . Monday night, and may be requested to dishonorably discharge them, just as he did the colored troops at Brownsville, Tex. . . . Foraker's friends claim that President Roosevelt has established a precedent."[62]

IN THE SPRING OF 1907 Roosevelt rewarded the Democratic leader in the Senate, Senator Joseph C. S. Blackburn, "by making him a member of the [Panama] Canal Commission . . . for standing by him during the Brownsville incident."[63] This was an even cushier job than being a senator. He would be "officially [the] Chief of Civil Administration," a job and title that meant almost nothing. (Blackburn's duties were once described unofficially as "attending commission meetings, signing cab licenses, and drawing $14,000 a year.")[64] He had almost no responsibilities. When he and other commissioners were appointed, Roosevelt told them, "It will be a position of ample remuneration and much honor."[65] The Panama Canal Commission evidently was what street and water departments were for city bosses: a dumping ground to reward cronies with soft, well-paying jobs at the public trough.

ON JANUARY 28, WHILE the Senate was debating Foraker's resolution and Roosevelt was working against it, Booker T. Washington, who knew a thing or two about rewarding supporters with government jobs, wrote to Francis E. Leupp, Commissioner of Indian Affairs, and mentioned "the feeling on the part of colored people against the President [over Brownsville]." But he still stood firmly with him. "Personally, I have the most implicit faith in everything the President does."[66]

The home Foraker built in Washington when he was in the Senate. Among other flourishes it had a Louis XVI ballroom. Mrs. Foraker called it a "big yellow house." *Used with permission from the Historical Society of Washington, DC.*

Harry C. Smith, editor of Cleveland's black newspaper. In the 1880s he believed Foraker had a greater concern for blacks than was commonly realized and urged Foraker to show it. Meanwhile, he promoted Foraker to his readers as a friend of the black race. *Used with permission from the Ohio History Connection, call no. AL03899.*

The Union recruits black soldiers for the Civil War. Note the reference to Port Hudson as an example of black valor. It was also where Sen. Francis E. Warren of Wyoming received his Medal of Honor. *Used with permission from the Library Company of Philadelphia.*

The Twenty-Fifth Infantry's Bicycle Corps training at Fort Missoula, Montana, in 1897. Lt. James A. Moss, "the Goat" in his West Point class, is its commanding officer. *Used with permission from the Archives and Special Collections, Mansfield Library, University of Montana–Missoula.*

Roosevelt, his Rough Riders, and Buffalo Soldiers of the Tenth Cavalry atop San Juan Heights after seizing them from the Spanish army. Roosevelt's triumph that day helped take him to the White House. Another photo of the moment with the black soldiers not shown is invariably used to show Roosevelt's victory, thereby erasing the Buffalo Soldiers from the famous charge. *Courtesy of the Theodore Roosevelt Collection, call no. R560.3.Scr7-037, Houghton Library, Harvard University.*

Brownsville residents armed and ready to defend their town from the soldiers. Note at least three of the rifles appear to be single shot, hardly a match for the soldiers' semiautomatic rifles. *Courtesy of the Texas State Library & Archives Commission.*

Senator Charles A. Culberson of Texas. He warned Secretary Taft not to send black soldiers to Brownsville, and he demanded their removal as soon as he heard about the shooting. *Courtesy of the Theodore Roosevelt Collection, call no. Roosevelt R570.P93p-085, Houghton Library, Harvard University.*

Texans said Texas Ranger William "Bill" McDonald would charge hell with one bucket of water. Ignoring being told he had no authority to investigate, he charged into Brownsville anyway to prove the soldiers' guilt. Before long, even Brownsvillites tired of him, and he left having proved nothing. *Courtesy of the Texas State Library & Archives Commission.*

Booker T. Washington with Robert C. Ogden, Secretary of War Taft, and steel magnate turned philanthropist Andrew Carnegie in front of the Carnegie Library built with Carnegie money and Tuskegee students' skills and labor. "The Wizard" was adept at gaining the confidence of important people and financial assistance for Tuskegee from men like Carnegie. *Photo by Frances Benjamin Johnston. From the Library of Congress.*

DISHONORABLY DISCHARGED

Cartoon in *Harpers Weekly* condemning the discharge of Mingo Sanders. The caption characterizes the discharge as Sanders and most people saw it, and the proud old soldier hangs his head in undeserved disgrace. *Image from Harper's Weekly, January 12, 1907, p.39. Used with permission from HarpWeek, LLC.*

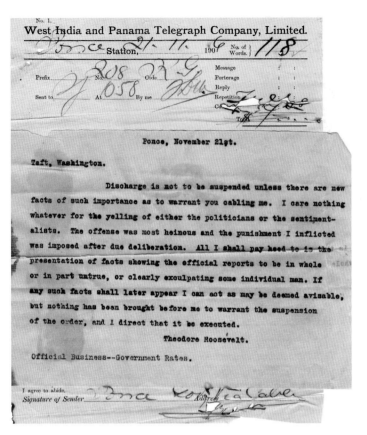

West India and Panama Telegraph Company, Limited.

Station, 1907

Ponce, November 21st.

Taft, Washington.

Discharge is not to be suspended unless there are new facts of such importance as to warrant you cabling me. I care nothing whatever for the yelling of either the politicians or the sentimentalists. The offense was most heinous and the punishment I inflicted was imposed after due deliberation. All I shall pay heed to is the presentation of facts showing the official reports to be in whole or in part untrue, or clearly exculpating some individual man. If any such facts shall later appear I can act as may be deemed avisable, but nothing has been brought before me to warrant the suspension of the order, and I direct that it be executed.

Theodore Roosevelt.

Official Business—Government Rates.

I agree to abide,
Signature of Sender
Address

Roosevelt's wire to Secretary of War Taft from Porto Rico, where Roosevelt stopped on his way back from Panama. His anger at Taft's suspension of the discharges while he was away from Washington almost bleeds through the paper. Two hours later, Roosevelt, wanting to make sure the message got through, sent a second and calmer—but equally direct—telegram to Taft. He did not know that Taft, on his own, already had rescinded the suspension order after a meeting with William Loeb and General Ainsworth. *Courtesy of Ruth Mildred "Millie" Duff and John Duff.*

Statue of Cornelia on the grounds of the Ohio Statehouse in Columbus. Beneath her are four of Ohio's "jewels." *Photo published by the Detroit Publishing Company. From the Library of Congress.*

President Roosevelt's cabinet. Secretary of War Taft is third from the left and Secretary of the Interior Hitchcock is at the extreme right. *Courtesy of the Theodore Roosevelt Collection, call no. 560.52 1906-071, Houghton Library, Harvard University.*

Secretary of the Interior Ethan Allen Hitchcock. He would be forced out of the cabinet, and his investigations of Senator Warren's alleged land fraud would be ignored to gain Warren's help in the Military Affairs Committee. *Courtesy of the Theodore Roosevelt Collection, call no. Roosevelt R570.P93p-010, Houghton Library, Harvard University.*

Senator John Spooner of Wisconsin. He disagreed with Roosevelt's discharge of the soldiers but went along and defended him. He spoke for black rights but more as a weapon against Democrats, who cared not at all about them. *Courtesy of the Theodore Roosevelt Collection, call no. Roosevelt R570.P93p-097, Houghton Library, Harvard University.*

Senator Benjamin "Pitchfork Ben" Tillman of South Carolina, one of the most vicious and outspoken racists ever to serve in the Senate. He hated President Roosevelt even more than he hated blacks and sided with the Black Battalion just to pick a fight with Roosevelt. His face, distorted by a missing eye, reflected his distorted sense of humanity. Just before Roosevelt left office, Tillman's racism trumped his feelings about Roosevelt and he switched sides and voted against the Court of Inquiry's consideration of reenlisting discharged soldiers. *Photo published by Bain News Service, 1915. From the Library of Congress.*

Cartoon from the Gridiron Club banquet program in January 1907, when President Roosevelt had to be physically restrained from leaping from his seat while Foraker was speaking. The cartoon and its poem suggests Foraker defended the soldiers to secure the Negro vote and enhance his White House hopes in 1908.

FORAKER

"All coons look alike to me,"
J. B. FORAKER, says he, says he,
"Even if they is black as kin be,
An' is dressed in blue or yaller
     khaki.
All coons look alike to me,
Since 'mancipation set 'em free,
Nigger vote hold de balance,
All coons look alike to me."

Senator Francis E. Warren was called "the Greatest Shepherd since Abraham" for how surely he protected his state's sheep industry (and his own herds) by seeing to it that wool tariffs remained high. His deal with President Roosevelt to avoid charges that he had fraudulently acquired government land in Wyoming helped doom the soldiers in the Senate Military Affairs Committee he chaired, and it caused Roosevelt to ask for the resignation of the man investigating him, Interior Secretary Ethan Allen Hitchcock. *Image from the Francis E. Warren Collection, American Heritage Center, University of Wyoming.*

President Roosevelt riding to Senator Warren's ranch in Cheyenne over land Warren later would be accused by Roosevelt's Interior Department of illegally fencing. *Image from the Francis E. Warren Collection, American Heritage Center, University of Wyoming.*

Senator Francis E. Warren of Wyoming presents a gift of spurs to President Roosevelt on Roosevelt's visit to Cheyenne. *Courtesy of the Theodore Roosevelt Collection, call no. 560.51 1903-149, Houghton Library, Harvard University.*

Pennsylvania's senator and "boss" Boies Penrose. Roosevelt's classmate, the two men disliked each other, but after Roosevelt came to his aid in the 1906 off-year elections, Penrose acted as his cat's paw in Brownsville. A very large man, Penrose had oversized furniture made to accommodate him and to intimidate visitors to his office. *From Wikimedia Commons.*

Buffalo Soldier monument at Warren Air Force Base in Cheyenne. The base was originally known as Fort Russell before being renamed Fort Warren to honor Francis E. Warren, the Wyoming senator who chaired the Senate Military Affairs Committee when it investigated the shooting. The committee's majority, including Warren, concluded that the soldiers took part in the shooting and the "conspiracy of silence" that followed. *Photo by Airman 1st Class Daryl Knee. Courtesy of the 90th Missile Wing Public Affairs, Warren Air Force Base, Wyoming.*

Cartoon showing puny Uncle Sam requiring help from J. P. Morgan to get through economic storms. At the 1907 Gridiron banquet, President Roosevelt shook his fist at Morgan, also a guest that evening. By the end of the year, he quietly accepted Morgan's help to end the Panic of 1907. *Puck Magazine*, April 26, 1907. *Painting by Udo J. Keppler. From the Library of Congress.*

Senator Joseph B. Foraker of Ohio. He looked every bit the senator. Foraker was the Black Battalion's most faithful and forceful advocate, and it cost him his Senate seat. *Courtesy of the Theodore Roosevelt Collection, call no. Roosevelt R570.P93p-071, Houghton Library, Harvard University.*

Black boxer Jack Johnson glaring down at the pummeled Jim Jeffries, the first "great white hope" seeking to take the world heavyweight championship away from Johnson. Johnson won the crown in 1908 during the Brownsville Incident. *Used with permission from the Nevada Historical Society.*

Senator Shelby Cullom from Illinois. He openly acknowledged that every senator knew Roosevelt was wrong. *Courtesy of the Theodore Roosevelt Collection, call no. Roosevelt R570.P93p-030, Houghton Library, Harvard University.*

Dorsie Willis, the only surviving soldier from the Black Battalion, in 1972, when he learned that the discharges of members of the Black Battalion would be changed to honorable. His was the only one not posthumously awarded. He was shining shoes in a Minnesota barbershop. Willis also received $25,000. *Photo by Boyd Hagen.*

"Begin with your most vivid memory."

Unidentified writer's advice for writing
memoirs

CHAPTER SEVENTEEN

"WHAT *DID* HAPPEN AT THAT GRIDIRON DINNER . . . ?"

JULIA FORAKER BEGINS HER memoirs with what was the most vivid memory of her life with her husband—the Gridiron Club dinner at which he and the Brownsville Incident became the evening's entertainment.

> One snowy night, January 1907, two or three hundred men sat down to dinner at a famous Washington club. The club was strictly a good-fellowship affair for chosen souls.
>
> That dinner never got beyond the quail. When the waiters appeared with those trifles they were frantically waved away. Something was happening that had startled the guests out of all thoughts of birds, bottles, and brotherly love:
>
> The President of the United States, reaching into the blue, had hurled a forensic bomb at the senior Senator from Ohio, and the Senator from Ohio was sending back at him from his own well-stocked arsenal, stinging shot; and Heaven knew how the affair would end.[1]

THE GRIDIRON CLUB WAS the gathering spot and watering hole of choice for Washington journalists. It took its name from the long handled cooking grill commonly called a gridiron in 1885, when the club was founded. At its dinners, the gridiron motif is repeated by setting the head table up against one end of the room and extending

273

the other tables perpendicularly away from it, so the grouping resembles the gridiron. On the real thing, meats are grilled; at a Gridiron Club dinner, it is politicians and office holders, and journalists apply the heat with their searing cartoons, songs, pokes, and sketches. Though not dangerous to life and limb, this can be unhealthy for the careers of those made fun of (one of the club's rules is that the Gridiron's heat singes but never burns). Since the club was formed, every sitting president but one, Grover Cleveland, has attended a Gridiron dinner, and though some will avoid its heat as long as they can, eventually they show up and endure the discomfort.[2] At the dinner in December 1906 both President Roosevelt and Senator Foraker were guests, and the journalists performed their usual hijinks and sang songs to well-known tunes but with words chosen to gently and slowly char the politicians, who took it with forced smiles and tried to look like they were having fun.[3] Roosevelt had to suffer a derisive lesson in the simplified spelling he ordered the government to use. Styled the Gridiron Dikshunary, it included *Demokrat*, an indivijual representing the Nth degree uv politikal hopelessness; *Obedientz*, a kwalifikashun for the Supreme Kort. For the December dinner, Brownsville was merely an appetizer when cartoons of Foraker and Mingo Sanders, along with those of John D. Rockefeller and other "disreputable" men, were forced to listen to a phonograph record of Roosevelt shouting derisive names at them, while the Senate was in the middle of debating the proposal to investigate the soldiers' discharges. The reporters seemed to leave Brownsville on the griddle's back burner that night for additional seasoning. By the January dinner, it was fully marinated.

THE PRESIDENT AS USUAL was the guest of honor. It had been a busy Saturday. In the morning he dealt with the seemingly endless Senate hearings over the expulsion of supposed polygamist Utah senator Reed Smoot. Roosevelt dismissed the tempest against Smoot as a sham and the polygamy problem as a fabrication. Using Idaho's large Mormon population as a point of reference, he noted that polygamy "was as sporadic there as, for instance, bigamy among the Gentiles."[4] The unmarried but philandering Senator Boies Penrose put the matter in a context only he could imagine. "As for me, I would rather have seated beside me in this chamber a polygamist who doesn't polyg than a monogamist who doesn't monag."[5] Smoot would win his case and stay in the Senate twenty-six more years.

Roosevelt's last event that day was the Gridiron Club dinner at the New Willard Hotel. He was tired and in no mood for the sharply sarcastic "entertainment" he knew was, along with quail, on the evening's menu.

"WHAT *DID* HAPPEN AT that Gridiron Dinner between the President and Foraker?" asked W. Sturgis Bigelow in an undated letter to Henry Cabot Lodge.[6] Bigelow was close to the Roosevelts and occasionally a guest in the White House. Roosevelt thought him "a delightful man, and as easy as an old shoe."[7] They shared an interest in Japan, and Bigelow was one of the few Americans of the time to have lived there. (He introduced Kaneko Kentaro to Roosevelt when Roosevelt was civil-service commissioner. They were at Harvard at the same time but never met. During the Russo-Japanese War, Kaneko was in Washington as Japan's special envoy, and it was he who asked Roosevelt to mediate an end to the war.) Bigelow read Boston newspaper accounts of the Gridiron dinner, and they made it sound, as one reporter would write, "as if the affair were a political convention instead of a dinner attended by gentlemen."[8] Bigelow wanted to learn the real story.

PRESIDENT ROOSEVELT TOOK HIS seat at the head table. Glancing down at the printed program, as much a part of the entertainment as a description of what it would be, he saw himself portrayed in caricature. The cartoon Roosevelt was writing with one hand, shooting a bear with another, and kicking a black man with his foot. Underneath was a jingle,

> "I'm busy with things night and day,"
> A Rough Rider was once heard to say.
> "Writing views, singing tunes,
> Killing Bears, firing coons,
> Or composing an Irish lay."

The reference to firing coons signaled Brownsville was to be in the center ring that evening.[9]

From the cartoons of other men attending the dinner, Roosevelt knew he was in for teasing for the dismissiveness he was thought to show too many important men. Looking around the room, he saw the banker J. P. Morgan. Almost five years earlier, when Roosevelt was still learning his way around the White House, he directed his attorney general to sue Morgan's railroad trust to break up its monopoly under the until then relatively toothless Sherman Antitrust Act. The surprised Morgan could not believe the government would do such a thing and tried to resolve the matter with Roosevelt in person. Unaware Roosevelt wanted a favorable court decision that would be a precedent to deter other monopolies, and not yet fully realizing just whom he was dealing with, at their meeting Morgan said exactly the wrong thing. As recounted by Edmund Morris, the meeting (attended by Attorney General Philander Knox) went something like this:

> *Morgan:* Why had the Administration not asked *me* to correct irregularities in the trust's charter?
> *Roosevelt:* That is just what we did not want to do.
> *Morgan:* If we have done anything wrong, send your man to my man and they can fix it up.
> *Roosevelt:* That can't be done.
> *Knox:* We don't want to fix it up, we want to stop it.
> *Morgan:* Are you going to attack my other interests, the Steel trust and others?
> *Roosevelt:* Certainly not—unless we find out that in any case they have done something that we regard as wrong.[10]

Morgan left the meeting not quite sure what to make of Roosevelt. When the US Supreme Court upheld Roosevelt, he found out.

Not far from Morgan sat H. H. Rogers of Standard Oil. Rogers and the financially inept Mark Twain were close friends, and Rogers guided the humorist's family finances. For Roosevelt, who thought Twain "a real genius . . . wholly without cultivation and without any real historical knowledge," Rogers's good deeds for Twain were a tepid endorsement of the financier.[11] (Twain was just as bipolar in his feelings for Roosevelt. In February 1910 he wrote to his daughter Clara of his "bitter detestation of him." At the same time, he thought Roosevelt was also "one of the most likable men that I am acquainted with."[12]) What really bothered Roosevelt was the enormous wealth Rogers had accumulated as an associate of John D. Rockefeller.

Turning his head to those at the table extending out in front of him, Roosevelt grimaced. Directly in his view, almost unavoidably so, sat Joseph Foraker. It was going to be a long night after what already had been a long day. But if entertainment was what the Gridiron Club wanted, he was gearing up to give it to them.

At his place setting, Senator Foraker read the evening's program that had made President Roosevelt's foul mood even more so. Along with cartoon images of Morgan, Rogers, and others to be maligned that evening (only in good fun of course), he saw one of himself, and beneath it was a jingle showing what the press thought of him and Brownsville. It was all about votes.

> "All coons look alike to me,"
> J. B. Foraker, says he, says he,
> Even they is black as kin be,
> An' is dressed in blue or yeller khaki.
> "All coons look alike to me,
> Since 'mancipation set 'em free,
> Nigger vote hold the balance,
> All coons look alike to me."

This ditty was a parody of the chorus of an immensely popular song of the day, "All Coons Look Alike to Me." Its original chorus was

> All coons look alike to me,
> I have got another beau you see.
> And he is just as good to me
> As you ever tried to be.
> He spends his money free,
> I know we can't agree
> So, I don't like you no how
> All coons look alike to me.[13]

Lyrics like these were commonplace in what were called "coon songs" with lyrics mimicking speech patterns of slaves and uneducated blacks. *Coon*, short for raccoon, was a disparaging term for blacks, who were thought to prefer their meat during slavery. The melodies were similar to ragtime in their structure and pace. Songwriter, composer, and music historian Arnold Shaw maintains "All Coons Look Alike to Me" is "one of the justly famous examples of true ragtime" and may be the first example of rock 'n' roll.[14] Before the days of records and radios, when the success of songs was measured by sales of sheet music, the song would sell more than one million copies, and its composer, Ernest Hogan, made $26,000 from it (almost $670,000 today). Hogan regretted writing it for the rest of his life because of the shame it would bring to his race.[15] By 1907 the song remained popular, but only with whites. Blacks hated it, and if they heard it whistled by a white man, they considered it a personal insult.

As the evening played out, Roosevelt and Foraker would engage in their own prize fight, at one point with fists punching the air.

IN ADDITION TO ITS prohibition against scalding its political prey, in 1906 the Gridiron Club had two other rules for these all-male dinners: ladies are always present (a reminder to the gentlemen to mind their language), but reporters never are (nothing seen or heard was on the record or to be reported). This time, as Julia Foraker put it, "the news was too good to keep."[16]

After the journalists' parodies and jokes it was not yet time for the speeches. After skits too pointed and cartoons too biting, President Roosevelt was at a boiling point surpassed only by the turtle soup, whose bowls had just been removed.[17] Unable to contain himself, Roosevelt told the club's president, Samuel G. Blythe, he wanted to speak right away.[18] The "raw encounter" was about to start.[19]

Roosevelt turned first to Morgan and Rogers. Raising his fist, he angrily told them to their faces they would have to learn to live with his administration's reform of corporate America, like it or not. He was the only thing preventing a takeover of Wall Street "by the mob."[20] This was not the usual levity and silliness masking true feelings. "The President was serious."[21]

Roosevelt turned to face straight ahead at Foraker. When he again spoke, he was "extremely strenuous in a vocal and gesticulatory way."[22] Just who did the senators think they were, presuming to question a decision of the army's commander in chief, he asked Foraker. It was none of their business, because "all" power in the matter was constitutionally his and only his. He could discharge the soldiers if he wished, and no one could review his actions. The Senate could discuss it all it wanted to, but "it served no good purpose, could have no result, was purely 'academic,'" and suggested Foraker's motives were political.[23] He went on like this for almost half an hour before taking his seat. The Gridiron Club had never heard anything like it.

Club president Blythe wondered what to do now. Another Gridiron Club rule was, "[The President's] Criticisms of all Matters, Public and Private, must be Respected.[24] By custom and protocol, therefore, no one spoke after he did. Should Blythe order the waiters to bring in the rest of the meal? Or, newspaperman that he was, get a good story? He chose the good story. "The hour for bloody sarcasm has arrived. I take the liberty of calling upon Senator Foraker for some remarks."[25]

Foraker rose, "stark white in the face."[26] He acknowledged his speaking after President Roosevelt was a breach of protocol, and he was embarrassed to be asked to do so, but since the attack was so clearly on him, he had no choice but to respond. He spoke without notes but as if he had an advance copy of Roosevelt's remarks. He addressed what Roosevelt said almost in the same order Roosevelt had expressed it but in a manner the *Washington Post* would characterize as "more serious."[27] Who was President Roosevelt to question the Senate's right to discuss his actions in the Brownsville matter? Such a discussion was not merely academic; it had significance. As a member of the Senate, he would ignore any direction to stay quiet and would continue to express his opinion on the Senate's floor. A few moments earlier, Roosevelt had said, "Well, all coons do not look alike to me." Now Foraker one-upped him by responding, "Not only all coons, but all *persons* look alike to me," substituting the word used in the Constitution.[28] No longer hesitant to confront

Roosevelt publicly, Foraker continued to give "the President the plainest talk he has probably ever listened to."[29] "I did not come to the Senate to take orders from anybody, either at this end of the line or the other." Using an expression common then but out of place for a man committed to equality, he added as a way to justify his independence from Roosevelt, "I am free born, white, over 30 years of age."[30] He brought up Sergeant Mingo Sanders. "In dismissing him [President] Roosevelt had violated a very plain law of Congress and thereby made himself amenable to the processes of law, besides laying himself open to a well-founded charge of having done the greatest injustice to a man who, it might be supposed, would have no powerful friends to assist him."[31]

"Champ Clark was seating some fifteen feet from Roosevelt and declares that while Foraker was speaking the President was gritting his teeth, clenching his fist, shaking his head and muttering 'That is not so; I am going to answer that; that is not true; I will not stand for it.' He was on his feet two or three times . . . and Justice Harlan with help from Blythe pulled him down."[32] Foraker took a different tack. "You know, Mr. President, I love you so."[33] And then, his face red as the stripes on the flag, he sat down to hubbub, cheering, and congratulations, with diners "rising from their places to get over to him."[34]

The show was too good to end there, and President Roosevelt certainly did not want it to. No longer restrained by Blythe and Justice Harlan, he jumped to his feet, but in the wild tumult for Senator Foraker, he had trouble getting the audience's attention. Blythe was equally frustrated trying to gavel the event back to order. Finally allowed to speak, Roosevelt called the Brownsville soldiers "bloody butchers . . . the only reason I didn't have them hung was because I couldn't find out which ones did the shooting."[35]

Nothing could top this, and Blythe, knowing everyone was eager to "catch their breath and gossip," called for the singing of "Auld Lang Syne," the signal that the evening was over.[36]

CHAMP CLARK SAID THE evening was a draw.[37] History gives the edge to Foraker, and so did many at the time. Cincinnati lawyer John Galvin believed "the whole country agrees that the President came out of that little mix-up second best."[38] Foraker scored points with calmness in the face of Roosevelt's provocation, command of the facts, and quick thinking. There was encouragement for the underdog senator taking on an aggressive president and sympathy for the battle Foraker undertook for the Black Battalion. Senator Albert Beveridge sent him a note, "I am against you, but I never so admired you as this instant. You are game, and you are masterful. You were altogether thoroughbred tonight."[39]

To Washington insiders Roosevelt seemed the clear winner, in spite of his bruising and pugnacious belligerence. Those in the president's official family were the most supportive. His new secretary of commerce and labor Oscar S. Straus was almost delusional in how recalled it. "[The President] referred incidentally, and in a somewhat humorous way to the Brownsville incident. . . . When President Roosevelt finished the President of the Gridiron Club called upon Senator Foraker. After a few pleasant preliminary remarks his face seemed to light up with a vindictive cast and he made an anti-President speech that I think jarred upon the sensibilities of everyone present. The President seemed to be very much agitated. Mr. Foraker's speech, while caustic and emphatic, certainly was out of place in the surroundings. At the end he moderated his language a little. The President stood up and replied, but he evidently did not make the reply that his face indicated he would like to make. He doubtless thought this was not the place to continue what developed into rather an unpleasant controversy."[40]

Even many of those who may have admired Foraker's moxie felt he had gone too far. Typical was a note from Senator Beveridge (who had written the complimentary note to Foraker) the next morning to Roosevelt, "I went down after the dinner, to spend an hour with the boys. . . . They said that Foraker was in damned bad taste." In a postscript, Beveridge added, "Still now, Foraker was 'nervy' wasn't he? How I love a fighter."[41] By then Roosevelt had cooled down, and he wrote back, "Foraker ought not to have been called upon to speak; but as he was called upon, I do not blame him much for the speech he did make." Having shifted the fault to Blythe and empathizing a bit with Foraker, he innocently suggested he intended nothing more than to "merely make a flat contradiction about what [Foraker said], point out the fact that I and not he would pass judgment upon the case, and that I should absolutely disregard anything except my own convictions, and let it go at that." A day later, while strolling with Gifford Pinchot and James Garfield along the Potomac River, Roosevelt told them the whole thing began when Foraker attacked him.[42] But he conceded what he said was perhaps a mite unrestrained: "I was in two minds what to say in answer; I was inclined to make a Berserker speech myself."[43] For Champ Clark it was berserk enough. "Of all the fantastic capers that President Roosevelt ever cut before high heaven, the most astounding and bizarre was his performance at the Gridiron Club in January, 1907."[44]

FORAKER REALIZED THE EVENT was historic, and at the "insistence of your mother," wrote an account of the dinner to his son Benson in Cincinnati. After an almost painfully detailed description of what "he said—I said—he said back" and the compliments those present paid to him, he wanted his son (and presumably posterity) "to know from me that I was not responsible for it. . . . I did not use a disrespectful word, or say anything to be regretted. . . . I am glad to believe that the overwhelming sentiment here is favorable to me."[45]

Perhaps it was. Perhaps it was the same outside Washington too. But if so, was it because Roosevelt's ill-mannered and almost hysterical behavior cost him points? From the moment the discharges were made public, Roosevelt had argued loudly, carelessly, and personally. He jeered his opponents and responded to their concerns with bombast and threats. His behavior was frightening. Six years later, the defeated and lame-duck President Taft chatted with *New York World* reporter Louis Seibold as they rode together on a special train to the funeral of Vice President James Sherman. Seibold asked him, "Beyond the personal ambition of Mr. Roosevelt, what do you think chiefly actuated him [to make the unsuccessful run for president in 1912, when] there was really no demand for him?" Taft hesitated to answer, but then said,

> Mr. Roosevelt is so constituted that it is impossible for him to go into controversy without becoming personal. What I mean is this: Mr.

Roosevelt is not a logician, and he never argues. His power of concentrated statement is that of a genius. His power of making a statement in such phrases as to give them currency is equal to that of any man I know. He never makes a sustained argument that appeals to you. He is not looking for an argument. Each blow he strikes is a hard one, because it calls attention to some defect in his enemy's armor, or some great claim to right on his part, but he does not establish a conclusion by one step and then another and another. He has not either patience or power to do that. He once said to me, "When I fight I like to get close up to a man." Well, by that he meant—he could not mean otherwise—that he fought not only the man's argument but the man himself. He could not ascribe to the man, differing from his radically, any other than an improper motive. He could not differ from a man in memory without imputing something more than a mistake of memory to him.[46]

Roosevelt's striking out against Foraker at the Gridiron dinner had little to do with defending his order to discharge the soldiers. When Foraker conceded Roosevelt's authority in the matter as part of a deal to get an investigation, Roosevelt knew the fight was won and the order could not be set aside. His public tongue-lashing that night was an act of anger and vindictiveness against Foraker. This was a shot across Foraker's bow to tell him to watch out, I'm coming after you. His anger at Foraker was as great—and as personal—as it was against the Black Battalion Foraker defended, and the consequences he wanted for him were the same: dismissal from the army for the soldiers and from public life for Foraker.

Foraker's reelection to the Senate in 1908 by the Ohio legislature was now in trouble.

"The Pres. Back—the Ohio appointment settled."

Secretary of the Interior James R. Garfield,
diary entry for May, 23, 1907

CHAPTER EIGHTEEN

FIRST-CLASS COLORED MEN

IT MAY HAVE BEEN at their White House meeting to discuss his annual message to Congress, when Booker T. Washington opened his eyes to Negro resentment, that Theodore Roosevelt started to think about mending fences with black Americans.[1] He had been able to avoid Brownsville's electoral repercussions by delaying the discharge order until after the 1906 elections. But he had to consider that Negroes had not gotten over Brownsville, and their simmering frustration over it and his hands-off policy during the Atlanta riots had reheated to a boil with his annual message in early December and what he said about lynching and conspiracies of silence. Roosevelt wondered if the collateral damage from all this might lay waste to Republican chances in 1908. Because of the black migration to electoral-vote-rich Northern states, where they could vote and where they could determine winners and losers, black loyalty had to be recaptured. A plan seemed to have gelled in his mind by Christmas Day, when he wrote Washington asking for "the names of . . . first-class colored men." They had to live in Ohio, preferably Cincinnati, and, signaling just what he was thinking of, "be up to the standard of an internal revenue collectorship."[2] Washington recommended Ralph Tyler, the Columbus journalist.[3]

Tyler was a clever man, fast thinking, active in the black civil rights movement but concerned for his own personal future. He had a talent for getting close to middle-level black political opera-

284

tives such as George Myers in Cleveland and ingratiating himself with white elected officials such as Ohio's senators Foraker and Dick. He always worked hard to get ahead in life and to prepare himself for opportunities that found him. His resourcefulness had impressed W. D. Brickell, owner of the *Columbus Dispatch*, when he needed a stenographer one night and the only person in the office was the young Ralph Tyler mopping the floor. Tyler volunteered to take his dictation. "You know shorthand, Ralph?" asked Brickell. "Yes sir." "And typing?" Ralph nodded he did. "You can put down that mop . . . for good," Brickell told him. Tyler had a second job waiting tables in the dining car of the Columbus–Cleveland train, and one night he overheard talk of a railroad merger. Surreptitiously writing down shorthand notes on his shirt cuffs, when the train got to Columbus he called the story in to the *Dispatch*, and the newspaper had a scoop.[4] When Robert F. Wolfe bought the *Dispatch* he continued to employ Tyler as a reporter and a writer and even made him his private secretary.

Tyler had hungered for a political appointment for some time. Shortly after the Ohio Republican Convention in Dayton the previous September, when Foraker seemed to have decisively turned back Theodore Burton, Tyler met with Ohio senator Charles Dick. Dick confided "he was glad the fight had been made on him and Senator Foraker" because with their triumph they now could "accomplish something for their friends. Ralph," Tyler quoted Dick as saying, "when this campaign is over I am going to secure you a consulship, or something equally as good, and Senator Foraker is with me. We . . . now believe we will secure something for you, as you deserve it."[5]

On Friday, January 4, Tyler got a letter from Roosevelt asking him to come to the White House. Traveling from Columbus through New York ("to throw the natives off the scent"), Tyler arrived at the White House on Monday at 11:00 a.m. to meet with President Roosevelt and his secretary William Loeb.[6] To George Myers in Cleveland, Tyler wrote, "Now in my interview with the President, he stated that he had an opportunity to appoint a colored man to the position of Collector of Customs at Cincinnati, and was going to do so; and that I was the man he had in view. He asked me if I thought that Foraker or Dick would oppose my confirmation. I advised him I could not see how they could, as our relations were of the most cordial. This pleased him, and turning to Loeb he said: 'Mr. Loeb this is our man. We will start with him.' At the conclusion of the conference, he asked me to go over and have a chat with Longworth, giving me a letter of introduction and saying that he did not want Longworth to think he was just sloughing over his head."[7]

From the beginning and the request to Washington for names of potential appointees, the entire affair might have been a charade, a trick played on Washington, Tyler, and the Negro community, with Roosevelt having no intention of following through.[8] A clue is Roosevelt's instruction to Tyler to go see Congressman Nicholas Longworth. Historian Emma Lou Thornbrough believed Longworth did not want Tyler, and neither did many other Ohio politicians.[9] But it made no sense for Longworth publicly to oppose Tyler's appointment. Why antagonize the black voters who made him the winner this past November? If Longworth told Tyler the appointment was fine with him, but it was all "the others" who opposed him that he was worried about, then Roosevelt and Longworth could use "the others" as an excuse not to close the deal with Tyler. The circle would be squared: blacks would be more favorably disposed to Roosevelt, Longworth, and Taft (perceived by blacks to be Roosevelt's hatchet man on Brownsville); this would peel black support away from Foraker; and Roosevelt would have an excuse to disappoint Tyler, who, understanding politics, would not raise a ruckus.

The story broke on January 30 in the *Cincinnati Enquirer*. Several problems worked against Tyler; one was that he was not from Cincinnati. The collector traditionally lived there. But what really mattered to Roosevelt was that Cincinnati was Foraker's hometown and where he wanted to show his friendship for Negroes. Roosevelt wanted to "hand Senator Foraker a lemon" with the appointment of a distinguished member of the colored race in Ohio.[10] When Foraker heard Ralph Tyler was being considered, his anger was "vigorous." According to the *New York Times* the only part of his comment that got past the censor was the sarcastic reference to "the Senator for Ohio, Booker Washington" for having been the patronage angel recommending Tyler to Roosevelt. In the end Roosevelt reappointed Amor Smith Jr., former mayor of Cincinnati and a man recommended by Foraker.[11]

Washington biographer Louis Harlan suggested Washington was just as happy Tyler was not appointed. He arranged for him to get a job as fourth auditor of the US Navy (actually in the Treasury Department) so he could keep an eye on the man whom Roosevelt, against Washington's recommendation of another man, made register of the US Treasury, the highest traditionally black-held position in Washington.[12] And the record suggests this is what Tyler did.[13]

GEORGE MYERS MOVED TO Cleveland from Baltimore when he was twenty years old to work in a hotel barber shop. He cut Senator Mark Hanna's hair, and on him Myers stropped his political skills. When a real estate developer built a new and lavish hotel, the Hollenden House, and wanted an equally lavish barber shop for its clientele, he loaned Myers the money to set one up. It thrived and soon became one of the places to go to talk politics—and get a shave and a haircut of course.[14]

Myers was a Republican fiercely loyal to the party and to Mark Hanna. He lost interest in actively working what he called "the game" after Hanna's death in 1904 but stayed close with Republican bosses in Cleveland and mentored the next generation of black leaders, including Ralph Tyler. Though Brownsville may have soured his opinion of Theodore Roosevelt, he remained a loyal Republican and worked to keep Negroes in the party and working for it. Because he would accept nothing less than full participation for Negroes in political, social, and economic America, he kept his distance from Booker T. Washington and his accommodation policies. On all other issues, he was "Old Guard" and already kindly disposed to Foraker. Foraker's support of the Black Battalion made him even better.[15]

On April 11, 1907, Myers wrote to Tyler ostensibly to congratulate him on his federal appointment but really to point out some of the facts of life as he saw them. "No action at this late day of any nature could stem the onward rush of the 'Black deluge' in Ohio for Foraker. . . . I am writing you . . . to demonstrate the futility of the President to corner or stop the stampede of the colored voters of Ohio by your appointment, and to show you what a gigantic and futile task you will have upon your hands if he contemplates using you as the means."[16] Myers's prediction to Tyler was wrong. He had been just as wrong back in January when he wrote Senator Foraker to say, "The President [thinking of appointing Tyler is] to embarrass you . . . and to regain the support of the colored voters of Ohio. In the first, he may be successful, but in the second, never."[17] By the spring of 1908, just in time for the Republican nominating convention, blacks were securely back in the party's fold.[18] But black factionalism was exhibiting itself in the Republican Party and inserting itself into the friendship between Myers and Tyler.

On May 23, 1907, Secretary of the Interior James Garfield would note in his diary "the Ohio appointment settled." Nine days later, Ralph Tyler was writing to George Myers on "Treasury Department" stationery.[19] And President Roosevelt was using small, mostly public-relations-type steps to regain black support. An eleventh-hour addition to a list of black army officers (there were only twelve in the entire army) added the name of "2nd Lt. John E. Green" and posted him to the Twenty-Fifth Infantry. He would be the regiment's first black infantry officer.[20] On January 28 Nick Longworth brought a delegation from the Colored Industrial Education Association to the White House to meet his father-in-law and ask him to attend its fair in Columbus the next summer. Roosevelt had a conflict and seemed sincerely regretful when he asked them to change the fair's date to accommodate his schedule. The delegation said it would try and left happy and delighted.[21]

ON DECEMBER 6, THE day the Senate voted for the Penrose and Foraker resolutions, Mingo Sanders presented himself at the War Department to apply for his own government job—as a reenlisted first sergeant in the Twenty-Fifth Infantry.[22] He hoped to see Secretary of War Taft but was unable to and had to leave disappointed.[23] The next day he returned accompanied by (former) Private Elmer

Brown. Both men wore their army uniforms with service stripes indicating twenty-six years for Sanders and sixteen for Brown. Secretary Taft, pleading his work on his annual report and having to be at the White House for a cabinet meeting, would not see them. But fifty more former soldiers had descended on Washington to apply for reenlistment. All filled in enlistment forms for first-time enlistees and were told they would be held until President Roosevelt decided what to do.[24]

On December 11 Taft distributed his guidelines for reenlistment applications, and the next day six more soldiers showed up at the War Department. They were allowed to file their applications when they gave assurances they subsequently would submit evidence to justify their innocence.[25] Accepting the applications was one thing; considering them was something else, and until President Roosevelt sent the information requested by the Foraker and Penrose resolutions, the War Department would do nothing.

On January 24, ten days after the president delivered the Brownsville information, Mingo Sanders was back at the War Department pursuant to a summons to meet with General George B. Davis, the army's judge advocate general. Sanders was hoping his reenlistment application had been approved and he would be welcomed back into the Twenty-Fifth Infantry.[26] This time he was accompanied by N. B. Marshall, a black lawyer. When General Davis asked Sanders to take an oath, Marshall refused to allow it. Inexplicably, Marshall would not permit Sanders to return to the army until the Senate Military Affairs Committee completed the investigation of Brownsville as ordered two days earlier. He feared the army would post Sanders to Alaska or some other faraway location to keep him from the committee. Marshall's logic is difficult to divine. The longer his client stayed out of the army, the harder it would be to get back in. Even if the army sent Sanders to Alaska, if the Senate committee wanted him to testify before it, the army would send him back to Washington right away. Marshall need not have worried. The application had not been approved, it was only now being looked at, and the oath was not the enlistment oath but one as part of an examination for evidence to consider his application. The army was mystified why Sanders was not cooperating in his own application. Meanwhile, Sanders and Marshall left the War Department to tell Senator Foraker the army wanted Sanders back in. Foraker was overjoyed, only to be disappointed when he learned the truth.

CAPTAIN EDGAR MACKLIN, FORMERLY commanding officer of Company C, was managing the Fort Reno Post Exchange (PX) while awaiting his scheduled court-martial. PXs generated a lot of cash receipts, and on December 21 Captain Macklin, unable to get to the bank in El Reno in time to make a deposit, had $1,500 of PX money in his quarters.

He and Mrs. Macklin were eating supper when someone tried to enter through a side door. "I have a message for you," whoever it was called into the quarters. Immediately, a black man wearing a mask broke in and, pointing a pistol, demanded "all the money you have got."[27] Macklin scuffled with the intruder to get the revolver away from him, but the man fired twice, and Macklin was wounded in his belly and jaw. Mrs. Macklin raced upstairs to get a pistol, but when she got back downstairs the intruder was gone. Her husband's wounds were serious but not fatal.[28]

Suspicion fell on the Brownsville soldiers. Was someone trying to prevent Macklin from testifying against the soldiers at his court-martial? This seemed unlikely. Macklin had defended them since the shooting, and there was no reason to think he would change his story. Besides, he was well liked by his troops and considered a good officer by them. The night he was attacked, an army campaign hat had been found outside Macklin's quarters with the number *25* and the letter *D* outlined on it. But such hats were for sale at shops in El Reno, and the soldiers of Company D had already been discharged and sent away. Because of this and the demand for money, few people believed the intruder was one of the discharged soldiers.[29]

Macklin's court-martial, scheduled for January 4, 1907, had to be postponed until February 4. That same day the Senate Military Affairs Committee began its hearings into the Brownsville Affair.

"My official interest in this matter will soon terminate, but I shall have the comfort in retiring from public service of a well founded conviction that the action of the President relative to this class of lawlessness will be sufficiently rigorous."

Secretary of the Interior Ethan Allen
Hitchcock in a letter to Theodore Roosevelt,
November 30, 1906

CHAPTER NINETEEN

GREATEST SHEPHERD

SENATOR FRANCIS E. WARREN was said to be the richest man in Wyoming.[1] He made money in every sort of venture, from real estate development to municipal utilities.[2] He built and owned opera houses, theaters, office buildings, and residential housing. His retail shops sold "carpet, sewing machines, works of art, pianos, and other furniture" to the wealthy living on Cheyenne's "Millionaires' Row."[3] In the US Senate he saw to it that practically every town in Wyoming got floods of federal funding for public works and army posts to protect them. When the army located Fort D. A. Russell near Cheyenne, the *Denver Post* noted "Denver would lose at least $2,000,000 per year."[4]

Ever more federal money was needed in Wyoming because Warren believed, even after statehood, the state was something akin to a ward of the federal government. Sparsely settled, its natural resources awaiting the technology of later generations to be profitably developed, and its economy imbalanced with ranching and agriculture, the state could not otherwise sustain itself. "Happily, Wyoming, like so much of the American West, did not have to rely solely on the personal resources of its citizens. The federal government stood ready, if solicited, to dispense its bounty through a variety of subsidizing devices." Francis Warren was ever unafraid to make the solicitation.[5] One "subsidizing device" was the tariff on imported wool, and for fighting to keep it at staggering heights, Senator Jonathan P. Dolliver of Iowa said Warren was the "greatest shepherd since Abraham."[6] With his own sheep ranches the foundation of his wealth, this profited his state and his wallet.

Warren was born and raised in the Berkshires of western Massachusetts about thirty miles from W. E. B. Du Bois's birthplace of Great Barrington. Sixteen when the Civil War began, he enlisted in the Forty-Ninth Massachusetts Volunteer Infantry, and at the battle of Port Hudson he was awarded the Medal of Honor for heroic bravery. After the war he tried to raise cattle back home but gave it up to move west and settle in the Wyoming Territory. After holding a series of local elective offices, he was appointed territorial governor by President Chester A. Arthur. With statehood in 1890 he was its first elected governor, and then its first US senator. When the Senate approved the Brownsville investigation, he chaired its Military Affairs Committee in charge of it.[7]

HIS CAREER HAD BEEN nagged by questions of impropriety, many the kind easily brushed under the carpet if the right political party happened to be in control. In 1905 Warren was accused of having his son and brother-in-law on the Senate's payroll, although neither lived in Washington or was seen doing any work. Senator Warren simply denied the charge and it went away.[8] There were allegations that through his influence his electric company secured the contract to provide electricity for Fort Russell in Cheyenne. He survived this one too.

Long whispered about were more-serious allegations that he illegally fenced government lands to graze his flocks. This was common in the high desert West, where raising cattle was a risky business. (If any man knew that, it was Theodore Roosevelt. The dreadful winter of 1886–87 devastated his herds in Dakota while he and Edith were enjoying their honeymoon in delightful Italy. It ended his ranching days.[9] That same cold winter affected Wyoming.) Lack of water was a constant problem.[10] While Warren was territorial governor he reported that "probably four times as many cattle die from want of water as for want of food."[11] To gain an edge ranchers grazed their herds on government land for the water on it and soon came to think the right to do so was their due. To keep other herds away, they saw no problem with fencing this government land. Anyone who tried to cut down the fences had better be "bulletproof."[12] It became a bitter political problem. In 1886 the Interior Department specifically named Warren as an illegal-fencing offender.[13] The next year, forty-six black soldiers came to remove his illegal fences, but they never were allowed to finish the job. Warren was still at it fifteen years later when it was reported there still was "illegal fencing of up to *hundreds of thousand of acres* of government [land] by the Warren Livestock Company, [including] a large pasture in which may be found the city of Cheyenne" (author's emphasis).[14]

Another problem aside from illegal fencing was illegal acquisition of land. The enormity of the fraud was spelled out by Democratic senator James H. Berry of Arkansas: "I wish to say that in my judgment there have been millions of acres of public land secured under the law by fraudulent acts of persons."[15] The Desert Land Act made 640 acres available for ownership if a settler lived on it for three years and showed an effort to irrigate it. In November 1884 Warren acquired a parcel swearing that he had lived continuously on it for the three years. A former associate justice of the territorial supreme court pointed out that Warren actually had been living in Cheyenne and was a member of its city council. (It didn't matter; his ownership stood.)

Warren was alleged to be involved up to his neck in the illegal acquisition of government land. Economics professor Benjamin Hibbard cites a newspaper article from 1904 stating Warren's companies acquired 125,000 acres using his employees as straw men.[16] Warren was indignant. "There has been fraud ever since there have been land laws, and there always will be. . . . Things have come to a pretty pass when it is assumed . . . that every man . . . must be considered a thief until he has proved himself innocent [and] must live on a homestead all of his natural life before he can be recognized as an honest man."[17]

Secretary of the Interior Ethan Allen Hitchcock had enough of this and ordered an investigation aimed at Warren and others in Wyoming.[18] It finished just as Warren's colleague from Ohio, Joseph Foraker, was taking aim at Roosevelt's actions in Brownsville.

IN MARCH 1903 PRESIDENT Roosevelt toured the western states and spent two nights as a guest at a Warren ranch near Cheyenne. On the way, the two men left the train at Laramie and rode the last fifty-six miles on horseback.[19] They sized each other up as their mounts trotted over land Warren later would be accused by Roosevelt's Interior Department of illegally fencing. Warren hoped Roosevelt would see for himself just what the territory was like and understand how badly ranchers needed to graze on it and how they might go about it. A few years later, as Secretary Hitchcock finished the investigation of Senator Warren's sheep grazing, fencing, and land acquisition and Senator Warren prepared to investigate the dismissals of the black soldiers, President Roosevelt and Senator Warren would remember this. Hitchcock, whom Roosevelt inherited from President McKinley, ran the Interior Department the way Roosevelt had run the Civil Service Commission: without concern for toes that might be stepped on, with little interest in bruised feelings, and with practically no allowance for misconduct. In 1901 Hitchcock curtly refused a "request" from Senator Mark Hanna, the man who got President McKinley into the White House, to remove a special inspector to make room for a man Hanna wanted. "I have not the slightest idea of removing [the man]. He has demonstrated his entire fitness for the office, during the last four years, and in the interest of the public service, he will be retained."[20] Five years later, when Hitchcock was hounding him, Warren would write Hitchcock had "gone from radical to wild, and from wild to crazy."[21]

As with most people who exhibited personality traits too much like his own, Roosevelt was uncomfortable with Hitchcock, and inevitably they got on each other's nerves. Hitchcock suggested Roosevelt's 1905 special message to Congress say, "The failure of justice to prevail in certain cases of violations of the law [is] due to lack of proper qualifications on the part of officers of the Government charged with the enforcement of the law. This [is the result of] selecting people for positions requiring confirmation by the Senate principally because they have rendered some political service." Roosevelt almost fell out of his chair and wrote back that this was like saying, "Men appointed by *me* in your Department are chosen in accordance with a policy which is against the interests of the Government, without regard to [their] fitness," and "implies the greatest dereliction of duty either in you or in *me*" (author's emphasis).[22] He ignored the recommendation.

SECRETARY HITCHCOCK SENT SPECIAL Investigator E. B. Linnen, one of his "ablest" inspectors, to investigate illegal fencing in Wyoming and Colorado.[23] The target was Senator Francis Warren.[24] Linnen's report, after almost nine months of digging into allegations and collecting evidence and sworn statements, damned Warren's company for illegally fencing 46,330 acres of federal land in Wyoming and another 1,120 acres in Colorado.[25] Even harsher allegations were made. "Persons who have settled on lands within enclosures have been harassed by stockmen and their employees and agents; their stock has been driven off; their pastures eaten out by the stockmen's sheep and cattle; their fences cut; windows broken in their houses. They have been threatened and intimidated and everything has been done . . . to make it uncomfortable and a hardship for such settlers . . . to continue to live there. There is at this point a strong coterie of politicians with Senator Warren at its head. . . . It seems unlikely that honest prosecutions can be had."[26] Warren knew what it said before it was released by Hitchcock; what had been for many years an annoyance was about to blow up in his face. Along with the federal land violations, he might face charges of corrupting federal officials to overlook what he had done—and still was doing.[27] He wasted no time turning to the onetime rancher who rode with him in Wyoming and was now in the White House. On October 4 he told Roosevelt that a leak from Hitchcock criticizing his position on the Oklahoma statehood bill showed Hitchcock was on a witch hunt against him. The next day he asked that Hitchcock not release any public statements about the Wyoming matters until he (Warren) had a chance to reply to them.[28] Warren warned the request was "for my protection and *for the honor and credit of your administration*" (author's emphasis). The day after that, President Roosevelt told Secretary Hitchcock to do as Warren asked.[29] "No publication of these facts should be made until they are submitted to me. . . . I desire you to take particular pains to see that not an allusion of any kind is allowed to get out . . . until I authorize whatever action is taken." For posterity Roosevelt added, "My one object is to have any investigation into any alleged misconduct thoro and impartial and I care not a rap whether the man hit be Democrat or Republican, Senator or private citizen."[30] In a second letter Roosevelt again engaged in a bit of future historical revisionism, "Let me emphasize, what should surely need no emphasis, that my aim in this matter is not to shield any man," but nevertheless again cautioned Hitchcock, "Until the matter is submitted to me no hint of it should be allowed to escape."[31]

Roosevelt had been putting his own pressure on Hitchcock. He had known what ranchers were doing but hoped they would remove the illegal fences on their own. Hitchcock's quest could reveal his naivety, but Roosevelt still hoped prosecution could be avoided.[32] Since any misstep in the Linnen investigations and subsequent enforcement might be a reason to quash them, on October 9 he wrote Hitchcock, "I should like you to give me a list of all the notices sent to the offending parties to remove their fences . . . the date of the request for removal in each case, and . . . what was done by the offending fence-owner in response. . . . I only want this for the State of Wyoming and of course only for the last few years. If no notice was sent I should like to know the names of the officials of your Department whose business it was to send them and who thus failed in their duty, and what excuse they have to give, and what their position now is."[33]

Roosevelt's Hitchcock fatigue was obvious to General Land Office Commissioner (and former Wyoming governor) W. A. Richards, a member in good standing of the Warren Machine, whose honesty was questioned in the Linnen Report. After a midnight meeting with Roosevelt he wrote to Warren, "I came away with the *very strong* conviction that your judgment [that after elections something might happen with Hitchcock] was correct"[34] (Richards' emphasis).

TWO DAYS AFTER THE off-year elections and the disclosure of Special Orders No. 266 discharging the Brownsville soldiers, Senator Joseph Foraker no doubt read in the *Cincinnati Enquirer*, "The Secretary of the Interior, Mr. Hitchcock, has informed the President that he would be unable to stay after March 4 [1907]."[35] The *New York Tribune* that day carried the same report, although it implied it was Hitchcock's idea that James R. Garfield replace him at the Interior Department and President Roosevelt agreed.[36]

In White House meetings on Monday and Wednesday, sandwiching election day, Roosevelt yielded to Warren's pressure to be rid of the unbendable Hitchcock and to his own exasperation with him. He asked for his resignation. Hitchcock would stay until March to see that his investigations into Wyoming land acquisitions and fencing were irreversibly on a path to cleaning things up and prosecuting offenders.[37] Roosevelt finally was acting against the illegal fencing.[38]

Warren agreed to remove his fences, and Roosevelt gave him time to get them down. Roosevelt would see that Hitchcock would not turn his attention back to Warren in his last four months as secretary, and during that time Warren would not backslide on his obligations nor would Hitchcock have reason to think he was.[39] After Hitchcock left office, Roosevelt would protect Warren against further difficulties with Garfield. The terms of the Roosevelt-Warren agreement took another month to iron out, but the parties shook hands in time for Roosevelt to leave for Panama.

ON NOVEMBER 30 SECRETARY Hitchcock sent the accusing Linnen Report to President Roosevelt and said he agreed with its conclusions. The White House passed it on to Senator Warren for "any comment he may desire."[40] On December 10, in a letter to W. W. Gleason, his man back in Cheyenne, Warren wrote of his agreement with Roosevelt. "I wish you would keep this letter under lock and key. . . . I do not wish to betray the confidences of the President." He instructed Gleason to check certain fencing. "You must go over and pull a lot of it down."[41] As for the damning Linnen Report, Roosevelt had said to Warren, "It is understood, of course, between us, that . . . your company has requested that [a new investigation] be made later on. [Meanwhile, we] have got to shift along with Hitchcock some way until the fourth of March." Warren asked that Hitchcock be "let out at once," and Roosevelt replied it was not worth "the blood and thunder. Later on, about April first maybe, we will have your matter looked over as per your request." Warren had made it clear, "I want a clean, new, fresh deal." Roosevelt told him, "You shall have it."[42]

Warren got his "clean, new, fresh" examination. On July 11, 1907, he received notice that the examination had found no "illegal enclosures,"[43] and he and his company were "absolutely cleared" of unlawfully enclosing "Government lands" and could ignore the previous order to remove fences. Alerted to this good news, the day before he wrote Secretary Garfield to say he made good on what he always said, "Warren Live Stock Company has not an acre of land illegally inclosed."[44]

WHILE WAITING FOR HITCHCOCK to leave, President Roosevelt had to alternatively scold him to see he did not wander off the reservation and coddle him to keep him quiet. On the evening James Garfield became Interior Department secretary, he and his wife were dinner guests at the Hitchcocks' home.[45] Hitchcock had no hard feelings.

ON FEBRUARY 4, 1907, Senator Warren, firmly in charge of the Senate's investigation of President Roosevelt and the soldiers of the Twenty-Fifth Infantry, his land irregularities satisfactorily dealt with, gaveled his committee to order.

"I am perfectly satisfied that no man in the Battalion fired a shot."

> Senator Joseph Foraker in a letter to
> Lieutenant Colonel Edwin F. Glenn,
> defense counsel for Major Charles Penrose,
> February 7, 1907

CHAPTER TWENTY

THE SOLDIERS' PATRON
AND PATRONAGE

A T 10:30 A.M., MONDAY, February 4, 1907, Senator Francis E. Warren brought the Senate Military Affairs Committee to order to begin its investigation of the Brownsville Incident. Over the next thirteen months—with a four-month break in the summer and fall of 1907—its members heard testimony from soldiers, civilians, investigators, and experts; read testimony from other hearings and trials; ordered sophisticated testing of rifles and other weapons, bullets, and shells found on the ground in Brownsville or dug out of walls, rooms, and trees; and endlessly discussed their differences. Its transcripts without exhibits are 3,411 pages long. When the committee issued its reports on March 11, 1908, nine senators—half its Republicans and all its Democrats—supported President Roosevelt's discharges.[1] In his memoirs Foraker would write, "All of [the Democrats on the committee] were against the Negroes before a word of testimony was heard," and enough of the Republican members would join with them to make a majority.[2] It claimed the evidence "clearly established" that the soldiers had shot up the town, but exactly which ones was still a mystery.[3]

299

Four Republican committee members, Senators Foraker, James A. Hemenway of Indiana, Morgan G. Bulkeley of Connecticut (who would sit with Joseph Foraker when he received the loving cup a year later), and Nathan Scott of West Virginia, who had stood by Foraker and defended the soldiers early in the Senate debates, disagreed with the committee's majority and said the case against the soldiers had not been proved. Their minority report said the testimony, "as thorough as it was possible to obtain," was nevertheless "very unsatisfactory, indefinite, and conflicting." It failed to show a motive for the soldiers to shoot up the town. Other persons, the owners of "eight gambling houses" who would not permit the black soldiers to come into their casinos and saloons and wanted the white troops back to recapture the wagering losses and bar bills that made their business so profitable, had better reasons to do it.[4] And all of the battalion's white officers believed the soldiers were innocent.[5] "Beyond a reasonable doubt . . . many of the men so discharged were innocent of any offense." Foraker and Bulkeley went a step further and flatly added to the minority report that "none of the soldiers participated in the shooting." In other words, all were innocent. They would submit an exhaustive seventy-four page memorandum justifying this position.[6]

In his almost 1,100-page memoirs, Senator Foraker devoted only thirty-four words to these hearings.[7] This may reflect regret was his lasting frustration. But in fact, he performed magnificently for the soldiers. The Senate committee was the wrong venue, and his skills as a lawyer were wasted.[8] He discredited testimony against the soldiers; committee members were unmoved. Katie Leahy said she saw from her window the soldiers shooting into the town from the Company B barracks. But she could not have. Foraker showed through Lieutenant Harry Leckie that a tree blocked her view.[9] George Rendall was sure he saw colored soldiers wearing army uniforms. But he was seventy-two years old, blind in one eye, had worn glasses for twenty-six years, and was not sure he had them on that night.[10] Later army tests taken under similar conditions indicated almost *none* of the witnesses could have distinguished soldiers or their race.[11] The committee's senators yawned.

Putting on his own case, Foraker established that the soldiers were not predisposed to act violently. Major Penrose said the battalion had an excellent reputation and that it was "the best drilled and best disciplined" he had ever seen in the army. Captain Lyon echoed his commanding officer, "The drill and discipline were excellent. I never saw better."[12] Even a white soldier in the departing Twenty-Sixth Infantry, who had served in the army for fifteen years, thought the black soldiers of the Twenty-Fifth Infantry, "were about the strictest soldiers that I had ever seen."[13] Evidence that men of the battalion's parent regiment may have been involved in "shooting affrays and difficulties of one kind or another" had nothing to do with the Black Battalion's soldiers. Their records showed "no stain." The troublemakers at Sturgis, Dakota Territory, in 1885 were with Company H, and a shooting in Winnemucca, Nevada, in 1899 was by soldiers in Companies L and M. These three companies were in different battalions. And those events were a long time ago. Company A, part of the First Battalion, was in a disturbance at Fort Bliss, Texas, but that company was not at Fort Brown and never would be. In the history of the First Battalion, only once was a man who was at Fort Brown even near trouble. Private Isaiah Raynor of Company B was wounded in a shooting at a "house of ill fame" outside Fort Niobrara, but he was the victim of a brawl by others and never thought to be anything but a hapless bystander.[14] Foraker was able to show there was no motive because of the racial-hostility problems of Privates Adair, Newton, and Reid. Adair "showed no resentment and made no threats," Newton "made no threats . . . and exhibited no special resentment," and Reid "laughingly remarked that he 'guessed he got about what he deserved.'"[15]

Foraker's biggest problem was that there were no logical suspects other than the soldiers, and the bullets, shells, and cartridges—army issue for the soldiers' Springfield rifles—found in Brownsville implicated them. Even Major Penrose changed his mind after he saw them.[16] If Foraker could show Brownsville civilians also had access to bullets like these and the weapons to fire them, it might refute everything else that pointed to the soldiers.

SENATOR FORAKER HAD BEEN in the army. He knew how often army gear, uniforms, and ammunition found their way into civilian hands.

He believed that while the soldiers may have been the only ones with Springfield rifles, they were not the only ones with Springfield rifle ammunition. To challenge the assumption they were, he acquired an education in military weapons and ammunition. He had to learn the differences among bullets; their size, composition, weight; and how they could be modified for different weapons. He found out the diameters of Springfield, Krag, and Mauser bullets were incredibly close in size, and the difference was obliterated after they struck an object and deformed (as had the Brownsville bullets). He found out a Springfield bullet can be fired by a different rifle.

All this education paid off when General William Crozier, the army's chief of ordnance, came before the Military Affairs Committee and Foraker handed him a Brownsville bullet and asked if it might have been fired from, say, a Krag rifle. Crozier said it could not because the Krag's chamber was too small for Springfield cartridges. But Foraker pressed him: Is it possible to do something to the Krag to accommodate the larger Springfield cartridges? Surprisingly, the general said yes. "The bore could be enlarged so as to get the cartridge in."

> [Foraker] Q: Now let me ask you if there is any difficulty whatever about boring that [Krag] barrel to accommodate this [Springfield] cartridge?
>
> [Crozier] A: I take it to be easily done.
>
> Q: Do you not know, General Crozier, that it is actually done by those who have Krag rifles, to accommodate the Springfield cartridge, since the Springfield rifle was brought into use?
>
> A: No, Sir, this is news to me.[17]

Now there were two rifles—the Springfield and the Krag—that could have fired the bullets.

What about the Mauser? "Yes, Sir," answered Crozier, "as far as my examination of it here in my hand, it might be a Mexican army Mauser." Crozier felt comfortable saying this because he could not tell from the bullet in his hand, distorted by being fired, what it originally weighed or how long was its length. But if it was a Mauser bullet, it would not have fit into the Springfield.

[Foraker] Q: You do not know that during the last two years [the Mexican army has] been issuing [a different size cartridge]?
[Crozier] A: No, sir; I am not aware of it.
Q: Made for the express purpose of accommodating our Springfield rifle caliber?
A: That I am not aware of.
Q: You have never heard of that at all, until it is suggested now?
A: No, sir.[18]

Now the Military Affairs Committee knew there were three kinds of rifles that could have fired this bullet, one of which was issued to the Mexican army just across the Rio Grande. There was another, the civilian Winchester. Although General Crozier failed to mention it to the committee, five months before he testified he was told 438 of the Winchester "model of 1805" rifles had been "chambered" for the Springfield ammunition and shipped to "dealers and others."[19]

Foraker therefore showed that the conclusion that the bullets had to have been fired by soldiers because they were army bullets and usable only in their Springfield rifles was false. But he was not finished. There were two types of Springfield ammunition: long-range, high-power "ball" ammunition for combat, and short-range, less powerful "guard" ammunition. The bullets retrieved in Brownsville were high power. Guided by the questions put to him by Foraker, Quartermaster Sergeant George McMurray of Company C told the committee that after arriving in Brownsville he had collected all high-power ammunition issued at Fort Niobrara and made sure it was all accounted for, then he had given each man ten rounds of guard ammunition. So the bullets like those dug out of Brownsville walls and fences had been returned by the soldiers before the shooting. And then, just before the committee excused McMurray, Foraker showed why he was a lawyer "in full":

Sergeant McMurray: One thing, there was a wood shed there, and I found in one of those woodsheds there a whole box of shells there, in the woodshed, that had been left there, I suppose, by the Twenty-sixth.

[Senator Foraker] Q: You were preceded at Brownsville by the Twenty-sixth Infantry?

[Sergeant McMurray] A: Yes, Sir.

Q: Two or three companies?

A: Yes, sir.

Q: And in a wood shed belonging to the barracks that you occupied?

A: Yes, sir; that had been used on target practice, as I would suppose.

. . .

Q: And how many were there?

A: There must have been a thousand or more. It was a box nearly full.

. . .

Q: No cover on the box?

A: No, Sir.

. . .

Q: And they had been standing there for how long a time before you got there?

A: I couldn't say how long. It looked like they had been there some time.[20]

So others had access to empty Springfield shells and could have scattered them on the ground. On the cold page of the transcript, this appears as an "oh, by the way" bit of information from Sergeant McMurray, eager to cooperate with the committee. It was really tenacious prospecting beforehand by Foraker to dig out this nugget of gold, the experience to know just where and how to use it, and the thespian skills of an experienced trial lawyer to mine the dramatic moment for its very best effect.

Throughout the hearings his preparation was thorough. He tracked down witnesses "from Boston to Winnemucca, Nev."[21] He contacted Dr. Edger, the army surgeon at Fort Brown, to find out what his testimony would be.[22] He wrote Captain Macklin asking him whether he made the statement in Crixell's bar, "These negroes might jump over the fence some night and shoot hell out of the town and that their officers could not prevent their doing it if they took such a notion." Captain Samuel Lyon responded, "Capt. Macklin has turned your letter of the 11th inst. over to me as his counsel."

The allegation "is unqualifiedly false in all material particulars."[23] Unsolicited suggestions and assistance came from the public. From "a friend" in Louisville: "I see through the paper you are asking for the names of the soldiers of the 25th." He gave Foraker J. H. Howard's address and employer in Louisville.[24] In December Foraker received a "Personal and Confidential" letter from Captain Ralph E. Gambell of the Porto Rico Infantry with information about Inspector General Garlington. "In Oct. 1877, Garlington was adjutant of the 7th Cavalry and with Gen. Sturges on an Indian chase on the Missouri river. Their steamer landed at a point where Gen. Miles was waiting with a command, among which were some colored troops. In passing up a narrow gangway as Garlington was coming down, an old Negro Sergeant accidentally touched elbows with the officer. Garlington stood him up by the rail, cursed and abused him shamefully. The Serg't reported it to his Captain, and the latter being a Civil War veteran carried it to Gen. Miles. Miles instantly sent his Adjutant Gen. on board the steamer with orders to Gen. Sturges to clap Lt. Garlington in close arrest, which was done. He remained there 48 hours and then made a public apology to Serg't. Coloredman. Garlington has been gunning for 'Niggers' ever since." When Garlington testified before the committee, Foraker never brought this up.[25]

When the black soldiers appeared before the committee, Foraker treated them softly and respectfully, always addressing them by their former ranks, thereby subtly reminding his senatorial colleagues what these men had been and reinforcing what President Roosevelt had taken from them. Jacob Frazier was first sergeant of Company D, a noncommissioned officer in the US Army, a man who gave orders and expected them to be obeyed; now he was a porter at the Elliott National Bank in Boston. Foraker was careful to call him "Sergeant." By contrast Democratic senator William Warner, having accepted the prosecutorial baton from the chastened Senator Lodge, insisted on using "Mr." to show Frazier was nothing more than a civilian and occasionally something less when he addressed him by only his last name.[26]

Foraker's skills showed themselves nowhere better than when

he cross-examined witnesses. Teofilo Martinez was sleeping on the rear gallery (another name for *porch* in Brownsville) of Francesco Yturria's home on Washington Street and directly across from Fort Brown. He told the committee the shots came from "the direction of the barracks" identified by him on a map as Company C's barracks. It took Foraker less than two minutes to show Martinez could not have seen a thing.

> *[Senator Foraker] Q:* Are there any trees between the rear part of
>   the Yturria house and the end of C barracks?
> *[Teofilo Martinez] A:* . . . A large tree.
> *Q:* Can you see C barracks from the rear part of the Yturria house?
> *A:* No, sir; on account of the trees.[27]

Major Blocksom was a tougher nut but he too cracked from the pressure of Foraker's cross-examination. Foraker persuaded Major Blocksom to change his mind about Sergeant James Reid, the sergeant of the guard at the time of the shooting, from saying he swore falsely about the incident's events to "I say now that my opinion is now that there is more of a chance he might be perfectly honest."[28]

"I am pretty familiar with the rules governing the interrogation of witnesses," Foraker immodestly said at the beginning of the hearings.[29] Later on Senator Warren agreed. "We all know he has to be a smooth examiner to follow the Senator from Ohio."[30]

Letters came into Foraker's Senate office thanking him for his efforts and congratulating him for how well he was doing. The Colored Foraker Club in Cadiz, Ohio, sent him resolutions of praise. W. W. Dudley, a lawyer in Washington, DC, wrote "how much I am pleased" and suggested he look up a helpful US Supreme Court decision. F. H. M. Murray, a founder of the Niagara Movement, advised him on strategy and who the raiders might have been. Charles P. Lincoln, a lawyer in El Reno, asked for a photo he could hang in the Republican headquarters there. Katie Leahy, who operated the Leahy Hotel in Brownsville and witnessed the shooting, invited him to be her guest at her hotel if he came to Brownsville ("I will do all in my power to make your stay in our city not only satisfactory but pleasant").[31]

Some federal employees were willing to risk Roosevelt's wrath to stand by Foraker. From E. N. Martin, US special pension examiner, came, "Your refusal to bend your knee and cringe your neck to the 'Big Stick' has intensified my admiration for your courage and genius."[32] Even the Twenty-Fifth Infantry's chaplain Theophilus Steward stuck his tongue out at his commander in chief when he said, "Senator Foraker is covering himself in glory."[33]

Joseph Foraker was more than anyone responsible for the headline in Monroe Trotter's *Guardian* of Boston: "Colored Soldiers Testifying Strongly."[34] Constitution League secretary A. B. Humphrey wrote, "Your magnificent conduct of the Brownsville case entitles you to the moral support of the world, and I believe you will get it when the facts are known."[35] John Milholland knew what it cost him. "[Had] the Senator not identified himself with the Brownsville Inquiry, he would have had no trouble in Washington, or in his own State."[36]

ON MARCH 18, 1908, there appeared a story in newspapers about a man in Galveston, Texas, named D. C. Gray. Gray said he had been a soldier in the Black Battalion's Company B, and on the night of the shooting he and other soldiers had been in their barracks playing cards. Suddenly a soldier not identified by Gray (nor were the card players) came into the room, angry from an insult to one of his friends (also not identified) from a white man. "He was going to fix that white [expletive] so that he will never fool with another soldier's friend." Quickly other soldiers joined with him and they rushed for the gun racks, "fixed the sentry," jumped the wall, and raced into Brownsville. They shot "in the house of Mr. Cowarts on Fourteenth street . . . into the Starcks house . . . as some of the boys did not like him and they wanted to kill him." Then they ran to Thirteenth Street where it joined Elizabeth Street and shot policeman Dominguez after he shot at them first. "Anyway, all of them said that when Major Penrose examined them." They shot into the saloon "run by Frank Natus" because they had had some trouble there. When they heard bugles sounding back at the fort, they knew the raid "was all off" and raced back to the barracks and got into their beds before anyone could see they had been out. One of the soldiers on guard came into the barracks and, in a loud whisper, told "any of you fellas in that dirty business" to get their guns in shape and back in the gun racks because "there will be inspection." When the first sergeant (which would have been Mingo Sanders) ordered them to fall in, they got dressed and went outside. When roll was taken, all the shooters were present.[37]

The Senate committee interrupted the testimony of Matias G. Tamayo, the post scavenger,[38] on March 18 to discuss Gray and his story. A telegram that day from the army's adjutant general advised the committee that Major Blocksom told him that the "Chief of Police, Galveston, has just wired me [that] confession of Gray, supposed discharged soldier, appearing in papers today, is a fake," and without much discussion all the committee members, regardless of their Brownsville position, agreed it must be so.[39] For a man who was not there, Gray was remarkably well informed about what happened. He identified the houses shot into (but misspelled the owners' names); knew Frank Natus's and Joe Dominguez's names and where they were shot; knew approximately what time the shooting took place, how many shooters were thought to have been involved, and how the bugle call might have been an alarm to get back to Fort Brown; and plausibly described what might have happened when the soldiers, had they been shooters, returned to the barracks.

But no one with the name D. C. Gray or anything like it was in company at Fort Brown. The D. C. Gray in question had lived in Galveston for the past seven years and never had been in the army.[40] Senator Foraker thought the committee should subpoena the editor of the Galveston newspaper that broke the story. Senator Warren suggested waiting a few days to "see what the developments are."[41] All agreed this made sense.

Foraker wanted to show the soldiers had nothing to do with the shooting and could not have planned a cover-up. Gray's statement showed otherwise. But if true, it would have helped Foraker and the innocent soldiers confirm their innocence and get them back in the army. It also would have helped Roosevelt because it confirmed the shooters were soldiers and, up until then, had not said anything.

The matter was dropped; the Gray confession was ignored.

FORAKER CLAIMED HE FOUND the "subject of patronage disagreeable" and that he attended to it only because he had a duty to recommend Ohioans to the White House for federal positions.[42] Supplying federal jobs rewarded deserving supporters and encouraged their future support. But it could be a pain in the neck. John Galvin was a Cincinnati lawyer who desperately wanted to be a federal judge. Only a week after the Senate voted to investigate the Brownsville shooting, and without invitation, he solicited Foraker's assistance. "I cannot refrain from extending to you my sincere and hearty congratulations upon the new evidence, not only of your courage, but of your matchless skill in debate. I read with much pleasure in the Enquirer this morning of the account at the Gridiron dinner." Galvin was just getting started. He mentioned the terrible ordeal Jim Foraker was going through and that he made a point of seeing poor Jim in the hospital in Philadelphia, who looked pretty good, all things considered. Then he got down to the matter of the federal judgeship. "When an opportunity to gratify the ambition of a lifetime presents itself, and it appears that it may possibly never come again, a man clings on tenaciously to the slightest hope, and is reluctant to hold his hands and do nothing, when by some activity he might accomplish something toward the gratification of that ambition." Galvin was saying, will you help me? Foraker merely thanked him "for his kind words." Galvin kept pressing. "Of course, as you can imagine that I am interested and watch everything in the papers. . . . Is there anything I can do to advance my own chances in any way." There was nothing. Foraker told him he planned to ask President Roosevelt to nominate Judge John J. Adams of Zanesville.

But federal appointments, even plums like judgeships, are like busses; there is always another one coming along, not quite as often but just as assuredly. Galvin kept in touch with the senator through late spring and early summer until news of Roosevelt's cold shoulder got through to him. Galvin realized Foraker was unable to rescue him from the practice of law, but that was no reason to burn bridges. He continued to send encouragement to Foraker, whose enemies "have seen fit to . . . demand your elimination from the face of the earth." He and others "are ready to go forth and fight with you as long as you give the word of command, and whether you command or not, we propose to fight against any attempt to eliminate you or injure you in any way. We are still with you and for you."[43] Most job seekers were just as pesky, but not as nice as the disappointed Mr. Galvin.

Judge Adams, the man Foraker wanted for the federal bench, never got the appointment either. On March 18 Roosevelt wrote Foraker, "I have come to the conclusion that Mr. John E. Sater . . . best meets the requirements . . . I shall give him a recess appointment." A recess appointment is made when the Senate is not in session, and, under the Constitution, Senate approval is not required until the end of the next calendar year. But individual senators have leverage over appointments, too; "senatorial courtesy" gives them something akin to a veto over any nominee for a federal position from that senator's state.[44] A clever president can work his way around this. In 1874 President Grant's man for the customs collector position in Boston was opposed by Senator George S. Boutwell of Massachusetts. Boutwell thought his position was perfectly clear to Grant when the Senate Committee on Commerce and Boutwell as its chairman voted against the nomination. But the careless senator neglected to inform President Grant personally and emphatically. If only Boutwell had "asked me to withdraw the nomination . . . , I would have acceded to his request."[45]

Foraker delayed Sater's donning judicial robes until March 1, 1909, simply by asking the Senate to accord him this senatorial courtesy.[46] He also gave Roosevelt some small payback by successfully engineering Senate rejection of four Taft supporters for postmasterships in Ohio.[47] Meanwhile, Roosevelt was working on other plans for Foraker that would have him out of the Senate at the end of 1908.

Foraker and Roosevelt had had an unsettled patronage relationship going back to 1905, when Foraker submitted newspaper editor Howard D. Mannington for surveyor of customs in Columbus. Roosevelt said no. A few months later Foraker objected to Roosevelt replacing an Ohio man as consul in Glasgow. Roosevelt did it anyway.[48] There was talk in the street that Roosevelt was asking James Garfield for names and not, as he should have been, Ohio's two senators, who were "mad because Mr. Garfield has been consulted by President Roosevelt as to Ohio appointments. Their version is that Mr. Garfield had 'butted in.'"[49] It was to get worse after Brownsville. On March 16, 1907, Roosevelt gave instructions to George Cortelyou, now secretary of the treasury (but with patronage still in his portfolio), "In any appointments of importance in Ohio I think it advisable now that the judgment of Secretary Taft should be obtained; and if there is any difficulty with either of the Senators you might mention that by my direction Mr. Taft is to be consulted as I feel a peculiar regard for his judgment and I think it wise to follow it."[50] Beyond simple job appointments, two months later Cortelyou's Treasury Department denied a request from a Cincinnati bank for "additional [Government] deposits" to bulk up its books during the economy's Panic of 1907.[51] The bank had made its request through Foraker.

Foraker's influence in Washington had evaporated and everyone knew it. "The conclusion cannot be escaped that Senator Foraker is not to be consulted as is the custom when the President prepares to distribute patronage."[52] After the Adams rejection, Foraker "never again made a recommendation to [Roosevelt] of anybody for anything." He knew it was a waste of time.[53]

ANOTHER MAN WAS WHISPERING into President Roosevelt's ear about Foraker and federal appointments. Foraker biographer Everett Walters suggests Congressman Theodore Burton, the man Foraker blew away at the state convention in Dayton the previous September, helped put the stakes through Judge Adams's and Foraker's hearts at a meeting on March 5, where he told Roosevelt that Foraker had recommended Adams as a reward for helping him outwit Burton.[54] Roosevelt was determined to help Burton win Foraker's Senate seat. That same day, Roosevelt made Burton chairman of the Inland Waterways Commission, which planned the use of rivers to move goods throughout the country while preserving them as natural resources.[55] This put Burton on the national stage and permitted him to say he did something important for Ohio. The Republican insurgents beaten by Foraker in Dayton were newly emboldened to cripple Foraker's chances in the Ohio Senate, which would select the next US senator in January 1909. It was not good news for Foraker.

IN THE SPRING OF 1907 Foraker was besieged. The Brownsville hearings were a full-time preoccupation. His Senate seat was under threat. He received worsening news from his niece Ethel Marie. "My dear Uncle Ben, I believe [Papa] has begun to realize that he can not live but a little while longer. The disease has eaten through his cheek to the right of his nose. He found it out Sunday for the first time. Of course it came as a shock to him. Try to see him as soon as it is convenient for you. Doctor Martin . . . gave him two months to live."[56] Jim bested the doctor's prediction by two weeks. When he died in April, his brother the senator had been unable to leave the committee hearings to see him.[57]

And now the presidential election forced itself on Foraker.

"He has done you dirt in the soldier business and the Ohio business, as he should not have dragged you into it."

T. Thomas Fortune in a letter to Booker
T. Washington, February 12, 1907

CHAPTER TWENTY-ONE

OTHER COALITIONS, OTHER FRONTS

BOOKER T. WASHINGTON HAD to rethink and regroup. Like Foraker, by the spring of 1907 he was under siege from different sides. President Roosevelt worked to cast Foraker out of public life, but to Washington he was merely indifferent. For a man called "the Wizard" because of his influence with powerful white men, this was just as cruel. The thanks for his support of Roosevelt in the Brownsville Incident was a resurgent effort by other black leaders to displace him, and little help came from the man he called "our friend" to deal with it. Unmoored from his patron in the White House, Washington was a man at sea.

He tried to show his worth to the administration, the Republicans, and the likely candidate in 1908, William Taft. When Charles Anderson, New York collector of customs, learned about a meeting in New York to protest Taft's nomination, Washington told Anderson to let Roosevelt know about it.[1] One of Anderson's accusations—that a Department of the Interior employee named L. M. Hershaw was the "head devil" inspiring newspaper attacks against Roosevelt—was false. But Roosevelt sent Anderson to Secretary James Garfield to do something about it. The pettiness, insignificance, and falseness of this "intelligence" so quickly and hopefully passed on to Roosevelt tell something of Washington's discouragement and despair. To get to Taft, he went through his Ohio campaign manager Arthur Vorys. He wrote there was "danger . . . to the Negro race in this Brownsville agitation and I am doing some quiet and effective work with colored newspapers in changing that tendency."[2]

He turned to blacks, including George Myers in Cleveland. Myers was already disenchanted with Washington and ready to help lead the former faithful out of the land of Tuskegee. In June 1907 Washington asked him to attend the upcoming meeting of his National Negro Business League. "The story of the success you have won, as a business man, as told by you, would inspire and help many other young men, who need some such stimulus as your story would give them."[3] Washington got nowhere with him. After Brownsville, Myers saw Washington as separated from the future of the Negro civil rights movement just as Roosevelt saw Foraker split from the Republican Party. Myers would stay a Republican, but not a Roosevelt man. For supporting the black soldiers, Foraker was entitled to the support of the black people and certainly had earned Myers's. Ralph Tyler, sitting comfortably at his desk, auditing the navy courtesy of Roosevelt, tried to make him see that it was still Roosevelt's party and black Republicans would recognize this and stay with him. As Washington was doing. "Fact is, George, you can't keep the colored man off the bandwagon. He sees it coming, the music grows louder."[4]

Myers understood that Brownsville could shift the balance in black factionalism from Washington to Du Bois. Would it provoke a factionalism for blacks within the Republican Party? Tyler thought not and for the moment was staying with Roosevelt. Myers saw things differently. Politics might mean going with the winner, but no longer with this winner. He was not with Roosevelt. Brownsville had done this to him.

It was becoming clear to Washington that the music from Tyler's oncoming bandwagon was disturbingly off-key and disorienting. A letter from Winfield Forrest Cozart of Manitou, Colorado, outlining the dilemma facing him, the Republican Party, and black Americans after Brownsville might have given him the compass points to find his sense of direction. Cozart was speaking for himself but made it clear his feelings represented where the race as a whole stood. He still admired Washington because his "great industrial movement . . . is beneficial to . . . both races," and he did not believe the criticisms and the "false light" shone on him by Negro newspapers (Cozart specifically mentioned Trotter's *Guardian*). He also believed "the President meant well [with the discharges] and we are still devoted to him, and do not question his honesty, and sincerity . . . because we have faith enough in him to believe that when he is thoroughly convinced of his mistake he will rectify" it. But "I have met only one Colored man who says the dismissal of the soldiers was right. . . . The race stands almost as a unit, in condemnation of their discharge without trial . . . nothing short of restoration will settle the matter." Meanwhile only party loyalty has kept him and "millions of others . . . silent [about] the effort of Senator Foraker." "If the administration and the [Republican] party wish to retain the support of the Colored Vote in the next National election, the time for action has come." If Washington too wished "to retain the support" of blacks, his time was at hand.[5]

Winfield Cozart was a western George Myers: smart, successful, solidly Republican, in touch with the street, and sounding a warning. But where Myers was barely deferential to Washington, Cozart still saw him as the Principal of Tuskegee and treated him with respect. But how the race saw Washington mirrored how they saw Roosevelt.[6] Whither will it drive the race?

SINCE 1905, WHEN HE feared it would interfere with his efforts to end the Russo-Japanese War, President Roosevelt was bedeviled by ongoing problems from the treatment of Japanese in the American West, particularly in California.[7] A good deal of this was based on race, but there was more to it than that. American workers did not want cheap Japanese labor competing for jobs, but California businesses wanted access to Japan for their goods and services. San Franciscans did not want Japanese children in their schools, and

California's governor and legislature did not want the federal government meddling with their schools, but Japan did not want its citizens unjustly treated by Americans and its self-image as a world power tarnished. Theodore Roosevelt wanted California and San Franciscans to calm down and not pass discriminatory legislation that would make matters worse and, most important, not interfere with his ability to soften Japan's aggressive tendencies.

In its war with Russia, Japan surprisingly and overwhelmingly defeated the hapless Russian military and its hopeless czar, but it required Theodore Roosevelt to help it negotiate the peace. He earned the Nobel Peace Prize for it. The victory gave the Japanese people a new sense of their potential, the taste of being a powerful nation, and feelings of envy, jealousy, and resentment of the West, including America, its former friend and teacher, now seen as a rival. According to historian Thomas A. Bailey, when the war ended, so did the golden age in Japanese-American relations.[8] There was a swagger to the Japanese leaders, especially its military, that did not go unnoticed by Roosevelt. Roosevelt the martinet admired these virtues; Roosevelt the president worried about them. In a letter to British General Ian Standish Monteith Hamilton, an observer with the Japanese army in Manchuria during the Russo-Japanese War, Roosevelt congratulated him for his book on the war, and noted, "Nothing in your book imprest me more than . . . that little play given by the Japanese soldiers." In it, a Japanese soldier murders his wife and children, lest concern for them back home hamper the enthusiastic and ruthless performance of his military duties in the war. Roosevelt thought the play "gruesome" but quickly added, "[It] gives one a thoro realization of what it is that makes them such formidable fighters." He speculated that these martial qualities could be enhanced only by "the extraordinary increase of industrialism" in Japan.[9] Roosevelt elevated Japan to a position of importance and respect accorded no other Asian nation and remained "profoundly friendly toward them."[10] Avoiding antagonisms, confrontation, even war itself became part of his and America's new foreign policy. Roosevelt saw America as a brake on Japanese hostility in Asia, as when he negotiated the treaty ending its war with Russia. California's bellicose and insulting actions made it harder for him and America to influence Japan to more peaceful behavior and to eliminate its aggression in Asia and elsewhere.[11] Roosevelt knew Japan and America would bump into each other in the Pacific Basin as each country extended its influence there, and he wanted Japan's reaction to be, "Excuse me," not "Get out of my way!" If he and the country did not handle Japan correctly, war between the two countries was not out of the question.

EVEN WHILE THE RUSSO-JAPANESE war was still going on, President Roosevelt got wind of what would be called "insolent" behavior by Japanese in Hawaii. In February 1905 he instructed his secretary of war to see "if a regiment or two of troops" might be needed there.[12] Back on the mainland, Californians felt there were too many Japanese slipping into their state, joining the already too many Chinese. They wanted something done about it and did not "give a rap" about the relations between the two countries.

Aware that the influx of Japanese to the West Coast was a problem, the Japanese government itself started to alleviate it. In August 1900 it stopped issuing passports to laborers for the mainland United States but continued issuing them for Hawaii. This cut the number of Japanese entering California directly but solved little.[13] Hawaii was American soil, and many Japanese workers who arrived there legally proceeded on to the mainland.[14] Foreshadowing later efforts in 1920 to limit worldwide immigration of people from elsewhere than northern Europe, bills were introduced in Congress to exclude specifically the Japanese. If such a law had been enacted, Roosevelt probably would have vetoed it. In his December 1904 annual message to Congress, Roosevelt made clear he had no sympathy for a discriminatory immigration policy, although he made no specific reference to the Japanese.[15]

But Californians had reached their limit. If they could not keep the Japanese out, they would be treated as Californians thought they deserved once they got in. On October 11, 1906, the San Francisco Board of Education set up a separate school just for Japanese students in the city's public schools.[16] Japan threatened a diplomatic crisis over it. President Roosevelt sent newly appointed Commerce and Labor Secretary Victor Metcalf, a native Californian, to San Francisco to persuade the school board to change its decision, but he was unable to. The problem was at an impasse: until the school order was rescinded, the Japanese refused to deal with the immigration problem; California officials would not reverse the school segregation plan until Japanese immigration was curtailed.

Stirring the pot, the California legislature started to work on discriminatory legislation, going beyond attendance at public schools and with statewide implications. On February 28, to increasing resentment in Japan, it passed a bill restricting Japanese ownership of land.[17] A week later it mimicked the San Francisco school plan and forbade Japanese children older than ten years from attending classes with whites. Roosevelt could understand why Californians and westerners might object to foreigners flooding in and believed it was not different from his own inclination to put reasonable limits on their entry. But once in, Roosevelt could not abide a denial of American rights, even citizenship. "We cannot afford to regard any immigrant as a laborer; we must regard him as a citizen."[18] Two years earlier he had written to Lodge, "The California Legislature and various other bodies have acted in the worst possible taste and in the most offensive manner to Japan. . . . How people can act in this way . . . I cannot understand. I do all I can to counteract the effects, but I cannot accomplish everything."[19] Since then the situation had gotten worse.

MEANWHILE, ROOSEVELT RECEIVED A confidential message from Kaiser Wilhelm of Germany that Japanese soldiers ready for war were in Mexico disguised as farm workers.[20] Roosevelt became more alarmed and came to believe war was possible between the two countries. To avoid it, he came close to declaring war on California.[21]

A FEW DAYS AFTER the Military Affairs Committee began its hearings, Senator Foraker received a letter from a man named George

V. S. Michaelis. Other than displaying the name "Michaelis & Ells-worth" on its letterhead and indicating the firm had offices in Boston, Chicago, and Washington, there was not a clue who the man was or what he did. He reminded Foraker that they had met before, "in company with the late Joseph Manley of Maine, whose daughter I married." Joseph Manley was someone Foraker surely knew. Manley was a Republican national committeeman and a close friend and political associate of James G. Blaine of Maine, whose decision not to seek the Republican presidential nomination in 1888 led to the middle-of-the-night offer of support to Foraker.[22] Manley was a delegate to that convention and almost certainly was one of the Blaine people there. If he was not, he knew of the offer to Foraker and agreed to it. He may even have been the one who asked Blaine, vacationing in Scotland, for permission to make the offer.

George Michaelis was one of the founders of the business of public relations or political consulting or both. He and two other men formed the Publicity Bureau in Boston in 1900 as the nation's first press agency. Its first client was Harvard University, but when its president Charles William Eliot decided its monthly retainer of two hundred dollars was an unnecessary expense and the prestige of having Harvard as a client was pay enough, the Publicity Bureau agreed to work for that. It soon added Harvard's neighbor in Cambridge, the Massachusetts Institute of Technology, as a client, along with the American Telephone Company.[23] Another client was a consortium of railroads hoping to defeat the Hepburn Bill. When the Hepburn Bill was passed, Michaelis & Ellsworth lost the client.[24]

Michaelis told Foraker his brother Francis Woodbridge, a lawyer with the prominent New York firm of Lord, O'Day & Lord, would like to come to Washington to discuss "a matter concerning the 25th U. S. Infantry."[25] Michaelis was ready to finance a lawsuit, "a test case," that would "lead to a judicial review" of the discharges. Two months earlier President Roosevelt dared the Senate to do anything about the discharges. He thundered he would veto any bill seeking to reinstate the soldiers, and if Congress passed it over his veto, he would pay no attention to it.[26] But he said nothing about a court order. Disregarding Congress was one thing; staring down a federal judge was something else entirely. Sixty-seven years later, when US District Court Judge John Sirica ordered President Richard M. Nixon to turn over White House tapes of conversations, Nixon had to do it. A generation after, when President William Jefferson Clinton lied under oath in front of US District Court Judge Susan Webber Wright to hide his sexual misadventures with Paula Jones, Judge Wright found him in contempt of court and he had to pay a fine. When US District Court Judge Norma Holloway Johnson ruled Clinton could not invoke executive privilege to keep his relationship with Monica Lewinsky under wraps, he had to disclose everything.[27] This latter Clinton case was more relevant to Roosevelt's defense. Clinton was claiming a right under the Constitution, as Roosevelt would have.[28]

Foraker immediately recognized the value of this collateral attack and the second front it would open. On Michaelis's letter he drafted his reply: "Your letter rec'd and will be very glad to see Mr. Woodbridge whenever he may call. J.B.F."[29]

HEEDLESS OF WHAT HE was hearing from men like Fortune, Myers, and Cozart, the Wizard kept with his old playbook and wooed wealthy and influential whites. Was Andrew Carnegie preparing a lecture to the Philosophical Society of Edinburgh on the progress of the American Negro? Washington would be pleased to help. (He assigned the task to Emmett Scott.)[30]

An approach to Oswald Garrison Villard, the respected and influential publisher of the *New York Evening Post*, was a disappointment. He had stood with Washington against Du Bois two years earlier, when W. E. B. Du Bois told him that Washington bribed black newspapers for his favorable coverage. Upset by the news, Villard nevertheless stood by Washington because of the great contributions he had made.[31] Now when Washington told him Secretary Taft turned away his suggestion that a black artillery regiment be created "when the Brownsville affair suddenly took a political turn," Villard responded, "Pray when did the Brownsville Affair take a fresh political turn? Was it not political from the start?" and added that Taft's action "confirms my own unfavorable impression of the man as a candidate."[32] The publisher saw Washington as a political naif for misunderstanding Brownsville, an increasingly ignored voice in the Roosevelt administration, and knew more was coming with Taft in the White House. If Villard was not supporting Taft, it would be something else they would differ over.

Ray Stannard Baker was a white journalist who was both progressive and something of a simpleton on the question of race. In his biography of Du Bois, David Levering Lewis repeated the assessment of someone else that Baker was "a young person whose mother didn't know he was out."[33] But he was influential and spoke often with Theodore Roosevelt at the White House. And he would be one of the few notables over whom Washington still held sway. While working on his *Following the Color Line* articles, Baker had sought his ideas and Washington was only too pleased to give them.[34] He politely corrected a statement Baker planned to write about Negroes being driven out of communities (Washington told him it happened in "very few communities in the South") and suggested he not ignore the problems of "the Convict System, the Public School System and Voting." It seemed to pay off. Washington happily wrote to Emmett Scott from New York, "It is a fine article, clear and clean-cut, and I am satisfied with his treatment of the subject. . . . When Du Bois, Trotter and his crowd read what Baker has written I think they will squirm."[35]

But if he was going to struggle with Du Bois, Washington needed the black newspapers on his side, and he renewed his efforts to use them to influence their readers. He wrote an editorial for the *New York Age*, poking fun at Du Bois's Niagara Movement, and had its new editor Fred Moore, for whom he had facilitated the newspaper's purchase, publish it.[36] Washington thought about investing in Max Barber's *The Voice* in Chicago when T. Thomas Fortune got involved with it after selling the *New York Age* to Moore. But Washington worried that the now-distant Fortune would reveal the truth about him and his manipulations, and he preemptively countered with a campaign of disinformation and denial. Most troubling was his portrayal of Fortune as mentally disturbed.[37] He was, as the playbook called for, continuing to use the Tuskegee Machine to gain information about those in the civil rights movement and pass it on the others.

Charles Anderson wrote to Emmett Scott with information about a Du Bois meeting in New York and rumors of Judge Robert H. Terrell's misdeeds.[38] Anderson also was on the receiving end of instructions. (Where did the busy Mr. Anderson find the time to collect custom duties for the federal government?) "[Constitution League secretary A. B.] Humphrey to have meeting tonight his headquarters. Think important you have friend on inside. B. T. W."[39] The "friend" was Roscoe Conkling Simmons, who reported directly back to "Uncle Booker" to tell him the Constitution League was planning a "huge demonstration" to arouse the country over Brownsville. In a postscript Simmons added, "If you want me to prevent Senator F.'s coming to this [Constitution League] meeting, let me know."[40] Simmons was a longstanding tripwire in the Washington–Du Bois clashes. As early as 1904 he was fanning Washington's suspicions and antagonism with news about an upcoming article in the *Colored American* critical of Washington and supportive of Du Bois and inflating his importance to the black race.[41]

Little was gained by Washington from all of this. Journalist T. Thomas Fortune sloughed off pressure from his former friend and former creditor. "I have lost faith in Roosevelt. . . . His action in the soldier business and appointment by threat in Ohio is bad policy, not based in sincerity. He has done you dirt . . . [and] should not have dragged you into it."[42]

The matter of any progress for Negro advancement seemed to have been put aside.

DU BOIS SAILED THROUGH Washington's dirty little war. After *The Souls of Black Folk*, Washington's weak response to the Atlanta riots, and his support for Roosevelt in Brownsville, there was no chance of any rapprochement. Du Bois biographer Lewis characterized the "civil estrangement" between them as "civil war within the race."[43] Du Bois preached that Negroes no longer could live in a nightmare while putting their trust in Washington's plea for patience until a better future that was coming, God only knew when. "Brownsville tore the veil of trust to shreds."[44]

In 1905 Du Bois called together like-minded Negroes to form the

Niagara Movement as a "militant alternative" to Washington.[45] At its meeting on the Canadian side of Niagara Falls (they were unable to find accommodations in Buffalo), they proclaimed their Declaration of Principles. These included the refusal to remain "submissive under oppression" and the declaration that "persistent manly agitation is the way to liberty."[46] Washington said he shrugged off this new organization. But he made sure to infiltrate it with his moles.[47]

Its 1906 meeting was held only two days after the Brownsville shooting, too soon to say or do anything about it. Booker T. Washington was another matter, and Reverdy Ransom, whose plan for achieving racial equality was an odd mixture of socialism and Christianity, blasted Washington's ideas (but not Washington himself by name) in his address "The Spirit of John Brown." To the delegates assembled on a hilltop at Harper's Ferry, West Virginia, Ransom said, "The spirit of John Brown beckons us to arise and seek the recovery of our rights." There was no going back to passivity. "Today, two classes of Negroes, confronted by a united opposition, are standing at the parting of the ways." "The one counsels patient submission to our present humiliations and degradations. . . . The other class believes that it should not submit to being humiliated, degraded, and remanded to an inferior place." Max Barber said this was "the most eloquent address this writer has ever listened to."[48]

At the Niagara Movement's annual meeting in 1907, Du Bois was ready to use Brownsville to spear Washington and Roosevelt. While the Senate committee's hearings were underway and in the news, he had prepared the ground with two pieces in the May issue of his recently inaugurated magazine *The Horizon*.[49] One criticized Washington for his shabby treatment of T. Thomas Fortune and used this portrait of Washington as "Arch Tempter" to trash him and, by inference, his ideas. Of Roosevelt, he wrote that Negroes, notwithstanding Brownsville, had little to thank Roosevelt for. "If the truth must be told, Theodore Roosevelt does not like black folk."[50]

The Wizard had his spy James A. Cobb, a Washington lawyer, registered at the August meeting in Boston. Cobb reported on the day he arrived, "There seems to be no Esprit de Corps . . . there is no definite program as yet. The leaders seem to be disgruntled among themselves." When the meeting ended, he wrote Emmett Scott, "The N. M. [meeting] seemed to have been beset with misgivings and discord. . . . I think the Movement has about met its 'watermellon-lou.'"[51] Cobb must have missed the session where Foraker was toasted as "the man of the hour for his condemnation of the evidence upon which the soldiers were dismissed from military service."[52] Or where Du Bois told "'500,000 free black voters of the North' to vote against Taft's nomination or that of any other 'Brownsville Republican' who had supported Roosevelt's dismissal of the soldiers." If one of them got the nomination, "I shall vote for Bryan."[53] Du Bois was taking on the Republicans as well as Booker T. Washington, and riding Brownsville he was preparing to upend both.

"There is probably not a doctor in the State who is not working overtime and after hours to beat Foraker, and the influence of a doctor, particularly a country doctor, is not to be despised."

"Sad Awakening Awaits Foraker,"
New York Times, April 7, 1907

CHAPTER TWENTY-TWO

A FACE TO GRACE THE WHITE HOUSE

I T IS GOSPEL TRUTH with Brownsville historians and commentators that Joseph Foraker defended the black soldiers because he thought it would help win the Republican presidential nomination. It would change his Old Guard image while attracting blacks and whites outraged over the discharges.[1] But accepted belief is not always historically correct, and this Foraker dogma may be particularly questionable. There are reasons to believe that very early in his Brownsville involvement he did not want to be in the White House, did not think he could get it, and was worried more about keeping his Senate seat in 1908.

Political insider Julius Chambers, whose column in the *Brooklyn Eagle* was thought to be influential, tried to get him into the presidential race just before the Brownsville shooting. In a May 1906 letter, he wrote Foraker that he and those he influenced would support him. "We have closed up all our other business affairs and are to concentrate our efforts on the new task. . . . Action is highly essential because other people are at work very actively."[2] Without any encouragement from Foraker, Chambers talked him up in his newspaper column. "Foraker was somebody in Ohio before Bill Taft was more than a 'cub' reporter for the *Cincinnati Star.*"[3] He told Foraker, "I believe matters are looking more favorable every day."[4] Foraker threw cold water on Chambers and his hopes. He wrote to Charles Kurtz, his secretary and confidant since his time as Ohio governor (he was in Foraker's hotel room in 1888 when Blaine supporters offered him their support), and who was Chambers's accomplice in the plotting, "The more I think of the matter the less I think of it, or rather the more I think it unwise and futile to undertake to do anything about it . . . it would be, I think, a mistake."[5] Two months later, as Foraker was thinking about Burton and the insurgents at the upcoming state Republican convention in Dayton, he told Kurtz, "Work such as you are doing is good at the right time, but just now it will hurt rather than help. I hope, therefore, that you will restrain."[6] Realizing this message was weaker than he intended, two days later he wrote directly to Chambers, "I do not want to be a candidate, and unless something wholly unforeseen should transpire to change the situation, I will not be."[7]

At the September 1906 convention in Dayton, Foraker thought he derailed Burton's hopes for the Senate. And he may have deliberately done the same for his chance at the White House. He told his people not to offer a resolution supporting him for president in 1908 even though "a blind man could see that it would have been adopted."[8] A serious candidate would never suppress such a show of strength. His stated reason in his memoirs—because the delegates had not been elected for that purpose—is simply not believable. More likely, as he wrote Chambers, "The results of the Dayton convention are entirely satisfactory in every way. . . . I do not want to be a candidate for 1908, and for that reason I would not allow the convention at Dayton to endorse me."[9] When Chambers warned the Taft Express was making steam, he replied, "I am not alarmed about Mr. Taft or anybody else. I simply don't want to be put in the attitude of a candidate and be for two years subjected to the annoyances and harassments that would arise in consequence." But he unlocked the door a mite. "*Another year might clear matters up, but that is only speculation*, and I am not willing to commit myself . . . to a proposition that in all probability would bring only disappointment" (author's emphasis).[10] When Chambers persisted in pestering, he made it very clear to stop bothering him. "I will not have anything to do with the subject," he wired on January 4, 1907. Chambers tried sympathy and guilt as bait: "[Another supporter] and I are both grieved and disappointed."[11] Foraker would not bite, and in what Foraker biographer Everett Walters correctly called a "rather sharp note," Foraker said, "I meant what I said when I told you that I would a great deal rather have you support Senator Knox or Vice President Fairbanks . . . kindly let the whole matter drop."[12] To John J. McCook, a New York lawyer and one of the army of ex-Ohioans now prominent in business and politics, and Foraker's fellow summer resident at Sea Bright, Foraker wrote the same day, "I prefer to have nothing more to do with [Chambers]."[13] Foraker's disdain for Chambers had become dislike. Two months later, the irrepressible Chambers was still at it. Foraker was forced to write him, "My feeling of aversion to become a candidate has not changed."[14]

Foraker was fibbing. He now had a reason to be a candidate, but it was not because he wanted to be president.

In January 1907, while he was dealing with Senate nitpicking to deny him and the Black Battalion any meaningful investigation, his political plight must have been obvious to him. He had stymied Theodore Burton's maneuver at the September state convention in Dayton to take his Senate seat from him, but that had been an opening gambit, and with two years until the election, Burton had plenty of time to regroup and keep working against him.[15] Then came Roosevelt's performance at the Gridiron dinner, and Ohio politicians quickly understood its meaning. Roosevelt wanted Foraker out of the Senate. As shown by his instructions to Kurtz and his letters to Chambers, Foraker concluded it would be a waste of time to run for president and it would crowd into the efforts for what were now more important, saving the Black Battalion and his seat in the Senate. But for the latter, he would be a candidate for the Republican presidential nomination, hoping Taft would accept his reelection to the Senate as a small price to pay for eliminating him as a rival for the White House. To make his feint believable, Foraker had to secure the support of the Ohio delegates to the national convention.

His first step came during the first week in January 1907 when
he tried to throw a scare into the Taft forces by denying the constitu-
tionality of the Ohio law requiring delegates to the 1908 Republican
nominating convention to be elected by Republican voters at primary
elections. This method gave Taft an edge because Foraker allies
were more likely to be delegates if selection was made at county conventions. But the Taft people preemptively and quickly obtained an
Ohio Supreme Court decision upholding the law Foraker objected
to. "The Foraker ruse had failed."[16]

For the time being, Foraker had to put 1908 politics aside to get
the Senate to OK an investigation and then prepare for the hearings. But a letter in February from Roosevelt saying he would need
a couple of days to think about Foraker's routine recommendation for a federal judgeship alerted him that Roosevelt had not been
sleeping.[17] Foraker turned his attention back to his reelection to the
Senate and his scheme to scare Taft. On March 26, three days *before*
he told Julius Chambers he had an "aversion" to becoming a candidate, he asked the Ohio Republican State Central Committee to
meet and issue a call for the election of delegates "to determine the
Ohio Republicans' choice for president and senator" at the primary
elections. Walters, accepting at face value that Foraker wanted to be
president, calls this the "virtual announcement of Foraker's presidential candidacy."[18]

Charles Taft, publisher and editorial writer for the *Cincinnati
Times-Star* and brother of William H. Taft, saw this as a Foraker
blunder that could get Foraker out of his brother's hair once and
for all. In his newspaper he accepted Foraker's proposal and argued
that whichever man lost "would be eliminated from the political situation."[19] If Charley Taft was reading the situation right, Foraker's
"virtual announcement" had failed.

Cincinnati's "Boss" Charles Cox saw nothing good coming out
of all of this. He was not a fan of Taft, especially since 1905, when
Taft "openly and virulently assailed" him and his organization.[20] But
he recognized Taft's stronger position because of Roosevelt's support
and the rumbles of discontent with Foraker echoing throughout
Ohio. He would be happy not to see Cleveland's Theodore Burton

in the Senate in place of his hometown's Joseph Foraker, whom he knew he could work with. At the beginning of April he proposed that Taft support Foraker for the Senate and Foraker agree to drop out of the presidential race and support Taft for the White House. Foraker raced to accept the "Cox Compromise." This was not the action of a man history later decided wanted to be president and used the Brownsville soldiers to help him. But Taft turned it down. And not for the first time. "[Murray Crane] told me when I was in Washington that he has tried to bring Foraker and Taft together," Henry Cabot Lodge wrote President Roosevelt, "and that Foraker was ready to support Taft for President if Taft would agree to leave Foraker alone for the Senate, but that Taft would have nothing to do with it."[21]

On April 4, congressman and first son-in-law Nicholas Long-worth announced he was for Taft, but added he was speaking only for himself.[22] Cox knew better and quietly began to separate himself publicly from Foraker, who all along had thought him an ally.[23] Charley Taft explained to his brother that Cox took his side because the "burden of Foraker" would break up his machine.[24] Cox also saw Taft would most likely be the winner and Ohioans were losing patience with Foraker. Medical doctors were angry when he supported legislation creating an examining board for their competing medical practitioners, osteopaths (who treated illness by manipulating and massaging bones, joints, and muscles).[25] Manufacturers in the heavily industrialized state had not forgiven him for voting against the Hepburn Act to reduce shipping rates. Most damaging to Foraker, political leaders throughout the state believed what Cox would express later on: "I never remember having read in history, nor do I recollect of any person who is posted in history telling me an instance of where any United States Senator has yet beaten a President of this country."[26] Two days earlier Roosevelt had written his son Kermit, "I believe [Foraker's] teeth are pretty well drawn nationally, altho locally he may cause trouble."[27] In spite of this upbeat assessment, his "haunting fear" of defeat would not loosen its grip, and in a letter the next day to Lodge he warned, "Foraker is a strong and adroit man. Taft *must* get into the fight in Ohio, if he intends to be a candidate"[28] (Roosevelt's emphasis). Taft got the message. A couple of weeks later, fellow Ohioan Jim Garfield took a few minutes from running the Interior Department to meet him early one morning "for full talks about the campaign. He is in for good no turning back and I am glad. We will win!"[29]

A few months later the State Central Committee met and lowered the boom on Foraker. It endorsed Taft for the presidency without endorsing Foraker for the Senate. Foraker found out a few days before the committee that Cox had again deserted him for Taft.[30] In his memoirs nine years later, he was still angry, writing he was "double-crossed by occult methods.[31] But not before one final attempt was made to bring about the "Cox Compromise" from April. Taft's Ohio campaign manager Arthur Vorys endorsed it to ensure no eleventh-hour surprise would stampede the State Central Committee away from Taft. Again Foraker agreed and Taft did not. "Rather than compromise with Foraker," wrote Taft, "I would give up all hope of the Presidency."[32] Taft's "no talking to, no compromising with Foraker" was still in effect, which he confirmed in a letter from his summer home in Canada to William R. Nelson, owner of the *Kansas City Star*. "I hope you think that the action which was taken in Ohio by the state central committee was favorable. *I distinctly declined to compromise with the Foraker forces*, and I hope that the vote as taken shows there was no compromise in the result" (author's emphasis).[33] Taft biographer Henry Pringle wrote of the committee vote, "The incident marked the virtual elimination of Foraker from public life."[34]

From Foraker's virtual announcement he was running for president to his virtual elimination from that office took only four months. The year that had started with such hopes for Foraker and the soldiers turned to ashes for Foraker before it was barely half over. And Foraker knew it. A race he did not want and a race he thought had been forced upon him by events had brought him disappointment and humiliation and ended in defeat. He knew he had to fight for an office he could not win to keep the other office he already had. And that is the more likely reason he ran for president.

He stayed in another fight too, the one for the Black Battalion.

Would he win that fight? More than likely not. Would it be worth the effort? Decidedly yes, because knew he was right and it was only he who could bring them the justice they deserved. He knew this fight for them would not help him in the Senate race any more than it had helped him win the White House. He stayed in it anyway because it was the right and just thing to do for the soldiers, for the country, and for himself. Any speculation that he began the fight to become President Foraker is not supported by anything he said, wrote, or did. It was never about that.

IN AN ARTICLE DATELINED April 6, 1907, the *New York Times* coldly, almost cruelly, told its readers how deep of trouble Joseph Foraker was in back in Ohio and how ignorant he was of this. "The nearest peanut stand man" knew more about Ohio politics than its senior senator. The *New York Times* was right about the trouble but as ignorant about Ohio politics as it claimed Foraker was. It was only slightly more observant when it stated the obvious, "The all-pervading personality in the White House throws a dark and deep shadow over Ohio politics." Fearing Roosevelt, people were running away from Foraker.[35] This was a drum the *Times* had been beating for some time now. On March 25 it had drawn a perfectly dismal picture of Foraker's problems. The Ohio rank and file were deserting him. When the toastmaster at a political dinner there mentioned his name, there was stone silence. Taft's name drew shouting, hand clapping, and feet stamping. In Ohio and Washington, Theodore Burton was being groomed as Foraker's successor. The *New York Times* described Burton as the ablest man in the House of Representatives, an intellect, a fighter with culture and polish, and perhaps most qualifying him to take Foraker's place in the Senate, "outspokenly a Taft man."[36] Now the *Times* told its readers those still with Foraker saw only one thing that might save him, as it had so often in the past, his ability to draw people to him when he speaks to them. "He can make men forsake their families and their home and their political principles and their bank accounts and anything else of value. He is a wizard and a hypnotist."

It is doubtful Foraker was that clueless. For the last two months he had been working constantly on the Senate's Brownsville investigation and getting precious little help from anybody. He could be forgiven for not tending to his political knitting. And then, on that April 6, he got a telephone call about Brownsville, and he wondered if at long last his crusade might be panning out.

IT WAS A SATURDAY, and a Mr. J. C. Williams, not otherwise identified, telephoned Foraker at his home in Washington to say a "Mr. H. J. Browne had just given him some very important information with respect to the Brownsville matter." That evening, Williams and Browne, a Washington journalist, came to Foraker's "big yellow house" to talk. Foraker, his instincts pummeled by the god-awful month of March that had just ended, was about to be taken by a con man. Browne played the exhausted Foraker like a fiddle. First he dangled the carrot. "A reliable source" told Browne that seven Brownsville residents had shot up the town. Three of them fled to Mexico, but the other four were still in Brownsville. Foraker had by then come to believe it had been Brownsville people, and he did not have to be convinced this made sense. Then Browne played the reluctant suitor. He had little interest in the matter, but purely in the interest of justice of course, he would be willing to go to Texas and meet the governor, who indicated he might be sympathetic to the idea, to see if he could secure clemency for these four men so they could turn state's evidence. Browne wasn't sure he could get away; he had some business in Washington to look after next week. He would know by Monday if he could go. Sure enough, Monday morning he called Foraker to say he'd taken care of his Washington business.

Browne's offer came on the heels of Taft's devastating rejection of Cox's offer. It is likely Foraker was vulnerable to any idea that might discredit Taft and his protector, President Roosevelt. The wits of normally shrewd Foraker seem to have deserted him. Without checking in to Browne and who he was, without questioning him to try to learn something about his "reliable source," without asking someone to see if the Texas governor knew anything about this, without any due diligence at all, Foraker put a check for $500 for "expenses" into Browne's hand and sent him off to Texas. Browne strung him along for another few weeks with "news" from stops in Texas. From Galveston on April 19: "Have been going over the Government's evidence. A flimsier lot of fabrications never was put together." From Austin the next day: "Have just left Governor Campbell after a very interesting confidential talk. . . . While reluctant to be put in the position of waiving the laws of Texas, he sees the greater importance of putting a curb on 'the most dangerous man in the history of America,' to use his own expression. . . . Saw Maj. Penrose at San Antonio. . . . He cleared up several minor difficulties." (Penrose warned Browne not to go to Brownsville, and when he did anyway, a worried Penrose wrote Foraker, "I have been particularly anxious regarding the Mr. Browne you sent to me, and who went to Brownsville against my best judgment. . . . I sincerely trust nothing may have happened to him.[37]) Five days later from Brownsville, where he was staying at the Leahy Hotel: "Louis Cowan, whose house was shot up, is the head devil in this business. He is a renegade Jew, Russian I am informed." From New Orleans on May 10: "Have cleaned up the Brownsville situation as far as possible there. *The Negro troops shot up the town. I can name four of them*" (author's emphasis).[38] A wiser Senator Foraker said good-bye to Mr. Browne and his $500 (more than $13,000 today). He was not interested in paying for information indicting the soldiers he was defending.[39]

Brownsville was taking its toll on this smart, resourceful, and accomplished man. He would not be the last to be taken in by Mr. Browne.

THE OTHER SIGNIFICANT EVENT in the history of the Brownsville Incident to take place on February 4, 1907, along with the opening of the Senate Military Affairs Committee hearings, was the court-martial of Major Charles Penrose, the commanding officer of the Black Battalion. Captain Edgar Macklin's trial was to have gone first but was postponed to allow him to heal from his shooting wound. Both men were charged with neglect of duty and both were found not guilty. Penrose was found guilty of a reduced charge of allowing, by failure to adequately direct Macklin to be especially vigilant on the night of the shooting, the shooting to take place, but the court-martial specifically found no criminality in this. Significantly, both courts-martial assumed it was the Negro soldiers who shot up Brownsville, and the Penrose court-martial recognized this as a fact in its finding.[40] Because no question was raised about who the shooters were, nothing came out of the courts-martial that would assist Senator Foraker at the committee hearings.

With a trial, the assistance of counsel, and the right to confront and cross-examine witnesses and present their own, none of which the 167 black soldiers had, their white officers were acquitted. Some of the witnesses who helped acquit them were the soldiers whose statements exonerating themselves were thought to be part of a conspiracy of silence and not believable, and therefore unable to keep them in the army.

After their acquittals, both officers would say they had changed their minds. They no longer believed their soldiers had anything to do with the shootings in Brownsville.[41]

"It is the law of human passion that friendship which lapses or seems to lapse begets the bitterest hate."

Kelly Miller, "Roosevelt and the Negro,"
in *Race Adjustment: Essays on the Negro in America*

CHAPTER TWENTY-THREE
BROWNSVILLE GHOULS

OVER THE WINTER AND spring of 1907 Foraker's attention could not focus solely on Brownsville. His presidential hopes, sincere or tactical, were dimming. He knew it and so did President Roosevelt, who fumed at the potential damage Foraker was doing to Taft in the November election. On June 26 he wrote to his son-in-law Nicholas Longworth to complain, "That scoundrel, Foraker, is doing all the damage he can with the negroes." But he saw a bright side to this. "When the report of the [Military Affairs] committee comes in the Democrats of the Committee will take such an extreme position as to make the colored men who have even the slightest shred of common sense realize where their true friends are."[1] By supporting Foraker on Brownsville, the Democrats were cutting their own throats in November. The next day Taft came to the summer White House in Oyster Bay for a little spine stiffening, and as soon as he left, Roosevelt wrote to Henry Cabot Lodge, "Taft, thank Heaven, is up to making an aggressive fight against Foraker, and anything you think he ought to say on the subject of Brownsville you can confidentially send him." Roosevelt was now so sure Brownsville was dealt with and safely put to rest, he added to Lodge, "I have half a mind, when I speak at Canton next October, to touch on the Brownsville case myself."[2]

FOR FORAKER'S CHANCES, OHIO'S summer was as cold as the winter and spring. Speaking at the Logan County (Ohio) Chautauqua at

the end of July, he denied he was a candidate, but not with any
finality. He made it clear he soon might be taking on his enemies
by name. For Roosevelt he had advice that seemed to apply to the
Brownsville soldiers and himself, "The big stick won't work with
any free-born American citizen." Obliquely referring to Brownsville, he took a moment to defend the Fourteenth and Fifteenth
Amendments as being part of "the great work of establishing the
doctrine of human equality before the law for all men." He pummeled both Taft and Burton on the tariff issue, trying to show there
was life in his political career yet.[3] But on July 30, the day after
his "virtual announcement," when the Ohio Republican State
Central Committee endorsed Taft for the White House but refused
to endorse Foraker for Senate, Foraker was a dead man walking.[4]
He campaigned throughout the state as if he did not know it. As
if to show he was not afraid of what President Roosevelt would
do to him, he picked every issue that divided him from Roosevelt
and Taft and defended himself. "In the Brownsville matter I had
no purpose except to secure for a lot of helpless men, who had been
branded as criminals and discharged without honor from the United
States army, a chance to be heard in their own defense, a right that
no American, no matter how humble he may be, should ever be
denied." He spiced this up with something more searing, "How
about then 10,000,000 black people in America who never drew a
disloyal breath, who are openly and defiantly being denied their constitutional rights of citizenship? What are the views of an aspirant
to the Presidency about the new rebellion that has broken out in the
Southern states, notably North Carolina and Alabama, in the form
of an open defiance of the authority of the United States Courts?"[5]
With these two issues sure to ring a bell with Ohio's black voters,
Foraker was trying to cleave them from Taft and the Republicans,
thereby hoping to gain back some of the ground from when the state
committee would not endorse him for the Senate. Foraker was a
man running for office, but not the same office Taft was going after.
He wanted not to be eliminated from public life and to stay in the
Senate. Shaking the trees in Ohio might shake Taft to his senses
and realize it was better to make sure people saw Ohio strongly sup-

ported him, and if he had to agree to support Foraker for the Senate, it was a reasonable price.

FORAKER'S POLITICAL CAREER WAS not the only thing stumbling through the summer and into autumn. The American economy was shakier than it had been since the Panic of 1893, and Roosevelt had few ideas for what to do about it. The term *Panic* was used to describe the aftermath of a sudden event generally not foreseen, such as a stock market crash or the failure of a large and influential bank that abruptly roiled financial institutions, such as banks as a group, brokerage companies, and underwriters, then quickly spread throughout the economy. When the stock market crashed a generation after Brownsville, *panic* seemed inadequate to describe the devastated economy it spawned and too frightening to the general public, and the more comforting *depression* was used in its place. That depression was so disruptive and so resistant to government efforts to cure it, it was transformed into the singular "The Great Depression," and thereafter what might have been a panic or a depression was called by the gentler and less disturbing term *recession*.[6] (The preference for soothing language made a sudden about-face in 2009, when the government felt *recession* would not justify what it wanted to do to the American economy wrecked by the subprime mortgage crisis, and it chose to call the resulting recession "The Great Recession.")

On January 4, 1906, the financier Jacob Schiff had addressed the New York Chamber of Commerce and "assailed in unequivocal language" how the US government handled the nation's money. Describing cash as "the nation's circulating medium," Schiff told his audience it has an "insufficient elasticity." Unless something was done soon, "a panic . . . with which the three which have preceded it would only be child's play" was inevitable. He called upon President Roosevelt to "put part of the energy which he has so admirably put into the attempt to regulate railroad rates into an attempt to cure this condition."[7] Possibly because finances puzzled him so much he was forced to rely on Mrs. Roosevelt to dole out his pocket money and entrust it with his valet for safekeeping, Roosevelt disregarded

Schiff's warning.[8] His ignorance of finances on the macro and micro levels persuaded him that "rich men" and their manipulations caused the sort of panic Schiff spoke about.[9] Roosevelt himself would bare his teeth to men like this at the 1907 Gridiron Club dinner and later that year on August 27 in a speech in Provincetown, Massachusetts, where he called them "malefactors of great wealth."[10]

It turned out both Roosevelt and Schiff were right. Either because banks trying to discredit trust companies that were threatening their business targeted the Knickerbocker Trust Company and so weakened it by silent runs that it failed; or because of continuing economic fallout from the San Francisco earthquake weakened Knickerbocker causing it to fail; or because President Roosevelt's speech in Provincetown caused distress throughout the financial industry and caused Knickerbocker and other banks and trust companies to fail; or because Knickerbocker was over its head with loans either to unscrupulous characters trying to corner the copper market or not-so-unscrupulous people simply trying to acquire control of copper mining companies—for whatever reason or reasons, the Knickerbocker Trust Company started to fail, leading to what is remembered as the Panic of 1907.[11] Long lines of panicked depositors formed outside banks to withdraw their deposits before their bank went bust. Wall Street needed the one man who could figure out a plan to save the situation and had the respect to influence others to agree to it. It was not President Roosevelt, who was hunting in Louisiana and taking his time returning to Washington. It was the financier J. P. Morgan, also out of town at a church conference in Richmond. On October 19, before the conference had ended, he rushed back to New York. In his mansion on Fifth Avenue and a private dining room at Sherry's Restaurant, he brought together financiers and bank presidents and decided which banks and brokerage companies could not be saved and would be allowed to fail and which could be rescued. For these he secured pledges of funding and then allowed his plan to unfold.[12] By the time Roosevelt returned to Washington, Treasury Secretary George B. Cortelyou was in New York, in effect relocating the Treasury Department there to serve J. P. Morgan. On October 25, Roosevelt,

responding to "much clamor for me to say something," sent Cortelyou a letter that expressed "calm confidence." He gave Cortelyou
extraordinary authority to publish the letter, to not publish it, or to
modify and then publish it. "I must trust to your judgment. . . . You
can judge better than any of us here."[13] That same day he sent a
second letter to Cortelyou to congratulate him "for the admirable
way in which you have handled the present crisis. *I congratulate
also those conservative and substantial businessmen who in this crisis
have acted with such wisdom and public spirit. . . . they did invaluable
service in checking the panic*" (author's emphasis). Roosevelt's meek-
ness in stepping aside to allow these "conservative and substantial
businessmen" to rescue the country's economy when he could not
and in thanking them for it contrasts with what he said to some of
these same men, including J. P. Morgan, to their faces the previous
January at the Gridiron Club dinner. No such consideration would
he give to Senator Joseph Foraker, his other target that night.

Nor did Roosevelt acknowledge Jacob Schiff had been right
in predicting the panic and identifying its causes. (The Dow Jones
Industrial Average lost 48 percent of its value from January 1906,
when Schiff made the speech, to November 1907, when the Panic
ended.[14]) Morgan had to find the money to save things because, as
Schiff pointed out, the federal government's monetary policy did not
have the flexibility to expand the money supply by putting more than
a pittance in the banks to cover the deposits. It had to depend on
Morgan, John D. Rockefeller (who put in $10 million), and other
malefactors of great wealth. Toward the end of November, Morgan
came to Washington to talk to Cortelyou and "pay my respects to
the President. Of course, we talked about the financial situation,
but I cannot go into details."[15] Less than two weeks later, Secretary Cortelyou did when he announced, using the very words Jacob
Schiff used the previous January, the nation's monetary system was
imperfectly organized and required a "greater elasticity."

MINDFUL OF GEORGE MYERS'S hostility when he got the Treasury
Department job, Ralph Tyler made a point of staying in touch and
ingratiating himself. In August he sent Myers a gift of Prussian coins

to add to his collection. There was no discussion of Brownsville or politics, an acknowledgment that the two men saw these things differently. In a postscript Tyler added, "It's HOT here," a reference no doubt to the weather and not Brownsville. About a week later Tyler wrote he had had a meeting with Secretary Taft regarding a favor Myers was doing for an army-chaplain friend who thought he was entitled to a promotion. Taft wanted to see the man's file, but it was late and the adjutant general who had possession of them had gone home. Tyler, sharp as ever, "thoughtfully brought the copies along you sent me and gave them to him." Taft said he would recommend a promotion to major. "I was received very cordially and was particularly pleased with my interview and the progress made."[16]

Two weeks later came the more important news. "Friend George: I have assumed additional charge of the N.Y. Age and will write its editorials. Watch them. [T. Thomas] Fortune is out. Has disposed of his interest." Unsaid in the letter was that the editing position was arranged for him by Booker T. Washington. Under its founder and publisher T. Thomas Fortune, the *New York Age* became one of the country's leading black newspapers. All the credit went to Fortune, a skilled writer of prose and poetry. The *Age* was more than a place for news of the black community in New York and elsewhere. It had social news, book reviews, gossip, and other special features. Washington quietly supported the newspaper and maintained his influence over its news articles and editorials, sometimes writing them himself, but always anonymously. Washington had emotional control over the emotionally fragile Fortune and could influence his behavior as well as the newspaper's. But Brownsville so irritated Fortune he no longer would toe the Washington line when it came to his editorials. They became anti-Roosevelt, and Washington knew Fortune had to go. He encouraged Fred Moore, a New York real estate investor, to buy the *Age*, and after a couple of false starts Fortune agreed to sell. The deal closed in September 1907.[17] Washington arranged Moore's financing—just as he had for Fortune—for the paper's operating and other expenses and thereby maintained his influence over the paper. He congratulated Moore and said he had in his hands "the greatest opportunity, in my opinion, that any individual has had in many years to influence and make public sentiment." Left unsaid was just how public sentiment should be influenced. Instead he cautioned Moore to "be more considerate of your health" and quit smoking.[18]

Moore was not the journalist or writer that Fortune was and someone had to be brought in for the editorials. The reliable Ralph Tyler, comfortably employed as an auditor for the navy in Washington thanks to the Wizard and Theodore Roosevelt, could be counted on to follow the party line. Energetic and resourceful as always, he took charge of more than the editorial page of the *Age*. He had hardly warmed his seat at the editorial desk when he arranged with his fellow Columbus resident Arthur Vorys to set up a Colored Press Bureau in Washington ("at their expense") to send "a newsy letter," pro-Taft of course, to black newspapers each week.[19]

Washington was solidifying his control over the newspaper and what it said. But not right away. Fortune had pulled the *Age* away from Roosevelt, and the move back had to be gradual so as not to seem too deliberate. Both Moore and Tyler understood it might take until December and January.[20] Nevertheless, for reasons not entirely clear, the timetable was moved up to October 17 when Tyler printed an incendiary editorial, "Brownsville Ghouls." It said those who supported Foraker and opposed Roosevelt were ghouls for making Brownsville a race issue not to obtain justice for the discharged soldiers but for "thirty pieces of silver coined for Judas." They were "worthless parasites who represent nothing but selfish avarice" and used the soldiers for their own political ends. The effect was explosive. Fortune was so angry he wrote a letter to the *Age*, which it refused to print.[21] He sent letters to other black newspapers, including Harry Smith's *Cleveland Gazette*, known to be the leading black newspaper to support Foraker. "Let Roosevelt-Taft ghouls howl. When God gets behind men, as He is behind Roosevelt and Taft he does not rest until he eats them up."[22]

"Brownsville Ghouls," as Washington wrote to Tyler soon after it was published, "proved a boomerang." It was printed "too quickly after [Moore's] taking charge of the paper" and changed the *Age*'s "attitude" too suddenly.[23] He told Fortune the same thing, but its damage would be to the newspaper, "as a business matter alone." (He also misled Fortune by saying, "I am absolutely sure that no one connected with this Institution *wrote* the 'Brownsville Ghouls'" [author's emphasis].)

Tyler had gone too far. And so had the Wizard.[24]

AT ITS THIRD ANNUAL meeting in Boston the Niagara Movement looked back to its Harper's Ferry meeting a year earlier and found it had been "A year of wrong and discrimination." W. E. B. Du Bois asked rhetorically, "Has not the man in the White House set [an] example by bowing before the brown and armed dignity of Japan and swaggering roughshod over the helpless black regiment whose bravery made him famous?"[25] His comparison between the benevolence Roosevelt displayed to Japanese in America and the hostility he showed to the "helpless black regiment" was telling.

There were, as already commented on, a series of antagonisms, prejudices, sensitivities, competing interests, and quasi-legitimate concerns boiling together in California and the AmericanWest.

Roosevelt knew he first had to show Japan he *could* resolve the problems before it would allow him the time to do so. His Harvard classmate and friend Japanese Baron Kaneko Kentaro, formerly Japan's minister of justice and a member of the Japanese House of Peers, became a back channel for getting messages to the Japanese government and sending back a reading of how it saw things. Kentaro told Roosevelt the Japanese government appreciated Roosevelt's attitude and sincerity.[26] Roosevelt knew he was on the right track.

San Francisco's exclusion of Japanese children was the flash point, California's discriminatory legislation the kindling, and Americans' belief Japanese should be kept out of the country entirely the lighter fluid that made the puzzle of how America would deal with a threatening Japan so combustible. They all came together to interfere with how Roosevelt wanted to deal with a foreign power. This made it a matter of foreign policy, a federal concern, and therefore he was entitled deal with it. But the overall problem would not be resolved until the San Francisco schools matter was straightened out.[27] He had instructed Metcalf to look at more than San Francisco schools; he was also "to confer with the authorities and the labor union people to point out the grave risk they are forcing the country to incur."[28] The "grave risk" he was worried about was nothing less than war, as he wrote to his son Kermit: "The infernal fools in California, and especially in San Francisco, insult the Japanese recklessly, and in the event of war it will be the nation as a whole which will pay the consequences."[29]

In California, Metcalf's visit was not favorably received at all.[30] On his first day there, he met with the San Francisco school board president, who told him the schools were only following California law, and if their exclusion of Japanese students violated any treaty provisions, "that is a matter . . . for persons other than the members of the School Board to pass upon."[31] A discouraged Metcalf wrote Roosevelt there was no chance the school board would modify or repeal its decision.[32] Roosevelt hoped his annual message to Congress, the same message in which he so antagonized Negro Americans with his talk of black crime and conspiracies of silence, would persuade Americans and especially Californians to reassess their opposition to the Japanese.[33] His target audience, however, was not just his own countrymen; he wanted to make sure his message got through to the Japanese government, and to this end he showed it to Japan's ambassador to the United States, giving him enough time to send it to Tokyo and measure its response.

Roosevelt began the Japan part of the message by saying there was "hostility . . . assumed toward the Japanese in this country," called it "most discreditable to us as a people," and warned, "it may be fraught with the gravest consequences to the nation." Using the bully pulpit as a classroom, he undertook to explain something about Japan and its people and why it could be a threat to America. "Her civilization is older than that of the nations of northern Europe."[34] But this civilization possessed the strength of Sparta as well as the humanities of Athens. The Japanese were "great in the arts of war . . . great in military. . . . Japanese soldiers and sailors have shown themselves equal in combat to any of whom history makes note. She has produced great generals and mighty admirals; her fighting men, afloat and ashore, show all the heroic courage, the unquestioning, unfaltering loyalty, [and] splendid indifference to hardship and death . . . and they show also that they possess the highest ideal of patriotism." Japan, in short, was not a country to pick on. It also was a friend to America. "Thru the Red Cross the Japanese people sent over $100,000 to the sufferers of [the] San Francisco [earthquake and fire], and the gift was accepted with gratitude by our people." "The Japanese have won in a single generation the right to stand abreast of the foremost and most enlightened peoples of Europe and America."

He turned to San Francisco. "To shut [Japanese schoolchildren] out from the public schools is a wicked absurdity. I ask fair treatment for the Japanese as I would ask fair treatment for Germans or Englishmen, Frenchmen, Russians, or Italians." To show the Japanese and California he meant business, he recommended Congress enact a law, "specifically providing for the naturalization of Japanese who come here intending to become American citizens."[35] (The dramatic effect of such a proposal is seen in the *New York Times* headline capturing what its editors thought was the most significant item in the address: "President Demands Citizenship for Japanese.") Roosevelt also wanted "the criminal and civil statutes of the United States be so amended and added to as to enable the President, acting for the United States Government, which is responsible in our international relations, to enforce the rights of aliens under treaties." Until then, "everything that is in my power to do will be done, and all of the forces, military and civil, of the United States which I may lawfully employ will be so employed."[36] Before leaving for Panama the previous month, Roosevelt ensured this would be done even in his absence. He gave Secretary of State Elihu Root a letter directing him "to use the armed forces of the United States to protect the Japanese in any portion of this country if they are menaced by mobs or jeopardized in the rights guaranteed them under our solemn treaty obligations."[37] Roosevelt showed his cleverness at laying the groundwork for taking action others might not accept as part of his authority. Enforcing treaties and granting citizenship are federal matters; two more reasons he was entitled to get involved with the Japanese problem.

The phenomenal success Roosevelt's message enjoyed in Japan can be measured by Baron Kaneko calling this the greatest "utterance by an American President since Washington's Farewell Address," thereby downgrading a gem such as Lincoln's Gettysburg Address.[38] San Franciscans were less impressed. Speaking for them and all Californians, Governor George Pardee, in language and tone milder than that heard on the street, said President Roosevelt "was not aware of conditions on this coast, especially in California."[39] When Roosevelt said he would employ "all of the forces, military and civil, of the United States," San Franciscans heard him say he would seat Japanese children in white schools with guns and bayonets. The schools matter remained at an impasse.

WHEN SAYING HE WOULD not hesitate to use the army in San Francisco, Roosevelt was showing he carried a big stick. He would display it again. On January 5, 1907, he met at the White House with Senator George C. Perkins of California and US District Attorney Robert Devlin, whom he summoned from San Francisco.[40] That same day it was reported Attorney General Charles Bonaparte was preparing the papers to go to court on behalf of the Japanese schoolchildren.[41] Two days after that, Roosevelt pressured Congressman Everis Hayes from California, who had introduced a Japanese exclusion bill in the House.[42] At the end of the month Roosevelt had the entire California congressional delegation come to the White House, and when they left it seemed a breakthrough had been made. The delegation issued a statement suggesting a solution was possible. It sent a telegram to the San Francisco school superintendent and president of the school board asking that they come to Washington to meet with Roosevelt and Secretary of State Root. A second wire was sent to Governor James Gillett, who had been newly inaugurated, requesting that he ask the California legislature to defer consideration of all Japanese matters before it. The invitation to the school officials was soon expanded to the entire school board, and with some further prodding by the members of Congress, they agreed to come. So did San Francisco's mayor. On February 3, only four days after receiving the first telegram from the congressional delegation, the Californians left on the long, cross-continent train trip to meet with President Roosevelt. It was time for him to speak softly.[43] By the middle of February, the mayor and school board gave in. Roosevelt had won.[44]

Roosevelt had protected the rights of Japanese children, most of whom were not American citizens. He saw to it they would attend schools with white children in California, something black school-children in the South would be *denied by law* until the Supreme Court ruled it unconstitutional almost half a century later.[45] Along the way he gave the Japanese ambassador approval rights to what he would say in his 1906 annual message, whereas Booker T. Washington had a right only to look at it and not, as T. Thomas Fortune put it, "blue pencil" Roosevelt's offensive and hurtful comments about blacks who were American citizens all.[46] Roosevelt muscled the San Francisco school board, its mayor, California's governor, and its legislature in a way thoroughly at odds with the American federalism he said tied his hands during the Atlanta riots.

Roosevelt went to these lengths to protect the country from war with Japan.[47] It was the foreign-policy element that made the difference to Roosevelt. It required he get involved to ensure "fair treatment" for schoolchildren and laborers. Unlike the Japanese schoolchildren, black Americans, their schoolchildren, and the soldiers of the Twenty-Fifth Infantry had no powerful foreign or domestic protector to ensure their fair treatment.

"Theodore Roosevelt was not lucky for Foraker; he was a disaster."

Julia Foraker, *I Would Live It Again*

CHAPTER TWENTY-FOUR

"DO YOU CARE TO SAY ANYTHING ON THE SUBJECT?"

T HE AUTUMN OF 1907 was an Indian summer of unexpected good news for Joseph Foraker and his fight to keep his Senate seat. The man yearning to seize it from him, Theodore Burton, had reluctantly accepted President Roosevelt's "suggestion" in the spring that he run for mayor of Cleveland, but, in what was seen as a direct blow to Roosevelt and Taft, a substantial majority of its voters elected the Democrat Tom Johnson.[1] More encouraging was the chatter that Foraker might control the Ohio delegation at the Republican nominating convention in June 1908. Taft's nomination effort would be crippled if his home state failed to support him, and he might have to endorse Foraker for the Senate just to keep him out of the presidential race.[2]

On November 20 Foraker extended his streak with the endorsement of the Ohio State League of Republican Clubs. In a slap at President Roosevelt the League declared it had no sympathy for the proposition Foraker should be eliminated from public life and supported him for president.[3] Foraker knew that he controlled the League, and this was no real achievement. But this public rejection might be another reason for Taft to relent. To further pressure Taft, Foraker made his virtual candidacy for the White House the real

347

thing. Interior Secretary (and fellow Ohioan) James Garfield saw this for what it was, "This is to my mind simply a desperate effort to compel an agreement by the Taft men not to oppose Foraker for the Senatorship."[4]

By the new year the glow was dimming. On January 2, 1908, the Republican State Central Committee voted to choose delegates to the nominating convention by primary elections, taking the decision out of the hands of county conventions Foraker was more likely to dominate. At the end of the month, Warren Harding, who had introduced the resolution supporting Foraker at the Ohio State League of Republican Clubs meeting in November, went over to Taft. He now saw Foraker's cause as lost.[5]

AFTER MEETING WITH FRANCIS Woodbridge, Foraker agreed to coordinate efforts with George Michaelis and his lawyers; Foraker would work in the Senate and with the lawyers in federal court. Michaelis became something of a gadfly, presuming he now was entitled to Foraker's ear whenever he had a thought or two to pass on. What was to have been a "second front" that would relieve some of Foraker's pressures was becoming a nuisance and sapping his energy. On June 18, 1907, Michaelis told Foraker who he thought shot up the town. Ignoring that policeman Joe Dominguez lost an arm and bartender Frank Natus lost his life, Michaelis smugly observed, "Veteran soldiers used to handling firearms would not have been such poor marksmen." Foraker thanked him for the "interesting and important information."[6] In August he wrote Foraker with his views on free trade ("Personally, I am a Republican free trader") and his opinion "from the alienist's point of view" that Roosevelt would be the candidate in 1908.[7] Foraker's secretary politely answered that he was "under general instructions to acknowledge receipt of your letter."[8]

By the end of 1907 Michaelis was getting down to business. He wrote Foraker that he hoped the Military Affairs Committee would not issue its reports before the lawsuits were filed. His colleagues in New England were "anxious to have the public realise that the legal actions . . . have not been inspired by any political motive. . . . We are working with you, and not for you . . . that I am anxious to have our actions precede the reports from the Committee." Foraker was trying to get the committee to recommend a bill allowing Browns-ville soldiers to reenlist and felt an earlier lawsuit might work against this. But if Michaelis and his group wanted to go to court sooner, "I will not have an objection. . . . I am anxious to see what the Supreme Court of the United States will say on the question you raise. Therefore do not like to even suggest any delay."[9]

The uncertainty Foraker wanted the Supreme Court to resolve grew out of his concession to senators unwilling to question President Roosevelt's authority. Foraker had to concede Roosevelt had the right to discharge the soldiers, and the resolution directing the investigation made Roosevelt's authority off-limits. Foraker would be confined to arguing Roosevelt's action was unjust because there was no proof of any soldier's guilt. Michaelis's lawyers indirectly would return to the question of authority by arguing the enlistment of the plaintiff, Private Oscar Reid, was a contract between him and the army, which the army (not President Roosevelt) breached when it discharged him without showing he did anything wrong, and he therefore was entitled to pay and benefits for the remainder of his enlistment term under contract law.[10] According to the *New York Times*, this was $122.26. But the hoped-for victory was that the Supreme Court would set aside his discharge because Roosevelt lacked the authority.[11]

MRS. JULIA FORAKER WAS a lively woman who could allow her imag-ination to get the best of her. So when she wrote that an Amer-ican journalist shadowed the Forakers at social events and spied on them for President Roosevelt, one would be forgiven skepticism. When she went on to say, "It took a little investigation to learn that Secret Service men . . . were keeping their eyes on our house," Mrs. Foraker sounds more believable.[12] Roosevelt using the Secret Service to snoop into a senator's privacy was not unknown.[13]

"Not suddenly, but subtly, a queer change came over the social atmosphere of our house. . . . People began to change their calling hours from daytime to evening. Men who worked for my husband,

and helping him collect information, called only after dark. . . . Sometimes . . . they sent their wives to see me. I would receive them and give to my husband the information they brought from their husbands. . . . Then we began to get it—we were being watched."[14] She recalled receptions she and her longtime friend Cornelia Fairbanks, wife of Vice President Charles Fairbanks, attended where Mrs. Fairbanks would "retreat to a far corner, stand with her back to the wall so that she could keep an eye on everybody, then signal me to come close to her and we would speak in whispers."[15]

Senator Foraker never mentioned any of this in his memoirs. But Napoleon B. Marshall, a lawyer assisting him in the committee hearings, told him Brownsville newspapers sent from Matamoros, Mexico, had a Post Office stamp on their wrapper, "Inspected at Washington."[16] Thereafter Foraker asked people to send correspondence (like a letter from Francis Woodbridge about the Reid lawsuit) to his home and not to his Senate office.

WITH THE NEW YEAR of 1908, Foraker and the soldiers had winter's cold blast blowing strongly against them. He was not able to a build a consensus on the Military Affairs Committee for nullifying the discharges. He submitted five different drafts of a majority report he hoped would do the trick, but it was no use.[17] He worked day and night to produce these five potential majority reports and, when they were rejected, he had to write the separate and lengthy Foraker-Bulkeley minority report. But he saw an opportunity to open a back door for readmission when President Roosevelt showed he was thinking about it by reviving the unwieldy December 1906 plan for reenlistment applications.[18] Three months later, all the Republicans (but no Democrat) concurred when Warren, Lodge, Warner, and Du Pont appended to the majority report a proposed reenlistment bill, because "it would seem but justice to restore to all the innocent men . . . their rights and privileges." Roosevelt approved it.[19] Senator Foraker had a different approach in mind.[20] The important difference between the two was how to weed out the guilty soldiers. Roosevelt's version permitted reenlistment "only on the presentation *of proof of innocence satisfactory to the President*" (Foraker's emphasis).[21] Foraker's required simply an oath from the soldiers denying guilt. He saw Roosevelt's as incurably hostile to the soldiers. Roosevelt thought Foraker's would "condone murder and perjury in the past and put a premium upon perjury in the future, by permitting any murderer or perjurer, who will again perjure himself, to be restored to the United States Army." Even if it passed over his veto, "it would simply be null [because it would usurp the appointing power of the President] and no reappointment would be made under it by me."[22] Their battle was still on.

HIS YEARS AS A trial lawyer trained Foraker to be more than a fire alarm when he spoke. He learned to marshal his thoughts and present his positions in a logical and persuasive argument. He spoke quietly so that listeners would shush their distracting neighbors and lean forward to hear better what he was saying. When he wanted to add emphasis to his words, he used a more assertive voice. He employed body language, facial expressions, and hand gestures to cosmetically add luster to his argument's strong points and camouflage its weaknesses.

On April 14, 1908, Foraker wanted to persuade the Senate to adopt his reenlistment bill and not the administration's. It would not be easy. The split in the Senate committee vote carried over to the full body, where the Democrats would vote against the black soldiers, the Republicans would be divided, and Roosevelt would therefore carry the day. Moreover, the Senate was like the country, and among some of its members there was what fifty years later would be called the "massive resistance" of Southern racism, while for others there would be an overall fatigue with the whole matter of civil rights and Brownsville. And President Roosevelt had, as Mrs. Foraker would grudgingly concede, "admirable dexterity in tight corners" that he would display until he got his way on Brownsville.[23] Finally, there was near unanimity that soldiers had been the shooters and escaped justice only because other soldiers kept quiet about it.

This last point Foraker could use to change minds. If President Roosevelt could not prove the charges, he could not discharge the soldiers. That was the American way of justice. Nothing—not the effect on the discipline of the Black Battalion and all other military units, not the fear in areas where these and other soldiers may in the future be posted, not the concern that some soldiers may have "gotten away with it," and not President Roosevelt's anger that his hands might be tied—nothing permitted disregarding Americans' constitutional rights and throwing the laws and foundation of a civilized nation out the window. Nothing.

This was something senators might listen to.

Still, on that April day, Foraker was a lonely man. Political allies had deserted him. Senate collegiality for him was a thing of the past, and members who formerly sought his help in Senate matters and his hand in friendship shunned him. His reputation was shattered by the relentless assault on him by President Roosevelt. He knew the Republican presidential nomination was Taft's, and its value as a wedge for him back into the Senate, if it ever existed, was gone, and indeed his Senate seat itself, with one more misstep, might be lost with it.[24] But he retained what Edmund Morris called "a passion for racial justice," an identification with the men of the Black Battalion, and an unshakable belief in their innocence. They no longer were a cause for their own sake; they were a battle for American justice. They ceased to be clients; they became his wards. He did not think of them as Negro soldiers; they were American soldiers, *his* soldiers. And if he lost his battle for them, he would lose his own for the soul of their and his country.

HIS ISOLATION FROM FELLOW senators and the politicians back in Ohio eased by Senate galleries, "packed with negroes, many of whom had been at the doors as early as 8 o'clock," Senator Foraker came out of his seat to be recognized.[25] "Mr. President," he addressed Fairbanks, "I ask that [reenlistment] bill 5729 may be laid before the Senate."[26]

He knew he must overcome the feeling that everything that could be said had been said. He must make this speech different and something important to his fellow senators. He began by noting he was speaking from a prepared manuscript. "I seldom make a speech in that way, but when I do it is, in my own mind at least, a compliment to the subject I am to discuss."[27] It is that important. Then he dispelled any display of unkindness toward President Roosevelt. He denied any intention of attacking him as a newspaper clipping he held in his hand suggests. Never had that been his purpose. He wanted "simply to present to the Senate, in so far as I might be able to do so, the facts in regard to this unfortunate affair."[28] Foraker would use President Roosevelt's words to support his own arguments and make Roosevelt a member of his team. He wanted "to give effect in a practical way *to the suggestions of the President himself*" to exempt from the discharges men "who were free from guilt" (author's emphasis). He told the Senate, "[It is now] commonly agreed upon, that, no matter who did the shooting there are many of the soldiers who are wholly innocent [who] have suffered disgrace, loss, and hardship from which they should be relieved, and that such relief can be granted only by an act of Congress. *Apparently no one appreciates this more keenly than the President*" (author's emphasis).[29] President Roosevelt and I want the same thing, Foraker was saying, only my bill accomplishes our common goal in a different way.

He turned to the theory that up to twenty soldiers formed a "preconcerted conspiracy," somehow got their hands on their weapons from the gun racks, fired into the town from the upper porch of Company B's barracks, then rushed down to and over the wall, shot up the town, killed one man and wounded another, then got back into the fort "without being detected by their officers, who were at that time wide-awake and engaged in the formation of the companies." This cannot be believed.[30]

He moved on to the evidence. There was no proof of a conspiracy of silence; even General Garlington, the army's inspector general admitted this and could only "suggest in a vague sort of way that the men had 'possibly' come to a common understanding" to say nothing.[31] The eyewitness testimony was "sufficiently contradictory to show that it is unreliable." More than that, the witnesses could not possibly have seen what they said they saw, and Foraker explained why. The most damaging evidence, the bullets and shells found on the street, prove nothing other than they might have been fired by the soldiers on the rifle range at their previous posting at Fort Niobrara and not in the streets of Brownsville.[32]

"No adequate motive—in fact, no motive whatever—is shown for such an assault upon the town." Frank Natus was shot in the Tillman saloon. If the soldiers were upset about the bars being closed to them, why did they shoot into it, the only one that served them?[33] The wounded policeman Dominguez had no trouble with the soldiers but had made many arrests of others who would have been more likely suspects. As for the assault on the Starck house, "There was not one scintilla of testimony to show that Newton or any other soldier of the battalion knew that Tate [the next-door neighbor supposed to have been the intended target] had a house, or on what street it stood, or at what point on any street it stood." Starck had arrested more than six hundred smugglers; maybe one of them shot up his house. Maybe it was one named Avillo, who lived in Brownsville and knew Starck's house. As for the assault on Mrs. Evans, this would be a motive for townspeople to shoot up the soldiers, not the other way around.[34]

Opposing this testimony was that of the soldiers. All said they are innocent and have done so "under oath." And their officers all believed them.[35]

If President Roosevelt's and his bills accomplished the same thing, if both "proceed from the assumption that some of the men, whether few or many, or all . . . were innocent and that justice requires that all such men should have the opportunity to reenlist," there are, nevertheless, differences. Foraker's voided the discharges without honor and thereby would have allowed pensions earned to be paid. More important, Foraker allowed them to prove their innocence by signing an oath that they are innocent. Why only this? Because it and testimony previously and repeatedly given by them was all they could give. "To require more is to require an impossibility, and to require a man to prove his innocence is to outrage justice by reversing the rule of evidence that obtains in every civilized country. . . . If these men are innocent, as they claim and as I believe, what else could they have said or done?"[36]

Before he ended, Foraker questioned President Roosevelt's judgment, but gently and logically. Roosevelt's messages of December 19, 1906, and January 14, 1907, had "assertions repeated over and over again [that] in the most extravagant language emphasize the President's unfit state of mind to act judicially in passing upon the applications of these men to reenlist as proposed in the [administration's] bill." Taking this decision out of Roosevelt's hands is no different from excusing a judge who expressed an opinion of the defendant's innocence or guilt.

> The vilest horse thief, the most dangerous burglar, or the bloodiest murderer would not be required either to prove his innocence or to submit to a trial before a judge who had in even the most casual way expressed the opinion that the defendant was guilty. . . . Who are these [soldiers] that it should be even suggested that they should be treated worse than common criminals? They are at once both citizens and soldiers of the Republic. . . . They are typical representatives of a race that has ever been loyal to America and American institutions; a race that has contributed to the nations tens of thousands of brave defenders, not one of whom has ever turned traitor or faltered in his fidelity. . . . Faithfully, uncomplainingly, with pride and devotion, they have performed all their duties and kept all their obligations. *They ask no favors because they are negroes, but only for justice because they are men.*[37]

THERE IS NO EMPHASIS shown to these final words in the printed *Congressional Record* and wherever else they appear. But it is hard to believe Foraker, theatrical as he was, would have delivered the punch line without some punch to it. The transcribing Senate clerk hints there was when he added at this point, "Applause in the galleries." Actually, it was a clamor unable to be stilled. Threats to clear the galleries were greeted with loud hooting followed by even more enthusiastic applause that lasted for several minutes. Senators ignored the clerk's attempt to read the next piece of legislation as they crowded around Foraker to congratulate him.[38]

In *Notes of a Busy Life*, Foraker recalled he received "hundreds of letters and telegrams of congratulation in addition to other hundreds that were orally extended." He printed one "I prize very highly." J. G. Schurman, the president of Cornell University, wrote as a concerned citizen, "The President has made a terrible mistake." As an educator he thought Foraker's speech was "overpoweringly conclusive." And as the proud teacher to a former student who had done well: "You have acquitted yourself with triumphant distinction. The speech . . . will long be remembered as the voice of a public conscience outraged by the injustice, dishonor, and tyranny to which American citizens have been exposed."[39]

THE CHEERS OF APPRECIATION and joy, the congratulatory letters and telegrams, even the praise from senators meant nothing. When it came down to the business of senators adopting his bill to readmit the soldiers, his speech did not persuade enough to vote for it. And it moved President Roosevelt not at all. In his letter to Senator William Smith ten days after Foraker spoke, Roosevelt called Foraker's bill "a purely academic measure." Displaying no doubt at all about his own actions, he told Smith, "Beyond all possible doubt, beyond all intelligent and honest opposition . . . the murderous assault was committed by [the] negro soldiers."[40] Now feeling the wind to *his* back, Roosevelt, if anything, was digging in and hardening his position.

But the game was not yet over for Foraker and his soldiers. Historian Elting Morison wrote that Foraker's speech "convinced many neutral observers that President Roosevelt and the majority of the Military Affairs Committee were wrong."[41] And it convinced some senators too. Foraker could not get his reenlistment bill passed, but as it turned out, neither could Roosevelt persuade enough senators to accept his. On this matter it was a draw. Short of the votes he needed, Foraker agreed to put the matter off until after the election.

An irritated John Milholland wrote Foraker, "I am bombarded with inquiries about the postponement. . . . Do you care to say anything on the subject?" Foraker answered, "It was simply a question of defeat in May or probable success in December, and I chose the latter, reluctantly as you may well imagine." A still unsatisfied Milholland pressed. "The Constitution League would be pleased to have you tell its members, at your convenience, why you deemed it better to postpone decisive action by the Senate until next December?" Foraker answered by quoting from a letter he sent to a man in Mas-

sachusetts. "It keeps the subject alive . . . during the present campaign." Besides, he added, more than a majority vote would be
needed to deal with Roosevelt's veto threat; to override the veto it
would take sixty-two votes.[42]

In his diary Milholland wistfully wrote, "Read letter from Sen.
Foraker explaining Brownsville or trying to explain it. . . . Fear he
had made a mistake."[43]

FORAKER WAS PHYSICALLY EXHAUSTED and close to a nervous breakdown. That's why two of his doctors, concerned he might collapse
while delivering his speech, were in the Senate chamber that day.
Burton was snapping at his heels. Taft, a man Foraker had never
spoken meanly about or acted unfriendly to, was destroying him
in Ohio. President Roosevelt, a man he had not been ashamed to
say he loved at the Gridiron banquet, was working to eliminate him
from public life. His brother lay dying a horrible death in a hospital less than three hours up the tracks in Philadelphia, and he was
unable to be with him, attend to him, and comfort him. The previous
August he had told Andrew Humphrey that he was "somewhat disappointed and depressed." Humphrey told Milholland, who wrote to
Foraker, "This is natural under the circumstances, but I attribute
your depression mainly to physical exhaustion." Foraker responded
the next day, "As to the matters which Mr. Humphrey talked to
you about . . . I have had so much disappointment and so much
exasperating experience."[44] When Napoleon Marshall had nagged
him about something, Foraker had brushed him off in a way so
uncharacteristic for him with its tone, self-pity, and anxiety. "I am so
engrossed with my contest [to retain the Senate seat] that I have no
time now for anything else. Later, if I am not eliminated, I will take
these subjects up again."[45] Since then, nothing had gone right for
him. The committee hearings had taken an enormous amount of his
time, requiring planning everything from the examination and cross-
examination of witnesses to scheduling their appearances, to complete attention at every hearing to what was said by witnesses and
other senators. Roosevelt's senators could let their minds wander
while others senators spelled them. Foraker could not. Other sena-

tors could skip this or that hearing; Foraker had to attend every one. He did not want to run for president, but he was forced to do so, "with full knowledge at that time I had no chance whatever to be nominated," and it competed with Brownsville for his time and attention.[46] In the end, he and his soldiers lost.

John Milholland understood and forgave him. On May 18 he wrote in his diary, "He was ill & Tired and felt alone."[47]

FOUR DAYS LATER ON December 14, 1908, President Roosevelt sent another special message about Brownsville to the Senate.[48] He announced a new investigation had with "tolerable definiteness" (a further retreat from "beyond a reasonable doubt") confirmed what he said all along and proved that "almost all the members of Company B must have been actively concerned in the shooting" and "practically every man" in the three companies knew it and covered for them.[49] In making this boast Roosevelt said he was relying on an investigation by Herbert J. Browne (the man who showed up on Foraker's door in 1907), whom Roosevelt called a Washington journalist, and his colleague "Captain" William Baldwin. They said they had the goods on the soldiers. Actually, Senator Foraker had the goods on them.

The previous April, Browne had sent a letter to Secretary Taft telling of his investigation a year earlier (but not that it had been for Foraker) and that it had convinced him soldiers from Company B had shot up the town. Taft, uncomfortable with the split decision by the Military Affairs Committee, aware that Foraker was planning his Black Battalion speech, and still not quite sure he had nailed down the Republican nomination, was about to be suckered as Foraker had been a year earlier. He recommended to Roosevelt that Browne and Baldwin, "a railroad detective" with "large experience and unusual ability" and recommended "by the presidents of several of the principal lines of railway in the South," be hired to get the evidence that had so frustratingly eluded the army. With the advice from the army's judge advocate general that their fee of $5,000 could be paid from an "emergency fund to meet unforeseen contingencies . . . at the discretion of the President" (and kept from the Senate and the public), Roosevelt told Taft to go ahead.[50] The agreement, signed only three days after Browne's letter to Taft, required the shooters' names, the names of those in the "subsequent conspiracy of [silence]," and, most important, "affidavits of witnesses" to back everything up. Crucial for candidate Taft, the final report had to be in "not later than June 15, 1908," the day before the Republican nominating convention convened in Chicago.[51]

On April 20 the first quarterly installment of the fee was paid, and the newspaperman and railroad sleuth were on their way. Tantalizing hints that they were making progress encouraged Taft, but nothing of value turned up by June 15. Taft easily won the nomination without it. By saying he and Baldwin were unable to locate the former members of the regiment, Browne coaxed a second agreement (for a second $5,000) out of the army on September 1 (by then Taft had resigned as secretary of war), which required a report by October 10. Browne missed that deadline too, but on December 5, 1908, he at last submitted a report to General Davis, the army's judge advocate general, "relative to the investigation of the Brownsville Raid."[52] In the report, Browne asked for additional time, which he got (and a third $5,000 payment).[53]

After Browne and Baldwin leveraged their ineptitude in finding soldiers and witnesses into a nine-month sinecure paying them a total of $15,000, they quickly located former Private Boyd Conyers of Company B in Monroe, Georgia, and along with their illiterate black employee named William Lawson they went down there to talk to him. They used everything from conversation to persuasion to threats to try to get him to sign a statement incriminating himself and the soldiers. Sure Conyers eventually would crack, Browne had written Taft back on July 10 saying that Conyers had confessed. Conyers never did and never would. Unknown to Browne, Baldwin, or anyone else in Washington, Conyers had written to Senator Foraker asking for his help.[54] Meanwhile, Browne continued to mislead Roosevelt and the new secretary of war, and Conyers and Foraker continued to correspond with each other.[55] The ex-soldier kept the senator up to date as he was pressured, and the experienced lawyer and senator kept a record of it all.[56]

In November, Browne went back to Monroe and told Conyers he might be sent to Texas to be tried for the Frank Natus murder. At the end of the month a new Browne-Baldwin investigator, who turned out to be Browne's brother, told Conyers that the detectives had obtained sworn statements from others nailing him. Conyers did not know this was a lie and wrote Foraker with this latest news.[57]

The agreement between Browne and the War Department required that he produce "affidavits of witnesses," and still Browne had none. His solution to that annoying omission was to have his illiterate employee Lawson sign one. This sort of hearsay evidence from a third party never in Brownsville was hardly what the agreement contemplated, but it was all Browne had. On December 9 Lawson signed his affidavit (with his X) swearing Conyers had confessed to him "as a criminal boasting to one of his own race of his crime and of his success in escaping discovery."[58] Now Browne had a witness and a sworn statement. But it was a lie.

IN JUNE THE REPUBLICANS nominated William Howard Taft. By then he had no effective competition for the prize he still was unsure he wanted. The only suspense at the convention was the hope by some and fear by others (especially Mrs. Taft) that Roosevelt would change his mind and snatch the nomination at the last minute, even though he had taken himself out of the race earlier in the year. On December 11, 1907, Roosevelt's secretary William Loeb, who by then had become more than a secretary, told him the only way put to rest all suspicions about his intention was to commit himself to someone else's candidacy. The next day Roosevelt wrote Taft he "decided to make one more public statement, quoting what I said the night after [the 1904] election, and adding that the decision was final and would not be changed."[59] But Mrs. William H. Taft for one never believed him.[60] When the demonstration by delegates at the mention of Roosevelt's name was louder, more boisterous, and almost twice as long as it was for her husband's (forty-one minutes versus twenty-two), she held her breath. But these convention hijinks meant very little. Taft won with 702 delegate votes; only 258 were scattered among five others. As Edmund Morris wrote, "The color returned to Helen Taft's high cheekbones."[61]

Joseph Foraker received only sixteen votes (eleven of which were Negro delegates thinking of Brownsville), fewer than any of the other names offered to the convention.[62] He immediately sent his good wishes to the victorious Taft. "Although I fear it may be unwelcome and probably misunderstood it is nevertheless my pleasure to avail myself of my privilege to send you heartiest congratulations and best wishes for success in November." He made no offer to help in the campaign. The decent Taft responded from his heart that same day, "I assure you that your kindly note of congratulation gave me the greatest pleasure and I thank you for it from the bottom of my heart. I have never ceased to remember that I owe to you my first substantial start in public life, and that it came without solicitation."[63] But he asked for no help in the campaign.

Foraker did little campaigning for Taft, and on one of the few times their paths crossed, Foraker was accused of deliberately turning it to his advantage by making it seem that the two men had reconciled and Taft was going to endorse him for the Senate. Taft's campaign denied this, and Taft himself immediately wrote to reassure Roosevelt that he "would take no part in the Ohio contest for Senator."[64] Taft knew whose support he really needed.

Black Americans played almost no role in the election campaign. Roosevelt had helped insulate Taft from Brownsville when he took the responsibility for what happened to the soldiers.[65] But it was not needed for Taft's victory in November and probably was more a gesture to clear the decks of Brownsville for Taft's presidency.[66] All blacks understood the Democrats did not want them and there was no place for them other than the Republican Party.[67] Booker T. Washington, aware that if Taft won without support from Negroes his race would be even deeper in the political wilderness, worked his diminished influence where he could.[68] Ralph Tyler formed a bureau to feed positive news about Taft to the black press and keep it in the Taft camp.[69] Remarkably, T. Thomas Fortune, who broke with the Tuskegee Machine over Brownsville, worked for the Republican

National Committee during the campaign.[70] W. E. B. Du Bois and his confrontational allies spoke against Taft and supported William Jennings Bryan and the Democrats. At the 1908 meeting of his Niagara Movement in Oberlin, Ohio, it was proclaimed, "We say to voters: Register and vote whenever and wherever you have a right. Vote not in the past, but in the present. Remember that the conduct of the Republican party toward Negroes has been a disgraceful failure to keep just promises. The dominant Roosevelt faction has sinned in this respect beyond forgiveness. We therefore trust that every black voter will uphold men like Joseph Benson Foraker, and will leave no stone unturned to defeat William H. Taft. Remember Brownsville, and establish next November the principle of Negro independence in voting, not only for punishing enemies, but for rebuking false friends."[71]

This appeal went unheeded. "Experience has shown that the negro, even in States where he possesses the power to overturn a Republican majority, has always remained true to the party. . . . There is every reason why this should be the case [in 1908]," predicted Henry Litchfield West, political editor of the *Washington Post*.[72] He was right. Taft won the black vote and the White House with 321 electoral votes to 162 for the Democrat Williams Jennings Bryan.

*"What a cleverly managed and malicious fraud the Browns-
ville business was."*

Senator Henry Cabot Lodge to
Theodore Roosevelt, September 21, 1908

CHAPTER TWENTY-FIVE

AN ACT OF TREASON

WITH THE PRESIDENTIAL ELECTION over, Joseph Foraker
had to get himself back in the Senate and get the innocent soldiers from the Black Battalion back in the army. The calendar dictated that the Senate would be decided first.

The day after Foraker's virtual announcement in March 1907
that he would try for the presidential nomination in Chicago,
Charles Taft wrote in his newspaper, the *Cincinnati Times-Star*, that
whichever man failed to be nominated by the Republicans for the
White House should be eliminated from politics. His brother never
contradicted him, and pundits wondered if, now that he was the
nominee, William Taft believed Foraker should be retired from the
Senate.[1] Other Republicans, considering how it would sound to
be greeted as "Senator," were thinking of getting in the race. Dr.
Charles Reed, a physician who led the medical community's opposition to Foraker, was an old friend of Taft's and was jumping in.
Arthur Vorys, who would become Taft's Ohio campaign manager,
expressed an interest.[2] Congressman Theodore Burton, hungering
to move to the other end of the Capitol since the Dayton Republican
convention in 1906, was rumored to be Taft's choice. But Taft held
his tongue. Foraker, on his way to Maine for his vacation, did the
same. Tranquility prevailed until August 7, when the Republicans,
for the first time in a generation, did not arrange for Foraker to

363

speak at the campaign's opening event in Youngstown. The local committee tried to calm the waters by ignoring the state committee and inviting Foraker on its own.³ Taft was forced to comment on the situation, and incautiously wondered aloud why someone who "only a short time ago, made a severe attack on the policies of President Roosevelt," was invited to be part of the campaign.⁴ What had been a restrained and awkward pas de deux became a more forceful and intentional stepping on toes accompanied by the atonal suite conducted by the retiring Maestro Roosevelt. By September Foraker's and Taft's seconds thought they had written a duet for their principals that would end the bickering. On September 10 Vorys told Foraker "it was the special desire of Mr. Taft" that he preside and introduce him at a Republican club meeting at the Music Hall in Cincinnati. Foraker accepted.⁵

FIVE DAYS EARLIER, PUBLISHING magnate and publicity magnet William Randolph Hearst found himself in Columbus where, according to Hearst biographer David Nasaw, he was tagging along with the campaign of "Honest Tom" Hisgen, a Massachusetts axle-grease manufacturer who was the presidential nominee of Hearst's Independence Party. Hisgen had no crowd appeal to speak of without Hearst and not much more with him. Finding himself unable to think of anything exciting to say, Hearst decided to draw attention to himself and, possibly only as an afterthought, to the hapless candidate Hisgen by reading portions of letters to Foraker from John D. Archbold, vice president and de facto chief operating officer of the Rockefeller-controlled Standard Oil Company.⁶ Hearst had acquired a sheaf of Archbold letters from a thief who stole them from Archbold's office four years earlier, and he had stashed them away for the right time to use them. The right time had come, and with no warning, Hearst decided to use them that night.

There are differing accounts about which letters Hearst used that night and what they said. Nor is it clear if he read the letters or only referred to them. Much of this is because Hearst deliberately said things in a misleading way for the most toxic effect. The general understanding is that however he did it, he accused the Republican

Party of being corrupted by big business trusts' money. Perhaps because he was in Ohio's capital at the time, he used Ohio's senior senator Joseph Foraker as an example.[7]

In his memoirs, Foraker wrote that Hearst "made it appear that I had some kind of improper relations with the Standard Oil Company, and he read a number of letters [written between 1900 and 1903] showing payments to me at different times of various sums of money."[8] Nasaw quotes from the next day's *New York Daily Tribune* describing the letters as "referring to legislation pending in Congress," with one of them enclosing $15,000.[9] The first letter mentioned by Hearst said, "In accordance with our understanding, I now beg to enclosure you certificate of deposit to your favor for $15,000. Kindly acknowledge receipt, and oblige." The next letter Hearst spoke of referred to "another very objectionable bill [that] needs to be looked after, and I hope there will be no difficulty in killing it."

Foraker responded the next day and admitted he had been one of Standard Oil's lawyers in Ohio, that it had nothing to do with federal government, and it "was common knowledge at the time. I was pleased to have people know that I had such clients. . . . It had not then become discreditable to be employed by such corporations."[10] Foraker thought he had adequately responded to the vague charges against him and that would be the end of it. But his political feelers had atrophied under the strain of Brownsville. Mrs. Foraker would later write, "The whole country was swept by a mad rage at [Standard Oil's] wealth. The most damaging thing that could be done to a public man was to link his name with the trusts."[11]

The next night in St. Louis, Hearst made his accusation clear. Referring to the disclosures in Columbus the night before, he told his audience, "Foraker admits part of the truth, but not all of it. . . . If he had seen the letters I am going to produce tonight, he would have denied the whole matter."[12] He then read two other letters from Archbold. The first one was about legislation before the Senate to "protect trade and commerce against unlawful restraint and monopolies," which Archbold thought was "unnecessarily severe" and hoped he and Foraker could "have a word" about.[13]

In the second letter, Archbold said somewhat cryptically, "Your letter states the conditions correctly, and I trust the transaction will be successfully consummated." With that letter was a certificate of deposit for $50,000. The conclusion was that *after* a Foraker-Archbold meeting at which they had "a word," Archbold sent Foraker $50,000. Foraker had been bribed. But this before-and-after cause and effect was only because *Hearst had reversed the order of two letters*. He read from a letter dated February 25, 1902, before one sent on January 27, 1902.

Foraker was stunned and appears to not have noticed that the letters were out of order. Potentially frightening for him, he had no memory of a legitimate $50,000 fee. ("A lawyer's memory for a fifty-thousand-dollar retainer is usually excellent," his wife would write.) After collecting his wits and hearing from a friend in Columbus, Foraker made a statement attempting to clear the matter up.[14] He pointed out the payment came before the letter about the disliked pending legislation, and there was no reason to infer any connection. Better yet, he knew what the $50,000 was all about. The friend in Columbus had an option to buy a newspaper there and wanted Foraker to invest with him. Foraker was able to "advance a part of it" and asked, among others, Standard Oil if it wanted some of the deal. It did (being one of the owners of a newspaper ensured its proper coverage), and its share was $50,000, which it covered with the certificate of deposit. When the "transaction" was not "consummated," Foraker returned the $50,000 to Standard Oil in a letter dated February 4, 1903. This was after Archbold sent him the money but three weeks before he asked to have "a word" about the antitrust legislation.

Despite what he showed, Foraker was unable to get ahead of the story. Two months later, after Taft won the White House, Foraker was still denying he did anything wrong.[15] To the public and to Theodore Roosevelt, being employed by Standard Oil (which Foraker admitted) was the same thing as being bribed by Standard Oil (which he denied).

ARCHBOLD AND STANDARD OIL were bipartisan dispensers of bounty to public men, and Hearst was an equal-opportunity exploiter of circumstances. The Democrats also nourished their "sinews for war" at the Standard Oil teat, with less sustenance, but they did not go away "empty-handed."[16] In St. Louis, Hearst also targeted Democratic governor Charles Haskell of Oklahoma, the treasurer of the Democratic National Committee. Theodore Roosevelt was quick to recognize an opportunity to make trouble, and he joined the attack on Haskell and the Democrat nominee William Jennings Bryan. Bryan hit back by demanding Roosevelt prove the charges against Haskell. Roosevelt could not and answered that Bryan's support of Haskell was a "scandal and disgrace." Haskell called Hearst "a liar" but meanwhile resigned as party treasurer.[17] Everyone seemed to be shocked by the allegations and counter-allegations, but to all appearances everyone was having a good old time. Especially publisher Hearst, who was selling a lot more newspapers.

PRESIDENT ROOSEVELT WAS JUST as quick to go after Senator Foraker as he was Governor Haskell. Three days after Hearst released the letters in St. Louis, Roosevelt wrote his friend Henry Cabot Lodge, "Those revelations about Foraker are very ugly. They of course show, what everyone on the inside knew, that Foraker was not really influenced in the least by any feeling for the Negro, but that he acted as agents for the corporations."[18] To his son-in-law Nick Longworth, Roosevelt suggested Taft "ought to throw Foraker over with a bump."[19] (Nothing in the Lodge and Longworth letters explained how defending the Negro soldiers was in the interest of Standard Oil.) Two days earlier he had wired Taft the same thing. Referring to the meeting of the National League of Republican Clubs meeting at Music Hall he advised, "If I were running for President, I should . . . decline to appear upon the platform with Foraker, and I would have it understood in detail what is the exact fact, namely, that Mr. Foraker's separation from you and from me has been due not in the least to a difference in opinion on the negro question, which was merely a pretense."[20] Taft got Roosevelt's message and indirectly sent his own to Foraker not to show up at Music Hall. Foraker took the hint and sent a note explaining he was bowing out "because I do not wish to do anything that might injure the cause or embarrass you personally." Taft gratefully accepted this gesture. Thereafter the Taft campaign cut all ties with Foraker.[21] Julia Foraker was particularly hurt by the Music Hall matter. "If the positions of the two men were reversed . . . I know what would happen. My husband would refuse to believe the charge brought against an intimate old friend. . . . He would insist that the Senator appear on the platform with him—or he would not appear."[22]

Maybe people saw Foraker's denial of wrongdoing not squaring with politics as it was practiced. In his biography of Boies Penrose, Robert Bowden lists eleven senators in 1906, including Foraker, as "representatives of corporate business." Their arrival in the Senate "had produced in Washington as commercial an atmosphere in its way as the atmosphere of Wall Street itself." Walter Davenport in his biography of Penrose reproduces a letter from John D. Archbold to Penrose enclosing the $25,000 that was what Davenport characterized as "Pennsylvania's quota of Mr. Archbold's contribution to the Republican party for favors done and expected." That letter and his letter to Foraker on January 27, 1902, both use the same shorthand explanation for why the money was sent; it was "in accordance with our understanding."[23]

Roosevelt sought to prove his pure politics by trumpeting that his 1904 campaign *returned* money from Archbold. In 1912 he denied any knowledge of a 1904 contribution at the time it was made and was able to produce letters to then chairman of the Republican National Committee George B. Cortelyou prohibiting the acceptance of any Standard Oil money and ordering the return of any already paid.[24] Of course, it is possible "these letters were written to be filed, but not otherwise respected," so-called posterity letters.[25] During the 1906 campaign, Standard Oil knew it was about to get whacked with an enormous antitrust lawsuit seeking to break the company into bite-sized entities. It remembered what happened to J. P. Morgan's Northern Securities Company (the Supreme Court broke it up) and was spreading its money around in 1904 to buy protection from a similar crusade against it. Its plan failed. On November 15, 1906 (like the order discharging the black soldiers, just after the off-year elections), Roosevelt's Justice Department sued it for conspiring to restrain trade under the Sherman Antitrust Act, and five years later the Supreme Court affirmed a lower court's order of dissolution.

THE HEARST–STANDARD OIL letters take up, as they do here, an important part of almost any narrative of the Brownsville Incident, despite their glancing connection with the Black Battalion. In his memoirs, Senator Foraker recalled that Champ Clark said Brownsville put him out of "the Presidency" and Senate.[26] But, Foraker insists, Clark was wrong about the Senate. His defeat there was because of the Hearst–Standard Oil letters.[27] Therein lies the link with Brownsville. Hearst's effort to get attention for himself grievously wounded Foraker's chance for reelection to the Senate. Few believed him when he said he did nothing wrong with Standard Oil, just as few believed the soldiers when they said they were innocent of the shooting. But knowing what Brownsville had cost him and not knowing what greater price might await him just ahead, he continued with his struggle for his soldiers.

And for reelection to the Senate. Until the Seventeenth Amendment to the Constitution in 1913, US senators were elected by state legislatures and not the direct vote of the people. A state legislature voted after it reassembled with its new members from the previous November election, thereby ensuring lame-duck legislatures would not make the decision. Exactly when was up to the states, so long as the decision was in time for senators to take their seats on March 4, the day their terms would begin.[28] In Ohio the senatorial choice would be made in early January 1908. Foraker still had time and still might have a chance.

ON SUNDAY AFTERNOON, DECEMBER 13, Foraker invited John Callan O'Laughlin to his home. One of Roosevelt's favorites in the Washington press corps (Roosevelt called him Cal), O'Laughlin had been, courtesy of Roosevelt, serving as secretary to the American Commission to the 1907 Tokyo Exposition intended by Japan to show it was now a world power. Roosevelt had promised to make O'Laughlin the assistant secretary of state after the 1908 elections to replace Robert Bacon, but only as a résumé builder, since the position came "with the distinct understanding" the job would end when Taft took the oath of office in two months.

At first O'Laughlin thought Foraker wanted an opinion on his latest answer to the Hearst charges. But Foraker wanted to talk about himself, President Roosevelt, and his Brownsville soldiers. In a memorandum, O'Laughlin said Foraker told him it still was possible he would be reelected and was "anxious to ascertain if the President proposed to take a part in [that] campaign. . . . Then he turned to Brownsville. 'I do not understand why the President has been so antagonistic to me. For years we were the closest friends, and then my opposition he construed as criticism.'" If O'Laughlin did not grasp that Foraker's grip on reality was loosening from his Alice-in-Wonderland belief that Ohio would send him back to the Senate, his failure to understand Roosevelt's antagonism surely put it in focus. Anyone who knew Theodore Roosevelt knew he did not tolerate criticisms of his programs and ideas. Foraker seems to have misplaced in some forgotten regions of his mind the joint statehood bill for Arizona and New Mexico, the Hepburn Act, the problems in Cuba in 1906, the Senate Brownsville investigation (which, if Foraker had not made the discharges an issue, would not have been approved), the stubborn defense the Ohioan put up for the soldiers in those hearings, the addresses to the Senate over and over again that made Roosevelt look sometimes like a madman, other times like a zealot, and still others like a fool, and his efforts, for whatever reason, to deny Taft the White House. Foraker's sad monologue went on: he always defended the president; he never said a bad word against him personally.

"Foraker closed by asking, 'Do you think there is any way a conference could be arranged with the President when we could talk over the Brownsville matter? I don't want to fight anybody. I am a man of peace. I do not believe the President wants the fight to continue. Could you find out for me if the President would care to see me and talk over the matter, perhaps the whole field?' I told Senator Foraker I would see what I could do."[29]

In the morning two days later, O'Laughlin met President Roosevelt and in the late afternoon he met again with Foraker to report Roosevelt's reaction. "If the Senator from Ohio wants to see me, I shall be glad to see him as I would a Senator from any other State." Foraker was crestfallen. "That means only he will see me officially. Now if he had said that he would see Senator Foraker, it would give the personal touch which I consider necessary." This perceptive observation of what Roosevelt said and what his words really meant suggests Foraker was reasserting a grip on himself. It also showed he understood very well his chances for getting back to the Senate. "It is probable I will not be reelected." He focused on Brownsville. "I would like to have a settlement of this Brownsville question . . . acceptable to the President and to me." It was becoming clear that when he said "to me" he meant not "to me for the benefit of my career" but "to me for my soldiers." In the context of his admission that he would not be reelected and his realization that Roosevelt had understood and disregarded why he wanted the meeting, there was nothing left for him but his commitment to the Black Battalion.

But Foraker thought there was still a chance. He repeated to O'Laughlin what he said two days ago, that "he was anxious . . . to effect a settlement [and] asked me to see the President that night, . . . that he was not wedded to the language of his bill . . . he was prepared to make numerous concessions."[30]

O'Laughlin ended his memorandum without any reference to a second meeting with Roosevelt, only, "I told Senator Foraker I would see what I could do." It is not likely he did anything. His meeting with Roosevelt that morning had been disappointing. Roosevelt would not ask Taft to keep O'Laughlin in the State Department. O'Laughlin had his own job now to worry about after Roosevelt left the White House. And he knew very well Roosevelt's reaction to a second Brownsville plea after the first was so coldly dismissed would not be pretty. What was Foraker's last attempt to find an accommodation with Roosevelt, more for his soldiers than for himself, had failed. And his hope for the Senate would soon be gone.

AT THE LAST MINUTE Charles Taft, President-elect Taft's brother, got into the Ohio Senate race, egged on by his wife, who wanted to move to Washington. According to a letter from Roosevelt to Taft on January 1, 1909, on December 17 Charley met with President Roosevelt to test his allegiance to Burton by telling him Burton might lose. Roosevelt's blood chilled at the thought Foraker would be returned and told Charley nothing was more important than defeating him. "Compared to the importance of [that] it was of no particular consequence at all what particular man was chosen to succeed him."[31] This was not what Charley wanted to hear. On December 28 he sent the Washington correspondent for his newspaper the *Cincinnati Times-Star* to the White House with a stronger hint. Burton had weakened and Foraker would win. Roosevelt knew where Charley Taft was going with this and had a message for him. He "thought Charley had grown weaker and Burton stronger."[32] Roosevelt added, "I thought it was outrageous from [President-elect Taft's] point of view . . . to consider any personal question whatever." The "one vital question" was getting rid of Foraker. But he would not tell him what to do.

For anyone without access to news of the outside world for the previous almost three years, Roosevelt made a statement to Gus Karger of the *Times-Star* to print the next day, and which was reprinted in Foraker's memoirs. "The one great issue involved in the Ohio Senatorial contest is now waged for the defeat of Foraker. . . . To support Foraker in this fight is to commit an ACT OF TREASON against the Republican Party."[33]

Foraker's end came two days later, on December 31, when Charley Taft withdrew from the race after getting the word from his brother to step aside. Only Burton was left standing. A few hours after his announcement, Foraker issued a statement of his own. "I would have been glad to be reelected . . . [but] there is a great compensation . . . in the result that has been reached. [Burton] is well-qualified by experience, ability and character."[34] The Republican caucus in the Ohio Senate confirmed the reality on January 2, and ten days later the Republicans in the Ohio General Assembly elected him the state's next United States senator.[35] When Foraker stood that day to make his final address to the Senate for his Brownsville soldiers, he was Ohio's senior senator. By the time he sat down, he was a lame duck.

DURING THE DECEMBER IN which Foraker's fate would be determined and the hopes of black Americans forsaken, thousands of miles away in Sydney, Australia, the promise of one black American was redeemed. On the day after Christmas, when President Roosevelt sent Kaiser Wilhelm II holiday greetings and said he hoped to visit German East Africa on his hunting trip to the Dark Continent in the coming year, a descendant of Africa was preparing to fight for boxing's heavyweight championship. Jack Johnson, a black American from Galveston, Texas, entered the ring to face Tommy Burns, a white Canadian. The odds were 5–4 that Burns, a little-regarded boxer, would win against the better boxer, and it may have been simply because Burns was white and Johnson was black. Whichever man won would capture the $35,000 purse.[36]

Johnson took command of the fight the moment he entered the ring. "Capable and confident, Johnson grinned, bantered and taunted Burns from the start of the fight to the finish." The writer Jack London, reporting on the fight for the *New York Herald*, wrote back to his newspaper, "Burns was a toy in his hands."[37]

There was never a doubt who the winner would be. Jack Johnson was declared the heavyweight champion. He had beaten a white man. Decisively. A black man was champion of the world.[38]

"It was because the Ninth Cavalry was my home, my real freedom, and my self-respect."

First Sergeant Braxton Rutledge,
Ninth United States Cavalry (Colored),
as played by Woody Strode in *Sergeant Rutledge*

CHAPTER TWENTY-SIX

ROOSEVELT FATIGUE

THE PREVIOUS MAY, THE US District Court, noting that the guilt or innocence of Private Oscar W. Reid or any of the soldiers was "beyond this judicial investigation," decided the enlistment contract was "terminable at will, if terminated [by the] President of the United States, as Commander in Chief."[1] Writing John Milholland, Foraker said, "This I hope is the last piece of bad luck we are to have. I hope the attorneys will take the case to the Supreme Court." They did, and the Court handed down its decision only twenty-one days after he appeared for his oral argument (considering the intervening Christmas/New Year holidays, perhaps no more than one working week). An opinion written by Justice Oliver Wendell Holmes Jr. turned Reid down. Federal courts could not hear Reid's claim because President Roosevelt was protected by the concept of sovereign immunity. That doctrine, absorbed by American jurisprudence from the English common law, and often characterized in both countries as "the king can do no wrong," protects the US government from claims such as Reid's.[2] Roosevelt had appointed Holmes to the court in 1902 after an intensive examination of his judicial rulings and questioning him on how he thought about the law.

Roosevelt wanted a man who would vote what Roosevelt considered the correct way. Holmes surprised him and dissented against the government in the *Northern Securities* antitrust case in 1904. Roosevelt was irritated and, as Holmes later remarked, "It broke up our incipient friendship."[3] But because the government had won the case anyway, he more or less shrugged it off.

Before the decision, Sturgis Bigelow (the man who in 1907 wondered what happened at the Gridiron dinner) sent Henry Cabot Lodge a newspaper clipping about the Korean emperor abolishing that country's supreme court. Lodge forwarded it Roosevelt, who sent it to Holmes with a note, "The merit of the suggestion is obvious." Holmes sent it back with the answer, "I shall have to remind [Cabot and Bigelow] that if I catch them [before him in court] I will lay them by the heels if they do not keep civil tongues in their heads. The King [Holmes meant Roosevelt], of course, can do no wrong." Later Holmes and his brethren applied that notion against Reid.

WHILE WAITING FOR THE Supreme Court decision, Foraker still had the Browne-Baldwin investigation to deal with. It had been made public by Roosevelt in his December 14, 1908, special message to the Senate.[4] Because of his own correspondence over the summer with Boyd Conyers, Foraker was prepared to answer Roosevelt in the time the Senate reserved for his reenlistment bill.[5] How the investigation was conducted was, he argued, so disturbing it showed why the soldiers deserved a proper tribunal, and that was what his reenlistment bill would give them. He described the investigation from the point of view of the soldier it targeted, Boyd Conyers, and the deceitful way Browne and his associates distorted the truth made it seem Conyers had confessed his guilt, when in reality he denied any involvement. "I am just as innocent of taking any part in that trouble that night as God is on high."[6]

Foraker had to bite his tongue that day because the day before he had asked John Callan O'Laughlin to speak with Roosevelt on his behalf, and O'Laughlin had not yet reported back to him. But he did well enough for the *Boston Herald* to speak for much of the

country and many in the Senate the next day when it titled an editorial "A Discredited Case."[7]

THE NEXT MORNING, FORAKER received a letter from Maurice Low,
the correspondent for the *London Morning Post*. Low had been in
Washington longer than Foraker and knew most of what went on
there, possibly too much for some people. Theodore Roosevelt could
not stand him. He called Low "an English Jew, an underhanded
fellow who has been blackballed in the Metropolitan Club here, who
dislikes America generally and hates me in particular, who knows
nothing whatever, and would misrepresent anything he did know, a
liar of bad character, utterly untrustworthy, untruthful little slander
monger, and circumcised skunk."[8] Foraker and Low had grown
close after Low's young son died and Foraker took a moment from
Brownsville and the election to send his condolences. Low now
questioned whether the War Department had a "secret service fund"
for hush-hush matters, and, if not, where did it get the money for
the Browne-Baldwin investigation? "Might not the public interests
be served by a resolution of enquiry eliciting this information?"[9] For
years Foraker the lawyer had used "fishing expeditions" to discover
weaknesses in the other side's case in lawsuits. You never knew
what sort of catch you might reel in. He took to Low's suggestion as
a hungry fish took to a wriggling worm on a hook and introduced in
the Senate a resolution asking for the details of the Browne-Baldwin
employment, the names of anyone else so employed, instructions
given to them, what had been paid and to whom, by what authority,
and where the money came from. As a sign that Roosevelt, with only
a few months left in the White House, no longer intimidated senators, the resolution easily passed a day later.[10]

While waiting for Roosevelt's answer, Foraker considered his
next move. Every Republican on the Military Affairs Committee
had said some sort of redress for the innocent soldiers was needed,
and even Roosevelt made minimally encouraging concessions to
this in his special message. The Senate was eager to be done with
Brownsville, and President Roosevelt was aware that at noon on
March 4, Inauguration Day for Taft, he would lose all control over

it. But he was not likely to sign any bill that permitted any soldier back in the army who to his mind was not absolutely free of the least hint of guilt. Foraker knew the time had come to abandon soldiers who were doomed, as in triage on a battlefield, to save those with a chance. Roosevelt would not come to an accommodation with him but might with the Senate. He would deal with Roosevelt through the Senate as "the Senator from Ohio," the term Roosevelt used in his answer to O'Laughlin, which Foraker took to mean without the empathy he hoped for.

ON JANUARY 12, 1909, Joseph Foraker rose before a Senate floor crowded with senators and with spectators jammed into gallery seats.[11] No one wanted to miss what was thought to be Foraker's last appearance on behalf of his Brownsville soldiers and possibly his last address to the Senate. Ostensibly speaking in support of his reenlistment bill, he quickly angled back to the Browne-Baldwin report. With his O'Laughlin hopes dashed, there was no reason to hold back, and he tore into Roosevelt and the investigation. He accused the detectives of using tactics just short of a rubber hose. Their evidence was "wholly false in every essential particular, being nothing more than malicious fabrications of the most villainous character."[12] He reminded senators that repeatedly since August 1906 Roosevelt had said with bombastic certainty the evidence overwhelmingly and conclusively showed the soldiers were guilty. Yet every time, he required more proof of what he said was already proved. Before the Senate in his special message on December 19, 1906, President Roosevelt had said it again with greater emphasis. But afterward Assistant Attorney General Milton D. Purdy and Major Augustus Blocksom had to go to Texas to investigate. In March 1908 a majority on the Senate Military Affairs Committee determined soldiers did it, and President Roosevelt said this confirmed their guilt. Within the month, though, he authorized Secretary Taft to hire private investigators to investigate one more time, and he kept this hidden and paid for with contingent funds only he controlled. And with not one soldier admitting guilt, still Roosevelt claimed he was right.

Time now was on Foraker's side. Roosevelt had only fifty-one days left in the White House; his ability to use the authority and respect of his office to persuade people was waning. The Senate was tired of Brownsville and tired of Roosevelt. Though not prepared to deny Roosevelt his discharges, senators were sure that for at least some soldiers an injustice had been committed and must be corrected. The president's blindness to the Browne-Baldwin investigation's shadiness and shabbiness was the best reason yet to give the soldiers a fair hearing and a real chance to get back in the army. Foraker would show little regard for the man who had treated him so cruelly. He had lost his cause in the Military Affairs Committee and his seat in the Senate. He had been humiliated and disgraced. What was left was his obligation to his soldiers. There would be no restraint in his speech today.

This speech put Brownsville back on the front pages. The *New York Times* called Foraker's speech his "swan song . . . a vigorous, vitriolic valedictory."[13] Senators turned from distractions on their desks and in the chamber to give him strictest heed. People in the galleries (including an unusual number of blacks) were too absorbed even to applaud. Spectators and listeners must have held their breath as the energized Senator Foraker accused President Roosevelt of behaving illegally; he cited an 1893 law expressly forbidding employment of private detectives by the government.[14] And why was such a thing even needed? Why the "determined effort . . . to again bolster the case [already] characterized as 'conclusive' and overwhelming"?[15] It was "monstrous," "revolting," "shocking to every sense of fairness, injustice, and every common decency."[16] "The President's methods cannot be fittingly characterized without the use of language which, if employed, might appear to be disrespectful to the Chief Executive. He has become utterly oblivious to all the restraints of law, decency, and propriety in his mad pursuit of these helpless victims of his ill-considered action."[17] The *New York Times* softened these indictments by calling them "flings of biting sarcasm."[18] But newspapers across the country had similar headlines: "President 'Oblivious to All Law and Decency.'"[19]

Foraker denied Conyers or any other soldier had confessed to any part in the shooting or cover-up and invited senators to look through letters from them bundled on his desk. He even had an affidavit from the white sheriff in Monroe, Georgia, who was present when Browne tried to get Conyers to confess, saying Conyers had made no confession and Browne's story was false. "*I desire*," swore Sheriff E. C. Arnold, "*to state further that the report of Mr. Herbert J. Browne . . . in so far as the same relates to these conversations with Boyd Conyers, is not true. To the contrary, and I say it under my solemn oath, it is the most absolute false, the most willful misrepresentation of the truth, and the most shameful perversion of what really did take place between them that I have ever seen over the signature of any person*" (emphasis in Foraker memoirs).[20] "Yet," Foraker editorialized, "a President of the United States . . . is continuing the employment of [this] man. . . . If I speak plainly . . . it is because we have reached the point where only plain talk would seem to properly meet the requirements of the case."[21]

But the matter before the Senate that day was his bill to get as many soldiers of the Black Battalion as possible back into the army. He might pummel Roosevelt with the Browne-Baldwin report, he might use it to purge himself of the frustration and bitterness built up over the almost two years since he took on what had become for him a crusade for justice, but he still had to convince the Senate to establish a tribunal to consider the reenlistments and to wall it off from Roosevelt's influence by naming its members in the legislation and not by presidential appointment.[22] He asked for a vote on his bill. The Senate postponed it. He sat down in his chair, depleted and disgusted.

THE MOOD OF THE Senate was reflected when it passed a resolution calling for an itemized accounting of the money spent from the so-called Emergency Fund as far back as 1898 under President McKinley.[23] The late McKinley was not its target. Roosevelt was. Two and a half years after the Brownsville shooting raid, almost a year after the Senate decided soldiers from the Black Battalion were the shooters, and less than a month after Roosevelt foisted on it a corrupt investigation with a scandalously unproven conclusion, the Senate was about to pay him back.[24] But this did little for the Black Battalion.

Roosevelt agreed to make a "full report." But the term *full report* had an elasticity to it, and there may have been more to this fund than Roosevelt wanted the Senate or the public to know. He wrote President-elect Taft that Taft "need not be under the least anxiety. I will see that the matter is put in such shape that no possible difficulty arises *from the disclosure of matters which ought to be kept confidential*" (author's emphasis). And just in case things should slip out nonetheless, he added language that would allow him to sidestep this commitment to Taft: "I knew *in a general way* of all that you did" (author's emphasis).[25]

TO SHOW HOW TOUGH he was, the day after the Senate voted for the accounting, the overweight, woefully out-of-shape, and blind in one eye Roosevelt left the White House at 3:40 a.m. for a round-trip ride of about one hundred miles on horseback to Warrenton, Virginia. He had ordered flabby army officers to condition themselves physically, and he was going to show them a thing or two. The last thirty miles were ridden through a blizzard that left him "covered with mud and ice from the brim of his Rough Rider hat to the tips of his riding boots." Leaping from his "steaming mount," he shook off the ice before entering the White House and declared to gathered reporters, "It was bully."[26]

IN FORAKER'S PAPERS IN Cincinnati is a letter from A. C. Stine, a white man from Monroe, Georgia. "We all know 'Buddie' [Boyd Conyers's nickname] here, and I do not believe there is a respectable white man here who believes for a moment that he" made that confession. Of Sheriff Arnold, who defended Conyers, Stine wrote, he belongs "to that class of the southern white people who do not make social equals of the negro, but who are willing and desire to see him treated right and fair at all times." Of Foraker he wrote, "I can say that you are doing simple justice."[27]

HANGING OVER THE SENATE and the Black Battalion were Roosevelt's and Foraker's differing bills to deal with reenlisting the innocent soldiers. As far as the Senate was concerned, the Brownsville Incident would be over once this matter was dealt with. Both Roosevelt and Foraker heard the clock ticking toward the end of their terms in office. One man who would still be there was Senator Nelson Aldrich, the Senate Republican leader. It was he who would have to protect President Taft and shepherd his legislation through, and he did not want Brownsville, which had tied the Senate in knots for more than two years, snarling things up. Unconsciously validating Foraker's thinking that it would have to be the Senate as a body to coax President Roosevelt into cooperation and accommodation, Aldrich was determined to close the matter and was the perfect man to do it. His intelligence, discretion, and charm could persuade and give cover to those eager to move away from Roosevelt on Brownsville. He had a reputation for thinking clearly and acting fairly. And because he was charming and reasonable, with none of the zealousness that characterized Foraker in Roosevelt's eyes, he would not elevate Roosevelt's blood pressure by walking into his office.[28]

He worked from Foraker's bill to make it more acceptable to all. It called for an authority called a Court of Inquiry with one year to do its work. The Court of Inquiry could only determine those "qualified for reenlistment," not reenlist any of them. Roosevelt especially liked that "the language is permissive and not mandatory and [the Court of Inquiry] is to be allowed to make eligible, and nothing more than eligible."[29] He also probably liked the fact that even though, as Senator Shelby Collum would later write, "it became perfectly clear to almost everyone in Congress that he was wrong," nothing the Court of Inquiry might do would embarrass him.[30] President Roosevelt was eager to get this compromise enacted, and to save time he encouraged Aldrich to show his letter of approval to Senators Warren and Warner, even to Foraker and the Democrats.

Foraker's memoirs make no reference to Aldrich or his compromise. They note only, "I succeeded in getting a vote on my bill, in an amended form" on February 23 with fifty-six Republicans for it and twenty-six Democrats against.[31] All the Republicans, in no small way moved by Foraker's eloquent presentations and perhaps angry at themselves for not doing it sooner, finally did *a* right thing, if not *the* right thing. The split in their party from Brownsville was mending. Not one Democrat showed such contrition. Every Democrat, more concerned with maintaining the support of what was then called "the Solid South," voted against the Black Battalion. Even Foraker's sometime-ally "Pitchfork Ben" Tillman. "As I did not want innocent men to be kicked out of the army, I do not want any guilty men back into the army."[32] It's just as possible he voted against the compromise because President Roosevelt was for it.

Four days later it was approved in the House. The pattern in the Senate repeated itself: Republicans voted for it, and Democrats, including John Nance Garner, Brownsville's congressman, were overwhelmingly against it. One Southern Democrat, however, Richard Hobson of Alabama, saw the shame of what was done to the Black Battalion. He voted to help the soldiers even though he unapologetically recognized that "the white man is supreme in this country. [Yet] that makes it only more sacred that he should give absolute justice to the black man who is in our midst. . . . We are standing here on the field of eternal justice, where all men are the same. It is justice that links man to the Divine. Whether the heavens fall or the earth melts away, while we live let us be just. (*Loud applause.*)"[33]

ON MARCH 2, 1909, with only one full day left in his term, President Roosevelt signed the bill creating the Court of Inquiry. For the Senate, this closed the Brownsville Incident. For Foraker, it remained an open wound never to heal. For the soldiers of the Black Battalion, there would be another investigation in the Court of Inquiry, where they wanted Captain Samuel Lyon, commanding officer of Company D, to represent them, but the army would not permit it. They then asked retired Brigadier General Aaron S. Daggett, their commanding officer at El Caney in Cuba. He accepted on the understanding he had complete sympathy for any soldier not involved in the Brownsville Incident, but none for those, if any, who were. They, he said, should be hanged. Napoleon B. Marshall, the black lawyer who had worked with Foraker in the Military Affairs Committee, would work now with Daggett. Marshall asked Foraker to join them but the exhausted Foraker backed off.[34]

IN THE LATE SPRING the Court of Inquiry began its work with a review of all the testimony and evidence from the earlier investigations (overwhelmingly critical of the soldiers), and then a visit to Brownsville to see for itself where it all happened and to talk to the townspeople (hearing only their side). By the time it got to new testimony and evidence back in Washington, its attitude was soured. This order of doing things helped crush any chance the soldiers had. Recycled soldier testimony and evidence was a trove to pick through for inconsistencies. Their memories had become hesitant. There were too many discrepancies and too many unanswered questions.[35] What should work in favor of a defendant in a court of law worked against the soldiers in the Court of Inquiry, where guilt was presumed. What Foraker had long feared had come to pass: the soldiers had to prove their innocence. General Daggett wrote Foraker that he and the soldiers faced a stacked deck.[36]

Within its one-year mandate, the Court of Inquiry issued its conclusions. It had considered the applications of eighty-two former soldiers (just shy of one-half of the 167 discharged), waded through a river of testimony from before it was created, and excavated a tributary of its own. Its report would take twelve volumes; its hearings alone would sprawl over 1,635 pages. It agreed with all the previous investigations, from the Citizens' Committee in Brownsville the day after the shooting to the Browne-Baldwin report completed just before the Court of Inquiry was created: unanimously its members said unidentified soldiers of the Black Battalion had shot up Brownsville, and other soldiers had protected them.

It decreed fourteen soldiers were eligible for reenlistment.[37] Excluded was every man above the rank of corporal, which meant every sergeant, including First Sergeant Mingo Sanders, a special target of Theodore Roosevelt.[38] How the fourteen were selected is not known. The Court of Inquiry gave the names but no reasons. Private Clifford Adair, the Company C private whose pen was confiscated as he crossed back into Brownsville from Matamoros, was one of the lucky few. The others, except for one, all seem to have been asleep when the shooting began, but so were most of the soldiers not on duty at midnight. The exception was Private John

Smith who was "in confinement," an ironclad alibi.[39] Five of the names were from Company C, the company generally thought to have done the shooting because of the harassment experienced by its soldiers. Six were with Company D, least likely to have been involved because its barracks were the farthest from where the shooting came from, and four were from Company B. Of these fourteen, eleven, including Adair, were readmitted to the army.[40] One hundred fifty-three soldiers never were.

ON WILLIAM HOWARD TAFT's Inauguration Day, Joseph Foraker, now a former senator, was packing for home in Cincinnati. His only engagement left was the loving cup reception at the Metropolitan AME Church, a short three blocks or so from his and Julia's "big yellow house."

"Prove to the world and to Mr. Foraker that we as a race are not a set of ingrates and that we are determined to support the men who dare contend for the full and fair enforcement of the Constitution."

Rev. J. Milton Waldron, treasurer of the
Niagara Movement, in an attachment to a letter from
Waldron to W. E. B. Du Bois, February 11, 1908

CHAPTER TWENTY-SEVEN

"NOT ONE PARTICLE OF REGRET"

ACCORDING TO THE *WASHINGTON Herald*, when people spotted Senator Joseph Foraker arriving at the Metropolitan AME Church for the presentation of the loving cup, "wild, mad cheers broke out, and the edifice fairly shook with the stamping of feet and the clapping of hands."[1] Three thousand people passed up the normal relaxation and pleasures of a Saturday evening and trudged through a cold, early-March rain to see him, honor him, and show him by their presence the gratitude they had for him. After the loving cup was presented, Armond Scott, its presenter, stepped back and, by a gesture toward the front of the podium, invited Foraker to come forward.

The cheering began anew, and when it subsided and quiet expectation took its place, Foraker began his remarks.[2] Associating himself with the previous speakers by addressing them as "Brother Grimké and Brother Scott" (and thereby strengthening his bond with his audience), he marveled at their oratorical skills. "Few men in the Senate of the United States, now or ever . . . could speak in favorable comparison." Keying off their eloquence, he said he would have only a few simple words about himself. But politician that he was, Foraker spoke longer to say thank you than anyone else that evening—easily twice as long as Archibald Grimké had in praising him.

Foraker got right to the question of why he took on Theodore Roosevelt. "Probably I ought to say in justice to myself that I never had a selfish thought in regard to the matter. It never once occurred to me that under any circumstances it would redound to my political benefit to champion that cause. I championed that cause because I could not help it." Foraker made it clear that, even if what he did cost him his Senate seat, "I can truthfully say that I have not one particle of regret. . . . I go back to my home carrying with me my own self-respect."

Before moving on to what he called the Brownsville "matter," he yielded to an irresistible urge and returned to the rhetoric of the "bloody shirt" to compare what he did with Brownsville to his fighting in the Civil War. "I hated and detested slavery. . . . We were engaged in a great struggle, for a great principle, to emancipate a race." Extending freedom for the slave to the rights of the Twenty-Fifth Infantry's soldiers as free men, he continued, "This is a land of the free . . . where no man can be convicted of a crime without first having had a chance to be heard in his own defense."[3] "It was our duty to ourselves as a great, strong and powerful nation to give every man a hearing, to deal fairly and squarely with every man, to see that justice was done to him, that he should be heard."

Getting down to specifics, Foraker made it clear the soldiers could not possibly have turned in any of their number, since none was a shooter. Who would know the men better than their white officers, he asked, and did not they believe their troops to be innocent? To suggest a conspiracy by 167 men to keep the identity of the guilty men a secret was impossible for an "unbiased mind possessing a knowledge of human nature." Raking up the testimony against the men, he again insisted eyewitnesses who said the shooters were black soldiers could not possibly have distinguished their race that dark, dark night. No army rifle had been fired in the affray, and none of the cartridges issued to the Black Battalion was unaccounted for.

The government had ordered further army investigations, sent the Secret Service to Texas to nail down the soldiers' guilt, even hired detectives to dig up whatever they could, but in the end it was inconclusive. What was worse, no investigator ever looked for others who could have done the deed. "I [remain] clearly convinced that not a man in that black battalion was guilty," Foraker cried out, and the crowd roared back its agreement. Each of these points had been made before, yet it was important that they be stressed again.

Foraker went on to link Brownsville to "a growing prejudice against the black man all over the country" and a denial of "his rights under the Constitution and the laws of the land," and added, "I want to see those rights protected and upheld." The audience responded, according to the transcript of the evening, with "applause."

Before ending, aware of the collateral bitterness many Negroes felt toward President Taft, who as Roosevelt's secretary of war formally issued the order of dismissal, Foraker graciously urged support for the man who bested him in the contest for White House. He admitted that after some of Taft's campaign speeches, he had shared Negroes' concerns about him. "But these fears were dispelled when I read his inaugural. . . . I am rejoiced to know he intends to do what he can to correct the wrongs of the race and bring about some acceptable adjustments of differences consistently with the [Fourteenth and Fifteenth] Amendments." There is no reference in the transcript to applause for this plea for patience. Perhaps it was the lingering resentment for Taft, maybe it was Foraker's reference to "the wrongs of the race" with no clear indication just which race he meant, or it might have been his implication that "adjustments of differences" should be only as consistent with the Constitution, with no moral component.

Foraker ended on a quiet, bittersweet note. "I will always cherish the recollections of this hour as among the most pleasing connected with my public service." To "applause," he took his seat.

William C. Beer, a white lawyer and seasoned behind-the-scenes player in the game of politics, was in the church that night.[4] Not one to stand fast with the wrong man, especially one so recently discarded by his party and his state, Beer was so moved by what he saw and heard, the next day he sent a letter to Foraker, by force of habit addressed in error to what formerly was his Senate office in Washington. He called the speech "prophetic."[5]

There was one last item on the evening's agenda. The three thousand people, "typical representatives of a race that has ever been loyal to America and American institutions," came to their feet and sang "America" to honor the country that had dishonored their—and its own—soldiers. "Let freedom ring."

After a reception hosted by Senator Foraker, the evening was over. It had been an important event for the black community. In below-freezing temperatures that lingered from the Inaugural Day blizzard, the people returned to their homes and the continuing struggle for equality. Foraker went back to his home in Cincinnati; he would never again hold elected office. At his home in Oyster Bay, ex-president Roosevelt went to sleep that night after an exhausting day of chopping trees behind the house, answering correspondence, and preparing for his upcoming big-game hunting trip to Africa, the ancestral home of the soldiers he had sent to their homes in America more than two years earlier.[6] The men of the Black Battalion were scattered across the country, and it was now clear that except for only a handful, they were never to return to the army. The battle was over and lost. Roosevelt's discharge order stood. Just as important to him, Roosevelt had seen to it that Foraker was thrown out of public life. "I have gotten [one of] the men I went after, Foraker."[7]

Oddly, not one speaker recalled that the evening was the anniversary of the US Supreme Court's infamous *Dred Scott* decision.[8] A slave who had been taken to the free state of Minnesota, Scott sued in federal court for his freedom. On March 6, 1857, the Supreme Court ruled his claim could not even be considered because he was not a citizen. Dred Scott and all people of African ancestry, said America's highest court, even free blacks, could never become citizens of the United States. Fifty-two years later, blacks were allowed to be citizens, but not quite so. Not yet.

> *"How many black people, with the memory of Brownsville,*
> *could support such a man passes our comprehension."*
>
> W. E. B. Du Bois, reacting to Roosevelt
> becoming a presidential nominee for the Progressive
> Party in 1912, in David L. Lewis, *W. E. B. Du Bois:*
> *Biography of a Race, 1868–1919*

EPILOGUE

WHAT HAPPENED LATER

THE ARMY ABANDONED FORT Brown shortly after the Black Battalion left, as it had been thinking of doing anyway.[1] Much of the land it sat on is now the campus of the University of Texas at Brownsville, and part of the rest is still a government reservation and used by civilian agencies. You can stand today where Elizabeth Street dead-ended at the Fort Brown gate, which is gone of course, and walk southeast (or south, as they say in Brownsville) along what is East University Boulevard. Continuing through what had been the gap between the Company B and Company D barracks and onto what was the post's parade ground, in a few minutes you come to where Captain and Mrs. Samuel Lyon's quarters were on a horseshoe body of water then called the Lagoon but now renamed the Fort Brown Resaca. Looking out their window, they would see the other side of the Lagoon and just beyond that the Rio Grande and Mexico. Today a bridge allows you to keep walking over the Resaca until, about half a mile from where you started, you come to Ringgold Road, not yet built in 1906. Walking a bit along Ringgold Road you come to where the National Cemetery was. Like Fort Brown, it too is gone. Those interred there (including Major Jacob Brown) were moved to Alexandria National Cemetery in Pinesville, Louisiana, in

1909. Where the cemetery was is now a condominium resort development called Fort Brown Condo Shares, described as "situated on the grounds of the historic battlefield of the Mexican-American War."[2] And, of course, on what was Fort Brown and the site of the Brownsville Incident, though the condominium does not mention that.

THE ARMY REBUILT THE Black Battalion with new recruits and transferred noncommissioned officers. In 1907, while the Brownsville investigations were taking place, the entire Twenty-Fifth Infantry returned to the Philippines, mostly for garrison duty but with some policing every now and then. In 1909 it returned to the continental United States and the Pacific Northwest for three years, then went to Hawaii, where it stayed through World War I. Some of its men received reassignments to Europe where, mainly with the French army, they saw action. In World War II the regiment arrived in the Pacific in 1944 and served mainly as a logistical unit. After the war it came home, and in early 1946 the Twenty-Fifth Infantry was deactivated.[3] It no longer exists.

THE 158 SOLDIERS OF the Black Battalion not reenlisted in the army soon faded into the vastness of America. Those called to Washington, DC, to testify before the Senate committee and later the Court of Inquiry resurfaced briefly, and then most were lost.[4] By 1970, when Brownsville historian John D. Weaver wrote *The Brownsville Raid* and brought the incident back into public awareness, all but two of the soldiers had died. The army they served in had remained segregated until President Harry Truman integrated the American armed forces in 1948.[5] Never again would America have military units designated "Colored." After Weaver's book was published, Augustus F. Hawkins, a black member of Congress from California, prodded the army into investigating the incident with the goal of correcting the injustice to the Black Battalion. In 1972 the now-renamed Defense Department amended the first paragraph of Special Orders No. 266 to replace "discharged without honor" with "honorably discharged from the army."[6] By then, only Private Dorsie Willis of Company D was still living, and on February 11,

1972, at the Zion Baptist Church in Minneapolis, on his eighty-seventh birthday, Dorsie Willis received his Certificate of Honorable Discharge attesting to his honest and faithful service.[7] (Private Edward Warfield of Company B also was still alive, but he was one of the soldiers readmitted to the army after the Court of Inquiry. He already had his honorable discharge.) A little less than a year later, Congress awarded Willis $25,000, and on January 11, 1974, an army general came to Minneapolis to present it.[8] When he died in 1977 at the age of ninety-one, he was buried at Fort Snelling, Minnesota, with the military honors he was entitled to. Congress awarded $10,000 to Black Battalion widows; there was only one of them, Bettye Conyers Hardeman, the wife of Boyd Conyers. "He never talked about it. The only thing he would say was he didn't do it." When she received the check she told the *New York Times*, "Big deal. There was no letter of apologies. This was in exchange, of course, for a man's whole life."[9]

FIRST SERGEANT MINGO SANDERS made his way to Washington very soon after leaving Fort Reno to get back into the army. President Roosevelt angrily and publicly refused even to consider letting him in. Sanders's last words to the Court of Inquiry weighing his eligibility for reenlistment came as he ended his testimony on February 8, 1910. "As I have been laboring three years or more, trying to prove my innocence to each individual person who has examined me, and now I am on my last examination, I suppose, by this grand court, and I am now passed half a century, and I am also pleading to this court for mercy for my sake, because when a man gets to be my age there is nobody wants him, and I wish that this court would consider my case to the bottom of their heart, to the full extent, and see that I do not die in agony, as I labored hard all my young life for the Government, honest and faithfully, and can prove it by a dozen or more officers, and I hope the Court will consider my case."[10] It turned him down.

In the summer of 1912, during his reelection campaign, President Taft ordered the Interior Department to hire Sanders as a messenger. Roosevelt accused Taft of hypocrisy for having his "campaign managers in Ohio" hire a man whom Taft, six years earlier, agreed was, because of his senior rank, "more responsible for what had occurred than any others."[11] Seventeen years later, still holding that job Taft gave him and Roosevelt would have denied him under Special Orders No. 266 as first written ("forever debarred . . . from employment in any civil capacity under the Government"), former First Sergeant Mingo Sanders entered Freedmen's Hospital at Howard University in Washington with a gangrenous infection of his foot. To save his life, the leg was amputated, but he died three days later on August 15, 1929.[12] His discharge without honor did not disentitle him to burial in Arlington National Cemetery, where he is today.

WITH TAFT ELECTED AND Foraker's Senate hopes on life support, on Christmas Day 1908 Roosevelt invited Booker T. Washington to attend a conference in Washington in January to consider ways to help destitute and orphaned children. It was a measure of the deterioration in their relationship that he now saw the Wizard as something of a social worker. Washington had always promptly responded to requests from the White House, and almost always said yes, but four days later the notation "No reply as yet" was penciled on the White House copy of the letter.[13] Washington's dependence on Roosevelt was also over; there was a new king to counsel and seek influence from, and he lost no time working to stay in the game. It started off well. During the campaign he wrote Taft strongly suggesting he modify how he planned to discuss state constitutions and black voting. "Negro newspapers will . . . misinterpret your meaning." Taft accepted the changes word for word.[14] But when safely elected and securely ensconced in the White House, Taft paid less and less attention to the man from Tuskegee.

As did black leaders. Booker T. Washington's failure to help the Black Battalion showed that his influence in politics and with white industrialists and business leaders was an illusion and his program of accommodation had little value. The conflict between Washington and W. E. B. Du Bois was increasingly shaded in Du Bois's favor. By 1911, the split was complete. There was an effort at reconciliation after a bizarre incident in which Washington was chased down Central Park West in New York and beaten up by a white man named Alfred Ulrich, who would tell police he thought Washington was a burglar. What Washington was doing in Ulrich's apartment building in a white neighborhood on West Sixty-Seventh Street, what his relationship may have been with a white woman who was somehow involved, and just what he may have done to merit a severe beating from Ulrich has never been completely understood. Washington's reluctance to press charges against Ulrich suggests he may have wanted to cover the matter up. The photos of a severely beaten and bandaged Washington and the anger among blacks that a well-dressed, well-spoken, and nonthreatening black man could be treated this way in a white neighborhood, regardless of why he was there, produced an outpouring of sympathy for him from those he would not have expected. Washington biographer Louis Harlan wrote that Washington was so moved he decided "this business of having a divided race" must cease, and he asked Oswald Garrison Villard, one of the founders of the NAACP, to help bring it about. The NAACP sent a mild expression of sympathy, written by Monroe Trotter, who detested Washington, but failed to give Washington a vote of confidence.[15] The moment for reconciliation passed.

On a trip to New York in 1915 Washington collapsed and was told he had only days to live. He announced, "I was born in the South, I have lived and labored in the South, and I expect to die and be buried in the South." He arrived in Tuskegee at midnight, November 14, 1915, and died in the South five hours later.

The movement away from Washington and accommodation became irreversible. Committed Bookerites now found themselves ignored as Du Bois firmly closed the door to any role in the new black leadership. But the Tuskegee Machine's divisiveness had passed away with him. In 1926 at John Milholland's funeral, Washington's aide Emmett Scott joined W. E. B. Du Bois to praise the man Washington scorned and bedeviled.[16]

W. E. B. DU BOIS CONTINUED to influence the more aggressive drive for civil rights, but not as the yang to Washington's yin. With Washington no longer a foil, Du Bois's philosophy to guide the Negro struggle had to ride on its own into the future.[17] In the obituary he wrote in the December 15, 1915, issue of *Crisis*, the magazine he founded for the NAACP in 1910 to articulate the crusade for civil rights, he continued his message of the Washington who did much good overshadowed by the Washington who did so much more wrong. But he did generously acknowledge the good.

In 1934 Du Bois broke with the NAACP after years of abrasive personal relations with others in the organization. He came back ten years later as its director of research but left for good in 1949. Increasingly convinced America would never acknowledge its own injustice, in 1961, when he was ninety-three years old, he joined the Communist Party. He surrendered his American citizenship and left his country for good, moving to Ghana, where he died on August 27, 1963, the day before the March on Washington. His death was noted by the executive director of the NAACP Roy Wilkins, standing before the Lincoln Memorial; many were surprised to realize he had still been alive, so far back had he been a leader, so far ahead had the struggle progressed.

In his late years in Ghana, Du Bois chastised a student who, as they were chatting on his porch, made an unkind comment about Booker T. Washington. "Don't say that. I used to talk like that." He remembered the words of an aunt to him, "Don't you forget that that man, unlike you, bears the mark of the lash on his back. He has come out of slavery. . . . You are fighting for the rights here in the North. It's tough, but it's nothing like as tough as what he had to face in his time and in his place."[18] The old Du Bois had softened, it seemed, and now was giving greater weight to Washington the good.

IT DID NOT TAKE Theodore Roosevelt long to lose patience with President Taft. Roosevelt kept his word and stayed away hunting big game in Africa to keep from overshadowing him, but word came from his acolytes back home that his successor had become a renegade. To the extent there was any truth to these charges, it was nothing more than a new man handling the job his own way. It was hardly a betrayal of Rooseveltian principles or the man who had put him in the White

House. Giving in to what Philander Knox called "whims" and "imperious, ambitious vanities and mysterious antipathies," Roosevelt took the bait, and inevitably the men clashed.[19] In 1912 Roosevelt tried to take the Republican nomination away from Taft, only to find out the rules favoring incumbency, rules he himself used (and in some cases wrote) in 1904 when he was the incumbent, still worked. Enraged when these rules denied credentials to his own delegates, he ran as the Progressive Party candidate against both President Taft and the Democrat Woodrow Wilson, thereby dividing the Republican Party and handing the White House to the Democrats. In January 1907, angry when the Senate acquiesced to Foraker's argument that some sort of Brownsville investigation was needed, Roosevelt had warned the Republicans "if they split off me [from the Republican Party] they would split the party neatly in two."[20] In 1912 Roosevelt did just that.[21]

FORMER PRESIDENT TAFT ACCEPTED an invitation to teach at Yale Law School. He was happy there, happier that he was out of the White House, and happiest when he finally got from President Warren Harding, an Ohioan not destined for Cornelia's statue in Columbus, what he always wanted, an appointment to the US Supreme Court. As chief justice he returned twice more to presidential inaugurations to administer the oath of office to two other Republicans, Calvin Coolidge in 1924 and Herbert Hoover in 1928.

Taft was puzzled, then bitter, then immensely saddened when Roosevelt turned against him in 1912. "I have a sense of wrong in the attitude of Theodore Roosevelt toward me which I doubt I can ever get over," he wrote his Aunt Delia. "I do not want to fight Theodore Roosevelt. But I am going to fight him," he said at a campaign stop. He told a reporter who saw him sitting alone with tears in his eyes, "Roosevelt was my closest friend." Eventually the two former friends reconciled at a chance meeting in the dining room of the Blackstone Hotel in Chicago, but Taft would weep again for his lost friend at Roosevelt's funeral in 1919.[22]

JOSEPH FORAKER RETURNED TO private life in Cincinnati and reestablished a successful law practice. He continued to receive letters from people praising and thanking him for what he did.[23] The most appreciated were from the Black Battalion and its officers who were sure their soldiers were innocent. "Your efforts in behalf of the 'Black Battalion' will cause your name to go down into history as the one man who braved every thing in behalf of justice and fair play and we . . . render you all honor and homage for your heroism and courage," wrote the battalion's commanding officer, Major Charles Penrose.[24] On the day Foraker received the loving cup, Captain Samuel Lyon's wife thanked him for his persistence in the creation of the Court of Inquiry and added, "I feel a love for and pride in the Regiment that such a close association with it must bring." She was a "proud member of our beloved Regiment."[25]

Foraker wrote his memoirs in 1916, and when Theodore Roosevelt, the man who tormented him over Brownsville, read it, he half admitted he may have been wrong ("There were some things told me against you, or in reference to you, which [when I consider what I now know of my informants] would have carried no weight with me at the time") and invited Foraker to visit him at Sagamore Hill.[26] Their tentative reconciliation actually started four years earlier when Roosevelt asked him for his views on the Sherman Antitrust Act, "of course merely for my private use." Roosevelt also asked him to "come around. . . . It will be a real pleasure to see you."[27] Foraker regretted he received the invitation too late in a letter that began, "Dear Colonel Roosevelt: That title does not seem just right but I guess it will have to answer for the present."[28]

Foraker never made a visit to Oyster Bay; a year after Roosevelt's unclearly expressed apology, he was dead. His friend and mentor Harry Smith of the *Cleveland Gazette* wrote, "Our people have lost their last great, aggressive white friend."[29] In reporting his death, the *New York Times* used the word *fight* or some variation of it six times in the first two paragraphs, making him appear to be antagonistic and pugnacious, something he was not. It highlighted his poor health since he left the Senate but did not link it to the brutal wear and tear he endured in the Brownsville Incident. In fact it did not mention Brownsville other than the indirect comment, "He . . . fought Roosevelt in [his] second term." [30] At a memorial service for him in the US Court of Appeals courtroom in Cincinnati, there were nine eulogists; not one mentioned Brownsville.[31] Six days earlier at a Foraker Memorial "under the auspices Cincinnati Branch, NAACP, assisted by Churches, Lodges, Clubs, etc.," the black community turned out to pay its respects to a man it knew to be great. Harry Smith sang a baritone solo of "Beyond the Gates of Paradise," and Gilchrist Stewart was the principal speaker. Brownsville was mentioned often.

Champ Clark, who did not like Foraker very much and was glad to see Theodore Burton take his Senate seat, may have written the most inappropriate obituary about him. "Foraker seems to me to be the most pathetic figure in Ohio politics. . . . More than once he appeared to be a presidential possibility; but something fatal to his ultimate ambition always happened."[32] Foraker would not have liked anyone to think he was pathetic; he probably would have preferred (though disagreed with) being thought pugnacious as described by the *New York Times*. Clark was wrong; Foraker was not pathetic. He took an action "expecting a useful reaction from his world, but instead the effect of his action [was] to provoke forces of antagonism."[33] Still he kept going to the very end. He was a man of character.

Unlike Theodore Roosevelt, who must share Mount Rushmore with three other men, Joseph Foraker has a mountain of his own. At 17,400 feet, Mount Foraker in Alaska is the third-highest mountain in the United States. (Mount Rushmore is only 5,725 feet.) Fourteen miles away is the highest, Mount McKinley, increasingly called Denali in the rush to multiculturalism. Should this movement overtake Mount Foraker, it would be called Sultana (meaning "the woman") or Menlale (meaning "Denali's wife"), and Foraker would lose that vestige of the memory of him.

THEODORE ROOSEVELT LIVED TEN years after leaving the White House. Still a young man, he continued to lead the strenuous life. He salved the wound from the 1912 election loss by exploring the Amazon River basin, almost dying there, and discovering a then-unknown river that today is called Rio Roosevelt.

And he worked to bind together Lincoln's party, the Republicans. In 1916 he turned aside efforts to get him to fight the progressive battle again. "We are beaten. There is only one thing to do and that is to go back to the Republican party."[34] He was aging rapidly and visibly. Ignoring his age and health, the Rough Rider tried to form another group of volunteers to fight in France in World War I, but President Wilson turned him down. Roosevelt was making plans for a political comeback in 1920, was considered the leading Republican candidate for the White House, and "was likely to be President again."[35] It was not to be. In January 1919, only sixty years old, he died at Sagamore Hill. The last man to hear his voice ("James, will you please put out the light?") and see him alive was his black valet, James Amos. In 1927 Amos wrote a memoir of his time with Roosevelt from the White House to his death. Its title makes clear how he felt about Theodore Roosevelt: *Hero to His Valet*.

WHEN ROOSEVELT LOST THE Republican nomination to Taft, Du Bois, still nursing anger over Brownsville, wrote in an editorial in the August 1912 issue of *Crisis*, "We thank God that Theodore Roosevelt was eliminated. How many black people, with the memory of Brownsville, could support such a man passes our comprehension." For him, Brownsville could never be forgiven.[36] Seven years later, when Roosevelt died, he softened a bit, as he had with Booker T. Washington when he died. "Even in our hot bitterness over the Brownsville affair we knew that he *believed* he was right, and he of all men had to act in accordance with his beliefs."[37] Others who bitterly opposed him in the Brownsville Incident would be just as charitable. Oswald Garrison Villard wrote, "No more remarkably engaging personality than Colonel Roosevelt has ever figured in American public life. However bitterly opposed one might be to his policies or to his political philosophy, however one might be convinced that his influence upon the national life was a baleful one, it was impossible to be near him and not be profoundly influenced by his charm and the force of his individuality. . . . Young men thronged about Colonel Roosevelt eager to be of his party, his entourage, and to bask in the warmth and geniality of his presence. . . . Many who deserted at times, returned later."[38]

POSTMORTEM EXPRESSIONS OF GENTLE admiration and tribute notwithstanding, neither of these eulogists forgave him for discharging the Black Battalion. But as even Du Bois conceded, Roosevelt did think he was right. Was he justified in thinking this?

Roosevelt believed that he had an intuitive sense of what was the right thing to do and that he was entitled, as commander in chief, to make his decision regarding Brownsville based on it. Pulitzer Prize–winning author and historian David Fromkin suggests, "Intimations of these moral issues—of the showdown between good and evil, and of the showdown struggle for survival in a lawless society" may have been deeply etched into him by his ranching days in Dakota.[39] His view of what was the morally right thing to do in Brownsville took in more than the soldiers. Convinced in his own mind they were guilty, he analyzed the problem considering the greater good, the nation's need for a disciplined army, and the soldiers' duty to turn in the guilty parties. Roosevelt and Taft biographer Henry Pringle identified this Rooseveltian capacity for taking the macro view as far back as when he was in the New York State Assembly. He used the young Roosevelt's "indignation" over cigars manufactured amid filth and disease in New York tenements to explain that his morality "did not spring from concern over the predicament of the workers; he looked at the problem in terms of public health."[40] While this global thinking may have led him to the right decision with cigars in New York City, it may have led him to the wrong one with soldiers in Brownsville.

We know he was persuaded by the letters from Mayor Combe's citizens in Brownsville that the soldiers had shot up the town and there was a real possibility they might do it again. With this, his initial inclination to let the army figure out what happened went out the window. He bought into the guilty-soldiers theory and then had to hold on to it. And do something about it. To do nothing about something never described Theodore Roosevelt, and in Brownsville he may have pulled the trigger too fast. "He was the most impulsive human being I ever knew," recalled Isaac L. Hunt, a member of the New York State Assembly when the neophyte Roosevelt was elected to it.[41] Former secretary of the navy John D. Long, who worked with him fifteen or so years later, also said his Brownsville action was "an honest, if a hasty impulse."[42] The more mature Roosevelt had not outgrown this habit, and Howard University professor Kelly Miller, a Roosevelt contemporary, wrote, "He reaches conclusions and settles issues with a swiftness and self-satisfying certainty that startle the more cautious statesmen who rely upon the slower processes of reason and deliberation. He has diagnosed the case, prescribed the remedy, and cured, or killed, the patient before the ordinary physician has finished feeling the pulse."[43] Henry Adams, another Roosevelt contemporary, but also his friend who had a closer look at him, put it more simply. "He was pure act."[44] And once he decided on a course of action, he was unable to change his mind.[45]

Roosevelt also may have been motivated by his uncontrolled anger at Foraker, which in full fury blinded him to the soldiers and focused him only on the man defending them. Roosevelt could be that way. "No man in American public life has ever been able to find for his personal animosities the sanctions from on high which strengthens Mr. Roosevelt's hatreds with a sort of inspired and holy zeal. . . . He sees in those who differ from him not merely mistaken persons, but moral offenders. To disagree with the President is not a sign of folly; it is an evidence of wickedness. To oppose him is to sin against God. Against the sinner, therefore, the hand of punishment must be stretched out, and stretched out, not to correct, but to slay. The eagerness with which the President pursues his enemies would, in any one of less moral earnestness, appear as intolerable vindictiveness."[46]

The simplest explanation for an action is usually the closest to the truth. Speaking only generally and not of Brownsville, toward the end of his life Roosevelt wrote to poet Edwin Arlington Robinson, "There is not one among us in whom a devil does not dwell; at some time, on some point, that devil masters each of us."[47]

ON JANUARY 31, 1919, less than a month after Theodore Roosevelt died, Mallie Robinson of Cairo, Georgia, gave birth to a son. She

and her husband Jerry were, as were all other black sharecrop-
pers in the South, struggling to get by in what Du Bois described as
"[Booker T.] Washington's impoverished, agrarian South, with its
monocrop economy and biracial demographics."[48] They wanted to
give their new son something more than poverty and hopelessness.
They wanted to give him an example of diligence, hard work, and
decency to guide him as he grew to adulthood and made his own way
in the world. They wanted his name to inspire him. They gave him
the middle name of Roosevelt, for the man who died just before their
son was born. Their son became the man they wanted him to be,
and he changed America. His impact on us can be measured by the
respect America pays to him. Once every year he is remembered and
honored by every major league baseball player wearing his number
on his jersey. That is the only time the number can be worn by a ball-
player, because in 1997 Major League Baseball retired it for every
major league team. No player will wear it again because no player
can ever do what Jerry and Mallie Robinson's son did for baseball
and for America. The number *42* worn by Jackie Roosevelt Robinson honors him as his middle name honors Theodore Roosevelt.
For them the Brownsville Incident, something they lived through,
could not tarnish what they knew Theodore Roosevelt to be.

ROOSEVELT'S AUTOBIOGRAPHY CONTAINS NO mention of the Brownsville Incident. The inference often made is that he realized he was
wrong and wanted to hide his mistake.[49] But W. E. B. Du Bois shoveled dirt on Brownsville too and left it out of his autobiography.

The Brownsville Incident is an unhappy story primarily about
a battalion of black soldiers, a senator from Ohio, and a president.
All were hurt—badly hurt—by it. So was our country. The happier
story is what happened to the country in the years since. Not right
away perhaps, but over time, painfully, often accompanied by
further tragedy and heartache, change came. To paraphrase Judy
Crichton in *America 1900: The Turning Point*, the American ideal and
promise surely were not realized in the Brownsville Incident, but
they remained alive until they could be, and they remain alive today.

"History can never be truthfully presented if the presentation is purely emotional. It can never be truthfully or usefully presented unless profound research, painful, laborious, painstaking has preceded the presentation. No amount of self-communion and of pondering on the soul of mankind, no gorgeousness of literary imagery, can take the place of cool, serious, widely extended study. The vision of the great historian . . . must be sane, clear and based on full knowledge of the facts and of their interrelations. Otherwise we get merely a splendid bit of serious romance writing."

Theodore Roosevelt, "History as Literature,"
the annual address of the president of the
American Historical Association,
delivered at Boston, December 27, 1912,
The American Historical Association Review 18, no. 3
(April 1913)

WHAT IF . . . ?

A BIZARRE BROWNSVILLE CONFESSION, believable because of its source, was never heard by the Senate committee or anyone else since it was not disclosed for twenty years, and then it was ignored. It comes by way of two men rarely mentioned in any Theodore Roosevelt narrative.

JAMES AMOS'S FATHER WAS a black policeman in Washington, DC, with a beat in Rock Creek Park, where President Roosevelt enjoyed riding his horse. Roosevelt would occasionally stop to chat with the senior Mr. Amos, who felt at ease enough with Roosevelt to ask one day if there might be an opening for his son at the White House. Roosevelt told him to send the boy to see the steward.[1] The younger Mr. Amos, then in his twenties, was given charge of handling the exuberant Roosevelt children and did the job so well that eventually Roosevelt asked him to be his own valet. He would be with Roosevelt day and night, traveling with him, even carrying Roosevelt's daily pin-money allowance from Mrs. Roosevelt.

In his memoirs of his service to Roosevelt, Amos wrote of what he called the Brownsville Shooting Affair. He recalled "big Republican leaders" warning Roosevelt he was making a mistake, but Roosevelt told them "he knew he was right."[2] According to Amos, one Republican leader in particular, Senator Joseph Foraker, made Roosevelt "very angry."[3] Because Roosevelt allowed Amos to enter the room when he was "discussing the most important matters with public men," he happened to be in the "President's Library" when "Senator Foraker was in a high temper and he spoke his mind very freely and in angry words to the President."[4]

According to Amos, Roosevelt had good reason to know he was

right. His access to discussions between Roosevelt and others permitted him to be present when, "through an army officer—I think it was Lieutenant Fortescue, a relative—the President got some of the accused troopers to call at the White House. They tried to hold out at first but under Mr. Roosevelt's questioning *they broke down and admitted the guilt of their companies* [author's emphasis]. The President never used this confession to justify the discharges he ordered. The soldiers had not made it willingly, but only under the influence of his dominating personality, and while it completely satisfied his mind he never felt at liberty to use it, though he might have hushed up the whole controversy by doing so."[5]

THE LIEUTENANT FORTESCUE TO whom Amos referred was Granville Roland Fortescue, and he was indeed a Roosevelt relative as Amos said, though no one seemed to know just how. As a young adult, stories about his bad-boy escapades made news, and he was described as Roosevelt's relative, sometimes his distant relative, occasionally his nephew, even as related through Mrs. Roosevelt. He was in fact Roosevelt's first cousin, who grew up in New York close to where Roosevelt lived as a boy. Because of their eighteen-year age difference they were not close in those days, but they were good friends when Roosevelt was in the White House.

Fortescue's mother was Minnie O'Toole Fortescue. His father was Robert Roosevelt, Theodore's Uncle Rob, the family Democrat, who, with his wife and family, lived in a mirror-image townhouse next door to the one Theodore grew up in.

But the family next door was not the family Uncle Rob had with Minnie O'Toole Fortescue. She was his longtime mistress, with whom he had a second family, and Granville Roland Fortescue, known as "Roly," was one of their five children. There never was a Mr. Fortescue. Uncle Rob made him up to give Minnie cover for her (and his own) children. Like an espionage agent fleshing out a counterfeit identity by salting his life with enough detail to make it plausible, he decided that she needed a husband, so he made one up for her—a lawyer named Robert F. Fortescue.[6] A lawyer needs an office, so Uncle Rob showed one for "Mr. Fortescue" at 65 Wall

Street in the New York City directory. Mr. and Mrs. Fortescue and their children (Uncle Rob's children) lived for a while at 3004 West Thirty-Fourth Street, then they moved to 214 East Thirty-Third Street. Not a word of this was true.[7] And Granville Roland Fortescue may have had a grandly British name, but there was not a lick of the Brit in him. His mother, Minnie O'Toole, immigrated from Ireland, and his father, Robert Roosevelt, was of Dutch descent.

When Uncle Rob's wife died, he never did the right thing by Minnie; that is, he didn't marry her. But he adopted their children, and Roly, already Theodore's cousin by birth, became his adopted cousin as well.

WHEN ROLY WAS TWENTY-THREE he followed his cousin Theodore and joined the Rough Riders. Roosevelt mentioned Roly in his Cuban memoirs and acknowledged Roly's courage when he refused to leave the line after being wounded. But he said nothing about the family connection. After Cuba, Fortescue joined the regular army, was commissioned a lieutenant in the Twenty-Sixth Volunteer Infantry, and fought with it in the Philippines.[8] But he was not a particularly good officer and had trouble persuading superiors that he was entitled to promotion.[9] Nor was he a particularly good man or good friend to his fellow officers. In 1904, he was named as co-respondent in a divorce by one of his fellow officers, Captain Elmore Taggart. There was nasty publicity about that.[10] He constantly lost his temper and got into fights, and there was unfortunate publicity about those too. These are the stories that made their way into the newspapers and identified him as President Roosevelt's relative.[11]

Theodore Roosevelt was indifferent to all this. They stayed close, and he kept an eye on Roly's career.[12] More than once this was what saved Roly from army discipline. When he was not promoted, Roosevelt took a personal interest and demanded to know why. In 1904 he plucked Fortescue out of the battle-ready army (and the military and personal discipline it demanded) and made him his military aide. In the White House he was Roosevelt's sidekick, boxing partner, dressed-up dandy at state dinners and other official White House functions, and go-to man for those jobs requiring absolute loyalty and a closed mouth. In 1905 Roosevelt sent him to the Russo-Japanese War as America's military observer. For this type of work, Roosevelt trusted him, and it was during this time he mentioned Fortescue by name—but not a word about their being family—often in his letters to his family.[13]

By 1906 the army wanted to be rid of Lieutenant Fortescue, but discharging an officer the commander in chief had an interest in required a light touch. When news came that Fortescue had resigned from the army, the published reports attributed it to the Taggart divorce and his history of troublemaking. But some saw the hand of President Roosevelt gently pushing him out.[14] As a civilian, Fortescue and President Roosevelt had a cordial relationship and stayed in touch mostly by letters (with the greeting in Fortescue's letters, "My Dear Colonel" and not "Dear Mr. President," which even Roosevelt's son-in-law Nicholas Longworth felt obligated to use). Occasionally Fortescue dropped in to the White House. He was there on January 30, 1907, for example, right around the time of the Gridiron banquet.[15]

IS THERE ANYTHING TO Amos's recollection about the unidentified soldiers' confessions? There is no record of either Roosevelt or Fortescue ever mentioning them. On its face the story seems incredible; soldiers mysteriously separated from their comrades and secretly taken to the White House, where they apparently were not seen coming or going, grilled so effectively by President Roosevelt they broke from an otherwise-unshakeable conspiracy of silence and confessed their guilt in—in what exactly? The shooting or the cover-up? Amos did not say precisely. What may be least believable is that Roosevelt kept it a secret, even if he did it to protect the confessing soldiers from the retribution of the men they peached on, and would not tell even Senator Foraker to persuade him to call off the dogs. It really makes little sense.

But it's possible.

Maybe Roosevelt never mentioned it to anyone because he told the confessing soldiers he wouldn't, and that would be a "gentle-man's word" Roosevelt would feel most honor-bound to keep.

Maybe he did tell one man, Foraker, and maybe that's why Foraker was so angry that night Amos caught him "in a high temper." There is no reason to question anything about Amos except possibly his memory, and there is really no reason to mistrust that. He does get some of the facts wrong in his Brownsville story, but they are small potatoes, the kinds of things easily confused after a few years; they are nothing as significant as this. Fortescue, on the other hand, was entirely unsavory, coarse, and thoroughly untrustworthy. Still, this would be the kind of "off-the-books" job he would do for Roosevelt. As a former army officer he would be able to handle soldiers and transport them to Washington and back. He had the time to help Roosevelt because during the Brownsville Incident he was at loose ends and, with little to do, available for an escapade such as this. Unreliability may have been his leitmotif in life, but Theodore Roosevelt, his cousin, mentor, and protector, could expect him to do what he was told and keep his mouth closed afterward. And to keep him away from the subpoena power of the Senate, Roosevelt could arrange for him to leave the country and go to Cuba with a commission in the Cuban Rural Guard and train police there.[16]

The ethically impaired Fortescue is an easily impeachable source. But he did not tell the story of the confession. That was James Amos. He would have seen Fortescue often in the White House when he was a military aide and known who he was. Amos had access to Roosevelt unlike many others, was so ubiquitous he became like the wallpaper. It's easy to imagine Roosevelt not noticing him entering the room at the wrong time. After his White House years he became a detective with the William Burns Detective Agency in New York and developed investigative skills (and may, as the son of a policeman, have already had a few), including assessing the reliability of what he heard and saw. His loyalty to President Roosevelt is unquestioned, but is it likely he created a story false from beginning to end for him? Or, as a black man, he lied in order to implicate other black men? What is possible is that twenty years later he was confused about the officer who showed up ("*I think* it was Lieutenant Fortescue"). It might have been Major Augustus Blocksom, the Brownsville investigator who met with

Roosevelt in the White House on December 9, 1906, in the middle of the Senate debate to investigate the incident, just when Roosevelt might want to question some of the soldiers themselves.[17] But does this call into question the rest of what Amos said?

Subsequent examinations of the Brownsville Incident, other than Edward Wagenknecht's, make no reference to any of this. It is not surprising historians would not have consulted Amos or his book. He was not a historian, not a Roosevelt adviser, not a member of his inner circle. He was merely his valet, he is not widely known, and his memoirs are not widely read. And he may be wrong, not intentionally, but still wrong.

On the other hand, President Roosevelt's cousin and his valet may have helped him crack the Brownsville mystery.

ACKNOWLEDGMENTS

I begin by expressing my gratitude and thanks to the archivists and librarians who guided me through their collections. From tips about a folder, box of letters, newspaper clipping or keepsake that might prove worthwhile to helping me thread the microfilm through the microfilm reader (no two readers work the same way, and most do not work at all), their assistance was invaluable. One in particular stands out. It has been said that no narrative on Theodore Roosevelt could have been written over the past thirty or more years without Wallace Dailey, former curator and fierce protector of the Theodore Roosevelt Collection at Harvard University, and I believe it. Future Roosevelt scholars may never know how immeasurably more difficult their tasks will be because he now enjoys the retirement he so deserves.

Unexpectedly, one of the most nettlesome, frustrating, and time-consuming tasks I encountered was obtaining the book's illustrations. There are no words to describe the patience, helpfulness, and friendliness of people across the country who held my hand and soothed my frustrations as they guided me through their collections and secured what I needed. Special thanks to John Anderson of the Texas State Library and Archives in Austin, Kia Campbell of the Library of Congress in Washington, Jillian Carney of the Ohio History Connection in Columbus, curator Heather Cole of the Theodore Roosevelt Collection at Harvard, Ayla Jaramillo of the Brownsville Historical Association, and Nicole Joniec of the Library Company of Philadelphia. One man, the photographer of the photo of the elderly Dorsie Willis, has become a friend. Boyd Hagen, you deserve a medal.

At a conference in Chicago the exceptionally talented writer and historian David McCullough recommended I speak to the Roosevelt family genealogist Timothy Beard, who then was kind enough to see me at his home in the most beautiful town in Connecticut

409

and share with me what he knew. Archibald Grimké biographer Dickson D. Bruce cordially and candidly spoke to me about Grimké and about the research room at Howard University. His Honor Judge James Cissell of the Hamilton County (Ohio) Probate Court invited me to his chambers to talk about the Forakers and to help with the Foraker probate file, long filed away and forgotten. Professors Emeritus Lewis Gould in Austin and John M. Blum in New Haven shared their insights on Theodore Roosevelt and the world of politics in the early twentieth century. They could not have been more gracious and helpful to a stranger whose only endorsement was a love of history.

James and Marjie Pehta, wonderful friends from the Theodore Roosevelt Association, remembered so often to give me encouragement. Fred Bateman, Doug Callander, and Rabbi Tom Liebschutz read chapters and were unafraid to point out the many parts that needed improvement. Heather Pudvin talked to me about the book, brightened many a day, and, on my "Book Mondays" devoted only to Brownsville, nourished me with her delicious treats. She is a special friend to me and my family.

To very dear friend Joanne Harrison, who read drafts of more chapters than anyone other than my wife and my editors and always asked for another, I give uncommon thanks and my special love. Her telephone calls to "my favorite writer" made the writing itself easier.

My family in Florida, Lee and Claire Hager, did more than encourage, although they did that too. The three weeks of solitude and concentration at their place in North Carolina gave me what I needed to surge, and it was there the narrative turned the corner. Without it there would have been no book. My brother Fred Lembeck, the first of us to write a book, was an inspiration.

Agent Don Fehr and Prometheus Books editor in chief Steven L. Mitchell took a chance on me when others would not.

From syntax to spelling to style sheet, my editor Jennifer Peterson. What the practice of law lost when she turned to editing is my and the book's gain. As I told my friends Sam and Lisa Olens, who were our matchmakers, "Wow, what a find!" Thanks, Jennifer.

Together, Mariel Bard, my copyeditor at Prometheus Books, and I weathered "the perfect storm" as cascading events fell upon us during the final editing. Together we got through it.

To my children and grandchildren, from now on there will be no more Little League games not gone to, family get-togethers postponed, memories not made because there will be no more "Grandpa's writing his Brownsville book."

Fourteen years ago the love of my life, my wife, Emily, told me I had a book in me and I should write it. After a few years she convinced me to get started, cheered me on, supported me throughout and comforted me by never failing to say at those times I needed to hear it the most, "Oh, this part is *really* good." For twenty-seven years she has given me all the love any man would want and has inspired me to be my best in all I do. As she is in all she does. This book is Emily's from cover to cover; she is on every page. For whatever value the book has, the credit is hers, and I accept its failures and lapses as my own. As its writing ends I dedicate *Taking on Theodore Roosevelt* to her with all my love.

Harry Lembeck

NOTES

PROLOGUE

1. Julia Foraker, *I Would Live It Again* (New York: Arno, 1975), p. 190. His biographer, Everett Walters, described the house as a "great yellow brick mansion," four stories high. "Inside, a wide stairway led from the first floor to the spacious Louis XVI ballroom and drawing room on the second floor [where there also was] a library and a large dining room, both finished with Flemish art effects." Everett Walters, *Joseph Benson Foraker: An Uncompromising Republican* (Columbus: Ohio History Press, 1948), p. 250. Its value was about $150,000 (about $3.5 million today).

2. Louis R. Harlan, *Booker T. Washington: The Wizard of Tuskegee, 1901–1915* (New York: Oxford University Press, 1983), p. 323.

3. It was Roosevelt's idea that his powers were more than those precisely delineated in the Constitution. Unless an action was specifically prohibited by the Constitution or Congress, he could take it. "I declined to adopt the view that what was imperatively necessary for the nation could not be done by the President unless he could find some specific authorization to do it." H. W. Brands, *TR: The Last Romantic* (New York: Basic Books, 1997), p. 420. Brands has a particularly well-written explanation of Roosevelt's thinking at pp. 420–21.

4. Lewis L. Gould, *Theodore Roosevelt* (New York: Oxford University Press, 2012), p. 73.

5. Henry R. Luce, "The American Century," *Life*, February 17, 1941, p. 61.

6. Jim Crow was a derisively stereotypical Negro character created by actor Thomas Rice. Rice got the idea when he saw an old black man in the street singing a simple ditty about a man with the name, and in 1828, Rice appeared on stage as "Jim Crow." Before the end of the nineteenth century, the term described laws and habits in the southern United States that oppressed blacks and denied them their rights and often their lives. See "What Was Jim Crow?," Jim Crow Museum of Racist Memorabilia, http://www.ferris.edu/jimcrow/what.htm (accessed June 1, 2014).

7. Owen Wister, *Roosevelt: The Story of a Friendship, 1880–1919* (New York: Macmillan, 1930), p. 6.

8. Quoted in TR, *Champion of the Strenuous Life: A Photographic Biography of Theodore Roosevelt* (New York: Theodore Roosevelt Association, 1948), p. 109.

9. Siena Research Institute, "American Presidents: Greatest and Worst," July 1, 2010, http://www2.siena.edu/uploadedfiles/home/parents_and_community/community_page/sri/independent_research/Presidents%20Release_2010_final.pdf (accessed September 12, 2014).

CHAPTER ONE: THE IRON OF THE WOUND ENTERS THE SOUL ITSELF

1. Ralph Tyler, letter to George Myers, February 6, 1909, George Myers Papers, Ohio History Connection (hereafter cited as Myers Papers).

2. Ralph Tyler, letter to Joseph Foraker, September 15, 1906, Joseph Foraker Papers, Cincinnati History Library and Archives (hereafter cited as Foraker Papers).

3. Ralph Tyler, letter to Joseph Foraker, September 27, 1906, Foraker Papers.

4. Ralph Tyler, letter to Joseph Foraker, December 6, 1906, Foraker Papers.

5. George Myers, letter to Ralph Tyler, April 17, 1907, Myers Papers.

6. 42 Cong. Rec. 4723 (1908).

7. "Presidency Foraker's Aim in Brownsville Inquiry," *Washington Times*, March 16, 1907, in Newspaper Clippings, Archibald Grimké Papers, Moorland-Spingarn Research Center, Howard University (hereafter cited as Grimké Papers).

8. Joseph B. Foraker, *Notes of a Busy Life* (Cincinnati: Stewart & Kidd, 1917), 1:278. It did not hurt that Wilson was a Democrat, not a Civil War veteran, and a populist. In Foraker's eyes, these were three strikes against him.

9. Earl R. Beck, "The Political Career of Joseph Benson Foraker" (PhD thesis, Ohio State University, 1942), p. 13.

10. *Cincinnati Commercial Gazette*, May 7, 1886, cited in Everett Walters, *Joseph Benson Foraker: An Uncompromising Republican* (Columbus: Ohio History Press, 1948), p. 43.

11. Cited in Walters, *Joseph Benson Foraker*, p. 115. As late as 1905, Foraker was saying the same thing, though in softer tones. See John R. Neff, *Honoring the Civil War Dead: Commemoration and the Problem of Reconciliation* (Lawrence: University Press of Kansas, 2005), p. 219.

12. In 1905, prodded by President Theodore Roosevelt, Congress authorized the return of Southern battle flags, but even this did not affect those held by the states, since it was limited to flags "now in the custody of the War Department." H.R.J. Res. 217, 59th Cong., 33 Stat. 1284 (1905). Even Foraker agreed with this action. He could change with the times when he needed to.

13. Ronald Fernandez, *The Disenchanted Island: Puerto Rico and the United States in the Twentieth Century* (New York: Praeger, 1992), p. 15.

14. Joseph B. Foraker (speech before the Canton Board of Trade, Canton, OH, April 10, 1907). See also "Foraker Opens Presidential Campaign by Speech at Banquet," *San Francisco Call*, April 11, 1907, p. 3.

15. "Presidential Inaugural Weather," National Weather Service, last modified January 10, 2013, http://www.erh.noaa.gov/er/lwx/Historic_Events/Inauguration/Inauguration.html (accessed September 12, 2014).

16. "Taft Is Sworn in Senate Hall," *New York Times*, March 5, 1909, quoted in Edmund Morris, *Theodore Rex* (New York: Random House, 2001), p. 551.

17. He would have to take the oath a second time the next day. Chief Justice Melville Fuller, administering his sixth presidential oath of office, bungled it when he

asked the new president to "execute the Constitution" instead of "execute the office of the President," and Taft dutifully repeated the error. "Taft Swore to 'Execute the Constitution,' Slip by Chief Justice," *Washington Sunday Star*, March 7, 1909.

18. William Howard Taft, "Inaugural Address," March 4, 1909, available online by Gerhard Peters and John T. Woolley, *The American Presidency Project*, http://www.presidency.ucsb.edu/ws/?pid=25830 (accessed September 12, 2014).

19. "Mr. Taft on the South," *New York Times*, December 9, 1908.

20. See Willard B. Gatewood, *Aristocrats of Color: The Black Elite, 1880–1920* (Bloomington: Indiana University Press, 1990), p. 38. A fictional treatment of the black high society in the nation's capital was written by Edward Christopher Williams and serialized in the literary magazine *The Messenger* in the 1920s as *The Letters of Davy Carr*. In 2003, it was published as the novel *When Washington Was in Vogue: A Love Story (A Lost Novel of the Harlem Renaissance)* (New York: Amistad, 2003). It has been compared to F. Scott Fitzgerald's *The Great Gatsby* in the way it captures the spirit of the 1920s. Its love story, beautifully written, knows neither race nor the intrusion of white discrimination.

21. The author acknowledges that much of this history was obtained from the Metropolitan AME Church's website, and he gives full credit to it. See "Who We Are," Metropolitan AME Church, http://www.metropolitanamec.org/history. asp (accessed April 28, 2014), and "About Us," Metropolitan AME Church, http:// www.metropolitanamec.org/aboutus.asp (accessed April 28, 2014).

22. Dickson D. Bruce, *Archibald Grimké: Portrait of a Black Independent* (Baton Rouge: Louisiana State University Press, 1993), p. 48.

23. Booker T. Washington did more than bless it; he actively—and secretly—worked for its approval. Using former senator Henry W. Blair as his lobbyist (and paying him three hundred dollars), Washington supported the amendment until he heard that the more militant W. E. B. Du Bois and W. Monroe Trotter opposed it for the same reason as Grimké. The normally astute Washington quickly realized his mistake and directed Blair to continue his lobbying, but now in opposition. Louis R. Harlan and Raymond W. Smock, *Booker T. Washington in Perspective: Essays of Louis R. Harlan* (Jackson: University Press of Mississippi, 1988), p. 116; and Booker T. Washington, *The Booker T. Washington Papers* (Urbana: University of Illinois Press, 1984), 9:xxvi.

24. See Daniel W. Crofts, "The Warner-Foraker Amendment to the Hepburn Bill: Friend or Foe of Jim Crow," *Journal of Southern History* 39, no. 3 (August 1973): 341–58.

25. Bruce, *Archibald Grimké*, p. 159.

26. What Grimké and others said that night was reprinted in full in a pamphlet, *Presentation of Loving Cup to Hon. Joseph Benson Foraker, United States Senator, in Appreciation of His Service on Behalf of the Members of Companies A, B, and C, Twenty-Fifth Infantry, by a Committee of Colored Citizens: The Ceremony and Addresses, March 6th, 1909, at Metropolitan A.M.E. Church, Washington, D.C.* (Washington, DC: Murray Brothers, 1909). A copy is in the Cincinnati Public Library.

27. "A Noble Roman. Metropolitan Church Filled. Hundreds Turned Away. Attorney Scott's Great Speech," *Washington Bee*, March 13, 1909.

28. "Race Honors Foraker," *Washington Post*, March 7, 1909.

29. *Presentation of Loving Cup to Hon. Joseph Benson Foraker.*

30. Archibald Grimké, "Why Independents Should Support Roosevelt for President," folder 416, box 39-21, Manuscripts, Grimké Papers.

31. Archibald Grimké, "The President's Message," folder 406, box 39-21, Manuscripts, Grimké Papers.

32. Grimké's use of "hoisted with their own petard" illustrates his command of the language and how he could sift more than one meaning from his words. A petard was an explosive device used to blow a hole in a wall. To "hoist on one's own petard" means to be caught in one's own trap. Grimké is continuing the military metaphor and, at the same time, reminding his audience that Roosevelt's evidence for the dismissal of the soldiers blew a hole in Roosevelt's own arguments.

33. *Presentation of Loving Cup to Hon. Joseph Benson Foraker.*

34. Morris, *Theodore Rex*, p. 465.

35. Percy E. Murray, "Harry C. Smith–Joseph B. Foraker Alliance: Coalition Politics in Ohio," *Journal of Negro History* 68, no. 2 (1983): 171.

36. Ibid., p. 172.

37. Kenneth J. Cooper, *Black Opinion in Early African American Newspapers in Boston* (Boston: William Monroe Trotter Institute, 2007), http://cdn.umb.edu/images/trotter/trotterblackpresspaper.pdf (accessed September 12, 2014).

CHAPTER TWO: "THEY ARE SHOOTING US UP"

1. Summary Discharge or Mustering Out of Regiments or Companies: Message from the President of the United States . . . , S. Doc. No. 59-155, vol. 11, pt. 2 (2d sess. 1907) (hereafter cited as SD-2), p. 144 (affidavit of Dr. Frederick J. Combe).

2. In 1906 the army's tactical units of interest in this narrative, going from the smallest to the largest, were companies, battalions, and regiments. There were four companies in a battalion, three battalions in a regiment. The "Twenty-Fifth Infantry" is properly the "Twenty-Fifth Infantry Regiment," but it was common then and now to drop the word "regiment" when referring to it. Not the entire Twenty-Fifth Infantry was transferred to Fort Brown, only its "First Battalion." Of the First Battalion's four companies, Company A was detached from the battalion and sent to Wyoming on a temporary assignment. Companies B, C, and D went ahead of it, and the soldiers of these three companies are the men of the Brownsville Incident. Even though these three companies are less than a full battalion, they were referred to as the "Black Battalion." And even though they were only a fraction of the complete Twenty-Fifth Infantry, at the time and in this narrative, they also are referred to as the Twenty-Fifth Infantry.

3. *Affray at Brownsville, Tex.: Hearings Before the Comm. on Military Affairs . . . ,* S. Doc. No. 60-402, pt. 6 (1908) (hereafter cited as SMAC-3), pp. 2380, 2392 (testimony of Combe).

4. Henry F. Pringle (whose biography of Roosevelt received the Pulitzer Prize) had an uncharitable opinion of Brownsville in his 1939 biography of William Howard Taft. He called it "the dismal city on the Rio Grande." Henry F. Pringle, *The Life and Times of William Howard Taft: A Biography* (Hamden, CT: Archon Books, 1964), 1:324. A lifelong New Yorker, Pringle, superb writer and biographer that he was, may have thought the same of any city west of the Hudson River.

5. SMAC-3, p. 2380 (testimony of Combe). Historically, they were barely any blacks in Brownsville because it was on the Mexican border. Before the Civil War, slave owners would not bring them where escape to freedom was nothing more than a quick swim across the Rio Grande. SMAC-3, p. 2521 (testimony of William Kelly). After emancipation, blacks would from time to time come to Brownsville, but Mexicans worked for less money, so the blacks would leave. Ibid., p. 2527.

6. The influence of Mexico was so great as late as 1905 that Mexican currency was the "circulating medium" in Brownsville. Ibid.

7. The 1900 census shows that in Cameron County, Texas (Brownsville was its county seat), there were only 177 Negroes out of a total population of 16,095, or slightly more than 1 percent. US Census Office, *Census Reports: Twelfth Census of the United States* (1900), General Tables, table 29, p. 222. Compare this with two Mississippi counties, in which Negroes were more than 79 percent of the residents. In Texas itself, blacks were 20.4 percent of the population, twenty times greater than in Cameron County. See also Ann J. Lane, *The Brownsville Affair: National Crisis and Black Reaction* (Port Washington, NY: Kennikat, 1971), p. 8, regarding the "decidedly Spanish quality to the town."

8. See "Brownsville Not Southern," Topic of the Times, *New York Times*, September 12, 1906, which cited a statistical survey by the *Houston Post*. Of seven thousand residents, only twenty-five were Southern. There were more Jews (one hundred) and vastly more Northerners (thirteen hundred), and all identified groups were greatly outnumbered by five thousand Mexicans. No group was identified by the *Post* as "Westerners."

9. S. Doc. No. 60-402, pt. 5 (1908) (hereafter cited as SMAC-2), pp. 1003–1004 (testimony of Capt. Dana Willis Kilburn, Twenty-Sixth Infantry).

10. At the 1893 Columbian Exposition in Chicago, held to celebrate four hundred years since Columbus discovered the new world for Europeans, and only three years after the census announced that the western frontier was closed, Frederick Jackson Turner spoke on how the advance of Americans through the frontiers of the American West helped form the distinctive character of the American nation and the American people. American self-reliance, individualism, swift acceptance of change, even what would be mistakenly referred to as "Yankee" ingenuity, came from this movement of the country to its "Manifest Destiny." Frederick J. Turner, *The Frontier in American History* (New York: Henry Holt, 1921), http://xroads.virginia.edu/~hyper/turner.

11. SMAC-2, pp. 1003–1004 (testimony of Kilburn).

12. SMAC-2, pp. 1193–94 (testimony of William Jacob Rappe).

13. SMAC-2, p. 1004 (testimony of Kilburn).

14. SMAC-3, pp. 2380–81 (testimony of Combe).

15. SMAC-2, p. 1071 (testimony of Lt. Edwin Potter Thompson).

16. SMAC-3, p. 2383 (testimony of Combe); and SD-2, p. 150 (affidavit of Combe).

17. SMAC-3, p. 2383 (testimony of Combe).

18. SMAC-3, p. 2381 (testimony of Combe). Mrs. Evans was not the only one who may have been assaulted that day. President Roosevelt, while attending church where he lived in Oyster Bay, New York, was bedeviled by a Mrs. Eliza Case, also known as Mrs. L. Esac ("Case" spelled backward). The evidently disturbed lady tried to approach him three times during the service only to be restrained by the Secret Service. John Duffy, one of the church's ushers, also stepped in to keep her back, and his reward was to have her later seek a warrant for his arrest for assault. In those simpler times—even when the incident involved a president who came to the White House after the assassination of his predecessor—because Mrs. Case/Esac apparently intended no physical harm, at the end of the service and when the Roosevelts were safely away, she was let go. "Woman Tried to Halt President at Church," *New York Times*, August 12, 1906, p. 1.

19. SMAC-3, p. 2383 (testimony of Combe).

20. This imprecise reference by witnesses to compass points caused no end of confusion to investigators not from Brownsville and to the author of this book.

[Senator Lodge] Q: This was on Elizabeth street, and near the corner of Elizabeth and Thirteenth streets?

[Dr. Charles H. Thorn] A: Yes, sir. It is about 15 or 20 feet from the lamp-post.

[Senator Warner]: Calling those streets, as we have been pleased to do here, running north and south—those are not the exact points on the compass.

A: No, Sir.

Q: It would be a half a block north and a block west of your house, where you found him?

A: No; that would not be north; it would be almost due west of my house.

Senator Foraker: You are counting from the alley?

[Senator Warner]: Pardon, I was facing your house on the alley. Your house faces on Elizabeth Street?

A: Yes, Sir.

Q: That is my mistake, Doctor. It was half a block west, or north as we are calling it now?

A: North would be up—

Q: We are calling these streets north and south *[indicating on map]*.

The Chairman [Senator Warren]: Gentlemen, let me say now all these witnesses are confused about the points of the compass, and if you would call attention to that [north] arrow there [on the map] it might save some trouble. What we call north is really northwest, and every witness has to have it explained to him.

SMAC-3, pp. 2105–2106.

21. Ibid., p. 2382 (testimony of Combe).

22. Ibid., p. 2383.

23. S. Doc. No. 59-155, vol. 11, pt. 1 (2d sess. 1907) (hereafter cited as SD-1), p. 441 (testimony of George Rendall before Brownsville Citizens' Committee).

24. SMAC-3, p. 2033 (testimony of G. Rendall).

25. Partial synopsis of SD-1, p. 440 (testimony of G. Rendall); and SMAC-3, pp. 2037–40 (same).

26. SMAC-3, p. 2037 (testimony of G. Rendall).

27. SD-2, p. 19 (testimony of Elizabeth Rendall).

28. Ibid.

29. SD-2, pp. 15–16 (testimony of G. Rendall).

30. Ibid., p. 16.

31. SMAC-2, p. 938 (testimony of Pvt. Joseph Howard).

32. Ibid., p. 939.

33. Ibid.

34. Ibid., p. 940.

35. Ibid. (response of Howard to question by Sen. Foraker).

36. John D. Weaver, *The Brownsville Raid* (College Station: Texas A&M University Press, 1992), p. 36, citing Penrose's testimony at his court-martial, *Affray at Brownsville, Tex. . . . Proceedings of a General Court-Martial . . . in the Case of Maj. Charles W. Penrose, Twenty-Fifth United States Infantry*, S. Doc. No. 60-402 (1908), p. 1153 (testimony of Penrose). Hairston remembered it differently: "I don't know; I think somebody is firing on the quarters." S. Doc. No. 60-402, pt. 4 (1908) (hereafter cited as SMAC-1), p. 742 (testimony of Pvt. Charley Hairston).

37. SMAC-1, pp. 740–42 (testimony of Hairston).

38. Ibid., p. 286 (testimony of 1st Sgt. Mingo Sanders).

39. Ibid., pp. 1281, 1208–84 (testimony of Pvt. Edward Johnson).

40. Ibid., pp. 1281–91.

41. SD-2, p. 36; and SMAC-3, pp. 2790–803.

42. SD-2, pp. 50–52. See also SD-1, p. 449 (testimony of Herbert Elkins before Brownsville Citizens' Committee).

43. SMAC-2, pp. 2304–5 (testimony of Dr. Charles H. Thorn).

44. Dr. Thorn's narrative and his quotes can be found at SMAC-3, pp. 2101–11, and SD-2, pp. 54–57.

45. SD-2, p. 73 (testimony of S. C. Moore).

46. Mrs. Moore heard the same words, except when she repeated them, she

said nothing about "on a horse" and refused to speak the words "son of a bitch" because "it was not very nice to be repeated." Ibid., p. 73.

47. Ibid.

48. SMAC-3, p. 2930 (testimony of Hale Odin).

49. Ibid. (testimony of H. Odin); SD-2, p. 83 (testimony of Ethel Odin).

50. SMAC-3, p. 2932 (testimony of H. Odin).

51. SD-2, pp. 75–88.

52. Ibid., pp. 88–93.

53. Ibid., p. 57.

54. This was the second time Dominguez had been shot in the line of duty. He was the policeman wounded years earlier, as remembered by Dr. Thorn.

55. SMAC-3, p. 2484 (testimony of Joe Crixell). But Crixell looked to get a piece of the action another way. He helped a soldier and a former soldier open their own bar, just for the soldier business. He advanced the cost of the business license and sold them beer. Ibid., p. 2486.

56. Paulino Preciado, one of the four men in the Ruby, remembers Crixell using the word "Negroes" and not "niggers." Ibid., p. 2301 (testimony of Paulino Preciado). It is likely Crixell's memory is the better one. He was a crude man, and when he testified before the Senate Military Affairs Committee, he used "nigger" quite freely. If he felt no constraint in this formal setting, it is likely he felt none when shouting across to the Ruby Saloon. It is an open question just how poorly Preciado spoke English (he had lived in Brownsville for twenty years). His testimony before the Senate Military Affairs Committee and in statements for other investigations required the assistance of an interpreter. "Negroes" may have been an imprecise translation or a hesitancy by the interpreter to say "niggers."

57. Preciado was sure Natus's last words were in Spanish. Ibid. Weaver quotes Natus in Spanish, "Ay Dios!" Weaver, *Brownsville Raid*, p. 47.

58. SMAC-3, pp. 2380–85 (testimony of Combe).

59. SD-2, p. 30 (testimony of James P. McDonnel).

60. SD-2, p. 45 (testimony of Katie Leahy).

61. SD-2, p. 24 (testimony of Jose Martinez).

62. SD-2, p. 46 (testimony of Leahy).

63. SD-2, p. 53 (testimony of Herbert Elkins).

64. SD-2, pp. 42–43 (testimony of Ygnacio Garza).

CHAPTER THREE: A SPECIAL REQUEST

1. "News from Washington. Our Special Washington Dispatches," *New York Times*, May 27, 1863.

2. "Black Sailors and Soldiers in the War of 1812," The War of 1812, PBS, http://www.pbs.org/wned/war-of-1812/essays/black-soldier-and-sailors-war/ (accessed April 28, 2014).

3. "The Fifty-Fourth Massachusetts Infantry," United States Civil War, accessed April 29, 2014, http://www.us-civilwar.com/54th.htm.

4. Oswald Garrison Villard, "The Negro in the Regular Army," *Atlantic Monthly* 91 (1903): 721.

5. "Brief History," Buffalo Soldiers National Museum, http://buffalosoldiers-museum.com/cms/?cat=9 (accessed April 29, 2014).

6. "7th Squadron, 10th Cavalry Regiment," GlobalSecurity.org, http://www.globalsecurity.org/military/agency/army/7-10cav.htm (accessed April 29, 2014).

7. Arlen L. Fowler, *The Black Infantry in the West, 1869–1891* (Norman: University of Oklahoma Press, 1996), p. 38.

8. Capt. N. H. Davis, letter to the inspector general, October 1875, Letters Received, Inspector General's Office, file D 113, Records of the Office of the Inspector General (Army), National Archives; and Col. G. L. Andrews, letter to the assistant adjutant general, Department of Texas, October 4, 1875, Letters Sent, Fort Davis, Texas, Records of United States Army Continental Commands, 1821–1920, National Archives, cited in Fowler, *Black Infantry in the West*, p. 22.

9. Fowler, *Black Infantry*, pp. 48–51.

10. William McNeil, *Black Baseball out of Season: Pay for Play outside of the Negro Leagues* (Jefferson, NC: McFarland, 2007), p. 52.

11. John H. Nankivell and Quintard Taylor, *Buffalo Soldier Regiment: History of the Twenty-Fifth United States Infantry, 1869–1926* (Lincoln: University of Nebraska Press, 2001), pp. 167–68. Between 1914 and 1920, Bullet Joe Rogan played for the Twenty-Fifth Infantry. He left the army to play ball with the Kansas City Monarchs of the Negro League (on the recommendation of a young Casey Stengel) until 1938. Like Babe Ruth, he was a top pitcher and a fantastic hitter. His win-loss record was 116–50, and his lifetime ERA was 2.59. His career batting average was .338, and in 1922 he led the Negro National League with sixteen home runs. With him, the Monarchs won three consecutive pennants between 1923 and 1925 and won the Negro League World Series in 1924. He played in the first night baseball game in history on April 29, 1930. In 1998, he was inducted into the Baseball Hall of Fame in Cooperstown, New York. "Rogan, Bullet," National Baseball Hall of Fame and Museum, http://baseballhall.org/hof/rogan-bullet (accessed April 29, 2014).

12. George Armstrong Custer turned down lieutenant colonel's rank in the black Ninth Cavalry for that of only captain in the Seventh Cavalry. Fowler, *Black Infantry*, pp. 115–16, cited in *An Officer and a Gentleman: The Military Career of Lieutenant Henry O. Flipper*, by Lowell D. Black and Sara H. Black (Dayton, OH: Lora, 1985), p. 4.

13. Nankivell and Taylor, *Buffalo Soldier Regiment*, p. 9.

14. Cited in Ibid., p. 62.

15. "Sgt. Mingo Sanders," *Riders of the Bicycle Corps* (blog), http://bicyclecorps-riders.blogspot.com/2009/01/mingo-sanders.html (accessed April 29, 2014).

16. Nankivell and Taylor, *Buffalo Soldier Regiment*, pp. 60–62; and William Hangen and Terra Hangen, "Steel Steeds," *Military Officer*, February 2004. These

resources were used extensively by the author for the story of the biking Buffalo Soldiers.

17. H. W. Brands, *TR: The Last Romantic* (New York: Basic Books, 1997), pp. 325–26.

18. Nankivell and Taylor, *Buffalo Soldier Regiment*, p. 65.

19. Otto J. Lindenmeyer, *Black and Brave: The Black Soldier in America* (New York: McGraw-Hill, 1970), pp. 69–70.

20. Moss the Goat went to Cuba with it, where he would receive commendations for bravery. In the subsequent Philippine Insurrection, the army awarded him the Silver Star. He finished his career as a soldier commanding the 367th Infantry in World War I. On April 14, 1941, he was killed in a traffic accident in New York and is buried at Arlington National Cemetery. "Lt. James A. Moss," *Riders of the Bicycle Corps* (blog), http://bicyclecorpsriders.blogspot.com/2009/01/lt-james-moss.html (accessed April 29, 2014).

21. See Edmund Morris, *The Rise of Theodore Roosevelt* (New York: Coward, McCann & Geoghegan, 1979), p. 612, for a sample of these reactions.

22. It took more than a century. The accepted story is that he badgered the army to get the Rough Riders, and indeed all other soldiers, out of Cuba quickly when the war ended. Too many of them were coming down with malaria and other tropical diseases and dying. Regular army officers in Cuba were reluctant to force the issue, fearing its effect on their military careers. Roosevelt, his time in the army over as soon as the Rough Riders would be disbanded, had no such qualms. Army brass was so irritated at Roosevelt, they slow-walked and then quietly killed the recommendation that he get the Medal of Honor.

23. Secretary of the Navy John D. Long, whose absence allowed Roosevelt to issue prewar orders to the navy, wrote in his diary, "He thinks he is following his highest ideal, whereas, in fact, as without exception every one of his friends advises him, he is acting like a fool. And yet, how absurd all this will sound if, by some turn of fortune, he should accomplish some great thing and strike a very high mark." Virgil C. Jones, *Roosevelt's Rough Riders* (Garden City, NY: Doubleday, 1971), p. 19.

24. According to the report of Captain Henry Rose Loughborough, Company B, Twenty-Fifth Infantry. T. G. Steward, *The Colored Regulars in the United States Army* (New York: Arno, 1969), p. 188.

25. "The Battles at El Caney & San Juan Hill," Home of Heroes, http://www.homeofheroes.com/wallofhonor/spanish_am/10_sanjuan.html (accessed April 30, 2014,). See also A. C. M. Azoy, *Charge! The Story of the Battle of San Juan Hill* (New York: Longmans, Green, 1961), pp. 34–35.

26. The unyielding officer was a white captain with the Ninth Cavalry, a Buffalo Soldier regiment. Azoy, *Charge!*, p. 136.

27. The author first saw this original photo at the annual meeting of the Theodore Roosevelt Association in Tampa, Florida, in October 2009 in a presentation by Prof. Quintard Taylor, University of Washington.

28. Steward, *Colored Regulars in the United States Army*, p. 132.

29. The pluckiness of the men of the Twenty-Fifth Infantry that day is shown in a story told by General Lawton. The morning after the fight for El Caney, he and another officer were watching soldiers marching past them as they redeployed for what was expected to be the advance on Santiago. Just before dawn, the men of the Twenty-Fifth Infantry came along, and one in particular, a tall corporal, was laughing and talking as he moved passed. With him was an injured soldier walking with a limp. The talkative corporal was carrying his own weapon, ammunition, blanket, and haversack, as well as those of the injured man. Lugging all of this weight, the corporal somehow found room to carry his company's mascot dog.

"Here, corporal," the other officer yelled out, "didn't you march all last night?"

"Yes, sir."

"And didn't you fight all day?"

"Sure, sir."

"And haven't you been marching since 10 o'clock tonight?"

"Yes, sir."

"Well then, what in thunder are you carrying that dog for?"

"Why, the dog is tired," the corporal answered.

Nankivell and Taylor, *Buffalo Soldier Regiment*, p. 83.

30. General Orders No. 19, Headquarters of the Twenty-Fifth Infantry, near Santiago de Cuba, August 11, 1898, folder 6, box 6, William Monroe Trotter/ *Guardian of Boston* Collection, Howard Gotlieb Archival Research Center, Boston University.

31. Lindenmeyer, *Black and Brave*, p. 70.

32. Ibid., p. 71.

33. Ibid.

34. Sanders mentions it in his reenlistment application affidavit after the Brownsville Incident. "Mingo Sanders out Now, Fed Roosevelt's Men," *New York Times*, December 22, 1906. See also Mary Church Terrell, "A Sketch of Mingo Sanders," *Voice of the Negro*, March 1907; and Affidavit J to Constitution League Report, *Brownsville Affray, Report of Secretary of War, and Additional Testimony*, S. Doc. No. 59-155, pt. 1 (1907) (hereafter cited as SD-1), p. 227, which says, "That upon the Twenty-Fifth day of June, about 9 or 10 miles from Siboney, in Cuba, Theodore Roosevelt came to him [Mingo Sanders], and at his [Roosevelt's] special request, his company shared their supply of hard-tack with his command."

35. His uneasiness was well-founded. Japan took its time but by the 1930s was well on its way to creating a Japanese empire in the Far East. Japan shared Roosevelt's foresight about the Philippines and coveted the islands for itself. While Pearl Harbor still was in flames, its forces began their assault on the Philippines. See also Philip J. McFarland, *Mark Twain and the Colonel: Samuel L. Clemens, Theodore Roosevelt, and the Arrival of a New Century* (Lanham, MD: Rowman & Littlefield, 2012), p. 129.

36. Nankivell and Taylor, *Buffalo Soldier Regiment*, pp. 90, 100.

37. Ibid., p. 101.

38. 1st Lt. William T. Schenck, letter to the *Denver Daily News*, undated, cited in ibid., p. 103.

39. SD-1, p. 227 (affidavit of Sanders); "Mingo Sanders, out Now, Fed Roosevelt's Men," *New York Times*, December 22, 1906.

40. Cited in Nankivell and Taylor, *Buffalo Soldier Regiment*, p. 115.

41. Roosevelt was a founder of the New York Zoological Society, the predecessor to the Bronx Zoo, where nascent herds of buffalo were bred and protected. Brinkley points out one of his reasons for forming the zoo was to have a place to put the buffalo. Noting Roosevelt's "enviable record as a promoter of measures for the protection of wildlife," the society mentioned his prohibition of hunting or trapping on Fort Niobrara. "Ex-President Roosevelt's Record in Wild-Life Preservation," *New York Zoological Society Bulletin*, nos. 30–36 (July 1908–October 1909): 510.

42. Brinkley's book is thorough and beautifully written and a "must-read" for anyone interested in the history of the American environmental movement.

43. Nankivell and Taylor, *Buffalo Soldier Regiment*, p. 119. Company A earlier had been sent to Wyoming to shepherd Indians onto the Washakie Reservation. See also SD-1, p. 309. It would never get to Brownsville. On September 7, 1906, it joined its sister companies at Fort Reno, Oklahoma.

44. Ulysses Simpson Grant, *Personal Memoirs of U.S. Grant* (New York: Dover, 1995), p. 29.

45. "Juneteenth," Texas State Library and Archives Commission, last modified January 15, 2013, https://www.tsl.state.tx.us/ref/abouttx/juneteenth.html (accessed September 18, 2014).

46. US War Department, Office of the Adjutant General, Military Secretary's Office, *Brownsville File*, July 7, 1906.

47. In his testimony before the Senate Military Affairs Committee, Dr. Edger thought Negro soldiers already had been there four times (which would make the Twenty-Fifth Infantry's turn the fifth time). *Affray at Brownsville, Tex.: Hearings Before the Committee on Military Affairs . . .* , S. Doc. No. 60-402 (1908), pt. 5, p. 1109. A sergeant in the departing Twenty-Sixth Infantry testified that an unidentified Brownsville resident told him it would be the fourth time. Ibid., pt. 6, p. 2949.

48. Wreford's letter is excerpted in Ann J. Lane, *The Brownsville Affair: National Crisis and Black Reaction* (Port Washington, NY: Kennikat, 1971), p. 14.

49. Benjamin J. Edger, letter to Joseph B. Foraker, February 16, 1907, box 63, Joseph Foraker Papers, Cincinnati History Library and Archives.

50. S. Doc. No. 60-402, pt. 4, pp. 1945–46.

51. Adair statement, Lovering, Report, SD-1, p. 479.

52. John D. Weaver, *The Brownsville Raid* (College Station: Texas A&M University Press, 1992), pp. 27–28.

CHAPTER FOUR: ON THE GROUND

1. *Affray at Brownsville, Tex.: Hearings Before the Comm. on Military Affairs . . .*, S. Doc. No. 60-402, pt. 5 (1908) (hereafter cited as SMAC-2), p. 1929 (testimony of Maj. Charles Penrose).

2. Ibid., p. 1925.

3. Ibid., p. 1926. The transcript misspells the sentry's name as "Herston."

4. Ibid., p. 1691.

5. Ibid., pp. 1927, 1929.

6. S. Doc. No. 60-402, pt. 6 (1908) (hereafter cited as SMAC-3), p. 2598 (testimony of Maj. Augustus Blocksom).

7. SMAC-2, p. 1930 (testimony of Penrose).

8. SMAC-3, p. 2384 (testimony of Dr. Frederick J. Combe).

9. Ibid., p. 2385.

10. Ibid.

11. Ibid., p. 2386.

12. SMAC-2, p. 1829 (testimony of Capt. Samuel Lyon).

13. SMAC-3, p. 2387 (testimony of Penrose).

14. SMAC-2, p. 2388 (testimony of Combe).

15. Ibid., p. 2389.

16. Ibid.

17. Ibid.

18. There was a street lamp on the southwest corner of Washington and Thirteenth Streets. Depending on where exactly Combe was standing, it was between 150 and 175 feet away. There was another street lamp on the southwest corner of Elizabeth and Thirteenth Streets, which would have been a little farther away. See map of Brownsville prepared for the Senate Committee on Military Affairs, in Summary Discharge or Mustering Out of Regiments or Companies: Message from the President of the United States . . . , S. Doc. No. 59-155, vol. 11 (2d sess. 1907).

19. SMAC-3, p. 2387 (testimony of Combe).

20. Ibid., pp. 2391, 2394.

21. Another was the dairyman Albert Billingsley, characterized by John Weaver as "loud talking [and] quick tempered." John D. Weaver, *The Brownsville Raid* (College Station: Texas A&M University Press, 1992), p. 172. He had been vocally upset since the alleged assault on Mrs. Evans, and the shooting made him even more so. In his own testimony before the Senate Committee on Military Affairs, Billingsley acknowledged he had been reprimanded and warned to stay quiet by Mayor Combe but quickly denied the allegation he wanted to attack the fort or any such action. He called the idea "foolishness." SMAC-3, p. 2479. He even claimed to welcome the black soldiers of the Twenty-Fifth Infantry when he heard they were coming. They would be good for business since "they were good milk customers" and did not spend their money in saloons. Ibid., p. 2482. Of course,

one reason for this might have been the saloons were segregated and they were not allowed in.

22. SMAC-3, p. 2392 (testimony of Combe).

23. SMAC-2, p. 1935 (testimony of Rentfro Creager). See also Weaver, *Brownsville Raid*, p. 86.

24. SMAC-3, p. 2340 (testimony of Combe).

25. Ibid., p. 2341.

26. Creager was a poor choice for Penrose to seek advice from about an impartial investigation, regardless of what Creager may have learned when he got back to Brownsville that morning. The day before, Creager acted as Lon Evans's lawyer and accompanied him to the meeting with Mayor Crowe and Penrose after Mrs. Evans accused a soldier of assault. Fred Tate, the customs official who used a pistol to crack the head of Private James Newton for not walking around Mrs. Tate on the sidewalk, also consulted with Creager. SMAC-3, p. 2840 (testimony of Rentfro B. Creager). As US Commissioner, Creager was a federal official appointed to the position by the US District Court, and the day after the shooting the potential involvement of the court could not be excluded. Penrose might not have realized the potential conflict of interest; Creager should have. Any presumption of impartiality on Creager's part was by the morning of August 14 a will-o'-the-wisp.

27. SMAC-3, p. 2392 (testimony of Combe).

28. Ibid.

29. SMAC-2, p. 1932 (testimony of Penrose).

30. Ibid., p. 1777 (testimony of Capt. Edgar Macklin).

31. Ibid., pp. 1777, 1770–71.

32. Ibid., p. 1778.

33. Ibid., p. 1933 (testimony of Penrose).

34. Ibid., pp. 1803, 1804 (testimony of Macklin).

35. Creager testified that Connor did as instructed, then turned everything over to the Mayor, who was keeping them at city hall.

36. SMAC-3, p. 2390 (testimony of Combe).

37. Ibid., p. 2387.

38. Ibid., p. 2386.

39. Ibid., p. 2393.

40. SMAC-2, pp. 2529–30, 2543, 2549 (testimony of William Kelly).

41. Ibid., p. 2525.

42. Ibid., p. 2520.

43. Ibid., p. 2530.

44. Ibid., p. 2525.

45. Ibid., p. 2558.

46. Ibid., p. 2531.

47. Ibid., pp. 2522, 2518, 2530–31, 3008, 3009.

48. SMAC-3, p. 2394 (testimony of Combe).

49. Ibid., p. 2531 (testimony of Kelly). Combe's recollection of Penrose's words was

even more damning: "I would give my right arm to find out the guilty parties." According to Combe, the army officer had tears in his eyes. Ibid., p. 2395 (testimony of Combe).

50. Maj. Charles Penrose, telegram to Military Secretary, Department of Texas, August 14, 1906, SMAC-2, p. 1938.

51. SMAC-3, p. 2395 (testimony of Combe).

52. The transcript of the testimony is at *Brownsville Affray, Report of Secretary of War, and Additional Testimony*, S. Doc. No. 59-155, pt. 1 (1907) (hereafter cited as SD-1), pp. 440–53, and additional statements given to explain incidents that led up to the shooting are at SD-1, pp. 454–55.

53. William Howard Taft, letter to Charles Culberson, June 4, 1906, SD-1, p. 301. It is not clear whether Colonel Hoyt, who a month earlier had made his request to the War Department that his regiment not be sent to Texas, was aware that Taft already had turned down Culberson's same request.

54. "Charles Culberson," GovTrack, http://www.govtrack.us/congress/members/charles_culberson/403074 (accessed May 6, 2014).

55. "Bailey, Joseph Weldon," *The Handbook of Texas Online*, http://www.tshaonline.org/handbook/online/articles/fba10 (accessed May 6, 2014).

56. "Senator Bailey," *New York Times*, July 2, 1902.

57. Charles Culberson and Joseph Bailey, telegram to William Howard Taft, August 15, 1906, SD-1, p. 19. Taft was vacationing, as he was every summer, at his summer retreat, what some years later the *New Yorker* magazine would call his "unpretentious estate" in Murray Bay, Quebec. "Mr. Taft's Murray Bay," The Talk of the Town, *New Yorker*, September 4, 1926, p. 7. His time at Murray Bay was so important to Taft that three years later, when he would be president only three months and by custom forced to remain in the United States, he would speculate on the consequences of not winning reelection in 1912. "One of the consolations would be that I could go to Murray Bay in the summers thereafter." William Howard Taft, letter to Charles P. Taft, June 28, 1909, quoted in *The Life and Times of William Howard Taft: A Biography*, by Henry F. Pringle (Hamden, CT: Archon Books, 1964), 1:123.

58. Theodore Roosevelt, *The Rough Riders: An Autobiography* (New York: Library of America, 2004), p. 329.

59. Roosevelt's orders to Taft and Bacon: see Henry F. Pringle, *Theodore Roosevelt: A Biography* (New York: Harcourt, Brace, 1984), p. 210; and Theodore Roosevelt, telegrams to Robert Bacon, September 12 and 13, 1906, in *The Letters of Theodore Roosevelt*, ed. Elting E. Morison, vol. 5, *The Big Stick: 1907–1909* (Cambridge, MA: Harvard University Press, 1952), pp. 408–409 and p. 409, respectively. Theodore Roosevelt, letter to Henry White, August 14, 1906, in Morison, *Letters of Theodore Roosevelt*, pp. 356–59; Theodore Roosevelt, letter to Joseph Cannon, August 15, 1906, in Morison, *Letters of Theodore Roosevelt*, pp. 359–61; Theodore Roosevelt, letter to Henry Cabot Lodge, August 15, 1906, in Morison, *Letters of Theodore Roosevelt*, p. 361; Theodore Roosevelt, letter to Charles Joseph Bonaparte, August 16, 1906, in Morison, *Letters of Theodore Roosevelt*, pp. 361–62.

60. SD-1, pp. 20–21.

61. There was no such testimony.

62. William Loeb, telegram to Gen. Fred C. Ainsworth, August 18, 1906, SD-1, p. 25. Gen. Fred C. Ainsworth, telegrams to Charles Culberson and Joseph Bailey, August 18, 1906, SD-1, p. 25.

63. Maj. Charles Penrose, telegram to the Department of Texas, August 14, 1906, SMAC-2, p. 1938.

64. Gen. Fred C. Ainsworth, telegram to Maj. Charles Penrose, August 15, 1906, SD-1, p. 19; and Maj. Charles Penrose, telegram to Gen. Fred C. Ainsworth, August 16, 1906, SD-1, p. 22.

65. Gen. Fred C. Ainsworth, telegram to William Loeb, August 17, 1906, SD-1, p. 23.

66. Charles Culberson, telegram to William Howard Taft, August 17, 1906, SD-1, p. 23.

67. "Fred Crayton Ainsworth," Arlington National Cemetery, http://www.arlingtoncemetery.net/fcains.htm (accessed May 7, 2014).

68. Gen. W. S. McCaskey, telegram to Gen. Fred C. Ainsworth, August 17, 1906, SD-1, p. 24. The next day, McCaskey again misconstrued Penrose's words. In the answer Penrose sent "at once," he reported, "Guard of one-third of garrison, one company, constantly on duty." McCaskey chose to report this as "One-third garrison guarding other two-thirds." Gen. W. S. McCaskey, telegram to Gen. Fred C. Ainsworth, August 18, 1906, SD-1, p. 22. Ainsworth forwarded this to Loeb— and by so doing to the president—in Oyster Bay.

69. Gen. Fred C. Ainsworth, telegram to William Loeb, August 18, 1906, SD-1, p. 24.

70. Telegram to the "Hon. Theodore Roosevelt, President of the United States," signed by John Bartlett, County Judge, and eighteen others, August 18, 1906, appearing in ibid., p. 26.

71. Charles Culberson, telegram to Gen. Fred C. Ainsworth, August 19, 1906, SD-1, p. 27; Gen. Fred C. Ainsworth, telegram to Maj. Charles Penrose, August 19, 1906, SD-1, p. 27; Maj. Charles Penrose, telegram to Gen. Fred C. Ainsworth (mistakenly identified as "Secretary of War"), August 19, 1906, SD-1, p. 28.

72. Gen. Fred C. Ainsworth, telegram to Maj. Augustus Blocksom, August 20, 1906, SD-1, p. 33; Maj. Augustus Blocksom, telegram to Gen. Fred C. Ainsworth, August 20, 1906, SD-1, p. 34.

73. "Texans Arm for Troops," *New York Times*, August 17, 1906.

74. See Gen. Fred C. Ainsworth, telegram to William Loeb, August 19, 1906, SD-1, p. 26.

75. "Mayor Saved Brownsville," *New York Times*, March 25, 1907.

76. William Loeb, telegram to Gen. Fred C. Ainsworth, August 20, 1906, SD-1, p. 34.

77. In World War I, Theodore Roosevelt's oldest son, Theodore Jr., served in

France with the Twenty-Sixth Infantry. At the beginning of World War II, he was its commanding officer.

78. Maj. Charles Penrose, telegram to adjutant general, Camp Mabry, August 21, 1906, SD-1, p. 40; and Gen. W. S. McCaskey, telegram to Gen. Fred C. Ainsworth, August 21, 1906, SD-1, p. 40.

79. William Loeb, telegram to Gen. Fred C. Ainsworth, August 21, 1906, SD-1, p. 38.

80. SMAC-3, p. 2545 (testimony of Combe).

81. Ibid., p. 2431.

82. Weaver, *Brownsville Raid*, p. 80.

83. SMAC-3, p. 3239 (testimony of John Kleiber).

84. SMAC-3, p. 2397 (testimony of Combe).

85. SMAC-3, pp. 2532, 2544 (testimony of Kelly).

86. SMAC-3, p. 2514 (testimony of Joe Crixell).

87. S. Doc. No. 60-402, pt. 4 (1908) (hereafter cited as SMAC-1), pp. 857–58 (testimony of Cpl. Willie Miller).

88. See Weaver, *Brownsville Raid*, pp. 254–58 and citations therein.

89. Quoted in Ann J. Lane, *The Brownsville Affair: National Crisis and Black Reaction* (Port Washington, NY: Kennikat, 1971), p. 20.

90. Later investigations of the shootings faced the puzzle of why some houses and buildings seemed targeted and others not. Most mystifying was the fusillade into the Starck house. It was not near the fort, and it was not along the path of shooting that started at the garrison wall and went to the Tillman and Crixell bars. The Starcks, especially Mr. Starck, had no run-in, problem, or difficulty with anyone, certainly not with the soldiers. When asked if they had an answer, both Starcks suggested their home might have been mistaken for that of Fred Tate, who lived next door and worked together with Fred Starck as a customs inspector. It was Tate who had confiscated Private Adair's pen and pistol-whipped Private Newton.

91. SMAC-3, p. 3112 (testimony of Penrose).

92. Maj. Charles Penrose, telegram to the adjutant general, Department of Texas; Gen. W. S. McCaskey, telegram to Gen. Fred C. Ainsworth, August 23, 1906, SD-1, p. 46; Capt. Samuel Lyon, telegram to the military secretary, Department of Texas, August 23, 1906, SD-1, p. 46.

93. Gen. Fred C. Ainsworth, telegram to Maj. Charles Penrose, August 24, 1906, SD-1, p. 47.

94. Ibid.

95. SMAC-3, p. 2397 (testimony of Combe).

96. Not knowing of Judge Welch's decision, Roosevelt said the battalion would go to Fort Reno, Oklahoma, but drop off the arrested men in San Antonio, Texas, where they would be within the reach of Texas authorities if he ever decided to turn them over.

CHAPTER 5: A MORE AGGRESSIVE ATTITUDE

1. Maj. Charles Penrose, telegram to Gen. Fred C. Ainsworth, August 24, 1906, in *Summary Discharge or Mustering Out of Regiments or Companies: Message from the President of the United States . . .* , S. Doc. No. 59-155, vol. 11, pt. 1 (2d sess. 1907) (hereafter cited as SD-1), p. 47.

2. *Affray at Brownsville, Tex.: Hearings Before the Comm. on Military Affairs . . .* , S. Doc. No. 60-402, pt. 6 (1908) (hereafter cited as SMAC-3), pp. 2404–2405 (testimony of Dr. Frederick J. Combe).

3. John D. Weaver, *The Brownsville Raid* (College Station: Texas A&M University Press, 1992), p. 87.

4. SMAC-3, p. 2596 (testimony of Maj. Augustus Blocksom).

5. Weaver, *Brownsville Raid*, p. 87.

6. Maj. Charles Penrose, telegram to the military secretary, Department of Texas, August 14, 1906, in S. Doc. No. 60-402, pt. 5 (1908) (hereafter cited as SMAC-2), p. 1938.

7. Four investigations were by local or state people or agencies, seven were by the army, three by federal agencies (one of which was jointly with the army), one by a private investigator hired by Senator Joseph Foraker, another (by this same investigator) retained for the government by Secretary of War William H. Taft, one by a court of inquiry, one informally by some of the soldiers, one by a civil rights organization, and the mammoth year-and-a-half-long hearing by the Senate Military Affairs Committee.

8. Maj. Charles Penrose, Report, August 15, 1906, SD-1, pp. 31, 32.

9. Maj. Charles Penrose, telegram to Gen. Fred C. Ainsworth, August 14, 1906, in S. Doc. No. 59-155, vol. 11, pt. 2 (2d sess. 1907) (hereafter cited as SD-2), p. 1345.

10. Maj. Charles Penrose, written report to Gen. Fred C. Ainsworth, August 15, 1906, SD-1, p. 30.

11. SMAC-2, p. 1803 (testimony of Capt. Edgar Macklin); SMAC-2, p. 1963 (testimony of Maj. Charles Penrose).

12. SMAC-3, p. 2584 (testimony of Macklin).

13. "Augustus P. Blocksom," Arlington National Cemetery, http://www.arlingtoncemetery.net/apblocksom.htm (accessed May 9, 2014); "Biography: Brig. Gen. Augustus P. Blocksom," US Army Pacific, http://www.usarpac.army.mil/history2/cg_blocksom.asp (accessed May 9, 2014).

14. SMAC-3, p. 2583 (testimony of Blocksom).

15. Ibid., p. 2597.

16. Ibid., pp. 2584, 2597.

17. Gen. Fred C. Ainsworth, telegram to Gen. Augustus Blocksom, August 20, 1906, SD-1, p. 33.

18. Gen. Augustus Blocksom, telegram to Gen Fred C. Ainsworth, August 20, 1906, SD-1, p. 34.

19. Blocksom Report, SD-1, p. 426.

20. See SD-1, p. 515 (affidavit of Pvt. Thomas Jefferson, Company C); and SMAC-1, p. 610 (testimony of Sgt. Francois L. Oltmans). And so did civilians, including Mayor Combe (SMAC-3, p. 2383). And George W. Randall (SD-1, p. 440), Jose Martinez (SD-1, p. 443), and A. Baker (SD-1, p. 445), all three of whom said so to the Citizens' Committee the morning after the shooting.

21. SMAC-3, p. 2459 (testimony of Ambrose Littlefield, former deputy sheriff of Cameron County).

22. SMAC-1, pp. 431–32 (testimony of Quartermaster Sgt. George McMurray); see also Philip J. McFarland, *Mark Twain and the Colonel: Samuel L. Clemens, Theodore Roosevelt, and the Arrival of a New Century* (Lanham, MD: Rowman & Littlefield, 2012), p. 331.

23. Blocksom Report, SD-1, p. 439 (affidavit of Pvt. Joseph Howard). See also SMAC-3, p. 2606 (testimony of Blocksom).

24. SMAC-3, p. 2642 (testimony of Blocksom).

25. See Sanders's service record given to the Senate Military Affairs Committee by the War Department and his responses to questions from Senator Foraker before the committee, SMAC-1, p. 285.

26. SMAC-3, p. 2633 (testimony of Blocksom).

27. Blocksom Report, SD-1, p. 427.

28. See experiments of Lieutenant H. A. Wiegenstein at Fort McIntosh, Texas, cited in Weaver, *Brownsville Raid*, pp. 151–52.

29. SMAC-3, p. 2644 (testimony of Blocksom).

30. Blocksom Report, SD-1, p. 428.

31. SMAC-3, p. 2642 (testimony of Blocksom).

32. Ibid., pp. 2641–42.

33. Ibid., p. 2629.

34. Blocksom Report, SD-1, p. 429.

35. Ibid., pp. 428–29.

36. Ibid., p. 430.

37. Gen. Fred C. Ainsworth, letter to William Howard Taft, August 28, 1906, SD-1, p. 59.

38. Gen. Augustus Blocksom, telegram to Gen. Fred C. Ainsworth, September 2, 1906, SD-1, p. 93; A. C. Hamilton, telegram to Attorney General William H. Moody, September 2, 1906, SD-1, p. 94.

39. Stanley Welch, telegram to Lt. Archer, September 27, 1906, SD-1, pp. 107–108.

40. William Loeb, letter to Gen. Fred C. Ainsworth, August 31, 1906, SD-1, p. 91; Martha A. Sandweiss, *Passing Strange: A Gilded Age Tale of Love and Deception across the Color Line* (New York: Penguin Press, 2009), p. 258.

41. Gen. Fred C. Ainsworth, letter to William Loeb, August 27, 1906, SD-1, p. 57; William Loeb, telegram to Gen. Fred C. Ainsworth, August 28, 1906, SD-1, p. 58. Loeb told Ainsworth, "[The President] thinks the action taken was excellent."

42. Gen. W. S. McCaskey, endorsement to Blocksom's report to Gen. Fred C. Ainsworth, September 4, 1906, SD-1, p. 65.

43. Gen. Fred C. Ainsworth, letter to William Loeb, September 12, 1906, SD-1, p. 97.

44. William Loeb, telegram to Gen. Fred C. Ainsworth, August 27, 1906, SD-1, p. 58.

45. Military secretary, Southwestern Division, written orders to Lovering, September 24, 1906, SD-1, p. 110.

46. Lovering Report, SD-1, p. 111.

47. Gen. Augustus Blocksom, statement to LTC Leonard A. Lovering, SD-1, p. 177.

48. Then again, this was not why Lovering was sent to Fort Reno. Before the Court of Inquiry a few years later, there was testimony that "In September, 1906, Lieut. Col. Lovering, inspector general, was sent to Fort Reno to investigate certain collateral matters. . . . [His] investigation was not calculated to determine the names of the participants in the raiding party." Report of the Proceedings of the Court of Inquiry Relative to the Shooting Affray at Brownsville, Tex. . . . , Senate Document No. 60-402 (1911), vols. 4–6 (hereafter cited as CI-2), pp. 1603–1604 (testimony of Capt. Charles R. Howland).

49. Gen. W. S. McCaskey, telegram to Gen. Fred C. Ainsworth, September 21, 1906, SD-1, p. 106.

50. Gen. W. S. McCaskey, first indorsement to Gen. Fred C. Ainsworth, September 24, 1906, SD-1, p. 106.

51. Secretary Taft was in Cuba and not available to deal with Brownsville. After more than two years as secretary of war, Taft had learned "the administration of the War Department was . . . an insignificant part of his work." Henry F. Pringle, *The Life and Times of William Howard Taft: A Biography* (Hamden, CT: Archon Books, 1964), 1:258.

52. Acting Secretary of War Robert Shaw Oliver, written order to Gen. Ernest A. Garlington, October 4, 1906, SD-1, p. 178.

53. "Roosevelt, Rain-Soaked and Exposed to Storm Gets Splendid Ovation at Capitol's Dedication," *Philadelphia Inquirer*, October 5, 1906, p. 1.

54. Gen. Ernest A. Garlington Report, SD-1, p. 528.

55. Ibid. Garlington displayed some investigative skills one might expect from the top man. Realizing the gulf between a white, general-grade officer and black enlisted men, he started his interrogations with general conversation, inquiries into their backgrounds, what sort of jobs they had in civilian life, what hometowns they came from. Remarkably, he found out one of the men had lived in the same home he once lived in.

56. Ibid., p. 530.

57. Ibid., p. 531.

58. Ibid., pp. 528–29.

59. Arthur W. Dunn, *From Harrison to Harding: A Personal Narrative, Covering a Third of a Century, 1888–1921* (New York: G. P. Putnam's Sons, 1922), p. 24.

60. Nettleton, letter to William Howard Taft, November 27, 1906, SD-1, p. 195.

61. Garlington Report, SD-1, p. 531.

62. Assistant Secretary of War Robert Shaw Oliver, cited in Weaver, *Brownsville Raid*, p. 102.

63. SMAC-3, p. 3192 (testimony of Gen. Andrew S. Burt).

64. Historians and later commentators agree. Referring to Taft's later defense of Roosevelt, Pringle writes there was "nothing whatever in proof that a conspiracy of silence existed." Pringle, *Life and Times of William Howard Taft*, 1:325.

65. Quoted in Weaver, *Brownsville Raid*, p. 105.

66. SMAC-3, p. 3192 (testimony of Burt).

67. Theodore Roosevelt, letter to Silas McBee, November 27, 1906, in *The Letters of Theodore Roosevelt*, ed. Elting E. Morison, vol. 5, *The Big Stick: 1905–1907* (Cambridge, MA: Harvard University Press, 1952), p. 509.

68. In fact, this is just what General Garlington would later tell the Senate Military Affairs Committee.

> *[Senator Foraker] Q:* Do you think colored people, generally, are truthful?
> *[General Garlington] A:* No, Sir; I do not.
> *Q:* You think a colored man might testify truthfully about the weather?
> *A:* He might have some difficulty.
> *[Earlier, Garlington traced his disbelief about black truthfulness to its logical if absurd conclusion.]*
> *Q:* You stood ready then to believe any man who would come forward and say, "I did not do it, but someone else did it?"
> *A:* I stood ready to follow up on any clew that any of those men gave me, and then to pass my opinion upon what I found.
> *Q:* But you would not have believed them without corroboration?
> *A:* No, Sir.

Had a black soldier done what Garlington asked him to do and identified a shooter, Garlington would not have believed him.

69. Theodore Roosevelt, letter to Ray Stannard Baker, March 30, 1907, in Morison, *Letters of Theodore Roosevelt*, 5:634.

70. Theodore Roosevelt, "Sixth Annual Message," December 3, 1906, available online by Gerhard Peters and John T. Woolley, *The American Presidency Project*, http://www.presidency.ucsb.edu/ws/index.php?pid=29547 (accessed September 23, 2014).

71. Bill Maxwell, "Code of Silence Corrodes Black Community," found in the *Marietta (GA) Daily Journal*, July 29, 2010.

72. See James A. Tinsley, "Roosevelt, Foraker, and the Brownsville Affray," *Journal of Negro History* 41, no. 1 (1956): 44.

73. Roosevelt had gotten to know Garlington, then a lieutenant colonel and

the division's inspector general, in Cuba and mentions him a few times in *The Rough Riders*. He includes Garlington in a grouping of "excellent officers." Theodore Roosevelt, *The Rough Riders: An Autobiography* (New York: Library of America, 2004), p. 148. Though not close by Roosevelt during the charge up San Juan Heights, Garlington had some part in it. See ibid., appendix D, pp. 230–31.

74. William Loeb, letter to Gen. Fred C. Ainsworth, September 13, 1906, SD-1, p. 99.

75. "Roosevelt and Taft Said to Have Clashed," *New York Times*, November 21, 1906.

76. "Inquiry in Congress," *New York Times*, November 23, 1906.

77. These matters are in the chronology compiled by Elting Morison and his colleagues. *The Letters of Theodore Roosevelt*, ed. Elting E. Morison, vol. 6, *The Big Stick: 1907–1909* (Cambridge, MA: Harvard University Press, 1952), p. 1603.

78. Theodore Roosevelt, letter to John St. Loe Strachey, October 25, 1906, in ibid., 6:468. Churchill came up twice in letters to Henry Cabot Lodge in September, "I dislike the father [Lord Randolph Churchill] and the son," September 12, 1906; "knowing the son I felt no inclination [to read his biography of Lord Randolph]," September 16; and again on November 14, while the president steamed to Panama. Theodore Roosevelt, letter to Henry Cabot Lodge, in *Selections from the Correspondence of Theodore Roosevelt and Henry Cabot Lodge, 1884–1918*, 2 vols. (New York: C. Scribner's Sons, 1925), 2:231, 232, 260. Churchill's American mother, the former Jennie Jerome, and Roosevelt grew up in the same New York society.

79. Theodore Roosevelt, letter to Winston Churchill, August 18, 1906, in Morison, *Letters of Theodore Roosevelt*, 5:378.

80. Barbara W. Tuchman, *Practicing History: Selected Essays* (New York: Alfred A. Knopf, 1981), p. 114.

81. Theodore Roosevelt, letter to Alice Roosevelt Longworth, October 16, 1906, Correspondence Photostats, box 27, October–December 1906, Theodore Roosevelt Collection, Houghton Library, Harvard University.

82. The *New York Times* said flat out that had his father-in-law not waited until after the election to make public the dismissal of the soldiers, and the Negro vote turned against him because of it, he would have lost. "Inquiry in Congress," *New York Times*, November 23, 1906. Maybe in his congratulatory letter, Roosevelt should have included himself.

83. Theodore Roosevelt, letter to Alice Roosevelt Longworth, November 7, 1906, Harvard Roosevelt Collection, MS Am 1541.9 (73), http://www.theodorerooseveltcenter.org/Research/Digital-Library/Record.aspx?libID=o283325 (accessed September 23, 2014).

84. "Plea of Roosevelt, Jr., Denied by Prosecutor," *New York Times*, October 4, 1906.

85. Theodore Roosevelt Jr., letter to Theodore Roosevelt, n.d., Henry Cabot Lodge Papers, Massachusetts Historical Society, Boston. His father asked Lodge to intercede on behalf of Ted Jr., and he did. Ted Jr. was hauled before the grand jury

to testify, and after he identified his friend (we don't know if this was at his father's urging or the insistence of the lawyer Lodge arranged for, was not charged with any offense. While all this was going on, the president defended his son's innocence in a letter to the Boston police commissioner, in which he recalled his days as New York police commissioner. Roosevelt turned the story into one of a bad cop (Roosevelt called him a brute, a fool, and a creature), and asked the Bostonian to consider charging the officer. Theodore Roosevelt, letter to Stephen O'Meara, October 2, 1906, Lodge Papers. The case against the friend ultimately was dismissed. "Shaun Kelley Exonerated," *New York Times*, October 17, 1906.

86. Theodore Roosevelt, letter to Kermit Roosevelt, December 5, 1906, in Morison, *Letters of Theodore Roosevelt*, 5:520n1.

87. Stacy A. Cordery, *Alice: Alice Roosevelt Longworth, from White House Princess to Washington Power Broker* (New York: Viking, 2007).

88. A few weeks after the election, the *New York Herald* suggested the results in the House of Representatives would have been a very greatly reduced Republican majority—from 59 to 14. Cited in Tinsley, "Roosevelt, Foraker, and the Brownsville Affray," p. 47.

89. *The Memoirs of Joseph Gurney "Uncle Joe" Cannon*, ed. Helen L. Abdill (Danville, IL: Vermilion County Museum Society, 1996), p. 56.

90. "On the whole, it is a little unfortunate for the Spartan purity of the order that it was 'held up' until election eve, but on the whole we ought to be thankful, for it was better late than never." Francis J. S. Darr (West Point graduate), letter to the editor, *New York Times*, November 26, 1906.

CHAPTER SIX: THE EDUCATIONS OF THE ROUGH RIDER AND THE WIZARD

1. Roosevelt had this fantasy he also was a man of the South through his mother from Roswell, Georgia. He expressed this mostly in a joking fashion, as when he and his military aide, Archie Butt, from Augusta, Georgia, played doubles tennis with two other army officers, and Roosevelt reported to his daughter Alice, "The two old Southern gentlemen whipped the two Yankees." Archie Butt, letter to his mother, October 2, 1908, in *The Letters of Archie Butt, Personal Aide to President Roosevelt*, ed. Lawrence F. Abbott (Garden City, NY: Doubleday, Page, 1924), pp. 108–109. But Roosevelt said it often enough to suggest there was more to it than humor.

2. Booker T. Washington, *Up from Slavery* (New York: Viking Penguin, 1986), pp. 24–25.

3. For supporters and admirers, it was a title of respect.

4. Louis R. Harlan, "Booker T. Washington in Biographical Perspective," in *Booker T. Washington in Perspective: Essays of Louis R. Harlan*, ed. Raymond W. Smock (Jackson: University Press of Mississippi, 1988), p. 7.

5. Rockefeller Jr., letter to Booker T. Washington, June 24, 1903, in *The Booker T. Washington Papers*, eds. Louis R. Harlan and Raymond W. Smock, vol. 7, *1903–4* (Urbana: University of Illinois Press, 1977), p. 183.

6. Louis Harlan, introduction to Washington, *Up from Slavery*, p. xxxix. Harlan cites a letter from Carnegie to Washington's admirer William H. Baldwin Jr., April 17, 1903, in *Booker T. Washington Papers*, 7:120–22. Carnegie made similar remarks in an address before the Philosophical Institution of Edinburgh, October 16, 1907, a copy of which is in box 39-37, Archibald Grimké Papers, Moorland-Spingarn Research Center, Howard University, Washington, DC.

7. See Louis R. Harlan, *Booker T. Washington: The Making of a Black Leader, 1856–1901* (New York: Oxford University Press, 1972), p. 135.

8. W. E. B. Du Bois, *The Souls of Black Folk* (New York: Barnes and Noble Classics, 2003), p. 35. Of course, one of Du Bois's gripes is that while Washington did ill for his race, he did well for himself.

9. Washington, *Up from Slavery*, pp. 26–27, 30–31.

10. Ibid., p. 34. "Washington" was his stepfather's last name.

11. Ibid., p. 44.

12. Ibid.

13. With today's more-direct highways, it is about 375 miles.

14. Washington, *Up from Slavery*, p. 50.

15. Samuel C. Armstrong, "Lessons from the Hawaiian Islands," *Journal of Christian Philosophy* (January 1884): 200–29, cited in *Booker T. Washington and W. E. B. Du Bois: A Study in Race Leadership, 1895–1915*, by Hae-sung Hwang (Seoul: American Studies Institute, Seoul National University, 1992), p. 11.

16. Harlan, *Booker T. Washington*, pp. 63–64, 65.

17. Before General Armstrong died, the by-then completely paralyzed man was invited to Tuskegee for his final days. Washington and his students honored him to the end.

18. Harlan, *Booker T. Washington*, p. 92; Harlan, introduction to Washington, *Up from Slavery*, p. xi.

19. Du Bois may not have liked Washington, but he was sincere when he said he started with so little before he achieved so much.

20. An old lady, a former slave, came to him one day. Walking with the use of a cane, she delivered six eggs. "Mr. Washington, God knows I spent de bes' days of my life in slavery. God knows I's ignorant an' poor; but I knows what you an' Miss Davidson is tryin' to do. I knows you is tryin' to make better men an' better women for de coloured race. I ain't got no money, but I want you to take dese six eggs, what I's been savin' up, an' I wants you to put dese six eggs into de eddication of dese boys an' girls." No gift, Washington wrote, ever "touched me so deeply as this one." Washington, *Up from Slavery*, p. 132.

21. Andrew Carnegie, who donated money for a library, realized it was student labor that enabled Tuskegee to get a lot of building for little money. Harlan, "Booker T. Washington in Biographical Perspective," p. 5.

22. These abolished slavery, granted US citizenship to former slaves and promised them equal protection of the laws, and guaranteed the vote regardless of race, color, or condition of previous servitude.

23. See Hodding Carter, *The Angry Scar: The Story of Reconstruction* (Garden City, NY: Doubleday, 1959), p. 22.

24. "What Was Jim Crow?," Jim Crow Museum of Racist Memorabilia, http://www.ferris.edu/jimcrow/what.htm (accessed May 14, 2014).

25. Henry E. Tremain, *Sectionalism Unmasked* (New York: Bonnell, Silver, 1907), p. 208.

26. According to the 1890 census, of the 7,488,788 Negroes in the continental United States, 6,143,876 lived in the eleven states of the Confederacy. In the border states and territories there were another 548,836. Altogether, in these areas lived almost 90 percent of Negro Americans.

27. Booker T. Washington, "The Educational Outlook in the South" (speech, National Educational Association, Madison, WI, July 16, 1894), in *The Booker T. Washington Papers*, ed. Louis R. Harlan, vol. 2, *1860–89* (Urbana: University of Illinois Press, 1972), pp. 259–60.

28. Washington, *Up from Slavery*, p. 153.

29. Washington's words and manner were calculated to calm and reassure both blacks and whites in his audience. A white teacher at the Alabama Female College in Tuskegee was surprised, and she wrote in the *Tuskegee Macon Mail*, "He spoke well.... He represented things as they are in the South, and said some nice things of the Tuskegee citizens." M.A.O., letter to the editor, *Tuskegee (AL) Macon Mail*, July 23, 1884, in *Booker T. Washington Papers*, 2:262.

30. Mitchell showed how disliked Bullock was by having Rhett invite the former governor to his and Scarlett's wedding. When news got out, "the Old Guard signified their disapproval by a sheaf of cards, regretting their inability to accept Scarlett's kind invitation . . . the party was utterly ruined for her." Margaret Mitchell, *Gone with the Wind* (New York: Scribner, 2006), p. 871.

31. Washington, "Chapter XIV: The Atlanta Exposition Address," *Up from Slavery*, available online at http://xroads.virginia.edu/~Hyper/washington/ch14.html (accessed September 29, 2014).

32. Ibid.

33. Harlan, *Booker T. Washington*, p. 223.

34. *The Autobiography of W. E. B. Du Bois: A Soliloquy on Viewing My Life from the Last Decade of Its First Century* (New York: International Publishers, 1968), pp. 234–35. Later on Du Bois would reflect on how even more deeply destructive the emotional degradation of Jim Crow could be. To explain it as a consequence of Reconstruction, white historians had to distort Negro behavior during Reconstruction. All blacks had to be seen as ignorant, lazy, dishonest, and extravagant, and all were responsible for bad government during Reconstruction. Whites believed it was true. So did blacks. See W. E. B. Du Bois, *Black Reconstruction in America, 1860–1880* (New York: Atheneum, 1992), pp. 711–13.

35. See Paul Grondahl, *I Rose Like a Rocket: The Political Education of Theodore Roosevelt* (New York: Free Press, 2004), p. 102.

36. Peter Collier and David Horowitz, *The Roosevelts: An American Saga* (New York: Simon & Schuster, 1994), p. 65.

37. Hermann Hagedorn, *Roosevelt in the Bad Lands* (Medora, ND: Theodore Roosevelt History and Nature Association, 1949), p. 411.

38. H. Paul Jeffers, *Commissioner Roosevelt: The Story of Theodore Roosevelt and the New York City Police, 1895–1897* (New York: John Wiley & Sons, 1994), p. 57.

39. Actually, it was written as the unofficial 1904 campaign biography.

40. These back-and-forth letters are in *Selections from the Correspondence of Theodore Roosevelt and Henry Cabot Lodge, 1884–1918* (New York: C. Scribner's Sons, 1925), 1:241, 243, 244, 253, 263.

41. Edmund Morris, *The Rise of Theodore Roosevelt* (New York: Coward, McCann & Geoghegan, 1979), p. 552.

CHAPTER SEVEN: ROOSEVELT DOES JUSTICE

1. Maj. Charles Penrose, telegram to Gen. Fred C. Ainsworth, September 20, 1906, in Summary Discharge or Mustering Out of Regiments or Companies: Message from the President of the United States . . . , S. Doc. No. 59-155, vol. 11, pt. 1 (2d sess. 1907) (hereafter cited as SD-1), p. 105.

2. Maj. Charles Penrose, telegram to Gen. Fred C. Ainsworth, August 27, 1906, SD-1, p. 59.

3. *Affray at Brownsville, Tex.: Hearings Before the Comm. on Military Affairs . . . ,* S. Doc. No. 60-402, pt. 4 (1908) (hereafter cited as SMAC-1), pp. 314, 330 (testimony of 1st Sgt. Mingo Sanders).

4. Originally First Sergeant Frazier thought the townspeople were attacking the fort. But when Captain Lyon told him government-issued Springfield rifle ammunition was used in the raid, he changed his mind and figured it had to be soldiers attacking Brownsville. Then he changed it again: "I do believe that if the soldiers had done it I would have heard them speak of it." SMAC-1, pp. 89–90 (testimony of 1st Sgt. Jacob Frazier).

5. Capt. Samuel Lyon, letter, December 20, 1906, SMAC-1, p. 90. Major Penrose did the same thing.

6. SMAC-1, p. 406 (testimony of Sgt. George McMurray).

7. "Sergeant Harley Tells of Brownsville Riot," *New York Times*, December 10, 1906.

8. SMAC-1, p. 130 (testimony of Pvt. Len Reeves).

9. Henry F. Pringle, *The Life and Times of William Howard Taft: A Biography* (Hamden, CT: Archon Books, 1964), 1:306.

10. *The Letters of Theodore Roosevelt*, ed. Elting E. Morison, vol. 5, *The Big Stick:*

1905–1907 (Cambridge, MA: Harvard University Press, 1952), pp. 408–409. Bacon, Roosevelt's Harvard classmate and lifelong friend, had been a partner of the most influential banker and financier of the day, J. P. Morgan. Although this made him a wealthy man, it was stressful, nerve-wracking, and killing him. In 1900 a concerned Theodore Roosevelt, as New York governor, urged him to give up banking for politics. (Roosevelt's counsel to Bacon had a fictional parallel in Edith Wharton's *The Age of Innocence*. Governor Roosevelt gave the same advice to the novel's protagonist, Newland Archer.) In 1905 President Roosevelt appointed Bacon assistant secretary of state under Elihu Root. Jean Strouse, *Morgan: American Financier* (New York: Random House, 1999), p. 443.

11. Quoted in Pringle, *The Life and Times of William Howard Taft*, 1:307.

12. Gen. Fred C. Ainsworth, written report to the commanding general, Southwestern Division, September 19, 1906, SD-1, p. 99.

13. While Taft was in Canada, the presumptuous General Ainsworth patronizingly encouraged Taft to stay detached. "I have been in close consultation with President," he wired Taft the day before the soldiers left for Fort Reno, without mentioning the impending move. "Believe no occasion for any anxiety on your part." The amiable Taft calmly disregarded this "jump" over his head by a subordinate and, by his quick answer the next day, made clear he expected more. "I think you might send me the papers and telegrams by mail. . . . I should like to keep up with the current information on the subject, as I presume some phase of the question may arise after I return." Gen. Fred C. Ainsworth, telegram to William Howard Taft, August 24, 1906, SD-1, p. 53; William Howard Taft, letter to Gen. Fred C. Ainsworth, August 25, 1906, SD-1, p. 53.

14. Pringle, *The Life and Times of William Howard Taft*, 1:258.

15. Ibid., 1:288.

16. Weaver claims the use of "discharge without honor" in Brownsville was "new and little-known." John Weaver, *The Brownsville Raid* (College Station: Texas A&M University Press, 1992), p. 133. The army's judge advocate general found that the discharge, with another name, had been used since the Civil War and was formally designated "discharge without honor" in 1893. "Report of the Judge-Advocate-General of the Army upon the Subject of Discharges without Honor," SD-1, p. 280.

17. "Report of the Judge-Advocate-General," SD-1, p. 280.

18. William Howard Taft, memorandum to Theodore Roosevelt, December 18, 1906, SD-1, p. 17.

19. Reel 343, Theodore Roosevelt Papers, Library of Congress.

20. Theodore Roosevelt, letter to his son Kermit Roosevelt, "On Board the U.S.S. *Louisiana*," November 11, 1906, in Morison, *Letters of Theodore Roosevelt*, 5:495.

21. See Henry Fowler Pringle, Research Notes for *Theodore Roosevelt: A Biography*, 7th year, p. 2, Houghton Library, Harvard University.

22. "Negroes Ask Roosevelt to Act in Race Fight," *New York Times*, October

11, 1906. See also John E. Milholland, Diary, October 9, 1906, John E. Milholland Papers (1887–1924), Ticonderoga (NY) Historical Society. (Milholland crammed a lot of his thoughts, some entered after October 9, onto this page.)

23. See Percy E. Murray, "Harry C. Smith-Joseph B. Foraker Alliance: Coalition Politics in Ohio," *Journal of Negro History* 68, no. 2 (1983): 177.

24. Ralph Tyler, letter to George Myers, August 28, 1906, folder 6, box 13, George A. Myers Papers, Ohio History Connection, Columbus.

25. The entire speech can be found in *The Booker T. Washington Papers*, ed. Louis R. Harlan and Raymond W. Smock, vol. 9, *1906–8* (Urbana: University of Illinois Press, 1980), pp. 62–67.

26. David L. Lewis, *W. E. B. Du Bois: Biography of a Race, 1868–1919* (New York: Henry Holt, 1993), p. 331.

27. "President Expels an Army Battalion," *New York Times*, November 7, 1906, cited in Dismissal of the Soldiers, Chronology, *The Brownsville Raid*, folder 10, box 17, John D. Weaver Papers, Earl Gregg Swem Library, College of William and Mary, Williamsburg, VA. Historians fudge the date the order was made public, generally by indicating only that it was after the election. Edmund Morris states it was November 7. Edmund Morris, *Theodore Rex* (New York: Random House, 2001), p. 721. If so, how did the *New York Times* get the story into its morning newspaper of November 7? No one disputes, however, that it was held back because of the election.

28. "President Expels an Army Battalion," *Washington Post*, November 7, 1906; *New York Sun*, November 24, 1906, cited in James A. Tinsley, "Roosevelt, Foraker, and the Brownsville Affray," *Journal of Negro History* 41, no. 1 (1956): 46–47.

29. Quoted in "Dishonorably Discharged Honorable Soldiers," *New York Age*, November 15, 1906.

30. Quoted in Emma Lou Thornbrough, "The Brownsville Episode and the Negro Vote," *Mississippi Valley Historical Review* 44, no. 3 (December 1947): 470.

31. Richard W. Thompson, letter to Emmett J. Scott, November 21, 1906, Washington Papers, cited in Thornbrough, "Brownsville Episode and the Negro Vote," p. 472.

32. Booker T. Washington, *My Larger Education: Being Chapters from My Experience* (Garden City, NY: Doubleday, Page, 1911), p. 181.

33. W. E. B. Du Bois, "The President and the Soldiers," *Voice of the Negro* 3 (December 1906): 553, http://www.library.umass.edu/spcoll/digital/dubois/WarPresident.pdf.

34. "Former Member of Twenty-Fifth Says President Acted Hastily," *Washington Post*, November 26, 1906.

35. In his commanding biography of Hearst, David Nasaw thoroughly and astutely discusses the 1906 New York gubernatorial election and emphasizes Roosevelt's fears Hearst could win and his dirty tricks on behalf of Hughes. Late in the campaign, he had Secretary of State Elihu Root say that Roosevelt "considered

Hearst complicit . . . in the assassination of President William McKinley." David Nasaw, *The Chief: The Life of William Randolph Hearst* (Boston: Houghton Mifflin, 2001), pp. 207–13.

36. Quoted in Tinsley, "Roosevelt, Foraker, and the Brownsville Affray," p. 47.

37. Ibid., p. 165.

38. *Washington Bee*, November 10, 1906, and November 16, 1906, respectively.

39. Ralph Tyler, letter to Booker T. Washington, November 23, 1906, microfilm reel 17, Booker T. Washington Papers, Library of Congress.

40. "Many Champion Negroes," *New York Times*, November 14, 1906.

41. Ibid.

42. Newspaper clipping, box 125, Joseph Foraker Papers, Cincinnati History Library and Archives. See also Weaver, *Brownsville Raid*, pp. 125–26.

43. "Negroes Meet and Protest," *New York Times*, December 7, 1906.

44. "Negro Pastor Doubts Washington's Loyalty," *New York Times*, December 18, 1906. See also "A Severe Criticism," *Washington Post*, December 18, 1906.

45. "Enemies to Two Races," *Atlanta Constitution*, November 27, 1906.

46. "Negro Pastor Doubts Washington's Loyalty," *New York Times*, December 18, 1906, cited in William H. Ferris, *The African Abroad; or, His Evolution in Western Civilization, Tracing His Development under Caucasian Milieu* (New York: Johnson Reprint, 1968), p. 379.

47. Booker T. Washington, letter to Oswald Garrison Villard, November 10, 1906, in *Washington Papers*, 9:122.

48. His biographer Pringle wrote in his notes, "[Brownsville] was a typical example of Roosevelt's inability to change his mind once he had adopted a course of action." Pringle, Research Notes for *Theodore Roosevelt: A Biography*, 7th year.

49. Booker T. Washington, letter to Charles W. Anderson, November 7, 1906, in *Washington Papers*, 9:122.

50. Du Bois, "President and the Soldiers," p. 552.

51. Milholland Diary, November 18, 1906, Milholland Papers.

52. Theodore Roosevelt, telegram to Curtis Guild Jr., November 7, 1906, in Morison, *Letters of Theodore Roosevelt*, 5:489.

53. Curtis Guild Jr., telegram to Theodore Roosevelt, November 7/8, 1906, Henry Cabot Lodge Papers, Massachusetts Historical Society, Boston.

54. "Plea for Colored Soldiers," *New York Times*, November 16, 1906.

55. Ibid. Stewart went back to the well a year later with a similar resolution, but this time the committee would not adopt it. Taking this losing effort very badly, he wrote Foraker, "The battle is over. In a moral sense it was a victory." Gilchrist Stewart, letter to Joseph Foraker, box 71, Foraker Papers.

56. "President Will Reconsider," *New York Times*, November 21, 1906.

57. Gen. Fred C. Ainsworth, telegram to Gen. W. S. McCaskey, November 9, 1906, SD-1, pp. 185–86.

58. CI-2, p. 1389 (testimony of Pvt. Boyd Conyers).

59. Affray at Brownsville, Tex. . . . Proceedings of a General Court-Mar-

tial . . . in the Case of Maj. Charles W. Penrose (hereafter cited as *Penrose Court-Martial*), S. Doc. No. 60-402 (1908), p. 1141 (testimony of Maj. C. J. T. Clarke).

60. "Not Surprised at Fort Reno," *New York Sun*, November 21, 1906.

61. *Penrose Court-Martial*, pp. 1141–43 (testimony of Maj. Charles Penrose).

62. Ann J. Lane, *The Brownsville Affair: National Crisis and Black Reaction* (Port Washington, NY: Kennikat, 1971), p. 23. After Roosevelt's death, his valet, James Amos, a black man, wrote that Roosevelt once told him he made sure to discharge the soldiers outside Texas. Otherwise, Texas authorities would have seized and jailed them, and he feared they would have been dragged from their cells and lynched. James E. Amos, *Theodore Roosevelt: Hero to His Valet* (New York: John Day, 1927), p. 65.

63. "President's Critics Called," *Washington Herald*, November 29, 1906.

64. "Mustering Out," *Washington Herald*, November 27, 1906.

65. Joseph B. Foraker, *Notes of a Busy Life* (Cincinnati: Stewart & Kidd, 1917), 2:249.

CHAPTER EIGHT: FRIENDS OF THE ADMINISTRATION

1. Booker T. Washington, letter to Charles W. Anderson, November 7, 1906, in *The Booker T. Washington Papers*, eds. Louis R. Harlan and Raymond W. Smock, vol. 9, *1906–8* (Urbana: University of Illinois Press, 1980), pp. 118–19.

2. Booker T. Washington, letter to Theodore Roosevelt, November 2, 1906, in Harlan and Smock, *Booker T. Washington Papers*, 9:113.

3. Theodore Roosevelt, letter to Booker T. Washington, November 5, 1906, in *The Letters of Theodore Roosevelt*, ed. Elting E. Morison, vol. 5, *The Big Stick: 1905–1907* (Cambridge, MA: Harvard University Press, 1952), p. 118.

4. Edmund Morris, *Theodore Rex* (New York: Random House, 2001), p. 467.

5. Booker T. Washington, letter to Oswald Garrison Villard, November 10, 1906, in Harlan and Smock, *Booker T. Washington Papers*, 9:122.

6. Theodore Roosevelt, letter to Kermit Roosevelt, November 20, 1906, in Morison, *Letters of Theodore Roosevelt*, 5:496.

7. Booker T. Washington, letter to William Howard Taft, November 20, 1906, in Harlan and Smock, *Booker T. Washington Papers*, 9:141.

8. Mary Church Terrell, *A Colored Woman in a White World* (Salem, NH: Ayer, 1998), p. 270.

9. Ibid., p. 205.

10. Ibid., pp. 211–12.

11. Ibid., p. 99.

12. Charles B. Flood, *Grant's Final Victory: Ulysses S. Grant's Heroic Last Year* (Boston: Da Capo, 2012), p. 86.

13. "Roosevelt and Taft Said to Have Clashed," *New York Times*, November 21, 1906.

14. William Howard Taft, letter to Helen H. Taft, November 21, 1906, cited in *The Life and Times of William Howard Taft: A Biography*, by Henry F. Pringle (Hamden, CT: Archon Books, 1964), 1:324–25.

15. "Roosevelt and Taft Said to Have Clashed."

16. "President Crosses Isthmus," *New York Sun*, November 16, 1906.

17. Terrell, *Colored Woman in a White World*, p. 270.

18. John D. Weaver is not the only one who credits Mrs. Terrell with getting Taft to act. So did the *Washington Post*, the *Washington Evening Star*, and the *St. Louis Globe-Democrat*. See ibid., pp. 271–72. And so did Milholland. "She did good work; she really does & deserves much credit." Milholland Diary, November 18, 1906, John E. Milholland Papers (1887–1924), Ticonderoga (NY) Historical Society.

19. William Howard Taft, telegram to Theodore Roosevelt, November 20, 1906, reel 320, William Howard Taft Papers, Ohio History Connection, Columbus. In the diary kept by Taft's secretary Fred W. Carpenter, the entry for that day describes the meeting, reel 603, p. 664, Taft Papers.

20. Taft's secretary got it backward. He told Taft his wire did not get to Roosevelt in Panama because of "atmospheric conditions," which makes no sense, since it was sent by undersea cable and not wireless. Carpenter, to William Howard Taft, November 19, 1906, reel 489, Taft Papers. Responding to the author's question about wireless ship-to-shore communication, Professor Emeritus James Reckner of Texas Tech University, an authority on the navy of that era, answered, "Clearly the Navy had wireless on board most, if not all, ships of the fleet. I would be very surprised if the President would go to sea—a precedent-setting trip—without the latest means of communication." The author expresses his thanks to Professor Reckner.

21. Theodore Roosevelt, three separate cables to William Howard Taft, November 21, 1906, reel 320, Taft Papers. Roosevelt would soon be forced to walk back, characterizing what he did as "punishment."

22. "Roosevelt Is Firm, and Taft Gives Way," *New York Times*, November 22, 1906.

23. William Howard Taft, to Helen H. Taft, November 21, 1906, cited in Pringle, *Life and Times of William Howard Taft*, 1:325.

24. Ibid.

25. William Howard Taft, letter to Richard Harding Davis, November 24, 1906, reel 603, Taft Papers.

26. Milholland Diary, November 22, 1906, Milholland Papers.

27. Terrell, *Colored Woman in a White World*, p. 271.

28. William Howard Taft, letter to Booker T. Washington, November 22, 1906, in Harlan and Smock, *Booker T. Washington Papers*, 9:146.

29. Report of Maj. Penrose, November 26, 1906, box 11, Records of United States Army Continental Commands, 1821–1920, National Archives.

30. Theodore Roosevelt, letter to Charles Joseph Bonaparte (on board USS *Louisiana*), November 12, 1906; Theodore Roosevelt, letter to Kermit Roosevelt (on board USS *Louisiana*), November 20, 1906; all found in Morison, *Letters of Theodore Roosevelt*, 5:496–98.

31. Roosevelt "knew very little about the law." "[He] had sampled a legal education, himself, many years before and had turned away from it in distaste. He never had much respect for the law or lawyers, particularly when they got in his path." Pringle, *Life and Times of William Howard Taft*, 1:256, 387.

32. The *New York* Times characterized this as "the fatal defect in the President's action" and predicted "the men of the negro regiments . . . will be likely to assume that [discharge from the army may be] the worst punishment which may overtake them." Untitled, *New York Times*, December 28, 1906.

33. The above text is an amalgamation of his arguments throughout Brownsville and gives an idea of why Roosevelt was so angry and vindictive.

34. Theodore Roosevelt, letter to Theodore Roosevelt Sr., June 22, 1873, in *The Letters of Theodore Roosevelt*, ed. Elting E. Morison, vol. 1, *The Years of Preparation, 1868–1898* (Cambridge, MA: Harvard University Press, 1951), p. 10, cited in *Theodore Roosevelt: Preacher of Righteousness*, by Joshua D. Hawley (New Haven, CT: Yale University Press, 2008), p. 14.

35. Henry F. Pringle, *Theodore Roosevelt: A Biography* (New York: Harcourt, Brace, 1984), p. 314.

36. Theodore Roosevelt, letter to Clark Howell, dated February 24, 1903, Henry Fowler Pringle, Research Notes for *Theodore Roosevelt: A Biography*, Houghton Library, Harvard University.

37. Theodore Roosevelt, letter to Richard Watson Gilder, February 7, 1903, Pringle Research Notes; Theodore Roosevelt, letter to Richard Watson Gilder, November 16, 1908, in *The Letters of Theodore Roosevelt*, ed. Elting E. Morison, vol. 6, *The Big Stick: 1907–1909* (Cambridge, MA: Harvard University Press, 1952), p. 1364.

38. Indianola was a higher-level post office requiring presidential appointment and Senate confirmation. Roosevelt himself confirmed those who supported her in a letter to John Graham Brooks. Theodore Roosevelt, letter to John Graham Brooks, November 13, 1908, in Morison, *Letters of Theodore Roosevelt*, 6:1343–48. This marvelous letter, in which Roosevelt discusses how he went about selecting people for federal appointments, considers the way a man with "none-too-abundant leisure" should decide which books to read in the limited time available to him, and dismisses Jack London's writing skills, is one of the reasons historians and others find Roosevelt so fascinating and why so many of his era found him irresistible. Brooks was a former Unitarian minister who studied the labor problem and become one of the Progressive Era's reformers. He studied labor-employer conflict, became a federal investigator of strikes, and organized consumer groups. He was thought to be a Socialist, and to the extent he was, his feelings could be understood by scanning the titles of some of his books: *The Social Unrest, The Conflict between Private Monopoly and Good Citizenship*, and *Labor's Challenge to the Social Order*. He was just the sort of man Roosevelt would seek out, enthrall, make his acolyte, and occasionally listen to.

39. Willard B. Gatewood, "Theodore Roosevelt and the Indianola Affair," *Journal of Negro History* 53, no. 1 (1968): 68–69, 67. The author credits Gatewood and his commentary for the author's treatment of the Cox matter.

40. Theodore Roosevelt, letter to James S. Clarkson, March 13, 1903, Pringle Research Notes. Clarkson was Roosevelt's link with Southern Republicans. Lewis L. Gould, *The Presidency of Theodore Roosevelt* (Lawrence: University Press of Kansas, 2011), p. 115.

41. Hawley, *Theodore Roosevelt: Preacher of Righteousness*, pp. xii, xiii.

42. Sidney M. Milkis, *Theodore Roosevelt, the Progressive Party, and the Transformation of American Democracy* (Lawrence: University Press of Kansas, 2009), p. 35.

43. Theodore Roosevelt, letter to Theodore Shonts, November 27, 1906, in Morison, *Letters of Theodore Roosevelt*, 5:504.

44. John A. Gable, *The Bull Moose Years: Theodore Roosevelt and the Progressive Party* (Port Washington, NY: Kennikat Press, 1978), p. 61.

45. See Gould, *Presidency of Theodore Roosevelt*, pp. 200–201.

46. Kelly Miller, "A Brief for the Higher Education of the Negro," in *Race Adjustment: Essays on the Negro in America* (New York: Neale, 1910), pp. 279–80.

47. Roosevelt Report to Civil Service Commission, January 24, 1894, in Morison, *Letters of Theodore Roosevelt*, 1:352.

48. Theodore Roosevelt, letter to Hugh McKittrick, February 21, 1895, in Morison, *Letters of Theodore Roosevelt*, 1:497.

49. Theodore Roosevelt, letter marked "Personal" to Elihu Root, August 18, 1906, in Morison, *Letters of Theodore Roosevelt*, 5:368.

50. See Lewis L. Gould, *The Progressive Era* (Syracuse, NY: Syracuse University Press, 1974), p. 193.

51. J. M. Holland, letter to Booker T. Washington, December 20, 1898, in *The Booker T. Washington Papers*, ed. Louis R. Harlan, vol. 4, *1895–98* (Urbana: University of Illinois Press, 1975), pp. 542–43.

52. Fortune, letter to Booker T. Washington, October 1, 1898, in ibid., 4:478–79.

53. See Pringle, *Theodore Roosevelt: A Biography*, pp. 161, 175. According to Pringle, the Washington acceptance is with the Roosevelt correspondence in the Theodore Roosevelt Papers at the Library of Congress.

54. Theodore Roosevelt, letter to Albion W. Tourgée, November 8, 1901, in *Theodore Roosevelt Cyclopedia*, eds. Albert B. Hart and Herbert R. Ferleger (New York: Roosevelt Memorial Association, 1941), p. 637.

55. Henry Cabot Lodge, letter to Theodore Roosevelt, October 19, 1901, in *Selections from the Correspondence of Theodore Roosevelt and Henry Cabot Lodge, 1884–1918*, 2 vols. (New York: C. Scribner's Sons, 1925) (hereafter cited as *Roosevelt-Lodge Correspondence*), 1:508. He was also consoled by Senator Joseph Foraker from Ohio, who, at a speech at Ohio Wesleyan University in Delaware, Ohio, may have been the first man publicly to defend Roosevelt, helping both Roosevelt and himself for his 1902 Senate campaign. Joseph B. Foraker, *Notes of a Busy Life*, 2 vols. (Cincinnati: Stewart & Kidd, 1917), 2:105.

56. Theodore Roosevelt, letter to Henry Cabot Lodge, October 28, 1901, in *Roosevelt-Lodge Correspondence*, 1:510.

57. Cited in *Mark Twain and the Colonel: Samuel L. Clemens, Theodore Roosevelt,*

and the Arrival of a New Century, by Philip J. McFarland (Lanham, MD: Rowman & Littlefield, 2012), p. 153.

58. Henry E. Tremain, *Sectionalism Unmasked* (New York: Bonnell, Silver, 1907), p. 131. Milholland confused upper-class Bourbons with working-class whites who were really running the show.

59. Oscar S. Straus, *Under Four Administrations: From Cleveland to Taft* (Boston: Houghton Mifflin, 1922), p. 184.

CHAPTER NINE: THESE ARE MY JEWELS

1. The others were William Henry Harrison, Benjamin Harrison (born in Ohio but elected from Indiana), and William McKinley. Two more (for a total of eight) would be elected in the future.

2. *Cincinnati Daily Enquirer*, August 16, 1869, roll 36166, Newspaper Archives, Ohio History Connection, Columbus.

3. The number of lawyers in Cincinnati appears in "Ohio's New Senator," *Munsey's Magazine*, April 1896, p. 61, in Joseph Benson Foraker Papers, Cincinnati History Library and Archives.

4. "Foraker himself was a bit staggered to learn" how many there were. Julia Foraker, *I Would Live It Again* (New York: Arno, 1975), p. 65.

5. "William Howard Taft: Life before the Presidency," Miller Center, http://millercenter.org/president/taft/essays/biography/2 (accessed May 16, 2014).

6. Henry F. Pringle, *The Life and Times of William Howard Taft: A Biography*, 2 vols. (Hamden, CT: Archon Books, 1964), 1:12, 14.

7. Ibid., 1:21.

8. "Abolitionist Orator Wendell Phillips Booed in Cincinnati," *This Day in History*, http://www.history.com/this-day-in-history/wendall-phillips-booed-in-cincinnati (accessed May 16, 2014).

9. Sidney Redner, "Population History of Cincinnati from 1810–1990," *Distribution of City Populations*, http://physics.bu.edu/~redner/projects/population/cities/cincinnati.html (accessed May 16, 2014); US Census Office, *Census Reports: Ninth Census of the United States* (1870), vol. 1, *Population of Civil Divisions Less Than Counties*, p. 231.

10. 5 Laws of Ohio 53 (passed January 25, 1807).

11. Population statistics found in *Frontiers of Freedom: Cincinnati's Black Community, 1802–1868*, by Nikki M. Taylor (Athens: Ohio University Press, 2005), p. 81.

12. Stephen Middleton, *The Black Laws: Race and the Legal Process in Early Ohio* (Athens: Ohio University Press, 2005), pp. 71–72.

13. Willard B. Gatewood, *Aristocrats of Color: The Black Elite, 1880–1920* (Bloomington: Indiana University Press, 1990), p. 118.

14. James W. Gordon, "Did the First Justice Harlan Have a Black Brother?,"

in *Critical White Studies: Looking behind the Mirror*, eds. Richard Delgado and Jean Stefancic (Philadelphia: Temple University Press, 1997), p. 449.

15. *Plessy v. Ferguson*, 163 U.S. 537, 559 (1896) (Harlan, J., dissenting).

16. Joseph B. Foraker, *Notes of a Busy Life* (Cincinnati: Stewart & Kidd, 1917), 1:5, 8.

17. Shakespeare, *Henry V*, act 3, sc. 1, lines 1–6, cited in ibid., 1:9.

18. Foraker, *Notes of a Busy Life*, 1:20.

19. Ibid., 1:35.

20. Ibid., 1:26. Foraker was referring to Lincoln's preliminary proclamation that he would order the freeing of all slaves in states that did not end their rebellion by January 1, 1863. None did, and on that date the Emancipation Proclamation was proclaimed.

21. Ibid.

22. Ibid., 1:78, 80.

23. Ibid., 1:79–80.

24. Foraker, *I Would Live It Again*, p. 55.

25. The Lyceum Circuit promoted learning through meetings at which notable speakers addressed the day's issues.

26. Everett Walters, *Joseph Benson Foraker: An Uncompromising Republican* (Columbus: Ohio History Press, 1948), p. 18.

27. Ibid., p. 20.

28. Foraker, *Notes of a Busy Life*, 1:85. Foraker does not say what was wrong with him. His biographer Everett Walters refers to it as a "breakdown." Walters, *Joseph Benson Foraker*, p. 250.

29. Foraker, *Notes of a Busy Life*, 1:105.

30. Walters, *Joseph Benson Foraker*, p. 25.

31. See Earl R. Beck, "The Political Career of Joseph Benson Foraker" (PhD thesis, Ohio State University, 1942), p. 40.

32. Pringle, *The Life and Times of William Howard Taft*, 1:33.

33. Ibid., 1:56–57.

34. Walters, *Joseph Benson Foraker*, pp. 25–26; Foraker, *I Would Live It Again*, p. 271.

35. Foraker, *I Would Live It Again*, p. 272.

36. From brother Charley Taft, "[The appointment] was a high honor and I hasten to add I appreciated it to the fullest extent. I trust you will have no cause to regret making this appointment." Foraker, *I Would Live It Again*, p. 305.

37. Charles P. Taft, letter to Joseph Benson Foraker, January 29, 1887, Foraker Papers.

38. Discussed in Middleton, *Black Laws*, p. 4.

39. Cited in Ibid., p. 324.

40. See Percy E. Murray, "Harry C. Smith-Joseph B. Foraker Alliance: Coalition Politics in Ohio," *Journal of Negro History* 68, no. 2 (1983): 174.

41. Cited in Beck, "Political Career of Joseph Benson Foraker," p. 99.

42. Mrs. James G. Blaine, letter to Walker Blaine, July 10, 1888, cited in *Andrew Carnegie*, by David Nasaw (New York: Penguin, 2006), p. 328.

43. See chapter one.

44. Had he won, he would have been another of Cornelia's Ohio jewels.

45. Foraker, *I Would Live It Again*, p. 107.

46. Ibid., pp. 108–109.

47. William Howard Taft, letter to Alphonso Taft, July 20, 1889, cited in Pringle, *Life and Times of William Howard Taft*, 1:106.

48. Ibid., 1:109.

49. Foraker, *I Would Live It Again*, pp. 307–308.

50. "William Howard Taft: Life before the Presidency."

51. Helen H. Taft, letter to William Howard Taft, June 9, 1890, cited in Pringle, *Life and Times of William Howard Taft*, 1:82.

52. See ibid., 1:161.

53. As Brownsville unfolded, Schurman would be a source of strength and encouragement to Foraker.

54. "William Howard Taft: Life before the Presidency."

55. William Howard Taft, letter to Theodore Roosevelt, October 27, 1902, cited in Pringle, *Life and Times of William Howard Taft*, 1:241.

56. James B. Morrow, "Foraker and His Early Struggles," *Washington Post*, June 18, 1905, reprinted in an unidentified magazine found in the Foraker Papers.

57. Champ Clark, *My Quarter Century of American Politics*, 2 vols. (New York: Harper & Brothers, 1920), p. 446; Henry Cabot Lodge, letter to Theodore Roosevelt, September 21, 1908, in *Selections from the Correspondence of Theodore Roosevelt and Henry Cabot Lodge, 1884–1918*, 2 vols. (New York: C. Scribner's Sons, 1925), 2:316–17; Paul F. Boller, *Presidential Campaigns: From George Washington to George W. Bush* (New York: Oxford University Press, 2004), p. 174; Margaret Leech, *In the Days of McKinley* (New York: Harper & Bros., 1959), pp. 493–94.

58. Foraker, *Notes of a Busy Life*, 2:92.

59. Joseph B. Foraker, letter to Robert McMurdy, August 27, 1888, cited in Walters, *Joseph Benson Foraker*, p. 80.

60. Walters, *Joseph Benson Foraker*, p. 181.

61. Foraker, *Notes of a Busy Life*, 2:205.

62. Ibid., 2:211–14; Joseph B. Foraker, Correspondence and Interviews concerning Railroad Rate Regulation, p. 48, cited in Walters, *Joseph Benson Foraker*, p. 214; Henry Cabot Lodge, letter to Joseph B. Foraker, September 22, 1905, cited in Walters, *Joseph Benson Foraker*, p. 214.

63. Foraker, *Notes of a Busy Life*, 2:227.

64. Justice Holmes, letter to Frederick Pollock, February 9, 1921, in *Holmes-Pollock Letters: The Correspondence of Mr. Justice Holmes and Sir Frederick Pollock, 1874–1932*, ed. Mark DeWolfe Howe (Cambridge, MA: Harvard University Press, 1942), 2:63–64, cited in *The Presidency of Theodore Roosevelt*, Lewis L. Gould (Lawrence: University Press of Kansas, 2011), p. 134.

65. Joshua D. Hawley, *Theodore Roosevelt: Preacher of Righteousness* (New Haven, CT: Yale University Press, 2008), p. 173.

66. "William Howard Taft: Life before the Presidency."

67. William Howard Taft, letter to H. C. Hollister, September 21, 1903, cited in Pringle, *Life and Times of William Howard Taft*, 1:236.

68. Ibid., 1:162.

69. Theodore Roosevelt, letter to George Otto Trevelyan, June 19, 1908, in *The Letters of Theodore Roosevelt*, ed. Elting E. Morison, vol. 6, *The Big Stick: 1907–1909* (Cambridge, MA: Harvard University Press, 1952), p. 1085. Once committed to the race, Taft certainly spoke as if he would do just that: "I agree heartily and earnestly in the policies which have come to be known as the Roosevelt policies." William Howard Taft, letter to C. M. Heald, December 25, 1907, cited in Gould, *Presidency of Theodore Roosevelt*, p. 272.

70. Theodore Roosevelt, letter to William Howard Taft, confidential, March 15, 1906, in *The Letters of Theodore Roosevelt*, ed. Elting E. Morison, vol. 5, *The Big Stick: 1905–1907* (Cambridge, MA: Harvard University Press, 1952), p. 183.

71. Ibid.

72. Herman H. Kohlsaat, *From McKinley to Harding: Personal Recollections of Our Presidents* (New York: C. Scribner's Sons, 1923), pp. 161–62.

73. William Howard Taft, letter to William R. Nelson, June 21, 1906, folder 1, box 1, William Howard Taft Papers, Ohio History Connection, Columbus.

74. William Howard Taft, letter to William R. Nelson, July 10, 1906, folder 1, box 1, Taft Papers.

75. Theodore Roosevelt, letter to William Allen White, August 11, 1906, in Morison, *Letters of Theodore Roosevelt*, 5:354. Also in series C, box 1, William Allen White Papers, Library of Congress.

76. Pringle, *Life and Times of William Howard Taft*, 2:318.

77. Ibid., 2:311.

CHAPTER TEN: TWO SETS OF AFFIDAVITS

1. Theodore Roosevelt, letter to Henry Cabot Lodge, September 27, 1906, in *Selections from the Correspondence of Theodore Roosevelt and Henry Cabot Lodge, 1884–1918*, 2 vols. (New York: C. Scribner's Sons, 1925) (hereafter cited as *Roosevelt-Lodge Correspondence*), 2:234–35. The day before, Roosevelt sent an "extremely polite but firm" reply to Foraker explaining, "for your private information only," he did not intend to act against the Cuban government. On September 27, Foraker answered, "Many thanks for your telegram. It is gratefully reassuring and dispels embarrassing apprehensions." A few days later, in a second letter to Lodge, Roosevelt characterized Foraker's reply as "much more friendly." Theodore Roosevelt, letter to Henry Cabot Lodge, October 1, 1906, in *Roosevelt-Lodge Correspondence*,

2:238. It would be many years before any exchange of correspondence between them could again be called "polite" or "friendly."

2. This constitutional argument continues today.

3. R. Taylor, letter to Joseph B. Foraker, September 1906, Joseph Foraker Papers, Cincinnati History Library and Archives, cited in *Joseph Benson Foraker: An Uncompromising Republican*, by Everett Walters (Columbus: Ohio History Press, 1948), pp. 256–57.

4. Roosevelt knew of the Burton insurgency before Burton's Cleveland address and understood the threat it posed to Foraker. "The Republicans of Ohio, for instance, want to down both Dick and Foraker." Theodore Roosevelt, letter to Henry Cabot Lodge, August 6, 1906, in *The Letters of Theodore Roosevelt*, ed. Elting E. Morison, vol. 5, *The Big Stick: 1905–1907* (Cambridge, MA: Harvard University Press, 1952), p. 347.

5. David F. Pugh, letter to Joseph B. Foraker, September 3, 1906, box 67, Foraker Papers.

6. "Foraker and Dick Capture Convention," *New York Times*, September 12, 1906.

7. Charles Fairbanks, letter to Joseph B. Foraker, September 15, 1906, box 49, Foraker Papers.

8. Milholland Diary, September 9 and 11, 1906, John E. Milholland Papers (1887–1924), Ticonderoga (NY) Historical Society.

9. "Pneumatic Tube System," *New York Times*, April 6, 1897.

10. Milholland Diary, undated 1906 entries, Milholland Papers.

11. August Meier and Elliott Rudwick, "The Rise of Segregation in the Federal Bureaucracy, 1900–1930," *Phylon* 28, no. 2 (1967): 181; Emma Thornbrough, *T. Thomas Fortune: Militant Journalist* (Chicago: University of Chicago Press, 1972), p. 270.

12. "Full of Virtue Just Now," *New York Times*, April 30, 1892.

13. See Thornbrough, *T. Thomas Fortune*, pp. 59–62.

14. John E. Milholland, letter to Booker T. Washington, January 17, 1905, cited in Thornbrough, *T. Thomas Fortune*, p. 270.

15. "Negroes Have an Inning at the Cooper Union," *New York Times*, February 2, 1906. Mary Terrell Church spoke that night with such bitterness, efforts by Milholland to tone her down got nowhere. The South was petty and mean. "But the silence of the North . . . is criminal. . . . It suffers from fatty generation of the brain. . . . Northern neutrality on the subject of negro disfranchisement in the South is criminal."

16. Meier and Rudwick, "Rise of Segregation in the Federal Bureaucracy," p. 181.

17. Theodore Roosevelt, letter to Henry Cabot Lodge, January 2, 1896, in *Roosevelt-Lodge Correspondence*, 2:206.

18. Milholland Diary, October 10, 1906, Milholland Papers. Also see *Crisis*, April 20, 1912, reproducing an article from *New York World*, October 16, 1906, E185.5.G82, *Guardian of Boston*/Trotter Collection, Howard Gotlieb Archival Research Center, Mugar Library, Boston University.

19. "Blackman's Progress," *Washington Post*, October 18, 1906.

20. Everett Walters, *Joseph Benson Foraker: An Uncompromising Republican* (Columbus: Ohio History Press, 1948), p. 236.

21. Elting Morison, who compiled *The Letters of Theodore Roosevelt*, is one of them. He believed Foraker's motivation was honest indignation over an "unjust order based on insufficient and spurious information." His enthusiasm sprang from a "chance to discredit Roosevelt and Taft" and improve his chances for the presidential nomination in 1908. Morison, *Letters of Theodore Roosevelt*, 5:524n2.

22. Julia Foraker, *I Would Live It Again* (New York: Arno, 1975), p. 3.

23. Lewis Gould (professor emeritus, University of Texas), in discussion with the author, April 2010.

24. Joseph B. Foraker, *Notes of a Busy Life*, 2 vols. (Cincinnati: Stewart & Kidd, 1917), 2:234.

25. Foraker, *I Would Live It Again*, p. 277.

26. Quoted statements by Foraker are in Foraker, *Notes of a Busy Life*, 2:234.

27. "Negro Troops Answer Inquiry under Path," *New York Times*, November 25, 1906.

28. "Negro Troops Answer Inquiry under Oath"; Edmund Morris, *Theodore Rex* (New York: Random House, 2001), p. 471; Theodore Roosevelt, letter to Herbert Parsons, April 10, 1908, *The Letters of Theodore Roosevelt*, ed. Elting E. Morison, vol. 6, *The Big Stick: 1907–1909* (Cambridge, MA: Harvard University Press, 1952), p. 999.

29. Charles W. Anderson, letter to Booker T. Washington, November 10, 1906, in *Booker T. Washington Papers*, ed. Louis R. Harlan, vol. 9, *1906–8* (Urbana: University of Illinois Press, 1980), pp. 123–24.

30. "President Will Reconsider," *New York Times*, November 21, 1906.

31. Gilchrist Stewart, telegram to Theodore Roosevelt, November 29, 1906, Summary Discharge or Mustering Out of Regiments or Companies: Message from the President of the United States . . . , S. Doc. No. 59-155, vol. 11, pt. 1 (2d sess. 1907), p. 196.

32. There is an empty envelope from Foraker to A. B. Humphrey, c/o Constitutional League, returned by the post office for a street address. Its postmark is May 30, 1906, when the proposed amendment to the Hepburn Bill to ban Jim Crow passenger cars was being discussed. Also see correspondence between Foraker and A. B. Humphrey, Constitution League secretary, regarding copies of the "The Affray at Brownsville" War Department Pamphlet and Foraker's analysis of the testimony it contained, and a letter from Foraker asking to meet with Gilchrist Stewart. Box 50, Foraker Papers.

33. A. B. Humphrey, letter to Joseph B. Foraker, November 25, 1906, box 50, Foraker Papers; Joseph B. Foraker, letter to A. B. Humphrey, November 29, 1906, box 50, Foraker Papers.

34. "President Will Reconsider."

35. Theodore Roosevelt, letter to Horace Voss, November 27, 1906, roll 343,

Theodore Roosevelt Papers, Library of Congress; Theodore Roosevelt, letter to Sen. John Kean, November 27, 1906, roll 343, Theodore Roosevelt Papers.

36. "President Will Reconsider."

37. Theodore Roosevelt, letter to William Howard Taft, n.d., reel 320, William Howard Taft Papers, Library of Congress.

CHAPTER ELEVEN: BETWEEN TWO STOOLS

1. Mary Church Terrell, letter to Mingo "Saunders [*sic*]," December 6, 1906, American Memory from the Library of Congress, http://memory.loc.gov/master/ipo/qcdata/qcdata7/naacp/tiffs/na0011_01.tif (accessed March 17, 2010).

2. *Affray at Brownsville, Tex.: Hearings Before the Comm. on Military Affairs . . .* , S. Doc. No. 60-402, pt. 4 (1908), p. 302 (affidavit of Mingo Sanders, May 16, 1886). Which would make him fifty-four years old when he came to Mrs. Terrell's home. She must not have asked him his age, but she was pretty close when she estimated he was "not much more than fifty years old."

3. Mary Church Terrell, "Sketch of Mingo Saunders," *Voice of the Negro*, May 1907. Both the letter and the article spelled Sanders's name as "Saunders." It is possible Mrs. Terrell was unaware of its spelling when she sent the letter, but it's odd that Sanders did not correct her in time for the article's publication five months later.

4. W. E. B. Du Bois, "To the Nations of the World" (speech, Pan African Convention, London, July 25, 1900), in *W. E. B. Du Bois: Biography of a Race, 1868– 1919*, by David L. Lewis (New York: Henry Holt, 1993), p. 251.

5. W. E. B. Du Bois, "Of the Faith of the Fathers," in *The Souls of Black Folk* (New York: Barnes & Noble Classics, 2003), p. 144.

6. In 1903 Du Bois described this in an essay titled "The Talented Tenth." The term referred to his belief that blacks needed and were entitled to what was then called a classical education, and those who received it would become leaders of their race and change its place in the world for the better. W. E. B. Du Bois, "The Talented Tenth," TeachingAmericanHistory.org, http://teachingamericanhistory.org/library/document/the-talented-tenth/ (accessed May 19, 2014).

7. See Thomas E. Harris, "The Black Leader's Rhetorical Dilemma: An Analysis of the Debate between W. E. B. Du Bois and Booker T. Washington" (paper presented at the Annual Meeting of the New York State Speech Association, Loch Sheldrake, NY, April 1974).

8. Elliott M. Rudwick, *W. E. B. Du Bois: A Study in Minority Group Leadership* (Philadelphia: University of Pennsylvania Press, 1960), p. 15.

9. *The Autobiography of W. E. B. Du Bois: A Soliloquy on Viewing My Life from the Last Decade of Its First Century* (New York: International Publishers, 1968), p. 64, cited in Lewis, *W. E. B. Du Bois: Biography of a Race*, p. 20.

10. Du Bois, *Souls of Black Folk*, p. 8.

11. See Thomas Allan Scott, *Cornerstones of Georgia History: Documents That Formed the State* (Athens: University of Georgia Press, 1995), pp. 141–42. A careful reading of Du Bois's petition suggests he made a "Washington-light" argument. Keeping lower-class blacks was not objectionable, so long as lower-class whites were treated the same. See Rudwick, *W. E. B. Du Bois: A Study in Minority Group Leadership*, p. 54.

12. See Lewis, *W. E. B. Du Bois: Biography of a Race*, pp. 231–37.

13. Rudwick, *W. E. B. Du Bois: A Study in Minority Group Leadership*, p. 58. He cites three letters in the Du Bois papers: W. E. B. Du Bois to G. R. Parkin, January 1, 1903; G. R. Parkin to W. E. B. Du Bois, January 28, 1903; and Booker T. Washington to W. E. B. Du Bois, February 3, 1903.

14. He was as outspoken and "in his face" with everybody he didn't like. He so angered President Woodrow Wilson at a White House meeting, he was thrown out of the building. "President Resents Negro's Criticism," *New York Times*, November 13, 1914.

15. August Meier, *Negro Thought in America, 1880–1915* (Ann Arbor: University of Michigan Press, 1988), p. 174.

16. *Boston Guardian*, November 8, 1902, shown as an illustration in *T. Thomas Fortune: Militant Journalist*, by Emma L. Thornbrough (Chicago: University of Chicago Press, 1972), p. 233.

17. "Solving the Race Problem," Session 2, National Afro-American Council, December 30, 1898, http://lcweb2.loc.gov/ammem/aap/aaprace.html (accessed September 28, 2014).

18. Alexander J. Opsahl, "Afro-American Council (1898–1907)," BlackPast.org, http://www.blackpast.org/aah/afro-american-council-1898-1907 (accessed May 19, 2014). Also involved was Congressman George Henry White of North Carolina, the only black member of Congress at the time, later a vice president of the organization. Members included Mary Church Terrell, former Louisiana governor Pinckney B. S. Pinchback, Professor William S. Scarborough, and Henry O. Flipper, the first black West Point graduate, who became a conservative Republican when Franklin Roosevelt was in the White House.

19. With Washington's recommendation, Lewis recently had been appointed by Roosevelt as assistant US attorney in Boston.

20. See Lewis, *W. E. B. Du Bois: Biography of a Race*, pp. 300–301; and Hae-sung Hwang, *Booker T. Washington and W. E. B. Du Bois: A Study in Race Leadership, 1895–1915* (Seoul: American Studies Institute, Seoul National University, 1992), pp. 99–100.

21. Du Bois, *Autobiography of W. E. B. Du Bois*, p. 248. One of the Niagara Movement's founders was John Milholland. Its name came from its inability to find a suitable place in the United States to hold a meeting, so it came together on the Canadian side of Niagara Falls.

22. The Niagara Movement is now the National Association for the Advancement of Colored People.

23. See Lewis, *W. E. B. Du Bois: Biography of a Race*, pp. 393, 341–42. He writes Brownsville would help them tear it "to shreds." Possibly, but not as quickly as this suggests.

24. The printed "programme" for the meeting indicates Du Bois was scheduled to speak that day, but Lewis writes the address was given later that evening and was read by a Du Bois loyalist. Ibid., p. 330. The handsomely printed "programme" is available at http://credo.library.umass.edu/view/full/mums312-b161-i230.

25. Du Bois's opposition to Washington had a personal component. He was frustrated with Washington's blocking his recognition and advancement. He also was irritated with the cool way his leadership ideas were treated by whites and jealous of the warmer relationships they had with Washington. These too were considerations in his developing a program of pressure and agitation. See Rudwick, *W. E. B. Du Bois: A Study in Minority Group Leadership*, p. 93.

26. W. E. B. Du Bois, "The Value of Agitation," *Voice of the Negro*, March 1907, in *The Social Theory of W. E. B. Du Bois*, ed. Phil Zuckerman (Thousand Oaks, CA: Sage, 2004), p. 115.

27. Lewis, *W. E. B. Du Bois: Biography of a Race*, p. 238.

28. It would take time. The next month H. G. Wells, the English science-fiction writer and dabbler in socialism, wrote a series of articles for *Harper's Weekly* that urged Booker T. Washington to fight Jim Crow and contrasted him favorably with W. E. B. Du Bois, who seemed to Wells "more like an artist, less the statesman." Chronology, September 1906, John D. Weaver Papers, Earl Gregg Swem Library, College of William and Mary, Williamsburg, VA.

29. Lewis, *W. E. B. Du Bois: Biography of a Race*, p. 227. See W. E. B. Du Bois, "On the Passing of the First-Born," in *Souls of Black Folk*, p. 147.

30. Each chapter in *The Souls of Black Folk* begins with poetry. Du Bois's prose comes close to poetry in its cadence and elegance. "On the Passing of the First-Born" is the most searing.

CHAPTER TWELVE: GRIM-VISAGED WAR

1. Garlington had begun his career with a fast promotion. In 1876, just out of West Point, he chose the Seventh Cavalry, beginning to rebuild its strength after the Sioux wiped out Custer and his men at the Battle of the Little Bighorn. Immediately he was promoted to first lieutenant. Edward M. Coffman, *The Old Army: A Portrait of the American Army in Peacetime, 1784–1898* (New York: Oxford University Press, 1986), p. 231.

2. 41 Cong. Rec. 1 (1906).

3. Robert A. Caro, *The Years of Lyndon Johnson: Master of the Senate* (New York: Alfred A. Knopf, 2002), p. 11.

4. "Penrose Scores First," *Washington Post*, December 4, 1906.

5. Paul B. Beers, *Pennsylvania Politics Today and Yesterday: The Tolerable*

Accommodation (University Park: Pennsylvania State University Press, 1980), p. 41; Edmund Morris, *Theodore Rex* (New York: Random House, 2001), p. 75.

6. Beers, *Pennsylvania Politics Today and Yesterday*, p. 37.

7. Ibid., p. 48.

8. Walter Davenport, *Power and Glory: The Life of Boies Penrose* (New York: G. P. Putnam's Sons, 1931), p. 13.

9. Beers, *Pennsylvania Politics Today and Yesterday*, p. 48.

10. Edmund Morris, *The Rise of Theodore Roosevelt* (New York: Coward, McCann & Geoghegan, 1979), p. 128.

11. Beers, *Pennsylvania Politics Today and Yesterday*, p. 49.

12. Robert D. Bowden, *Boies Penrose: Symbol of an Era* (New York: Greenberg, 1937), p. 210.

13. Ibid., p. 154.

14. Ibid., p. 155.

15. "Senator Penrose Here," *Washington Herald*, November 5, 1906.

16. "About People and Social Incidents," *New York Tribune*, November 6, 1906.

17. White House visitor log, September 20, 1906, Theodore Roosevelt Papers, Library of Congress.

18. Theodore Roosevelt, report to Boies E. Penrose, September 20, 1906, reel 342, Roosevelt Papers.

19. Theodore Roosevelt, letter to Philander Knox, September 22, 1906, box 2, Philander C. Knox Papers, Library of Congress.

20. Theodore Roosevelt, letter to Philander Knox, November 5, 1906, box 2, Knox Papers.

21. "Roosevelt, Rain-Soaked and Exposed to Storm Gets Splendid Ovation at Capitol's Dedication," *Philadelphia Inquirer*, October 5, 1906.

22. "Results of the Election," *Washington Herald*, November 7, 1906; "Stuart's Plurality is 70,000," *Washington Herald*, November 8, 1906.

23. Julia Foraker, *I Would Live It Again* (New York: Arno, 1975), pp. 295–96.

24. "The President of the United States, especially such a figure as Roosevelt, cannot be successfully withstood by any individual." Quoted in *The Memoirs of Joseph Gurney "Uncle Joe" Cannon*, ed. Helen L. Abdill (Danville, IL: Vermilion County Museum Society, 1996), p. 130.

25. See "Dismissal of Negro Troops," *New York Tribune*, December 2, 1906.

26. See chapter nineteen.

27. Gen. Fred C. Ainsworth, report to Headquarters, Southwestern Division, December 1, 1906, Summary Discharge or Mustering Out of Regiments or Companies: Message from the President of the United States . . . , S. Doc. No. 59-155, vol. 11, pt. 1 (2d sess. 1907) (hereafter cited as SD-1), p. 200.

28. Ainsworth Memorandum for Secretary of War, December 5, 1906, Summary Discharge or Mustering Out of Regiments or Companies: Message from the President of the United States . . . , S. Doc. No. 59-155, vol. 11, pt. 2 (2d sess. 1907), pp. 311–12.

29. Private Secretary, instructions to Mr. Young, Foreman of Printing, Government Printing Office, December 2, 1906, reel 489, William Howard Taft Papers, Library of Congress.

30. "Congress Meets Again; Negro Troops Issue Up," *New York Times*, December 4, 1906; 41 Cong. Rec. 2 (1906). In *I Would Live It Again*, Julia Foraker mistakenly recalls the debate that day. She writes, at page 278, "The Vice-President was on the point of proposing adjournment when Senator Penrose sprang upon the Senate a message from the President of the United States. This message was a request that the Brownsville matter be left wholly in the President's hands. The Senate would be so good as not to concern itself with Brownsville."

31. 41 Cong. Rec. 2 (1906).

32. "Penrose Scores First."

33. See "In Foraker's Favor," *Dayton Evening News*, December 18, 1906; John D. Weaver, Notes on the Debate on a Senate Investigation, John D. Weaver Papers, Earl Gregg Swem Library, College of William and Mary, Williamsburg, VA.

34. John Milholland Diary, December 3, 1906, John E. Milholland Papers (1887–1924), Ticonderoga (NY) Historical Society.

35. "Dismissal of Negro Troops," *New York Sun*, December 4, 1906.

36. John D. Weaver, *The Brownsville Raid* (College Station: Texas A&M University Press, 1992), p. 113. "Foraker, *by chance*, happened to have in his coat pocket a draft of a similar resolution he had dictated to his stenographer and intended to introduce *the following day*" (author's emphasis). John D. Weaver, *The Senator and the Sharecropper's Son: Exoneration of the Brownsville Soldiers* (College Station: Texas A&M University Press, 1997), p. 120. Foraker biographer Walters believes Foraker was prepared to ask the Senate to look into the discharges, but he planned first to consult with other senators about when. Penrose forced him to act that day. See Everett Walters, *Joseph Benson Foraker: An Uncompromising Republican* (Columbus: Ohio History Press, 1948), p. 235.

37. "Congress Meets Again; Negro Troops Issue Up."

38. "Dismissal of Negro Troops."

39. "Senate after Roosevelt on Negro Troops," *New York Evening World*, December 3, 1906.

40. "Congress and the President," *New York Times*, December 4, 1906.

41. Abdill, *Memoirs of Joseph Gurney "Uncle Joe" Cannon*, pp. 55–56.

42. Theodore Roosevelt, letter to "Nannie" Lodge, December 3, 1906, Roosevelt Papers.

43. "Resolutions Go Over," *New York Tribune*, December 6, 1906.

44. "Dismissal of Negro Troops," *New York Sun*, December 4, 1906.

45. "In Foraker's Favor," *Dayton Evening News*, December 3, 1906.

46. "The Brownsville Affair as a Political Weapon," *Literary Digest* 33, no. 24 (December 15, 1906): 895, 896.

47. *New York World*, December 4, 1906, cited in Henry Fowler Pringle, Research Notes for *Theodore Roosevelt: A Biography*, 7th year, p. 4, Houghton Library, Harvard University.

48. Joseph B. Foraker, *Notes of a Busy Life*, 2 vols. (Cincinnati: Stewart & Kidd, 1917), 2:234–35.

49. *Gregory (Scotland Yard detective):* "Is there any other point to which you would wish to draw my attention?"
     Sherlock Holmes: "To the curious incident of the dog in the night-time."
     Gregory: "The dog did nothing in the night-time."
     Holmes: "That was the curious incident."

Arthur Conan Doyle and Leslie Klinger, *The New Annotated Sherlock Holmes* (New York: W. W. Norton, 2005), see specifically "Silver Blaze, p. 411.

50. "Taft Defends Penalty on Negro Battalion," *New York Times*, December 6, 1906.

51. Ibid.

52. SD-1, pp. 301–307. Examples of enlisted soldiers who denied either hearing about mistreatment or harassment by Brownsville civilians or hearing any soldier upset about it include Private Jones A. Coltrane of Company B, SD-1, p. 466; Corporal Wade Harris of Company B, SD-1, p. 468; Corporal Wade H. Watlington of Company B, SD-1, p. 469; Private Thomas Jefferson of Company C, SD-1, p. 475; and Private Erasmus T. Dabbs of Company C, SD-1, p. 478.

53. "Taft Defends Penalty on Negro Battalion."

54. The Senate's procedures can be baffling. The reader will recall that on December 3, after Penrose jumped ahead of him, Foraker did in fact "offer as a substitute" his own resolution. On December 5, it was treated as "an amendment in the nature of a substitute." To disentangle it from Penrose's, Foraker first had to have it declared "independent." 41 Cong. Rec. 2, 55 (1906).

55. David McCullough, *The Path between the Seas: The Creation of the Panama Canal, 1870–1914* (New York: Simon and Schuster, 1977), p. 261.

56. 41 Cong. Rec. 83–97 (1906).

57. 41 Cong. Rec. 97.

58. 41 Cong. Rec. 99.

59. He confirmed it years later when he told this same story "at a Patriotic Race Service, Held by the Negroes of Philadelphia" and made himself sound like a hero. Boies Penrose, "The Progress of the Negro Race" (speech, Philadelphia, March 1, 1914), http://digital.lib.lehigh.edu/eb/supp/4890/index.pdf (accessed September 28, 2014).

60. 41 Cong. Rec. 101 (1906).

61. 41 Cong. Rec. 102.

62. Ibid.

63. "In Foraker's Favor," *Dayton Daily News*, December 18, 1906.

64. "Call for the Facts," *Washington Herald*, December 7, 1906.

CHAPTER THIRTEEN: STRANGE FRUIT

1. "Strange Fruit" is the name of a poem by Abel Meeropol that later was made into a song recorded by, among others, Billie Holiday. Though the words *lynch* and *lynching* do not appear in its lyrics, the title refers to lynched bodies swinging from trees, a strange fruit. In 1999 *Time* magazine proclaimed it the song of the century. When he wrote the poem, Meeropol was a teacher in New York City and an active member of the Communist Party (years later he would leave it). He and his wife adopted the sons of Julius and Ethel Rosenberg, who stole secrets of the atom bomb to help the Soviet Union develop one of its own and were executed for it.

2. Washington very early on was given an advance copy of Roosevelt's address and circulated it among trusted members of the Tuskegee Machine for their thoughts. He warned Roosevelt his comments on lynching would not go over well, but Roosevelt ignored him. See Booker T. Washington, letter to Whitefield McKinlay, October 25, 1906, in *The Booker T. Washington Papers*, eds. Louis R. Harlan and Raymond W. Smock, vol. 9, *1906–8* (Urbana: University of Illinois Press, 1980), p. 103; Whitefield McKinlay, letter to Booker T. Washington, November 2, 1906, in Harlan and Smock, *Booker T. Washington Papers*, 9:113–14; also see T. Thomas Fortune, letter to Booker T. Washington, December 8, 1906, in Harlan and Smock, *Booker T. Washington Papers*, 9:156–58.

3. Kelly Miller, *The Everlasting Stain* (Washington, DC: Associated Publishers, 1924), pp. 329–30.

4. Mark Twain, *Autobiography of Mark Twain: The Complete and Authoritative Edition*, eds. Benjamin Griffin and Harriet Elinor Smith, vol. 2 (Berkeley: University of California Press, 2013), pp. 133, 524. A search of the online archives of the *New York Times* did not find this article.

5. Between six million and seven million Ukrainians are estimated to have died in two years. "Ukrainian Famine," *Revelations from the Russian Archives*, http://www.loc.gov/exhibits/archives/ukra.html (accessed May 21, 2014). The Russian successor government to the Soviet Union continues to deny the Ukrainian Famine as genocide. The government of Ukraine does, and it has made denial illegal. "Ukraine Famine," United Human Rights Council, http://www.unitedhumanrights.org/genocide/ukraine_famine.htm (accessed May 21, 2014).

6. Theodore Roosevelt, letter to Jacob Schiff, July 26, 1906, in *The Letters of Theodore Roosevelt*, ed. Elting E. Morison, vol. 5, *The Big Stick: 1905–1907* (Cambridge, MA: Harvard University Press, 1952), p. 336. Questioning America's inaction came from Russia itself. In a letter from one of the survivors, "We are considering why you in America, who are constantly doing so much good in the world, remain idle now. You made peace for Japan. Why are you not doing something for us?" "Bombs Sold Openly on Bialystok Streets," *New York Times*, June 17, 1906.

7. "William Lynch (Lynch Law)," *Wikipedia*, last modified August 19, 2013, http://en.wikipedia.org/wiki/William_Lynch_(Lynch_law) (accessed September 30, 2014), citing "Lynch, Charles," *American National Biography* and *Southern Lit-*

erary Messenger 2 (May 1836): 389. Mark Gado, "Carnival of Death: Lynching in America," Crime Library, http://www.crimelibrary.com/notorious_murders/mass/lynching/lynching_2.html (accessed May 21, 2014). "Lynch Law," *Daily Alta California* (San Francisco), July 20, 1887, available online at http://cdnc.ucr.edu/cgi-bin/cdnc?a=d&d=DAC18870720.2.48.

8. Miller, *Everlasting Stain*, pp. 324–28.

9. Theodore Roosevelt, letter to John M. Parker, October 3, 1906, box 27, Correspondence Photostats, Theodore Roosevelt Collection, Houghton Library, Harvard University.

10. Theodore Roosevelt, Address to the Proceedings of the New York State Conference of Charities and Correction at the First Annual Session, pp. 7–8, cited in *Roosevelt Cyclopedia*, eds. Albert B. Hart and Herbert R. Ferleger (New York City: Roosevelt Memorial Association, 1941), p. 321.

11. Theodore Roosevelt, letter to Philander Knox, July 24, 1903, in *The Letters of Theodore Roosevelt*, ed. Elting E. Morison, vol. 3, *The Square Deal: 1901–1903* (Cambridge, MA: Harvard University Press, 1951), p. 528.

12. Theodore Roosevelt, letter to Winfield Taylor Durbin, August 6, 1903, in Morison, *Letters of Theodore Roosevelt*, 3:540.

13. "The Wilmington Lynching," *New York Times*, October 29, 1903.

14. *Negro* with a lowercase *n* was in the transcript of the message. See, for example, Miller Center, http://millercenter.org/president/speeches/detail/3778, and the *New York Times*, December 5, 1906. The author used the transcript in these two sources for quoted material from the annual message.

15. The theory of "conspiracy of silence" seems never to have been applied to lynching. Lynchers were rarely caught and arrested, more rarely tried, and most rare of all, ever convicted, because a conspiracy of silence was between more than the lynchers and their abettors; it included sheriffs, local police, and other authorities. Lynchings took place with their knowledge, consent, and help. Lynching was worse than a perversion of a system of justice; it was a tool for terrorizing and controlling blacks—and occasionally others, such as Leo Frank, a Jew, in Atlanta.

16. Theodore Roosevelt, letter to Silas McBee, November 27, 1906, in Morison, *Letters of Theodore Roosevelt*, 5:509.

17. Booker T. Washington (address, National Negro Business League, Atlanta, August 29, 1906), in Harlan and Smock, *Booker T. Washington Papers*, 9:65, 62. The text has *negro* with a lowercase *n*, though it may not have been in the original. By 1906, Washington had been spelling *Negro* with an uppercase *N* for some years.

18. Donald L. Grant, *The Way It Was in the South: The Black Experience in Georgia* (New York: Birch Lane, 1993), p. 208.

19. Milholland Diary, September 23, 1906, John E. Milholland Papers (1887–1924), Ticonderoga (NY) Historical Society.

20. James Krohe Jr., "Reading: Anatomy of a Race Riot," *Chicago Reader*, September 13, 1990, http://www.chicagoreader.com/chicago/reading-anatomy-of-a-race-riot/Content?oid=876322 (accessed September 30, 2014).

21. "Atlanta Views on Riots," *New York Times*, September 24, 1906.

22. On the day of the riot, newspapers told of *four* assaults of women by Negroes. Journalist Ray Stannard Baker investigated and learned only two *may* have been assaults. The other two "were nothing more than fright on the part of both the white woman and the Negro." Ray Stannard Baker, *Following the Color Line: An Account of Negro Citizenship in the American Democracy* (Williamstown, MA: Corner House, 1973), pp. 9–10.

23. "Rioting Goes On, Despite Troops," *New York Times*, September 24, 1906 (with the subheadline "Exodus of Black Servants Troubles City"); "The Atlanta Riots," editorial, *New York Times*, September 25, 1906; Kathy Lohr, "Century-Old Race Riot Still Resonates in Atlanta," *National Public Radio*, September 22, 2006, transcript available online at http://www.npr.org/templates/story/story.php?storyId=6106285 (accessed September 30, 2014)·

24. "Atlanta Riots."

25. See Russell S. Bonds, *War Like the Thunderbolt: The Battle and Burning of Atlanta* (Yardley, PA: Westholme, 2009), for a superb narrative of the Battle of Atlanta. The expulsion of its residents and the city's burning are in chapters 11 and 12. Ray Stannard Baker makes the point that both races were bound by fear of the other race. Whites were afraid of Negro crime, especially rape. Negroes also feared Negro crime, for they, more than whites, were hurt by it. But Negroes also feared whites and the brutal consequences of what otherwise would be innocent encounters with them. Baker tells of an unnamed white woman who described how she was bumped by a Negro man who didn't see her on the street as he came out of a building. "When he turned and found it was a white woman he had touched, such a look of abject terror and fear came into his face as I hope never again to see on a human countenance. He knew what it meant if I was frightened, called for help, and accused him of insulting or attacking me. . . . It shows, doesn't it, how little it might take to bring punishment upon an innocent man!" Baker, *Following the Color Line*, p. 8.

26. Francis J. Grimké, "The Atlanta Riot" (speech, Washington, DC, October 7, 1906), University of Georgia Library.

27. See Edmund Morris, *Theodore Rex* (New York: Random House, 2001), pp. 451–52.

28. Harlan and Smock, *Booker T. Washington Papers*, 9:73.

29. Theodore Roosevelt, letter to Booker T. Washington, October 8, 1906, box 27, Correspondence Photostats, Theodore Roosevelt Collection.

30. "An Account of a Speech in New York," *New York Times*, September 21, 1906, reprinted in Harlan and Smock, *Booker T. Washington Papers*, 9:74–75.

31. See S. Laing Williams, letter to Booker T. Washington, October 7, 1906, in Harlan and Smock, *Booker T. Washington Papers*, 9:91. "I note your going to Atlanta in the midst of the anarchy down there. It was an exceedingly courageous thing for you to do and, like thousands of others I thank you for this exhibition of that sort of courage which counts in trying affairs."

32. David L. Lewis, *W. E. B. Du Bois: Biography of a Race, 1868–1919* (New York: Henry Holt, 1993), p. 335. The wife of John Hope, the president of Atlanta Baptist College, now Morehouse College, remembered the mob turning back from its campus rather than having to go through a "notoriously tough black ghetto" nearby (Lewis, *W. E. B. Du Bois: Biography of a Race*, p. 333).

33. Theodore Roosevelt, letter to Ray Stannard Baker, "Personal and Private," March 30, 1907, in Morison, *Letters of Theodore Roosevelt*, 5:634–35. Baker had been traveling the South to study the Negro "problem" there when Atlanta broke apart. The following spring, he wrote a series of articles titled "Following the Color Line" in the *American Magazine*. Roosevelt read the articles, and it was what they said about the causes of the Atlanta riots that he said he now agreed with. Baker later converted the articles into a book with a similar title, *Following the Color Line: American Negro Citizenship in the Progressive Era*.

34. Baker damns the white community. And he reveals that the foreman of the jury who tried (and acquitted) Negroes charged with crimes during the riot did too. Baker, *Following the Color Line*, pp. 14–16.

35. "Atlanta Views on Riots."

36. Lewis, *W. E. B. Du Bois: Biography of a Race*, p. 335.

37. Ibid., p. 337.

38. Ibid., p. 342.

39. Louis R. Harlan, introduction to *Up from Slavery*, by Booker T. Washington (New York: Viking Penguin, 1986), p. xiii.

40. Ann J. Lane, *The Brownsville Affair: National Crisis and Black Reaction* (Port Washington, NY: Kennikat, 1971), p. 77.

41. T. Thomas Fortune, letter to Booker T. Washington, December 8, 1906, in Harlan and Smock, *Booker T. Washington Papers*, 9:156–58. Fortune never liked Roosevelt. Just after he was elected governor of New York, Fortune told Washington, "He is no good, and you will find it out." T. Thomas Fortune, letter to Booker T. Washington, November 30, 1898, cited in *T. Thomas Fortune: Militant Journalist*, by Emma L. Thornbrough (Chicago: University of Chicago Press, 1972), p. 220. The feeling was mutual. While Roosevelt was in the White House, Fortune tried time and again for a federal appointment but never got one.

CHAPTER FOURTEEN: A DIFFERENT BURDEN OF PROOF

1. See "Washington Begged President Not to Dismiss Troops," *New York Age*, November 15, 1906. In this article is the related story about Pitcher: "There is reason to believe that Booker T. Washington is at the bottom of Col. Pitcher's trouble, though this cannot be established definitely."

2. "President Expels an Army Battalion," *New York Times*, November 6, 1906.

3. U. S. Grant, letter to Mary B. Pitcher, July 12, 1869, in *The Papers of*

Ulysses S. Grant, ed. John Y. Simon, vol. 19, *July 1, 1868–October 31, 1869* (Carbondale: Southern Illinois University Press, 1995), p. 204.

4. "Cadet Smith," *New York Times*, August 2, 1872.

5. "Censures Lieut. Col. Pitcher," *New York Times*, November 18, 1904.

6. "Race Feeling Rampant among Negro Soldiers," *New York Times*, November 7, 1906.

7. One was the *Brownsville Herald*. "Dismissed by President," *Brownsville Herald*, November 8, 1906.

8. "Grants in Washington," *New York Times*, February 25, 1907. Pitcher immediately denied the charges against him. The *New York Age* reported on November 15, 1906, his statement that "he had never entertained and never expressed such sentiments. He explained that he had served with colored troops in the past and had seen them do heroic fighting" ("Pitcher, of Course, Denies").

9. "Infantry's Officers Remiss; Did Not Examine Rifles until Day after the Brownsville Riot," *New York Times*, November 15, 1906.

10. "May Punish Officers of Negro Battalion," *New York Times*, November 13, 1906; "Officers to Be Tried for Brownsville Riot," *New York Times*, November 15, 1906.

11. Maj. Augustus P. Blocksom Report, Summary Discharge or Mustering Out of Regiments or Companies . . . , S. Doc. No. 59-155, vol. 11 (2d sess. 1907) (hereafter cited as SD-1), p. 425; A. B. Nettleton Letter, SD-1, p. 533.

12. "Negro Troops Praised," *New York Times*, November 27, 1906. The *Washington Post* stories of November 27 and 29 are included in Henry Fowler Pringle, Research Notes for *Theodore Roosevelt: A Biography*, 7th year, p. 4, Houghton Library, Harvard University.

13. A. B. Nettleton, letter to William Howard Taft, SD-1, p. 535. Nettleton said nothing about Captain Macklin drinking beer while officer of the day. When Garlington later was questioned about Macklin going to sleep while on duty, he said it was no concern; "this was the usual custom in the service."

14. Fred W. Carpenter (Taft's private secretary), memorandum to the general staff, December 6, 1906, SD-1, p. 291.

15. Theodore Roosevelt, letter to William Howard Taft, December 5, 1906, SD-1, p. 291; Fred W. Carpenter, letter to the general staff, December 6, 1906, SD-1, p. 291; statement that matter was "very much a question," SD-1, p. 291; Macklin's response, SD-1, p. 296; Garlington's response, SD-1, p. 292; Roosevelt approves court-martial, SD-1, p. 299. The genesis of the courts-martial may have been a statement Maj. Charles Penrose made to Gilchrist Stewart on the day the last soldier was mustered out at Fort Reno. "There goes the last of the best disciplined, best behaved and regulated battalion in the entire United States Army." Stewart asked him if this was for publication. "Yes, indeed, I would say that anywhere." Stewart told it to the *Washington Post*, which published it on November 27, the day Roosevelt returned from Panama. On Thanksgiving, Roosevelt would have read in the *Post* that morning that Penrose's statement had caused indignation at

the War Department. "It was flagrantly insubordinate, and his court-martial would surely follow." The *Washington Post* stories of November 27 and 29 are included in Pringle, Research Notes, 7th year, p. 4. President Roosevelt may have seen this was a message to him. The *New York Times* ran with the story that same day. "Negro Troops Praised," *New York Times*, November 27, 1906.

16. See Frederick Funston, Commanding General, Southwestern Division, to Military Secretary, December 5, 1906, Summary Discharge or Mustering Out of Regiments or Companies: Message from the President of the United States . . . , S. Doc. No. 59-155, vol. 11, pt. 2 (2d sess. 1907) (hereafter cited as SD-1), p. 201.

17. Maj. Augustus Blocksom, letter to Capt. William Kelly and Frederick Combe, December 4, 1906, SD-1, pp. 202–203.

18. See Report of the Judge-Advocate General of the Army upon the Subject of Discharge without Honor, SD-1, pp. 279–82.

19. *Stewart Report* may be a complete misnomer. What was given to President Roosevelt and Senator Foraker was signed by officers of the Constitution League and referred to as a "Petition." Properly it should be referred to as the *Constitution League Report*. Stewart made the investigation on which it was based and had the major role in writing it, and to keep its continuity with his investigation clear, it will be referred to from this point on as the *Stewart Report*.

20. The date of Roosevelt's telegram (actually Loeb's on his behalf) to Stewart was December 8, 1906, and is referenced in Humphrey's cover letter with the report on December 10, 1906. SD-1, p. 205. Stewart, reply telegram, December 8/9, 1906, Theodore Roosevelt Papers, Library of Congress.

21. Milholland Diary, December 9, 1906, John E. Milholland Papers (1887–1924), Ticonderoga (NY) Historical Society. They had been working on it since the first of the month, as indicated by Milholland's diary for that date, when Stewart got back from Fort Reno.

22. James A. Tinsley, "Roosevelt, Foraker, and the Brownsville Affray," *Journal of Negro History* 41, no. 1 (1956): 50.

23. See *Stewart Report*, SD-1, pp. 229–30. Frazier's correctly spelled name is in the army record at SD-1, p. 266.

24. According to the *New York Times*, Stewart "was assisted by a Mr. Barbour," a local attorney. "Negro Troops Answer Inquiry under Oath," *New York Times*, November 25, 1906.

25. The affidavits appear at SD-1, pp. 216–34.

26. "Short Evening with Gilchrist Stewart on Roosevelt Telegram," diary entry, Milholland Diary, December 8, 1906, Milholland Papers.

27. It is not certain when Smith left for Brownsville. Milholland wrote in his diary, "I'm preparing to send for Joe Smith to investigate the shameful actions of the Administration in dealing with the Black Soldiers at Brownsville and Oh let me be free, Good Lord, that I may free others!" This probably was sometime in September, possibly September 10, because it is sandwiched between the September 9 and September 11 entries. We know for sure the draft of the report was ready on November

24, because on that date Milholland wrote, "Spent entire day in the house scouring [illegible] from Smith and Stewart. Smith's . . . was superb, *better* than I expected & my expectations were lofty. Stewart's was good but his appeal to Washington premature and a mistake." Milholland Diary, November 24, 1906, Milholland Papers. Milholland's praise for both men and failure to comment on the faulty affidavits suggests he had only the report interpreting the affidavits and other evidence but not the affidavits themselves.

28. *Stewart Report*, SD-1, pp. 205–35. For this argument, see pp. 205–206 and p. 209. Stewart may have brought this up to Taft before he left Fort Reno. Brownsville historian John Weaver wrote that he wired Taft from Fort Reno, "[Soldiers] not allowed to present their side and investigation a farce." In his report he modified this argument to say they had such an opportunity but whatever they said had not been considered or even received by the War Department until after their guilt was presumed. Weaver's citation of authority is "National Archives." John D. Weaver, *The Brownsville Raid* (College Station: Texas A&M University Press, 1992), pp. 109, 301.

29. Constitution League Report, SD-1: Residents' bias, p. 209; shooters wore khaki, p. 211; witnesses were unable to identify, p. 208; mixed arms, p. 214; rifle in common use, p. 217; and prejudging case, p. 220.

30. Milholland Diary, December 7, 1906, Milholland Papers.

31. See ibid., December 9, 1906. On December 2 Milholland's diary reflected his mounting frustration with the investigation's costs and his acceptance of them. "Our report on the Negro Battalion Discharge in preparation by Gil Stewart and Joe Smith wired from San Antonio for $50 I think making to him $200. This Negro Soldier [illegible] will cost me more than $500 and I don't begrudge a cent of it. This is for the Republic."

32. The time and date are fixed by Loeb's cover letter to Taft forwarding the report. William Loeb, forward letter to William Howard Taft, December 11, 1906, SD-1, p. 204. There was no mention of the telegrams exchanged between Stewart and the White House in November when Roosevelt was in Panama. The report was to have been ready and delivered on November 27; perhaps the Constitution League did not want to remind Roosevelt it was late.

33. "Keep your eyes on the stars and your feet on the ground" was a Roosevelt aphorism.

34. "Roosevelt Sees Payn and Wins Approval," *New York Times*, July 1, 1906.

35. "Noted Men Demand We Arm for War," *New York Times*, December 2, 1914. Theodore Roosevelt was another. See Peter Collier and David Horowitz, *The Roosevelts: An American Saga* (New York: Simon & Schuster, 1994), pp. 182–87.

36. "Soldiers Have Chance. President Tempers His Order against Negro Troops," *Washington Post*, December 12, 1906.

37. Gen. Ernest A. Garlington, letter to Gen. Fred C. Ainsworth, December 14, 1906, SD-1, pp. 242–43; Maj. Augustus Blocksom, letter to Gen. Fred C. Ainsworth, December 12, 1906, SD-1, pp. 236–37.

38. Maj. Augustus Blocksom, letter to Gen. Fred C. Ainsworth, December 12, 1906, SD-1, p. 236.

39. SD-1, p. 204.

CHAPTER FIFTEEN: CORDIAL COOPERATION

1. "Roosevelt to Explain," *New York Times*, December 7, 1906.

2. This was in accordance with Section 2 of the Fourteenth Amendment to the Constitution: "Representatives shall be apportioned among the several states according to their respective numbers, counting the whole number of persons in each state, excluding Indians not taxed. But when the right to vote . . . is denied . . . or in any way abridged, . . . the basis of representation therein shall be reduced in the proportion which the number of such male citizens shall bear to the whole number of male citizens twenty-one years of age in such state."

3. 22 Cong. Rec. 730 (1890) (address of Sen. Spooner). The purpose was as much to protect the Negro as a sure Republican voter as to protect the Negro's rights as an American. Republican votes and Negro equality both were marginalized when Lodge's bill was traded away to gain passage of the McKinley Tariff Act and its increased tariffs on imported materials and goods. The fatigue from the continuing fight for black rights could no longer be questioned.

4. James R. Parker, "Paternalism and Racism: Sen. John C. Spooner and American Minorities, 1897–1907," *Wisconsin Magazine of History* 57, no. 3 (1974).

5. John C. Spooner, letter to T. L. Rosser, March 1, 1904, John C. Spooner Papers, Library of Congress.

6. Dorothy Ganfield Fowler, *John Coit Spooner: Defender of Presidents* (New York: University Publishers, 1961), p. 361. This is not confirmed by the chronology in *The Letters of Theodore Roosevelt*, ed. Elting E. Morison, vol. 6, *The Big Stick: 1907–1909* (Cambridge, MA: Harvard University Press, 1952), p. 1604.

7. Fowler cites as authority letters from the Spooner Papers: William Loeb, letter to John C. Spooner, December 6, 1906; William Howard Taft, letters to John C. Spooner, December 22, 1906, January 4, 1907, and January 5, 1907.

8. In his message's first paragraph, Roosevelt seems to taunt the Senate by calling it simply "several documents." This report makes up what is referred to in this book as SD-1. Volume 11 of S. Doc. No. 59-155 contains another 201 pages of testimony taken and other evidence, photos, and maps prepared after December 19, plus President Roosevelt's second Special Message on January 14, 1907, all of which is designated as SD-2.

9. Taft's memo answered three resolutions: Penrose's, Foraker's and a third asking for the history of riots, raids, or other disturbances between the Twenty-Fifth Infantry and civilians at posts before Brownsville. All three are "inclosures" to Roosevelt's Special Message.

10. Summary Discharge or Mustering Out of Regiments or Companies: Message from the President of the United States . . . , S. Doc. No. 59-155, vol. 11, pt. 1 (2d sess. 1907) (hereafter cited as SD-1), p. 15.

11. Its full text is at SD-1, pp. 1–9.

12. Would the timidity fostered by the political correctness of the twenty-first century permit anyone to use "black" as often as Roosevelt did to color a crime said to be committed by black men?

13. SD-1, p. 5.

14. SD-1, pp. 5, 2.

15. "Public interest" could take in and act as a defense of just about anything.

16. SD-1, p. 203.

17. SD-1, p. 6.

18. SD-1, pp. 8–9.

19. Roosevelt's message referred to the letter from General A. B. Nettleton. On November 18 its full text was published on page 1 of the *Brownsville Daily Herald* in an article that referred to the shooting as "the infamous outrage upon Brownsville." A yellowing copy is at the National Archives in file 1135832, box 4499, Records of the Adjutant General's Office, 1780s–1917.

20. "Foraker Leads Fight," *Washington Post*, December 20, 1906; "The Brownsville Affair," *Washington Post*, December 20, 1906.

21. Joseph B. Foraker, *Notes of a Busy Life*, 2 vols. (Cincinnati: Stewart & Kidd, 1917), 2:236. Roosevelt biographer Henry Pringle wonders if Foraker received any joy in seeing how irritated Roosevelt was. Henry Fowler Pringle, Research Notes for *Theodore Roosevelt: A Biography*, 7th year, p. 5, Houghton Library, Harvard University.

22. 41 Cong. Rec. 551 (1906).

23. Ibid.

24. Ibid.

25. Ibid.

26. Ibid.

27. Ibid.

28. 41 Cong. Rec. 552.

29. 41 Cong. Rec. 552–53.

30. "The Brownsville Affair."

31. Milholland Diary, December 20 and 21, 1906, John E. Milholland Papers (1887–1924), Ticonderoga (NY) Historical Society.

32. "Foraker's Attack," *Washington Post*, December 21, 1906. The prominence given to Foraker's address, reflecting in great part how much was expected from it, can be seen in the placement of news stories about it in the *Washington Post* and in the *New York Times*. The former put it on page 1 and the latter on page 2. Both newspapers put Roosevelt's special message on p. 5.

33. Roosevelt had thundered, "I refer to Major Blocksom's report for proof of the fact that certainly some, and probably all, of the non-commissioned officers in

charge of the quarters who were responsible for the gun racks and had keys thereto in their personal possession knew what men were engaged in the attack," SD-1, p. 4. What Blocksom's report actually said was, "Many of its old soldiers who had nothing to do with the raid must have known something tangible as to the identity of the criminals," SD-1, p. 428. In later testimony, to a man every noncommissioned officer would deny it.

34. 41 Cong. Rec. 568.

35. U.S. Constitution, art. 1, sec. 8.

36. 41 Cong. Rec. 571.

37. 41 Cong. Rec. 568.

38. 41 Cong. Rec. 569.

39. 41 Cong. Rec. 571. Lodge came to the Senate that day angry at Foraker. The day before, Senator Warren wrote his daughter that he noticed "Foraker and Lodge are a bit belligerent." Francis Warren, letter to Frances "Frankie" Warren Pershing, December 19, 1906, Francis E. Warren Papers, American Heritage Center, University of Wyoming.

40. The counting of witnesses and the elimination of those not eyewitnesses are at 41 Cong. Rec. 571–73.

41. 41 Cong. Rec. 573.

42. 41 Cong. Rec. 576.

43. Ibid.

44. SD-1, p. 4.

45. 41 Cong. Rec. 577.

46. Ibid.

47. 41 Cong. Rec. 577–78. At its next reunion, the "surviving members of the 60th O. V. I." thanked Foraker "for defending, on the floor of the United States Senate, our record as soldiers in the war of rebellion." Resolution, September 18, 1907, box 69, folder 1907-M (cont.), Foraker Papers.

48. 41 Cong. Rec. 578–79.

49. 41 Cong. Rec. 579.

50. 41 Cong. Rec. 592.

51. "Foraker's Attack."

52. Everett Walters, *Joseph Benson Foraker: An Uncompromising Republican* (Columbus: Ohio History Press, 1948), p. 237, citing "The Brownsville Affray," *Literary Digest*, December 29, 1906, p. 967.

53. Milholland's reaction to this: "Roosevelt broke loose again on Col. Soldiers matter, telling press he would defy Congress and even hazard impeachment before he would surrender and—[Milholland editorializes] do right." Milholland Diary, December 23, 1906, Milholland Papers.

54. "Mr. Roosevelt Defies Negro Troops' Friends," *New York Times*, December 23, 1906.

55. John D. Weaver, *The Brownsville Raid* (College Station: Texas A&M University Press, 1992), p. 118. Weaver has no citation of authority.

56. William Howard Taft, letter to Milton D. Purdy, December 22, 1906, SD-2, p. viii.

57. SD-2, pp. vii–viii.

58. Roosevelt's orders are contained in the report Taft sent him on January 12, 1907, SD-2, p. vii. The reason for the investigation is in "Purdy Goes to Texas," *Washington Post*, December 23, 1906.

59. "Mr. Roosevelt Defies Negro Troops' Friends."

60. Joseph B. Foraker, letter to Sen. W. A. Clark, December 29, 1906, box 47, Foraker Papers.

61. Henry F. Pringle, *Theodore Roosevelt: A Biography* (New York: Harcourt, Brace, 1984), p. 325.

62. Theodore Roosevelt, letter to Booker T. Washington, November 5, 1906, in *The Booker T. Washington Papers*, eds. Louis R. Harlan and Raymond W. Smock, vol. 9, *1906–8* (Urbana: University of Illinois, 1980), p. 118. See Hae-sung Hwang, *Booker T. Washington and W. E. B. Du Bois: A Study in Race Leadership, 1895–1915* (Seoul: American Studies Institute, Seoul National University, 1992), p. 139.

63. Booker T. Washington, letter to James A. Cobb, November 13, 1906, in Harlan and Smock, *Booker T. Washington Papers*, 9:124–25.

64. Booker T. Washington, letter to Ralph Tyler, December 5, 1906, in ibid., 9:153–54.

65. Emmett Scott, letter to William Howard Taft, December 12, 1906, in ibid., 9:163–64.

66. Hwang, *Booker T. Washington and W. E. B. Du Bois*, p. 141.

67. Milholland Diary, December 23, 1906 ("Senator Foraker arrived from Washington and decided to confer at 10 a.m. Monday."), and December 24, 1906, Milholland Papers.

68. Joseph Foraker, letter to Creighton Foraker, November 24, 1906, box 49, Foraker Papers. All letters dealing with James Foraker's illness are in box 49.

69. Milholland Diary, December 24, 1906, Milholland Papers.

70. See "Secret Service Aiding," *Washington Post*, December 27, 1906; and "To Improve President's Case against Negroes," *New York Times*, December 27, 1906. The newspapers may have gotten the story from a leak by Foraker; the *Post* article claims its sources were "Senators insisting upon an investigation by the Senate."

71. Gen. Fred C. Ainsworth, telegram to William Loeb, August 25, 1906, SD-1, p. 94; and William Loeb, telegram to Gen. Fred C. Ainsworth, SD-1, p. 100.

72. Gen. Fred C. Ainsworth, letter to John E. Wilkie, September 12, 1906, SD-1, pp. 98–99.

73. Kathleen Dalton, *Theodore Roosevelt: A Strenuous Life* (New York: Alfred A. Knopf, 2002), p. 341.

74. Theodore Roosevelt, Eighth Annual Message (address, Washington, DC, December 9, 1908), available online from the Miller Center at the University of Virginia, http://millercenter.org/president/speeches/detail/3780 (accessed September 30, 2014); Morison, *Letters of Theodore Roosevelt*, 6:1424n3. See also Theodore Roo-

sevelt, letter to Eugene Hale, February 19, 1909, in Morison, *Letters of Theodore Roosevelt*, 6:1527.

75. Emma L. Thornbrough, *T. Thomas Fortune: Militant Journalist* (Chicago: University of Chicago Press, 1972), p. 264.

76. T. Thomas Fortune, letter to Booker T. Washington, December 8, 1906, in Harlan and Smock, *Booker T. Washington Papers*, 9:156–58.

77. Washington was worried about Fortune's drinking. Booker T. Washington, letter to Frederick Randolph Moore, August 20, 1906, in ibid., 9:61. Fortune went to Atlanta anyway.

78. Charles Anderson, letter to Booker T. Washington, January 21, 1907, in ibid., 9:197.

79. According to what Stewart told Anderson, it was $375 Milholland gave Stokes for his expenses, not the $175 in Milholland's diary.

80. Booker T. Washington, letter to George Cortelyou, January 28, 1907, Booker T. Washington Papers, Library of Congress, cited in *The Brownsville Affair: National Crisis and Black Reaction*, by Ann J. Lane (Port Washington, NY: Kennikat, 1971), p. 97. Cortelyou coldly answered Washington, "The gentleman you mention is not an employee of this Department" and "is not actively connected" with the pneumatic-tube companies that had a contract with it. George Cortelyou, letter to Booker T. Washington, February 16, 1907, in Harlan and Smock, *Booker T. Washington Papers*, 9:219.

81. Joseph B. Foraker, letter to William Howard Taft, December 26, 1906, box 24, Foraker Papers. Taft quickly and courteously responded with the requested material.

82. Milholland Diary, December 31, 1906, Milholland Papers.

CHAPTER SIXTEEN: MOST IMPLICIT FAITH

1. "Must Vote on Legality of President's Action," *New York Times*, January 4, 1907.

2. "Shielding the President," *New York Times*, January 5, 1907.

3. "Urge Lodge to Give Way," *New York Times*, January 7, 1907. See "Roosevelt Is Defeated on Brownsville Issue," *New York Times*, January 8, 1907, for a discussion of Sen. Winthrop Crane's objections. Crane's family owned Crane & Co., which manufactured quality paper for correspondence and other uses. When he was involved in its business, he landed the government contract to supply paper for US currency. It still does.

4. The dread saturating the Republicans' Senate cloakroom was strong enough to register in the *Washington Post* newsroom. A week earlier it noted, "nowhere can be found a Republican member of [the Senate], recognized as a lawyer of ability, who is willing to come to the front as the defender of the President." "No Champion Appears," *Washington Post*, December 12, 1906.

5. "Roosevelt Is Defeated in Brownsville Issue," *New York Times*, January 8, 1907. That evening a sobered President Roosevelt held a meeting at the White House with senators to discuss Brownsville. Elting E. Morison, ed., *The Letters of Theodore Roosevelt*, vol. 6, *The Big Stick: 1905–1907* (Cambridge, MA: Harvard University Press, 1952), p. 1605.

6. Robert La Follette, letter to Belle Case La Follette, January 7, 1907, box A6, La Follette Family Papers, Library of Congress.

7. "Angry Negro Debate, Tillman Rouses Senate," *New York Times*, January 13, 1907.

8. "Fire from Tillman," *Washington Post*, January 13, 1907.

9. Francis Butler Simkins, *Pitchfork Ben Tillman, South Carolinian* (Baton Rouge: Louisiana State University Press, 1944), p. 45.

10. The missing eye kept him out of the Confederate Army.

11. See Philip J. McFarland, *Mark Twain and the Colonel: Samuel L. Clemens, Theodore Roosevelt, and the Arrival of a New Century* (Lanham, MD: Rowman & Littlefield, 2012), p. 161.

12. See Simkins, *Pitchfork Ben Tillman*, p. 441.

13. Just a few months earlier, Tillman allied himself with his archenemy Roosevelt on the Hepburn Bill. When Roosevelt turned on Republicans in the Senate, Tillman became his floor leader to get the bill passed.

14. Stephen David Kantrowitz, *More Than Freedom: Fighting for Black Citizenship in a White Republic, 1829–1889* (New York: Penguin Press, 2012), p. 67.

15. It never recovered, and today Hamburg exists only as a street name in North Augusta, Georgia.

16. David L. Lewis, *W. E. B. Du Bois: Biography of a Race, 1868–1919* (New York: Henry Holt, 1993), p. 255.

17. See Simkins, *Pitchfork Ben Tillman*, pp. 62–64.

18. None of the perpetrators of the Hamburg murders was ever tried.

19. It was during that campaign that he acquired his nickname when he said he was going to take his pitchfork to Washington and use it to prod fellow Democrat President Grover Cleveland, "the old bag of beef," in his "old fat ribs." See McFarland, *Mark Twain and the Colonel*, p. 161.

20. Kantrowitz, *More Than Freedom*, p. 259.

21. The *Atlanta Constitution* was upset that he did. "Senator Tillman throws little light on or the reasons for his attitude [of helping the soldiers]. . . . It appears from his argument that [he] rather sought to turn the facts of the Brownsville case to his own ends." "Tillman and the President," *Atlanta Constitution*, January 14, 1907.

22. Quoted items in 41 Cong. Rec. 1030–32 (1907) (statements of Sen. Tillman).

23. Ibid.

24. Simkins, *Pitchfork Ben Tillman*, p. 443.

25. 41 Cong. Rec. 1033.

26. The transcript of his comments in the *Congressional Record* does not match all that was attributed to him in the *Washington Post*. The *Post* seems to have used

prepared remarks it had a copy of but that in some places were disregarded or for-gotten in the heat of the debate. The reference to President Roosevelt's responsibility was one example. It might have been better that he omitted some comments; there was enough anger that day.

27. 41 Cong. Rec. 1042.

28. 41 Cong. Rec. 1040.

29. 41 Cong. Rec. 1047 (statement of Sen. Tillman).

30. Theodore Roosevelt, letter to Kermit Roosevelt, January 1, 1909, in Morison, *Letters of Theodore Roosevelt*, 6:1472.

31. Summary Discharge or Mustering Out of Regiments or Companies: Message from the President of the United States . . . , S. Doc. No. 59-155, vol. 11, pt. 2 (2d sess. 1907) (hereafter cited as SD-2), p. vii.

32. The message and its attachments make up SD-2. They are: Roosevelt's message, pp. i–vi; Taft's letter transmitting the Purdy-Blocksom evidence, pp. vii–xviii; a second Taft letter commenting specifically on the testimony of one witness, Paulino Preciado, p. xix; Taft's preliminary statement on the evidence, pp. 5–6; Major Blocksom's report and Mr. Purdy's concurrence, p. 7; the witnesses' affida-vits, pp. 11–200 (except for other documentary evidence scattered within the affida-vits and shown in the table of contents, pp. 3–4).

33. Theodore Roosevelt, Special Message, January 12, 1907, SD-2, p. ii.

34. A rifle's barrel has grooves on its inside that cause the bullet to rotate as it passes through. This gives it spin to make it more accurate and gives it greater range. In between the grooves are "lands" that leave marks on the bullet. The barrel of the Springfield rifle had four lands; the Winchester's had six. A "cartridge" is the combined bullet and shell that contains the powder that explodes and propels the bullet down and out of the barrel. When the rifle is fired, the empty shell separates from the bullet, is ejected, and falls to the ground.

35. Roosevelt, Special Message, SD-2, pp. iii–iv.

36. Ibid., pp. ii, v.

37. Ibid., p. v.

38. Ibid., p. vi.

39. "Roosevelt Modifies Negro Dismissal Order," *New York Times*, January 15, 1907.

40. 41 Cong. Rec. 1131–32 (statement of Sen. Spooner). See also Dorothy Ganfield Fowler, *John Coit Spooner: Defender of Presidents* (New York: University Publishers, 1961), pp. 361–62.

41. 41 Cong. Rec. 1137.

42. Ibid.

43. 41 Cong. Rec. 1142.

44. Cited in John D. Weaver, *The Brownsville Raid* (College Station: Texas A&M University Press, 1992), p. 137.

45. 41 Cong. Rec. 1435 (statement of Sen. Blackburn). See also "A Break on Brownsville," *Boston Evening Transcript*, January 18, 1907.

46. "A Break on Brownsville." See also "Roosevelt Beats down Enemies in the Senate," *New York Times*, January 21, 1907.

47. For Blackburn's reaction to Republicans, see "Senate Democrats Trap the Republican Leaders," *New York Times*, January 18, 1907.

48. "Senate Hesitates at Amendments," *San Francisco Call*, January 18, 1907.

49. Theodore Roosevelt, letter to Kermit Roosevelt, January 19, 1907, in *The Letters of Theodore Roosevelt*, ed. Elting E. Morison, vol. 5, *The Big Stick: 1905–1907* (Cambridge, MA: Harvard University Press, 1952), pp. 557–58.

50. "Roosevelt Beats Down Enemies in the Senate." The newsworthiness of Roosevelt's counterattack against fellow Republicans is shown by the placement of this story on page 1, when three days earlier Brownsville was on page 8.

51. "Surrender to Roosevelt," *New York Times*, January 21, 1907.

52. 41 Cong. Rec. 1501. The debate touched upon Mormon religious practices and beliefs, Mormon Church history, and Smoot's "heresies" (a lawyer in Provo said one was being a member of the Republican party), but it kept coming back, as everyone knew it would, to the problem of polygamy.

53. 41 Cong. Rec. 1511.

54. "Brownsville Inquiry Voted by Senate," *New York Times*, January 23, 1907.

55. 41 Cong. Rec. 1512.

56. Joseph B. Foraker, *Notes of a Busy Life*, 2 vols. (Cincinnati: Stewart & Kidd, 1917), 2:248–49.

57. Theodore Roosevelt, letter to George Spinney, January 22, 1907, in Morison, *Letters of Theodore Roosevelt*, 5:559–60. In this letter, Roosevelt refers to having had a "comic time" with the Senate, which surely was not so, especially when Republicans threatened to support Senator Blackburn's amendment in the debate's final days.

58. Henry Cabot Lodge, letter to W. Sturgis Bigelow, January 23, 1907, P-525, reel 24, Henry Cabot Lodge Papers, Massachusetts Historical Society, Boston. Sturgis was close enough to Roosevelt to have him as his houseguest in December 1912, when Roosevelt was in Boston to give his address "History as Literature" to the American Historical Association meeting there. See Edmund Morris, *Colonel Roosevelt* (New York: Random House, 2010), p. 262.

59. H.R. 22591, 59th Cong. (1906); 41 Cong. Rec. 436.

60. File 1135832, box 4499, Records of the Adjutant General's Office, 1780s–1917, National Archives.

61. Michael Lee Lanning, *The African-American Soldier: From Crispus Attucks to Colin Powell* (Secaucus, NJ: Carol, 1997), p. 115.

62. "May Fire Soldiers," *Columbus Citizen*, January 22, 1907, microfilm roll 8950, Ohio History Connection.

63. Clipping dated March 18, 1907, from an unidentified newspaper in box 70, Joseph Foraker Papers, Cincinnati History Library and Archives. From other articles on the yellowing page, it appears to have been a black paper.

64. David McCullough, *The Path between the Seas: The Creation of the Panama Canal, 1870–1914* (New York: Simon and Schuster, 1977), p. 568.

65. Ibid.

66. Booker T. Washington, letter to Francis E. Leupp, January 18, 1907, in *The Booker T. Washington Papers*, eds. Louis R. Harlan and Raymond W. Smock, vol. 9, *1906–8* (Urbana: University of Illinois Press, 1980), pp. 190–91.

CHAPTER SEVENTEEN: "WHAT *DID* HAPPEN AT THAT GRIDIRON DINNER . . . ?"

1. Julia Foraker, *I Would Live It Again* (New York: Arno, 1975), p. 3.

2. Cleveland disliked reporters, but after leaving the White House he attended at least one Gridiron dinner. Brayman, Harold. *From Grover Cleveland to Gerald Ford . . . The President Speaks Off-the-Record. Historic Evenings with America's Leaders, the Press, and Other Men of Power, at Washington's Exclusive Gridiron Club* (Princeton: Dow Jones Books, 1976), p. 33.

3. "Wits Hold Revels," *Washington Post*, December 9, 1906.

4. Theodore Roosevelt, letter to Lyman Abbott, January 3, 1907, in *The Letters of Theodore Roosevelt*, ed. Elting E. Morison, vol. 5, *The Big Stick: 1905–1907* (Cambridge, MA: Harvard University Press, 1952), p. 536.

5. Paul B. Beers, *Pennsylvania Politics Today and Yesterday: The Tolerable Accommodation* (University Park: Pennsylvania State University Press, 1980), p. 51.

6. W. Sturgis Bigelow, letter to Henry Cabot Lodge, n.d., P-525, p. 24, Henry Cabot Lodge Papers, Massachusetts Historical Society, Boston.

7. Theodore Roosevelt, letter to Kermit Roosevelt, June 9, 1906, in Morison, *Letters of Theodore Roosevelt*, 5:296.

8. Washington dispatch filed by a Pittsburg (as it was then spelled) correspondent, reprinted in "Cheers for Foraker," *Washington Post*, January 29, 1907.

9. Brownsville had a passing mention at the dinner a month earlier. In one skit, an officer from the Twenty-Fifth Infantry explained that Taft had to rescind his suspension of Roosevelt's order "because he found that Fairbanks had bagged the coons." "Gridiron in Round of Mirth," *Washington Times*, December 9, 1906.

10. Edmund Morris, *Theodore Rex* (New York: Random House, 2001), pp. 91–92.

11. Theodore Roosevelt, letter to Kermit Roosevelt, February 16, 1907, in Morison, *Letters of Theodore Roosevelt*, 5:589–90.

12. Mark Twain, *Autobiography of Mark Twain: The Complete and Authoritative Edition*, eds. Benjamin Griffin and Harriet Elinor Smith, vol. 2 (Berkeley: University of California Press, 2013), pp. 552, 259.

13. These lyrics can be found at http://clio.lib.olemiss.edu/cdm/ref/collection/sharris/id/1122 (accessed October 1, 2014).

14. The discussion of coon songs and "All Coons Look Alike to Me" was distilled from Arnold Shaw, *Black Popular Music in America: From the Spirituals, Minstrels, and Ragtime to Soul, Disco, and Hip-Hop* (New York: Schirmer Books, 1986),

pp. 30–39; and Dave Wondrich, "The First Rock 'n' Roll Record," *Lowest Common Denominator* 25, https://wfmu.org/LCD/25/firstrock1.html (accessed May 27, 2014).

15. "Ernest Hogan, 'All Coons Look Alike to Me,'" Yah's People, http://www.yahspeople.com/bloglounge/ernest-hogan-all-coons-look-a-like-to-me (accessed December 30, 2012).

16. Foraker, *I Would Live It Again*, pp. 280–81.

17. Everett Walters, *Joseph Benson Foraker: An Uncompromising Republican* (Columbus: Ohio History Press, 1948), p. 239.

18. Morris, *Theodore Rex*, p. 478.

19. "Gridiron Fires Nation's Great on Hot Griddle," *Washington Post*, December 9, 1934.

20. Morris, *Theodore Rex*, p. 479.

21. "Roosevelt in Tilt," *Washington Post*, January 29, 1907.

22. Ibid.

23. Ibid.; Morison, *Letters of Theodore Roosevelt*, 5:571n1.

24. Arthur W. Dunn, *Gridiron Nights: Humorous and Satirical Views of Politics and Statesmen as Presented by the Famous Dining Club* (New York: Frederick A. Stokes Company, 1915), p. 167.

25. Morris, *Theodore Rex*, p. 479; Walters, *Joseph Benson Foraker*, p. 239.

26. Champ Clark, *My Quarter Century of American Politics* (New York: Harper & Brothers, 1920), p. 445; "Loosed the Dogs of Wrath to Tear the Vitals of His Bitterest Foes," *Cincinnati Enquirer*, January 29, 1907.

27. "Roosevelt in Tilt." Roosevelt had been darn serious. Perhaps the *Washington Post* was trying to say Foraker was less angry.

28. Morris, *Theodore Rex*, p. 479.

29. Walters, *Joseph Benson Foraker*, p. 239.

30. Clark, *My Quarter Century of American Politics*, p. 447.

31. "Cheers for Foraker," *Washington Post*, January 29, 1907.

32. Henry Fowler Pringle, Research Notes for *Theodore Roosevelt: A Biography*, 7th year, p. 12, Houghton Library, Harvard University. As excited as Pringle's notes were, for some reason his finished biography never mentioned the Gridiron Club dinner. Morris, *Theodore Rex*, p. 725n480; Clark, *My Quarter Century in American Politics*, p. 447.

33. "Roosevelt in Tilt." Roosevelt biographer Edmund Morris quotes Foraker as expressing this love in the past tense, having at that moment only an "affectionate regard for him." Morris, *Theodore Rex*, p. 480.

34. Clark, *My Quarter Century in American Politics*, p. 446; "Cheers for Foraker"; Morris, *Theodore Rex*, p. 725n480; H. W. Brands, *TR: The Last Romantic* (New York: Basic Books, 1997), p. 592.

35. Clark, *My Quarter Century in American Politics*, p. 446.

36. "Loosed the Dogs of Wrath to Tear the Vitals of His Bitterest Foes."

37. Clark, *My Quarter Century in American Politics*, p. 443.

38. John Galvin, letter to Joseph B. Foraker, box 64, Joseph Foraker Papers, Cincinnati History Library and Archives.

39. Joseph B. Foraker, *Notes of a Busy Life*, 2 vols. (Cincinnati: Stewart & Kidd, 1917), 2:252.

40. Oscar S. Straus Diary, box 22, Oscar S. Straus Papers, Library of Congress.

41. Albert Beveridge, note to Theodore Roosevelt, January 27, 1906, Theodore Roosevelt Papers, Library of Congress.

42. James R. Garfield Diary, January 28, 1906, James Rudolph Garfield Papers, Library of Congress.

43. Theodore Roosevelt, note to Albert Beveridge, January 27, 1906, in Morison, *Letters of Theodore Roosevelt*, 5:571.

44. Clark, *My Quarter Century in American Politics*, p. 442.

45. Joseph B. Foraker, letter to Joseph Benson Foraker Jr., January 29, 1907, in Foraker, *Notes of a Busy Life*, 2:249–54.

46. Henry F. Pringle, *The Life and Times of William Howard Taft: A Biography* (Hamden, CT: Archon Books, 1964), 2:838–39.

CHAPTER EIGHTEEN: FIRST-CLASS COLORED MEN

1. See Booker T. Washington, letter to Whitefield McKinlay, October 25, 1906, in *The Booker T. Washington Papers*, ed. Louis R. Harlan and Raymond W. Smock, vol. 9, *1906–8* (Urbana: University of Illinois Press, 1980), p. 103.

2. Theodore Roosevelt, letter to Booker T. Washington, December 25, 1906, microfilm reel 70, p. 72, Theodore Roosevelt Papers, Library of Congress.

3. See Percy E. Murray, "Harry C. Smith-Joseph B. Foraker Alliance: Coalition Politics in Ohio," *Journal of Negro History* 68, no. 2 (1983): 177.

4. See "The Tyler Legacy—A Good Name," *Columbus Sunday Dispatch Magazine*, March 20, 1949.

5. See Tyler's letter to Foraker around this time. "It is only my great admiration for you . . . and my desire to see you victorious in everything that prompted my writing . . . . You know, Senator, I am a REAL Foraker man, and am always with you and for you, whether in defeat or in victory." September 27, 1906, Joseph Foraker Papers, Cincinnati History Library and Archives.

6. The White House visitor log does not show Tyler that day. But it shows Booker T. Washington, his champion.

7. Ralph Tyler, letter to George Myers, January 12, 1907, box 69, folder 1907 M (cont.), Foraker Papers.

8. There is something else that suggests Roosevelt's offer was not serious. There is great confusion about what job he was offering. In its January 30 article the *Cincinnati Enquirer* said he was being considered for "Surveyor of Customs" for the port. In his earlier letter to George Myers, Tyler said it was "Collector of Customs." There was a difference. The collector was in charge of the office; the surveyor was number two. It may be Roosevelt dangled the top job in front of Tyler, because he was not going to get it anyway.

9. Emma Lou Thornbrough, "The Brownsville Episode and the Negro Vote," *Mississippi Valley Historical Review* 44, no. 3 (December 1947): 479.

10. "One Spot," *Cincinnati Enquirer*, January 30, 1907. This newspaper clipping was attached to a letter dated January 30, 1907, from George H. Jackson, former member of the Ohio legislature, asking for the job. Container 1, Nicholas Longworth Papers, Library of Congress.

11. It seems first son-in-law Nicholas Longworth's aspiration to remain in Congress and daughter Alice's craving not to live in Cincinnati overcame his concern for the black vote. "Roosevelt Names Foraker's Choice," *New York Times*, March 1, 1907. "[Longworth was] pleading with his father-in-law to send Ralph Tyler to Cleveland or some place as far as possible from Cincinnati."

12. Washington biographer Harlan calls Roosevelt's slight of Washington here "ominous." Louis R. Harlan, *Booker T. Washington: The Wizard of Tuskegee, 1901– 1915* (New York: Oxford University Press, 1983), pp. 29–30.

13. See Ralph Tyler, letter to Booker T. Washington, in Harlan and Smock, *Booker T. Washington Papers*, 9:504–5.

14. Elbert Hubbard, the American writer and artist, called it "the best barber shop in America," and it probably was. Nothing was overlooked; even individual telephones were installed at each barber chair.

15. Biographical information from Thomas J. Reider, ed., introduction to George A. Myers Papers, Ohio History Connection, http://memory.loc.gov/ammem/award97/ohshtml/myers/overview.html (accessed October 1, 2014).

16. The quoted portion of the letter is reproduced as Myers wrote it. Either he was in a hurry or was very irritated with Roosevelt and Tyler. George Myers, letter to Ralph Tyler, April 11, 1907, Myers Papers.

17. George Myers, letter to Joseph B. Foraker, January 30, 1907, Myers Papers.

18. The *New York Age* reported on March 12, 1907, at least with "Washington Negroes . . . [Tyler's] appointment appeared to establish friendly feelings toward Roosevelt." Cited in John D. Weaver, *The Brownsville Raid* (College Station: Texas A&M University Press, 1992), p. 241.

19. Ralph Tyler, letter to George Myers, June 1, 1907, Myers Papers.

20. Fred C. Ainsworth, List of Colored Officers in the Military Service of the United States, January 21, 1907, William Howard Taft Papers, Library of Congress. The different ink and handwriting for Green show he was not on the list when it was prepared on January 21, the day before the Senate voted to investigate Brownsville.

21. See "Roosevelt Wants to Talk," *New York Times*, January 29, 1907.

22. Mary Church Terrell knew Sanders was in Washington that day and sent him the letter asking to meet her. See chapter eleven.

23. "Discharge Stigma Burns," *Washington Post*, December 8, 1906. Sanders's name is mistakenly shown as "Saunders."

24. "Negro Case to Roosevelt," *New York Times*, December 9, 1906.

25. "Negro Soldiers Apply to Taft," *Atlanta Constitution*, December 13, 1906.

26. "Mingo Sanders Scents a Plot in Washington," *New York Times*, January 25, 1907.

27. "Attempt to Murder Captain Macklin," *Brownsville Daily Herald*, December 24, 1906.

28. Four years later Macklin had not fully recovered from the shooting, and the army medically discharged him. "Capt. Macklin Retired," *New York Times*, August 19, 1910.

29. "Negro Shot Capt. Macklin," *New York Times*, December 22, 1906.

CHAPTER NINETEEN: GREATEST SHEPHERD

1. See Agnes W. Spring, *William Chapin Deming of Wyoming: Pioneer Publisher, and State and Federal Official: A Biography* (Glendale, CA: Arthur H. Clark, 1944), p. 316. But not the richest in the Senate. In 1908, sixteen other senators were worth more than his $2 million. Also with $2 million, Foraker tied. Lodge had $1.5 million, and "Boss" Boies Penrose just barely made it into the millionaire's club with $1 million. "Millionaires in Hall of Congress," *Philadelphia Press*, March 8, 1908, clipping found in Francis E. Warren Papers, American Heritage Center, University of Wyoming.

2. See G. B. Dobson, "Cheyenne Continued," *Wyoming Tales and Trails*, http://www.wyomingtalesandtrails.com/cheyenne4a.html (accessed May 29, 2014).

3. T. A. Larson, *History of Wyoming* (Lincoln: University of Nebraska Press, 1965), p. 197.

4. "Splendid Work of Senator Warren of Wyoming Wins For His State," *Denver Post*, November 9, 1906. Newspaper clipping in Warren scrapbook at the American Heritage Center, University of Wyoming.

5. Lewis L. Gould, *Wyoming: A Political History, 1868–1896* (New Haven, CT: Yale University Press, 1968), pp. 15, 49.

6. 44 Cong. Rec. 2943 (1909).

7. "Warren, Francis Emroy, 1844–1929," Biographical Directory of the United States Congress, http://bioguide.congress.gov/scripts/biodisplay.pl?index=w000164 (accessed May 29, 2014).

8. "Senator Warren Accused," *New York Times*, February 9, 1905; and "Senator Rests under Charges," *San Francisco Call*, February 9, 1905.

9. His losses were such that for the rest of his life he had to earn a living.

10. After Dakota, Roosevelt developed a "passionate interest . . . in reclamation of arid western lands by irrigation." Henry F. Pringle, *Theodore Roosevelt: A Biography* (New York: Harcourt, Brace, 1984), p. 302.

11. Cited in Larson, *History of Wyoming*, p. 191.

12. Benjamin H. Hibbard, *A History of the Public Land Policies* (Madison: University of Wisconsin Press, 1965), p. 476.

13. Larson, *History of Wyoming*, p. 180.

14. *Labor News*, January 25, 1902.

15. 38 Cong. Rec. 1182 (1904), cited in Robert F. Jones, "The Political Career of Senator Francis E. Warren, 1902–1912 (master's thesis, University of Wyoming, 1949), p. 75.

16. Hibbard, *History of the Public Land Policies*, p. 432.

17. 41 Cong. Rec. 3191 (1907). Senator Warren's complaint was much like that of the Brownsville soldiers and Senator Foraker, who wondered why they were presumed guilty and had to prove their innocence.

18. Hitchcock was the great-grandson of Ethan Allen, whose Green Mountain Boys seized Fort Ticonderoga from the British in the Revolutionary War.

19. Larson, *History of Wyoming*, p. 318. Roosevelt finished the ride, but Warren could not. "We shed three [riders] including Warren." *Selections from the Correspondence of Theodore Roosevelt and Henry Cabot Lodge, 1884–1918*, 2 vols. (New York, Charles Scribner's Sons, 1926), 1:23.

20. Ethan Allen Hitchcock, letter to Mark Hanna, July 18, 1901, Ethan Allen Hitchcock Papers, National Archives, College Park, MD.

21. Francis E. Warren, letter to William E. Chaplin, December 31, 1906, Warren Papers.

22. Theodore Roosevelt, letter to Ethan Allen Hitchcock, October 10, 1905, in *The Letters of Theodore Roosevelt*, ed. Elting E. Morison, vol. 5, *The Big Stick, 1905–1907* (Cambridge, MA: Harvard University Press, 1952), p. 51. In this letter Roosevelt put Hitchcock to his proof. He asked him for the names of each Department of Interior employee Hitchcock was referring to and "whether he holds office by your appointment or by mine."

23. Ethan Allen Hitchcock, letter to Alford W. Cooley, US Civil Service Commission, June 30, 1906, Hitchcock Papers. Also see Morison, *Letters of Theodore Roosevelt*, 5:445n1.

24. And the senator knew it. "Linnen and Hintze are now in Denver. There is no doubt but they mean the ugliest kind of ugliness." Francis E. Warren, letter to W. A. Richards, September 22, 1906, Warren Papers.

25. Warren was a piker compared to others. A man named H. J. Weare was alleged to have illegally enclosed 149,000 acres. G. F. Pollock, Acting Commissioner, General Land Office, letter to Ethan Allen Hitchcock, October 15, 1906, Warren Papers.

26. E. B. Linnen, letter to Ethan Allen Hitchcock, September 7, 1906, p. 8. Warren Papers. The United States District Attorney for Wyoming, Timothy F. Burke, was alleged, as the administrator for an estate, to be "maintaining an illegal inclosure; and that he was, in fact, obstructing the enforcement of the public land laws instead of bring the offenders to justice." E. B. Linnen, letter to Ethan Allen Hitchcock, November 15, 1906, Warren Papers.

27. The most damning was his relationship with Special Agent M. A. Meyendorff. See "Amazing Tale of Land Fraud Told in Detail," *Washington Times*, November 29, 1906.

28. Francis E. Warren, two letters to Theodore Roosevelt, October 5, 1906, Warren Papers.

29. See Francis E. Warren, letter to W. W. Gleason, January 19, 1907, Warren Papers. "The President promised me it should be as I asked, and on the next day, October 6th, he wrote a letter to the Secretary."

30. Theodore Roosevelt, letter to Ethan Allen Hitchcock, October 6, 1906, in Morison, *Letters of Theodore Roosevelt*, 5:445.

31. Theodore Roosevelt, letter to Ethan Allen Hitchcock, October 27, 1906, in ibid., 5:481.

32. "Roosevelt has waited, so far as he is concerned—year after year for the people to get their fences down or for Congress to legislate." Francis E. Warren, letter to William E. Chaplin, December 31, 1906, Warren Papers.

33. Theodore Roosevelt, letter to Ethan Allen Hitchcock, October 9, 1906, box 27, Correspondence Photostats, Theodore Roosevelt Collection, Houghton Library, Harvard University.

34. W. A. Richards, letter to Francis E. Warren, November 1, 1906, Warren Papers.

35. "Son of Martyred Ohio President Will Become a Member of the Nation's Cabinet," *Cincinnati Enquirer*, November 8, 1906, in box 156, James Rudolph Garfield Papers, Library of Congress.

36. "Garfield to Cabinet," *New York Tribune*, November 8, 1906.

37. Roosevelt was not so cooperative with other stockmen (none as powerful as Warren), many of whom were taken to court in Cheyenne in an event called locally the "Roosevelt Roundup." Some were fined; others given a short time in jail. All were respected men. Spring, *William Chapin Deming of Wyoming*, p. 123.

38. "*By direction of the President*, Secretary Hitchcock to-day [January 4, 1907] issued an order to Commissioner Richards" to notify interested parties that the law against enclosing public lands "will be rigidly enforced after April 1, 1907" (author's emphasis). "Ultimatum to Cattle Men," *New York Times*, January 5, 1907.

39. "I, for one, am feeling no resentment because my company has had 100 miles or more of fence to pull down, and to be at vast expense arranging other matters." Francis E. Warren, letter to William E. Chaplin, December 31, 1906, Warren Papers. Chaplin was yet another part of the Warren Machine. Between 1893 and 1895 he was the register of the US Land Office in Cheyenne and knew all about the land acquired by Warren. Roosevelt told Hitchcock that Linnen's judgment and findings with reference to Warren were discredited. Theodore Roosevelt, letter to Ethan Allen Hitchcock, January 24, 1907, in Morison, *Letters of Theodore Roosevelt*, 5:564–65. Note this was two days after the Senate approved the Brownsville investigation by Warren's Military Affairs Committee.

40. William Loeb, letter to Francis E. Warren, December 4, 1906, Warren Papers. Also referred to in Theodore Roosevelt, letter to Ethan Allen Hitchcock, December 4, 1906, in Morison, *Letters of Theodore Roosevelt*, 5:519; and William Loeb, letter to W. H. Moody, Attorney General, December 4, 1906, Warren Papers.

41. Francis E. Warren, letter to W. W. Gleason, December 10, 1906, Warren Papers.

42. Francis E. Warren, letter to W. W. Gleason, January 19, 1907, Warren Papers.

43. "Senator Warren Exonerated," *New York Sun*, July 12, 1907.

44. Francis E. Warren, letter to James R. Garfield, July 10, 1907, Warren Papers. This "new" report carefully spoke in the present tense, stating that *in July* there were none. By then Gleason had them torn down. In 1913, when the Democrats took control of Congress, a House committee determined by a vote of 5–2 (one dissenter being Franklin W. Mondell, another gear in the Warren Machine) "that Senator Warren had been guilty of the illegal enclosure of public lands." See commentary in Morison, *Letters of Theodore Roosevelt*, 5:445–46.

45. Garfield Diary, March 5, 1907, Garfield Papers.

CHAPTER TWENTY: THE SOLDIERS' PATRON AND PATRONAGE

1. The Republicans were Warren, relieved of his concerns about Wyoming land irregularities, and Lodge, President Roosevelt's best friend who doubted the need for an investigation in the first place, William Warner, and Henry A. Du Pont. Four of the Democrats in the majority were from the South: James P. Taliaferro (Florida), Murphy J. Foster (Louisiana), Lee S. Overman (North Carolina), and J. B. Frazier (Tennessee), and one from a border state, James B. McCreary (Kentucky).

2. Joseph B. Foraker, *Notes of a Busy Life*, 2 vols. (Cincinnati: Stewart & Kidd, 1917), 2:260. He never changed his mind either; his quote beginning this chapter and asserting the soldiers' innocence was written three days after the hearings began.

3. Ibid., 2:260. The majority's report is at pp. 23–27 of *The Brownsville Affray*, Part I, S. Doc. No. 60-309 (1908); the number of witnesses is at p. 23. The three volumes of hearings are *Affray at Brownsville, Tex.: Hearings Before the Comm. on Military Affairs . . .* , S. Doc. No. 60-402, pts. 4, 5, 6 (1908) (hereafter cited as SMAC-1 [pt. 4], SMAC-2 [pt. 5], and SMAC-3 [pt. 6]).

4. The saloon owners bore losses disproportionately greater than other businesses. And they made up a smaller group and were therefore more likely to successfully pull off such a thing and keep it a secret. Their Jim Crow discrimination had turned on them, and they were losing money. First Sergeant Jacob Frazier thought this. See SMAC-1, pp. 78–79 (answer of 1st Sgt. Frazier to Sen. Warner).

5. "Officer's Belief Shaken," *New York Times*, March 30, 1907. See SMAC-2, pp. 1747–48 (testimony of 2nd Lt. Harry S. Grier). "Major Penrose Acquits Blacks," *Atlanta Constitution*, April 5, 1907. Capt. Sam Lyon had always believed the men were innocent.

6. The minority Foraker-Hemenway report is at S. Doc. No. 60-309, pp. 27–30; and the Bulkeley-Foraker memorandum is at pp. 31–107.

7. Foraker, *Notes of a Busy Life*, 2:260.

8. The American system of justice protects persons accused of crime by making the trial not a determination of guilt or innocence but a test of the prosecution's evidence. The verdict is either "guilty" (the prosecution's evidence showed "beyond a reasonable doubt" that the defendant committed the crime) or "not guilty" (the prosecution did not). There is never a verdict of "innocent." If a jury believes the defendant did the crime but the prosecution did not prove it beyond a reasonable doubt, it must acquit the defendant. In the Military Affairs Committee the soldiers had no such protection.

9. See John D. Weaver, *The Brownsville Raid* (College Station: Texas A&M University, 1992), p. 151.

10. SMAC-3, pp. 2032, 2035, 2037, 2059 (testimony of George Rendall).

11. See testimony of Lt. Henry Wiegenstein, Twenty-Fifth Infantry, given at the Penrose court-martial. *Affray at Brownsville, Tex. . . . Proceedings of a General Court-Martial . . . in the Case of Maj. Charles W. Penrose*, S. Doc. No. 60-402 (1908), pp. 989–99.

12. Foraker-Hemenway Report, S. Doc. No. 60-309, p. 31; SMAC-3, p. 1936 (testimony of Maj. Penrose); SMAC-3, p. 1836 (testimony of Capt. Lyon).

13. SMAC-2, p. 1350 (testimony of Henry Watson).

14. SD-1, pp. 315–31 (Sturgis), 331–41 (Winnemucca), 352–60 (Fort Bliss), 361–64 (Fort Niobrara). Nothing about this was noted in Raynor's official records. See SMAC-2, p. 1757.

15. Foraker-Hemenway Report, S. Doc. No. 60-309, p. 43.

16. See chapter four; see also SMAC-3, p. 2392 (testimony of Mayor Combe) and SMAC-2, p. 1933 (testimony of Penrose).

17. SMAC-3, pp. 2853, 2862–63 (testimony of Gen. Crozier).

18. SMAC-3, p. 2862.

19. J. H. Rice, Captain, Ordnance Department, US Army, letter to Gen. William Crozier, January 10, 1907, S. Doc. No. 59-155, vol. 11, pt. 2 (hereafter cited as SD-2), p. 177.

20. SMAC-1, pp. 395–96, 404, 405 (testimony of Sgt. McMurray).

21. Joseph B. Foraker, letter to John E. Milholland, January 30, 1907, box 68, Foraker Papers.

22. Joseph B. Foraker, letter to Benjamin J. Edger, February 11, 1907, box 63, Foraker Papers.

23. This took place while Macklin awaited his court-martial. Joseph B. Foraker, letter to Capt. Edgar Macklin, March 11, 1907, and Capt. Samuel Lyon, letter to Joseph B. Foraker, March 14, 1907, box 68, Foraker Papers.

24. Unidentified correspondent, letter to Joseph B. Foraker, February 23, 1907, box 63, Foraker Papers.

25. Capt. Ralph E. Gambell, letter to Joseph B. Foraker, December 21, 1906, box 49, Foraker Papers. Foraker answered Gambell, "No one will know that you have written me on the subject." Joseph B. Foraker, letter to Capt. Ralph E.

Gambell, January 6, 1907, box 64, Foraker Papers. Not all the correspondents were encouraging or supportive. S. L. French of Plymouth, Pennsylvania, wrote, "I am addressing you to express my sincere regret at your course in opposition to the President." From Z. Preston Fuller of Brooklyn, "I have always voted the Republican ticket . . . but if you were the Republican candidate and W. R. Hearst were the democratic I should vote for him . . . because of your attitude against the President on the troop question & I am no Southerner being born & raised in N. Y. City." To Mr. French, Foraker wrote politely, "I have no desire with respect to the matter except only to secure for these unfortunate men a chance to be heard somewhere, sometime, some way, in their defense." Mr. Fuller merited no explanation, only politeness: "I appreciate very highly your acquainting me with your views." S. L. French, letter to Joseph B. Foraker, December 26, 1906; Joseph B. Foraker, letter to S. L. French, December 28, 1906; Z. Preston Fuller, letter to Joseph B. Foraker, December 31, 1906; Joseph B. Foraker, letter to Z. Preston Fuller, January 2, 1907; all in box 49, Foraker Papers.

26. See SMAC-1, pp. 77 and 74, respectively. Senator Lodge, possibly still wounded from his disappointing performance during the Senate investigation debate, remained surprisingly quiet during the hearings and rarely said anything that might have invited a clash with Foraker. However, he remained Roosevelt's not-so-hidden mole on the committee and alerted him to opportunities to defend his position as they came up. On the last of the hearings before the committee's summer recess, he wrote Roosevelt about a visit Lieutenant Harry G. Leckie of the Twenty-Sixth Infantry made to Mexico. "Leckie's going to Mexico seems to me very improper." Henry Cabot Lodge, letter to Theodore Roosevelt, June 14, 1907, in *Selections from the Correspondence of Theodore Roosevelt and Henry Cabot Lodge, 1884–1918*, 2 vols. (New York: C. Scribner's Sons, 1925), 2:270.

27. SMAC-1, pp. 2472, 2474.

28. SMAC-3, pp. 2608–2609. Blocksom thought Sergeant Reid lied when he denied sounding the "Call to Arms" on his own. If he had it might have been warning the raiders to get back to the fort. When Foraker pointed out Major Blocksom had ordered Private Charley Hairston to instruct Reid to sound the alarm, Blocksom changed his mind. This created some doubt the shooting was planned by the soldiers.

29. SMAC-1, p. 63.

30. SMAC-2, p. 1184.

31. W. H. Lucas, letter to Joseph B. Foraker, April 16, 1907; W. W. Dudley, letter to Joseph B. Foraker, December 26, 1906; F. H. M. Murray, letter to Joseph B. Foraker, December 29, 1906; Katie Leahy, letter to Joseph B. Foraker, March 18, 1907; all in Foraker Papers. Lincoln and Foraker became pen pals. When he wrote Foraker to caution him not to accept at face value news reports about Negro crime in El Reno, especially during the Macklin and Penrose courts-martial, Foraker asked him to send him facts. Charles P. Lincoln, letter to Joseph B. Foraker, December 29, 1906, Foraker Papers; Joseph B. Foraker, letter to Charles P. Lincoln, December 31, 1906, Foraker Papers.

32. E. N. Martin, letter to Joseph B. Foraker, June 18, 1907, Foraker Papers.

33. Theophilus Steward, letter to John Cromwell, March 3, 1907, cited in *Unveiled Voices, Unvarnished Memories: The Cromwell Family in Slavery and Segregation, 1692–1972*, by Adelaide M. Cromwell (Columbia: University of Missouri Press, 2007), p. 312. John Cromwell was on the executive committee of the AME churches.

34. "Colored Soldiers Testifying Strongly," *Boston Guardian*, February 23, 1907, *Guardian of Boston*/Trotter Collection, Howard Gotlieb Archival Research Center, Mugar Library, Boston University.

35. A. B. Humphrey, letter to Joseph B. Foraker, March 28, 1907, folder 4, box 17, Fox section, *Guardian*/Trotter Collection.

36. John E. Milholland, letter to N.B. Marshall, May 16, 1907, folder 5, box 4, Foraker Papers.

37. SMAC-2, pp. 1292–93.

38. A civilian whose job it was to remove refuse from the post.

39. Maj. Augustus Blocksom, telegram to the adjutant general, March 17, 1907, SMAC-2, p. 1292; "Pronounced a Fake," *Washington Evening Star*, March 18, 1907.

40. "Army Rifles Fired at Brownsville," *New York Times*, March 19, 1907.

41. SMAC-2, p. 1295.

42. Foraker, *Notes of a Busy Life*, 2:259.

43. John Galvin, letter to Joseph B. Foraker, January 29, 1907; Joseph B. Foraker, letter to John Galvin, February 1, 1907; John Galvin, letter to Joseph B. Foraker, May 14, 1907, all in box 67, Foraker Papers.

44. See Robert A. Caro, *The Years of Lyndon Johnson: Master of the Senate* (New York: Alfred A. Knopf, 2002), pp. 27–28.

45. "General Grant on Senatorial Courtesy," *Sacramento Daily Record-Bulletin*, June 23, 1881.

46. Roberta Sue Alexander, *A Place of Recourse: A History of the U.S. District Court for the Southern District of Ohio, 1803–2003* (Athens: Ohio University Press, 2005), pp. 230–32.

47. Roosevelt confirmed these disappointments at the hand of Foraker. Theodore Roosevelt, letter to William Dudley Foulke, February 7, 1908, in *The Letters of Theodore Roosevelt*, ed. Elting E. Morison, vol. 6, *The Big Stick: 1907–1909* (Cambridge, MA: Harvard University Press, 1952), pp. 927–33. The reference to Foraker is at p. 930.

48. Weaver, *Brownsville Raid*, pp. 227–28.

49. "Trouble Brews on Every Hand," *Cleveland Plain Dealer*, December 23, 1905, box 25, James Rudolph Garfield Papers, Library of Congress. "I now find myself obliged to give Ohio a second appointment in the shape of Jim Garfield. For reason I will explain, the announcement was made earlier than I expected, which is the reason I did not write you in advance." Theodore Roosevelt, letter to Joseph B. Foraker, November 8, 1906, Foraker Papers. President Arthur did not consult Ohio senator John Sherman about his appointment for the vacant col-

lector of revenue for Cincinnati. On his own he appointed William H. Taft. Henry F. Pringle, *The Life and Times of William Howard Taft: A Biography*, 2 vols. (Hamden, CT: Archon Books, 1964), 1:61.

50. Theodore Roosevelt, letter to George B. Cortelyou, March 16, 1907, box 37, George B. Cortelyou Papers, 1871–1948, Library of Congress. Roosevelt sent a virtually identical letter to George von L. Meyer, who had succeeded Cortelyou as postmaster general. Theodore Roosevelt, letter to George von L. Meyer, March 16, 1907, in *The Letters of Theodore Roosevelt*, ed. Elting E. Morison, vol. 5, *The Big Stick: 1905–1907* (Cambridge, MA: Harvard University Press, 1952), p. 625. Well into the twentieth century, the postmaster general's most important job was patronage.

51. George B. Cortelyou, letter to Joseph B. Foraker, May 20, 1907, box 64, Foraker Papers.

52. *Cincinnati Enquirer*, January 30, 1907, container 1, Nicholas Longworth Papers, Library of Congress.

53. Foraker, *Notes of a Busy Life*, 2:258.

54. Everett Walters, *Joseph Benson Foraker: An Uncompromising Republican* (Columbus: Ohio History Press, 1948), p. 259. Walters cites a report of the Roosevelt-Burton meeting in the *Cincinnati Enquirer*, March 6, 1907.

55. Theodore Roosevelt, letter to Theodore Burton, March 14, 1907, in Morison, *Letters of Theodore Roosevelt*, 5:619–21.

56. Ethel Marie Foraker, letter to Joseph B. Foraker, February 15, 1907, box 49, Foraker Papers.

57. "James R. Foraker Dead," *New York Times*, April 28, 1907.

CHAPTER TWENTY-ONE: OTHER COALITIONS, OTHER FRONTS

1. Charles W. Anderson, letter to Booker T. Washington, "(Personal) Private & Confidential," May 27, 1907, in *The Booker T. Washington Papers*, ed. Louis R. Harlan and Raymond W. Smock, vol. 9, *1906–8* (Urbana: University of Illinois Press, 1980), 9:274–77. Occasionally Washington personally "dished the dirt." He took a moment to reinforce Anderson's information about Hershaw in his own letter to Garfield. Booker T. Washington, letter to James Garfield, May 27, 1907, in Harlan and Smock, *Booker T. Washington Papers*, 9:278.

2. Booker T. Washington, letter to Arthur Vorys, July 8, 1907, in ibid., 9:301.

3. Booker T. Washington, letter to George Myers, June 11, 1907, George A. Myers Papers, 1890–1929, Ohio History Connection, Columbus. This letter was sent on National Negro Business League stationery, so that Myers would see the names of its officers and executive committee.

4. Ralph Tyler, letter to George Myers, September 17, 1907, Myers Papers.

5. Winfield Forrest Cozart, letter to Booker T. Washington, July 29, 1907, in Harlan and Smock, *Booker T. Washington Papers*, 9:305–307.

6. Cozart may have expressed his feelings calmly and respectfully. But his anger at the discharges and what he was capable of doing to show it was also conveyed. He was being considered by the State Department for "an appointment in the Consular Service." Because of Brownsville, he withdrew his name. Winfield Forrest Cozart, letter to Booker T. Washington, July 29, 1907, in ibid., 9:306.

7. Henry F. Pringle, *Theodore Roosevelt: A Biography* (New York: Harcourt, Brace, 1984), p. 280.

8. Thomas A. Bailey, *Theodore Roosevelt and the Japanese-American Crises: An Account of the International Complications Arising from the Race Problem on the Pacific Coast* (Gloucester, MA: P. Smith, 1964), p. v.

9. Theodore Roosevelt, letter to Gen. Ian Standish Monteith Hamilton, May 8, 1907, in *The Letters of Theodore Roosevelt*, ed. Elting E. Morison, vol. 5, *The Big Stick: 1905–1907* (Cambridge, MA: Harvard University Press, 1952), p. 663. Hamilton commanded British and Empire forces in the apocalyptic Gallipoli campaign in World War I. It ended his military career and for a time the political career of Winston Churchill, who left the government and went to France and combat with the Grenadier Guards Second Battalion. See William Manchester, *The Last Lion: Winston Spencer Churchill*, vol. 1, *Visions of Glory, 1874–1932* (Boston: Little, Brown, 1983), pp. 546–71, 575; and Robert K. Massie, *Castles of Steel: Britain, Germany, and the Winning of the Great War at Sea* (New York: Random House, 2003), pp. 496–97.

10. See Pringle, *Theodore Roosevelt: A Biography*, pp. 280–81.

11. See Henry F. Pringle, *The Life and Times of William Howard Taft: A Biography*, 2 vols. (Hamden, CT: Archon Books, 1964), 1:296.

12. Bailey, *Theodore Roosevelt and the Japanese-American Crises*, p. 7, n. 16, citing *Roosevelt and the Russo-Japanese War*, by Tyler Dennet (Garden City, NY: Doubleday, Page, 1925), p. 160.

13. "In strict confidence, I am endeavoring to secure what I am sure we must have; that is, preferably by mutual agreement, the exclusion of Japanese laborers from the United States just as we should not object to the Japanese excluding our laborers from Japan." Theodore Roosevelt, letter to Harrison G. Otis, January 8, 1907, cited in ibid., pp. 155–56.

14. Japan's government said not giving passports to Hawaii would be embarrassing and suggested it was America's business to take care of travel within its borders (which included Hawaii). Historian William Tilchin cites a letter from Roosevelt to Arthur Hamilton Lee, in which Roosevelt wrote the Canadian Commissioner of Labor and said he had Japanese documents proving the Japanese government tightly controlled immigration and "deliberately overissued" passports. Theodore Roosevelt, letter to Arthur Hamilton Lee, February 2, 1908, in *The Letters of Theodore Roosevelt*, ed. Elting E. Morison, vol. 6, *The Big Stick: 1907–1909* (Cambridge, MA: Harvard University Press, 1952), pp. 919–21. William N. Tilchin, *Theodore Roosevelt and the British Empire: A Study in Presidential Statecraft* (New York: St. Martin's, 1997), p. 175.

15. "There is no danger of having too many immigrants of the right kind. It

makes no difference from what country they come. If they are sound in body and in mind, and, above all, if they are of good character, so that we can rest assured that their children and grandchildren will be worthy fellow-citizens of our children and grandchildren, then we should welcome them with cordial hospitality." Theodore Roosevelt, Annual Message to Congress, December 6, 1904, HR 58A-K2, Records of the U.S. House of Representatives, Center for Legislative Archives, National Archives. See also Theodore Roosevelt, letter to Henry Cabot Lodge, May 15, 1905, in *Selections from the Correspondence of Theodore Roosevelt and Henry Cabot Lodge, 1884–1918* (New York: C. Scribner's Sons, 1925), 2:122.

16. "On November 10, 1906," On This Day, https://www.nytimes.com/learning/general/onthisday/harp/1110.html (accessed May 31, 2014).

17. See Bailey, *Theodore Roosevelt and the Japanese-American Crises*, p. 169.

18. Theodore Roosevelt, letter to Lawrence F. Abbott, January 3, 1907, in Morison, *Letters of Theodore Roosevelt*, 5:536–38.

19. Theodore Roosevelt, letter to Henry Cabot Lodge, May 15, 1905, in *Roosevelt-Lodge Correspondence*, 2:122.

20. Pringle believed in hindsight the stories were not credible and the fear was an overreaction. Pringle, *Theodore Roosevelt: A Biography*, pp. 284–85. Nevertheless, coming from credible sources, Roosevelt had to deal with it.

21. Paraphrased from Edward Wagenknecht, *The Seven Worlds of Theodore Roosevelt* (New York: Longmans, Green, 1958), p. 273.

22. See chapter nine.

23. Ronald D. Smith, "Pioneers in Public Relations," Buffalo State College, http://faculty.buffalostate.edu/smithrd/PR/pioneers.htm (accessed May 31, 2014).

24. See Adam Sheingate, "Progressive Publicity and the Origins of Political Consulting," http://users.polisci.wisc.edu/apw/archives/sheingate.pdf (accessed May 31, 2014).

25. Woodbridge was born Francis Woodbridge Michaelis two years after his brother George. Their parents, Ortho and Kate Michaelis, had nine children, seven of which were born at six different army arsenals where Ortho was stationed during his military career with the army's ordnance corps. There is no record of when or why he dropped Michaelis as his last name, but in 1894 (four years after his father died) when he was nineteen and applying to Harvard for financial aid, he was Francis Woodbridge. His mother's name on the application is shown as Kate K. (for Kerchival) Woodbridge Michaelis, suggesting he was born in an earlier marriage. But in an affidavit among her pension records she indicated she and Ortho were married seven years before Francis was born. See Edward Winter, "Ortho Ernst Michaelis," *Chess Notes*, April 2011, http://www.chesshistory.com/winter/winter81.html (accessed October 2, 2014). See also Harvard University Application for Aid from the Price Greenleaf Fund, April 28, 1894, Harvard University Archives.

26. "Mr. Roosevelt Defies Negro Troops' Friends," *New York Times*, December 23, 1906.

27. See *United States v. Nixon*, 418 U.S. 683 (1974); Robert Suro and Joan

Biskupic, "Judge Finds Clinton in Contempt of Court," *Washington Post*, April 13, 1999; Peter Baker and Susan Schmidt, "President Is Denied Executive Privilege," *Washington Post*, May 6, 1998.

28. Though Clinton's case may have been weaker. Roosevelt's authority as commander in chief is explicitly part of the Constitution. Clinton's claim of executive privilege is recognized only as implied by the Constitution's separation of powers among the three branches of government. Both, however, are derived from the Constitution.

29. George Michaelis, letter to Joseph B. Foraker, February 7, 1907, Joseph Foraker Papers, Cincinnati History Library and Archives.

30. Andrew Carnegie, letter to Booker T. Washington, January 5, 1907, in Harlan and Smock, *Booker T. Washington Papers*, 9:182–83; Booker T. Washington, letter to Emmett Scott, January 31, 1907, in Harlan and Smock, *Booker T. Washington Papers*, 9:205–206.

31. See Hae-sung Hwang, *Booker T. Washington and W. E. B. Du Bois: A Study in Race Leadership, 1895–1915* (Seoul: American Studies Institute, Seoul National University, 1992), p. 122.

32. William Howard Taft, letter to Booker T. Washington, February 5, 1908, in Harlan and Smock, *Booker T. Washington Papers*, 9:451; Oswald Garrison Villard, letter to Booker T. Washington, February 25, 1908, in Harlan and Smock, *Booker T. Washington Papers*, 9:457.

33. David L. Lewis, *W. E. B. Du Bois: Biography of a Race, 1868–1919* (New York: Henry Holt, 1993), p. 363.

34. "Mr. Baker came here day before yesterday and is going to remain several days. We have just gone over the Atlanta situation thoroughly." Booker T. Washington, letter to Oswald Garrison Villard, November 9, 1906, in Harlan and Smock, *Booker T. Washington Papers*, 9:120.

35. Booker T. Washington, letter to Ray Stannard Baker, May 23, 1907, July 23, 1907, and August 21, 1907, in ibid., 9:272, 303, 333. Booker T. Washington, letter to Emmett Scott, March 2, 1908, in ibid., 9:459.

36. Unsigned letter to Moore, September 7, 1908, in ibid., 9:619. See Emma L. Thornbrough, *T. Thomas Fortune: Militant Journalist* (Chicago: University of Chicago Press, 1972), pp. 225–26, 255, 307–309. See also T. Thomas Fortune, letter to Emmett Scott, September 7, 1907; and Booker T. Washington, letter to Fred Moore, October 5, 1907, in Harlan and Smock, *Booker T. Washington Papers*, 9:619.

37. See Thornbrough, *T. Thomas* Fortune, pp. 310–13.

38. Charles Anderson, letter to Emmett Scott, February 25, 1907, in Harlan and Smock, *Booker T. Washington Papers*, 9:223.

39. Booker T. Washington, letter to Charles Anderson, September 30, 1907, in ibid., 9:223.

40. Roscoe Conkling Simmons, letter to Booker T. Washington, October 2, 1907, in ibid., 9:347.

41. Roscoe Conkling Simmons, letter to Booker T. Washington, December

12, 1904, in *The Booker T. Washington Papers*, ed. Louis R. Harlan and Raymond W. Smock, vol. 8, *1904–6* (Urbana: University of Illinois Press, 1979), pp. 154–56. Roscoe Conkling Simmons should not be confused with Roscoe Conkling Bruce. Both were card-carrying members of the Tuskegee Machine. Simmons became Washington's nephew when Washington married his third wife, Margaret Murray Washington, who was Simmons's aunt. Both were named after the New York senator who, among other things, helped draft the Fourteenth Amendment. Bruce was the son of Reconstruction Mississippi senator Blanche K. Bruce and figured in another irritant between Washington and Du Bois. Du Bois wanted to be the Colored Superintendent of the District of Columbia schools and wanted Washington's support. Instead Washington recommended Bruce, and he got the job. See Lewis, *W. E. B. Du Bois: Biography of a Race*, p. 246. Another once-famous-but-now-forgotten man named after Conkling was Roscoe Conkling "Fatty" Arbuckle, the silent movie comedian and star.

42. T. Thomas Fortune, letter to Booker T. Washington, February 12, 1907, in Harlan and Smock, *Booker T. Washington Papers*, 9:217–19.

43. Lewis, *W. E. B. Du Bois: Biography of a Race*, p. 246.

44. Ibid., pp. 341–42.

45. "Niagara Movement (1905–10)," *The Rise and Fall of Jim Crow*, http://www.pbs.org/wnet/jimcrow/stories_events_niagara.html (accessed May 31, 2014).

46. See "Niagara's Declaration of Principles, 1905," Gilder Lehrman Center for the Study of Slavery, Resistance, and Abolition, http://www.yale.edu/glc/archive/1152.htm (accessed May 31, 2014).

47. The efficient Tuskegee Machine even learned of the first meeting in spite of Du Bois's efforts to keep it secret. Harry Smith of the *Cleveland Ledger* suggested a Buffalo real estate agent for finding meeting and housing facilities. That man was a confidant of Washington's man, Charles Anderson. He told Anderson, who passed it on to Washington. It was too late for the 1905 meeting. See Christopher E. Forth, "Booker T. Washington and the 1905 Niagara Conference," *Journal of Negro History* 72, nos. 3–4 (Summer–Autumn 1987): 44–56.

48. "Ransom, Reverdy C., 1861–1959," *American Decades*, http://www.encyclopedia.com/doc/1G2-3468300612.html (accessed February 25, 2014). See also Susan D. Carle, *Defining the Struggle: National Racial Justice Organizing, 1880–1915* (New York: Oxford University Press, 2013), pp. 193–94.

49. Its coeditor was Lafayette M. Hershaw, Washington's target at the Department of the Interior.

50. See Lewis, *W. E. B. Du Bois: Biography of a Race*, p. 339.

51. James A. Cobb, letter to Booker T. Washington, August 26, 1907; and James A. Cobb, letter to Emmett Scott, September 5, 1907, both found in Harlan and Smock, *Booker T. Washington Papers*, 9:334.

52. Elliott M. Rudwick, *W. E. B. Du Bois: A Study in Minority Group Leadership* (Philadelphia: University of Pennsylvania Press, 1960), p. 109. On October 11, 1907, Du Bois wrote to Foraker (on Atlanta University stationery), "By direction of the Third Annual Meeting of the Niagara Movement . . . I beg to congratulate

you upon the firm stand which you have taken for justice." Foraker sent his thanks on seven days later and added, "Be assured of my high appreciation for [the Niagara Movement]." Both letters found in Foraker Papers.

53. Lewis, *W. E. B. Du Bois: Biography of a Race*, p. 341.

CHAPTER TWENTY-TWO: A FACE TO GRACE THE WHITE HOUSE

1. John D. Weaver, *The Brownsville Raid* (College Station: Texas A&M University Press, 1992), p. 110; Everett Walters, *Joseph Benson Foraker: An Uncompromising Republican* (Columbus: Ohio History Press, 1948), p. 236; Edmund Morris, *Theodore Rex* (New York: Random House, 2001), p. 471; H. W. Brands, *TR: The Last Romantic* (New York: Basic Books, 1997), pp. 496–97; Henry F. Pringle, *Theodore Roosevelt: A Biography* (New York: Harcourt, Brace, 1984), p. 274 ("when he shaved he saw a face that would grace the White House in 1908").

2. Julius Chambers, letter to Joseph B. Foraker, May 1, 1906, folder 2, box 2, Joseph Foraker Papers, Cincinnati History Library and Archives.

3. Julius Chambers, "Walks and Talks," *Brooklyn Eagle*, June 22, 1906, folder 2, box 2, Foraker Papers.

4. Julius Chambers, letter to Joseph B. Foraker, June 23, 1906, folder 2, box 2, Foraker Papers.

5. Joseph B. Foraker, letter to Charles Kurtz, June 28, 1906, folder 5, box 2, Foraker Papers.

6. Joseph B. Foraker, letter to Charles Kurtz, August 30, 1906, folder 5, box 2, Foraker Papers.

7. Joseph B. Foraker, letter to Julius Chambers, September 1, 1906, folder 2, box 2, Foraker Papers.

8. Joseph B. Foraker, *Notes of a Busy Life*, 2 vols. (Cincinnati: Stewart & Kidd, 1917), 2:377.

9. Joseph B. Foraker, letter to Julius Chambers, September 14, 1906, folder 2, box 2, Foraker Papers.

10. Joseph B. Foraker, letter to Julius Chambers, September 19, 1906, folder 2, box 2, Foraker Papers.

11. Julius Chambers, letter to Joseph B. Foraker, January 7, 1907, Foraker Papers.

12. Joseph B. Foraker, letter to Julius Chambers, January 8, 1907, Foraker Papers. Foraker knew he was sending them to two men who had no chance and were no threat to him.

13. Joseph B. Foraker, letter to John J. McCook, January 8, 1907, Foraker Papers.

14. Joseph B. Foraker, letter to Julius Chambers, March 29, 1907, Foraker Papers.

15. See "Loosed," *Cincinnati Enquirer*, January 9, 1907. "Possibly the sting of the President's remarks [at the Gridiron dinner] was intensified by the knowledge the friends of the Administration in Ohio are trying to destroy him politically."

16. See Walters, *Joseph Benson Foraker*, pp. 258–59.

17. Roosevelt, letter to Joseph B. Foraker, February 21, 1907, in *The Letters of Theodore Roosevelt*, ed. Elting E. Morison, vol. 5, *The Big Stick: 1905–1907* (Cambridge, MA: Harvard University Press, 1952), p. 595–596. The next month Roosevelt made it clear he was serious. He refused to appoint Foraker's man, Judge John J. Adams. See footnote 1 to this letter at p. 596.

18. Walters, *Joseph Benson Foraker*, p. 260.

19. *Cincinnati Times-Star*, March 30, 1907, cited in ibid., p. 260.

20. Foraker, *Notes of a Busy Life*, 2:383. See also "Taft May Get Ohio Machine," *New York Times*, April 5, 1907.

21. Henry Cabot Lodge, letter to Theodore Roosevelt, April 13, 1907, in *Selections from the Correspondence of Theodore Roosevelt and Henry Cabot Lodge, 1884–1918* (New York: C. Scribner's Sons, 1925), 2:266. This letter from Lodge answered Roosevelt's handwritten letter the day before, in which Roosevelt wrote that Crane "has been in touch with Foraker and [Boies] Penrose and . . . the whole opposition and reactionary crowd" and suggesting Crane was not acting so much as a peacemaker as he was a Foraker advocate. Theodore Roosevelt, letter to Henry Cabot Lodge, April 12, 1907, Henry Cabot Lodge Papers, Massachusetts Historical Society, Boston.

22. Pringle, *Theodore Roosevelt: A Biography*, p. 352.

23. Foraker, *Notes of a Busy Life*, 2:383.

24. See William Howard Taft, letter to C. P. Snow, May 8, 1907, William Howard Taft Papers, Library of Congress.

25. After medical doctors could not cure Foraker's son Arthur of a bone disease and an osteopath did, Foraker became their advocate. One osteopath, unfortunately for Foraker not practicing in Ohio, was grateful for Foraker's support of his profession and the soldiers. Dr. S. S. Still in Iowa wrote, "I do not profess to be a 'negro lover' and have great respect for the President; but I feel in this case he was wrong." S. S. Still, letter to Joseph B. Foraker, December 20, 1906, box 55, Foraker Papers.

26. See "Sad Awakening Awaits Foraker." For Cox quote, see *Cincinnati Enquirer*, March 28, 1908, cited in Walters, *Joseph Benson Foraker*, p. 268.

27. Theodore Roosevelt, letter to Kermit Roosevelt, April 11, 1907, in Morison, *Letters of Theodore Roosevelt*, 5:647.

28. Theodore Roosevelt, letter to Henry Cabot Lodge, April 12, 1907, Lodge Papers. For "haunting fear" of defeat, see chapter five.

29. Garfield Diary, May 2, 1907, James Rudolph Garfield Papers, Library of Congress.

30. See Earl R. Beck, "Joseph B. Foraker and the Standard Oil Charges," *Ohio Archeological and Historical Quarterly* 56 (1947): 159, citing a letter from Foraker to C. B. McCoy, July 29, 1907; and Foraker, *Notes of a Busy Life*, 2:383–84. "Taft's

endorsement was taken at the specific behest of George B. Cox of Cincinnati, who had been vigorously denounced by Taft in 1905 as a political boss. The loss of Cox's support was a bitter and unexpected blow to Foraker, for the Senator well knew of the power of the political machine which the municipal boss had constructed. Foraker was to declare that Taft owed his nomination to Cox more than any other single individual."

31. Foraker, *Notes of a Busy Life*, 2:383. He found out how Cox planned the double cross more than four years later, when he received a letter spelling it out. Foraker confronted Charles D. Hilles, by then the secretary to President Taft, who confirmed the details. Hilles expressed his "deep regret" for any offense. See the series of correspondence at ibid., 2:384–86.

32. William Howard Taft, letter to Theodore Roosevelt, July 23, 1907, cited in Walters, *Joseph Benson Foraker*, p. 264. Naturally, this is exactly what Roosevelt wanted to hear. In that same letter, Taft also told Roosevelt it would be "for the benefit of the country to remove [Foraker from the Senate because he was] a man so reactionary, so unscrupulous, and so able."

33. William Howard Taft, letter to William R. Nelson, July 31, 1907, William Howard Taft Papers, folder 1, box 1, Ohio History Connection, Columbus.

34. Henry F. Pringle, *The Life and Times of William Howard Taft: A Biography*, 2 vols. (Hamden, CT: Archon Books, 1964), 1:323. See also Zane L. Miller, *Boss Cox's Cincinnati: Urban Politics in the Progressive Era* (New York: Oxford University Press, 1968), p. 197.

35. "Sad Awakening Awaits Foraker."

36. "Depend on Burton to Smash Foraker," *New York Times*, March 25, 1907.

37. Maj. Charles Penrose, letter to Joseph B. Foraker, May 7, 1907, box 70, Foraker Papers.

38. H. J. Browne, letters to Joseph B. Foraker, April 19, 20, and 25, as well as May 10, 1907; copies of which were attachments to Joseph Foraker, memorandum, April 9, 1907, Report of the Proceedings of the Court of Inquiry Relative to the Shooting Affray at Brownsville, Tex. . . . , S. Doc. No. 60–701, vols. 4–6 (1911) (hereafter cited as CI-2), pp. 1393–98.

39. All references to Foraker's employment of Browne are in CI-2, beginning at p. 1393.

40. *Proceedings of a General Court-Martial . . . in the Case of Maj. Charles W. Penrose . . .* , S. Doc. No. 60–402 (1908), p. 1248 (acquittal of Maj. Penrose); *Proceedings of a General Court-Martial . . . in the Case of Capt. Edgar A. Macklin . . .* , S. Doc. No. 60–402 (1908), p. 247 (acquittal of Capt. Macklin).

41. *The Brownsville Affray*, S. Doc. No. 60–389 (1908), pp. 56–58.

CHAPTER TWENTY-THREE: BROWNSVILLE GHOULS

1. Theodore Roosevelt, letter to Nicolas Longworth, June 26, 1907, in *The Letters of Theodore Roosevelt*, ed. Elting E. Morison, vol. 5, *The Big Stick: 1905–1907* (Cambridge, MA: Harvard University Press, 1952), p. 695.

2. William Howard Taft, letter to William R. Nelson, June 26, 1906, folder 2, box 1, William Howard Taft Papers, Ohio History Connection, Columbus; Theodore Roosevelt, letter to Henry Cabot Lodge, June 27, 1907, in *Selections from the Correspondence of Theodore Roosevelt and Henry Cabot Lodge, 1884–1918* (New York: C. Scribner's Sons, 1925), 2:272–73. Roosevelt never mentioned Brownsville when he spoke in Canton; Lodge talked him out of it. See Everett Walters, *Joseph Benson Foraker: An Uncompromising Republican* (Columbus: Ohio History Press, 1948), p. 263.

3. "Foraker Assails All His Enemies," *New York Times*, July 28, 1907.

4. See Walters, *Joseph Benson Foraker*, p. 264; and Henry F. Pringle, *The Life and Times of William Howard Taft: A Biography* (Hamden, CT: Archon Books, 1964), 1:323.

5. "Foraker Wants to Know about Suffrage in the South," *Washington Post*, August 22, 1907.

6. See Murray N. Rothbard, *Economic Depressions: Their Cause and Cure* (Auburn, AL: Ludwig von Mises Institute, 2009), p. 8, http://books.google.com/books?id=R87hqJk42T0C.

7. "Schiff Predicts Panic Unless Money Is Freed," *New York Times*, January 5, 1906.

8. See chapter sixteen. See also H. W. Brands, *TR: The Last Romantic* (New York: Basic Books, 1997), p. 601. "No man in an important position ever handled as little money or paid as little attention to money as he did." James E. Amos, *Theodore Roosevelt: Hero to His Valet* (New York: John Day, 1927), p. 103.

9. See Edmund Morris, *Theodore Rex* (New York: Random House, 2001), p. 488.

10. He went on to say, "[These men] combine to bring about as much financial stress as possible, in order to discredit the policy of the government and thereby secure a reversal of that policy, so that they may enjoy unmolested the fruits of their own evil-doing. . . . I regard this contest as one to determine who shall rule this free country—the people through their governmental agents, or a few ruthless and domineering men whose wealth makes them peculiarly formidable because they hide behind the breastworks of corporate organization."

11. David Fettig, "F. Augustus Heinze of Montana and the Panic of 1907," *Region*, August 1989, https://www.minneapolisfed.org/publications_papers/pub_display.cfm?id=3807&TC=1&DPR=1 (accessed October 2, 2014); Christopher Gray, "Stanford White's Backdrop for the Panic of 1907," *New York Times*, March 5, 2009; Abigail Tucker, "The Financial Panic of 1907: Running from History," Smithsonian.com, October 9, 2008, http://www.smithsonianmag.com/history/the-financial-panic-of-1907-running-from-history-82176328 (accessed October 2, 2014); see Jean Strouse,

Morgan: American Financier (New York: Random House, 1999), p. 575; "The 1907 Crisis in Historical Perspective," Center for History and Economics, http://www.fas. harvard.edu/~histecon/crisis-next/1907/ (accessed May 31, 2014).

12. On October 22, Knickerbocker Trust was allowed to fail. Strouse, *Morgan: American Financier*, p. 577.

13. Theodore Roosevelt, letter to George Cortelyou, October 25, 1907, in Morison, *Letters of Theodore Roosevelt*, 5:821–22. See also Morison, *Letters of Theodore Roosevelt*, 5:822n1. Others felt Morgan was entitled to more than one line of anonymous thanks. "Morgan should be represented as buttressing up the tattering fabric of finance the way Giotto painted St. Francis holding up the falling Church with his shoulder." Bernard Berenson to Isabella Stewart Gardner, cited in Strouse, *Morgan: American Financier*, pp. 588–89. A first-class discussion of the Panic of 1907 and Morgan's decisive role in it is in Strouse, *Morgan: American Financier*, pp. 573–89.

14. "Knickerbocker Trust Panic," *InvestmentNews*, http://www.investment-news.com/gallery/20120716/FREE/716009999/PH (accessed May 31, 2014).

15. "Morgan Visits the President," *New York Times*, November 23, 1907.

16. Ralph Tyler, letters to George Myers, August 8 and 16, 1907, George A. Myers Papers, 1890–1929, Ohio History Connection, Columbus.

17. T. Thomas Fortune, letter to Emmett Scott, September 7, 1907, in *The Booker T. Washington Papers*, ed. Louis R. Harlan and Raymond W. Smock, vol. 9, *1906–8* (Urbana: University of Illinois Press, 1980), p. 335.

18. Booker T. Washington, letter to Fred Moore, October 5, 1907, in ibid., 9:363–64.

19. Ralph Tyler, letter to Booker T. Washington, October 5, 1907, in ibid., 9:365–66.

20. See Emma L. Thornbrough, *T. Thomas Fortune: Militant Journalist* (Chicago: University of Chicago Press, 1972), p. 314.

21. Moore in a letter to Washington said he had no objection to publishing it after deleting a reference to a Roosevelt letter to Washington just before he went to Panama. Fred Moore, letter to Booker T. Washington, October 19, 1907, in Harlan and Smock, *Booker T. Washington Papers*, 9:378–79. Moore added, "Fortune is bitter. Dont you send him any more money." But two days later Charles Anderson, whom Moore showed a copy, tried to spike it on Washington's behalf. "I advised Moore not to print any of it." Charles Anderson, letter to Booker T. Washington, October 21, 1907, in Harlan and Smock, *Booker T. Washington Papers*, 9:384–86.

22. Cited in Thornbrough, *T. Thomas Fortune*, p. 316. See also August Meier, *Negro Thought in America, 1880–1915* (Ann Arbor: University of Michigan Press, 1966), p. 229.

23. Booker T. Washington, letter to Ralph Tyler, November 4, 1907, in Harlan and Smock, *Booker T. Washington Papers*, 9:394–95.

24. It is not clear who authorized the editorial's publication in the first place. Washington did not admit to it. Thornbrough said it was "with Scott's approval." See Thornbrough, *T. Thomas Fortune*, p. 314.

25. W. E. B. Du Bois, "Address to the Country" (speech, Annual Meeting of the Niagara Movement, Boston, August 1907), cited in *W. E. B. Du Bois: Biography of a Race, 1868–1919*, by David L. Lewis (New York: Henry Holt, 1993), p. 339.

26. See Thomas A. Bailey, *Theodore Roosevelt and the Japanese-American Crises: An Account of the International Complications Arising from the Race Problem on the Pacific Coast* (Gloucester, MA: P. Smith, 1964), p. 86.

27. Theodore Roosevelt, letter to Victor Metcalf, October 27, 1906, cited in ibid., p. 92.

28. Theodore Roosevelt, letter to Senator Eugene Hale, October 27, 1906, in Morison, *Letters of Theodore Roosevelt*, 5:473–75.

29. Theodore Roosevelt, letter to Kermit Roosevelt, October 27, 1906, in ibid., 5:475–76.

30. "Japan's Demand Heeded," *Los Angeles Herald*, October 27, 1906.

31. "Metcalf Starts Investigation," *San Francisco Call*, November 2, 1906. Unwittingly the school board president was subscribing to Roosevelt's shouldering the school problem because it dealt with the country's foreign policy, "a matter . . . for persons other than the members of the School Board to pass upon."

32. See Bailey, *Theodore Roosevelt and the Japanese-American Crises*, p. 88.

33. See chapter thirteen.

34. In the hierarchy of races as seen by Roosevelt, northern Europeans were the most advanced. (His ancestors came to America from Holland, firmly anchored in northern Europe.)

35. "President Demands Citizenship for Japanese," *New York Times*, December 5, 1906.

36. Theodore Roosevelt, Sixth Annual Message (address, Washington, DC, December 3, 1906), available online from the Miller Center at the University of Virginia, http://millercenter.org/president/speeches/detail/3778 (accessed October 2, 2014); and *New York Times*, December 5, 1906. The author used the transcript in these two sources for quoted material from the annual message.

37. Theodore Roosevelt, letter to Elihu Root, October 29, 1906, in Morison, *Letters of Theodore Roosevelt*, 5:484.

38. See Bailey, *Theodore Roosevelt and the Japanese-American Crises*, p. 95.

39. "Pardee Tells of Year's Prosperity in California," *Los Angeles Tribune*, January 9, 1907.

40. *The Letters of Theodore Roosevelt*, ed. Elting E. Morison, vol. 6, *The Big Stick: 1907–1909* (Cambridge, MA: Harvard University Press, 1952), p. 1605; Bailey, *Theodore Roosevelt and the Japanese-American Crises*, p. 127; "Roosevelt Discusses Japanese Situation," *Los Angeles Herald*, January 6, 1907.

41. Morison, *Letters of Theodore Roosevelt*, 6:1605; Bailey, *Theodore Roosevelt and the Japanese-American Crises*, p. 127; "Roosevelt Discusses Japanese Situation," *Los Angeles Herald*, January 6, 1907.

42. "Hayes and Kahn See Roosevelt about Japs," *San Francisco Call*, January 8, 1907.

43. "I have always been fond of the West African proverb, 'Speak softly and carry a big stick. You will go far.'" Theodore Roosevelt, letter to Henry Sprague, January 26, 1900, American Treasures of the Library of Congress, http://www.loc. gov/exhibits/treasures/trm139.html (accessed May 31, 2014). This is probably Roosevelt's most famous and often repeated comment and is used to describe his foreign policy.

44. See Bailey, *Theodore Roosevelt and the Japanese-American Crises*, pp. 126–45, for the entire story and what it took the make the deal.

45. *Brown v. Board of Education*, 347 U.S. 483 (1954).

46. T. Thomas Fortune, letter to Booker T. Washington, December 8, 1906, in Harlan and Smock, *Booker T. Washington Papers*, 9:157.

47. But only temporarily. Thirty-four years later the Japanese bombed Pearl Harbor.

CHAPTER TWENTY-FOUR: "DO YOU CARE TO SAY ANYTHING ON THE SUBJECT?"

1. "The Election in Ohio," *Outlook*, November 16, 1907, pp. 549–50. "Foraker Now Leads Taft in Ohio Fight," *New York Times*, November 17, 1907.

2. "Foraker Now Leads Taft in Ohio Fight."

3. See Everett Walters, *Joseph Benson Foraker: An Uncompromising Republican* (Columbus: Ohio History Press, 1948), p. 265; and "Foraker Indorsed by the Ohio League," *New York Times*, November 21, 1907. Fifteen months later it changed its collective mind and "jumped out of the [Foraker] bandwagon" and endorsed Roosevelt's administration while criticizing those in Congress who did not. "Home Blow to Foraker," *New York Times*, February 23, 1909.

4. Garfield Diary, November 29, 1907, James Rudolph Garfield Papers, Library of Congress.

5. Walters, *Joseph Benson Foraker*, pp. 266–67.

6. George Michaelis, letter to Joseph B. Foraker, June 18, 1907, box 68, Joseph Foraker Papers, Cincinnati History Library and Archives; Joseph B. Foraker, letter to George Michaelis, June 26, 1907, Foraker Papers.

7. In the early twentieth century, *alienist* was the term for psychiatrist.

8. George Michaelis, letter to Joseph B. Foraker, August 1, 1907, Foraker Papers; unsigned copy of letter to Michaelis, August 3, 1907, Foraker Papers.

9. George Michaelis, letter to Joseph B. Foraker, December 6, 1907, Foraker Papers; Joseph B. Foraker, letter to George Michaelis, December 7, 1907, Foraker Papers. Michaelis's letter speaks of two "actions in Washington and New York." Only the one in New York would be filed.

10. Reid was the soldier shoved into the Rio Grande by a customs inspector when returning from Mexico. See chapter three.

11. "Negro Troops Case Taken into Court," *New York Times*, December 27, 1907; "Rights of Soldiers," *Washington Post*, December 27, 1908. The US District Court's file and the petition filed by his lawyers, which would show the relief he wanted, cannot be found. According to the district court's published decision, his petition asked only "to recover the pay and emoluments which would have accrued to him" and made no demand for reenlistment. If Reid's lawyers thought he was entitled to reenlistment, they would have asked for it.

12. Foraker, *I Would Live It Again*, p. 286.

13. See chapter fifteen. See also Henry F. Pringle, *Theodore Roosevelt: A Biography* (New York: Harcourt, Brace, 1984), pp. 339–41; and Willard B. Gatewood, *Theodore Roosevelt and the Art of Controversy* (Baton Rouge: Louisiana State University Press, 1970), pp. 237–39.

14. Foraker, *I Would Live It Again*, p. 286.

15. Ibid., p. 288.

16. Napoleon B. Marshall, letter to Joseph B. Foraker, July 24, 1907, Foraker Papers. Julia Foraker seems to confirm the postal spying. She wrote that Senator Foraker was told by a friend from northern Ohio, "Be careful what you say in your letters. I have learned that they are being opened in the Post Office at Washington." Foraker, *I Would Live It Again*, p. 286. She does not identify the friend and may have been referring to Marshall's letter. "Senator Foraker told me, when he was having his difficulties with Roosevelt, that his letters were opened in transit. A man I knew, who had a great deal of difficulty with the Postoffice Department, resorted to every method to keep the contents of his letters from the department officials, using sealing wax and other protective measures, but it was no use. One of the officials told him to save his time as the inspectors had the art down fine, and could open any letter and reseal it so that nothing could be actually proved." Arthur W. Dunn, *From Harrison to Harding: A Personal Narrative, Covering a Third of a Century, 1888–1921* (New York: G. P. Putnam's Sons, 1922), p. 89.

17. These were the discussions he referred to in his December 7, 1907, letter to Michaelis. See "Democratic Votes Uphold Roosevelt," *New York Times*, February 26, 1908.

18. Theodore Roosevelt, message to the Senate, March 11, 1908, *The Brownsville Affray*, S. Doc. No. 60-389 (1908), p. 22.

19. "I am entirely in accord with the bill you showed me." Theodore Roosevelt, letter to Francis E. Warren, March 9, 1908 (two days before the majority report and the appended bill were presented to the Senate), in *The Letters of Theodore Roosevelt*, ed. Elting E. Morison, vol. 6, *The Big Stick: 1907–1909* (Cambridge, MA: Harvard University Press, 1952), pp. 966–67. Roosevelt made a significant (for him) concession. He no longer required a reenlisted soldier first to assist in finding the guilty soldiers.

20. The Warner and Foraker bills are at S. Doc. No. 60-389, pp. 27 and 106–108, respectively. The reference to "justice" is at S. Doc. No. 60-389, p. 26.

21. Joseph Foraker, *Notes of a Busy Life*, 2 vols. (Cincinnati: Stewart & Kidd, 1917), 2:293.

22. Ibid., 2:292–93; Theodore Roosevelt, letter to Francis E. Warren, March

9, 1909, in Morison, *Letters of Theodore Roosevelt*, 6:966–67; see also Theodore Roosevelt, letter to Sen. William Alden Smith, April 24, 1908, in Morison, *Letters of Theodore Roosevelt*, 6:1016–17 ("[Foraker's] would be clearly unconstitutional and I should pay not the slightest heed to it. . . . [It] is simply to replace murderers in the public armed forces of the United States on the sole condition that to the crime of murder in the past they add the crime of perjury in the future."). It is interesting to note that not only did Roosevelt not require assistance in ferreting out the guilty soldiers, in his letter to Warren, by saying "no reappointment would be made under it by me," he realized his successors might do just that.

23. Foraker, *I Would Live It Again*, p. 270.

24. He knew it. During the debate that day he addressed Vice President Fairbanks as "Your Honor," and then with a bow and smile-joked, "Coming events cast their shadows before them. I suppose it will not be long before I must become accustomed to the phrase, 'May it please the court.'" Walters, *Joseph Benson Foraker*, p. 250, citing an article in the *New York Times* and reprinted in *New York Age*, March 14, 1908. See also Joseph B. Foraker, letter to D. H. Moore, April 4, 1908, Foraker Papers, in which he suggests he has given up hopes for nomination.

25. "Negroes Wild over Foraker in Senate," *New York Times*, April 15, 1908.

26. 42 Cong. Rec. 4709 (1908) (address of Sen. Foraker).

27. 42 Cong. Rec. 4710.

28. Ibid.

29. 42 Cong. Rec. 4720.

30. 42 Cong. Rec. 4711.

31. Ibid.

32. 42 Cong. Rec. 4715, 4716, 4718.

33. It was segregated service, but the other bars would not permit even that.

34. 42 Cong. Rec. 4714.

35. 42 Cong. Rec. 4715.

36. 42 Cong. Rec. 4722. Foraker might have pointed out they also tried to find the guilty parties.

37. 42 Cong. Rec. 4723.

38. "Negroes Wild over Foraker."

39. J. G. Schurman, letter to Joseph B. Foraker, April 27, 1908, cited in Foraker, *Notes of a Busy Life*, 2:298.

40. Theodore Roosevelt, letter to William Smith, April 24, 1908, in Morison, *Letters of Theodore Roosevelt*, 6:1016–17.

41. Ibid, 6:966.

42. John E. Milholland, letter to Joseph B. Foraker, May 14, 1908; Joseph B. Foraker, letter to John E. Milholland, May 16, 1908; John E. Milholland, letter to Joseph B. Foraker, May 18, 1908; and Foraker, letter to John E. Milholland, May 20, 1908, all in box 81, Foraker Papers.

43. Milholland Diary, May 18, 1908, John E. Milholland Papers (1887–1924), Ticonderoga (NY) Historical Society.

44. John E. Milholland, letter to Joseph B. Foraker, August 22, 1907, Foraker Papers; John B. Foraker, letter to John E. Milholland, August 23, 1907, Foraker Papers.

45. John B. Foraker, letter to Napoleon B. Marshall, July 26, 1907, Foraker Papers.

46. Foraker, *Notes of a Busy Life*, 2:376.

47. Milholland Diary, May 18, 1908, Milholland Papers, cited in "The Political Career of Joseph Benson Foraker," by Earl R. Beck (PhD diss., Ohio State University, 1942), p. 96.

48. Only six days earlier he had sent Congress his last annual message. There was no mention of Brownsville. See "Last Message of Roosevelt," *New York Times*, December 9, 1908.

49. 43 Cong. Rec. 185, 185.

50. Letter from the Secretary of War Transmitting a Report, S. Doc. No. 60-626 (1909), p. 2.

51. Appendix A, Letter from the Secretary of War, S. Doc. No. 60-626.

52. S. Doc. No. 60-587 (1908), p. 9.

53. Appendix C, Letter from the Secretary of War, S. Doc. No. 60-626.

54. 43 Cong. Rec. 191–92.

55. Luke Wright, who had replaced Taft in 1904 as governor of the Philippines, now took his seat as secretary of war.

56. 43 Cong. Rec. 190, 194.

57. 43 Cong. Rec. 194.

58. Ibid.

59. Theodore Roosevelt, letter to William Howard Taft, December 12, 1908, in Morison, *Letters of Theodore Roosevelt*, 5:864. Morison added Roosevelt's statement, released that same day, did the trick. It "ended the continuing talk of a [Roosevelt] third term" and "strengthened Taft's position."

60. See Henry F. Pringle, *The Life and Times of William Howard Taft: A Biography*, 2 vols. (Hamden, CT: Archon Books, 1964), 1:318, 353.

61. See Edmund Morris, *Theodore Rex* (New York: Random House, 2001), pp. 526–27.

62. Walters, *Joseph Benson Foraker*, p. 268. In *Notes of a Busy Life*, 2:394, Foraker imperfectly remembers the vote count of the candidates other than Taft. He wrote his sixteen votes were "probably as many as any other candidate . . . except Taft." Actually, each of the other candidates had more than sixteen.

63. Joseph B. Foraker, letter to William Howard Taft, June 18, 1908, folder 1, box 24, Foraker Papers; William Howard Taft, letter to Joseph B. Foraker, June 19, 1908, in Foraker, *Notes of a Busy Life*, 2:394.

64. Walters, *Joseph Benson Foraker*, p. 272. Walters also cites Taft's letter to Roosevelt, September 4, 1908, quoted in Pringle, *Life and Times of William Howard Taft*, 1:271.

65. See "Roosevelt Frees Taft of Censure," *New York Times*, August 8, 1908.

66. "Roosevelt Helps Taft with Negroes," *New York Times*, August 9, 1908. See also "Negro Voters Will Swing to Taft," *New York Times*, May 18, 1908.

67. See Emma Lou Thornbrough, "The Brownsville Episode and the Negro Vote," *Mississippi Valley Historical Review* 44, no. 3 (December 1947): 469–93. See also August Meier, "Booker T. Washington and the Rise of the NAACP," *Crisis* 61, no. 2 (February 1954): 75.

68. As much to transfer to a Taft administration some semblance of the influence he once had with Theodore Roosevelt. See Booker T. Washington, letter to William Howard Taft, July 7, 1908, in *The Booker T. Washington Papers*, ed. Louis R. Harlan and Raymond W. Smock, vol. 9, *1906–8* (Urbana: University of Illinois Press, 1980), pp. 365–66.

69. Ralph Tyler, letter to Booker T. Washington, October 5, 1907, in ibid., 9:589.

70. Emma L. Thornbrough, *T. Thomas Fortune: Militant Journalist* (Chicago: University of Chicago Press, 1972), p. 328. For discussion of black vote for Taft, see Thornbrough, "Brownsville Episode and the Negro Vote," pp. 487–93.

71. "The Niagara Movement," Electronic Oberlin Group, http://www.oberlin.edu/external/EOG/Niagara%20Movement/niagaramain.htm (accessed June 1, 2014). Booker T. Washington knew that by then the Niagara Movement barely had a pulse. "We can safely say the movement is practically dead." Booker T. Washington, letter to the editor of the *New York Age*, September 7, 1908, in Harlan and Smock, *Booker T. Washington Papers*, 9:619. Earlier that year its treasurer reported to Du Bois that it was broke. Members were not paying their dues. Rev. J. Milton Waldron, letter to W. E. B. Du Bois, February 11, 1908, W. E. B. Du Bois Library, University of Massachusetts, http://credo.library.umass.edu/view/full/mums312-b004-i190 (accessed October 3, 2014).

72. Henry Litchfield West, "American Politics," *Forum*, July 1902, p. 3.

CHAPTER TWENTY-FIVE: AN ACT OF TREASON

1. See *Cincinnati Times-Star*, March 27, 1907, for Charles Taft's statement. See John D. Weaver, *The Brownsville Raid* (College Station: Texas A&M University, 1992), p. 269, for its postconvention effect on Foraker.

2. "Taft Will Make No Set Speeches," *New York Times*, April 8, 1908.

3. See Everett Walters, *Joseph Benson Foraker: An Uncompromising Republican* (Columbus: Ohio History Press, 1948), p. 269.

4. See ibid., p. 270.

5. Joseph B. Foraker, *Notes of a Busy Life*, 2 vols. (Cincinnati: Stewart & Kidd, 1917), 2:395.

6. See David Nasaw, *The Chief: The Life of William Randolph Hearst* (Boston: Houghton Mifflin, 2001), pp. 220–21.

7. Maybe it was not spur of the moment. Why else would he have the letters with him?

8. Foraker, *Notes of a Busy Life*, 2:328.

9. Nasaw, *The Chief*, p. 221.

10. Foraker, *Notes of a Busy Life*, 2:329.

11. Julia Foraker, *I Would Live It Again* (New York: Arno, 1975), p. 300.

12. Foraker, *Notes of a Busy Life*, 2:329.

13. John D. Archbold, letters to Joseph B. Foraker, January 27, 1902, and February 25, 1902, both cited in Foraker, *Notes of a Busy Life*, 2:329–30.

14. "Foraker Makes Attack on Taft," *New York Times*, September 26, 1908.

15. "Foraker Defends Standard Oil Fees," *New York Times*, November 16, 1908.

16. "Newspaper Comment on Campaign Contributions," *Outlook*, September 14, 1912, p. 68.

17. "The Standard Oil Scandal," HarpWeek, http://elections.harpweek.com/1908/Overview-1908-4.htm (accessed June 1, 2014).

18. Theodore Roosevelt, letter to Henry Cabot Lodge, September 19, 1908, in *Selections from the Correspondence of Theodore Roosevelt and Henry Cabot Lodge, 1884–1918*, 2 vols. (New York: C. Scribner's Sons, 1925), 2:316. Theodore Roosevelt, letter to William Howard Taft, September 19, 1908, in *The Letters of Theodore Roosevelt*, ed. Elting E. Morison, vol. 6, *The Big Stick: 1907–1909* (Cambridge, MA: Harvard University Press, 1952), p. 1244. Roosevelt came back to Foraker's Standard Oil troubles again with Lodge just a few days later. "Foraker is a brilliant man; he was a gallant soldier. . . . He was also a corrupt man and [struck through by Roosevelt] but [handwritten in] as this was so I am glad that he was exposed." Lodge replied, "Foraker's downfall appears complete and his letter was one of the feeblest productions I have ever read." Theodore Roosevelt, letter to Henry Cabot Lodge, September 25, 1908; Henry Cabot Lodge, letter to Theodore Roosevelt, September 29, 1908, both found in Henry Cabot Lodge Papers, Massachusetts Historical Society, Boston.

19. Theodore Roosevelt, telegram to Nicolas Longworth, February 21, 1908, in Morison, *Letters of Theodore Roosevelt*, 6:1244–45.

20. Theodore Roosevelt, letter to William Howard Taft, September 19, 1908, in Morison, *Letters of Theodore Roosevelt*, 6:1244.

21. See Archibald Butt, letter to Pamela Butt, September 23, 1908, in *The Letters of Archie Butt, Personal Aide to President Roosevelt*, ed. Lawrence F. Abbott (Garden City, NY: Doubleday, Page, 1924), p. 95. Butt was military aide to both Presidents Roosevelt and Taft. In 1912 Taft gave him leave to visit Europe with a friend. Their passage home was booked on the *Titanic*; both were lost.

22. Foraker, *I Would Live It Again*, p. 311.

23. Robert D. Bowden, *Boies Penrose: Symbol of an Era* (New York: Greenberg, 1937), pp. 178–79; Walter Davenport, *Power and Glory: The Life of Boies Penrose* (New York: G.P. Putnam's Sons, 1931), p. 177.

24. "George B. Cortelyou (1907–1909): Secretary of the Treasury," *American President: Theodore Roosevelt*, Miller Center, University of Virginia, http://miller-

center.org/president/roosevelt/essays/cabinet/422 (accessed June 1, 2014). Pringle writes Roosevelt did not order the Standard Oil money returned until October 26, less than two weeks before the election, and it was not paid back until after Election Day. Henry F. Pringle, *Theodore Roosevelt: A Biography* (New York: Harcourt, Brace, 1984), p. 251.

25. Cited in "Newspaper Comment on Campaign Contributions," p. 68.

26. Clark's statement is cited in Foraker, *Notes of a Busy Life*, 2:312.

27. Clark's comment about the Senate is that Brownsville "contributed largely" to what happened to Foraker's run for reelection. It is cited in ibid., 2:312. Foraker's response is at ibid., 2:328.

28. Robert Dove, The Term of a Senator—When Does It Begin and End?, S. Doc. No. 98-29 (1984), http://www.senate.gov/reference/resources/pdf/termofasenator.pdf (accessed October 3, 2014).

29. Memorandum of Conversation Held with Senator Foraker, December 13, 1908, John Callan O'Laughlin Papers, Houghton Library, Harvard University.

30. Memorandum of Conversation Held with Senator Foraker, December 15, 1908, O'Laughlin Papers.

31. Theodore Roosevelt, letter to William Howard Taft, January 1, 1909, in Morison, *Letters of Theodore Roosevelt*, 6:1454–56. Roosevelt delayed the letter until after Charley Taft withdrew. It was marked "Personal," and in it he cautioned Taft, "This letter is to be shown to no one excepting of course Mrs. Taft."

32. Theodore Roosevelt, letter to William Howard Taft, January 1, 1906, in Morison, *Letters of Theodore Roosevelt*, 6:1454–56.

33. Foraker, *Notes of a Busy Life*, 2:349. Foraker is a bit misleading here. The words *act of treason* were not in uppercase in the newspaper. Foraker gave them added punch by capitalizing them. It was commonly believed Roosevelt dictated the article word for word. See "C. P. Taft May Quit Ohio Senate Race," *New York Times*, December 31, 1908.

34. "Burton for Senator; Taft, Foraker Out," *New York Times*, January 1, 1909.

35. See Walters, *Joseph Benson Foraker*, pp. 283–84.

36. "Burns Favorite over Negro Fighter," *New York Times*, December 25, 1908.

37. Thomas R. Hietala, *The Fight of the Century: Jack Johnson, Joe Louis, and the Struggle for Racial Equality* (Armonk, NY: M. E. Sharpe, 2002), pp. 29–30.

38. Two years later when Johnson defended his title against Jim Jeffries (the "great white hope") in Reno, Nevada, as he walked to the ring a brass band played "All Coons Look Alike to Me," the lyrics of which were used to taunt Foraker at the Gridiron banquet in January 1907 (see chapter seventeen). The crowed joined in singing, but if they wanted to rattle the champ, it didn't work. Johnson walloped Jeffries and kept the crown. "July 4, 1910: Great White Hope vs. the Galveston Giant: The Jack Johnson 'Fight of the Century,'" US History Scene, http://www.ushistoryscene.com/1901-1950/july-4-1910-great-white-hope-vs-the-galveston-giant-the-jack-johnson-%E2%80%9Cfight-of-the-century%E2%80%9D/ (accessed June 1, 2014). Johnson historian Thomas R. Hietala writes the band intended to play "All

Coons Look Alike to Me" but at the last minute changed to "Dixie." Hietala, *Fight of the Century*, pp. 13–47.

CHAPTER TWENTY-SIX: ROOSEVELT FATIGUE

1. *Reid v. United States*, 161 F. 469, 470 (S.D.N.Y. 1908).

2. *Reid v. United States*, 211 U.S. 529 (1909). See William Blackstone, *Commentaries on the Laws of England* 1:*242: "No suit or action can be brought against the king, even in civil matters, because no court can have jurisdiction over him. For all jurisdiction implies superiority of power: authority to try would be vain and idle, without an authority to redress; and the sentence of a court would be contemptible, unless that court had the power to command the execution of it: but who . . . shall command the king?"

3. Holmes's comment cited in *TR: The Last Romantic*, by H. W. Brands (New York, NY: Basic Books, 1997), p. 542.

4. Roosevelt had hinted to a few people something was in the wind but did not say what. See Theodore Roosevelt, letter to Booker T. Washington, November 5, 1908, in *The Booker T. Washington Papers*, eds. Louis R. Harlan and Raymond W. Smock, vol. 9, *1906–8* (Urbana: University of Illinois Press, 1980), p. 686.

5. Foraker had a second source for information. In September, Napoleon Marshall wrote that a man who identified himself as "Col. Brown from the War Department" came to Mingo Sanders's home and tried to get him to confess. Foraker, recognizing the name "Brown," immediately thought of Boyd Conyers down in Georgia. Napoleon B. Marshall, letter to Joseph B. Foraker, September 15, 1908; and Joseph B. Foraker, letter to Napoleon B. Marshall, September 17, 1908, both found in Joseph Foraker Papers, Cincinnati History Library and Archives.

6. Boyd Conyers, letter to Joseph B. Foraker, July 24, 1908, cited by Foraker at 42 Cong. Rec. 192 (1908).

7. "A Discredited Case," *Boston Herald*, December 15, 1908.

8. The quoted language appears in the following correspondence: Theodore Roosevelt, letter to Whitelaw Reid, April 26, 1906, in *The Letters of Theodore Roosevelt*, ed. Elting E. Morison, vol. 5, *The Big Stick: 1905–1907* (Cambridge, MA: Harvard University Press, 1952), pp. 230–51; Theodore Roosevelt, letter to Arthur Hamilton Lee, October 22, 1906, in Morison, *Letters of Theodore Roosevelt*, 5:476; Theodore Roosevelt, letter to Arthur Hamilton Lee, in *The Letters of Theodore Roosevelt*, ed. Elting E. Morison, vol. 6, *The Big Stick: 1907–1909* (Cambridge, MA: Harvard University Press, 1952), pp. 918–21. Lee was the British military attaché to the US army in Cuba, where he and Roosevelt became such close friends Roosevelt made him an honorary member of his Rough Riders. "Lord Lee of Fareham (1868–1947)," *The Roaring Twenties: An Encyclopaedia*, http://homepages.warwick.ac.uk/~lysic/1920s/leelord.htm (accessed June 1, 2014).

9. Maurice Low, letter to Joseph B. Foraker, December 14, 1908, Foraker Papers.

10. Letter from the Secretary of War Transmitting a Report, January 2, 1909, S. Doc. No. 60-626 (1909), p. 1.

11. Except for those reserved for the White House. They were empty.

12. 43 Cong. Rec. 805.

13. "Foraker Scorns Official Spying," *New York Times*, January 13, 1909.

14. 43 Cong. Rec. 806–8.

15. 43 Cong. Rec. 805.

16. "Says President Violated Law," *Marysville (OH) Evening Tribune*, January 13, 1909.

17. 43 Cong. Rec. 797.

18. "Foraker Scorns Official Spying."

19. "Says President Violated Law"; "President 'Oblivious to All Law and Decency.'" *Daily Saratogian*, January 12, 1909.

20. Joseph B. Foraker, *Notes of a Busy Life*, 2 vols. (Cincinnati: Stewart & Kidd, 1917), 2:305–306. See also "President 'Oblivious to All Law and Decency.'"

21. Foraker, *Notes of a Busy Life*, 2:306. Foraker also had affidavits supporting Conyers from the assistant cashier of the leading bank in Monroe and the captain of the local company of the Georgia National Guard, both white men.

22. The next month, when the final Browne-Baldwin report was delivered to the War Department, Roosevelt told the secretary of war, "It is not necessary to send this report to Congress." Whatever new information it might have, he saw no reason to provide further fodder for Foraker to turn against him. Theodore Roosevelt, letter to Luke Edward Wright, February 7, 1909, in Morison, *Letters of Theodore Roosevelt*, 6:1507.

23. 43 Cong. Rec. 805.

24. Roosevelt sensed the antagonisms in Congress. On January 14, two days after Foraker tore apart the Browne-Baldwin investigation, Roosevelt wrote his son Kermit, "Congress of course feels that I will never again have to be reckoned with and that it is safe to be ugly with me. Accordingly, in one way I am not having an easy time." Theodore Roosevelt, letter to Kermit Roosevelt, January 14, 1909, in Morison, *Letters of Theodore Roosevelt*, 6:1475–76.

25. "Roosevelt Will Make Full Report to the Senate," *Atlanta Constitution*, January 17, 1909. Theodore Roosevelt, letter to William Howard Taft, January 16, 1909, in Morison, *Letters of Theodore Roosevelt*, 6:1476.

26. "98-Mile Ride Bully, President Declares," *New York Times*, January 14, 1909.

27. A. C. Stine, letter to Joseph B. Foraker, February 8, 1909, box 94, Foraker Papers.

28. Nathaniel W. Stephenson, *Nelson W. Aldrich, A Leader in American Politics* (New York: C. Scribner's Sons, 1930), pp. 48–51.

29. Theodore Roosevelt, letter to Nelson W. Aldrich, January 27, 1909, in Morison, *Letters of Theodore Roosevelt*, 6:1486–87.

30. Collum, cited in Foraker, *Notes of a Busy Life*, 2:470.

31. Ibid., 2:310. This was Roosevelt's second celebration in two days. The day before, he was in Hampton Roads, Virginia, to welcome back his Great White Fleet after its fourteen-month cruise around the world. It had been received everywhere with acclaim, especially in Japan. Roosevelt had worked his magic with his sure handling of the Japanese-workers problem. See James B. Reckner, "The Fleet Triumphant," *Theodore Roosevelt Association Journal* 29, no. 2 (Summer 2008): 5–16.

32. Foraker, *Notes of a Busy Life*, 2:311.

33. 42 *Cong*. Rec. 3391 (1909).

34. Not completely; he helped Daggett and Marshall locate soldiers who might want to apply for reenlistment. Senator Francis Warren obtained a list from the army, and on March 13, 1909, he forwarded it, with forty-one names and addresses, to Foraker. Mingo Sanders was on the list. So were five others later found by the Court of Inquiry eligible for reenlistment.

35. Mingo Sanders testified the shooting came from the town and into the fort. Why then, he was asked, did he form his company with their backs to the town? Why were there no bullets in any of the fort's buildings? And why was none of the soldiers shot? His confused answer seems to have been something Daggett or Marshall prepared him to say in response to a different question: Why would the fort be under attack? "My reason is this, to get the soldiers away from [Brownsville and Fort Brown]." See Report of the Proceedings of the Court of Inquiry Relative to the Shooting Affray at Brownsville, Tex. . . . , S. Doc. No. 61-701, vols. 4–6 (1911) (hereafter cited as CI-2), pp. 1062, 1069, 1078–79 (testimony of Sanders).

36. Aaron S. Daggett, letter to Joseph B. Foraker, November 16, 1909, Foraker Papers, cited in *The Brownsville Raid*, by John D. Weaver (College Station: Texas A&M University, 1992), p. 225.

37. See "Its Conclusions," CI-2, p. 1635; Weaver, *Brownsville Raid*, p. 247; "Brownsville Case Settled," *New York Times*, April 7, 1910.

38. Sanders was the only soldier mentioned by name in messages he sent to Congress. As late as February 1909 Roosevelt wrote to Secretary of War Luke Wright (in the letter telling him not to send the Browne-Baldwin report to Congress) that Sanders was "as thoroughly dangerous, unprincipled and unworthy a soldier as ever wore the United States uniform." Theodore Roosevelt, letter to Luke Wright, February 7, 1909, in Morison, *Letters of Theodore Roosevelt*, 6:1507.

39. See Summary Discharge or Mustering Out of Regiments or Companies: Message from the President of the United States . . . , S. Doc. No. 59-155, vol. 11, pt. 1 (2d sess. 1907), p. 486 (statement of John Smith to Lt. Col. Lovering).

40. Ann J. Lane, *The Brownsville Affair: National Crisis and Black Reaction* (Port Washington, NY: Kennikat, 1971), p. 168.

CHAPTER TWENTY-SEVEN: "NOT ONE PARTICLE OF REGRET"

1. "Negroes Present Loving Cup to Foraker," *Washington Herald*, March 7, 1909.

2. Foraker's remarks were reprinted in full in a pamphlet, *Presentation of Loving Cup to Hon. Joseph Benson Foraker, United States Senator, in Appreciation of His Service on Behalf of the Members of Companies A, B, and C, Twenty-Fifth Infantry, by a Committee of Colored Citizens: The Ceremony and Addresses, March 6th, 1909, at Metropolitan A.M.E. Church, Washington, D.C.* (Washington, DC: Murray Brothers, 1909).

3. In referring to crime and conviction, Foraker was splitting hairs, but Roosevelt had done the same in crafting a plan against the soldiers. If Roosevelt could sharpen the distinction between disobedience and murder to throw the soldiers out, Foraker could dull it to argue they should have been kept in.

4. His son Thomas Beer would write a well-received biography of that other Ohioan Mark Hanna.

5. William C. Beer, letter to Joseph B. Foraker, March 7, 1909, Joseph Foraker Papers, Cincinnati History Library and Archives.

6. "Roosevelt with Ax in Wood," *New York Times*, March 7, 1909.

7. Theodore Roosevelt, letter to Kermit Roosevelt, January 14, 1909, in *The Selected Letters of Theodore Roosevelt*, ed. H. W. Brands (Lanham, MD: Rowman & Littlefield, 2001), p. 509.

8. *Scott v. Sandford*, 60 U.S. (19 How.) 393 (1857).

EPILOGUE: WHAT HAPPENED LATER

1. "The President supposes [Fort Brown] will eventually be abandoned." William Loeb, letter to Gen. Fred C. Ainsworth, August 20, 1906, Summary Discharge or Mustering Out of Regiments or Companies: Message from the President of the United States . . . , S. Doc. No. 59-155, vol. 11, pt. 1 (2d sess. 1907) (hereafter cited as SD-1, p. 34. See also Fred C. Ainsworth, letter to William Loeb, August 20, 1906, SD-1, p. 35; William Loeb, letter to Gen. Fred C. Ainsworth, August 21, 1906, SD-1, pp. 38–39; Gen. Fred C. Ainsworth to William Loeb, August 21, 1906, SD-1, p. 39.

2. "Fort Brown Condo Shares," RedWeek.com, http://www.redweek.com/resort/P700-fort-brown-condo-shares (accessed June 1, 2014).

3. See John H. Nankivell and Quintard Taylor, *Buffalo Soldier Regiment: History of the Twenty-Fifth United States Infantry, 1869–1926* (Lincoln: University of Nebraska Press, 2001), pp. 120–44.

4. Surprisingly, some were entitled to some veterans' benefits from service in the Spanish-American War (or because they were the eleven who reenlisted), and so long as they lived, the government could locate them. John D. Weaver, *The*

Senator and the Sharecropper's Son: Exoneration of the Brownsville Soldiers (College Station: Texas A&M University Press, 1997), p. 204.

5. Exec. Order No. 9981, 13 Fed. Reg. 4313 (July 26, 1948).

6. Box 4499, Records of the Adjutant General's Office, 1780s–1917, National Archives.

7. Weaver, *Senator and the Sharecropper's Son*, p. xx. Andrew H. Malcolm, "Army Returns Honor to Discharged Black," *New York Times*, February 12, 1973.

8. Andrew H. Malcolm, "67 Years after Discharge, Black Soldier Is Honored," *New York Times*, January 11, 1974.

9. Frank N. Schubert, *On the Trail of the Buffalo Soldier: Biographies of African Americans in the U.S. Army, 1866–1917* (Wilmington, DE: Scholarly Resources, 1995), pp. 476–77. Nan Robertson, "Family of Black Veteran in 1906 Texas Raid Recalls Stigma," *New York Times*, February 8, 1977.

10. Report of the Proceedings of the Court of Inquiry Relative to the Shooting Affray at Brownsville, Tex. . . . , S. Doc. No. 61-701, vols. 4–6 (1911) (hereafter cited as CI-2), pp. 1111–12. The court reporter transcribing First Sergeant Sanders's testimony that morning was Mr. H. B. Weaver. His son, John Weaver, is the Brownsville historian most responsible for the correction of Special Orders No. 266 to an honorable discharge. By then, Sanders had been in his grave forty-four years.

11. "Post for Mingo Sanders," *New York Times*, August 4, 1912; "Roosevelt on Way; Sounds a Warning," *New York Times*, August 5, 1912.

12. Schubert, *On the Trail of the Buffalo Soldier*, pp. 367–68.

13. Theodore Roosevelt, letter to Booker T. Washington, December 25, 1908, with pencil notation dated December 29, 1908, box 36, Correspondence Photostats, Theodore Roosevelt Collection, Houghton Library, Harvard University.

14. Booker T. Washington, letter to William Howard Taft, July 18, 1908; Booker T. Washington, letter to William Howard Taft, July 20, 1908; William Howard Taft, letter to Booker T. Washington, July 22, 1908; all found in *The Booker T. Washington Papers*, ed. Louis R. Harlan and Raymond W. Smock, vol. 9, *1906–8* (Urbana: University of Illinois Press, 1980), pp. 600–601. In the July 18 letter the greeting to Taft was "Dear Secretary Taft." In the July 20 letter it was "My Dear Judge." Washington had moved Taft out of the shadow of Theodore Roosevelt. See Ralph Tyler, letter to Emmett Scott, July 21, 1908, in Harlan and Smock, *Booker T. Washington Papers*, 9:601–602.

15. Louis R. Harlan, *Booker T. Washington: The Wizard of Tuskegee, 1901–1915* (New York: Oxford University Press, 1983), p. 393.

16. Program for Memorial Service held March 14, 1926, at St. James Presbyterian Church, New York, found in John E. Milholland Papers (1887–1924), Ticonderoga (NY) Historical Society.

17. "Du Bois and Washington, in speaking for two dissimilar socioeconomic orders, were really speaking past each other rather than to the same set of racial problems and solutions; but Du Bois . . . had the advantage of speaking to the future, while Washington . . . spoke . . . for the early industrial past." David L.

Lewis, *W. E. B. Du Bois: Biography of a Race 1868–1919* (New York: Henry Holt, 1993), p. 502.

18. Cited in David L. Lewis, *W. E. B. Du Bois: The Fight for Equality and the American Century, 1919–1963* (New York: Henry Holt, 2000), p. 569.

19. Cited in Henry F. Pringle, *Theodore Roosevelt: A Biography* (New York: Harcourt, Brace, 1984), p. 393.

20. Theodore Roosevelt, letter to George Spinney, January 22, 1907, in *The Letters of Theodore Roosevelt*, ed. Elting E. Morison, vol. 5, *The Big Stick: 1905–1907* (Cambridge, MA: Harvard University Press, 1952), pp. 359–60.

21. Pretty close. Roosevelt received 4,120,609 votes to Taft's 3,487,937.

22. William Howard Taft, letter to Aunt Delia, cited in *The Life and Times of William Howard Taft: A Biography*, 2 vols., by Henry F. Pringle (Hamden, CT: Archon Books, 1964), 2:787; "Roosevelt Grips Hand of Taft; Diners in Chicago Hotel Cheer as the Ex-Presidents End Six-Year Quarrel," *New York Times*, May 27, 1918; Edmund Morris, *Colonel Roosevelt* (New York: Random House, 2010), p. 558.

23. He sometimes got gifts. One of the most unusual and more expensive was a watch fob of solid Alaskan gold from eleven black miners in Fairbanks. "Present from Far-Away Alaska," *Cincinnati Enquirer*, October 24, 1909. Two years earlier Roosevelt received his own expensive gift from the residents of Brownsville. It was a walking stick, "silver mounted, set with forty-five precious stones for the States," and hand-carved from Mexican coffee wood, "treasured" by the family of Sam Houston, with "nearly 400 figures and emblems. . . . The engraver spent nearly six months in the work." "Big Stick for Roosevelt," *New York Times*, April 14, 1907.

24. Maj. Charles Penrose, letter to Joseph B. Foraker, marked "Confidential," November 1, 1908, Joseph Foraker Papers, Cincinnati History Library and Archives. Foraker wrote back, "I shall never regret that I championed the cause of poor, helpless soldiers, who were, in my opinion, unjustly discharged without honor." Joseph B. Foraker, letter to Maj. Charles Penrose, December 1, 1908, Foraker Papers.

25. Cited in John D. Weaver, *The Brownsville Raid* (College Station: Texas A&M University Press, 1992), p. 264.

26. If this is an apology, Foraker may be the only public man Roosevelt ever apologized to. Edward Wagenknecht, *The Seven Worlds of Theodore Roosevelt* (New York: Longmans, Green, 1958), p. 144.

27. Theodore Roosevelt, letter to Joseph B. Foraker, January 19, 1912, Foraker Papers.

28. Joseph B. Foraker, letter to Theodore Roosevelt, January 24, 1912, Foraker Papers. When these letters were exchanged, Roosevelt was beginning his campaign to unseat Taft. It is impossible to believe Joseph Foraker, who knew Roosevelt's wrath and what he was capable of, did not see what he would do to President Taft. It is impossible to believe his comment about "Colonel" being a temporary title suggested anything but a polite witticism to show no hard feelings. Politeness and forgiveness were qualities Foraker possessed.

29. Percy E. Murray, "Harry C. Smith-Joseph B. Foraker Alliance: Coalition Politics in Ohio," *Journal of Negro History* 68, no. 2 (1983): 181.

30. "Joseph B. Foraker, Ex-Senator, Dead," *New York Times*, May 11, 1917.

31. *Memorial to Joseph Benson Foraker: Meeting of the Bench and Bar Held in the Court Room of the United States Circuit Court of Appeals* . . . , Public Library of Cincinnati and Hamilton County.

32. Champ Clark, *My Quarter Century of American Politics* 2 (New York: Harper & Brothers, 1920), 1:419.

33. Robert McKee, *Story: Substance, Structure, Style, and the Principles of Screenwriting* (New York: HarperCollins Books, 1997), pp. 144–45.

34. Cited in Pringle, *Life and Times of William Howard Taft*, 2:888.

35. Peter Collier and David Horowitz, *The Roosevelts: An American Saga* (New York: Simon & Schuster, 1994), p. 239; H. W. Brands, *TR: The Last Romantic* (New York: Basic Books, 1997), pp. 811–12. Pringle thought it doubtful; Pringle, *Theodore Roosevelt: A Biography*, p. 424.

36. Lewis, *W. E. B. Du Bois: Biography of a Race*, p. 422.

37. Kathleen Dalton, *Theodore Roosevelt: A Strenuous Life* (New York: Alfred A. Knopf, 2002), pp. 523–24, citing W. E. B. Du Bois, "Theodore Roosevelt," *Crisis* 17, no. 4 (February 1919): 163.

38. Oswald Garrison Villard, obituary, *Nation*, January 18, 1919, folder 3312, Oswald Garrison Villard Papers, Houghton Library, Harvard University.

39. David Fromkin, *The King and the Cowboy* (New York: Penguin Press, 2008), p. 151. Another way of expressing this is to say he distrusted the law, and lawyers and courts, particularly when they got in his path. Pringle, *Life and Times of William Howard Taft*, pp. 256, 387. Joshua Hawley called these "warrior values." Joshua D. Hawley, *Theodore Roosevelt: Preacher of Righteousness* (New Haven, CT: Yale University Press, 2008), p. 114. Having earned his right to assert them and protect them, how could Roosevelt permit the soldiers to sully them?

40. Pringle, *Theodore Roosevelt: A Biography*, p. 55.

41. Ibid., p. 49.

42. Quoted in *Brooklyn Daily Eagle*, January 20, 1907, and cited in James A. Tinsley, "Roosevelt, Foraker, and the Brownsville Affray," *Journal of Negro History* 41, no. 1 (1956): 63.

43. Kelly Miller, "Roosevelt and the Negro," in *Race Adjustment: Essays on the Negro in America* (New York: Neale, 1910), p. 276.

44. Henry Adams, *The Education of Henry Adams* (New York: Penguin Books, 1995), p. 396.

45. Henry Fowler Pringle, 7th year, Research Notes for *Theodore Roosevelt: A Biography*, Houghton Library, Harvard University.

46. "Senator Foraker and His Fight on the President," *New York Times Sunday Magazine*, May 19, 1907, p. 4.

47. Cited in Arthur Stanley Link, "Theodore Roosevelt in His Letters," *Yale Review* 43, no. 4 (1954): 594.

48. Lewis, *W. E. B. Du Bois: The Fight for Equality and the American Century*, p. 502.

49. In his "biography" of the Twenty-Fifth Infantry, Nankivell repays Roosevelt for his omission; he ignores him and his Rough Riders when writing about Cuba and El Caney.

AFTERWORD: WHAT IF . . . ?

1. James E. Amos, *Theodore Roosevelt: Hero to His Valet* (New York: John Day, 1927), p. 5.

2. Ibid., p. 63.

3. Ibid., p. 59.

4. Ibid., p. 62.

5. Ibid., p. 64.

6. Might the same first name—Robert—have been chosen to avoid confusion when she referred to one when meaning the other?

7. Uncle Rob's lifestyle was decidedly "bohemian." See David McCullough, *Mornings on Horseback* (New York: Simon & Schuster, 1981), p. 22. He was an endlessly fascinating man and counted among his friends and correspondents General George Custer; the writer Bret Harte; both Gilbert (the librettist) and Sullivan (the composer) of *HMS Pinafore* and other comic operas; and Irish playwright Oscar Wilde, who signed letters to him "Affectionately." M. Fortescue Pickard, *The Roosevelts and America* (London: H. Joseph, 1941), pp. 249–50, 245–46, 257–59, 261–62. In his autobiography, Theodore Roosevelt recognized his uncle for writing the B'rer Rabbit stories long before Joel Chandler Harris. *Theodore Roosevelt, An Autobiography*, in *The Rough Riders / An Autobiography*, ed. Louis Auchincloss (New York: Library of America, 2004), p. 264.

8. The Twenty-Sixth *Volunteer* Infantry is not to be confused with the Twenty-Sixth Infantry, the regiment the Twenty-Fifth Infantry replaced at Fort Brown.

9. Fortescue Efficiency Record; Acting Secretary to the President to Assistant Secretary of War, July 30, 1902, file 258313, Records of the Adjutant General's Office, 1780s–1917, National Archives. "By direction of the President . . . make a report to him of this case. At the bottom, in Roosevelt's handwriting, "Please look into this personally," (signed) Theodore Roosevelt.

10. "Capt. Taggart Wins His Divorce Case," *New York Times*, October 15, 1905. The divorce action had been filed a year earlier. Evidently Mrs. Taggart may have initiated her dalliance with Fortescue and possibly two other officers, one a general. A year later, Captain Taggart died of fever in the Philippines. "Major Taggart Dying in Far Off Philippines," *Newark (Ohio) Daily Advocate*, October 25, 1906.

11. "Teddy's Nephew a Scrapper," *San Francisco Call*, October 26, 1904. Fortescue was drunk, punched a hack driver, and was arrested. He told the arresting

officer he was Roosevelt's nephew. Newspaper clipping, file 429833, Records of the Adjutant General's Office.

12. "Both Edith and I are very fond of Roly," Theodore Roosevelt, letter to Robert Roosevelt, April 20, 1905. Pickard, *Roosevelts and America*, p. 232. See also *Letters to Kermit from Theodore Roosevelt, 1902–1908*, ed. Will Irwin (New York: C. Scribner's Sons, 1946), p. 267.

13. "Roly Fortescue is here as an Aide. I have had him riding and walking with me." Theodore Roosevelt, letter to Kermit Roosevelt, December 5, 1903, in Irwin, *Letters to Kermit from Theodore Roosevelt*, p. 52. "By the way, Roly Fortescue insisted upon boxing with me the other day. I did not exactly want to box; I was afraid I would hurt him, and I did, giving him a most gorgeous pair of black eyes." Theodore Roosevelt, letter to Kermit Roosevelt, February 5, 1905, in Irwin, *Letters to Kermit from Theodore Roosevelt*, p. 93.

14. "Lieut. Fortescue Resigns," *Washington Evening Star*, November 17, 1905.

15. White House visitor log, January 30, 1908, Theodore Roosevelt Papers, Library of Congress.

16. See "Washington News," *Washington National Tribune*, November 14, 1907. See also Allan R. Millett, "The Rise and Fall of the Cuban Rural Guard," *Americas* 29, no. 2 (October 1972): 191–213, for a discussion of the organization Fortescue escaped to.

17. White House visitor log, December 9, 1906, Roosevelt Papers.

BIBLIOGRAPHY

BOOKS & ARTICLES

Adams, Henry. *The Education of Henry Adams*. New York: Penguin Books, 1995.

Aldrich, Nelson W. *Old Money: The Mythology of Wealth in America*. New York: Allworth Press, 1996.

Alexander, Roberta Sue. *A Place of Recourse: A History of the U.S. District Court for the Southern District of Ohio, 1803–2003*. Athens: Ohio University Press, 2005.

Amos, James E. *Theodore Roosevelt: Hero to His Valet*. New York: John Day, 1927.

Arthur, Anthony, and John J. Broesamle. *Twelve Great Clashes That Shaped Modern America: From Geronimo to George W. Bush*. New York: Pearson/Longman, 2006.

Ascoli, Peter M. *Julius Rosenwald: The Man Who Built Sears, Roebuck and Advanced the Cause of Black Education in the American South*. Bloomington: Indiana University Press, 2006.

Azoy, A. C. M. *Charge! The Story of the Battle of San Juan Hill*. New York: Longmans, Green, 1961.

Bailey, Thomas A. *Theodore Roosevelt and the Japanese-American Crises: An Account of the International Complications Arising from the Race Problem on the Pacific Coast*. Gloucester, MA: P. Smith, 1964.

Baker, Leonard. *Brandeis and Frankfurter: A Dual Biography*. New York: Harper & Row, 1984.

Baker, Ray Stannard. *Following the Color Line: An Account of Negro Citizenship in the American Democracy*. Williamstown, MA: Corner House, 1973.

Barry, David S. *Forty Years in Washington*. Boston: Little, Brown, 1924.

Beck, Earl R. "Joseph B. Foraker and the Standard Oil Charges." *Ohio Archaeological and Historical Quarterly* 56 (1947): 154–78.

———. "The Political Career of Joseph Benson Foraker." PhD diss., Ohio State University, 1942.

Beer, Thomas. *The Mauve Decade*. New York: Carroll & Graf, 1997.

Beers, Paul B. *Pennsylvania Politics Today and Yesterday: The Tolerable Accommodation*. University Park: Pennsylvania State University Press, 1980.

Bishop, Joseph Bucklin. *Theodore Roosevelt and His Time: Shown in His Own Letters*. 2 vols. New York: C. Scribner's Sons, 1920.

Black, Lowell D., and Sara H. Black. *An Officer and a Gentleman: The Military Career of Lieutenant Henry O. Flipper*. Dayton, OH: Lora, 1985.

Blackmon, Douglas A. *Slavery by Another Name*. New York: Anchor Books, 2009.

Blaesser, Brian W. "John E. Milholland." PhD diss., Brown University, 1969.

Blaine, James G., Mrs. *Letters of Mrs. James G. Blaine*. Edited by Harriet S. B. Beale. 2 vols. New York: Duffield, 1908.

Blum, John M. "Editors' Camera: 'The Letters of Theodore Roosevelt.'" *American Documentation* 1, no. 4 (October 1950): 181–84.

———. "Theodore Roosevelt and the Hepburn Act: Toward an Orderly System of Control." In *The Letters of Theodore Roosevelt*, ed. Elting E. Morison. Vol. 6, *The Big Stick: 1907–1909*, pp. 1558–71. Cambridge, MA: Harvard University Press, 1952.

Boller, Paul F. *Presidential Campaigns: From George Washington to George W. Bush*. New York: Oxford University Press, 2004.

Bonds, Russell S. *War Like the Thunderbolt: The Battle and Burning of Atlanta*. Yardley, PA: Westholme, 2009.

Bowden, Robert D. *Boies Penrose: Symbol of an Era*. New York: Greenberg, 1937.

Brands, H. W. *The Man Who Saved the Union: Ulysses Grant in War and Peace*. New York: Doubleday, 2012.

———. *TR: The Last Romantic*. New York: Basic Books, 1997.

Brayman, Harold. *From Grover Cleveland to Gerald Ford . . . The President Speaks Off-the-Record. Historic Evenings with America's Leaders, the Press, and Other Men of Power, at Washington's Exclusive Gridiron Club*. Princeton: Dow Jones Books, 1976.

Brinkley, Douglas. *The Wilderness Warrior: Theodore Roosevelt and the Crusade for America*. New York: HarperCollins, 2009.

Bruce, Dickson D. *Archibald Grimké: Portrait of a Black Independent*. Baton Rouge: Louisiana State University Press, 1993.

Buecker, Thomas R. "Prelude to Brownsville, the Twenty-Fifth Infantry at Fort Niobrara, Nebraska, 1902–06." *Great Plains Quarterly* 16, no. 2 (Spring 1996): 95–106. http://digitalcommons.unl.edu/greatplainsquarterly/1087.

Burns, James MacGregor, and Susan Dunn. *The Three Roosevelts: Patrician Leaders Who Transformed America*. New York: Atlantic Monthly Press, 2001.

Butt, Archibald W. *The Letters of Archie Butt, Personal Aide to President Roosevelt*. Edited by Lawrence F. Abbott. Garden City, NY: Doubleday, Page, 1924.

————. *Taft and Roosevelt: The Intimate Letters of Archie Butt, Military Aide.* Port Washington, NY: Kennikat, 1971.

Cannon, Joseph G. *The Memoirs of Joseph Gurney "Uncle Joe" Cannon.* Edited by Helen L. Abdill. Danville, IL: Vermilion County Museum Society, 1996.

Caro, Robert A. *The Years of Lyndon Johnson: Master of the Senate.* New York: Alfred A. Knopf, 2002.

Carroll, Rebecca, ed. *Uncle Tom or New Negro? African Americans Reflect on Booker T. Washington and "Up from Slavery" 100 Years Later.* New York: Harlem Moon, 2006.

Carter, Hodding. *The Angry Scar: The Story of Reconstruction.* Garden City, NY: Doubleday, 1959.

Cash, Kevin. *Who the Hell Is William Loeb?* Manchester, NH: Amoskeag, 1975.

Chernow, Ron. *Alexander Hamilton.* New York: Penguin Books: 2004.

Chessman, G. W. *Theodore Roosevelt and the Politics of Power.* Boston: Little, Brown, 1969.

Christian, Garna L. "The Brownsville, Texas, Disturbance of 1906 and the Politics of Justice." *Trotter Review* 18, no. 1 (2009): 23–28. http://scholarworks.umb.edu/trotter_review/vol18/iss1/4.

Clark, Champ. *My Quarter Century of American Politics.* 2 vols. New York: Harper & Brothers, 1920.

Clemens, William M. *The Ancestry of Theodore Roosevelt: A Genealogical Record from 1649, with Notes on the Families of Baillee, Bulloch, Douglas, Elliott, Irvine, Stewart, Van Schaack, with Complete Name Index.* New York: W. M. Clemens, 1914.

Coffman, Edward M. *The Old Army: A Portrait of the American Army in Peacetime, 1784–1898.* New York: Oxford University Press, 1986.

————. *The Regulars: The American Army, 1898–1941.* Cambridge, MA: Belknap Press of Harvard University Press, 2004.

Collier, Peter, and David Horowitz. *The Roosevelts: An American Saga.* New York: Simon & Schuster, 1994.

Cordery, Stacy A. *Alice: Alice Roosevelt Longworth, from White House Princess to Washington Power Broker.* New York: Viking, 2007.

Crichton, Judy. *America 1900: The Turning Point.* New York: Henry Holt, 1998.

Cromwell, Adelaide M. *Unveiled Voices, Unvarnished Memories: The Cromwell Family in Slavery and Segregation, 1692–1972.* Columbia: University of Missouri Press, 2007.

Cullom, Shelby M. *Fifty Years of Public Service.* Chicago: McClurg, 1911.

Dalton, Kathleen. *Theodore Roosevelt: A Strenuous Life.* New York: Alfred A. Knopf, 2002.

Darrow, Clarence. *The Story of My Life.* New York: C. Scribner's Sons, 1932.

Davenport, Walter. *Power and Glory: The Life of Boies Penrose.* New York: G. P. Putnam's Sons, 1931.

Douglas, Davison M. "The Struggle for School Desegregation in Cincinnati before 1954." *University of Cincinnati Law Review* 71 (2003): 979–1030. http://scholarship.law.wm.edu/facpubs/114.

Downey, Fairfax. *Richard Harding Davis: His Day.* New York: C. Scribner's Sons, 1933.

Du Bois, W. E. B. *The Autobiography of W. E. B. Du Bois: A Soliloquy on Viewing My Life from the Last Decade of Its First Century.* New York: International Publishers, 1968.

———. *Black Reconstruction in America, 1860–1880.* New York: Atheneum, 1992.

———. "Booker T. Washington." *Crisis* 11, no. 2 (December 1915): 82.

———. "Politics." *Crisis* 4, no. 4 (August 1912): 180–81.

———. "The President and the Soldiers." *Voices of the Negro* 3 (December 1906): 552–53.

———. *The Social Theory of W. E. B. Du Bois.* Edited by Phil Zuckerman. Thousand Oaks, CA: Pine Forge Press, 2004.

———. *The Souls of Black Folk.* New York: Barnes & Noble Classics, 2003.

———. "Theodore Roosevelt." *Crisis* 17, no. 4 (February 1919): 163.

———. *Writings.* Edited by Nathan Irvin Huggins. New York: Literary Classics of the United States, 1986.

Dunbar-Nelson, Alice M., ed. *Masterpieces of Negro Eloquence: The Best Speeches Delivered by the Negro from the Days of Slavery to the Present Time.* New York: G. K. Hall, 1997.

Dunn, Arthur W. *From Harrison to Harding: A Personal Narrative, Covering a Third of a Century, 1888–1921.* New York: G. P. Putnam's Sons, 1922.

———. *Gridiron Nights: Humorous and Satirical Views of Politics and Statesmen as Presented by the Famous Dining Club.* New York: Frederick A. Stokes Company, 1915.

Egan, Timothy. *The Worst Hard Time: The Untold Story of Those Who Survived the Great American Dust Bowl.* Boston: Houghton Mifflin, 2006.

Fernandez, Ronald. *The Disenchanted Island: Puerto Rico and the United States in the Twentieth Century.* New York: Praeger, 1992.

Ferris, William H. *The African Abroad; or, His Evolution in Western Civilization, Tracing His Development under Caucasian Milieu.* New York: Johnson Reprint, 1968.

Flipper, Henry O. *Black Frontiersman: The Memoirs of Henry O. Flipper, First Black Graduate of West Point.* Edited by Theodore D. Harris. Fort Worth: Texas Christian University Press, 1997.

Flood, Charles B. *Grant's Final Victory: Ulysses S. Grant's Heroic Last Year.* Boston: Da Capo, 2012.

Foraker, Joseph B. *Notes of a Busy Life.* 2 vols. Cincinnati: Stewart & Kidd, 1917.

Foraker, Julia. *I Would Live It Again.* New York: Arno, 1975.

Fortescue, Granville R. *At the Front with Three Armies: My Adventures in the Great War.* London: A. Melrose, 1915.

———. *Fore-Armed: How to Build a Citizen Army.* Philadelphia: John C. Winston, 1916.

———. *Front Line and Deadline: The Experiences of a War Correspondent.* New York: G. P. Putnam's Sons, 1937.

Forth, Christopher E. "Booker T. Washington and the 1905 Niagara Conference." *Journal of Negro History* 72, nos. 3–4 (Summer–Autumn 1987): 44–56.

Fortune, Timothy Thomas. *Dreams of Life: Miscellaneous Poems.* Miami: Mnemosyne, 1969.

Foster, Gaines M. *Ghosts of the Confederacy: Defeat, the Lost Cause, and the Emergence of the New South, 1865 to 1913.* New York: Oxford University Press, 1987.

Fowler, Arlen L. *The Black Infantry in the West, 1869–1891.* Norman: University of Oklahoma Press, 1996.

Fowler, Dorothy Ganfield. *John Coit Spooner: Defender of Presidents.* New York: University Publishers, 1961.

Fradella, Sal. *Jack Johnson.* Boston: Branden, 1990.

Friedman, Milton, and Anna J. Schwartz. *A Monetary History of the United States, 1867–1960.* Princeton, NJ: Princeton University Press, 1963.

Fromkin, David. *The King and the Cowboy.* New York: Penguin Press, 2008.

Gable, John A. *The Bull Moose Years: Theodore Roosevelt and the Progressive Party.* Port Washington, NY: Kennikat Press, 1978.

Gatewood, Willard B. *Aristocrats of Color: The Black Elite, 1880–1920.* Bloomington: Indiana University Press, 1990.

———. *Theodore Roosevelt and the Art of Controversy.* Baton Rouge: Louisiana State University Press, 1970.

———. "Theodore Roosevelt and the Indianola Affair." *Journal of Negro History* 53, no. 1 (1968): 48–69.

Goodwin, Paul George. "Theodore Roosevelt: The Politics of His Candidacy, 1904, 1912." PhD diss., Syracuse University, 1961.

Gordon, James W. "Did the First Justice Harlan Have a Black Brother?" In *Critical White Studies: Looking behind the Mirror*, edited by Richard Delgado and Jean Stefancic, pp. 444–57. Philadelphia: Temple University Press, 1997.

Gould, Lewis L. *The Most Exclusive Club: A History of the Modern United States Senate.* New York: Basic Books, 2005.

———. *The Presidency of Theodore Roosevelt.* Lawrence: University Press of Kansas, 2011.

———. *The Progressive Era.* Syracuse, NY: Syracuse University Press, 1974.

———. *Theodore Roosevelt*. New York: Oxford University Press, 2012.

———. *Wyoming: A Political History, 1868–1896*. New Haven, CT: Yale University Press, 1968.

Grant, Donald L. *The Way It Was in the South: The Black Experience in Georgia*. New York: Birch Lane Press, 1993.

Grant, Ulysses S. *The Papers of Ulysses S. Grant*. Edited by John Y. Simon. Vol. 19, *July 1, 1868–October 31, 1869*. Carbondale: Southern Illinois University Press, 1995.

———. *Personal Memoirs of U.S. Grant*. New York: Dover Publications, 1995.

Greeley, Horace, John F. Cleveland, F. J. Ottarson, Alexander J. Schem, Edward McPherson, and Henry E. Rhoades. *The Tribune Almanac and Political Register*. New York: Tribune Association, 1838.

Grondahl, Paul. *I Rose Like a Rocket*. New York: Free Press, 2004.

Grossman, Lawrence. "In His Veins Coursed No Bootlicking Blood: The Career of Peter H. Clark." *Ohio History* 86, no. 2 (1977): 79–95.

Habegger, Alfred. *Gender, Fantasy, and Realism in American Literature*. New York: Columbia University Press, 1982.

Habibuddin, Syed. "Theodore Roosevelt's Attitude toward Civil Rights and Civil Liberties." PhD diss., University of Pennsylvania, 1968.

Hagedorn, Hermann. *The Roosevelt Family of Sagamore Hill*. New York: Macmillan, 1954.

———. *Roosevelt in the Bad Lands*. Medora, ND: Theodore Roosevelt History and Nature Association, 1949.

Hakim, Joy. *An Age of Extremes*. New York: Oxford University Press, 1994.

Haney, James E. "Blacks and the Republican Nomination of 1908." *Ohio History* 84, no. 4 (1975): 207–21.

Hangen, William, and Terra Hangen. "Steel Steeds." *Military Officer*, February 2004, pp. 68–75.

Hansen, Anne C. "The Congressional Career of Senator Francis E. Warren from 1890 to 1902." Master's thesis, University of Wyoming, 1942.

Harlan, Louis R. *Booker T. Washington: The Making of a Black Leader, 1856–1901*. New York: Oxford University Press, 1972.

———. *Booker T. Washington: The Wizard of Tuskegee, 1901–1915*. New York: Oxford University Press, 1983.

———. *Booker T. Washington in Perspective: Essays of Louis R. Harlan*. Edited by Raymond W. Smock. Jackson: University Press of Mississippi, 1988.

Harris, Thomas E. "The Black Leader's Rhetorical Dilemma: An Analysis of the Debate between W. E. B. Du Bois and Booker T. Washington." Paper presented at the Annual Meeting of the New York State Speech Association, Loch Sheldrake, NY, April 1974.

Hawley, Joshua D. *Theodore Roosevelt: Preacher of Righteousness*. New Haven, CT: Yale University Press, 2008.

Hayes, Rutherford B. *Hayes: The Diary of a President, 1875–1881.* Edited by T. Harry Williams. New York: David McKay, 1964.

Helicher, Karl. "The Brahmin Scholar: The Formative Years of Theodore Roosevelt." *Presidential Studies Quarterly* 15, no. 3 (1985): 541–48.

Hibbard, Benjamin H. *A History of the Public Land Policies.* Madison: University of Wisconsin Press, 1965.

Hietala, Thomas R. *The Fight of the Century: Jack Johnson, Joe Louis, and the Struggle for Racial Equality.* Armonk, NY: M. E. Sharpe, 2002.

Hodgson, Godfrey. *The Colonel: The Life and Wars of Henry Stimson, 1867–1950.* New York: Knopf, 1990.

Holmes, Oliver Wendell, Jr., and Frederick Pollock. *Holmes-Pollock Letters: The Correspondence of Mr. Justice Holmes and Sir Frederick Pollock, 1874–1932.* Edited by Mark DeWolfe Howe. 2 vols. Cambridge, MA: Harvard University Press, 1942.

Hwang, Hae-sung. *Booker T. Washington and W. E. B. Du Bois: A Study in Race Leadership, 1895–1915.* Seoul: American Studies Institute, Seoul National University, 1992.

Jeffers, H. Paul. *Commissioner Roosevelt: The Story of Theodore Roosevelt and the New York City Police, 1895–1897.* New York: John Wiley & Sons, 1994.

Jeffreys-Jones, Rhodri. *The FBI: A History.* New Haven, CT: Yale University Press, 2007.

Jenny, George F. "Joseph B. Foraker as Governor of Ohio, 1886–1890." Master's thesis, Ohio State University, 1936.

Johnson, Donald B. *National Party Platforms.* Urbana: University of Illinois Press, 1978.

Johnston, William D. *TR, Champion of the Strenuous Life: A Photographic Biography of Theodore Roosevelt.* New York: Theodore Roosevelt Association, 1958.

Jones, Robert F. "The Political Career of Senator Francis E. Warren, 1902–1912." Master's thesis, University of Wyoming, 1949.

Jones, Virgil C. *Roosevelt's Rough Riders.* Garden City, NY: Doubleday, 1971.

Kantrowitz, Stephen. *More Than Freedom: Fighting for Black Citizenship in a White Republic, 1829–1889.* New York: Penguin Press, 2012.

Kaplan, Fred. *Lincoln: The Biography of a Writer.* New York: HarperCollins, 2008.

Kendrick, Benjamin B. "McKinley and Foraker." *Political Science Quarterly* 31, no. 4 (1916): 590–604.

Kerr, Winfield S. *John Sherman: His Life and Public Services.* Boston: Sherman, French, 1908.

King, Lucy Jane. *Madame President 1901–1905: Nellie Fairbanks, Path Finder to Politics for American Women.* Bloomington, IN: AuthorHouse, 2008.

Knightley, Phillip. *The First Casualty: The War Correspondent as Hero and Myth-Maker from the Crimea to Iraq.* Baltimore: Johns Hopkins University Press, 2004.

Kohlsaat, Herman H. *From McKinley to Harding: Personal Recollections of Our Presidents.* New York: C. Scribner's Sons, 1923.

Lane, Ann J. *The Brownsville Affair: National Crisis and Black Reaction.* Port Washington, NY: Kennikat, 1971.

Lanning, Michael Lee. *The African-American Soldier: From Crispus Attucks to Colin Powell.* New York: Citadel, 1997.

Larson, T. A. *History of Wyoming.* Lincoln: University of Nebraska Press, 1965.

Latham, Aaron. "Can the Pistol-Packing Publisher Win It for the Cowboy Star?" *New York Magazine* 9, no. 5 (1976): 32–41.

Leckie, William H. *The Buffalo Soldiers: A Narrative of the Negro Cavalry in the West.* Norman: University of Oklahoma Press, 1967.

Leech, Margaret. *In the Days of McKinley.* New York: Harper & Brothers, 1959.

Leiker, James N. *Racial Borders: Black Soldiers along the Rio Grande.* College Station: Texas A&M University Press, 2002.

Leslie, Kent A. *Woman of Color, Daughter of Privilege: Amanda America Dickson, 1849–1893.* Athens: University of Georgia Press, 1995.

Leupp, Francis E. *The Man Roosevelt: A Portrait Sketch.* New York: D. Appleton, 1904.

Lewis, David L. *W. E. B. Du Bois: Biography of a Race, 1868–1919.* New York: Henry Holt, 1993.

———. *W. E. B. Du Bois: The Fight for Equality and the American Century, 1919–1963.* New York: Henry Holt, 2000.

Lincoln, Abraham. *The Collected Works of Abraham Lincoln.* Edited by Roy P. Basler. Vol. 1, *1824–1848.* New Brunswick, NJ: Rutgers University Press, 1953.

Lindenmeyer, Otto J. *Black & Brave: The Black Soldier in America.* New York: McGraw-Hill, 1970.

Link, Arthur Stanley. "Theodore Roosevelt in His Letters." *Yale Review* 43, no. 4 (1954): 589–98.

Linn, Brian M. A. *The Echo of Battle: The Army's Way of War.* Cambridge, MA: Harvard University Press, 2007.

Lipsey, John J. *General Palmer's Half-Brother-in-Law, Chase Mellen: His Colorado Adventures, 1871–1881.* Colorado Springs: Western Books, 1958.

Literary Digest. "The Brownsville Affair as a Political Weapon." Topics of the Day, December 15, 1906, pp. 895–96.

———. "How the President's Message Is Received." Topics of the Day, December 15, 1906, pp. 889–90.

————. "Lynching and the Negroes." *Topics of the Day*, December 15, 1906, pp. 891–92.

Logan, Rayford W. *The Betrayal of the Negro, from Rutherford B. Hayes to Woodrow Wilson.* New York: Da Capo, 1997.

Malbrew, Ricardo Purnell. "Brownsville Revisited." Master's thesis, Louisiana State University, 2007.

Manchester, William. *American Caesar: Douglas MacArthur, 1880–1964.* Boston: Little, Brown, 1978.

————. *The Last Lion: Winston Spencer Churchill.* Vol. 1, *Visions of Glory, 1874–1932.* Boston: Little, Brown, 1983.

Marshall, S. L. A. *World War I.* New York: American Heritage, 1971.

Massie, Robert K. *Castles of Steel: Britain, Germany, and the Winning of the Great War at Sea.* New York: Random House, 2003.

McCullough, David. *John Adams.* New York: Simon & Schuster, 2001.

————. *Mornings on Horseback.* New York: Simon & Schuster, 1981.

————. *The Path between the Seas: The Creation of the Panama Canal, 1870–1914.* New York: Simon & Schuster, 1977.

McFarland, Philip J. *Mark Twain and the Colonel: Samuel L. Clemens, Theodore Roosevelt, and the Arrival of a New Century.* Lanham, MD: Rowman & Littlefield, 2012.

McKee, Robert. *Story: Substance, Structure, Style, and the Principles of Screenwriting.* New York: HarperCollins Books, 1997.

McNeil, William. *Black Baseball Out of Season: Pay for Play outside of the Negro Leagues.* Jefferson, NC: McFarland, 2007.

McPherson, James M. *Tried by War: Abraham Lincoln as Commander in Chief.* New York: Penguin Press, 2000.

Meier, August. "Booker T. Washington and the Rise of the NAACP." *Crisis* 61, no. 2 (February 1954): 69–79, 117–23.

————. *Negro Thought in America: 1880–1915.* Ann Arbor: Ann Arbor Paperbacks, University of Michigan Press, 1966.

Meier, August, and Elliott Rudwick. "The Rise of Segregation in the Federal Bureaucracy, 1900–1930." *Phylon* 28, no. 2 (1967): 178–84.

Meltzer, Milton. *Theodore Roosevelt and His America.* New York: Franklin Watts, 1994.

Merrill, Horace S., and Marion Merrill. *The Republican Command, 1897–1913.* Lexington: University Press of Kentucky, 1971.

Michaelis, David. *N. C. Wyeth: A Biography.* New York: Knopf, 1998.

Middleton, Stephen. *The Black Laws: Race and the Legal Process in Early Ohio.* Athens: Ohio University Press, 2005.

Milkis, Sidney M. *Theodore Roosevelt, the Progressive Party, and the Transformation of American Democracy.* Lawrence: University Press of Kansas, 2009.

Millard, Candice. *Destiny of the Republic: A Tale of Madness, Medicine and the Murder of a President.* New York: Anchor Books, 2012.

Miller, Kelly. *The Everlasting Stain*. Washington, DC: Associated Publishers, 1924.

——. *Race Adjustment: Essays on the Negro in America*. New York: Neale, 1910.

Miller, Zane L. *Boss Cox's Cincinnati: Urban Politics in the Progressive Era*. New York: Oxford University Press, 1968.

Millett, Allan R. "The Rise and Fall of the Cuban Rural Guard." *Americas* 29, no. 2 (October 1972): 191–213.

Minnesota Board of Commissioners. *Minnesota in the Civil and Indian Wars, 1861–1865*. 2 vols. St. Paul: Pioneer Press, 1890.

Mitchell, Margaret. *Gone with the Wind*. New York: Scribner, 2006.

Moon, Henry L. *Balance of Power: The Negro Vote*. Garden City, NY: Doubleday, 1949.

Moore, J. H. *Roosevelt and the Old Guard*. Philadelphia: Macrae Smith, 1925.

Morris, Edmund. *Colonel Roosevelt*. New York: Random House, 2010.

——. *The Rise of Theodore Roosevelt*. New York: Coward, McCann & Geoghegan, 1979.

——. *Theodore Rex*. New York: Random House, 2001.

Morrison, Gayle. *To Move the World: Louis G. Gregory and the Advancement of Racial Unity in America*. Wilmette, IL: Bahá'í Publishing Trust, 1982.

Morrow, James B. "Foraker and His Early Struggles." *Washington Post*, June 18, 1905.

Murray, Percy E. "Harry C. Smith-Joseph B. Foraker Alliance: Coalition Politics in Ohio." *Journal of Negro History* 68, no. 2 (1983): 171–84.

Muzzey, David S. *James G. Blaine: A Political Idol of Other Days*. New York: Dodd, Mead, 1934.

Nalty, Bernard C. *Strength for the Fight: A History of Black Americans in the Military*. New York: Free Press, 1986.

Nankivell, John H., and Quintard Taylor. *Buffalo Soldier Regiment: History of the Twenty-Fifth United States Infantry, 1869–1926*. Lincoln: University of Nebraska Press, 2001.

Nasaw, David. *Andrew Carnegie*. New York: Penguin Press, 2006.

——. *The Chief: The Life of William Randolph Hearst*. Boston: Houghton Mifflin, 2001.

Neale, Walter. *Life of Ambrose Bierce*. New York: W. Neale, 1929.

Neff, John R. *Honoring the Civil War Dead: Commemoration and the Problem of Reconciliation*. Lawrence: University Press of Kansas, 2005.

"Newspaper Comment on Campaign Contributions." *Outlook*, September 14, 1912, pp. 68–70.

Norrell, Robert J. *Up from History: The Life of Booker T. Washington*. Cambridge, MA: Belknap Press of Harvard University Press, 2009.

Norton, Aloysius A. *Theodore Roosevelt*. Boston: Twayne, 1980.

Noyes, Edward. "Ohio G.A.R. and Politics from 1866 to 1900." *Ohio State Archeological and Historical Quarterly* 55 (1946): 79–105.

Okrent, Daniel. *Great Fortune: The Epic of Rockefeller Center*. New York: Penguin Books, 2004.

Oren, Michael B. *Power, Faith, and Fantasy: America in the Middle East, 1776 to the Present*. New York: W. W. Norton, 2007.

Parker, James R. "Paternalism and Racism: Sen. John C. Spooner and American Minorities, 1897–1907." *Wisconsin Magazine of History* 57, no. 3 (1974): 195–200.

Patton, Eugene B. "Secretary Shaw and Precedents as to Treasury Control over the Money Market." *Journal of Political Economy* 15, no. 2 (1907): 65–87.

Pickard, M. Fortescue. *The Roosevelts and America*. London: H. Joseph, 1941.

Pringle, Henry F. *The Life and Times of William Howard Taft: A Biography*. 2 vols. Hamden, CT: Archon Books, 1964.

———. *Theodore Roosevelt: A Biography*. New York: Harcourt, Brace, 1984.

Rampersad, Arnold. *The Art and Imagination of W. E. B. Du Bois*. Cambridge, MA: Harvard University Press, 1976.

Reckner, James B. "The Fleet Triumphant." *Theodore Roosevelt Association Journal* 29, no. 2 (Summer 2008): 5–16.

Reid, Whitelaw. *Ohio in the War: Her Statesmen, Her Generals, and Soldiers*. Cincinnati: Moore, Wilstach & Baldwin, 1868.

Reilly, John C. *Ships of the United States Navy: Christening, Launching, and Commissioning*. Washington, DC: Naval History Division, Department of the Navy, 1975.

Riis, Jacob A. *Theodore Roosevelt: The Citizen*. New York: Outlook, 1904.

Robinson, Charles M. *The Fall of a Black Army Officer: Racism and the Myth of Henry O. Flipper*. Norman: University of Oklahoma Press, 2008.

Roosevelt, Robert B. *Progressive Petticoats; or, Dressed to Death: An Autobiography of a Married Man*. New York: G. W. Carleton, 1874.

Roosevelt, Theodore. *Letters and Speeches*. Edited by Louis Auchincloss. New York: Library of America, 2004.

———. *Letters from Theodore Roosevelt to Anna Roosevelt Cowles, 1897–1918*. New York: Charles Scribner's Sons, 1924.

———. *The Letters of Theodore Roosevelt*. Edited by Elting E. Morison. 8 vols. Cambridge, MA: Harvard University Press, 1951–1954.

———. *Letters to Kermit from Theodore Roosevelt, 1902–1908*. Edited by Will Irwin. New York: C. Scribner's Sons, 1946.

———. *The Rough Riders / An Autobiography*. Edited by Louis Auchincloss. New York: Library of America, 2004.

———. *The Selected Letters of Theodore Roosevelt*. Edited by H. W. Brands. Lanham, MD: Rowman & Littlefield, 2001.

——. *Theodore Roosevelt Cyclopedia.* Edited by Albert Bushnell Hart and Herbert R. Ferleger. New York: Roosevelt Memorial Association, 1941.

——. *Theodore Roosevelt's Letters to His Children.* Edited by Joseph Bucklin Bishop. New York: Charles Scribner's Sons, 1919.

Roosevelt, Theodore, and Henry Cabot Lodge. *Selections from the Correspondence of Theodore Roosevelt and Henry Cabot Lodge, 1884–1918.* 2 vols. New York: C. Scribner's Sons, 1925.

Roosevelt, Theodore, and Brander Matthews. *The Letters of Theodore Roosevelt and Brander Matthews.* Edited by Lawrence J. Oliver. Knoxville: University of Tennessee Press, 1995.

Rothbard, Murray N. *Economic Depressions: Their Cause and Cure.* Auburn, AL: Ludwig von Mises Institute, 2009. http://books.google.com/books?id=R87hqJk42T0C.

Rudwick, Elliott M. "Race Leadership Struggle: Background of the Boston Riot of 1903." *Journal of Negro Education* 31, no. 1 (1962): 16–24.

——. *W. E. B. Du Bois: Propagandist of the Negro Protest.* New York: Atheneum, 1968.

——. *W. E. B. Du Bois: A Study in Minority Group Leadership.* Philadelphia: University of Pennsylvania Press, 1960.

Russell, Thomas H. *Life and Work of Theodore Roosevelt: Typical American, Patriot, Orator, Historian, Sportsman, Soldier, Statesman and President.* Chicago: Homewood Press, 1919.

Sandweiss, Martha A. *Passing Strange: A Gilded Age Tale of Love and Deception across the Color Line.* New York: Penguin Press, 2009.

Savage, B. L., and C. D. Shull. *African-American Historic Places.* Washington, DC: Preservation Press, 1994.

Sawyer, Logan Everett, III. "Constitutional Principle, Partisan Calculation, and the Beveridge Child Labor Bill." *Law and History Review* 31, no. 2 (2013): 325–53.

Scarborough, W. S., and Michele V. Ronnick. *The Autobiography of William Sanders Scarborough: An American Journey from Slavery to Scholarship.* Detroit: Wayne State University Press, 2004.

Schubert, Frank N. *On the Trail of the Buffalo Soldier: Biographies of African Americans in the U.S. Army, 1866–1917.* Wilmington, DE: Scholarly Resources, 1995.

——. *Voices of the Buffalo Soldier: Records, Reports, and Recollections of Military Life and Service in the West.* Albuquerque: University of New Mexico Press, 2003.

Scott, Thomas Allan. *Cornerstones of Georgia History: Documents That Formed the State.* Athens: University of Georgia Press, 1995.

Shaw, Arnold. *Black Popular Music in America: From the Spirituals, Minstrels, and Ragtime to Soul, Disco, and Hip-Hop.* New York: Schirmer Books, 1986.

Shaw, Irwin. "Act of Faith." In *The Bar Mitzvah Treasury*, edited by Azriel Louis Eisenberg, pp. 235–56. New York: Behrman House, 1952.

Sheingate, Adam. "Progressive Publicity and the Origins of Political Consulting." Unpublished manuscript, n.d. http://users.polisci.wisc.edu/apw/archives/sheingate.pdf.

Simkins, Francis Butler. *Pitchfork Ben Tillman, South Carolinian*. Baton Rouge: Louisiana State University Press, 1944.

Sponholtz, Lloyd. "Harry Smith, Negro Suffrage and the Ohio Constitutional Convention: Black Frustration in the Progressive Era." *Phylon* 35, no. 2 (1974): 165–80.

Spring, Agnes W. *William Chapin Deming of Wyoming: Pioneer Publisher, and State and Federal Official: A Biography*. Glendale, CA: Arthur H. Clark, 1944.

Stannard, David E. *Honor Killing: How the Infamous "Massie Affair" Transformed Hawai'i*. New York: Viking, 2005.

Stephenson, Nathaniel W. *Nelson W. Aldrich: A Leader in American Politics*. New York: C. Scribner's Sons, 1930.

Steward, T. G. *The Colored Regulars in the United States Army*. New York: Arno, 1969.

Stone, Candace. *Dana and the Sun*. New York: Dodd, Mead, 1938.

Straus, Oscar S. *Under Four Administrations: From Cleveland to Taft*. Boston: Houghton Mifflin, 1922.

Strouse, Jean. *Morgan: American Financier*. New York: Random House, 1999.

Sullivan, Mark. *Our Times: The United States, 1900–1925*. New York: Charles Scribner's Sons, 1926.

Swift, Leonard W. *Index to the Heritage of Hinsdale: An Anthology*. Pittsfield, MA: Berkshire Family History Association, 2006.

Taylor, Henry L., Jr., ed. *Race and the City: Work, Community, and Protest in Cincinnati, 1820–1970*. Urbana: University of Illinois Press, 1993.

Taylor, Nikki M. *Frontiers of Freedom: Cincinnati's Black Community, 1802–1868*. Athens: Ohio University Press, 2005.

Terrell, Mary Church. *A Colored Woman in a White World*. Salem, NH: Ayer, 1998.

———. "A Sketch of Mingo Saunders." *Voice of the Negro*, March 1907.

Thornbrough, Emma Lou. "The Brownsville Episode and the Negro Vote." *Mississippi Valley Historical Review* 44, no. 3 (December 1947): 469–93.

———. *T. Thomas Fortune: Militant Journalist*. Chicago: University of Chicago Press, 1972.

Tilchin, William N. *Theodore Roosevelt and the British Empire: A Study in Presidential Statecraft*. New York: St. Martin's, 1997.

Timberlake, Richard H., Jr. "Mr. Shaw and His Critics: Monetary History in the Golden Era Reviewed." *Quarterly Journal of Economics* 77, no. 1 (1963): 40–54.

Tinsley, James A. "Roosevelt, Foraker, and the Brownsville Affray." *Journal of Negro History* 41, no. 1 (1956): 43–65.

Tremain, Henry E. *Sectionalism Unmasked*. New York: Bonnell, Silver, 1907.

Tuchman, Barbara W. *Practicing History: Selected Essays*. New York: Alfred A. Knopf, 1981.

Turner, Frederick J. *The Frontier in American History*. New York: Henry Holt, 1921. http://xroads.virginia.edu/~hyper/turner.

Twain, Mark. *Autobiography of Mark Twain: The Complete and Authoritative Edition*. Edited by Harriet Elinor Smith and Benjamin Griffin. 2 vols. Berkeley: University of California Press, 2010–2013.

Tweedy, John. *A History of the Republican National Conventions from 1856 to 1908*. Danbury, CT: J. Tweedy, 1910.

US Congress. *Congressional Record*. 159 vols. Washington, DC: Government Printing Office, 1873–2013.

US Department of State. *Papers Relating to the Foreign Relations of the United States*. Vol. 2. Washington, DC: Government Printing Office, 1889.

Vaughn, Leroy. *Black People and Their Place in World History*. Inglewood, CA: Leroy Vaughn, 2002. http://www.computerhealth.org/ebook/.

Villard, Oswald Garrison. "The Negro in the Regular Army." *Atlantic Monthly* 91 (1903): 721–29.

Wagenknecht, Edward. *The Seven Worlds of Theodore Roosevelt*. New York: Longmans, Green, 1958.

Wagner, Leopold. *Manners, Customs, and Observances: Their Origin and Signification*. New York: MacMillan, 1895.

Walters, Everett. *Joseph Benson Foraker: An Uncompromising Republican*. Columbus: Ohio History Press, 1948.

———. "The Ohio Delegation at the National Republican Convention of 1888." *Ohio State Archaeological and Historical Quarterly* 56 (1947): 228–41.

Washington, Booker T. *The Booker T. Washington Papers*. Edited by Louis R. Harlan. 14 vols. Urbana: University of Illinois Press, 1972–89.

———. *My Larger Education: Being Chapters from My Experience*. Garden City, NY: Doubleday, Page, 1911.

———. *The Story of My Life and Work: An Autobiography*. Toronto: J. L. Nichols, 1901.

———. *Up from Slavery*. New York: Viking Penguin, 1986.

Watts, Sarah L. *Rough Rider in the White House: Theodore Roosevelt and the Politics of Desire*. Chicago: University of Chicago Press, 2003.

Weaver, John D. *The Brownsville Raid*. College Station: Texas A&M University Press, 1992.

——. *The Senator and the Sharecropper's Son: Exoneration of the Brownsville Soldiers.* College Station: Texas A&M University Press, 1997.

West, Henry Litchfield. "American Politics." *Forum*, July 1902, pp. 3–17.

Williams, Edward C., Adam McKible, Emily Bernard, and Edward C. Williams. *When Washington Was in Vogue: A Love Story (A Lost Novel of the Harlem Renaissance).* New York: Amistad, 2003.

Wister, Owen. *Roosevelt: The Story of a Friendship, 1880–1919.* New York: Macmillan, 1930.

Wolters, Raymond. *Du Bois and His Rivals.* Columbia: University of Missouri Press, 2002.

Woodward, C. Vann. *Reunion and Reaction: The Compromise of 1877 and the End of Reconstruction.* Boston: Little, Brown, 1951.

Works Progress Administration. *The Berkshire Hills.* New York: Funk & Wagnalls, 1939.

Wynne, Lewis N. "Brownsville: The Reaction of the Negro Press." *Phylon* 33, no. 2 (1972): 153–60.

Young, Elliott. "Red Men, Princess Pocahontas, and George Washington: Harmonizing Race Relations in Laredo at the Turn of the Century." *Western Historical Quarterly* 29, no. 1 (Spring 1998): 49–85.

DOCUMENTS & ARCHIVES

Affray at Brownsville, Tex., August 13 and 14, 1906: Proceedings of a General Court-Martial Convened at Headquarters, Department of Texas, San Antonio, Tex., April 15, 1907 in the Case of Capt. Edgar A. Macklin, Twenty-Fifth United States Infantry. S. Doc. No. 60-402 (1908), pt. 3, cited in this book as "Macklin Court-Martial."

Affray at Brownsville, Tex.: Hearings Before the Committee on Military Affairs, United States Senate, Concerning the Affray at Brownsville, Tex., on the Night of August 13 and 14, 1906. S. Doc. No. 60-402 (1908), pts. 4, 5, and 6, cited in this book as "SMAC-1," "SMAC-2," and "SMAC-3."

Affray at Brownsville, Tex., August 13 and 14, 1906: Proceedings of a General Court-Martial Convened at Headquarters, Department of Texas, San Antonio, Tex., February 4, 1907 in the Case of Maj. Charles W. Penrose, Twenty-Fifth United States Infantry. S. Doc. No. 60-402 (1908), pt. 2, cited in this book as "Penrose Court-Martial."

Archibald Grimké Papers. Moorland-Spingarn Research Center, Howard University.

Booker T. Washington Papers. Ford Motor Company Library. Tuskegee University, Tuskegee, Alabama.

Booker T. Washington Papers. Library of Congress.

Charles W. Fairbanks Papers, 1819–1839. Lilly Library, Indiana University.

Elihu Root Papers. Library of Congress.

Ethan Allen Hitchcock Papers. National Archives, College Park, MD.

Francis E. Warren Papers. American Heritage Center, University of Wyoming.

George A. Myers Papers, 1890–1929. Ohio History Connection, Columbus.

George B. Cortelyou Papers, 1871–1948. Library of Congress.

Guardian of Boston/Trotter Collection. Howard Gotlieb Archival Research Center, Mugar Library, Boston University.

Henry Cabot Lodge Papers. Massachusetts Historical Society, Boston.

Henry Fowler Pringle. Research Notes for *Theodore Roosevelt: A Biography*. Houghton Library, Harvard University.

Homecoming Dinner for Sen. Foraker, Neil House, Columbus, March 12, 1909. PA Box 340/37e, Ohio History Connection, Columbus.

John C. Spooner Papers. Library of Congress.

John Callan O'Laughlin Papers. Houghton Library, Harvard University.

John Callan O'Laughlin Papers. Library of Congress.

John D. Weaver Papers. Earl Gregg Swem Library, College of William and Mary, Williamsburg, VA.

John E. Milholland Papers (1887–1924). Ticonderoga (NY) Historical Society.

Joseph Foraker Papers. Cincinnati History Library and Archives.

Joseph Benson Foraker Papers. Library of Congress.

Joseph Benson Foraker Papers. Ohio History Connection, Columbus.

James Rudolph Garfield Papers. Library of Congress.

La Follette Family Papers. Library of Congress.

Mellen Family Papers. Bowdoin College, Brunswick, ME.

Memorial to Joseph Benson Foraker: Meeting of the Bench and Bar Held in the Court Room of the United States Circuit Court of Appeals, Federal Building, Cincinnati, Ohio . . . Saturday Morning, June Sixteenth, in the Year One Thousand Nine Hundred and Seventeen. Public Library of Cincinnati and Hamilton County.

Nicholas Longworth Papers. Library of Congress.

Oscar S. Straus Papers. Library of Congress.

Oswald Garrison Villard Papers. Houghton Library, Harvard University.

Philander C. Knox Papers. Library of Congress.

Presentation of Loving Cup to Hon. Joseph Benson Foraker, United States Senator, in Appreciation of His Services on Behalf of the Members of Companies A, B and C, 25th Infantry, by a Committee of Colored Citizens: The Ceremony and Addresses, March 6th, 1909, at Metropolitan A.M.E. Church, Washington, DC. Washington, DC: Murray Brothers, 1909.

Records of the Adjutant General's Office, 1780s–1917. National Archives.

Report of the Proceedings of the Court of Inquiry Relative to the Shooting Affray at Brownsville, Tex., August 13 and 14, 1906, by Soldiers of Companies B, C, and D, Twenty-Fifth United States Infantry. S. Doc. No. 61-701 (1911), vols. 1–3, 4–6, 7–9, and 10–12, cited in this book as "CI-1," "CI-2," "CI-3," and "CI-4."

Steven Elkins Collection. West Virginia University.

Summary Discharge or Mustering Out of Regiments or Companies: Message from the President of the United States Transmitting a Report from the Secretary of War, Together with Several Documents, Including a Letter of General Nettleton, with Memoranda as to Precedents for the Summary Discharge or Mustering Out of Regiments or Companies. S. Doc. No. 59-155, vol. 11 (2d sess. 1907), pts. 1 and 2, cited in this book as "SD-1" and "SD-2."

Theodore Roosevelt Collection. Houghton Library, Harvard University.

Theodore Roosevelt Papers. Library of Congress.

William H. Scott Family Papers. Manuscript, Archives, and Rare Book Library, Emory University.

William Howard Taft Papers. Library of Congress.

William Howard Taft Papers. Ohio History Connection, Columbus.

INDEX